# Scholars' Guide to
# Washington, D.C.,
# for
# PEACE AND INTERNATIONAL
# SECURITY STUDIES

SCHOLARS' GUIDES TO
WASHINGTON, D.C.

Zdeněk V. David, Series Editor

# Scholars' Guide to Washington, D.C., for PEACE AND INTERNATIONAL SECURITY STUDIES

## Robert W. Janes

with the assistance of Katherine R. Tromble

Consultants:
James H. Laue,
George H. Quester,
and George Weigel

WOODROW WILSON INTERNATIONAL
CENTER for SCHOLARS

UNITED STATES
INSTITUTE of PEACE

THE WOODROW WILSON CENTER PRESS
Washington, D.C.

THE JOHNS HOPKINS UNIVERSITY PRESS
Baltimore and London

Scholars' Guide to Washington, D.C., no. 15


Editorial Office:
The Woodrow Wilson Center Press
370 L'Enfant Promenade, S.W., Suite 704
Washington, D.C. 20024-2518
Telephone 202-287-3000, ext. 218


Order from:
The Johns Hopkins University Press
Hampden Station
Baltimore, Maryland 21211
Telephone 1-800-537-5487

9 8 7 6 5 4 3 2 1


Library of Congress Cataloging-in-Publication Data

Janes, Robert W.
      Scholars' guide to Washington, D.C., for peace and international security studies / Robert W. Janes ; with the assistance of Katherine R. Tromble ; consultants, James H. Laue, George H. Quester, and George Weigel.
      p.   cm. — (Scholars' guide to Washington, D.C. ; no. 15)
      "Woodrow Wilson International Center for Scholars."
      "United States Institute of Peace."
      Includes bibliographical references and index.
      ISBN 0-8018-5218-8 (cloth : alk. paper). — ISBN 0-8018-5219-6 (paper : alk. paper)
      1. Peace—Societies, etc.—Directories.   2. Security, International—Societies, etc.—Directories.   I. Tromble, Katherine R.
II. Woodrow Wilson International Center for Scholars.   III. United States Institute of Peace.   IV. Title.   V. Series.
JX1905.5.J36   1995
016.3271—dc20
                                                                                                                              95-14677
                                                                                                                                    CIP

# Contents

# List of Entries

Entry symbols correspond to the following sections of the text:

A—Libraries (Government, Academic, Public, and Special)
B—Archives and Manuscript Repositories
C—Museums, Galleries, and Art Collections
D—Map Collections
E—Collections of Sound Recordings
F—Film Collections (Still Photographs and Motion Pictures)
G—Data Banks
H—Research Centers and Information Offices
J—Academic Programs and Departments
K—United States Government Agencies
L—International Government Organizations
M—Associations (Academic, Professional, and Cultural)
N—Cultural-Exchange and Technical-Assistance Organizations

## Libraries
### (Government, Academic, Public, and Special)

A1  Agency for International Development (AID) (International Development Cooperation Agency)—Development Information Center (DIC)
A2  American Federation of Labor and Congress of Industrial Organizations (AFL-CIO)—Library
A3  American Society of International Law (ASIL)—Library
A4  American University (AU)—Bender Library
A5  Arms Control and Disarmament Agency (ACDA)—Technical Reference Center
A6  Carnegie Endowment for International Peace—Library
A7  Catholic University of America (CUA)—Mullen Library
A8  Census Bureau Library (Commerce Department)
A9  Center for Strategic and International Studies (CSIS)—Library
A10  Commerce Department Library
A11  Education Department—Research Library
A12  Energy Department (DOE)—Library
A13  European Union—Delegation of the European Commission—Press and Public Affairs Office
A14  Export-Import Bank of the United States—Library
A15  Federal Emergency Management Agency—Library
A16  Federal Reserve System (FRS)—Library
A17  Food and Agriculture Organization (FAO) (United Nations)—Liaison Office for North America—Library
A18  George Mason University (GMU)—Fenwick Library
A19  George Washington University (GWU)—Gelman Library
A20  Georgetown University—Lauinger Library
A21  House of Representatives—Library
A22  Howard University—Founders Library
A23  Inter-American Defense College Library
A24  Inter-American Development Bank (IDB)—Library
A25  International Labor Organization (ILO) (United Nations)—Washington Branch Office—Library
A26  International Trade Commission (ITC)—National Library of International Trade
A27  Joint Bank-Fund Library (Library of the International Bank for Reconstruction and Development [World Bank] and the International Monetary Fund [IMF])

## Archives and Manuscript Repositories

## Museums, Galleries, and Art Collections

## Map Collections

## Collections of Sound Recordings

## Film Collections
## (Still Photographs and Motion Pictures)

## Data Banks

## Research Centers and Information Offices

## Academic Programs and Departments

## United States Government Agencies

## International Government Organizations

## Associations (Academic, Professional, and Cultural)

## Cultural-Exchange and Technical-Assistance Organizations

# Foreword

This Guide on peace and international security studies is the fifteenth volume in a reference series locating and describing the scholarly resources of the Washington, D.C., area. This series, sponsored by the Woodrow Wilson International Center for Scholars seeks to facilitate connections between the astonishing and often unexpected scholarly resources of the nation's capital and those who have scholarly or practical needs for them—or simply a desire to satisfy intellectual curiosity.

In creating the Woodrow Wilson Center, the founders envisioned a place that, in addition to developing its own scholarly role, would perform a special "switchboard" function to assist others in using the rich resources of the city. These Guides serve as tangible evidence that this idea was not forgotten, but has given birth to a precious research tool for the 20,000 or more visiting scholars who come to Washington each year, both from the Americas and abroad to pursue serious research. Publication of the Guides began in 1977, largely on the initiative of the center's second director (now Librarian of Congress), James H. Billington (1973–87), and of Zdeněk V. David, the Wilson Center Librarian since 1974. Dr. David, who devised the basic format, has been responsible for the general editorship role.

Peace and international security studies are pursued at the Center mainly in the Division of International Studies, directed by Robert S. Litwak. The Division focuses particular attention in its meetings and publications on major issues, such as nuclear proliferation and ethnic conflicts, at the heart of the post-Cold War international agenda. Through the use of history and a multidisciplinary perspective, the Division, often working in conjunction with other Center programs, has attempted to bring the underlying dynamics of these and other pressing global problems into sharper focus and thereby pro-vide important background to current policy concerns. This approach reflects the Woodrow Wilson Center's congressional mandate to strengthen "the fruitful relations between the world of learning and the world of public affairs."

The Guides cover the resources of the metropolitan area of Washington, D.C., and are designed as scholarly Baedekers of local organizations and institutions to inform researchers, many of them from outside the major university research centers in the United States, about the availability of specific collections on particular topics in Washington. In the city's libraries, archives, and data banks, in its universities and research centers, and perhaps more unexpectedly in the federal agencies and international organizations concentrated here, Washington holds resources that are of worldwide significance.

The planning of this Guide was undertaken largely by Jeanne Bohlen, until February 1994 the Director of the Jeannette Rankin Library Program at the United States Institute of Peace, and by Zed David. Subsequently, Robert A. Farina assumed Ms. Bohlen's liaison role on behalf of the Institute of Peace. The author, Robert W. Janes, who holds the degree of Master of International Affairs from Columbia University and Ph.D. in government and politics from the University of Maryland, was responsible for the researching and writing of entries for this Guide and, jointly with Zed David, for the preparation of the manuscript for the press. Katherine R. Tromble helped with the research and drafting of entries on academic institutions, U.S. government agencies, and international government organizations. Although most of the information was newly prepared for this volume, for a few categories the author and the editor also relied on updated sections, relevant to peace and international security studies, from previous volumes, namely *Scholars' Guide to Washington, D.C., for Cartogra-*

*phy and Remote Sensing Imagery,* by Ralph E. Ehrenberg (1987), *Scholars' Guide to Washington, D.C., for Audio Resources,* by James R. Heintze (1985), and *Scholars' Guide to Washington, D.C., Media Collections,* by Bonnie G. Rowan and Cynthia J. Wood (1994).

Serving as consultants for this volume were James H. Laue, professor of conflict resolution at the Institute for Conflict Analysis and Resolution, George Mason University; George H. Quester, professor in the Department of Government and Politics, University of Maryland; and George Weigel, president, Ethics and Public Policy Center, Washington, D.C. Sadly, we have to report the untimely death of Professor Laue on September 25, 1993, before the completion of the project. Staff members of the Woodrow Wilson Center providing advice and assistance were Dean W. Anderson, Joseph Brinley, and Richard Rowson.

The Center thanks the United States Institute of Peace for its indispensable financial support of the Guide's preparation.

Previous Guides for scholars have been issued in the fields of Russian, Central Eurasian, and Baltic (3d rev. ed., 1994), Latin American and Caribbean (2d rev. ed., 1992), East Asian (1979), African (1980), Central and East European (1980), Middle Eastern (1981), South Asian (1981), Southeast Asian (1983), Northwest European (1984), and Southwest European studies (1989), as well as Guides covering film and video collections (1980), audio resources (1985), cartography and remote sensing imagery (1987), and media collections (1994).

Charles Blitzer, Director
Woodrow Wilson International Center for Scholars
Washington, D.C.

# Preface

The United States Institute of Peace is pleased to have initiated and funded the *Scholars' Guide to Washington, D.C., for Peace and International Security Studies*. This project was a collaborative effort between the Institute's Jeannette Rankin Library Program and the Woodrow Wilson International Center for Scholars. Grateful acknowledgment is due, in particular, to the contributions in preparing the guide of Zdeněk V. David at the Woodrow Wilson Center and to Jeanne Bohlen and Robert A. Farina of the Institute's library program.

This publication has drawn upon the expertise and cooperation of specialists of varied backgrounds and viewpoints. Their contributions have helped to ensure the accuracy, timeliness, and high quality of the information. For their assistance in developing this project and in selecting, reviewing, and commenting on the data included, the Institute gives special thanks to Robert W. Janes, the late James H. Laue, George H. Quester, and George Weigel. Thanks are also due Institute specialists Kenneth Jensen and Hrach Gregorian.

The Institute of Peace is mandated by Congress to expand and make available to the public and to academic specialists knowledge about ways of dealing with international conflicts without resort to violence or war. We believe that this publication will help advance scholarship and public understanding of peace and international security studies.

Richard H. Solomon, President
United States Institute of Peace

# Introduction

## PURPOSE

This volume is intended to serve as a basic reference aid for scholars interested in utilizing the diverse and often unique resources of the nation's capital for research in peace and international security studies. Although the Guide is intended for the serious researcher, those with a more casual interest in these regions will also find much of value within its pages. Washington is unsurpassed as a resource for research on international political, economic, and military relations, as well as peace issues. Its numerous libraries and archives contain not only some of the most extensive book, document, and manuscript holdings in the fields of interest to the users of this Guide, but likewise boast major specialized collections of maps, sound recordings, photographs, and films. The city also is the home of one of the largest and most comprehensive museum collections in the United States: the Smithsonian Institution. The scholars, diplomats, government employees, journalists, politicians, and activists who work in Washington, D.C. represent an additional source of expertise on issues of peace and international relations. Finally, Washington is the home of numerous think tanks and foreign policy centers that compete for government funds and research grants to study international security affairs. The purpose of this Guide, therefore, is to indicate the research possibilities of Washington, D.C., in the fields of peace and international security studies by exploring and describing the many collections and organizations available in this capital city. It seeks to provide the essential facts researchers need in deciding which institutions to examine, and how to use their resources.

## SCOPE

The Guide seeks to cover the fields traditionally subsumed under peace studies and international security studies, namely arms control; arms production and acquisition; collective security; conflict management and resolution (including behavioral approaches, and unofficial and nongovernmental approaches); defense conversion; deterrence; development issues; diplomacy and negotiations; disarmament; energy; ethnic and religious conflict; foreign policy; global environmental issues; humanitarian issues; human rights; international economics (especially, international finance and international trade); international law; international organizations; international politics; low-intensity conflict; military history; military science; military spending; national security; naval science; pacifism and peace movements; peacekeeping; peace theory and research; political systems and ideologies; proliferation; psychological aspects of war and peace; refugees; regional conflict; religious, philosophical, and ethical concepts of war and peace; rule of law; terrorism; transnationalism; war and violence; and war crimes.

Scholars who are interested in international political, economic, and military relations affecting individual countries and world regions, or in additional map or audiovisual resources, should consult other volumes in the series of Scholars' Guide to Washington, D.C. These include Guides devoted to particular geographic areas: Africa, Latin America and the Caribbean, East Asia, South Asia, Southeast Asia, Central and Eastern Europe, Northwestern Europe, Southwestern Europe, the Middle East, and Russia, Central Eurasia and the Baltic states. Additional Guides are available for audio resources, map collections, film and video resources, and media collections.

## CONTENTS

More than 750 collections, organizations, and agencies have been surveyed as part of the preparation of this volume. Although it provides such basic directory information as names, addresses, telephone numbers, and details about individual collections, the Guide is primarily a descriptive and evaluative survey of Washington's scholarly resources. It is divided into two sections. The first part examines Washington-area resource collections: libraries; archives and manuscript depositories; collections of art objects and museum artifacts, maps and remote sensing imagery, sound recordings, and still pictures and films; and data banks. Each entry describes the size, content, and organizational format of a particular collection's relevant holdings and quantitatively evaluates subject strengths and unique materials within those holdings. The second part of the Guide is comprised of Washington-based organizations, public and private, that deal with issues of international security, peace maintenance, or both, and are potential sources of information or assistance to researchers. Included are research centers and information offices; academic programs at local universities; U.S. and international government agencies; private academic, professional, and cultural associations; and technical-assistance and cultural-exchange programs. Each entry describes the organization's specific functions; delineates its pertinent research activities, materials, and products (published and unpublished, classified and unclassified); and discusses the restriction on scholarly access to unpublished and classified materials. Brief introductions highlight special features of each section and provide related supplemental information. At the back of the book, readers will find a series of appendixes, a bibliography, and relevant indexes.

## METHODOLOGY

The preparation of this volume began with compiling a list of all Washington-area collections and organizations that were thought to be potential sources of information or assistance for scholars. The bibliography in this volume lists the published sources that were examined. The actual suitability of institutions for inclusion was then determined by

telephone calls, personal visits, or both. Once a collection or organization was chosen for inclusion, information was collected through its publications and staff, and in on-site examinations. Relevant information available in the earlier volumes of the Scholars' Guide series was also consulted, updated (if necessary), and utilized, particularly in the areas of cartography, sound recordings, still pictures, and films. The author, with the editor's assistance, then prepared the individual entries. The process of data gathering and entry writing took place from February 1993 to April 1994. All the information was reviewed by the consultants, as well as the staff at the United States Institute of Peace, rechecked for accuracy, updated, and reedited between May and August 1994. Readers' comments and suggestions, for possible future revisions of this Guide, would be most appreciated. Please notify the Librarian, Woodrow Wilson Center, 1000 Jefferson Drive, SW, Washington, D.C. 20560.

## ACKNOWLEDGMENTS

The author and the editor extend their appreciation for support and advice to the consultants James H. Laue, George H. Quester, and George Weigel, as well as Jeanne Bohlen, Robert A. Farina, and their associates at the United States Institute of Peace. The preparation of this volume benefited substantially from the accumulated experience and findings of the authors of the other Guides in this series, above all, Ralph E. Ehrenberg, James R. Heintze, Bonnie G. Rowan, and Cynthia J. Wood, as well as Purnima M. Bhatt, Kenneth J. Dillon, Steven R. Dorr, Steven A. Grant, Michael Grow, Joan F. Higbee, Hong N. Kim, Patrick M. Mayerchak, Louis A. Pitschmann, William E. Pomeranz, and Enayetur Rahim. Peter Ammirati, Carla A. Bosco, and Robyn Goldstein provided research assistance. Grateful appreciation is also extended to the hundreds of men and women on the staffs of the institutions here described who contributed their time and knowledge to this project. Many, but by no means all, of these individuals are mentioned in the pages that follow.

# How to Use This Guide

The following comments provide a general guide for using this reference work. For additional explanations concerning particular types of collections and organizations (libraries, U.S. government agencies, research centers, etc.) see the introductory note to each section.

FORMAT. The main body of the volume is divided into two parts: Collections, which contains seven sections (A-G); and Organizations, which contains six sections (H, J-N). Within each section, entries are arranged alphabetically by the name of the individual collection or organization. In the section containing U.S. government agencies (K), functional descriptors precede the generic name (e.g., State Department rather than Department of State).

STANDARD ENTRY FORMAT. A brief introductory paragraph to each section is preceded by a standard entry format (see also Appendix VII), which outlines the categories and sequence of information contained within each entry. The numbers of the entry format correspond to the numerical arrangement of each entry. If a particular number does not appear in an entry, that category of information was either not applicable or not available. If a single institution or organization has more than one entry in the Guide, references to all entries are gathered under the main entry and also in the Organizations and Institutions Index.

INDEXES. Four indexes provide access to information in the text from several perspectives. The Personal Papers Index includes the names of individuals whose papers and manuscripts are located in libraries and other depositories in the Washington, D.C., area. The Library Subject-Strength Index ranks the major library collections in the area by subject and by region. The scale of evaluation used to rank these libraries is explained in the introduction to the library section (A) and preceding the index. (See also Appendix II for size estimates of the major library collections relevant to peace and international security studies.) The Subject Index is based on subject headings that designate the established topics for peace and international security studies. The Organizations and Institutions Index includes the names of all organizations and institutions covered in the Guide; subdivisions of highly differentiated agencies are grouped under the main entry in the index. Names of individuals are not included in this index.

NAMES, ADDRESSES, AND TELEPHONE NUMBERS. This information is subject to frequent changes, particularly for U.S. government agencies and highly differentiated organizations where reorganization and personnel changes occur often. Such information in this Guide is valid up to August 31, 1994. All telephone numbers include area codes (202 for the District of Columbia, 301 for the Maryland suburbs, and 703 for the Virginia suburbs).

# Collections

# A

# Libraries
# (Government, Academic,
# Public, and Special)

## Libraries Entry Format (A)

1. *General Information*
   a. address; telephone number(s)
   b. hours of service
   c. conditions of access (including availability of interlibrary loan service and photocopying facilities)
   d. name/title of director and heads of relevant divisions

2. *Size of Collection*
   a. general
   b. peace and international security studies

3. *Description and Evaluation of Collection*
   a. narrative assessment of peace and international security studies holdings—subject strengths/weaknesses
   b. notable holdings/collections
   c. tabular evaluation of subject strength:

| Subject | Number of Titles | Rating (A–C)* |
|---|---|---|
| Philosophy—War and Peace | | |
| Psychology—War and Peace | | |
| Ethics—War and Peace | | |
| Religion—War and Peace | | |
| World History | | |
| History—Military Science | | |
| Geography—Military | | |
| Anthropology—War and Peace | | |
| Economic History and Conditions | | |
| Commercial Policy | | |
| International Finance | | |
| Sociology | | |
| Political Theory | | |
| Constitutional History and Administration | | |
| Colonies and Emigration | | |
| International Relations | | |
| International Organizations | | |
| International Law | | |
| Education—International Relations and Military | | |
| Music—Military | | |
| Art and War | | |
| Military Science | | |
| Naval Science | | |
| Bibliography and Reference | | |

*A—comprehensive collection of primary and secondary sources (Library of Congress collection to serve as a standard of evaluation)

B—substantial collection of primary and secondary sources; sufficient for some original research (holdings of roughly one-tenth those of the Library of Congress)

C—substantial collection of secondary and some primary sources; sufficient to support graduate instruction (holdings of roughly one-half those of a B collection)

4. *Special Collections* (periodicals; newspapers; government documents; vertical files; archives and manuscripts; maps and remote sensing imagery; sound recordings [including oral history]; prints, photographs, and motion pictures)

5. *Bibliographic Aids Facilitating Use of Collection*

6. *Index Terms* (relevant subject specialties)

## Introductory Note

One could justifiably call Washington, D.C., a City of Libraries as no fewer than 400 separate and distinct libraries can be found in the metropolitan area. Those described in this section were selected on the basis of their scholarly value to specialists in peace and international security studies. The single most important repository of printed resources for these fields is, to be sure, the Library of Congress (A29). Otherwise, the largest collections for international security studies are in the National Defense University (A33), Navy Department Library (A36), and Pentagon Library (A41). American University Library (A4) and George Mason University's Fenwick Library (A18) hold the most notable collections for peace theory and research. The most substantial holdings in the areas of development and international economics are in the Joint Bank-Fund Library (A27) and in the International Trade Commission's National Library of International Trade (A26).

In the descriptions that follow, interlibrary loan service usually means (a) most of the materials, except periodicals, will be loaned to most outside institutions but not to individuals, and (b) the library will borrow materials for its own institutional community.

Most large and general collections, plus some smaller or more specialized ones, are evaluated on a scale of A to C. These rankings are based on quantity and quality of holdings for 24 subject categories. The Library of Congress was taken as a standard for A collections: comprehensive collections of primary and secondary sources. A collection receiving a B ranking was defined as a substantial collection (roughly one-tenth the size of holdings in the Library of Congress) of primary and secondary sources, sufficient for original research. A substantial collection

of secondary and primary sources (about one-half the size of a B collection), sufficient for graduate instruction, was considered a C collection. Collections with fewer holdings than those in the C category were not rated.

For the large and general libraries, numbers of titles in the various subject categories were derived primarily through the measurement of shelflists, on the basis of a Library of Congress formula of 33.8 titles per centimeter of shelflist catalog cards.

Library of Congress classification numbers, used for the measurement of the number of titles in the individual subject categories, covered the various topics and subtopics germane to peace and international security studies. *Guide to Library of Congress Subject Headings and Classification on Peace and International Conflict*, edited by Judith A. Kessinger (Washington, D.C.: United States Institute of Peace, 1990) served as an important source for the identification of these numbers. For a table of the relevant Library of Congress classification numbers used in the shelflist measurements, see Appendix IV.

In addition to the libraries with substantive resources for peace and international security studies, which have separate entries in section A, there are smaller library resources within individual organizations, especially in sections H (research centers), K (U.S. government agencies), and M (associations), which are described under their parent institutions and cross-referenced in section A.

Some seminary libraries and military libraries in the Washington, D.C., area may have holdings of interest to users of this Guide but are not substantial enough to merit separate entries in section A. The following seminary libraries may hold relevant materials for scholars concerned with the religious, philosophical, or ethical aspects of war and peace:

Atonement Seminary Library
145 Taylor Street, NE
Washington, D.C. 20017
(202) 529-1114

Capuchin College Library
4121 Harewood Road, NE
Washington, D.C. 20017
(202) 529-2188
Fax: (202) 526-6664

De Sales School of Theology
721 Lawrence Street, NE
Washington, D.C. 20017
(202) 269-9410
Fax: (202) 526-2720

Dominican House of Studies—Dominican College
  Library
487 Michigan Avenue, NE
Washington, D.C. 20017
(202) 529-5300
Fax: (202) 636-4460

Friends Meeting of Washington—Library
2111 Florida Avenue
Washington, D.C. 20008-1912
(202) 483-3310
Fax: (202) 483-3312

Marist College Library
220 Taylor Street, NE
Washington, D.C. 20017
(202) 529-2821
Fax: (202) 635-4627

Oblate College Library
391 Michigan Avenue, NE
Washington, D.C. 20017-1587
(202) 529-6544

St. Paul's College Library
3015 4th Street, NE, Suite 540
Washington, D.C. 20017
(202) 832-6262
Fax: (202) 269-2507

Virginia Theological Seminary—Bishop Payne
  Library
3737 Seminary Road
Alexandria, Va. 22304
(703) 370-6602
Fax: (703) 370-6234

Washington Bible College/Capital Bible Seminary—
  Oyer Memorial Library
6511 Princess Garden Parkway
Lanham, Md. 20706
(301) 552-1400 ext. 231
Fax: (301) 552-2775

Washington Theological Union—Library
9001 New Hampshire Avenue
Silver Spring, Md. 20903
(301) 439-0551
Fax: (301) 445-4929

Wesley Theological Seminary—Library
4500 Massachusetts Avenue, NW
Washington, D.C. 20016-5690
(202) 885-8691

The following libraries, maintained mainly by the
U.S. armed forces, may hold relevant materials for
scholars interested in military history, military law,
and military science:

Air Force Legal Services Agency—Library
172 Luke Avenue, Suite 343
Bolling Air Force Base
Washington, D.C. 20332-5113
(202) 767-1558
Fax: (202) 767-3201

Army and Navy Club—Library
901 17th Street, NW
Washington, D.C. 20006-2503
(202) 628-8400
Fax: (202) 296-8787

Army Department—Fort Myer—Library
Building 469
Fort Myer, Va. 22211-5050
(703) 696-3555
Fax: (703) 696-8587

Army Department—Medal of Honor Library
Post Library, Building 4418
Fort Meade, Md. 20755-5086
(301) 677-4509
Fax: (301) 677-6228

Army Department—Van Noy Library
5966 12th Street
Fort Belvoir, Va. 22060-5554
(703) 806-3323
Fax: (703) 806-3422

Army Materiel Command—Headquarters
  Technical Library
5001 Eisenhower Avenue
Alexandria, Va. 22333-0001
(703) 274-8152
Fax: (703) 274-5588

Navy Department—Office of General Counsel Law
  Library
2211 Jefferson Davis Highway, Room 450
Arlington, Va. 22202
(703) 602-2750
Fax: (703) 602-4532

Navy Judge Advocate General—Law Library
200 Stovall Street
Alexandria, Va. 22332-2400
(703) 325-9565
Fax: (703) 325-9152

Soldiers' and Airmen's Home—King Health Care
  Patient Library
3700 North Capitol Street, NW
Scott Building
Washington, D.C. 20317
(202) 722-3319

Veterans Affairs Department—Central Office
Library
810 Vermont Avenue, NW
Washington, D.C. 20420
(202) 523-1612
Fax: (202) 535-7539

---

## AI Agency for International Development (AID) (International Development Cooperation Agency)—Development Information Center (DIC)

1.a. Center for Development Information and
Evaluation
1601 North Kent Street
Rosslyn, Va. 22209
(703) 875-4849
Fax: (703) 875-5269
Mailing Address:
CDIE/DI Room 209, SA-18

Agency for International Development
Washington, D.C. 20523-1802

b. 10:00 A.M.–4:00 P.M. Monday–Friday

c. The AID Development Information Center
(*formerly* AID library) is primarily for the use of
AID staff and current contractors. Local scholars
and development professionals may visit the library
to use the self-service reference collection of AID
materials and self-service terminals offering menu-
driven on-line access to the AID Development Information System (DIS) of documents and projects. Assistance from on-site reference staff is available. Dis-
tant users may request expert search services by
writing to the above address. Interlibrary loan service is available. On-site photocopying facilities are
limited and arrangements with the staff must be
made for more than 10 copies.

d. Maury Brown, Chief, Development Information Division
John E. Butsch, Coordinator, Development Information Center

2. The Development Information Center's holdings consist primarily of 100,000 documents on microfiche, 9,000 books, and 450 journal subscriptions. All of these materials are tightly focused on
development issues.

3.a. AID project documents, evaluations, and technical and research reports, produced since 1974 in
microfiche, are the bulk of the center's holdings.

These are accessed through DIS, an on-line
database. A brief search on the on-line system of the
following categories yielded the following numbers,
which represent titles: development assistance:
3,229; economic development: 2,901; economic
policy: 1,377; foreign assistance: 550; foreign trade:
237; environmental economics: 49; technical assistance: 2,763. The collection ranks in the B range for
the fields of economic history and conditions, and
international finance.

b. The center also holds a small but focused collection of books, reports, addresses, and occasional
papers on the history of AID and its predecessor organizations. This material covers major reports on
economic assistance and the organization of aid
agencies such as Mutual Security Agency (MSA) and
the International Cooperation Administration
(ICA). Considerable material relates to Point Four of
the Marshall Plan. These items are contained in a
bibliography, *Agency for International Development, Historical Materials at the AID Development
Information Center.* The center also holds miscellaneous records such as annual budget submissions,
congressional hearings back to the MSA (1951), reports, program evaluations, and other historical
information.

5. The center's material is accessed through DIS.
There is a thesaurus that provides key words used in
indexing AID documents.

6. Index Terms: Development Issues—Aid and
Investment

See also entries G2, G3, and KI

### American Association of University Women (AAUW)—Educational Foundation Library
See entry N4

### American Bar Association (ABA)—Section of International Law and Practice Library See entry M4

---

## A2 American Federation of Labor and Congress of Industrial Organizations (AFL-CIO)—Library

1.a. 10000 New Hampshire Avenue
Silver Spring, Md. 20903
(301) 431-5445
Fax: (301) 431-0385

b.  9:00 A.M.–4:30 P.M. Monday–Friday

c.  Open to the public for on-site use. Photocopying facilities available.

d.  Ruby U. Tyson, Librarian

2.  The library contains 10,000 volumes. Its principal relevance lies in international economics. Concerning the archival, audio, and film and photograph resources of the AFL-CIO's George Meany Memorial Archives, see entries B2, E2, and F3.

3.  The library's relevant holdings relate to international trade and economic relations, and international labor activity. The collection ranks in the B range for international organizations, and in the C range for commercial policy.

4.  The library receives approximately 175 general, policy, and economic periodicals; 83 union periodicals; and 40 newsletters and reports. Material of international relevance may be found in a vertical file that covers labor history and current topics pertaining to the period 1916 to present, labor union constitutions and proceedings.

5.  There is an on-line catalog, IME-Information Navigator.

6.  Index Terms: Conflict Management and Resolution—Unofficial and Nongovernmental Approaches; International Economics; International Organizations—Labor

See also entries B2, E2, and F3

---

## A3  American Society of International Law (ASIL)—Library

---

1.a.  2223 Massachusetts Avenue, NW
      Washington, D.C. 20008
      (202) 939-6005
      Fax: (202) 797-7133

b.  9:00 A.M.–4:00 P.M. Monday–Friday

c.  Open to the public. Interlibrary loan service is restricted to special circumstances and by annual fee. Photocopying facilities available.

d.  Jill Watson, Librarian

2.a–b.  The society's library contains an estimated 22,000 volumes on all aspects of public international law with virtually all the holdings directly relevant to the scope of this Guide.

3.a.  Although relatively small, the library is fully concentrated on international law and deals with the international legal aspect of many issues relevant to this Guide. The holdings rank in the A range for international law and international organizations, and in the C range for philosophical, psychological, and ethical aspects of war and peace, as well as for commercial policy and international relations.

The library contains a large selection of basic and classic texts of international law, including translations of Grotius, Alberico Gentili, Suárez, and others. The holdings also include a substantial number of general histories, perspectives, analyses, and essays regarding international law. Of particular interest is the complete set of *Collected Courses of the Hague Academy of International Law, 1923–1992*, with an index to 1960. The library contains an extensive collection on human rights, *The Israeli Yearbook on Human Rights, 1971–1990*, and the three-volume *Human Rights International Documents*, by James Avery Joyce (1978). Another substantial section relates to works on international organization, with over 100 volumes on the United Nations. Also well covered is the European Union and the International Court of Justice. There is another section that relates to enforcement of international sanctions, the law of war, laws of armed conflict, neutrality, and terrorism. Specific topics covered, in addition to general warfare, are nuclear weapons, biological warfare, and naval engagements.

There are also a number of works on how law relates to foreign policy and national security, such as, *National Security Law,* by John Norton Moore, Frederick S. Tipson, and Robert F. Turner (1990) and various works on arms control. There is also a section covering international trade and investment, and multinational corporations. Another section covers international environmental legal issues.

4.  The library receives over 200 journals, bulletins, reviews, and proceedings from around the world. The majority of these relate directly to international law or the legal affairs of particular countries. A number of them bear on international and political affairs more generally, such as, *International Studies, Journal of International Affairs,* and *Middle East Journal.* The library has a narrow selection of international organization documents; these include: *Yearbook of the International Law Commission of the United Nations; United Nations Resolutions,* Series I (General Assembly) and II (Security Council); *Yearbook of the European Convention on Human Rights (1955–1982).* It is a depository for documents of the General Agreement on Trade and

Tariffs (GATT). There are also documents of the Organization of American States (L13); European Union (L2); and Council of Europe. In addition, the holdings include a fairly wide selection of State Department (K37) documents.

5. The primary bibliographic aid is a card catalog. There is an in-house computerized index on which the librarian can locate works, including international law articles.

6. Index terms: Human Rights—and International Law; International Law; International Organizations; Religious, Philosophical, and Ethical Concepts of War and Peace; Terrorism

See also entry M9

---

## A4  American University (AU)—Bender Library

1.a.  4400 Massachusetts Avenue, NW
Washington, D.C. 20016
(202) 885-3238
Fax: (202) 885-1317

b.  Academic Year
8:00 A.M.–Midnight Monday–Thursday
8:00 A.M.–10:00 P.M. Friday
9:00 A.M.–9:00 P.M. Saturday
11:00 A.M.–Midnight Sunday
Summer Hours
9:00 A.M.–10:00 P.M. Monday–Thursday
9:00 A.M.–5:00 P.M. Friday
11:00 A.M.–6:00 P.M. Saturday and Sunday as posted

c.  The library's stacks and reading rooms are open to the public for on-site use. Interlibrary loan (to reciprocating libraries) and photocopying services are available.

d.  Patricia A. Wand, University Librarian

2.a.  Bender Library holdings total 550,000 volumes and it currently receives 4,500 periodicals and 80 newspapers.

b.  Based on measurements taken of the general collection, the holdings pertinent to peace studies and international security are estimated at 93,890 volumes. Among university libraries in the Washington, D.C., area, these holdings fall in the middle range, close to those of George Washington University (A19) and are exceeded only by those of George-

town University (A20) and the University of Maryland (A47).

3.a.  Bender Library's strengths pertinent to peace studies and international security are in the fields of international relations, and religious aspects of war and peace.

b.  In addition, the Peace and Conflict Resolution Studies program of the university (J1) has a small but select library of approximately 800 volumes focusing on conflict management.

c.  Subject categories and evaluations:

| Subject | Number of Titles | Rating |
| --- | --- | --- |
| Philosophy—War and Peace | 2,477 | B |
| Psychology—War and Peace | 3,422 | B |
| Ethics—War and Peace | 847 | B |
| Religion—War and Peace | 14,264 | B |
| World History | 7,237 | C |
| History—Military Science | 230 | C |
| Geography—Military | 5 | — |
| Anthropology—War and Peace | 324 | C |
| Economic History and Conditions | 10,595 | B |
| Commercial Policy | 2,254 | C |
| International Finance | 489 | B |
| Sociology | 5,366 | B |
| Political Theory | 2,601 | B |
| Constitutional History and Administration | 5,712 | B |
| Colonies and Emigration | 547 | B+ |
| International Relations | 2,454 | B+ |
| International Organizations | 2,954 | B |
| International Law | 669 | — |
| Education—International Relations and Military | 319 | C |
| Music—Military | 4 | — |
| Art and War | 14 | — |
| Military Science | 2,576 | C |
| Naval Science | 352 | C |
| Bibliography and Reference | 11 | — |

4. The Government Documents Room receives *Foreign Broadcast Information Service* in microform. The Media Services Department maintains a collection of over 2,000 titles in audio, video, and film formats. Approximately 200 of these are relevant to international security, international relations, or human rights. Video holdings include: "Vietnam: A Television History," and "Eyes on the Prize." Also relevant to international relations is the Drew Pearson Collection, including 897 broadcasts of his radio series "Washington Merry Go Round" from the period 1953–67. For information on access

and availability of transcripts contact James R. Heintze at (202) 885-3205.

5. In addition to ALADIN, the on-line catalog located throughout the library, there is a detailed printed catalog to the Non-Print Media Collection available in Non-Print Media on the lower level. The *Library Guide* offers a good introduction to the collections and is available without charge upon request at the Reference Desk.

6. Index Terms: Arms Control; Conflict Management and Resolution; Development Issues; Foreign Policy; Human Rights; Humanitarian Issues; International Organizations; Military Science; Peace Theory and Research

*Note:* The Washington College of Law Library (Patrick E. Kehoe, Director; John Heywood, Law Librarian; 202/885-2627), located at 4400 Massachusetts Avenue, NW, Washington, D.C., 20016-8087, is open to the public. Within its total collection of over 300,000 volumes, the Washington Law Library maintains an extensive collection of works on international law. In particular it encompasses the Richard Baxter Collection, which contains extensive material on the International Court of Justice. Other strengths include European Union material, especially from France and Great Britain, and human rights law, especially relating to humanitarian issues and law of war. The library maintains a complete set of United Nations documents on CD-ROM.

See also entry J1

---

## A5 Arms Control and Disarmament Agency (ACDA)—Technical Reference Center

1.a. 320 21st Street, NW, Room 5840
Washington, D.C. 20451
(202) 647-5969
Fax: (202) 647-6928

b. 8:00 A.M.–4:00 P.M. Monday–Friday

c. Open to researchers by appointment. Interlibrary loan and photocopying services are available.

d. Diane A. Ferguson, Librarian

2.a. The library holds 4,000 volumes, and subscribes to 200 serials. In the early 1980s a large proportion of earlier holdings was transferred to the George Washington University Library (A19).

b. All the library's material is pertinent to this guide, especially in regard to arms control.

3.a. The holdings rank in the A range for the field of international relations and in the B range for international organizations.

b. The library holds full sets of ACDA's annual publications: *Arms Control Impact Statements, World Military Expenditures and Arms Transfers,* and the *ACDA Annual Report.* The library collection also includes external research reports, agency reports, *Documents on Disarmament,* (1986) congressional reports on arms control, and arms control impact and budget statements.

This collection also contains conference reports from many United Nations arms control conferences and from conferences of parties to the nuclear nonproliferation treaty. There are dissertations, in microform, written under the Hubert H. Humphrey Fellowship. In addition, a small collection of books relates to arms control, international security, NATO, and related subjects.

4. The library receives approximately 200 periodicals; most recent issues circulate throughout the State Department. A vertical file contains speeches and miscellaneous reports in microform.

5. A card catalog registers items up to 1987; since 1987 the catalog has been computerized. Relevant journal articles are indexed up until 1992.

6. Index Terms: Arms Control; Diplomacy and Negotiations; International Organizations

See also entry K4

---

**Army Center of Military History (Army Department)—Library    See entry B3**

**Brookings Institution Library    See entry H8**

---

## A6 Carnegie Endowment for International Peace—Library

1.a. 2400 N Street NW
Washington, D.C. 20037-1153
(202) 862-7970
Fax: (202) 862-2610

b. 9:00 A.M.–5:00 P.M. Monday–Friday

c. The library is not open to the public. Interlibrary loan is available.

d. Jennifer L. Little, Librarian

2.a–b. The library contains 7,000 volumes and receives 220 periodicals. All of these are pertinent to peace and international security studies.

3.a. The library has a small but very focused collection of peace and international security books. The primary subjects are international relations, international law, and peace studies in support of the research interests of the endowment. The collection ranks in the A range for the field of international relations and in the C range for international law. Research focuses on countries and geographical regions including Cyprus, Turkey, Central Asia, the Caribbean, Germany, Europe, South Asia, East Asia, Russia, and the former Soviet republics. Subject areas of research include: nonproliferation, multilateral international institutions, arms control in the Middle East, immigration, and national security law.

b. The library does not maintain a collection of reports done for Carnegie Endowment by its associates. Such reports are maintained within departments, which will mail them out. For further information, contact the endowment, (202) 862-7900.

5. There is an on-line catalog of books in the collection.

6. Index Terms: Arms Control; International Law; International Organizations; Peace Theory and Research

See also entry H9

---

# A7 Catholic University of America (CUA)— Mullen Library

1.a. 620 Michigan Avenue, NE
Washington, D.C. 20064
(202) 319-5055 (Administrative Offices)
(202) 319-5070 (Reference)
Fax: (202) 319-6101

b. Academic Year
9:00 A.M.–10:00 P.M. Monday–Thursday
9:00 A.M.–6:00 P.M. Friday–Saturday
Noon–10:00 P.M. Sunday
Summer and holiday hours vary considerably. Visitors should call (202) 319-5077 for current hours.

c. Open to public for on-site use; borrowing privileges are restricted. Visiting researchers should in-

quire at the Office of the Director (202/319-5055) about temporary borrowing arrangements. Interlibrary loan and photocopying services are available.

d. Adele R. Chwalek, Director

2.a. The total collection numbers over 1,277,000 volumes and the library receives some 7,000 periodicals.

b. Based on measurements taken of the general collection, holdings pertaining to international security and peace studies are estimated at 65,020 volumes.

3.a. The primary relevant strengths of this collection are in philosophy and theology especially relating to the medieval period. Among area university libraries Mullen is strongest in philosophical, psychological, and ethical aspects of war, just war doctrine, and liberation theology. It also contains major Roman law and canon law collections.

b. The Rare Books and Special Collections section of the library is a unique source for research on the history of international law and theology. The 9,800-volume Clementine collection, comprising part of the library of the Italian Clementine family (which included among its members Pope Clement XI), features a wide range of rare books on church law and history, 1473–1870. Included in this collection are complete original editions of the writings of the Spanish theologian and legal theoretician Francisco Suárez (1548–1617). The 1,000-volume canon law collection features original editions of works by Aquinas, Erasmus, and other major church writers. The rare book holdings also include:
Francisco de Vitoria (1486–1546), a theorist on natural law and the rights of nations.
A considerable number of works by Hugo Grotius (1583–1645) on international law along with commentaries based on Grotius, notably by John Selden (1584–1654), about dominion and ownership of the sea.
The *Foedera* (1727), by Thomas Rymer, a source book for diplomatic agreements between England and other powers, especially France and the Vatican.
Further relevant material can be found in the Knights of Malta collection.

c. Subject categories and evaluations:

| Subject | Number of Titles | Rating |
|---|---|---|
| Philosophy—War and Peace | 11,141 | B+ |
| Psychology—War and Peace | 4,992 | B+ |
| Ethics—War and Peace | 1,937 | B+ |

| Subject | Number of Titles | Rating |
|---|---|---|
| Religion—War and Peace | 5,099 | B |
| World History | 5,594 | C |
| History—Military Science | 127 | — |
| Geography—Military | 4 | — |
| Anthropology—War and Peace | 167 | C |
| Economic History and Conditions | 2,505 | — |
| Commercial Policy | 635 | — |
| International Finance | 247 | C |
| Sociology | 4,691 | C |
| Political Theory | 2,217 | B |
| Constitutional History and Administration | 2,822 | B |
| Colonies and Emigration | 69 | C |
| International Relations | 943 | B |
| International Organizations | 1,007 | C |
| International Law | 409 | — |
| Education—International Relations and Military | 111 | — |
| Music—Military | 8 | — |
| Art and War | 4 | — |
| Military Science | 712 | — |
| Naval Science | 51 | — |
| Bibliography and Reference | 21 | — |

4. The Department of Archives and Manuscripts holds the following pertinent items:

The 1919–70 records of the National Catholic Welfare Council, predecessor to the United States Catholic Conference (NCWC/USCC). These include the papers of the Legal Department General Counsel covering congressional matters such as national defense and wartime measures, and foreign and international relations (1929–62). The archives also holds the records of the NCWC/USCC Office of UN Affairs (1946–70); the NCWC/USCC Executive Department Latin American Bureau records (1928–70); and the National Catholic War Council Papers (1917–33). Holdings also include the annual reports of the NCWC Social Action Department; the *Minutes of the Annual Meeting of the Bishops* (1919–65); and the *Minutes of the Administrative Board of the NCWC* (1930–66). The latter two items are indexed by subject matter.

The Rev. Charles W. Perrier Papers. Perrier was bishop of Matanzas, Cuba, during World War I; his papers also contain scattered materials on the Mexican Revolution.

The Rev. Donald A. McClean Papers. McClean was Professor of International Relations and Political Science at Trinity College and was interested in the Catholic Church, disarmament, and world peace.

Generally, finding-aids for archive materials are exceedingly rudimentary. For information, contact archivist Anthony Zito (202/319-5065).

5. On the second floor of the Mullen Library is located the central dictionary card catalog. Equally important works, however, are only described in small, separate catalogs located in other parts of the building. Significant early holdings cataloged under the Decimal Classification System appear to have escaped contemporary record keeping.

Today the Mullen Library follows the Library of Congress classification schedules, modified in some areas, for its collection, except for materials on ecclesiastical literature, theology, canon law, and church history. For literature in these subjects, *An Alternate Classification for Catholic Books* is used. For current periodicals received by the library, separate mimeographed lists on humanities, social sciences, and theology-philosophy are available in the respective divisions. A useful pamphlet, *General Library Handbook,* is provided.

6. Index Terms: Diplomacy and Negotiations; Foreign Policy; Human Rights; Humanitarian Issues; International Law; Religious, Philosophical, and Ethical Concepts of War and Peace; Peace Theory and Research; Psychological Aspects of War and Peace

*Note:* Catholic University's Robert J. White Law Library (Stephen G. Margeton, Director, 202/319-5155), located at 620 Michigan Avenue, NW, Room 102, Washington, D.C., 20064, is closed to the public. Scholars wishing to use the library must contact it. White Library contains 200,000 volumes. Its emphasis is primarily on domestic law with relatively light holdings on international law.

See also entry J2

---

## A8 Census Bureau Library (Commerce Department)

---

1.a. Federal Office Building 3, Wing 4, Room 2455
Suitland Road and Silver Hill Road
Suitland, Md.
(301) 763-5042 (Reference)
Fax: (301) 763-7322

Center for International Research (CIR)
Washington Plaza II, Room 109
8905 Presidential Parkway
Upper Marlboro, Md. 20772
(301) 457-1390

Mail: Bureau of the Census Library
Room 2455, FOB 3
Washington, D.C. 20233

b. 8:00 A.M.–5:00 P.M. Monday–Friday

c. Open to the public. Interlibrary loan and photocopying services are available.

d. Jeane Bothe, Project Manager
Grace Barnas, Library Technician, CIR

2.a. Total holdings are approximately 300,000 volumes and 4,000 serials divided between the Census Bureau Library and the CIR. The bulk of the material consists of U.S. and foreign statistical materials (censuses, yearbooks, bulletins) and monographs on statistics and demography.

b. Materials pertinent to the scope of this Guide, aside from foreign population data, include holdings on ethnic minorities, emigration and immigration, and economic development. Approximately 150,000 volumes pertain to these areas.

3.a. In 1993 the collection was split between the Census Bureau Library and the CIR; all foreign census material was transferred to the CIR. The library retained domestic census data and the general collection. Foreign demographic material at the CIR includes national censuses, yearbooks, statistical abstracts, country studies, gazetteers, United Nations publications, foreign serials, and annuals. This material is arranged by country.

The general collection contains books on population growth and forecasting by country with fairly comprehensive global representation. Other strengths are population policy and research. Material on legal status, policy, and statistical information regarding refugees, emigration, and immigration is moderately well represented according to various countries.

For the fields of economic history and conditions, commercial policy, and colonies and emigration the materials rank in the A range.

b. Most foreign census materials are kept in the CIR library, but there are two exceptions. Chinese census data are held in the China Branch (Lorraine West, Chief, Room 117, 301/763-4012) of the CIR; census data pertaining to the successor states of the former Soviet Union are in CIR's Eurasia Branch (Mark Rubin, Chief, Room 114, 301/763-4020).

5. All cataloging, processing, and technical services are still done at the library. The card catalog is divided into two sections: one covering authors and titles; the second covering subjects. The pre-1976 records have been published as the *Catalogs of the Bu-*

*reau of the Census Library* (Boston: G. K. Hall, 1976). The five-volume *Supplement* (1979) contains records for titles processed up to 1979. Lists of current acquisitions and current periodicals are also available.

6. Index Terms: Development Issues—Population Policy; Ethnic and Religious Conflict; International Economics

See also entries G6 and K7

## Center for Defense Information (CDI) Library See entry H11

## Center for Naval Analysis (CNA) Library See entry H16

---

## A9 Center for Strategic and International Studies (CSIS)—Library

1.a. 1800 K Street, NW, Suite 400
Washington, D.C. 20006
(202) 887-0200
Fax: (202) 775-3199

b. 9:00 A.M.–5:00 P.M. Monday–Friday

c. Access to non-CSIS researchers is by appointment only and primarily in cases where material cannot be located at other libraries. Interlibrary loan is available. Access to photocopying facilities must be arranged with library staff.

d. Kari Anderson, Librarian

2.a. The CSIS library contains approximately 4,500 volumes and receives 200 periodicals.

b. The library focuses on international security issues and area studies.

3.a. The library was started in 1989 to serve as a central reference facility for CSIS researchers. The collection ranks in the A range for the field of international relations and promises to grow further. Aside from holding standard reference works, the library attempts to provide center researchers access to a wide variety of data. In addition to programs covering most regions of the globe, the center maintains programs in the following areas: energy, economic and business policy, international communications, international economic and social development, political-military studies, and science and technology. The library maintains a comprehensive collection of CSIS publications. It also attempts to collect CSIS conference proceedings and materials.

5. An on-line catalog is available.

6. Index Terms: Arms Control; Defense Policy, National; Deterrence; Military Science—Strategy and Tactics; Peace Theory and Research

See also entry H18

**Central Intelligence Agency (CIA) Library**
**See entry K6**

## A10  Commerce Department Library

1.a. 14th Street and Constitution Avenue, NW,
Room 7046
Washington, D.C. 20230
(202) 482-5511
Fax: (202) 482-5685

b. 9:00 A.M.–4:30 P.M. Monday–Friday

c. Open to the public for on-site use: 1:00 P.M.–4:30 P.M. Monday–Friday. Photocopying services and interlibrary loan are available.

d. Anthony J. Steinhauser, Director

2.a. Holdings total approximately 55,000 volumes on economics and trade. The library receives over 600 periodicals.

b. Approximately 5 percent of the collection is international in scope. It is relevant to this Guide principally in terms of international finance, international trade, and international organization. It ranks in the B range for the fields of commercial policy, international finance, and international organizations.

3.a. The collection primarily focuses on economics, industry, marketing and trade. It has light holdings in international relations, organization, and law. Its holdings on economic history and conditions worldwide and on commercial policy rank in the B range, and international finance in the C range. Included are reports and statistical bulletins of government ministries, trade bureaus, tariff commissions, commercial agencies, and central banks, along with scattered research reports and country studies by U.S. government agencies, the World Bank (L8), Organization of American States (L13), and other international organizations. Holdings of Commerce De-

partment publications—current and retrospective—are strong.

4. Researchers who desire specific, current information about foreign trade statistics may consult the Foreign Trade Reference Room (Room 2233), a division of the International Trade Administration (ITA).

5. The library has a CD-ROM catalog.

6. Index Terms: Development Issues; International Economics—International Finance—International Trade; International Organizations

*Note:* Several bureaus and subagencies of the Commerce Department maintain separate libraries, reference collections, or both.

See also entries A8, K7, and K29

**Commerce Department—Patent and Trademark Office—Scientific and Technical Information Center    See entry K7**

**Consortium of Universities of the Washington Metropolitan Area—Washington Research Library Consortium    See entry J4**

**Consortium on Peace Research, Education, and Development (COPRED) Library    See entry M24**

## A11  Education Department—Research Library

1.a. 555 New Jersey Avenue, NW, Room 101
Washington, D.C. 20208-1239
(202) 219-1884
Fax: (202) 219-1696

b. 9:00 A.M.–4:00 P.M. Monday–Friday

c. The library is open to the public. Interlibrary loan and photocopying services are available.

d. Robert Leestma, Acting Director

2.a. The library holds some 216,000 volumes. The library's 650 serial subscriptions relate mostly to education.

b. Approximately 3,200 volumes in the collection pertain to security and peace studies primarily in terms of cognitive psychology.

3.a. For research on international security and peace studies the library has C-ranked holdings in psychological aspects of war and peace, sociology, and constitutional history and administration.

b. The holdings include a large number of bibliographic and reference works.

5. Researchers must consult two separate finding-aids: for recent acquisition, a CD-ROM catalog (updated monthly); for older materials, a 20-volume publication, *National Institute of Education, Subject Catalog of the Department Library* (Boston: G. K. Hall, 1965) with a four-volume supplement (1973). The library staff includes specialists in the fields of education and statistics.

6. Index Terms: Conflict Resolution and Management; Political Systems and Ideologies; Psychological Aspects of War and Peace

See also entry K11

## A12 Energy Department (DOE) — Library

1.a. Germantown Branch
Routes 270 and 118
Germantown, Md. 20545
(301) 903-4166
Fax: (301) 903-3960

Forrestal Branch (D.C.)
Forrestal Building GA-138
1000 Independence Avenue, SW
Washington, D.C. 20585
(202) 586-9534
Fax: (202) 586-9534

b. 8:30 A.M.–5:00 P.M. Monday–Friday

c. Direct access is restricted to agency employees and authorized contractors. However, limited telephone reference, as well as interlibrary loan and photocopying services, are available to the general public.

d. Jeanne M. Perrone, Supervisor, Germantown Branch
Norman N. Barbee, Supervisor, Forrestal Branch

2.a. The combined library holdings total more than 55,000 book volumes and 2,500 periodical titles. There are also 1 million uncataloged technical reports.

b. About 10 percent of the library's holdings pertain to arms control and deterrence and to economic development.

3.a. The combined holdings of the library rank in the B range for international relations and economic history and conditions.

b. The Germantown Branch collects the bulk of the technical material and some economic literature. Here are housed international reports and proceedings of international conferences. The Forrestal Branch maintains an international collection on energy statistics.

5. The library's catalogs are fully automated with all bibliographic records stored on-line. A complete listing of cataloged books is updated annually and is available for on-site use at each branch. Access to the on-line catalogs (the Power File) is commercially available from ORBIT, 8000 West Park Drive, Suite 400, McLean, Va. 22102 (703/442-0900).

6. Index Terms: Arms Control; Development Issues; Energy; Environmental Issues, Global

See also B5 and K12

**Environmental Protection Agency (EPA) Library** See entry K13

## A13 European Union — Delegation of the European Commission — Press and Public Affairs Office

1.a. 2100 M Street, NW, 7th Floor
Washington, D.C. 20037
(202) 862-9565
Fax: (202) 429-1766

b. 10:00 A.M.–4:00 P.M. Monday–Thursday

c. The library is open to the public by appointment only. Interlibrary loan and photocopying services are available.

d. Barbara Sloan, Head of Public Inquiries

2.a. The library houses more than 50,000 titles including all public European Union publications.

b. Virtually the entire collection of the library lies in the relevant fields of economic development and the environment, international law, and international organizations.

3.a–b.  The collection ranks in the A range for international organizations and in the B range for commercial policy, international finance, international relations, and international law. It is strongly focused on the areas of international trade, monetary policies, environmental studies, European Community (EU) legal affairs, and all other areas in which the EU has worked. Researchers will find extensive data on all European countries that are EC members. These data are contained in comparative studies of member nations and studies devoted solely to individual countries.

4.  Vertical files are maintained for articles, pamphlets, documents, etc. These are arranged into 1,000 subject files, providing a valuable resource on EU activities. The library maintains a small collection of maps that indicate nuclear power plants, oil resources, and land use, among other topics.

5.  A highly detailed catalog analyzes the holdings according to author, title, series, and subject. Holdings are classified according to the Universal Decimal Classification (UDC) system.

6.  Index Terms: Collective Security—Regional Alliance Systems; Development Issues; International Economics—Integration; International Organizations—Regional

See also entries F9 and L2

---

## A14  Export-Import Bank of the United States — Library

1.a.  811 Vermont Avenue, NW
Washington, D.C. 20571
(202) 566-8320
Fax: (202) 566-7524

b.  8:30 A.M.–5:00 P.M. Monday–Friday

c.  The library is open to the public on a limited basis by appointment only. Interlibrary loan service is available. Photocopying facilities are not available.

d.  Eugene H. Ferguson, Librarian

2.a.  Holdings total 15,000 books and 1,000 periodicals, as well as 25,000 documents.

b.  Virtually the entire collection is relevant to this Guide for the fields of international economics and economic development.

3.a.  The collection ranks in the A range for commercial policy and international finance. Holdings emphasize statistical data, central bank reports, and the subject areas of commerce, finance, international banking, developmental economics, and trade. The library holds a considerable number of general serials relating to international economics and political affairs. The majority relate to economic conditions, including statistical sources, of specific countries or regions. The library has various country studies, including the *Economist Intelligence Unit*, and receives approximately a dozen political affairs journals. Periodicals are retained for approximately two years.

b.  An impressive collection of 25,000 documents, both public and private, concerns foreign trade, finance, international economy, and business. The arrangement is by country.

5.  An on-line catalog is being prepared. A periodicals list is available upon request.

6.  Index Terms: Development Issues; International Economics—International Finance; International Economics—International Trade

See also entry K14

---

## A15  Federal Emergency Management Agency—Library

1.a.  500 C Street, SW, Room 123
Washington, D.C. 20472
(202) 646-3768
Fax: (202) 646-4255

b.  8:30 A.M.–4:30 P.M. Monday–Friday

c.  The library is open to the public with restrictions, by appointment only. For interlibrary loan information contact Arlett H. Leigh. Photocopying facilities are available.

d.  Mercedes L. Emperado, Librarian

2.a.  The collection holds 6,000 volumes and receives 150 serials.

b.  Within the collection, 3,500 volumes concern civil defense and 2,500 disaster-related problems. The primary relevance of this library lies in arms control and deterrence, and military science.

3.a.  In the fields of psychological aspects of warfare and of military science the library's holdings rank in the B range. The collection provides very thorough information on all aspects of civil defense, including history, budgeting, social and psychological studies, and postattack research. There are also research reports on Soviet civil defense.

4. The library receives 50 periodicals. There are 5,000 photographs and 3,000 slides on disaster-related subjects. In addition, the holdings include over 300 video cassettes on security education relating to terrorism and espionage.

5. There is a card catalog.

6. Index Terms: Military Science—Civil Defense and Effects of Nuclear War; Terrorism

---

## AI6 Federal Reserve System (FRS)— Library

1.a. 20th and C Streets, NW, Room BC-241
Washington, D.C. 20551
(202) 452-3332
Fax: (202) 452-3819

b. 9:00 A.M.–5:00 P.M. Thursday

c. The library is open, with restrictions, Thursday only. Call before 2:30 P.M. on Wednesday for appointment. Local area interlibrary loan and limited photocopying facilities are available.

d. Susan R. Vincent, Chief Librarian

2.a. The library's collection contains 60,000 volumes and 2,000 periodicals.

b. About one-third of the library's holdings fall within the scope of this Guide, concerning international economics.

3.a. The subject strengths of the library are banking, finance, and monetary policy of the U.S. and foreign governments. The collection ranks within the A range for international finance and within the B range for commercial policy. A lesser strength is the area of economic history and conditions.

b. A special collection covers the history of the Federal Reserve System.

4. Included among the serials are bank bulletins and newsletters, general statistical bulletins, central-bank annual reports, bank superintendents' reports, government financial reports, foreign trade reports, treasury bulletins, national development corporation reports, and national development plans. Some

of the periodical holdings are retained by the library for only one or two years. Holdings of major bank bulletins from some countries, however, extend back to the 1930s. The library has U.S. government documents on monetary policy since 1913.

5. With a few exceptions, the collection is searchable electronically.

6. Index Terms: Development Issues; International Economics—International Finance; International Economics—International Trade

See also entry K15

---

## AI7 Food and Agriculture Organization (FAO) (United Nations)—Liaison Office for North America—Library

1.a. 1001 22nd Street, NW, Suite 300
Washington, D.C. 20437
(202) 653-2402
Fax: (202) 653-5760

b. 10:00 A.M.–5:00 P.M. Monday–Friday

c. The library is open to researchers by appointment only. Interlibrary loan is not available; limited photocopying services are available.

d. Marva Coates, Librarian

2.a. The FAO's Washington office library contains a small, but useful, reference collection.

b. The library's chief relevance lies in the fields of economic development and international organizations.

3. The holdings, which rank in the B range for the field of international organizations and the C range for commercial policy, include reports and papers of the regional conferences and FAO budget and conference reports, as well as other documents issued by the organization. These include: a regional trade outlook for the Uruguay Round of GATT; statistical yearbooks on world agriculture production and trade, fisheries, forest products, and livestock health; the organization's nutritional and agricultural studies, world agricultural commodity reviews and projections; FAO's *Monthly Bulletin of Statistics;* the bimonthly *Ceres: FAO Review on Agriculture and Development;* the organization's series *Food and Agriculture Legislation;* an index to FAO documents; and a bulletin, *FAO at Work,* published by the Washington office.

5. FAO documents' indexes are available in the library. Also see the sales pamphlet *FAO New and Most Recommended Titles,* which contains information on how to order FAO publications from the sales agent, Unipub, 4611-F Assembly Drive, Lanham, Md. 20706; telephone (301) 459-7666.

6. Index Terms: Economic Development—Agriculture; International Economics; International Organizations

See also entry L3

### Fort George G. Meade Army Museum (Army Department)    See entry C3

### General Accounting Office (GAO) Library    See entry K18

---

# A18    George Mason University (GMU)— Fenwick Library

---

1.a.  4400 University Drive
Fairfax, Va. 22030
(703) 993-2210
Fax: (703) 993-2229

b.  7:30 A.M.–Midnight Monday–Thursday
7:30 A.M.–9:00 P.M. Friday
9:00 A.M.–9:00 P.M. Saturday
9:00 A.M.–Midnight Sunday
Hours vary during intercession.

c.  Fenwick Library is open to the public for on-site use. Interlibrary loan and photocopying facilities are available.

d.  Charlene S. Hurt, Director
Laura O. Rein, Associate Director and Head of Reference

2.a.  The library's holdings total about 432,500 volumes, and the library receives approximately 4,700 periodicals.

b.  Based on measurements taken of the general collection, holdings related to international security and peace studies consist of approximately 47,540 volumes and 444 periodicals.

3.a.  Fenwick Library's overall holdings are somewhat smaller than other universities in the area, but there is significant strength in the fields of international relations, ethical, philosophical, and psychological aspects of war and peace, and military music.

b.  In addition, since 1990 the library has been building a collection to support the university's conflict resolution and mediation program. These books focus on techniques and facilitation of the mediation process and are integrated into the general collection. This collection is expected to grow substantially every year from its current (1994) 1,000 titles.

c.  Subject categories and evaluations:

| Subject | Number of Titles | Rating |
|---|---|---|
| Philosophy—War and Peace | 2,801 | B |
| Psychology—War and Peace | 4,302 | B+ |
| Ethics—War and Peace | 712 | B |
| Religion—War and Peace | 2,579 | C |
| World History | 3,136 | C |
| History—Military Science | 161 | — |
| Geography—Military | 4 | — |
| Anthropology—War and Peace | 186 | C |
| Economic History and Conditions | 3,664 | — |
| Commercial Policy | 1,067 | C |
| International Finance | 426 | C |
| Sociology | 5,223 | B |
| Political Theory | 1,931 | B |
| Constitutional History and Administration | 3,475 | B |
| Colonies and Emigration | 47 | — |
| International Relations | 997 | B |
| International Organizations | 757 | C |
| International Law | 373 | — |
| Education—International Relations and Military | 158 | — |
| Music—Military | 53 | A |
| Art and War | 7 | — |
| Military Science | 1,116 | — |
| Naval Science | 84 | — |
| Bibliography and Reference | 25 | — |

4.  Periodicals relevant to peace studies are broken down as follows: public affairs, 110; policy, 21; economics, 96; history, 107; philosophy and religion, 100.

Fenwick Library's Special Collections and Archives (703/993-2220) holds the following relevant archival collections:

Milton Barnes Civil War Correspondence (1 lin. ft.) contains dispatches, photos, and personal observations.

Herbert Feis/Arline Pratt Manuscript Collection (2 lin. ft.).

Alexander Haight Civil War Collection (118 lin. ft.) consists of journals, household records, and military records.

Edwin Lynch Collection contains material relating to Vietnam protests in Fairfax County.

John P. Shacochis Collection (9 lin. ft.) consists primarily of reports from naval career and campaign material.

Saundra Moore Memorial Library on Vietnamese-American Cultural Relations (6 lin. ft.).

Fenwick Library's Special Collections and Archives also holds significant photographic collections bearing on international security, particularly the Ollie Atkins Photographic Collection, which contains more than 15,000 negatives, contact sheets, and photographs from the period 1946–68. Atkins was an international and war photographer for the *Saturday Evening Post* and White House photographer under Richard M. Nixon. The collection includes files for Dwight D. Eisenhower, John F. Kennedy, Robert Kennedy, and Lyndon B. Johnson.

The library's Audiovisual Resource Center (703/993-2205) has films relating to the following topics: conflict resolution, 11 titles; history, 57 titles; mediation, 9 titles; war, 12 titles; Vietnam, 113 titles (fiction and nonfiction); World War II, 24 titles (fiction and nonfiction).

5. Fenwick Library uses the on-line NOTIS system. There is also a large collection of CD-ROM databases available.

6. Index Terms: Arms Control; Conflict Management and Resolution; Development Issues; Foreign Policy; International Organizations; Military Science; Peace Theory and Research; Psychological Aspects of War and Peace

See also entry J5

---

## AI9  George Washington University (GWU)—Gelman Library

---

1.a. 2130 H Street, NW
Washington, D.C. 20052
(202) 994-6558 (Information)
(202) 994-6047 (Reference)
Fax: (202) 994-2645

b. For most of the academic year the building is open:
7:00 A.M.–Midnight Monday–Friday
9:00 A.M.–10:00 P.M. Saturday
9:00 A.M.–Midnight Sunday
Service desks do not open until 9:00 A.M. on weekdays and 10:00 A.M. on weekends.

Hours vary during examination periods, summer sessions, and at certain other times. For information regarding library hours, call (202) 994-6845.

c. Open to the public for on-site use except on weekends or evenings during examination periods. Visitors are required to present currently valid photo identification and register at the entrance. Interlibrary loan service and photocopying facilities are available.

d. Jack Siggins, University Librarian

2.a. The library collection totals 1,257,432 volumes. It currently receives over 11,000 periodicals.

b. Based on measurements taken of the general collection, approximately 91,420 volumes pertain to peace studies and international security. Among university libraries in the Washington, D.C., area, these holdings fall by size into the middle range, close to those of American University (A4), and are exceeded only by those of Georgetown University (A20) and the University of Maryland (A47).

3.a. The library is strong in philosophy, psychology, political theory, constitutional history and administration, and international relations and organization. In the 1950s the library purchased a substantial collection, numbering more than 3,500 volumes, mainly in the field of international law, from the Carnegie Endowment for International Peace Library (A6) and integrated it into the general collection. These volumes constitute a substantial source relevant to peace and international security studies within the larger Gelman collection. In the early 1980s, Gelman library acquired a substantial number of volumes from the library of the Arms Control and Disarmament Agency (A5), dealing mainly with arms control and deterrence.

b. The Special Collections Division houses a small number of works by Hugo Grotius relating to international law. There is a 1689 copy of *De jure belli ac pacis* printed in Amsterdam, along with a 1715 English translation. There are also editions of *De mare libero* (1633) and *Epistolae ad Gallos* (1648). There is a French edition (1926) in the main collection of Grotius's letters to family and friends.

The Information Center for the Former Soviet Union, Eastern Europe, and East Asia (Cathy Zeljak, Subject Specialist for Slavic, East European, and East Asian Studies; Craig H. Seibert, Coordinator; 202/994-7105) is part of Gelman Library and maintains a noncirculating reference and research collection. The collection is housed in Room 603 of the library and focuses primarily on post–World War II political, economic, military, and social issues of the successor states of the former Soviet Union, Eastern Europe, and East Asia. It contains approximately 2,500 reference volumes, 17,750 microfiche, 600 microfilm roles, and 1,150 feet of bound periodical volumes.

c.  Subject categories and evaluations:

| Subject | Number of Titles | Rating |
|---|---|---|
| Philosophy—War and Peace | 4,091 | B |
| Psychology—War and Peace | 4,452 | B+ |
| Ethics—War and Peace | 4,299 | A |
| Religion—War and Peace | 1,369 | — |
| World History | 8,596 | B |
| History—Military Science | 218 | C |
| Geography—Military | 13 | — |
| Anthropology—War and Peace | 163 | C |
| Economic History and Conditions | 8,628 | B |
| Commercial Policy | 3,713 | B |
| International Finance | 813 | B |
| Sociology | 7,013 | B |
| Political Theory | 2,619 | B |
| Constitutional History and Administration | 4,522 | B |
| Colonies and Emigration | 165 | B |
| International Relations | 5,089 | A |
| International Organizations | 3,179 | B |
| International Law | 1,615 | C |
| Education—International Relations and Military | 471 | B |
| Music—Military | 2 | — |
| Art and War | 75 | B |
| Military Science | 2,321 | C |
| Naval Science | 317 | C |
| Bibliography and Reference | 252 | C |

4.  The Information Center for the Former Soviet Union, Eastern Europe, and East Asia maintains a large collection of foreign newspapers and periodicals. All are relevant to peace and international security studies, with a heavy emphasis on economics, politics, and foreign relations. Titles of particular note include: *Foreign Broadcast Information Service (FBIS)* (in hardcopy since 1962 and with its own current index on CD-ROM), *Joint Publications Research Service (JPRS),* and Radio Free Europe and Radio Liberty publications. The center currently subscribes to 175 periodicals relating to the successor states of the former Soviet Union and Eastern Europe, and approximately 80 focusing on East Asia, especially China and Japan. Eight periodicals focus specifically on peace or security studies.

Gelman Library's map collection is described in entry D2. In addition, the center holds 1,400 relevant maps and atlases.

The Media Resources Department (Gerald Phillips, 202/994-6378) can assist researchers in accessing the Vanderbilt University News Archives. The Vanderbilt Archives maintains and lends its collection of evening newscasts and special events from ABC, NBC, and CBS dating from 1968. The center also provides referral services on the archive collections of National Archives and Records Administration, ABC, NBC, CBS, and the Library of Congress. For finding broadcasts relevant to peace studies and international security, researchers should consult *Television News Index and Abstracts: A Guide to the Videotape Collection of the Network Evening News Programs* (1968–) published monthly by the Vanderbilt Television News Archives.

5.  Gelman Library is part of the Washington Research Library Consortium and shares the on-line ALADIN system with the six other consortium members. As of fall 1992, the ALADIN system had more than 2.2 million catalog records out of a total of more than 5 million volumes throughout the consortium. All materials of the Sino-Soviet Information Center are included on ALADIN.

6.  Index Terms: Arms Control; Conflict Management and Resolution; Development Issues; Deterrence; Diplomacy and Negotiations; Foreign Policy; Human Rights; International Organizations; Military Science; Naval Science; Political Systems and Ideologies; Psychological Aspects of War and Peace; Religious, Philosophical, and Ethical Concepts of War and Peace

*Note:* George Washington University's Jacob Burns Law Library (Paul Zarins, International Law Librarian, 202/676-6648), located at 716 20th Street, NW, Washington, D.C. 20052, is open to the public. Burns library, although smaller than Georgetown's, for example, still offers a substantial collection. It is particularly strong on international human rights. It has moderate strengths on international organizations.

See also entries D2 and J6

## A20  Georgetown University—Lauinger Library

1.a.  37th and N Streets, NW
Washington, D.C. 20057-1006
(202) 687-7452 (Reference)
Fax: (202) 687-1215

b. Hours of operation vary for the multiple services offered by Lauinger Library. Reference help is available and the book stacks are open during the following periods:

8:30 a.m.–Midnight Monday–Thursday
8:30 A.M.–10:00 P.M. Friday
10:00 A.M.–10:00 P.M. Saturday
11:00 a.m.–Midnight Sunday
Holiday and summer hours may differ.

c. The library is open to the public. Interlibrary loan and photocopying services are available.

d. Susan K. Martin, University Librarian

2.a. The library collection numbers some 1,175,000 volumes, and the library currently receives 11,940 periodicals.

b. Based on measurement taken of the general collection, Lauinger Library holds approximately 121,170 volumes pertaining to peace studies and international security, making it the strongest collection in these fields among the university libraries in the Washington, D.C., area. (Outside the university libraries, it is, of course, exceeded in size by the Library of Congress [A29], as well as the relevant holdings of the State Department Library [A43], and those of several specialized military libraries, attached to the National Defense University [A33], Navy Department [A36], and Pentagon [A41].)

3.a. Lauinger Library's holdings in peace and security studies are integrated into the general collection and they reflect the strengths of the overall holdings. There are substantial collections on philosophy, ethics, psychology, history, international finance, political theory, constitutional history and administration, and international relations. Geographic areas in which the collection is strong are the United States, Europe, including Russia, Latin America, and the Middle East.

b. Located on the lower level of Lauinger Library, Woodstock Theological Library (202/687-7513, open 8:30 A.M.–5:30 P.M. Monday–Friday) contains approximately 180,000 volumes. Only about 100 of these volumes deal strictly with the issues of war and peace, but many other volumes discuss the morality of war and peace. Woodstock's collection consists mostly of Catholic theology, although Protestant and Jewish theology are also represented. Similarly, Woodstock has a substantial collection of ethical and philosophical works, as well as its theological works.

c. Subject categories and evaluations:

| Subject | Number of Titles | Rating |
|---|---|---|
| Philosophy—War and Peace | 9,807 | B+ |
| Psychology—War and Peace | 5,168 | B+ |
| Ethics—War and Peace | 1,870 | B+ |
| Religion—War and Peace | 6,715 | B |
| World History | 12,108 | B |
| History—Military Science | 463 | B |
| Geography—Military | 25 | C |
| Anthropology—War and Peace | 165 | C |
| Economic History and Conditions | 12,498 | B |
| Commercial Policy | 3,550 | B |
| International Finance | 1,170 | B+ |
| Sociology | 7,126 | C |
| Political Theory | 4,644 | B+ |
| Constitutional History and Administration | 6,313 | B+ |
| Colonies and Emigration | 191 | B |
| International Relations | 2,795 | B+ |
| International Organization | 2,752 | B |
| International Law | 1,589 | C |
| Education—International Relations and Military | 454 | B |
| Music—Military | 8 | — |
| Art and War | 15 | C |
| Military Science | 4,317 | B |
| Naval Science | 200 | C |
| Bibliography and Reference | 881 | B |

4. Lauinger Library has been a selective depository library for U.S. government documents since 1969. Its holdings total more than 400,000 government publications. The Government Documents Room has the *Congressional Information Service Index,* 1789 to the present. It also holds *Foreign Relations of the United States;* major studies and issue briefs of the Congressional Research Service (K9) with a cumulative index, 1916–89, and supplemental indexes, 1989–90; the *Declassified Documents Catalog* and accompanying microfiche set; and numerous Arms Control and Disarmament Agency (K4) titles.

The library also has extensive microform holdings, including United Nations Documents (1946–present) and the International Population Census Publications Microfilm Series.

For a description of archival holdings in the library's special collections, see entry B6.

The Foreign Affairs Oral History Program is described in entry E6.

For a description of the photograph and film collections in the library's special collections, see entry F10.

5. The Lauinger Library has an on-line catalog, known as GEORGE, that contains records of all the books and periodicals in the general collection in Western languages. Books in Chinese, Japanese, and Korean (CJK) can be located using vernacular script in the CJK card catalog on the lower level. Holdings for the Special Collections Division are found through its own card catalog on the fifth floor.

6. Index Terms: Arms Control; Conflict Management and Resolution; Diplomacy and Negotiations; Deterrence; Development Issues; Foreign Policy; Human Rights; International Economics; International Law; International Organizations; Military Science; Naval Science; Psychological Aspects of War and Peace; Religious, Philosophical, and Ethical Concepts of War and Peace

*Note:* Georgetown University's Edward Bennett Williams Law Library (Robert L. Oakley, Director; Ellen Schaefer, International Law Librarian; 202/662-9131), located at 111 G Street, NW, Washington, D.C. 20001-1417, is closed to the public. Scholars interested in gaining access must contact the library. Williams Law Library, with 660,000 volumes, is the largest and most complete collection on law and international law among area law school libraries. It is strong in all areas of public international law, with particular strengths in international trade, environmental law, and human rights.

See also entries B6, E6, F10, and J7

## Heritage Foundation Library    See entry H35

## Historical Evaluation and Research Organization (HERO) Library    See entry H37

---

### A21  House of Representatives—Library

---

1.a. Cannon House Office Building, B-18
New Jersey and Independence Avenues, SE
Washington D.C. 20515
(202) 225-0462

b. 9:00 A.M.–5:30 P.M. Monday–Friday

c. The library is open to the public for limited on-site use. Researchers should call before visiting the library.

d. E. Raymond Lewis, Librarian

2.a. Library holdings contain approximately 100,000 volumes, largely of legislative materials

generated by the House of Representatives and the Senate.

b. About one-third of the holdings pertains to international economic, military, and political affairs.

3. This collection can be of value to researchers studying U.S. relations with foreign countries. The holdings are in the B range for the legislative backgrounds of U.S. commercial policy, international finance, international relations, international organizations, international law, military science, and naval science. The library contains complete sets of House and Senate reports, the *Congressional Record, House Bills and Debates, House and Joint Committee Hearings, Supreme Court Reports, Statutes at Large,* and many other congressional documents. Of special interest are holdings germane to hearings of the House Committee on Foreign Affairs. The House of Representatives Library is independent of the Library of Congress.

5. The library has no catalog. A descriptive flyer is available.

6. Index Terms: Arms Control; Defense Policy, National; Deterrence; Diplomacy and Negotiations; Development Issues; International Economics; International Law; Military History

See also entries K8 and K9

---

### A22  Howard University—Founders Library

---

1.a. 500 Howard Place, NW
Washington, D.C. 20059
(202) 806-7253 (Reference)
(202) 806-7234 (Administrative Offices)
Fax: (202) 806-4622

b. 8:00 A.M.–Midnight Monday–Thursday
9:00 A.M.–5:00 P.M. Friday–Saturday
12:30 P.M.–9:00 P.M. Sunday
Hours vary during the summer semester.

c. Open to serious researchers for on-site use. Interlibrary loan and photocopying facilities available.

d. Ann K. Randall, Director of University Libraries

2.a. Howard University Library is a major research library holding approximately 1,528,000 books and bound periodicals. The library also receives 23,784 current serial titles.

b. Based on measurements taken of the general collection, publications pertaining to peace studies and international security are estimated at 77,540 volumes. For archival and oral history holdings in the university's Moorland Spingarn Research Center see entries B7 and E7.

3.a. The peace studies and international security holdings show strengths in philosophical, psychological, ethical, and religious aspects of war and peace, international finance, political theory, constitutional history and administration, and international relations.

b. Founders Library formerly housed the Bernard B. Fall Collection, consisting of Southeast and East Asian materials with a focus on the Indochina and Vietnam conflicts. The collection was transferred in the mid-1980s to the Harvard University Library, Cambridge, Mass. 02138.

c. Subject categories and evaluations:

| Subject | Number of Titles | Rating |
|---|---|---|
| Philosophy—War and Peace | 3,634 | B |
| Psychology—War and Peace | 6,279 | B+ |
| Ethics—War and Peace | 1,063 | B |
| Religion—War and Peace | 5,049 | B |
| World History | 6,407 | C |
| History—Military Science | 181 | — |
| Geography—Military | 7 | — |
| Anthropology—War and Peace | 306 | C |
| Economic History and Conditions | 6,311 | C |
| Commercial Policy | 1,955 | C |
| International Finance | 829 | B |
| Sociology | 7,996 | B |
| Political Theory | 2,784 | B |
| Constitutional History and Administration | 4,866 | B |
| Colonies and Emigration | 159 | B |
| International Relations | 1,267 | B |
| International Organizations | 1,248 | C |
| International Law | 553 | — |
| Education—International and Military | 425 | C |
| Music—Military | 4 | — |
| Art and War | 16 | C |
| Military Science | 2,364 | C |
| Naval Science | 307 | C |
| Bibliography and Reference | 273 | C |

5. Access to library materials processed since 1976 is through STERLING, an integrated, on-line library information system. Materials acquired before 1976 are identifiable through the union card catalog of holdings in the university libraries processed prior to January 1, 1981. It is located on the second floor of Founders Library. The card catalog is divided into two parts: author/title and subject.

Older materials in the Founders Library are classified according to the Dewey Decimal System; more recent acquisitions have been assigned Library of Congress classification numbers.

Selected W. H. Wilson databases have been loaded on the NOTIS multiple database system and are, therefore, searchable through the on-line catalog. Several social science-related CD-ROM workstations are available for searching.

6. Index Terms: Development Issues; Diplomacy and Negotiations; Foreign Policy; Human Rights; International Economics—International Finance; Political Systems and Ideologies; Psychological Aspects of War and Peace; Religious, Philosophical, and Ethical Concepts of War and Peace

*Note:* Howard University's Law School Library (202/806-3045), located at 2900 Van Ness Street, NW, Washington, D.C. 20008, is open to the public. Howard University Law School Library is relatively weak on international law. Among its 237,000 volumes, several hundred relate to international public law.

See also entry B7 and E7

**Inter-American Defense Board Library** See entry L5

---

## A23 Inter-American Defense College Library

---

1.a. Fort Lesley J. McNair, Building 52
Washington, D.C. 20319-6100
(202) 646-1330
Fax: (202) 287-9567

b. 7:30 A.M.–4:00 P.M. Monday–Friday

c. The library is primarily for the use of the students and faculty of the college. Permission to use the library may be granted upon request. Interlibrary loan service and photocopying facilities are available.

d. Gioconda M. Vallarino, Librarian

2.a. The total collection numbers approximately 20,000 volumes. The library receives almost 300 current periodicals, a significant number of which are military-related journals.

b. International security and peace studies holdings amount to approximately 12,000 volumes (50 percent in Spanish or Portuguese).

3. The library's holdings do not concentrate on Latin American military affairs as might be expected. They are eclectic, with a worldwide focus designed to support the wide-ranging curriculum of abstract and global, as well as hemispheric, topics taught at the Inter-American Defense College (L6). The peace and international security studies holdings are strongest in history, politics, economics, ethnic relations, human rights, and international organizations within the Latin America system. Holdings are weak in international law, conflict resolution, and peace theory. Holdings on Latin American military affairs, internal security, and military civic-action, while not extensive, may include titles not available elsewhere in the area. Overall holdings on international relations, international organizations, and military science rank in the B range.

4. Back issues of periodicals are retained for five years. Approximately 90 percent of the articles are indexed in a PROCITE database. Most of the records have abstracts.

5. An on-line public access catalog was installed in 1991. Two commercial bibliographic databases from Latin America are available on CD-ROM.

6. Index Terms: Collective Security—Regional Alliance Systems; Human Rights; International Organizations; Military Science

See also entry L6

---

**A24** Inter-American Development Bank (IDB)—Library

---

1.a. 1300 New York Avenue, NW
Washington, D.C. 20577
(202) 623-3211
Fax: (202) 623-3183

b. 9:00 A.M.–5:30 P.M. Monday–Friday

c. Open to qualified researchers with proper identification. Interlibrary loan service and photocopying facilities are available.

d. Benita Weber Vassallo, Chief of the Library
Rolland Lamberton, Public Inquiries

2.a. The library contains 70,000 volumes on Latin American socioeconomic matters and a separate 8,000-volume collection on Latin American cultural topics.

b. Its relevance to peace and international security studies centers on international organizations and international economic affairs.

3.a. The topics on which the IDB currently focuses are debt, foreign trade, women in development, financial institutions, and third-world issues generally. The collection ranks in the A range for the fields of economic history and conditions, and international finance, and in the B range for international organizations.

b. The library has extensive holdings of serial publications from every Latin American government: statistical bulletins, censuses, the annual reports of central banks, development corporations, and a wide range of governmental ministries. The official publications of international economic organizations, regional-integration bodies (such as Central American Common Market [CACM], Latin American Free Trade Association [LAFTA], and Sistema Económico Latinoamericano [SELA]), and regional development banks are also well represented, as are periodicals from the major Latin American research centers.

4. The library has a periodicals collection of some 1,200 titles and receives 40 Latin American newspapers. The library's photographs collection is described in entry F11.

5. An on-line catalog covers books and reports held by the library. In addition, the library prepares occasional bibliographies on topics of interest to the bank staff (e.g., finance, land reform, financing of higher education).

6. Index Terms: Development Issues—Aid and Investment; International Economics—International Finance; International Organizations

*Note:* The bank's Law Library (Luz Sadak, Librarian, 202/623-2164) has a 10,000-volume collection of current Latin American legal codes, constitutions, commercial and financial legislation, international treaties, and related materials. The library also subscribes to the official gazettes from every Latin American country.

See also entry F11

**Interior Department—Geological Survey Library** See entry K21

**Interior Department—Natural Resources Library** See entry K21

## **A25** International Labor Organization (ILO) (United Nations)—Washington Branch Office—Library

1.a. 1828 L Street, NW, Suite 801
Washington, D.C. 20036
(202) 653-7652
Fax: (202) 653-7687

b. 9:00 A.M.–4:30 P.M. Monday–Friday

c. Open to the public for on-site use by appointment. Interlibrary loan service is not available. Photocopying services are available at a nominal charge.

d. Jean Decker Mathews, Technical Information Officer

2. The International Labor Organization (ILO) Washington Branch Office library collection consists of between 3,000 and 4,000 ILO documents and publications dating from 1919 to the present.

3.a. The ILO, a specialized agency of the United Nations with 150 member countries, seeks to improve working conditions, create employment, and promote human rights globally. The collection ranks in the B range for international organizations and in the C range for economic history and conditions, and for international relations. Issues addressed by the ILO include: setting international labor standards; fostering economic development and employment growth in developing countries through technical assistance, in conjunction with other United Nations agencies; promoting human rights through the right of free association (UN Human Rights Convention No. 87, adopted 1948).

3.b. Among the holdings are ILO conference documents; the minutes of the ILO Governing Body; reports, resolutions, and proceedings of ILO regional and industrial (mining, petroleum, plantations, etc.) conferences; the ILO *Yearbook of Labour Statistics;* the ILO *Legislative Series* of national laws and regulations on labor and social security (in English), as well as its successor, since 1990, *Labor Law Documents;* ILO studies and reports on international labor conditions, trade unionism, labor-management relations, social security, occupational health and safety, etc.; International Social Security Association publications; and documents from International Conferences of Labour Statisticians.

4. Separate files are maintained by country of national laws and regulations on labor and social security. Through 1989 the contents were extracted from issues of the ILO *Legislative Series.* For information concerning ILO photographic collection see entry F13.

5. There is no card catalog. The key finding-aids for identifying documents and publications are the ILO's *Catalogue of ILO Publications in Print, 1991–92* (1991); *Bibliography of Published Research of the World Employment Programme* (1988); *Subject Guide to Publications of the International Labor Office, 1980–1985* (1987); and LABORDOC, a database that contains over 145,000 bibliographic references since 1965.

6. Index Terms: Development Issues; Human Rights; International Organizations—Labor—United Nations

See also entries F13 and L10

## **A26** International Trade Commission (ITC)—National Library of International Trade

1.a. 500 E Street, SW, Room 300
Washington, D.C. 20436
(202) 205-2630
Fax: (202) 205-2316

b. 9:00 A.M.–5:00 P.M. Monday–Friday

c. The library is open to the public. Interlibrary loan and photocopying services are available.

d. Katherine Loughney/Elizabeth Root, Chiefs, Library Services

2.a–b. The ITC's National Library of International Trade holds approximately 100,000 volumes. Virtually the entire collection is relevant to the scope of this Guide under the rubric of international trade.

3.a. The commission's library is an excellent source on international commerce, tariffs, and customs. The collection ranks in the A range for the fields of commercial policy and international finance. It has all ITC reports dealing with antidumping measures, countervailing trade, surveys of industries, and trade disputes in general. Statistical holdings include international trade data and tariff schedules from around the world. It receives official foreign trade serials and statistical yearbooks, and has commerce, census, and monthly exchange rate information on CD-ROM (e.g., the National Trade Data Bank). Foreign trade statistics on microfiche extend back to

1950 for many countries. For the period since 1992 the data are available on CD-ROM as U.S. Exports of Merchandise Trade and U.S. Imports of Merchandise Trade.

3.b. The library also features a full set of International Customs Journal, listing tariff schedules from around the world.

4. The library receives about 2,000 periodicals, mostly commodity and economic journals, but many are routed through commission departments and only about 1,000 may be in the library.

5. The on-line catalog permits author, title, and subject access to holdings.

6. Index terms: Development Issues; International Economics—International Trade

See also entry K22

---

## A27 Joint Bank-Fund Library (Library of the International Bank for Reconstruction and Development [World Bank] and the International Monetary Fund [IMF])

---

1.a. 700 19th Street, NW
Washington, D.C. 20431
(202) 623-7054
Fax: (202) 623-6417

b. 9:00 A.M.–5:00 P.M. Monday–Friday

c. The library is for the staff of the IMF and the World Bank. Outside visitors must make an appointment. There is a three to four week delay for appointments. Contact the reference desk (202/623-7054) for procedures. Interlibrary loan and photocopying facilities are available at a charge.

d. Peter Hegedus, Chief Librarian

2.a. The library holds more than 150,000 volumes and receives approximately 4,000 journals.

b. Almost the entire collection is relevant to peace and international security studies in the areas of economic development, international economics, and international organizations.

3. The library's holdings rank in the A range for economic history and conditions, commercial policy, international finance, and international organizations. The collection consists primarily of economic data on individual member countries: banking, commerce, finance, industry, labor, economic policy, planning production, and develop-

ment. The library is particularly strong in periodical holdings, such as annual reports and statistical bulletins from central banks, government ministries, and private research centers. International and regional organization publications include statistical bulletins, newsletters, and journals. Publications of the World Bank (L8) and the International Monetary Fund (L11) are neither held nor distributed by the library. They are available through the publication offices of those organizations.

5. All books cataloged in the Joint Bank-Fund Library, working papers, bound periodicals, and an index to selected journal articles can be accessed through an automated catalog available to on-site users. A compact disc version of the journal/working paper index, called INTLEC, may be purchased from Chadwyck-Healey, 1101 King Street, Alexandria, Va. 22314 (703/683-4890).

6. Index terms: Development Issues—Aid and Investment; International Economics—International Finance; International Organizations

See also entries D3, F12, G8, G9, L8, and L11

## Justice Department Library    See entry K23

---

## A28 Labor Department Library

---

1.a. 200 Constitution Avenue, NW, Room N-2445
Washington, D.C. 20210
(202) 219-6993 (Reference)
Fax: (202) 219-6354

b. 8:15 A.M.–4:45 P.M. Monday–Friday

c. The library is open to the public for on-site use. Interlibrary loan and photocopying facilities are available.

d. Sabina Jacobson, Manager

2.a. The Labor Department Library holds some 500,000 volumes; approximately 2,500 periodicals are received.

b. About 20 percent of the library's holdings pertain to foreign labor issues. Approximately 10 percent of the total collection is relevant to the scope of this Guide in the fields of conflict resolution, economic development, human rights, and peace studies.

3.a. Library holdings cover a wide range of subjects in labor and industrial relations, economic conditions, and labor economics. The collection ranks in the B range for the fields of economic history and conditions, and commercial policy.

b. Approximately 1,000 volumes concern peace studies and conflict resolution. The bulk of peace studies material relates to industrial arbitration, which includes general industrial arbitration, arbitration techniques, and arbitration worldwide (including within the United States). Approximately 250 titles are related to this topic. There are approximately 20 titles related specifically to international arbitration and peaceful resolution of disputes. Another 20 titles relate to mediation and conciliation in general. Other relevant subjects include: general international relations, human rights, and negotiation.

4. A special "Foreign Trade Union Periodicals" collection is arranged alphabetically by country. The library is the repository for a complete set of the major publications of the Labor Department. Other strengths are International Labour Organization publications.

5. Material acquired prior to 1988 is cataloged in a card catalog. For later material, the library's online system must be consulted.

6. Index terms: Conflict Resolution and Management; Development Issues; Human Rights; Peace Theory and Research

See also entry K24

---

## A29 Library of Congress (LC)

1.a. Thomas Jefferson Building
1st Street, SE
(between Independence Avenue and East Capitol Street)

John Adams Building
2nd Street, SE
(between Independence Avenue and East Capitol Street)

James Madison Building
Independence Avenue, SE
(between 1st and 2nd Streets)

Mail
10 First Street, SE
Washington, D.C. 20540
(202) 707-5000 (main number)

b. General Reading Room
8:30 A.M.–9:30 P.M. (stack service to 8:30 P.M.)
Monday–Friday

8:30 A.M.–5:00 P.M. (stack service to 4:00 P.M.)
Saturday

1:00 P.M.–5:00 P.M. (stack service to 4:30 P.M.)
Sunday

Closed on New Year's Day, Memorial Day, the Fourth of July, Labor Day, Thanksgiving, and Christmas. Summer hours may vary. Division hours are noted below.

c. Open to all researchers over high school age for on-site use. Members of the public do not have access to a small group of classified or confidential materials housed in the library for the use of Congress. The public is not normally allowed access to the stacks. Interlibrary loan service (exclusive of periodicals, newspapers, genealogical, and rare materials) is available to the public through their local library. Self-service, coin-operated photocopying machines are available in the General Reading Rooms. The Photoduplication Service, room G-1009, John Adams Building (202/707-5640), can supply microfilms and photocopies of library materials including copies of items not available on interlibrary loan. A brochure listing photocopying charges is available upon request.

d. James H. Billington, Librarian of Congress
Division Chiefs are listed below.

2.a. Library of Congress holdings are in excess of 100 million items, probably the largest of any library in the world.

b. On the basis of measurements of the shelflists the library holds about 963,550 volumes relevant to the scope of this Guide. They represent by far the largest library collection for peace and international security studies in the Washington, D.C., area, and next to the National Archives and Records Service (B11) the most valuable resource for the study of these fields. In fact, LC's holdings are the criterion against which relevant holdings of other major libraries in the area are measured in this Guide.

3.a–b. It is difficult to discuss the Library of Congress without a certain ambivalence. On one hand, LC undoubtedly possesses the largest and most comprehensive collection of peace studies and international security research materials in the United States, and probably in the world. On the other hand, the identification and retrieval of those materials can be rather complicated. Holdings are so massive, and so diffused among various divisions of the library, that it is often difficult to identify everything that is available for research on a given topic. Cataloged materials are divided, frequently at random, among several divisions. For international relations and peace studies one must look in the main book collection, the Serial and Government Publications Division, the Law Library, the Microform Reading Room, and the Rare Book and Special Collections Division. To be thorough, researchers must visit the various divisions described below, explore the catalogs and other finding-aids available in each division, and discuss their research projects with as many library staff members as possible. In addition, see the following divisions with separate entries in this Guide: Manuscript Division (B8), Geography and Map Division (D4), Motion Picture, Broadcasting, and Recorded Sound Division (E8 and F14), and Print and Photographs Division (F15).

3.b. Subject categories and evaluations:

| Subject | Number of Titles |
|---|---|
| Philosophy—War and Peace | 29,411 |
| Psychology—War and Peace | 17,625 |
| Ethics—War and Peace | 9,029 |
| Religion—War and Peace | 56,466 |
| World History | 96,687 |
| History—Military Science | 5,419 |
| Geography—Military | 701 |
| Anthropology—War and Peace | 4,747 |
| Economic History and Conditions | 111,201 |
| Commercial Policy | 33,894 |
| International Finance | 5,483 |
| Sociology | 69,126 |
| Political Theory | 20,209 |
| Constitutional History and Administration | 34,638 |
| Colonies and Emigration | 1,445 |
| International Relations | 9,478 |
| International Organization | 22,908 |
| International Law | 36,300 |
| Education—International Relations and Military | 6,353 |
| Music—Military | 42 |
| Art and War | 212 |
| Military Science | 50,851 |
| Naval Science | 8,362 |
| Bibliography and Reference | 10,200 |

4. Divisions of the Library of Congress Research Services

See also entries B8, D4, E8, F14, and F15

## GENERAL READING ROOMS DIVISION

Thomas Jefferson Building, Room 144
(202) 707-5530

Suzanne E. Thorin, Chief
Main Reading Room (MRR)
Thomas Jefferson Building
(202) 707-5522 or 705-5523
Victoria C. Hill, Head
Larry Boyer, Assistant Head

Located here are 70,000 reference sources, LC hardcopy catalogs, and a computer catalog center that offers on-line access to a wide variety of in-house databases. Instruction in the use of LC automated systems is available on-site from librarians familiar with retrieval strategies appropriate for diverse needs. On the floor of the Main Reading Room (MRR) and in the balconies above are bibliographies, handbooks, encyclopedias, dictionaries, and indexes to facilitate research. Several of the commercially produced bibliographic databases in social sciences, covering international and military affairs, are also available on-line via computer terminals in the MRR. The European Reading Room (ERR) is located adjacent to the MRR. In addition to its own holdings on European military affairs, including materials on Russia and the other succession states of the former Soviet Union, the ERR is a good place to begin searching general peace studies and international security reference works in the MRR, which number approximately 70.

The stacks are closed to the public, but all items in the general collections may be requested for use in the General Reading Rooms. Depending on the time of day, paging items from the stacks can take from 30 minutes to an hour or more. Should a call slip be returned with the notation NOS (not on shelf), researchers may request the book service staff to check the Central Charge File. If this procedure does not locate the material, contact the Special Search Section in the Center Room, Adams Building, Fifth Floor, adjacent to the Social Science Reading Room. Staff in this section have a good record for tracking down NOS items.

To assist scholars whose projects require extensive use of the collections, the General Reading Rooms provide study shelves and desks on a limited basis. Applications for these services should be addressed to the Research Facilities Office, General Reading Rooms Division (202) 707-5211. Space is limited and waiting lists exist for desks. For short-term projects the reading rooms provide ample seating. Scholars in need of typists, translators, or research assistants should contact the General Reading Rooms Division, which maintains a list of persons offering these services on a freelance basis.

## SERIAL AND GOVERNMENT PUBLICATIONS DIVISION

Newspaper and Current Periodical Room
James Madison Building, First Floor, Room LM133
(202) 707-5690

8:30 A.M.–9:30 P.M. Monday, Wednesday, Thursday
(Stack service closes at 7:30 P.M.)
8:30 A.M.–5:00 P.M. Tuesday, Friday, Saturday
(Stack service closes at 4:00 P.M.)

Donald F. Wisdom, Chief
Irene Schubert, Head, Government Publications and
    Periodical Section
Frank Carroll, Head, Newspaper Section
Robert Schaaf, Senior Specialist in United Nations
    and International Documents

LC's Newspaper and Current Periodical Room receives and retains for 24 months approximately 70,000 publications. Unless the researcher arrives with specific titles in mind, however, adequate catalogs or indexes to the comprehensive body of these materials do not always exist.

(1) The division receives 359 U.S. newspapers and 1,134 foreign newspapers that are retained on a permanent basis. An additional 120 U.S. and 43 foreign newspapers are retained on a current basis only. Many newspapers are available to visitors in full-text CD-ROM.

For identification and retrieval, the staff relies on *A Checklist of Foreign Newspapers in the Library of Congress* (1929), with loose-leaf supplementary updates through the 1960s, and *Newspapers Currently Received in the Library of Congress* (1990). All newspaper acquisitions since 1962 have been microfilmed and are available for interlibrary loan. A card catalog of the holdings on microfilm is available in the Newspaper and Current Periodical Reading Room, as is an LC publication *Newspapers in Microform: Foreign Countries, 1948–1983* (1984). Regrettably the Library has not published any supplements to *Newspapers in Microform.* The entire pre-1962 retrospective collection is scheduled to be microfilmed within the next decade.

(2) The Newspaper and Current Periodical Room also receives an impressive range of government serial publications and some 60,000 periodicals from around the world. The reading room maintains a regularly updated dictionary card catalog to its collections of periodicals and government publications. The reading room also maintains a collection of major periodical indexes currently received, which are arranged by subjects.

The reading room subscribes to the *Monthly Catalog of Government Publications,* published by the

Government Printing Office (GPO), which indexes publications from 1941 to the present. There is a CD-ROM version of this publication, entitled *MARCIVE,* from July 1976 to present. This does not include Department of Defense documents. Other relevant CD-ROM indexes include: the *Congressional Record;* Environmental Protection Agency's *Toxic Release Inventory (TRI)* and *National Economic, Social, and Environmental Data Bank (NESE);* the National Trade Data Bank's *Foreign Trade Index (FTI);* and the *Ethnic Newswatch.* The reading room also has *CIS: Congressional Information Service Index to Congressional Publications and Legislative Histories,* since 1970, and *ASI: American Statistics Index,* also by CIS.

(3) The Library of Congress receives publications from about 60 international and intergovernmental organizations to most of which the United States belongs. These include: the United Nations; the United Nations Educational, Scientific, and Cultural Organization (UNESCO); the European Community (EC); the Food and Agricultural Organization (FAO); the General Agreement on Trade and Tariffs (GATT); the World Health Organization (WHO); and the World Intellectual Property Organization (WIPO). The library receives over 10,000 United Nations documents a year. The *Readex Index to United Nations Documents and Publications* on CD-ROM, an index of United Nations documents that gives the UN document number, is available. The division houses a large reference section that includes, for example, the United Nations *Yearbook,* the UNESCO *Yearbook on Peace and Conflict Studies,* the *World Directory of Peace Research and Training Institutions,* and *Basic Documents on United Nations and Related Peace-Keeping Forces.* Division staff member Robert Schaaf specializes in the publications and documents of international organizations. He can aid researchers in locating these materials in LC and elsewhere.

(4) Among its special collections, the division holds the *Alternative Press Collection,* which contains 350 titles of underground newspapers, mid-1960s to present. Access is via the *Alternative Press Index, 1972–present.*

## RARE BOOK AND SPECIAL COLLECTIONS DIVISION

Thomas Jefferson Building, Room 256
(202) 707-5434

8:30 A.M.–5:00 P.M. Monday–Friday

Larry Sullivan, Chief

The Rare Book and Special Collections Division holds about 500,000 books; 200,000 broadsides, pamphlets, theater bills, title pages, prints, manuscripts, posters, photographs; and nearly 6,000 incunabula. Scattered among these are various works relating to peace and security. The chief finding-aids are a card catalog and the library's computerized catalog. The peace and international security studies subject headings reflected most strongly in the catalog are military and naval science, diplomacy, and economic history. These items are extremely diverse and range from *Publications of the American Peace Society* (1916) to *Archives Diplomatiques et Consulaires* from Zurich (undated).

There are a number of collections held by the Rare Books and Special Collections Division that include pertinent security and peace studies material. Most important is the John Boyd Thacher Collection, which contains primary and secondary sources regarding the French Revolution. It includes a set of letters written by members of the ancien régime prior to the Revolution. Another set of letters written during the Revolution consists of letters from legislators who belonged to the States General, the Legislative Assembly, and other bodies. There are also documents from the Committee of Public Safety, Committee of General Security, Committee of Legislation, Commune of August 10, 1792, Revolutionary Tribunal, 9 Thermidor, and the Jacobin Club.

Other collections that contain relevant material are the Anarchism Collection, consisting of 341 books relating to the study of anarchy between 1850 and 1970; the Confederate States of America Collection, 1,812 titles of publications issued in the South during the Civil War; the Martin Hertz Gift, two scrapbooks of World War II propaganda ephemera; the House Un-American Activities Committee (HUAC) Collection of 4,000 pamphlets; and the Radical Pamphlets Collection containing 2,000 items concerning American communism, anarchism, and socialism 1870–1980 (especially 1930–49); the Third Reich Collection, 1,019 publications and photographs from the libraries of Nazi leaders; the Underground Movement Collection, 16,162 items pertaining to World War II resistance activity; and the World War II Propaganda Collection, 6,700 items of propaganda material distributed in Europe in World War II.

General information brochures, *Some Guides to Special Collections in the Rare Books Division* (1974) and *Library of Congress Rare Books and Special Collections: An Illustrated Guide* (1992), can be obtained from the division.

## LAW LIBRARY

James Madison Building, Second Floor
(202) 707-5065

8:30 A.M.–4:30 P.M. Monday–Friday

Kathleen Price, Law Librarian
James Madison Building, Room Second Floor
(202) 707-5070

The Law Library contains approximately 2 million volumes divided into five geographic subdivisions. There is no specific division for international legal materials, so the roughly 36,300 volumes in international law are spread out among the geographic divisions. A large portion of these books relate to international relations and international organization. They are now being transferred to the general collection. The library receives 30 yearbooks of international law.

There is a large section of international law reference books in the Law Library reading room. These include: *Digest of U.S. Practice in International Law; The Canadian Yearbook of International Law; International Legal Materials; The Consolidated Treaty Series; UN Treaty Series; Statement of Treaties and International Agreements; U.S. Treaties and Other International Agreements; U.S. Treaty Index; U.S. Department of State Bulletin; Digest of Commercial Laws of the World; International Environmental Reporter; Constitutions of Countries of the World; Human Rights; Digest of International Law; Encyclopedia of Public International Law; Encyclopedia of European Country Law; Court of Justice of the European Community Reports; International Court of Justice: Pleadings, Oral Arguments, and Documents;* and *New Directions in the Law of the Sea.*

## MICROFORM READING ROOM

Main Building, Room 137
(202) 707-5471

8:30 A.M.–9:30 P.M. Monday–Friday
8:30 A.M.–5:00 P.M. Saturday
1:00 P.M.–5:00 P.M. Sunday

Betty M. Culpepper, Head

The Microform Reading Room contains, among its nearly 1.5 million titles, a heterogeneous but significant collection of international security and peace studies materials on microform. These include full microform runs of United Nations and League of Nations official publications; Foreign Broadcast Information Service (K16), and Joint Publications Research Service (K16) transcripts; substantial quantities of British state papers from the Public Record Office in London; and an estimated 98 percent of all U.S. doctoral dissertations, which appear in *Dissertation Abstracts*. Records for most microforms cataloged after 1980 have been entered in the library's on-line catalogs. However, researchers should not fail to explore the Microform Reading Room's card catalog, as most of these microform holdings are available nowhere else in the Library of Congress in any format and many are not cataloged in the general collection on-line database. Reading machines and reader/printers are available.

Many of the collections of the Microform Reading Room are listed in the guide *Microform Collections and Selected Titles in Microform* in the Microform Reading Room. Below are selected relevant titles from this guide:

Allied Powers Reparation Commission—Documents 1922–30

Arab Bureau Papers (1911–19)

Archive of Mexican Revolution

Asia, Special Studies (1980–82)

British Parliamentary Papers on Central and South America, 1800–99

British War Art of the 20th Century

Bulletins and Other Ephemera Relating to the Fourth International: 1930–40

China and India (O.S.S./State Department intelligence and research reports) filmed holdings of the National Archives; also China and India: 1950–61 Supplement; China, 1911–41 (filmed holdings of National Archives, Series: U.S. Military intelligence reports); China: Special Studies, 1970–80 (monographs commissioned by the White House and other Executive Branch agencies)

Confidential U.S. diplomatic post records (filmed holdings of the National Archives, Record Groups 59 and 84):
Japan, 1914–41
Middle East, 1925–41
Russia and the Soviet Union, 1914–41

Confidential U.S. State Department central files (filmed holdings of the National Archives, Record Group 59):
Argentina: internal affairs, 1945–49; foreign affairs, 1945–49
China: internal affairs, 1940–49
Cuba, internal and foreign affairs, 1945–54
Germany: foreign affairs, 1930–44; internal affairs, 1930–44
Great Britain: foreign affairs, 1940–44; internal affairs, 1930–44

Indochina: internal affairs, 1945–54
Iran: foreign and internal affairs, 1950–54
Italy: foreign and internal affairs, 1940–44
Japan: internal affairs 1945–54
Nicaragua: internal and foreign affairs, 1945–54
Palestine and Israel: foreign and internal affairs 1945–54
South Africa: foreign and internal affairs, 1945–54
Soviet Union: foreign and internal affairs, 1950–54
Spain: foreign and internal affairs, 1930–39

Crises in Panama and the Dominican Republic: National Security files and NSC histories, 1963–69

Diplomatic Correspondence of British Ministers to the Russian Court at St. Petersburg, 1704–76

Documents of the National Security Council

Documents on British Policy Overseas—Series I, v. 1, Conferences at Potsdam, July–August 1945

Papers of John Foster Dulles and Christian A. Herter, 1953–61

Dutch Underground Press, 1940–45

Europe, 1946–76 (CIA research reports)

Europe, 1950–51 Supplement (O.S.S./State Department intelligence and research reports)

European Contributions to the History of World War II, 1939–45: The War in the Air (in German and English)

Files of the National Socialist Party Chancellery (Akten der Partei-Kanzlei der NSDAP: Rekonstruktion eines verlorengegangenen Bestandes)

German Army High Command, 1938–45

Germany and Its Occupied Territories during World War II (O.S.S./State Department intelligence reports)

Germany, 1919–41 (filmed holdings of National Archives) U.S. military intelligence reports on strength and capacities of Germany military and social and political developments

Germany, clippings regarding July 20, 1944 attempted assassination of Hitler.

Great Britain, Foreign Office: Japan correspondence, 1856–1905, 1930–45

History of the Ministry of Munitions—Official 12 vol. history of the British Ministry of Munitions, 1915–21

Imperial War Museum (Great Britain), Women at Work Collection, Relief Efforts and participation in war efforts during World War I

Israel, National Security Files, (U.S. government files written between 1963–69)

Japan, Korea, and the security of Asia, 1970–80 (special studies series produced by government agencies and private organizations)

Japan, Korea, Southeast Asia, and the Far East generally (O.S.S./State Department research reports, 1950–61)
U.S. State Department: American Foreign Policy Current Documents
Vietnam War (filmed holdings of Indochina Archive at the University of California, Berkeley)

5. Computer terminals located at the Computer Catalog Centers provide free automated access to files in the Library's Multiple Use MARC System (MUMS) and Subject-Content-Oriented-Retriever-for-Processing-Information-On-Line (SCORPIO) system. MUMS facilitates access to bibliographic information about most books and maps cataloged by the library since 1968 and serials cataloged since 1973. However, earlier publications have been retrospectively added in the so-called pre-MARC file. SCORPIO includes the following databases: Library of Congress Computerized Catalog (LCCC), which permits author, title, and subject searches of the book file; Bibliographic Citation File (BIBL), which indexes periodicals, pamphlets, and U.S. government and United Nations publications; the Legislative Information Files for the 94th to the present Congresses (1975–).

For items cataloged before January 1, 1981, the Main Card Catalog, located adjacent to the Main Reading Room, is still heavily used. The Main Card Catalog contains more than 23 million cards alphabetically interfiled by author, title, and subject. Even for the period before January 1, 1981, however, this catalog does not include records for some items maintained by the various special divisions (manuscripts, microforms, rare books, periodicals, maps, prints, photographs, motion pictures, and sound recordings). Researchers must consult the card files in the appropriate divisions in order to determine locations and the extent of holdings for certain items. Thus, the Main Catalog should serve as a point of departure when searching for items at LC.

*Note:* If you cannot find an entry for what you need, seek out the aid of a reference librarian before assuming that it is not available.

Major LC catalog publications:
*The National Union Catalog, Pre-1956 Imprints. A Cumulative Author List Representing Library of Congress Printed Cards and Titles Reported by Other American Libraries.* Published by the Mansell Company in England in 754 vols.
*The National Union Catalog: A Cumulative Author List Representing Library of Congress Printed Cards and Titles Reported by Other American Libraries.* Cumulation for 1956–67, 125 vols., available from Rowman and Littlefield; cumulation for 1968–72, 119 vols., available from J. W. Edwards; cumulation for 1973–77, 135 vols., available from Rowman and Littlefield; cumulations for individual years 1978–82 available from LC Cataloging Distribution Service.
*National Union Catalog. Books* [Microform]. Washington, D.C.: Library of Congress, 1983–. Published monthly in microfiche, it supersedes the preceding entry. It represents entries for works cataloged by LC together with catalog entries prepared by about 1,100 contributing libraries.
*National Register of Microform Masters,* annual, 1969 and later years available from LC Cataloging Distribution Service. It lists and locates microfilm masters from which libraries may acquire prints.
*Library of Congress Subject Headings,* 16th ed. (1993) 4 vols., contains the subject listing the library uses to organize and access its collections. Consulting this reference work can make finding information faster, easier, and much more accurate.
*New Serial Titles: A Union List of Serials Commencing Publication After December 31, 1949,* based on reports from some 800 U.S. and Canadian libraries; cumulation for 1950–70, 4 vols., available from R. R. Bowker Co.; cumulations for 1971–75, 1976–80, 1981–85, and 1986–88, available from LC Cataloging Distribution Service. Currently published in eight monthly and four quarterly issues with an annual cumulation (annuals cumulate up to 5- or 10-year periods). This work is a supplement to *Union List of Serials in Libraries of the United States and Canada,* ed. Edna B. Titus, 5 vols., 3d ed. (New York: Wilson, 1965).
*Combined Indexes to the Library of Congress Classification Schedules,* comp. Nancy Olson, 15 vols., (Washington D.C.: U.S. Historical Documents Institute, 1974). An aid to locating call numbers for materials by authors, names, geographic areas, subjects, and key words.
*Library of Congress Publications in Print,* biennial. Available without charge from LC Cataloging Distribution Service.
*Annual Report of the Librarian of Congress.*
*Quarterly Journal of the Library of Congress* (1943–83), particularly useful for the description of acquisitions of the various divisions. Though no longer published, back issues continue to provide valuable research material.

6. Index Terms: Arms Control; Collective Security; Conflict Resolution and Management; Defense Policy, National; Deterrence; Development Issues; Diplomacy and Negotiations; Foreign Policy; Human Rights; Humanitarian Issues; International

Economics—International Finance; International Economics—International Trade; International Law; International Organizations; Military History; Military Science; Naval Science; Pacifism and Peace Movements; Political Systems and Ideologies; Psychological Aspects of War and Peace; Religious, Philosophical, and Ethical Concepts of War and Peace

See also entries B8, D4, E8, F14, and F15

**Marine Corps Museum (Navy Department— Marine Corps Historical Center)    See entry C5**

---

**A30   Marine Corps University (Navy Department)—James Carson Breckinridge Library**

---

1.a.  Quantico, Va. 22134-5050
(703) 640-2248

b.  8:00 A.M.–4:30 P.M. Monday–Friday

c.  The library is open to the public for on-site use. Interlibrary loan and photocopying facilities are available.

d.  David C. Brown, Librarian

2.a.  The library holds approximately 75,000 volumes and receives about 400 periodicals.

b.  About one-half the collection is pertinent to the scope of this Guide, primarily for the fields of military history, planning and strategy (with an emphasis on the marines), and secondarily for the field of international relations.

3.a.  The holdings rank in the A range for military and naval science. The bulk of the collection centers on general military science (2,419 titles); organization and structure of armies (2,400); military administration (913); transportation (440); infantry (220); artillery (338); military engineering (1,359); naval science, administration, and organization (3,346); and the marines (372).

b.  The library has a small collection related to international and general political affairs ranking in the C range for international relations. It has a fairly complete set of congressional hearings on military budgeting, approximately 40 volumes, dating from the 1820s to the present.

4.  Approximately 50 percent of the 400 periodicals are military related. The library's government

documents include Defense Department, State Department, General Accounting Office, and congressional foreign affairs reports in microform. The library also receives Foreign Broadcast Information Service. The holdings include a small collection of maps.

5.  The library's card catalog is currently 75 percent on-line.

6.  Index Terms: Arms Control; Deterrence; Military History; Military Science; Naval Science

See also entries B9, C5, D5, E9, E10, and K30

**National Academy of Sciences (NAS)— National Research Council (NRC) Library See entry M36**

---

**A31   National Agricultural Library (NAL) (Agriculture Department)**

---

1.a.  Main Library
10301 Baltimore Boulevard
(at U.S. Route 1 and Interstate 495, Beltway Exit North)
Beltsville, Md. 20705-2351
Director's Office
(301) 504-5248
General Information of Activities and Services
(301) 504-5755
Fax: (301) 504-5472
Reference Service
(301) 504-5479
D.C. Reference Center

U.S. Department of Agriculture, South Building
Independence Avenue and 14th Street, SW, Room 1052
Washington, D.C. 20250
(202) 720-3434

b.  Main Library: 8:00 A.M.–4:30 P.M. Monday–Friday
Reference Service: 8:30 A.M.–4:30 P.M. Monday–Friday
D.C. Reference Center: 8:30 A.M.–5:00 P.M. Monday–Friday

c.  Open to the public. Interlibrary loan and photocopying services are available. Access to the book stacks may be granted to visiting scholars with a demonstrated, specific need.

d. Pamela André, Acting Director

2.a. The library maintains more than 2.1 million bound volumes pertaining to agriculture and related sciences. In addition, the library holds 434,000 microforms, and it currently receives 22,000 periodicals.

b. The NAL's primary relevance to international security and peace studies lies in its extensive economic holdings of over 60,000 volumes, including material on trade, economic development and assistance, and international organizations.

3.a. Because it serves as the research library of the Agriculture Department, its collection reflects thorough acquisitions in all areas of agricultural sciences. The D.C. Reference Center provides materials on statistics, economics, the social sciences, journalism, and industrial and office management. The library collection ranks in the B range for the fields of economic history and conditions, and commercial policy, and in the C range for international organizations.

b. The significant holdings in international security and peace studies are primarily in economics, trade, and economic development. Under economic history and conditions by country there are 8,794 titles. There are 1,568 titles relating to commercial policy. Cataloged separately under the library's own classification system, from 1862 until 1965, are 48,368 titles. These latter volumes cover agriculture, national resources, and national production comprehensively by country for most countries of the world.

A brief search of the on-line system found 210 citations on development; 594 on development assistance; 148 on economic assistance; 362 on technical assistance. The library also has a small collection relative to international organizations. It holds 2,100 food and agricultural reports and documents. An on-line search produced 116 citations on international cooperation, which includes works on agriculture in GATT, alliances and American foreign policy, and the European Free Trade Association, among others.

5. Bibliographic access to the collections is via the NAL card catalogs, published catalogs and bibliographies, on-line data bases, and various computer-produced printouts of microforms.

The library maintains two primary card catalogs of its holdings: a catalog of material processed from 1862 through 1965, and a catalog of items acquired from 1966 to 1987 arranged by author, and subject. These inactive catalogs are also available in printed form: *Dictionary Catalog of the National Agricultural Library, 1862–1965* (New York: Rowman and Littlefield, 1967–70) 73 volumes, and the *National Agricultural Library Catalog, 1966–1987,* in 12 volumes for 1966–70, and in annual cumulations 1971–87. *The Bibliography of Agriculture,* an index of periodical articles, symposia papers, etc., appears monthly and has annual cumulations with author, subject, and geographic indexes. Other publications include *Guide to Manuscripts in the National Agricultural Library* (USDA Miscellaneous Publication, No. 1374, 1979) compiled by Alan Fusonie; and *Journal of NAL Associates,* a quarterly devoted to agricultural topics.

The library's bibliographic on-line database, AGRICOLA, now stores in machine-readable form records for more than 3 million books, journals, journal articles, government reports, and conference papers acquired by the library since 1970. NAL users can search the database by author, title, subject headings (including geographic names), and other search keys. Terminals are available at all library branches. The system may also be accessed at most research libraries in the United States through national data networks.

In addition to on-line access, the AGRICOLA database is also available on CD-ROM from Silver Platter Information (1970–present).

6. Index Terms: Development Issues—Agriculture; International Economics—International Trade; International Organizations

See also entries G4, G5, and K2

## A32 National Air and Space Museum (NASM) (Smithsonian Institution) — Library

1.a. 6th Street and Independence Avenue, SW, Room 3100
Washington, D.C. 20560
(202) 357-3133
Fax: (202) 786-2835

b. 10:00 A.M.–4:00 P.M. Monday–Friday

c. Open to serious researchers by appointment only. Interlibrary loan and photocopying facilities are available.

d. David Spencer, Librarian

2.a. The National Air and Space Museum Library, part of the Smithsonian Institution Libraries, serves the research and exhibit programs of the museum. The library holds 30,000 book volumes, 10,000 volumes of bound periodicals, and 170 current subscriptions. Museum artifacts are described in entry C6; the museum's general archives in entry B10, and film and photographic archives in entries F18 and F19, respectively.

b. The principal relevance of this museum to peace and international security studies centers on the development of aviation as a part of military science. About 20 percent of the collection, or 8,000 volumes, are devoted entirely to military aviation.

3.a. The library collection ranks in the B range for military science. The primary strength of the library lies in its extensive holdings relating to specific models of aircraft or manufacturers. There are numerous books on Boeing, Lockheed, Grumann, the B-1 bomber, the F-16, etc. These volumes range from technical descriptions and design characteristics to histories of development as well as more general military capabilities. Holdings also include considerable material on military aviation generally, as well as air power during World Wars I and II, and the Korean and Vietnam wars. There is proportionally more material on World War II than other wars. Much of the relevant material on general topics relating to military aviation is historical. For example, there are contemporary sources on the development of bombardment capabilities in the 1940s.

b. A quick search of the on-line catalog found 30 titles on air defense, a number of them unique volumes dating from the 1930s. There are smaller holdings on contemporary military aviation and SDI. The library also holds the annual reports of the National Advisory Committee for Aeronautics (NASA's predecessor) from 1915–58.

4. Among the periodicals received, most of which relate to aeronautics and space flight, are at least a dozen specifically on military aviation, such as, *Air Wars 1919–1939: Army Aviation* and *Military Space*. The library also has an extremely strong collection of early aviation periodicals. For archival and manuscript holdings see entry B10. Film and photograph archival holdings are described in entries F18 and F19, respectively.

5. The library's holdings are on the Smithsonian Institution Library's on-line system.

6. Index Terms: Military History—Air Force; Military Science

See also entries B10, C6, F18 and F19

**National Conference of Catholic Bishops (NCCB) Library    See entry N38**

## A33    National Defense University (Defense Department)—Library

1.a. Fort Lesley J. McNair, Building 62
4th and P Streets, SW
Washington, D.C. 20319-6000
(202) 287-9111
Fax: (202) 287-9102

b. September–mid-June
7:00 A.M.–5:30 P.M. Monday–Friday
Mid-June–August
8:00 A.M.–4:30 P.M. Monday–Friday

c. The library is open to visitors with access to Fort McNair or who are sponsored by faculty or staff. Interlibrary loan and photocopying services are available.

d. Sarah A. Mikel, Director
Ann Parham, Chief, Resources and Information Services
Susan Lemke, Chief, Special Collections

2.a. The library holds approximately 250,000 volumes of books, as well as an additional 250,000 items, mainly technical reports, microforms, and compact discs. Subscriptions consist of 1,300 serial publications.

b. Virtually the entire collection is relevant to the scope of this Guide.

3.a. The library's subject strengths lie primarily in military science, military history, and international relations with a rating of A, and in political theory and constitutional history with a B rating. The library supports the curricula and the research interests of the three component colleges of the university: the Industrial College of the Armed Forces, the Information Resources Management College, and the National War College.

b. Special collections include classics on the art of war; Fort McNair History; and Alfred H. Hausrath Collection on Wargaming.

4. The library holds a substantial collection of technical reports. Archival holdings consist of collections, such as documents on industrial mobilization, including Bernard Baruch's papers; the Hudson Institute Archives; the papers of General Frank S. Besson, first commander of the Army Materiel Command; the papers of Fred Hoffman, a former defense correspondent of the Associated Press; papers from the Presidential Commission on the Assignment of Women in the Armed Forces; and archives of Na-

tional Defense University and its constituent colleges.

There are also several more recent collections of diplomatic and military papers, some of which may require clearance. These include the papers of Gen. Andrew J. Goodpaster (1968–74); Gen. Maxwell Taylor (World War II to 1981); Gen. Lyman L. Lemnitzer (1952–69); Dr. Ralph L. Powell (papers on modern China); Dr. Richard W. Van Wangenen (a member of the Allied Control Authority of Germany, 1945–47).

5. There is a card catalog. The library staff includes specialists in the fields of government and politics, military history, military art and science, strategic planning, World War I, and World War II.

6. Index Terms: Collective Security; Defense Policy, National; Diplomacy and Negotiations; Military History; Military Science; Political Systems and Ideologies

See also entry K10

**National Endowment for the Humanities (NEH) Library   See entry K26**

**National Firearms Museum Library   See entry C7**

**National Institute for Dispute Resolution (NIDR) Library   See entry N42**

## A34   National Labor Relations Board — Library

1.a. 1099 14th Street, NW
Washington, D.C. 20570
(202) 273-3720
Fax: (202) 273-4286

b. 8:30 A.M.–5:00 P.M. Monday–Friday

c. The library is open to the public for on-site use. Interlibrary loan and photocopying facilities are available.

d. Kenneth E. Nero, Administrative Librarian

2.a. The library holds a total of 50,000 volumes and receives approximately 60 periodicals.

b. Though the number of directly relevant volumes does not amount to more than 1,000, their value to the users of this Guide rests in their specific

focus on the limited but crucial field of arbitration and mediation, and conciliation.

3.a. The library's holdings pertain to labor history, labor-management relations, and legislative histories. Approximately half the collection consists of law reviews, public interest journals, federal regulatory codes, and some state regulations.

b. Approximately 180 titles relate to negotiation, labor bargaining, and industrial arbitration. Another 50 titles deal with dispute resolution and mediation, and conciliation.

5. There are subject, and name and title card catalogs.

6. Index Terms: Conflict Management and Resolution; Peace Theory and Research

## A35   National Library of Medicine (Health and Human Services Department — Public Health Service — National Institutes of Health)

1.a. 8600 Rockville Pike
Bethesda, Md. 20894
(301) 496-6095 (Reference Service)
(301) 496-5405 (History of Medicine Division)
Fax: (301) 496-2809

b. 8:30 A.M.–5:00 P.M. Monday, Friday
8:30 A.M.–9:00 P.M. Tuesday–Thursday
8:30 A.M.–12:30 P.M. Saturday
Summer hours (Memorial Day to Labor Day) vary.

c. The library is open for on-site use, but access to the stacks is restricted to employees. Visitors may request that materials be brought to the reading room as needed. All first-time users are required to obtain a registration number at the circulation desk. Photocopying and interlibrary loan services are available.

d. Donald A. B. Lindberg, Director

2.a. The collection numbers about 1.9 million volumes, approximately 25,000 serial titles are received annually.

b. Only a small part of the library's holdings, probably no more than 25,000 volumes, pertain to peace and international security studies. Relevant holdings relate to international organizations, principally the World Health Organization (WHO), international relations, economic development and foreign assistance, and the medical effects of nuclear war. The collection ranks in the B range for the field of international organizations and the C range for international relations.

3.a. A search of the on-line system produced 796 citations for developing countries; 633 citations on foreign aid, which covers international cooperation between industrialized and developing countries; 32 citations on disease control in developing countries; and 52 citations on health and welfare planning in developing countries. The areas of international relations and international law (relevant also to economic development and humanitarian issues) are represented by foreign nations' statistical materials (vital and health statistics), with holdings often extending back into the 19th century; legislation and international treaties pertaining to health and sanitation; and government nutrition and mortality studies.

b. Some 250 volumes relate to the medical effects of nuclear war. These include, among other topics, specific aspects of treating victims of nuclear disaster, diseases associated with nuclear fallout, protection from fallout, psychological dimensions of nuclear conflict, and prospects for nuclear war.

4. Serials of foreign governments are well represented, particularly the annual reports and bulletins of national, state, and municipal public health agencies; reports of national disease-control agencies; and the publications of military medical services. The library holds 1,124 World Health Organization (WHO) reports and proceedings, as well as 240 WHO serial titles.

5. For the library as a whole (including historical collections) there is an on-line catalog. Records for monographs can also be located in the printed catalog covering acquisitions processed between 1950 and 1965 and in *National Library of Medicine Current Catalog (1965 to 1993)*. *Index Medicus* provides access to articles in over 2,500 journals.

Since the mid-1960s, the National Library of Medicine (NLM) has proven to be an international trailblazer in the burgeoning realm of bibliographic and information databases for the health sciences. NLM delivers literature retrieval services through a computerized system known as MEDLARS (Medical Literature Analysis and Retrieval System) that contains some 8 million references to books and journal articles in the health sciences published since 1965. Although based at the NLM campus in Bethesda, Md., MEDLARS and its many subsystems are available to a network of more than 80,000 universities, medical schools, hospitals, government

agencies, and commercial organizations and individuals in the United States and 17 foreign countries.

6. Index Terms: Arms Control; Development Issues—Health; Humanitarian Issues; International Law; International Organizations; Military Science—Civil Defense and Effects of Nuclear War

See also entry K19

**National Museum of American History (NMAH) (Smithsonian Institution)  See entry C8**

**National Science Foundation (NSF) Library  See entry K27**

---

## A36  Navy Department Library

---

1.a. Washington Navy Yard, Building 44
901 M Street, SE
Washington, D.C. 20374-5060
(202) 433-4131
Fax: (202) 433-9553

b. 8:30 A.M.–4:30 P.M. Monday–Friday

c. The library is open to the public for on-site use. Interlibrary loan and photocopying facilities are available.

d. Frances Q. Deel, Director
Jean Hort, Head, Reference and Readers' Services

2.a. The library holds more than 170,000 volumes, as well as some 10,000 microfilm rolls. Approximately 325 periodicals are received.

b. Approximately 90 percent of the holdings are oriented toward international security studies pertaining to the fields of naval history, planning, and strategy, arms control and deterrence, diplomacy and negotiations, and international law. See also entries for the holdings of the Naval Historical Center, B13, D9, E13, and F23.

3.a. The collection ranks in the A range for the subjects of naval science, military science, and international relations, and the B range for international law. There may be specialized titles in these fields that are not available at the Library of Congress. Aside from naval and military affairs, the Navy Department Library emphasizes general history (14,692 titles by on-line search), international law, diplomacy, and government. The library's primary strength lies in naval history, with particular emphasis on U.S. and British navies. Military science and strategy, in general, are very well represented in the collection, particularly regarding naval and combined operations. Specific strengths are in naval art and science, naval tactics, naval aviation, naval warfare, and the marines. Arms control, deterrence, and nuclear warfare also are well represented. In addition, the library has major holdings on the Soviet navy, especially post-World War II. Histories of individual wars and specific sea battles are extensively covered.

Similarly, the collection has substantial holdings on many subjects specific to naval affairs such as naval architecture and shipbuilding; naval customs and traditions; and naval regulations, orders, and instructions.

b. The Navy Department Library maintains a rare book section, which is separately cataloged, of approximately 5,000 volumes dating primarily from 1699 to 1820. These holdings, in various languages, all relate to naval affairs. Predominant topics include accounts of cruises, exploration, and major battles and naval engagements.

4. The library is a selective depository for government documents. Its holdings selectively cover all armed services and focus especially on congressional reports, hearings and legislation, and reports of the Secretary of the Navy and naval boards and panels. It has on microfilm significant portions of the navy's archives from the National Archives.

The library holds roughly 1,600 vertical files dating from 1955. These are primarily on naval subjects. Topics include aviation history, African-Americans in the military, navy SEALs, navies of the world, biographies of naval personnel (mostly obituaries of flag officers), intelligence material, environmental health reports, and some special reports on Pearl Harbor.

The library also has a large collection of manuscripts, many regarding cruises and explorations. A special collection of unpublished unit histories, produced by naval historians on active duty during World War II, includes studies of wartime U.S. naval operations in the South Atlantic, the Caribbean, and the Canal Zone. The histories are described in William C. Heimdahl and Edward J. Marolda (comps.), *Guide to United States Naval Administrative Histories of World War II* (1976), published by the Naval History Division of the Naval Historical Center. The library holds an extensive collection of doctoral dissertations on naval and military history.

For a description of the archival holdings of the Naval Historical Center see entry B13. The library's map collection is described in entry D10.

5. The library has an on-line catalog. Special collections are cataloged in separate card catalogs. A descriptive pamphlet is available.

6. Index Terms: Arms Control; Deterrence; Diplomacy and Negotiations; International Law; Military History—Navy; Naval Science

See also entries B13, D9, D10, E13, F23, K30

---

## A37 Nitze School of Advanced International Studies (SAIS) (Johns Hopkins University)—Library

---

1.a. 1740 Massachusetts Avenue, NW
Washington, D.C. 20036
(202) 663-5900 (Reference)
Fax: (202) 663-5916

b. Academic Year
8:30 A.M.–11:00 P.M. Monday–Thursday
8:30 A.M.–7:00 P.M. Friday
10:00 A.M.–10:00 P.M. Saturday
11:00 A.M.–11:00 P.M. Sunday
When classes are not in session
8:30 A.M.–5:00 P.M. Monday–Friday

c. Open with restrictions. Limited access granted to scholars needing to consult materials not readily available in other area libraries. Scholars should call to arrange for access. Interlibrary loan and photocopying services are available.

d. Peter J. Promen, Director

2.a. The total collection numbers 105,000 volumes, and the library currently subscribes to 900 periodicals.

b. Based on measurements taken of the general collection, the international security and peace studies holdings amount to 26,970 volumes.

3.a–b. The collection consists largely of English-language secondary literature published since 1950. From the viewpoint of peace and international security studies the subject strengths are international finance and international relations.

c. Subject strengths and evaluations:

| Subject | Number of Titles | Rating |
|---|---|---|
| Philosophy—War and Peace | 166 | — |
| Psychology—War and Peace | 61 | — |
| Ethics—War and Peace | 23 | — |
| Religion—War and Peace | 403 | — |
| World History | 2,329 | — |
| History—Military Science | 63 | — |
| Geography—Military | 4 | — |
| Anthropology—War and Peace | 24 | — |
| Economic History and Conditions | 4,587 | C |
| Commercial Policy | 1,656 | C |
| International Finance | 534 | B |
| Sociology | 1,308 | — |
| Political Theory | 872 | C |
| Constitutional History and Administration | 1,075 | C |
| Colonies and Emigration | 54 | C |
| International Relations | 1,321 | B |
| International Organizations | 1,398 | C |
| International Law | 625 | — |
| Education—International Relations and Military | 173 | — |
| Music: Military | 0 | — |
| Art and War | 0 | — |
| Military Science | 1,859 | C |
| Naval Science | 108 | — |
| Bibliography and Reference | 239 | — |

4. The library receives a wide array of journals related to international relations and economics.

5. Library holdings are classified according to the Library of Congress classification scheme. All holdings are included in the library's CD-ROM catalog.

6. Index Terms: Arms Control; Collective Security; Defense Policy, National; Deterrence; Diplomacy and Negotiations; Foreign Policy; International Organizations; Military History; Military Science

See also entry J11

---

# A38 Organization of American States (OAS)—Columbus Memorial Library

1.a. Constitution Avenue and 19th Street, NW
Washington, D.C. 20006
(202) 458-6040 (Director)
(202) 458-6037 (Reference)
Fax: (202) 458-3914

b. 9:30 A.M.–4:30 P.M. Monday–Friday
(Stack service until 4:30 P.M.)

c. Open to the public (stack access restricted). Interlibrary loan service is available, as is a relatively expensive photocopying service. There are no individual photocopying machines.

d. Virginia Newton, Director
Lucilia Harrington, Reference Librarian

2.a. The collection totals more than 300,000 Latin American—related volumes, some 4,560 serial titles (currently received and retrospective), and approximately 150,000 government (largely OAS) documents.

b. The primary relevance of this library lies in economic history and conditions, among Latin American countries, including developmental issues. A shelflist count revealed approximately 10,550 volumes directly pertinent to peace and international security studies. For a description of the archival and audio holdings in OAS's Records Management Center, see entries B14 and E14, respectively.

3.a. The OAS library has the second strongest Latin American collection in the Washington area after the Library of Congress. Holdings are strongest in works produced between 1890 and 1950, with some major post-1950 titles in international relations, the social sciences, history, and literature. Within the scope of this Guide the main strength of the holdings lies in the documents collection (see point 4 below) rather than in the book collection, where the number of directly relevant items (mainly in international relations and organizations) is relatively modest.

c. Subject categories and evaluations:

| Subject | Number of Titles | Rating |
|---|---|---|
| Philosophy—War and Peace | 278 | — |
| Psychology—War and Peace | 67 | — |
| Ethics—War and Peace | 47 | — |
| Religion—War and Peace | 77 | — |
| World History | 442 | — |
| History—Military Science | 5 | — |
| Geography—Military | 7 | — |
| Anthropology—War and Peace | 14 | — |
| Economic History and Conditions | 1,461 | — |
| Commercial Policy | 663 | — |
| International Finance | 0 | — |
| Sociology | 375 | — |
| Political Theory | 563 | — |

| Subject | Number of Titles | Rating |
|---|---|---|
| Constitutional History | 181 | — |
| Administration | | |
| Colonies and Emigration | 64 | — |
| International Relations | 653 | B |
| International Organizations | 844 | C |
| International Law | 1,397 | C |
| Education—International | 0 | — |
| Relations and Military | | |
| Music—Military | 1 | — |
| Art and War | 0 | — |
| Military Science | 71 | — |
| Naval Science | 7 | — |
| Bibliography and Reference | 169 | — |

4. Serial holdings include government statistical publications and ministerial reports, and major academic and scholarly journals from every Latin American nation. The approximately 700 Latin American periodicals currently received focus largely on government statistics, social and economic development, and international relations. The library has a substantial collection of Latin American newspapers on microfilm, mainly for the 1940s and 1950s.

The library maintains a separate collection of some 150,000 documents and publications of the OAS and specialized inter-American agencies. The primary finding-aid for this collection is an ongoing annual OAS accumulation, *Documentos Oficiales de la Organización de los Estados Americanos*.

The library is also a depository for United Nations documents and has strong collections of Economic Commission for Latin America (ECLA), United Nations Conference on Trade and Development (UNCTAD), and General Agreement on Tariffs and Trade (GATT) materials.

The library administers a small archive containing copies of Pan American Union and OAS documents from 1890 to the present. Included are the minutes, proceedings, and reports of inter-American conferences and congresses (and many collections of related newspaper clippings), the minutes of the Governing Board of the Pan American Union, and the records of OAS council sessions. Miscellaneous materials include World War II records of the Inter-American Defense Board and the Inter-American Emergency Advisory Committee for Political Defense, and copies of the records of the first meeting (1960) of the Board of Governors of the Inter-American Development Bank. Many of these archival copies are not duplicated in the library's general collection or documents collection.

The library's map collection is described in entry D11. The library's photograph collection is described in entry F24.

5. The principal finding-aids are the main card catalog (a dictionary catalog) and the periodicals card catalog. Separate shelflists are available for OAS and UN documents and for the rare book collection. A quarterly *List of Recent Accessions* is published. The quarterly *Inter-American Review of Bibliography*, prepared by the OAS Department of Cultural Affairs, also contains bibliographic information on the library's accessions.

Researchers should note that the Department of Educational Affairs of the OAS General Secretariat maintains its own separate Documentation and Information Library. The Columbus Memorial Library's card catalog does not reflect the holdings of this collection.

6. Index Terms: Development Issues; International Law; International Organizations—Regional

See also entries B14, D11, E14, F24, and L13

---

## A39 Organization for Economic Cooperation and Development (OECD)— Information and Publications Center

1.a. 2001 L Street, NW, Suite 700
Washington, D.C. 20036
(202) 785-6323
Fax: (202) 785-0350

b. 9:00 A.M.–5:00 P.M. Monday–Friday

c. Open to the public for on-site use. The center does not participate in interlibrary loan. Self-service photocopying is available.

d. Denis Lamb, Washington Representative

2.a. The center maintains one of the most complete libraries of OECD publications in the United States. Holdings also include publications of the following corporate bodies: OECD's predecessor, the Organization for European Economic Cooperation (OEEC); International Energy Agency (IEA); Nuclear Energy Agency (NEA); and the European Conference of Ministers of Transport (ECMT). The collection numbers approximately 2,500 monographs.

b. The pertinence of the center's holdings lies in OECD publications on migration, international economic relations, development issues, and international organization.

3. The collection ranks in the B range in the fields of international finance, colonies and emigration, and international organizations. General holdings pertain to general economic analysis and forecasting, energy, development and aid, labor and social issues, science and technology, financial markets, multinational enterprises and foreign investment, agriculture, transportation, tourism, industrial issues, education, environmental and urban problems, taxation, consumer protection, and internationally standardized statistical studies. The OECD also publishes the *Economic Survey* series on an annual or biennial basis, which includes member and nonmember countries.

Recent examples of relevant titles on emigration and immigration include *Trends in International Migration.* Titles on development include *Debt Relief and Growth, Redefining the State in Latin America, From Trade-Driven Growth to Growth-Driven Trade,* and *Development Co-operation: Efforts and Policies of the Members of the Development Assistance Committee,* 1993 report. This last volume contains information on foreign assistance flows from donor countries. The OECD in the past several years has started to publish material on economic transition and privatization in Eastern Europe and the republics of the former Soviet Union (some of these countries are also covered by the *Economic Survey* series). This series includes *Integrating Emerging Market Economies into the International Trading System.* The center also has a limited selection of unpublished OECD working documents.

4. The center retains vertical file copies of OECD and IEA press releases as well as information pertaining to the activities of OECD and its affiliated bodies. The center routinely provides details about major OECD meetings.

5. No card catalog is maintained. For titles still in print, the OECD *Catalog of Publications* is a useful guide. The OECD *Index,* a bibliographical database of OECD publications and documents, is available to visitors.

6. Index Terms: Development Issues; International Economics—Integration; International Organizations—Regional

**Overseas Development Council (ODC) Library   See entry H60**

**Overseas Private Investment Corporation (OPIC) (International Development Cooperation Agency) Library   See entry K32**

## A40   Peace Corps—Library

1.a. 1990 K Street, NW, Room 5353
Washington, D.C. 20526
(202) 606-3307
Fax: (202) 606-3108

b. 8:30 A.M.–5:00 P.M. Monday–Friday

c. The library is open to the public for on-site use. Interlibrary loan and self-service photocopying facilities are available.

d. Terry Cappuccilli, Librarian

2.a. The Peace Corps Library holds some 12,000 books and subscribes to approximately 150 periodicals from around the world.

b. The holdings' pertinence to the scope of this Guide lies chiefly in the fields of economic development, human rights, and peace studies.

3. The collection ranks in the B range for the field of education and in the C range for international relations, and economic history and conditions. Relevant holdings consist largely of country studies and secondary literature in the areas of history, economics, development, and general culture, as well as training materials.

4. The Peace Corps Library's major research resource is its collection of Peace Corps program documents and legislative history dating from the agency's inception to the present. Included are country training manuals, project reports, country program evaluations, volunteers' newsletters, and speeches. The library's vertical file collection contains approximately 1,400 folders about topics related to Peace Corps programs, developing countries, organizations dealing with development, and special subjects.

5. The library has a card catalog. All books and documents are shelved by region and country. The library compiles bibliographies of all countries in which the Peace Corps operates, which include general citations about those countries.

6. Index Terms: Economic Development; Human Rights; Humanitarian Issues; Peace Theory and Research

See also entries F25 and K33

## A41 Pentagon Library (Army Department)

1.a. Pentagon, Room 1A518
Washington, D.C. 20310-6605
(703) 697-4301 (Reference)
Fax: (703) 693-6543

b. 9:00 A.M.–4:00 P.M. Monday–Friday

c. Entrance to the Pentagon is restricted to Defense Department personnel. Researchers who can gain access to the building may use the library, but the library cannot provide escort service into the building. Self-service photocopying and interlibrary loan service are available.

d. Louise Nyce, Director

2.a. Library holdings total 164,000 book volumes and 9,000 technical reports. The library subscribes to about 1,500 periodicals and 7,225 other serials.

b. About 90 percent of the library's holdings are relevant to peace and international security studies in the fields of military science, diplomacy and negotiations, international economics, and international law.

3. The collection ranks in the A range for the fields of military science and international relations and in the B range for economic history and conditions, political theory, and constitutional history and administration. The library has significant holdings in military history, current events, economics, biography, law, and international relations.

4. Of major interest to researchers are the library's holdings of military documents dating back to World War I and originating from the army and the Defense Department. The library also serves as a partial depository for Government Printing Office publications.

5. There is an on-line public catalog. A list of currently received periodicals is issued annually.

6. Index Terms: Collective Security; Defense Policy, National; Diplomacy and Negotiations; International Economics; International Law; Military History—Army; Military Science; Political Systems and Ideologies

See also entries B3, B4, C2, C3, E3, and K5

## Population Action International (PAI) (*formerly* Population Crisis Committee) Library   See entry M48

**Population Reference Bureau Library**   See entry H62

**Resources for the Future (RFF) Library**   See entry H67

## A42 Senate Library

1.a. Capitol Building, Room S-332
Washington, D.C. 20510-7112
(202) 224-7106 (Reference)
(202) 224-2971 (Legislative Status)
Fax: (202) 224-0879

b. 9:00 A.M.–5:30 P.M. Monday–Friday (and whenever the Senate is in session)

c. The library is restricted to the use of senators and their staff. Private researchers may, however, make use of the library with a letter of introduction from a senator. There is no interlibrary loan service, but photocopying facilities are available.

d. Roger K. Haley, Librarian

2.a. The collection holds 150,000 volumes.

b. About one-third of the holdings pertains to international economic, military, and political affairs.

3.a. The holdings are in the B range for the legislative background of commercial policy, international finance, international relations, international law, military science, and naval science. The library is primarily a legislative and general reference collection with comprehensive holdings of congressional publications. Operated under the direction of the Secretary of the Senate, it is not part of the Library of Congress. Holdings include Senate and House bills and resolutions, reports, hearings, and other publications. U.S. foreign relations and congressional activities bearing on those relations are covered. The reference staff of the library specializes in compiling legislative histories. U.S. treaties and related documentation are available.

b. Since 1979 the Senate Library has been a selective depository for U.S. government documents. Among items received are State Department publications that provide in-depth treatment of individual countries. The library also has a complete set of U.S. treaties and all committee reports regarding foreign affairs.
The library has described its micrographics center as having an extensive microform collection of congressional documents, popular periodicals, and

newspapers, which now totals about 500,000 microfiche and over 2,500 reels of microfilm.

4. The library receives the following journals that are relevant to peace and international security studies: *Defense and Foreign Affairs Weekly* (on-line), *Defense and Foreign Affairs Daily* (on-line), *Department of State Newsletter, European Community Foreign Affairs, Foreign Policy, Highlights of U.S. Import-Export Trade, International Economic Indicators, International Energy Statistical Review, International Financial Statistics, Weekly Compilation of Presidential Documents, White House Press Releases,* and *World Financial Markets* (on-line). The library subscribes to *Summary of World Broadcasts* (on-line). Among wire services received are UPI World and National Wires.

The following congressional publications are available in the Senate Library. Proceedings are given in the *Journals of the Continental Congress* (1774–89), *Senate Journal* (1789–present), *Senate Executive Journal* (1789–present), *House Journal* (1789–present), *Annals of Congress* (1789–1824), *Debates in Congress* (1824–1938), *Abridgment of the Debates of Congress* (1789–1850), *Congressional Globe* (1833–73), *Congressional Record* (1873–present). Further documentation is provided by *Bills and Resolutions of Senate and House* (1789–present), *Committee Hearings of Senate and House* (1839–present), *Committee Prints of Senate and House* (1830–present), *American State Papers* (1789–1833), *Serial Set* (reports and documents of Senate and House, 1817–present).

The library also has a large collection of documents from the Executive Branch including the *Federal Register,* White House press releases, and the annual reports of many executive agencies.

5. The library has an on-line catalog to its collection.

6. Index terms: Arms Control; Deterrence; Diplomacy and Negotiations; Development Issues; Human Rights; Humanitarian Issues; International Economics; International Law; Military History; Peace Theory and Research

See also entries K8, K9, and K35

---

## A43 State Department Library

1.a. State Department Building, Room 3239
2201 C Street, NW
Washington, D.C. 20520

(202) 647-1099 (Reference)
Fax: (202) 647-2971

b. 8:15 A.M.–5:00 P.M. Monday–Friday

c. Access is limited to employees of the department. However, scholars who have not been able to locate needed materials elsewhere in the Washington, D.C., area may request permission to use the collection. Interlibrary loan and photocopying services are available.

d. Dan O. Clemmer, Head Librarian
Lucinda Conger, Chief, Reader Services

2.a. The library holds nearly 750,000 volumes and receives approximately 1,000 periodicals.

b. On the basis of measurements taken of the general collection, the library holds approximately 143,410 volumes pertaining to peace and international security studies. In the Washington, D.C., area, these holdings rank second, after the Library of Congress collection, in offering a broad and diversified coverage in both peace and international security studies. In size, however, they are exceeded by specialized military collections of the National Defense University (A33), Navy Department (A36), and Pentagon (A41) libraries.

3.a–b. Peace and international security holdings are strongest in economic history and conditions, international trade and finance, constitutional and administrative history, international relations, international organizations, international law, and military science.

c. Subject categories and evaluations:

| Subject | Number of Titles | Rating |
|---|---|---|
| Philosophy—War and Peace | 420 | — |
| Psychology—War and Peace | 179 | — |
| Ethics—War and Peace | 213 | — |
| Religion—War and Peace | 1,369 | — |
| World History | 8,810 | B |
| History—Military Science | 155 | — |
| Geography—Military | 36 | C |
| Anthropology—War and Peace | 41 | — |
| Economic History and Conditions | 22,115 | B+ |
| Commercial Policy | 8,230 | B+ |
| International Finance | 2,079 | B+ |
| Sociology | 6,851 | B |
| Political Theory | 3,211 | B |
| Constitutional History and Administration | 6,811 | B+ |
| Colonies and Emigration | 355 | B+ |
| International Relations | 12,763 | A |

| Subject | Number of Titles | Rating |
|---|---|---|
| International Organizations | 8,605 | B+ |
| International Law | 8,602 | B+ |
| Education—International Relations and Military | 727 | B |
| Music—Military | 0 | — |
| Art and War | 2 | — |
| Military Science | 7,020 | B |
| Naval Science | 718 | B |
| Bibliography and Reference | 1,080 | B |

4. The library's collections of international treaty materials and State Department publications (notably foreign service and consular lists and State Department press releases) are the most comprehensive in the area.

5. There is an on-line Public Access Catalog, covering from 1978 to the present. In addition, the library has undertaken a retrospective conversion of its English-language titles to machine-readable form.

The library publishes a monthly acquisitions list as well as an irregular series of bibliographies on topical foreign affairs issues. In addition, the library prepares short subject- and country-oriented bibliographies for publication each month in the State Department newsletter, *State*. A brief guide, *Department of State Library* (1988), is available without charge.

6. Index Terms: Arms Control; Collective Security; Defense Policy, National; Deterrence; Conflict Resolution and Management; Diplomacy and Negotiations; Development Issues; Human Rights; Humanitarian Issues; International Economics; International Law; International Organizations; Military Science; Naval Science; Political Systems and Ideologies

See also entry K37

## Trade and Development Agency (TDA) (International Development Cooperation Agency) Library    See entry K38

## Transportation Department (DOT) Library    See entry K39

## Treasury Department Library    See entry K40

## United Nations Development Programme (UNDP)—Washington Office Library    See entry L14

## A44    United Nations—Information Center—Library

1.a. 1775 K Street, NW
Washington, D.C. 20006
(202) 331-8670
Fax: (202) 289-4267

b. 9:00 A.M.–1:00 P.M. Monday–Friday

c. Open to the public for on-site use. Telephone inquiries accepted until 5:00 P.M. Interlibrary loan and photocopying facilities are available.

No publications are sold at the center in Washington, D.C. Documents may be borrowed through interlibrary loan. Those of general interest may be borrowed for a period of one week. Reference materials circulate for one day only. Individuals may place their names on the center's mailing list to receive the *Weekly News Summary*, the *Monthly Chronicle*, and *Notes and Documents* (issued by the Center against Apartheid).

d. Jeanne Dixon, Reference Assistant

2.a. The collection totals approximately 10,000 items.

b. All the holdings are pertinent to the topics of this Guide, particularly to the fields of arms control, conflict resolution, economic development, human rights, international law, international organizations, and peacekeeping.

3.a. The collection ranks in the A range for the fields of international relations and international organizations, and the B range for international law. The Information Centre Library maintains an up-to-date reference collection of UN documents and publications. This includes the official record of the General Assembly, Security Council, Economic and Social Council, and Trusteeship Council from 1946 until the present, as well as records from the International Court of Justice. Particularly valuable is a complete collection of the UN Treaty Series. Also included among its holdings are council and committee proceedings, statistical references on issues ranging from nuclear energy to world women contributions to economic development, and reports of special conferences such as UN Conference on Trade and Development (UNCTAD) and Law of the Sea. Documents from UN regional commissions, such as the Economic Commission for Latin America and the Caribbean (ECLAC) (L15), are incomplete but the center can provide liaison with the United Nation's New York City documents library and with ECLAC/CEPAL headquarters in Santiago, Chile.

b. Of particular interest to the users of this Guide are documents on current UN peacekeeping and conflict resolution efforts. Contained in loose-leaf binders, they cover International Atomic Energy Agency Inspection Reports, Yugoslavia, 1993 (4 volumes); Security Council Resolutions, 1991–Current; Cambodia; Somalia; Truth Commission Report, 1993 (and annex); the Iraq-Kuwait Situation, 1990 (3 volumes), 1991 (3 volumes, 2 miscellaneous files), 1991–92 (miscellaneous file); the Iraq-Kuwait Compensation Commission, 1990–91; and Iraq-Kuwait Resolutions, 1990–91, 1993. The information center distributes *Peace-Keeping Information Notes,* which gives a brief overview of UN peacekeeping activity worldwide.

4. The library's film and video collection is described in entry F27.

5. The library has the Readex United Nations document index.

6. Index Terms: Conflict Resolution and Management; Development Issues; Human Rights; Humanitarian Issues; International Law; International Organizations—United Nations; Peacekeeping

See also entries F27 and H69

---

## A45 United States Holocaust Research Institute—Library

1.a. 100 Raoul Wallenberg Place, SW
Washington, D.C. 20024-2150
(202) 488-0400
Fax: (202) 479-9726

b. 10:00 A.M.–5:30 P.M. Daily
Closed Christmas and Yom Kippur.

c. The library is open to the public for on-site use. Interlibrary loan is not available; photocopying facilities are available.

d. Elizabeth Koenig, Director

2.a. The collection is currently at more than 20,000 volumes.

b. The entire collection pertains to the subject matter of this Guide, especially in terms of human rights.

3.a. The collection ranks in the A range for international relations and in the B range for world history and international law. The library is part of the

United States Holocaust Research Institute. The primary focus of the library is the Holocaust, although it aims to collect material on war crimes and human rights more generally. The library was established in 1993 and the eventual goal is for at least 100,000 volumes. Current acquisitions focus on the past 50 years, especially regarding out-of-print books. Future acquisitions will be more concerned with contemporary human rights and war crime issues. Although English is the primary language there are also works in Czech, German, Polish, Hebrew, Rumanian, French, Latvian, Danish, Italian, and Spanish among others. Much of the library's holdings relate to the prosecution of war crimes trials. It holds a set of the 1948 Nuremberg proceedings, *International Military Tribunal, Trial of the Major War Criminals* (known as the "Blue Series") and the subsequent trial proceedings on Nazi conspiracy and aggression (the "Green Series"). The library holds a copy of *The Holocaust,* by Jacob Robinson, which provides a very rare index to these series and other Holocaust material.

b. Considerable library material traces the history of anti-Semitism (e.g., the Dreyfus affair is well covered).

4. The library has a vertical file of clippings, articles, and miscellaneous material relating to the Holocaust. The institute's archives are described in entry B16. The institute's film and photography departments are described in entry F29.

5. The library has an on-line catalog system. Available is *Subject Heading Authority List, United States Holocaust Memorial Museum,* which will assist with key word searches. The library primarily uses Library of Congress headings with some specific subject headings of its own.

6. Index Terms: Ethnic and Religious Conflict; Human Rights; Humanitarian Issues; International Law; War Crimes

See also entries B16, C11, F29, and H72

**United States Information Agency (USIA) Library   See entry K41**

---

## A46 United States Institute of Peace (USIP)—Library

1.a. 1550 M Street, NW, Suite 700
Washington, D.C. 20005-1708

(202) 457-1700
Fax: (202) 429-6063

b. 9:00 A.M.–5:00 P.M. Monday–Friday

c. Open to the public by appointment for on-site use. Interlibrary loan and photocopying facilities are available.

d. Margarita S. Studemeister, Director, Jeannette Rankin Library Program

2.a. The library contains 4,500 books and receives 165 periodicals.

b. The entire collection pertains to peace and international security studies with special strength in arms control, international law, and conflict resolution.

3. The collection ranks in the A range in the field of international relations. The library primarily supports the work and research of practitioners in the field and of the United States Institute of Peace (H73) whose chief focus is the pacific settlement of international disputes. The library has a strong orientation toward conflict resolution, as well as international relations and peace studies.

4. All periodicals received relate to international studies and conflict resolution. Six foreign newspapers are received. The library maintains an archive of legislative and historical materials relating to the institute. The library's video collection is described in entry F30.

5. The library's collection is cataloged on an on-line system.

6. Index Terms: Arms Control; Conflict Management and Resolution; International Law; Peace Theory and Research

See also entries F30 and H73

### United States Trade Representative Library
See entry K42

---

## A47 University of Maryland at College Park — McKeldin Library

---

1.a. College Park, Md. 20742-7011
    (301) 405-9075 (Reference)
    (301) 405-9127 (Administration)
    Fax: (301) 314-9416

b. 8:00 A.M.–11:00 P.M. Monday–Thursday
   8:00 A.M.–6:00 P.M. Friday
   10:00 A.M.–6:00 P.M. Saturday
   Noon–11:00 P.M. Sunday

c. Open to the public. Interlibrary loan and photocopying facilities are available.

d. H. Joanne Harrar, Director of Libraries
   Wilson Plunkett, Head, Government Documents
   Lauren Brown, Curator, Archives and Manuscript Department

2.a. Campus libraries hold some 2.1 million volumes. More than 22,000 periodicals are currently received, as well as 168 newspapers.

b. On the basis of measurements taken on the general collection, the McKeldin Library holds approximately 114,300 volumes pertaining to peace studies and international security. These holdings rank only marginally behind Georgetown University (A20) in breadth and depth, making them the second largest in size and importance among university libraries in the Washington, D.C., area. (Outside the university libraries, however, its holdings are exceeded in size by the relevant collections in the Library of Congress [A29] and the State Department Library [A43], as well as several specialized military libraries, namely those of the National Defense University [A33], Navy Department [A36], and Pentagon [A41].)

3.a–b. From the viewpoint of peace and international security studies the collection is particularly strong in philosophical, psychological, ethical, and religious aspects of war and peace, international economics and finance, political theory, constitutional and administrative history, international relations, international organizations, and military and naval science.

c. Subject categories and evaluations:

| Subject | Number of Titles | Rating |
|---|---|---|
| Philosophy—War and Peace | 7,831 | B+ |
| Psychology—War and Peace | 7,237 | B+ |
| Ethics—War and Peace | 1,676 | B |
| Religion—War and Peace | 5,780 | B |
| World History | 10,552 | B |
| History—Military Science | 458 | B |
| Geography—Military | 17 | C |
| Anthropology—War and Peace | 422 | B |
| Economic History and Conditions | 11,047 | B |
| Commercial Policy | 2,282 | B |
| International Finance | 961 | B |
| Sociology | 10,760 | B |
| Political Theory | 4,334 | B+ |

| Subject | Number of Titles | Rating |
|---|---|---|
| Constitutional History and Administration | 5,993 | B |
| Colonies and Emigration | 390 | B+ |
| International Relations | 1,858 | B+ |
| International Organizations | 2,143 | B |
| International Law | 1,163 | C |
| Education—International Relations and Military | 546 | B |
| Music—Military | 25 | B |
| Art and War | 69 | B |
| Military Science | 3,433 | B |
| Naval Science | 498 | C |
| Bibliography and Reference | 540 | C |

4. McKeldin Library is a regional depository for U.S. government documents. Its documents collection—in excess of 500,000 items—is virtually complete for the period 1925–present, with a substantial holding of earlier series. The library also has impressive holdings of the publications of international organizations, in particular the United Nations and the League of Nations, International Monetary Fund (L11), and the Organization of American States (L13).

The Archives and Manuscripts Department (301/405-9058), housed on the third floor of McKeldin Library (10:00 A.M.–5:00 P.M., Monday–Friday), is open to the public, with photocopying services available. Research guides are available, including *Guide to Historical Manuscript Collections*. The primary holdings of interest are the papers of Millard Tydings, U.S. Senator from Maryland and member of the Armed Services Committee. Also housed on the third floor is the Marylandia Rare Book Collection.

Concerning map holdings see entry D12. For descriptions of the National Public Broadcasting Archives in the Non-Print Media Services, see entries E16 and F31.

5. The library has an on-line system named VICTOR.

6. Index terms: Arms Control; Conflict Resolution and Management; Deterrence; Development Issues; Diplomacy and Negotiations; Foreign Policy; Human Rights; Humanitarian Issues; International Economics; International Law; International Organizations; Military History; Military Science; Naval Science; Political Systems and Ideologies; Psychological Aspects of War and Peace

See also entries D12, E16, F31, and J13

## University of the District of Columbia (UDC) Library    See entry J14

## Urban Institute Library    See entry H74

## Woodrow Wilson International Center for Scholars (WWICS) Library    See entry H76

## World Wildlife Fund (WWF) Library    See entry N61

# B

# Archives and Manuscript Repositories

**Archive and Manuscript Repositories Entry Format (B)**

1. *General Information*
   a. address; telephone number(s)
   b. hours of service
   c. conditions of access
   d. photocopying facilities
   e. name/title of director and heads of relevant divisions

2. *Size of Holdings Pertaining to Peace and International Security Studies*

3. *Description of Holdings Pertaining to Peace and International Security Studies*

4. *Bibliographic Aids Facilitating Use of Collection*

5. *Index Terms* (relevant subject specialties)

**Introductory Note**

The archival materials stored in the repositories of the Washington, D.C., area are among the world's most extensive, offering scholars virtually limitless research possibilities in many fields, including peace and international security studies. In this section an effort has been made to highlight the holdings of the most important collections in order to apprise researchers of the nature and extent of materials that await their consideration and investigation. The largest archive in the city is the National Archives and Records Administration (NARA) (B11), which contains documentation on virtually all the subjects within the scope of this Guide. Washington's second largest archival collection is housed in the Manuscript Division of the Library of Congress (B8). Researchers will find there, in addition to presidential papers and papers of notable American families, a rich source of documentation on international political, military, economic, and humanitarian affairs. Major sources for diplomacy and international relations can also be found in the Special Collections of Georgetown University's Lauinger Library (B6), the National Security Archive (B12), and the Records Management Center of the Organization of American States (OAS) (B14). The military archives (B1, B3, B4, B9, B13) contain considerable data on military and naval history, as do the Energy Department Archives (B5), and the Manuscript Division of Howard University's Moorland-Spingarn Research Center (B7).

Many of the libraries in the Washington, D.C., area hold archival or manuscript material, usually of individuals. These items are described in Section A (Libraries) under point 4, with cross-references in this section. Furthermore, many vertical file collections consisting primarily of printed matter are described in entries for sections A (Libraries), H (Research Centers), K (Government Agencies), and M (Associations).

---

## BI Air Force History Office (Air Force Department)

1.a. 170 Luke Avenue, Suite 400
Bolling Air Force Base, Building 5681
Washington, D.C. 20332
(202) 767-5764
Fax: (202) 404-7915

b. 9:00 A.M.–4:15 P.M. Monday–Friday

c. Open by appointment to qualified researchers for on-site use. Many of the holdings are classified.

d. Microfilming and photocopying facilities are available.

e. Richard P. Hallion, Air Force Historian
William C. Heimdahl, Chief, Historical Services Division

2. The principal relevance of this collection is with regard to military history, especially World War II, national defense, and military science generally.

3. The Office of Air Force History possesses an extensive collection of microfilm copies of official air force archival records housed in the Air Force Historical Research Agency at Maxwell Air Force Base, Alabama 36112-6678. Included are air force unit histories, strategic assessments, policy and planning documents, intelligence reports, end-of-tour reports, attaché debriefings, records of air force commands and units, and intelligence studies prepared by the Central Intelligence Agency, Defense Intelligence Agency, State Department, and Defense Department. Also available are microfilm copies of materials from personal papers and oral history collections (see E1) located at the Air Force Historical Research Agency. The bulk of the collection dates from World War II to the present, with some earlier coverage. Much of the post-World War II material is restricted. Staff members, however, can assist researchers in obtaining declassification of classified documents.

The following are some of the personal papers within the collection:

Maj. Gen. Elmer E. Adler. Papers contain official correspondence concerning the maintenance and supply of U.S. aircraft, personnel, and equipment furnished to the British from September–November 1941 (2 vols.) and data on the Anglo-American offer to provide aid to the Russians in the Caucasus.

Lt. Gen. Arthur C. Agan Jr. Includes copies of official reports on operations of the 8th Air Force and a copy of Lt. Gen. Ira Eaker's report on U.S. Air Force activities in the United Kingdom, 1942–43.

Gen. Charles Pearre Cabell. Cabell served as Director of Plans, Headquarters, U.S. Strategic Air Forces in Europe, 1944, and Director of Operations and Intelligence, Headquarters, Mediterranean Allied Air Forces, 1944–45. He retired as Deputy Director of the CIA in 1962. The papers cover the period 1925–63 and incorporate material pertaining to early Allied strategy in World War II. Some restrictions apply.

Gen. John Kenneth Cannon. Cannon served as Deputy Commanding General, Allied Tactical Air Force, Sicilian Campaign and Invasion of Italy, 1943. He was the Commanding General, U.S. Air Forces in Europe, 1945–46. His papers cover the period 1936–46 and include material on the U.S. Strategic Air Forces in Europe, 1942–45.

Gianni Caproni, Count di Taliedo. Caproni was an Italian aircraft engineer and builder whose papers cover the period 1913–70. They illuminate the role of the Caproni aircraft in World War I and present ideas on the development of air power.

Maj. Gen. Grandison Gardner. These are miscellaneous materials relating to SHAPE Air Defense Technical Center, The Hague, Netherlands, 1955–65.

Bernhard Hougen. The Hougen Papers cover the period 1943–46. They present visual and narrative information about targets of the 322nd Bomb Group in France.

Gen. Laurence S. Kuter. Included here are notes on effectiveness of flying bomb attacks on London as compared with bombing raids over German cities in 1944.

Gen. William Wallace Momyer. Includes in part personal recollections and views on air warfare in North Africa during World War II. Classified documents only.

Col. Peter S. Rask. Items include miscellaneous papers, operations bulletins, and reports concerning USAF in North Africa during World War II. Classified documents only.

Brig. Gen. Martin F. Scanlon. Included are personal and official papers relating to Scanlon's embassy duties in London; personal diaries (1937–40) written in England; British Air Ministry propaganda leaflets from World War II in German and French.

Capt. Benjamin F. Watson. Among these papers are bulletins from Britain, 1941–42 and materials relating to the Battle of the North Atlantic and the defense of Iceland, 1941.

The facility also has a reference library, open by appointment to qualified researchers for on-site use. It contains a collection of air force historical studies and a multivolume collection of "Selected Statements" by principal air force or Defense Department officials, 1958–present. The primary resource of this library consists of air force unit, squadron, and headquarters histories from World War II stored on approximately 6,000 rolls of microfilm. The library also contains a large number of air force studies on a wide range of topics and the personal papers of many air force officers, as well as diaries and rare books on early air power.

4.   There is an index (on microfilm) to the microfilmed records collection, arranged alphabetically by subject as well as by individual countries. This index contains detailed references to both classified and unclassified documents and should prove useful to researchers in compiling data for Freedom of Information Act requests. Also useful in working with the collection is the *Air Force Historical Archives Document Classification Guide* (1971). For materials in the personal papers, consult *Personal Papers in the U.S. Air Force Historical Research Center* (1980).

Two Office of Air Force History publications will also be of interest to researchers: *United States Air Force History: A Guide to Documentary Sources* (1973) and *An Aerospace Bibliography* (1978).

5.   Index terms: Collective Security; Defense Policy, National; Military History—Air Force; Military Science

See also entries C1, E1, F2, and K3

## American Association of University Women (AAUW)—Educational Foundation Archives   See entry N4

---

**B2**   **American Federation of Labor and Congress of Industrial Organizations (AFL-CIO)—George Meany Memorial Archives (GMMA)**

---

1.a.   10000 New Hampshire Avenue
Silver Spring, Md. 20903

(301) 431-5452
Fax: (301) 431-0385

b.   9:00 A.M.–4:30 P.M. Monday–Friday

c.   Open to researchers with prior appointment.

d.   Photocopying services available.

e.   Lee Sayrs, Archivist

2.   The AFL-CIO established the George Meany Memorial Archives in 1980 to honor the memory of its first president, to provide a program to preserve its historical records and those of its predecessor organizations, and to make those records available for research. In 1987 the archives moved from AFL-CIO headquarters to the 47-acre campus of the George Meany Center for Labor Studies in Silver Spring, Md., an educational institution for labor officers, representatives, and staff of AFL-CIO and its affiliates. The archives pertinence lies in international organizing activities.

3.   In addition to holdings relating to U.S. labor leaders Samuel Gompers, William Green, and George Meany, there are records dealing with the international activities of the AFL and AFL-CIO. These include the AFL Executive Council Minutes, Vote Books, and Correspondence, 1892–1955 (in some cases to 1965). Other available records are: Office of the President International Affairs and International Affiliations, 1949–67; International Affairs Department, Country Files, 1945–71; and AFL Advisors to United Nations Economic and Social Council, 1945–52.

Other records dealing with international affairs will be opened in the future, such as those of the internationally oriented organizations sponsored by the AFL-CIO's Department of International Affairs (see entry N7): African-American Labor Center (AALC), American Institute for Free Labor Development (AIFLD), Asian-American Free Labor Institute (AAFLI), and Free Trade Union Institute (FTUI).

4.   Processed collections are available for research subject to terms and restrictions set by donors or the AFL-CIO. In general, records are released 20 years after their creation, and unprocessed collections are closed. For specific information on the availability of records, contact the archives. A brochure on the archives is available free of charge.

5.   Index Terms: Conflict Resolution and Management—Unofficial and Non-Governmental Approaches; International Organizations—Labor

See also entries A2, E2, F3, and N7

## B3 Army Center of Military History (Army Department)

1.a. 1099 14th Street, NW
Building 159, Room 538
Washington, D.C. 20005-3402
(202) 504-5420
Fax: (202) 504-5390

b. 8:00 A.M.–4:30 P.M. Monday–Friday

c. Hours for visitors are 8:00 A.M. to 3:30 P.M. Researchers should make an appointment with the appropriate office within the center prior to their visit. Foreign nationals are required to apply through the military attaché at their embassy in Washington, D.C., for permission from the Deputy Chief of Staff for Intelligence for permission to visit the center.

d. Limited photocopying services are available for 15 cents per page.

e. Harold W. Nelson, Chief, Military History
Jeffrey Clarke, Deputy Chief Historian
Hannah Zeidlik, Chief, Historical Records Branch

2. The material found in the Army Historical Center is immediately relevant to military science. The center maintains extensive published and unpublished materials on the history of the U.S. Army at home and abroad. The material includes copies of manuscripts (approximately 2,500 lin. ft.), as well as war diaries, dispatches, telegrams, radio news broadcasts, press releases, operation reports, statistics, and historical reference files of clippings and unpublished reports (600 lin. ft.). It holds approximately 2,000 unpublished histories dealing with the U.S. Army. Holdings also go back to the colonial militia. In addition, the center also serves as a repository of army unit histories, of which there are more than 10,000.

3. The center's materials are maintained and serviced by two branches. They are the Historical Resources Branch and the Organizational History Branch.

### HISTORICAL RESOURCES BRANCH

(202) 504-5416
Fax: (202) 504-5393

The branch maintains collections of published and unpublished material dealing with the history of the U.S. Army and related activities worldwide. The center produces several ongoing multivolume series of U.S. Army historical studies including *United States Army in World War II, United States Army in the Korean War,* and an *Army Lineage* series. Almost all aspects of World War II are well represented in the center's collection of published and unpublished works. Examples of well-documented campaigns include the Normandy invasion, the Battle of the Bulge, and the liberation of Belgium.

The materials dealing with East and Southeast Asia from 1941 through the 1970s are also impressive. There is considerable material relating to the war with Japan and the U.S. occupation of Japan, 1945–52. Examples include historical reports on major battles such as Okinawa and Saipan; various U.S. Army staff studies of Japanese operations on the Jolo Islands, Leyte and Cebu, Mindanao Island, Negros Island, and others. The center maintains records of the 8th U.S. Army in Japan during the occupation period. This material covers the administration of the occupation; trials of war criminals; constitutional revision; development of political parties; and other topics. There are 53 titles covering these topics in the collection *History of the Non-Military Activities of the Occupation of Japan.* There are two major collections of Japanese documents, *List of Japanese Monographs and Studies,* containing 185 monographs and studies prepared by the Japanese Research Division of the Military History Section, General Headquarters, Far East.

On Southeast Asia the center holds approximately 100 lin. ft. of historical source materials that include situation reports; reports on U.S. operations in Vietnam and Thailand; U.S. casualty and strength figures for the Vietnam war period; Allied and Japanese operations during World War II; historical background information on the war in Vietnam; Military Advisory Group (M.A.G.) monthly reports; lessons learned in Vietnam; the Vietnamization program; Pentagon papers; and the U.S. Army historical program in Vietnam.

Also relevant to Vietnam are the personal papers of Gen. Samuel Williams, Chief, M.A.G., 1955–60 (restricted); copies of the papers of Gen. William C. Westmoreland, commander, U.S. Military Assistance Command, Vietnam, 1964–68; and the papers of Thomas Thayer, who served as director of the Southeast Asia (SEA) Intelligence and Force Effectiveness Division of the SEA Programs Office under the assistant secretary of defense for systems analysis.

In addition, the center is in possession of considerable material dealing with the armed forces and military experience of other nations. British materials relating to World War II are very well represented: maps showing portions of Britain during the war;

information on British forces in Normandy; Lend-Lease data; statistics on British casualties; and miscellaneous pamphlets. Records confiscated from Germany in 1945 detail Finnish operations against the Soviet army during the winter war, 1939–40. Other German documents outline plans drawn up by Third Reich military heads for an invasion of Sweden. Also captured by the U.S. Army in World War II were Mussolini's private papers and official Italian records.

**Library**

A military history library contains some 40,000 volumes and is maintained adjacent to the Historical Records Branch. Highly specialized in army and related activities, the collection consists of government and commercial publications including the center's publications, army regulations, Department of the Army pamphlets, technical and training manuals.

## ORGANIZATIONAL HISTORY BRANCH

(202) 504-5413
Fax: (202) 504-5416.

The branch maintains Table of Organization and Equipment (TO&E) files on army units that support the lineage and honors of these units. The basic collection was started after World War I. Some cross-indexed files are available to track the units through various changes in their designations. Bibliographies are maintained, but primarily for combat organizations at the battalion level and above. The branch also has custody of a collection of historical data cards on the Table of Distribution and Allowances (TD&A) for army units, with some dating from World War II. From the adoption of the Unit Identification Code (UIC) system in mid-1960s to about 1990, the TD&A historical data card collection is basically complete.

4.   The library's holdings are accessible through author/title and subject catalogs. The center's other materials are accessible through a geographic file. There is no published guide to the collections. Researchers should contact Hannah Zeidlik (202/504-5416) or a member of her staff, who can assist in verifying historical information and locating military source materials at the National Archives and Records Administration (B11) and at the Army Military History Research Collection at Carlisle Barracks, Pa. 17013.

*Publications of the U.S. Army Center of Military History* is available free upon request.

5.   Index Terms: Collective Security; Defense Policy, National—History; Intelligence; Military History—Army; Military Science

See also entries A41, B4, C2, C3, E3, and K5

---

**B4**   **Army Corps of Engineers (Army Department)—Office of History**

---

1.a.  Kingman Building
      7701 Telegraph Road
      Alexandria, Va. 22315-3865
      (703) 355-2543
      Fax: (703) 355-8172

b.  8:00 A.M.–4:00 P.M. Monday–Friday

c.  Scholars must call in advance to arrange to see the collection.

d.  Photocopying facilities are available.

e.  Paul K. Walter, Chief
    Martin K. Gordon, Historian/Curator

2.   Established in 1942, the Historical Division prepares historical monographs and bibliographies chronicling the activities of the Corps of Engineers, provides reference service related to engineering history, and maintains an extensive research collection that is germane to the scope of this Guide with respect to military history and planning. The holdings are divided into nine record groups and one miscellaneous collection (biography). For the office's oral history collection, see entry E3.

3.   The following record groups contain information relevant to security and peace studies:
**RG 2:**  *General Files.*
These contain published and unpublished histories, historical outlines, lectures, newspaper clippings, movie scripts, and articles relating to the Corps of Engineers (67 file folders) and the Corps of Topographical Engineers (1 folder). The latter contains historical and operational reports for the 64th Engineer Battalion (Base Topographic).
**RG 3:**  *Military Files.*
These consist primarily of memoranda, correspondence, and reports prepared by officers of the Corps of Engineers and other government agencies; published and unpublished articles and monographs prepared by historians of the History Division; and other materials (including some maps) relating to the military activity of the corps. The file is arranged

chronologically according to major military epochs with some topical categories. There are 25 such divisions within the RG. Within the larger divisions, files are divided into boxes and folders. The following categories contain material particularly relevant to this guide.

I. General. Box 1: "The Air Force and Strategic Deterrence, 1951–60" and "The Air Force and the Concept of Deterrence." Folder 6: Patterns of Air Base Development. Box 3: History and Development of U.S. Strategy and Capabilities for Strategic Warfare. Box 9: Indian Wars. Box 15A: Mine and countermine warfare, 1914–70; submarine mines and movable torpedoes.

II. 18th and 19th Centuries. Boxes 1–6: Research documents on "Engineers of Independence"; map of early amphibious operations, 1745. Boxes 7–10: Army engineering in the War of 1812. Box 11: Fortifications, 1815–39. Box 13: Mexican War. Boxes 14–17: Civil War, including, reports on activities in Georgia; maps of the Battle of Gettysburg; and "The Corps of Engineers and American Civil War" (draft). Box 18: Indian Wars. Box 19: Spanish-American War and Mexican Punitive Expedition, 1916 (1 folder).

III. World War I. Boxes 1–7: Allied Expeditionary Force (AEF) construction; some aerial reconnaissance maps. Box 10: Historical reports on corps in World War I.

IV. World War II—General. There are numerous items of interest among the general records relating to construction, airfields, logistics, public relations, training, and units. These include: Box 1: "Report on the Defence of Airbases (1941)." Box 5: Casualties; chemical warfare; and a chief of staff report. Box 15: "Industrial Mobilization Plan, 1939"; "Key Issues in Management and Allocation of Construction Resources during World War II" (draft, 1985); National Defense Program—Senate Investigative Report, 1941. Box 24: Amphibious forces, engineers, training, and equipment. Box 42: War Production Board.

VIII. Manhattan Engineer District. The seven boxes in this set of records deal with the Manhattan Project, including construction of the Clinton Engineer Works and Los Alamos.

X. World War II—Theaters of Operation. This set of records contains extensive material on all theaters of the war. Examples of relevant material include: Box 17: European Theater: AEF combat interviews; reports, articles, press releases about the AEF. Box 22: Engineering support at Omaha Beach; D-Day engineering operations. Box 23: D-Day after-action reports. Box 24: Battle of the Bulge; crossing the Rhine.

XI. Foreign Military Construction, 1945–. This group of files contains manuscripts of the Historical Division and comments on drafts. Topics include: overseas military operations of the corps, 1945–70; post-World War II occupations; informal comments on arctic defenses, North African airfields, NASA, the intercontinental ballistic missile (ICBM) program, and the Vietnam War; and formal comments on the manuscript "Military Activities of the Corps of Engineers in the Cold War, 1945–1972."

XII. Overseas Military Operations. Box 1: Occupation of Germany, Austria, and Italy; interview with Averell Harriman (1980) regarding Truman, MacArthur, and the European Recovery Plan; reconstruction work in Austria; historical manuscripts on the Berlin Airlift. Boxes 2 and 4: Construction and other corps activity in Greece and Turkey. Boxes 5–7: Occupation of Japan, Korea, and Okinawa; general historical reportage; construction program in Japan, 1952–54; history of 6th Army occupation of Japan. Boxes 8–24: Korean War; general information on Korean War; a draft article and notes on limited war and civil military projects; enemy field defenses; intelligence on enemy construction projects; logistics, mapping, and mobilization. Also in this set of records is material through the 1960s on Greenland, Iceland, Morocco, Libya, France, Germany, and the military buildup in the Near East in the early 1950s.

XIII. Southeast Asia Military Files. There are 52 boxes of records in this group, which cover a wide range of corps activity. The material reflects corps activity on all levels: assessments of overall priorities and construction troop estimates; base development; plans for specific ports; drilling wells in the Mekong Delta. Also included are unit records, headquarters down to detachment level; construction and nonconstruction engineering activities; general information on Vietnam, its communications, cantonments, and bridge defense systems; Thai military construction, 1966–68; lessons learned (indexed); and material on the Agency for International Development.

XIV. American Overseas Operations, 1980s. This group of records consists of five boxes. There is material on arms control; corps activity in Egypt, Israel, Saudi Arabia, and the Pacific; National Guard road building in Ecuador, 1987; corps activity in Honduras, 1984–88.

XVIII. Space and Missile File. This set of records concerns the Corps of Engineers Ballistic Missile Construction Office (CEBMCO) and consists of 38 boxes of material. There is general information on the historical background of the corps ballistic missile program. Boxes 4–8: ICBM development, including "Chronological Summary of Events Associated with Establishment of Corps of Engineers—Air Force Missile Operations." Boxes 9–13: Minuteman missile development, sites and facilities. Boxes 14–20: Atlas missile site development. Boxes 33–34: Nike missile site development. Boxes 21–26: Titan missiles I and II development. Boxes 37–38: MX missile development and deployment; SDI program (2 folders).

With the exception of photographs of Southeast Asia and the Vietnam conflict, the History Division's photo collection has been transferred to the National Archives and Records Administration (F21, RG 77). The division also holds a cartographic collection of several hundred maps that are photostatic copies of maps in the National Archives and Records Administration.

4. The General and Military Files have been inventoried and a detailed guide exists for the Military Files. These files can be searched by key word on the History Division's database.

5. Index Terms: Arms Production and Acquisition; Collective Security; Defense Policy, National—History; Deterrence; Military History—Army; Military Science—Engineering, Logistics, and Support

See also entry A41, B3, C2, C3, E3, and K5

**Catholic University of America—Mullen Library   See entry A7**

---

**B5   Energy Department (DOE) Archives**

1.a.   U.S. Department of Energy
      Germantown Branch
      Routes 270 and 118
      Germantown, Md. 20545
      (301) 586-5230

b.   9:00 A.M.–5:00 P.M. Monday–Friday

c.   Because many of the documents are classified, access to them requires Freedom of Information Act procedures. DOE advises prior consultation. For information contact Chief Historian, History Division AD-35, Department of Energy, Washington, D.C. 20851; (301/903-5431).

e.   Francis G. Gosling, Chief Historian

2.   Archival materials are relevant to arms control and national defense.

3.   Atomic Energy Commission (AEC) records from 1947–58 are in the National Archives and Records Administration (B11, RG 326), but AEC records from 1958–75, are stored in the Germantown archive of the Energy Department. They contain considerable national security related material, principally AEC reports on nuclear weapons, nonproliferation treaties and conferences, and defense programs.

5.   Index Terms: Energy; Military Science—Civil Defense and Effects of Nuclear War; Proliferation

See also entries A11 and K12

**George Mason University—Fenwick Library   See entry A18**

---

**B6   Georgetown University—Lauinger Library—Special Collections—Manuscripts**

1.a.   37th and O Streets, NW
      Washington, D.C. 20057-1006
      (202) 687-7444

b.   9:00 A.M.–5:00 P.M. Monday–Friday

c.   Open to the public, but the collection does not circulate.

d.   Photocopying facilities are available.

e.   Nicholas B. Scheetz, Manuscripts Librarian

2.   The Special Collections Division has materials on European and American alliances, international political and military affairs, international economics, and intelligence.

3.   Relevant collections include the following:
   David M. Abshire Papers, 1962–83 (27 lin. ft.). Papers contain material relating to his State Department service in the 1970s, with the Murphy Commission (Commission for the Organization of Government for the Conduct of Foreign Policy), and to the history and operations of the Center for Strategic and International Studies. (Restricted)
   Garret G. Ackerson Jr. Papers, 1923–76 (4.5 lin. ft.). A long series of descriptive letters from this diplomat to his family, written from his various foreign postings, including Hungary at the outbreak of World War II.
   Archives of the American Committee on United Europe, 1948–60. The committee was established

to promote public discussion and understanding regarding European national integration.

Archives of the Carlucci Commission on Security and Economic Assistance, 1983–84 (10.5 lin. ft.).

Archives of the Society for Historians of Foreign Relations, 1967–74 (3.75 lin. ft.).

Samuel D. Berger Papers, 1937–79 (2 lin. ft.). Papers relate to Berger's service on the Lend-Lease Commission in New Zealand, as ambassador to Korea 1961–64), and as deputy ambassador to South Vietnam (1968–72).

Russell J. Bowen Collection. More than 14,000 titles on intelligence, spying, covert activities. A bibliography, *Scholar's Guide to Intelligence Literature,* covers the first 5,300 titles.

Richard Crane Papers, 1915–38 (37.5 lin. ft.). Papers, correspondence, and diaries of the first American ambassador to former Czechoslovakia. Crane was also private secretary to Secretary of State Robert Lansing (1915–19).

Laurence D. Egbert Papers, 1943–46 (8.5 lin. ft.). Colonel Egbert served as military liaison officer in Rouen (1943–44) and on the staff of the U.S. chief counsel at the Nuremberg War Crimes Trials.

Edwin Emerson Papers, 1898–1952 (4.5 lin. ft.). Emerson was a journalist who covered the Spanish-American War, the Russo-Japanese War, and World War I.

Cornelius Van H. Engert Papers, ca. 1917–65 (12.5 lin. ft.). Materials include papers from Ambassador Engert's career postings in Kabul, Beirut, Teheran, Havana, Santiago, and the Hague. Papers also include material relating to Arab-Israeli struggle for Palestine.

The Franco-American Alliance Collection.

Dino Grandi Papers, 1925–37 (22 reels). Part of the papers of the former Italian foreign minister and ambassador to Great Britain that include papers relating to the United States and selections from his diary (1929–32). Positive copies of microfilm may be ordered from Georgetown University Library.

Otto E. Guthe Papers, 1906–83 (3 lin. ft.). Guthe served as a geographer for the State Department and the CIA; some of the papers deal with remote sensing and satellite photography.

Martin F. Herz Papers, 1942–76 (9 lin. ft.). The collection includes printed propaganda leaflets from World War II and Vietnam as well as unpublished reports on psychological warfare.

Harry L. Hopkins Papers, 1932–46 (29.5 lin. ft.). Material of primary interest includes extensive correspondence with Franklin Roosevelt, Harry Truman, Dwight Eisenhower, Lyndon Johnson, Averell Harriman, Winston Churchill, George C. Marshall, Bernard Baruch, and Anthony Eden. Other material includes his World War II work as head of Lend-Lease and in policy matters, especially regarding Roosevelt's negotiations with Churchill and Stalin.

Joseph John Jova Papers, 1945–88 (19.5 lin. ft.). Jova served as Deputy Chief of Mission in Chile and as ambassador to Honduras, the Organization of American States, and Mexico.

Robert F. Kelley Papers, 1922–72 (7.5 lin. ft.). Kelley served as chief of the Division of Eastern European Affairs, Department of State, and played a role in the founding and early years of Radio Liberty. Also included are papers dealing with American-Russian relations leading up to recognition of the Soviet government.

Hamilton King Papers, 1898–1915 (10.25 lin. ft.). King served as American minister to Siam, 1898–1912.

Jeane J. Kirkpatrick Papers, 1984–85 (ca. 30 lin. ft.). Material from her ambassadorship at the United Nations. (Restricted)

Cecil B. Lyon Papers, 1930–71 (30 lin. ft.). Before World War II Lyon served with the U.S. Foreign Service in Cuba, Japan, China, and Chile. After the war he was assigned to Poland and Germany. Subsequently, he was ambassador to Chile, minister in Paris, and ambassador to Ceylon. His papers, including an extensive correspondence, document all aspects of his long career.

McCarthy Historical Project Archive, 1967–70 (445 lin. ft.). This project documents the 1968 primary campaign of presidential candidate Sen. Eugene J. McCarthy.

Jack K. McFall Papers, 1925–90 (3.25 lin. ft.). Materials primarily from his time as the U.S. Assistant Secretary of State for Congressional Relations and his ambassadorship to Finland.

George C. McGhee Papers, 1942–76 (101.5 lin. ft.). McGhee was U.S. ambassador to Turkey (1950–53) and West Germany (1963–68). Included are papers relating to McGhee's work on official and informal boards and groups.

James D. Mooney Papers, 1924–55 (9 lin. ft.). Mooney, an industrialist, carried out informal diplomatic contacts with Adolf Hitler on behalf of President Roosevelt.

Panama and the Canal Collections: Endicott Panama Collection. This collection includes several scores of rare volumes about Panama and the Canal from the library of Mordecai Endicott, a member of the Nicaragua Canal Commission. Also present are the extensive papers of engineer John F. Stevens; Henry Chauncey, partner in the Panama Railroad Company; diplomat Tomás Herrán; and various other collections all dealing with Panama and the Canal.

James Brown Scott Papers, 1906–46 (38.5 lin. ft.). Papers cover Scott's activities as special adviser to the State Department; his participation, at the Second Hague Conference and the Paris Peace Conference, among other international conferences; and his work as secretary of the Carnegie Endowment for International Peace.

Carroll Spence Papers, 1853–1858 (1.75 lin. ft.). Papers regarding Spence's tenure as the U.S. envoy extraordinary and minister plenipotentiary to the Sublime Porte (Turkey).

University Publications of America Collection, 3,800 reels of microfilm and more than 1,000 microfiche sheets. Included are records of American diplomats, including State Department central files on Formosa, Saudi Arabia, and Iran; confidential United States diplomatic posts on the Middle East and Cuba; and the diplomatic papers of John Moore Cabot.

Sen. Robert F. Wagner Papers, 1912–49 (588 lin. ft.). Personal and official papers of long-term U.S. senator from New York that in part cover his work on immigration, especially from Nazi Germany, and the recognition of a Jewish state in Palestine.

Rev. Edmund A. Walsh, S.J., Papers, 1885–1956 (22.5 lin. ft.). Rev. Walsh was founder of Georgetown University School of Foreign Service and served as the head of the Papal Relief Mission to Russia in the early 1920s. He also served as president of the Catholic Near East Welfare Association, as a representative of the Catholic Church in Mexico, and as a consultant at the Nuremberg War Crimes Trials.

Leonard S. Wilson Collection, 1944–60 (12 lin. ft.). This collection deals with American geographic intelligence during and after World War II, including OSS work, and a small number of items up to 1960.

Thomas Murray Wilson Papers, 1899–1942 (5 lin. ft.). Papers include typescript diaries of his service as consul general in Australia, American commissioner to India, and as minister to Iraq.

William A. Wilson Papers, 1980–92 (6.50 lin. ft.). The papers generally concern his tenure as President Reagan's personal representative to the Vatican and later as the United States ambassador to the Holy See, the first since 1867.

4. The collections in this division are described in *Special Collections at Georgetown* (1989).

5. Index Terms: Collective Security; Defense Policy, National—History; Development Issues; Human Rights; Humanitarian Issues; Intelligence; International Organizations; Military Science; Peace Theory and Research

See also entries A20, E6, F10, and J7

# B7 Howard University — Moorland-Spingarn Research Center — Manuscript Division

1.a. Founders Library Building, Room G-2
500 Howard Place, NW
Washington, D.C. 20059
(202) 806-7479
Fax: (202) 806-6405

b. 9:00 A.M.–1:00 P.M. and 2:00–4:30 P.M. Monday–Friday

c. Open to all qualified researchers by appointment. Some collections are not yet or completely classified. Some collections are open but donors have placed specific restrictions on their use.

d. Photocopy, microfilm, and photographic services are available.

e. Thomas C. Battle, Director
Joellen Elbashir, Curator, Manuscript Division
Esme Bhan, Research Associate, Manuscript Division

2. The Manuscript Division's holdings total more than 600 manuscript collections with more than 160 collections available for research. These holdings are relevant to the scope of this Guide in terms of human rights and humanitarian assistance and diplomacy.

3. Many of the collections in the Manuscript Division are the papers of Afro-Americans who had a direct or an indirect interest in Africa. Relevant holdings deal primarily with the Civil War, abolition, and international politics pertaining to Africa. These collections are listed below:

Cape Verdean Collection. Photocopies of the collection of papers in New Bedford Free Public Library, 613 Pleasant Street, New Bedford, Mass. 02740-6203. Contains correspondence and manuscripts about Cape Verdean immigrants to the United States, support given by them to liberation movements in Africa, periodicals, bibliographies, organizational affairs.

Thomas Clarke Papers, 1904–55 (1.5 lin. ft.). Clarke was an author and columnist; included is material on China, Japan, and the Russo-Japanese War.

Thomas Clarkson Papers. Clarkson was an English abolitionist, and his letters from 1814–46 deal with slavery. Letters from Thomas Fowell Buxton to Clarkson deal with the need to organize against the effort to recruit so-called free labor in Africa.

Mercer Cook Papers, 1890–1985 (8 lin. ft.). Cook was a scholar and U.S. diplomat to Nigeria, Senegal, Gambia, and the United Nations.

Paul Cuffe Collection. Microfilm of papers held in the New Bedford Free Public Library, 613 Pleasant Street, New Bedford, Mass. 02740-6203. Materials include correspondence relating to Sierra Leone and Cuffe's efforts to transport African-Americans there as settlers; scrapbooks concerning Cuffe's sea ventures; passenger lists of families going to Sierra Leone in 1815; and Cuffe's writings concerning settlement in Africa.

John W. Davis Papers, 1920–75 (24 lin. ft.). Davis was U.S. director of the Technical Cooperation Administration in Liberia from 1953 to 1954.

Charles Diggs Papers (800 lin. ft.). A member of Congress from Michigan, Diggs was chairman of the House International Relations Subcommittee on Africa. The bulk of his papers have been turned over to the center.

Frederick Douglass Collection. 11 boxes, 400 items. The collection contains speeches, photos, and correspondence.

Archibald Grimke Papers, 1822–1930 (23 lin. ft.). Grimke was consul to Santo Domingo from 1894 to 1898, vice-president of the NAACP, and president of the American Negro Academy from 1903 to 1916.

Edwin Bancroft Henderson Papers, 1915–76 (5 lin. ft.). Some of this material deals with African Americans in World War II.

Howard University Men and Women in the Armed Forces, 1941–46 (1.5 lin. ft.).

William H. Hunt Papers, 1898–1941 (6 lin. ft.). Hunt was American consul to Madagascar, and in 1931 he was secretary of legation in Liberia. Some correspondence, clippings on Madagascar, and a manuscript "Our Duty to Liberia."

Campbell C. Johnson, 1940–55 (15 lin. ft.). These papers deal with armed services and national defense.

Edward Kinsley Papers, 1862–65 (0.5 lin. ft.). This material concerns recruitment of African-Americans during the Civil War and commentary on the valor of African-American officers.

John M. Langston Papers, 1870–91. Langston was a U.S. diplomat.

Rayford W. Logan Papers, 1917–82 (43.5 lin. ft.). Logan was an important African-American historian who served as secretary to first Pan-African Congress in Paris and who wrote and taught at Howard University. Items in collection concern African Studies Association, American Committee on African Affairs, Njala University in Sierra Leone, and Friends of Africa in America.

Walter Howard Loving Papers, 1872–1983 (0.5 lin. ft.). Loving worked in military intelligence. Some material deals with African-American unrest in the armed forces during World War II.

Charleston Martin Papers, 1860–65 (1 lin. ft.). Papers dealing with the Civil War.

William Stuart Nelson Papers. Restricted. Vice-president of Howard University and dean of the School of Religion, Nelson was deeply involved in the nonviolence movement around the world. The collection is unprocessed and very large.

Kwame Nkrumah Papers, 1955–87 (26 lin. ft.). This material includes correspondence, cables, and reports relating to Nkrumah's leadership of Ghana. About one half of the records relate to books Nkrumah wrote.

Prometheans Records, 1945–50 (0.5 lin. ft.). The Prometheans is an organization formed by 300 African-American recruits in the Army Specialized Training Program in 1942, most of whom served in the 92d Division during World War II. The collection contains the original constitution; correspondence of members stationed in the Pacific and European campaigns with the organization's coordinator and president; application forms for membership; newsletters; financial reports and statements; postcards.

William Steen Papers. Restricted. Steen was an African area specialist in the Department of Labor. As such he helped plan visits to America of African leaders and arrange for labor training programs for Africans.

Stewart-Flippin Papers. Thomas McCants Stewart lived in Africa, 1883–86, where he was associate justice of the Supreme Court of Liberia. Box 1 contains papers on the "Liberia Controversy." There is also a scrapbook about his career, 1874–1921.

Mary Church Terrell Papers. Terrell was the first president of the National Association of Colored Women. Box 2 contains letters concerning the International Council of the Women of Darker Races.

U.S. Colored Troops in the Civil War. This collection contains 429 items, principally clothing account books.

Max Yergan Papers. Restricted. Twenty-three large storage boxes and 2 file drawers. With Paul Robeson, Yergan worked on the Council on African Affairs.

The 160,000-volume research center library also specializes in works written by or about persons of African descent. It has an extensive collection on African politics and economics. It is particularly strong on works dealing with slavery. One of the principal original donations that helped establish the collection was the 1873 bequest of Lewis Tappan, a noted abolitionist and organizer of American and Foreign Anti-Slavery Society, of more than 1,600 books, pamphlets, newspapers, letters, pictures, clippings, and periodicals. Other strengths include ethnology; race relations; development; colonization; development issues; and human rights.

4. The principal finding-aid for the collection is the *Guide to Processed Collections in the Manuscript Division of the Moorland-Spingarn Research Center* (1983) and the *Update to the Guide to Processed Collections in Manuscript Division of the Moorland-Spingarn Research Center* (1993). In addition, many of the unprocessed collections have inventories. The library has a card catalog. See also *Dictionary Catalog of the Arthur B. Spingarn Collection of Negro Authors, Howard University Library, Washington, D.C.* (Boston: G. K. Hall and Co., 1970) and *Dictionary Catalog of the Jesse E. Moorland Collection of Negro Life and History, Howard University Library, Washington, D.C.* (Boston: G. K. Hall and Co., 1970) plus three-volume supplement.

5. Index Terms: Ethnic and Religious Conflict; Foreign Policy; Human Rights; Humanitarian Issues; Peace Theory and Research

See also entries A22, E7, and J8

---

## B8 Library of Congress (LC)—Manuscript Division

---

1.a. James Madison Building, Room LM-101
Independence Avenue, SE
(between 1st and 2nd Streets)
Washington, D.C. 20540-4780
(202) 707-5387
Fax: (202) 707-6336

b. 8:30 A.M.–5:00 P.M. Monday–Saturday
(Stack service ends at 4:15 P.M.)

c. Open to persons engaged in research. Identification (preferably bearing the applicant's photograph) and formal registration are required. Undergraduates are normally not permitted to consult the division's holdings. Restrictions on the use of certain items have been imposed by donors or by the federal government for reasons of national security. With few exceptions, microfilms of manuscripts are available on interlibrary loan (202/707-5441). Most collections are stored in the Madison Building and can be delivered upon ordering, but some collections are

stored off-site and require one to two days for delivery of material to the Manuscript Reading Room.

d. Subject to copyright, donor restrictions, and preservation restraints, many items may be photocopied for research use. The reading room maintains photocopying machines and microprinters. Scholars who wish to use the services of the library's Photoduplication Service may call (202) 707-5640 for information. Subject to the restrictions mentioned above, the service will produce for purchase copies of original manuscripts held by the division. Telephone orders are not accepted.

e. James H. Hutson, Chief
   Mary M. Wolfskill, Head, Reference and Reader Service Section

2. The Manuscript Division of the Library of Congress has, scattered among its massive holdings of documents and personal papers, a large and exceedingly heterogeneous collection of peace and international security studies materials.

3. Peace and international security studies source materials are found primarily in individual and family papers, with a few collections on specific topics (e.g., World War I). These papers deal principally with international relations, peace negotiations, and foreign and military policy matters. The list presented below is not exhaustive but is indicative of the Manuscript Division's extremely large holdings:

U.S. Presidential Papers: Chester Arthur, James Buchanan, Calvin Coolidge, Dwight D. Eisenhower, Millard Fillmore, James Garfield, Ulysses S. Grant, Warren G. Harding, Benjamin Harrison, William Henry Harrison, Rutherford B. Hayes, Herbert Hoover, Andrew Jackson, Thomas Jefferson, Andrew Johnson, John F. Kennedy, Abraham Lincoln, James Madison, James Monroe, Franklin Pierce, James K. Polk, Franklin D. Roosevelt, Theodore Roosevelt, William H. Taft, Zachary Taylor, John Tyler, Martin Van Buren, George Washington, Woodrow Wilson.

Papers of U.S. Secretaries of State: John Quincy Adams, Thomas Bayard, James G. Blaine, William Jennings Bryan, James Buchanan, John C. Calhoun, Lewis Cass, Henry Clay, John Clayton, Bainbridge Colby, William Day, William Evarts, Edward Everett, Hamilton Fish, John Forsyth, John Foster, Frederick Frelinghuysen, Walter Gresham, John Hay, Charles Evans Hughes, Cordell Hull, Thomas Jefferson, Frank Kellogg, Philander C. Knox, Robert Lansing, Hugh Swinton Legare, James Madison, William Marcy, John Marshall, Louis McLane, James Monroe, Richard Olney, Timothy Pickering,

Edmund Randolph, Elihu Root, William Seward, John Sherman, Robert Smith, Henry Stimson, Martin Van Buren, Daniel Webster.

Papers of U.S. Secretaries of War: John Armstrong, Newton Baker, James Barbour, William Belknap, John Bell, John Calhoun, Simon Camron, Lewis Cass, Charles Conrad, George Crawford, Henry Dearborn, George Dern, John Eaton, Stephen Elkins, William Eustis, John Floyd, Joseph Holt, Henry Knox, Daniel Lamont, Benjamin Lincoln, Robert Todd Lincoln, William Marcy, James McHenry, James Monroe, Robert Patterson, Timothy Pickering, Joel Poinsett, Peter Porter, Alexander Ramsey, Elihu Root, John Schofield, John Spencer, Edwin Stanton, Henry Stimson, John Weeks, William Wilkins.

Papers of U.S. Secretaries of the Navy: George Bancroft, Charles Bonaparte, Benjamin Butler, William Chandler, Benjamin Crownshield, Josephus Daniels, Mahlon Dickerson, James Dobbin, Paul Hamilton, David Enshaw, William Hunt, William Jones, Franklin Knox, John Long, John Mason, George von Lengerke Meyer, William Moody, James Paulding, George Robeson, Robert Smith, Samuel Southard, Benjamin Stoddert, Richard Thompson, Smith Thompson, Benjamin Tracy, Abel Upshur, Gideon Welles, William Whitney, Curtis Wilbur.

Papers of Journalists: Joseph and Stewart Alsop, 1969–75 (79,000 items), nationally syndicated columnists. Raymond Clapper, 1913–44 (79,000 items), political columnist during the Roosevelt years. Elmer Davis, 1893–1957 (7,800 items), radio commentator and member of the Office of War Information during World War II. Bess Furman, 1728–1967 (47,000 items), White House reporter for AP and the Office of War Information. Horace Greeley, 1826–1928 (1,500 items), editor of the *New York Herald Tribune*. Roy Howard, 1911–66 (115,000 items), journalist with Scripps-Howard newspapers. Henry R. Luce, 1917–67 (35,000 items), editor of *Time* magazine. John B. Martin, 1900–1986 (150,000 items), investigative journalist. Edward R. Murrow, 1927–73 (microfilm of collection held elsewhere), CBS correspondent, director of United States Information Agency (USIA). Joseph Pulitzer, 1897–1958 (67,500 items), publisher of the *St. Louis-Post Dispatch*. Carl Schurz, 1842–1932 (23,110 items), journalist and official in the Hayes administration. Arnold Eric Sevareid, 1930–57 (20,500 items), CBS correspondent and news analyst. Lawrence Spivak, 1945–1975 (30,000 items), host of National Broadcasting Company's "Meet the Press." Dorothy Wayman, 1862–1971 (6,000 items), journalist and librarian. William Allen White

Papers, 1859–1944 (136,800 items), editor of the Emporia *Gazette*.
Other Collections of Papers:

American Peace Society Records, 1825–1928. Contains roughly 500 items including those from the Conference on Justice held in Cleveland, 1928.

Chandler P. Anderson Papers, ca. 1896 (18,300 items). Anderson was a legal adviser to the State Department.

Anglo-Dutch War Collection, 1780–83. Consists of one anonymous journal of war in the Netherlands.

Hannah Arendt Papers, 1906–75 (28,000 items). Contains correspondence, family papers, speeches, and articles.

Ray Stannard Baker Papers, 1936–46. Baker, a journalist and biographer of Woodrow Wilson, attended the Paris Peace Conference.

Tasker Howard Bliss Papers, 1870–1930 (116 lin. ft.; 3 reels of microfilm). Bliss was an army officer, scholar, and diplomat who served in the Spanish-American War, World War I, and also attended the Paris Peace Conference.

Boer Republic, Miscellaneous Papers.

Chester Bohlen Papers, 1969–70.

William E. Borah Papers, 1865–1940. Senator Borah was active in foreign policy.

Omar N. Bradley Papers, 1948–53 (83 items). Collection contains mostly addresses, statements, and articles pertaining to the Cold War, NATO, the Military Assistance Plan, and the budget.

Breckinridge Family Papers, 1752–1965 (205,000 items). Especially pertinent in this collection are the papers of William Campbell Breckinridge (1837–1904), a cavalry commander in the Civil War, Joseph Cabell Breckinridge (1842–1920), and Henry Breckinridge (1886–1960), who served in the American Expeditionary Force and was assistant secretary of war.

Jacob J. Brown Papers, 1812-28. Brown was a U.S. army officer and took part in several northern battles of the War of 1812.

William Jennings Bryan Papers, 1877–1926 (30 lin. ft.). Collection consists of correspondence, memoranda, diaries, books, and other material.

Edmund Byrne Papers, 1825–50 (33 items). Byrne was commander of the USS *Decatur*. These papers are originally from the Naval Historical Foundation.

Andrew Carnegie Papers, 1809–1935 (67,000 items). Some of these papers deal with the establishment of the Carnegie Endowment for International Peace.

Joseph H. Choate Family Papers, 1745–1927 (20 lin. ft.). Choate was a lawyer, author, and diplomat;

material pertains to crisis in China, 1900, Hay-Paun-cefote Treaty, and Hague conferences.

Ray S. Cline Papers. Cline is a political scientist who served as deputy director of the CIA.

Norman Davis Papers, 1918–42 (43 lin. ft.). Davis was an expert economist, diplomat, and consultant to numerous international conferences.

Frederick Douglass Papers, 1841–1967 (7,300 items).

Ira C. Eaker Papers, 1918–60 (30,000 items). Eaker was an air force officer, aviation pioneer, and a member of VIII Bomber Command during World War II.

George F. Eliot Papers, 1939–71 (5,000 items). Eliot was a military analyst.

Thomas Ewing Family Papers, 1759–1941 (94,000 items). Ewing was a U.S. senator, treasury and interior secretary. Some of the material deals with 1861 peace conference, the role of Sherman in the Civil War, the conduct of the war in Kansas, Missouri, Arkansas, and the assassination of Lincoln.

Ford Peace Plan Papers, 1915–18 (5 lin. ft.). The papers in this collection are taken from the Henry Ford Peace Expedition, the Ford International Commission, and the Neutral Conference for Continuous Mediation.

James Guthrie Harbord Papers, 1886–1938. The bulk of the material pertains to World War I service. Harbord was chief of the American Mission to Armenia, 1919.

Leland Harrison Papers, 1915–47 (50 lin. ft.). Harrison was a diplomat, and the bulk of the collection pertains to the Paris Peace Conference, 1918–21.

Edith Helm Papers, 1918–53 (7 lin. ft.). Helm was White House social secretary. This collection contains many notes on President Wilson's trip to the Paris Peace Conference.

Loy Henderson Papers, 1892–1986. Henderson was posted in Russia during annexation of the Baltic states, the Russo-Finnish War, and the signing of the Molotov-Ribbentrop pact.

Robert Lansing Papers, 1914–20. Lansing was a State Department counsel.

George von Lengerke Meyer Papers, 1901–9 (50 items). Meyer was U.S. ambassador to Italy and Russia, and Secretary of the Navy.

David Miller Papers 1917–32. Miller, an international lawyer, took part in several peace conferences and activities of the League of Nations. Emphasis of the collection is on legal aspects of international relations.

National Board for Historical Services Papers, 1917–19 (16 lin. ft.). Collection largely consists of articles, extracts, summaries, outlines, and correspondence.

Paris Peace Conference Papers, 1917–19 (17 lin. ft.). Papers of the American Peace Commission to Versailles.

Paul Robinett Papers, 1943–57 (2 lin. ft.). Material pertains to military campaigns in World War II in which Robinett served as general.

Henry White Papers 1851–1937. White was a diplomat and served in Austria, Great Britain, Italy, and France.

World War I collection, 1914–35 (59 lin. ft.; 1 roll of microfilm). Collection consists of miscellaneous soldiers' letters, scrapbooks, clippings, reports prepared for the Paris Peace Conference, and other items.

4. No comprehensive finding-aid to the Manuscript Division's material related to peace and international security exists. The above lists were taken from a variety of catalogs. A two-part computer printout, known as the Master Record of Manuscript Collections, serves as the basic guide to all collections. Master Record I provides a checklist of all collections arranged alphabetically by name of individual or organization. Master Record II contains summary descriptions of collections. It is augmented by a name and key word index. Unpublished registers or other finding-aids exist for most individual collections. A card file of collections for which such aids are available is maintained in the division. Some relevant guides are *German Captured Documents on Microfilm Index, Papers of the Nixon White House,* and *Iran-Contra Papers.* Relevant guides for individual collections include Ray S. Cline, W. Averell Harriman, Theodore Roosevelt, and Woodrow Wilson.

The ongoing annual publication *National Union Catalog of Manuscript Collections* (1959–) describes many of the division's holdings. Manuscript accessions are also described in published annual acquisitions reports of the Manuscript Division, the *Annual Report of the Librarian of Congress* (1897–), and between 1943 and 1983 in the *Quarterly Journal of the Library of Congress* (originally the *Library of Congress Quarterly Journal of Acquisitions*).

Dated but still useful inventories include the *Handbook of Manuscripts in the Library of Congress* (1918); Curtis W. Garrison, *List of Manuscript Collections in the Library of Congress to July 1931* (1932); C. Percy Powell, *List of Manuscript Collections Received in the Library of Congress, July 1931 to July 1938* (1939); and Philip Hamer, *A Guide to*

*Archives and Manuscripts in the United States* (New Haven: Yale University Press, 1961).

5.   Index Terms: Arms Control; Collective Security; Conflict Management and Resolution; Defense Policy, National; Human Rights; Humanitarian Issues; Intelligence; International Law; International Organizations; Pacifism and Peace Movements; Political Systems and Ideologies

See also entries A29, D4, E8, F14, and F15

---

## B9   Marine Corps Historical Center (Navy Department)

1.a.   Washington Navy Yard, Building 58
9th and M Streets, SE
Washington, D.C. 20374
(202) 433-3439 (Archives Section)
(202) 433-3396 (Personal Papers Collections)
(202) 433-3837 (Historical Branch)
(202) 433-3447 (Library)
Fax: (202) 433-7265

b.   8:00 A.M.–4:30 P.M. Monday–Friday

c.   Open to the public for on-site use. Researchers should notify the Reference Section (202/233-3483) of their intent to use the center's facilities up to two weeks before their arrival.

d.   Photocopying facilities are available.

e.   Frederick J. Graboske, Head, Archives Section
Amy Cantin, Personal Papers Curator
Benis M. Frank, Chief Historian

2.   The Archives Section contains approximately 5,000 cubic feet of Marine Corps records. The relevance of this collection lies primarily in military science, naval science, and national defense. The center's cartographic holdings are covered in entry D5 and the Oral History Section in entry E10.

3.   The archives' records consist chiefly of combat operational reports, command diaries and chronologies, after-action reports, field reports, operational plans, and intelligence estimates dating from 1940–present. Most earlier records are held by the National Archives and Records Administration (B11). Examples of earlier records include material on Marine Corps activities in Nicaragua, 1912–36; Haiti, 1914–34; and the Dominican Republic, 1920–21. Many of the post-World War II records are stored in the Washington National Records Center (Suitland, Md.) but will be retrieved for researchers.

A separate personal papers collection contains manuscript material currently filling 1,500 manuscript boxes. The program solicits historically significant manuscripts, maps, photographs, and memorabilia from active and retired marines. Examples of the personal papers collection are given below:

Martha R. Allen Papers contain a seven-page manuscript entitled "Memorial Day in Belleau Wood."

David Bellamy. Photocopy of a diary entitled "World War I Diary of David Bellamy, 1888–1960." The author served as adjutant of the 3d Battalion, 6th Marines until January 1919.

Smedley D. Butler. Butler won two Congressional Medals of Honor—for service in occupation of Vera Cruz, Mexico, and for repelling attacks by Caco rebels in Haiti.

Clifton B. Cates Holdings. Includes diaries that cover Cates's tour with the American Expeditionary Forces in France during World War I. Letters describe actions at Belleau Wood, Soissons, St. Mihiel, and Argonne.

Henry Clay Cochrane. This collection contains among other items a correspondence file on the Philippine Expedition. Cochrane served as District Commander of Peninsula of Cavite, Philippines, 1900.

George C. Connor. Includes scenes of World War I obtained from soldiers in France.

John A. Daly. This collection is composed entirely of World War I materials including items pertaining to France.

Robert Deckert. These papers contain information about the battle of Belleau Wood.

Lester A. Dessez. These papers include a report on courses at the Ecole de Guerre, Paris, France, dated August 20, 1937.

Joseph W. Duermit. Includes coverage of his involvement in the major campaigns in France.

Barbara J. Dulinsky. The personal recollections of the first woman marine to serve on active duty in Vietnam during the period of hostilities, 1967–68, form the basis of this collection.

Frank E. Evans. Contains information about the 6th Marines Regiment on the war front of France in June 1918 and a description of the battle of Belleau Wood.

Wallace M. Greene Jr. Greene was Commandant of the Marine Corps, 1964–67, and this file contains official and personal correspondence, daily journals, subject files, speeches, and other documentary material. There is considerable material on Vietnam. Permission of donor required for researchers.

Robert W. Huntington. This collection contains material on the Spanish-American War.

Harold Kinman. Thirty-one letters in this collection chronicle Pvt. Kinman's participation in the marine action against the Aguinaldo insurgency in the Philippines.

Victor H. Krulak. Some 160 photocopies of letters, reports, memoranda, speeches, transcripts, and newspaper articles dating from November 1952 to May 1977 are included here. Dealing primarily with General Krulak's far-ranging activities during the Vietnam War, a small portion of the early entries record the general's views of the role of the Marine Corps; a similar portion of the more recent entries reflect his position as editor-journalist for the Copley News Service.

Keith B. McCutcheon. This is a significant collection that provides insight into the role and mission of Marine Corps aviation during the Korean and Vietnam conflicts. Many top policy proposals and decisions pertaining to Marine involvement are explored.

Merwin Silverthorn. In addition to a manuscript entitled "Men in Battle" (1936), the holdings include 12 photograph albums that cover the general's long career in the Marine Corps. Of note are the photo albums of the Okinawa campaign, April–June 1945, and assignments at Mare Island, Tinian, Peleliu, and Guadalcanal during World War II.

William W. Stickney. During World War II General Stickney participated in the Guadalcanal-Tulagi landings, the eastern New Guinea and Bismarck archipelago operations, Saipan, and the postwar occupation of Japan.

Helen Stote. The collection centers on materials relating to the Marine Corps' role in the siege of Peking, 1900.

Mclane Tilton. As senior marine officer with the Asiatic squadron, 1870–72 he led the U.S. marine contingent in the Korean Expedition of 1871.

The Historical Branch of the Marine Corps Historical Center has published a wide range of works on Marine Corps activities around the world. These include general histories, unit histories, bibliographies, catalogs, chronologies, personal papers, and special publications. Historical publications, 1920–present, cover a wide range of topics. A *Marine Corps Historical Publications Catalog* is available on request. Staff members of the Histories Section and Reference Section will consult with private researchers.

The Marine Corps Historical Center's 30,000-volume reference library (Evelyn A. Englander, Librarian, 202/433-3447) includes biographies, academic dissertations, journals, and Marine Corps post and station newspapers from the 1930s. There is also a separate reference section that houses several files: the "Subject File," which contains articles, reports, documents, and general information of research value; the "Geographical File," which contains information on geographical areas where marines have been stationed; the "Biographical File," which has information on more than 1,500 individuals (including non-marines who were associated with the corps); and the "Unit File," which maintains a working file on all units, past and present, in the corps.

4. There is a card index to documents in the Archives Section (both classified and unclassified), arranged by geographic area. For a detailed description of the personal papers collection's contents, see the Marine Corps Historical Reference Pamphlet *Marine Corps Personal Papers Collection Catalog*, compiled by Charles A. Wood (1974, rev. 1980).

In addition to a brochure describing the center, the *Guide to the Marine Corps Historical Center* (1979), scholars should also consult *An Annotated Bibliography of the United States Marine Corps in the Second World War*, by Michael O'Quinlivan and Jack B. Hilliard (1970), which includes a geographical index.

5. Index Terms: Defense Policy, National—History; Military History—Marine Corps; Military Science; Naval Science

See also entries A30, C4, C5, D5, E9, E10, and K30

---

**BIO  National Air and Space Museum (NASM) (Smithsonian Institution)—Archives Division**

---

1.a.  6th Street and Independence Avenue, SW, Room 3100
Washington, D.C. 20560
(202) 357-3133
Fax: (202) 786-2835

b.  10:00 A.M.–4:00 P.M. Monday–Friday

c.  Open to serious researchers by appointment only.

d.  Photocopying facilities are available. Microfilm and other holdings will be duplicated on request at cost plus a handling charge.

e.  Thomas Soapes, Archivist

2.  The National Air and Space Archives contains roughly 10,000 cubic feet of documents dating from the 19th century to the present. The holdings are

relevant to the development of military science, specifically in regard to aviation. For film and photographic archives see entries F18 and F19. Library holdings are described in entry A32 and museum artifacts in entry C6.

3. The archives principally contains technical records, although different collections are sources of considerable interest in the study of international security as it pertains to the history of military aviation. The archives holds Personal and Professional Papers; Corporate and Organizational Records; and Artificial Collections.

Personal and Professional Papers Collection. Includes papers of aircraft designers, engineers, corporate figures, aviation pioneers, and a significant number of individuals involved in military aviation. At least 15 of the more than 50 collections, usually the papers of army air corps or air force officers, have direct relevance to military affairs. Collections of other individuals should not be neglected since many either served in or had other contact with the military. Below are some representative examples of sources found in these collections.

Raymond Arthur Brooks, ca. 1917–18 (12 cubic feet). Brooks was a World War I ace credited with shooting down six enemy aircraft. A SPAD XIII C.1 *Smith IV* he flew is now part of the museum's collection.

Charles W. Chillson, ca. 1950–56 (3 cubic feet). Chillson was an expert in air and rocket propulsion.

Andrew G. Haley, 1939–67 (43 cubic feet). Haley, a major influence on space law, was active in the American Rocketry Society and helped found the International Academy of Astronautics and International Institute of Space Law.

Frank Purdy Lahm, ca. 1899–1974 (2 cubic feet). Lahm was the first balloon pilot, the first airship pilot, and the first airplane pilot in the United States, and was trained by the Wright brothers. He had a distinguished career in the U.S. Army until 1941.

William Mitchell: Court Martial Collection, 1925–26 (2 cubic feet). Brig. Gen. "Billy" Mitchell was an early advocate of an independent air service. He was court martialed in 1925 on grounds of insubordination for his promotion of air power and criticism of the government.

Corporate and Organizational Records. The majority of these corporations also had some connection with the military aspect of aeronautics and space industry. Some examples include:

Defense Advisory Committee on Women in the Services Collection, 1975–87 (6 cubic feet). This committee was established in 1951 by the Defense Department to advise the Secretary of Defense on policy relating to women in the armed forces.

Fairchild Industries, 1919–80 (277 cubic feet). Fairchild developed and built a wide variety of militarily significant aircraft. Files include joint venture efforts with Fokker (Netherlands), Pilatus (Switzerland), and other aircraft manufacturers.

Fairchild KS-25 High-Acuity Camera System Documentation, 1956–67 (2 cubic feet). Material relates to Defense Department request for improved aerial photography capabilities.

Collections Relating to the Apollo-Soyuz Test Project. Two collections relate to the first effort at space cooperation (July 1975) between the United States and the USSR: Apollo-Soyuz Test Project Earth Observation and Photography Experiment (4 cubic feet), which contains documents of efforts to photograph features of scientific interest on the Earth's surface; and Apollo-Soyuz Test Project Images Collection (32 cubic feet), which contains photographs of test project activities.

Collections Related to the U.S. Army Air Forces/ U.S. Air Force. Among these eight separate collections are: Freeman Field Reports, 1936–46 (0.5 cubic feet), which pertain to the examination and evaluation of captured enemy aircraft during World War II; Nike-Ajax Antiaircraft Missile System Technical Manuals, 1957–59; and Southwest Pacific Theater Intelligence Reports, 1942–45 (10 cubic feet), which contains weekly intelligence summaries from Allied air forces including information on effects of Allied attacks.

Artificial Collections. These are either compiled by some party other than the documents' creator or published material gathered from different sources. Two collections are of particular interest:

Aerial Photographic Reconnaissance (Samuel L. Batchelder), 1914–45 (8.4 cubic feet). Contains historical information on aerial photographic reconnaissance compiled by Samuel Batchelder, who served at the U.S. Army Air Force Intelligence School (Harrisburg, Penn.).

American Volunteer Group (Larry Pistole), 1938–44 (2 cubic feet). Contained here are copies of historical documentation on American Volunteer Group (AVG), better known as the Flying Tigers. This documentation includes operational records (fragmentary), correspondence, diaries, logs, news clippings, and photos. Compiled by Larry Pistole.

4. There are few formal finding-aids available. The archives has published *Guide to the Collections of the National Air and Space Archives* (April 1991). It contains brief descriptions of many of the collections.

5. Index Terms: Military History—Air Force; Military Science

See also entries: A32, C6, FI8, and FI9

---

## BII National Archives and Records Administration (NARA)

1.a. 8th Street and Pennsylvania Avenue, NW
Washington, D.C. 20408
(entrance from Pennsylvania Avenue only)
(202) 501-5405 (Central Research Room)
(301) 457-7010 (Reference Services Branch)

b. Central Research Room (and Microfilm Research Room)
8:45 A.M.–5:00 P.M. Monday, Wednesday
8:45 A.M.–9:00 P.M. Tuesday, Thursday, Friday
8:45 A.M.–4:45 P.M. Saturday

National Archives at College Park
8:45 A.M.–5:00 P.M. Monday–Friday

Suitland Annex Research Room
8:00 A.M.–4:30 P.M. Monday–Saturday

c. Open to researchers over the age of 16. Users must obtain a National Archives research pass (available in room 207), for which appropriate identification is required. Some material may be restricted.

d. Extensive photocopying facilities are available. Extensive material is available on microfilm. Researchers should check *Catalog of National Archives Microfilm Publications* (rev. 1989) to see if the particular record groups they want are listed.

e. Trudy Peterson, Acting Archivist of the United States

2. One hardly knows where to begin with a resource as large and important but relatively "unorganized" as NARA. In Washington it must share equal billing with the Library of Congress as a scholarly research facility in almost every field. Recent estimates of its size are that it contains more than 1.5 million cubic feet of material, equaling some 4.5 billion records. Among these holdings are 7 million photographs, 5 million maps and charts, almost 250,000 sound recordings, and 300,000 reels of film and video recordings. NARA's extensive holdings of cartographic, audio, and visual resources, and electronic records are examined in entries D6, EII, F20, F21, and GIO. Deposited here are the past records (from 1774) of all branches of the federal government and materials collected by them as well. NARA has been accurately described as "the nation's memory."

3. Holdings are distributed among some 400 record groups (RG). NARA defines a record group as a body of organizationally and functionally related records established with particular regard for the administrative history, complexity, and volume of the records and archives of an agency. Typically, a record group contains the records of individual government units (e.g., agencies, bureaus, departments). The filing arrangement within each group reflects the filing arrangement in which the records were originally kept by the government body that generated them. There are three variations of this record group control:

(1) record groups with the title "general records," which are composed of records of the office of the head of the department or agency, records of other units that are concerned with matters that affect the department or agency, and records of other units that are concerned with matters that affect the department as a whole;

(2) collective record groups, which contain functionally or administratively related records of small, short-lived agencies; and

(3) record groups consisting of documents not created by a single agency or group of agencies but gathered from a variety of sources.

Many records were also deposited in lot files. Many State Department records, in particular, relating to the topics of this Guide are found in lot files. There are over 400 State Department lot files dating from the 1940s and 1950s. These lot files should be examined in conjunction with RG's 59 and 84, the two principal groups of State Department records. It is advisable first to consult the series *Foreign Relations of the United States* as a considerable amount of the State Department material has been published there. For further information on State Department lot files, see *A Reference Guide to United States Department of State Special Files*, by Gerald K. Haines, Greenwood Press (1985).

Most records at the archives are available to researchers, but access to some documents is restricted. Scholars researching national and international security matters, especially since the 1940s, may find that some records or portions of records have not yet been declassified. Reasons for range from national security to donors' restrictions placed on personal papers. In some cases, restrictions have not yet been removed simply because staff cannot keep pace with incoming materials. Scholars should, therefore, keep careful lists of identifying information on restricted records (i.e., author, date, and file number). Such data are necessary should a scholar wish to initiate Freedom of Information Act procedures. Whether certain materials are restricted can be ascertained by writing or phoning the appropriate division.

The enormous holdings of NARA pertinent to peace and international security studies makes any comprehensive account impossible. Listed below are the most prominent record groups and lot files, with brief summaries about the collection's pertinence to the subjects of this Guide. Holdings within the archives are in no way evenly distributed among these subjects. Because many record groups are very old or are still being added to, material relevant to peace and international security studies occur among a wide range of other topics. Military records are vast, to say the least. Emphasis in this guide has been placed on military operations, strategic planning, and accounts of military engagements. Human rights, on the other hand, is a considerably more recent issue and correspondingly less material has been turned over to the archives. The most prominent international organization that appears in these records is the United Nations, although references to others are scattered through various record groups. The principal subject areas and the relevant record group or lot file are as follows:

Arms Control: RG 11, RG 43, RG 46, RG 233, RG 326, LF 66 D 428, LF 388, LF 57 D 688

Conflict Resolution, Arbitration, and Peace Negotiations: RG 11, RG 59, RG 75, RG 76, RG 233, RG 256, RG 353

Diplomacy and Alliances: RG 43, RG 46, RG 59, RG 61, RG 84, RG 220, RG 233, RG 353, RG 360, Lot File (LF) 64 D 563, LF 54 D 195, LF 67 D 237

Economic Aid: RG 220, RG 250, RG 353

Economic Development: RG 5, RG 46, RG 169, RG 179, RG 220, RG 233, RG 250, RG 253, RG 286, RG 353, RG 469, LF 64 D 21

Human Rights: RG 46, RG 60, RG 75, RG 153, RG 238, RG 242, LF 60 D 400

Intelligence: RG 59, RG 226, RG 243, RG 457

International Organizations: RG 43, RG 330, RG 333, LF 64 D 21, LF 60 D 400

Military Planning, Strategy, and Operations: RG 43, RG 46, RG 74, RG 128, RG 218, RG 226, RG 250, RG 260, RG 273, RG 330, RG 331, RG 334, RG 360, RG 374, RG 457; Army: RG 77, RG 94, RG 107, RG 120, RG 165, RG 319, RG 335, RG 338, RG 395, RG 407; Air Force: RG 18, RG 340, RG 341; Navy and Marine Corps: RG 38, RG 45, RG 72, RG 80

Terrorism and Low Intensity Conflict: RG 65, RG 153, RG 338

War Crimes: RG 153, RG 238, RG 239

War Economy: RG 61, RG 154, RG 182, RG 250, RG 253, RG 261, RG 304

War Propaganda: RG 63, RG 208

The record groups are arranged by the division or branch that has custody of them. The record groups (RG) and lot files (LF), discussed in this Guide, are covered under the following branches:

Civil Reference Branch: RG 11, RG 43, RG 56, RG 59, RG 60, RG 63, RG 65, RG 75, RG 76, RG 84, RG 220, RG 239, RG 250, RG 256, RG 262, RG 273, RG 286, RG 326, RG 353, RG 360, LF 54 D 195, LF 57 D 688, LF 64 D 21, LF 64 D 563, LF 67 D 237, LF 388

Legislative Reference Branch: RG 46, RG 128, RG 233, RG 287

Suitland Reference Branch: RG 5, RG 61, RG 153, RG 154, RG 169, RG 182, RG 200, RG 208, RG 253, RG 260, RG 261, RG 331, RG 335, RG 338, RG 340, RG 341, RG 374, RG 407, RG 469, LF 60 D 400, LF 66 D 428, Donated Materials (*formerly* RG 200)

Military Reference Branch: RG 18, RG 38, RG 45, RG 72, RG 74, RG 77, RG 80, RG 94, RG 107, RG 120, RG 165, RG 179, RG 218, RG 226, RG 238, RG 243, RG 304, RG 319, RG 330, RG 331, RG 333, RG 334, RG 395, RG 457

Captured German Records Staff: RG 242

The following divisions and branches hold relevant archival materials:

## TEXTUAL REFERENCE DIVISION (INTERNAL DESIGNATION: NNR)

(301) 713-7230
R. Michael McReynolds, Director

### Civil Reference Branch (NNRC)
(301) 713-7250
Milton Gustafson, Chief

**RG 11:** *General Records of the United States Government.*
This RG contains international treaties and related records, 1778–1969, including, for example, the SALT I treaty. See *Preliminary Inventory* (PI) 159.

**RG 43:** *Records of the United States Participation in International Conferences, Commissions, and Expositions.*
This RG contains considerable material on World War II and postwar political and military diplomatic activity. These records are divided into geographical and topical subgroups. Relevant subcollections in RG 43 are:

Special Military and Political Collections: Records of the Policy Committee on Arms and Armaments, 1945–49; the Tripartite Naval Commission, 1945–47; and Records of Southeast Asia Policing (SEAC), 1950–53.

Europe and British Commonwealth: Records of Allied Control Council, 1945–50; Reports of the Allied Forces Headquarters Germany Psychological Warfare Branch received from the American Embassy in Italy, 1944–45; Records of Charles E. Bohlen, 1942–52; Records of Central Europe, 1944–45; Records of the European Advisory Commission and Philip E. Mosely, U.S. Policy Adviser Thereto, 1943–46; Records of the Office of European Affairs, 1935–47; Records of Office of West European Affairs Relating to Italy, 1943–51; Records Relating to the Establishment of NATO, 1948–49; Records Relating to the Establishment of the Office of the Assistant Secretary of State for Occupied Affairs, 1946–49.

Near East, Asia, and Africa: Records of the Office of African Affairs; Records of Four Powers Commission of Investigation (Former Italian Colonies), 1934–50; Records of the Military Adviser to the Office of the Near East, South Asia, and African Affairs, 1945–50; Records of the Anglo-American Inquiry Regarding Palestine, 1944–46; Records of the Office Near Eastern Affairs Relating to Palestine, 1946–49.

East Asia and the Pacific: Records of the U.S. Element of the Allied Control Council for Japan, 1946–52; Records of the Office of Chinese Affairs; Records of the Office of Far Eastern Division, 1932–41; Records of the Office of the Far Eastern Commissioner, 1945–51; Reports on the Japanese Economy, 1938–46; Records of the American Delegation, U.S.-USSR Joint Commission on Korea and Records Relating to the United Nations Temporary Commission on Korea, 1946–48; Records of the Marshall Mission to China, 1945–47; Records of Assistant Secretary of State for Occupied Areas, 1946–49; Records of Philippines and South Asia Division, 1944–52; Records of U.S. Reparations and Restitutions Delegations to Tokyo, 1947–49; Records Relating to the South Pacific Commission, 1946–51; Records of the Wedemeyer Mission to China, 1947.

United Nations: Records Relating to U.N. Conference on Freedom of Information, Geneva, 1948; Records of Secretary of State's Advisory Committee on the 1972 U.N. Conference on the Human Environment, 1971–72; Background Files on the Establishment of the U.N., 1941–45; Records of the U.S. Mission to the United Nations, 1945–49.

Economic Records: Records of the Division of World Trade Intelligence and Its Successor the Division of Economic Security Controls: Proclaimed List of Certain Blocked Nationals, 1941–46.

Intelligence Records: Reports of Research and Analysis Branch, Office of Strategic Services and Bureau of Intelligence and Research, 1941–61.

Also included in this RG are State Department records of the First Panama Congress, 1825–27; State Department records to the Paris Peace Commission, 1898, which brought an end to the Spanish-American War. Included are materials on several conferences with references to the USSR (e.g., the Third World Power Conference, 1936; Moscow Conference of Foreign Ministers, October 19–30, 1943; and the Tehran Conference, 1943). See PI 76 and supplement.

**RG 56:** *General Records of the Department of the Treasury.*

Records of the Bureau of War Risk Insurance, 1917–20, contains material related to the Trading with the Enemy Act of 1917 and reports of the War Trade Board.

**RG 59:** *General Records of the Department of State.*

This record group, the main concentration of the department's records, extending back to 1789, is of primary interest for peace and international security studies. In the course of accumulating these records, they have been divided into four major parts: pre-1906 records, 1906–10 central files, 1910–49 central files, and lot files. The National Archives, as part of a larger program of publishing specific groups of records, has made most of RG 59 available on microfilm. The chief finding-aid is PI 157. For microfilmed records see: *Diplomatic Records, A Select Catalog of National Archives Microfilm Publications.*

The pre-1906 central files are mostly department correspondence and are divided according to type: diplomatic, consular, and miscellaneous. The records contain instructions to and dispatches from American diplomatic and consular officers around the world. Instructions go back to foreign letters of the Continental Congress that transmit policy and actions to be taken regarding relief and protection of U.S. seamen, commercial matters, and administration of consulates. The consular and diplomatic dispatches are a great source of information regarding conditions in foreign countries as well as responses to diplomatic matters. The dispatches are published in chronological order by country (diplomatic) or by city (for consular).

From 1906–10 the State Department grouped files according to a numerical filing system that proved to be cumbersome and difficult for research purposes. In 1910, the decimal file system was adopted, which is basically a subject file system with nine major categories. The categories are: (0) general and miscellaneous; (1) administration of the U.S. government; (2) extradition and treaty cases; (3) protection of private and national interests; (4) international claims treaties and cases; (5) multilateral treaties; (6) international conferences and organizations, commerce, customs, and trade agreements; (7) political and treaty relations of states; (8) internal affairs of states.

Other records within this RG that are relevant to security and peace studies include:

Records Relating to Special Agents: Dispatches from special agents of the Department of State, 1794–1906 includes a journal from Commodore Perry's 1853–54 expedition to Japan.

Correspondence Relating to Filibustering Expedition against the Spanish Government of Mexico, 1811–16 (unsanctioned incursions against Mexico from U.S. territory).

"Journal of the Voyage of the USS *Nonsuch* up the Orinoco," 1819, which was an attempt to have Venezuela's government stop supporting privateers who threatened U.S. shipping.

"Record of the Department of State Special Interrogation Mission to Germany, 1945–46."
Miscellaneous records include:

Copybooks of George Washington's Correspondence with Secretaries of State, 1789–1796; "War of 1812 Papers" of the State Department, 1789–1815; Records of the Negotiation of the Treaty of Ghent, 1813–1815; Minutes of Treaty Conference between the United States and Japanese Representatives; and Treaty Drafts, March 11–July 22, 1872.
Records of the World War I Period include:

Records of the Department of State Relating to World War I and Its Termination, 1914–29 (518 rolls of microfilm). Specific subjects within this file include: neutrality, neutral commerce, enemy property, prisoners of war, civil prisoners and enemy noncombatants, illegal and inhumane warfare, hospital ships, military and civilian observers, peace negotiations and the armistice.

Correspondence of Secretary of State William Jennings Bryan with President Wilson, 1913–15. Topics include: Mexican Revolution, China, Japan, Nicaragua, beginning of World War I.

Personal and Confidential Letters from Secretary of State Lansing to President Wilson, 1915–18.
Records of the World War II and Postwar Periods include:

Records of the Department of State Relating to World War II, 1939–45 (252 rolls of microfilm).

Records of the Office of European Affairs, 1934–47.

State Department Documents of the Interdivisional Country and Area Committee, 1943–46, including Japan, Germany, problems of disarmament, occupation, political reorganization, boundary adjustment.

Minutes of Meetings of the Interdivisional Area Committee on the Far East, 1943–46. Committee analyzed specific problems relating to U.S.-Asian policy, including types of governments to be formed following Japanese surrender.

State Department Documents of the Post-War Programs Committee, 1944. Problems this committee dealt with include terms of surrender, occupation, displaced persons, minorities, foreign petroleum policy, and reconstruction financing.

Policy Planning Staff Numbered Papers 1–63, 1947–49. These papers deal with a wide variety of postwar policy issues: reconstruction, geopolitical reorganization, the new balance of power, relations with newly created governments, and the spread of communism into Eastern Europe and the Far East.

Records of Assistant Secretary of State and Under Secretary of State Dean Acheson, 1941–50. These records refer to U.N. Relief and Rehabilitation Administration; Lend-Lease; the Bretton Woods Conference; Leith-Ross Committee; Board of Economic Warfare.

Records of Assistant Secretary of State for Occupied Areas, 1946–49.

Palestine Reference Files of Dean Rusk and Robert McClintock, 1947–49. Rusk was director of the Office of Special Political Affairs and then Assistant Secretary of State for United Nations Affairs. McClintock was special assistant in the Offices of Political Affairs and United Nations Affairs.

Intelligence Reports, 1941–61 (approximately 9,000 microfiche cards). These reports were from the Research and Analysis Branch of the Office of Strategic Services and, after 1945, from the Bureau of Intelligence and Research in the State Department. Reports cover international relations and internal affairs of foreign countries, including political, military, economic, and social topics. The Diplomatic Branch of the National Archives has a card index to these reports.

There are also Research and Analysis Reports not in the decimal file that have separate indexes in the Civil Reference Branch.

Lot files for the State Department contain important information not included in record groups. These records include memoranda from Secretaries of State, Under and Deputy Secretaries; records of the Policy Planning Staff, the National Security Council. Lot File 68 contains Special Politico-Military Collections. This lot contains files of the Special Assistant Secretary of State for Politico-Military Affairs, 1950–67.

**RG 60:** *General Records of the Department of Justice.*

Attorney General's Records, 1790–1870. Among other topics, these records cover treaty interpretations; neutrality laws during the Napoleonic wars; Latin American struggles for independence; the Crimean War; nonintercourse legislation of the Jefferson-Madison period; the War of 1812; piracy; slavery and the slave trade; the Civil War and Reconstruction, including the Enforcement Act of 1870, the Ku Klux Klan of 1871, and the Civil Rights Act of 1875.

**RG 63:** *Committee on Public Information.*

This committee (known as the Creel Committee) was established to release government news during World War I, sustain morale, and administer voluntary press censorship. The Russian Division of the foreign section of this committee dealt with American propaganda campaigns in the Soviet Union, 1918–19. Among these are leaflets, bulletins, and news clippings from the Russian and Siberian press and photostats on the "German-Bolshevik conspiracy."

**RG 65:** *Federal Bureau of Investigation.*

The largest series of records in this RG are microfilmed FBI investigative case files, 1908–22, which consist of 955 rolls of microfilm and are divided into four subseries: Miscellaneous, Mexican, Bureau Section, and Old German. Investigation case files contain information on persons and organizations associated with socialist, communist, anarchist, and Russian activities in the U.S.

**RG 75:** *Bureau of Indian Affairs.*

This record group includes records of the office of the Secretary of War relating to Indian affairs (1800–1824) concerning negotiation of treaties. It also contains records relating to Indian removal (1817–1906).

**RG 76:** *Boundary and Claims Commissions and Arbitrations.*

These records include international boundary claims by and against the United States as well U.S. arbitration in international disputes.

**RG 84:** *Foreign Service Posts of the Department of State.*

Some records in this group duplicate documents in RG 59 (e.g., instructions sent to consulates and dispatches sent to the State Department). Thus should items be missing from RG 59, they might be found here. There is also original material, and a thorough search of Consular Records will often reveal considerable data on economic and political conditions in the host country. To a large extent, relevant data are contained in the correspondence between the Foreign Service posts and local governments, businesses and individuals. Although records date from the 1790s, records for many posts are incomplete, especially from the early years. See PI 60, "Records of Selected Foreign Service Posts."

**RG 220:** *Presidential Committees, Commissions, and Boards.*

These are records of temporary committees and commissions, 1924–70. Included are records of the President's Commission for the Study and Review of Conditions in the Republic of Haiti, 1930, which investigated the U.S. intervention, the effectiveness of American administration, and social and economic conditions. Records of the National Defense Advisory Commission, 1940–42. Other series include the Records of the President's Soviet Protocol Committee, 1941–45, responsible for overall lend-lease assistance to Russia, and the Records of the American War Production Mission in China, 1944–45.

**RG 239:** *American Commission for the Protection and Salvage of Artistic and Historic Monuments in War Areas.*

Documents in this record group include memoranda and reports pertaining to art collections and monuments in war areas in France and Italy.

**RG 250:** *Office of War Mobilization and Reconversion, 1942–47.*

Included are materials on war relief in the USSR and on U.S. agricultural goods sent to the Soviet Union, 1941–45. See PI 25.

**RG 256:** *American Commission to Negotiate Peace.*

The commission was appointed by President Wilson to accompany him to Paris at the end of World War I. A group of experts (known as the "Inquiry") prepared information on a wide range of problems following the war. Included are the general records of the commission, 1918–31, covering its activities, and the "Inquiry Document," which includes about 1,000 reports on virtually every international question facing the negotiators. See PI 9 and PI 89.

**RG 262:** *Foreign Broadcast Intelligence Service, 1940–47.*

Included are transcripts of foreign broadcasts related to economic, military, and other matters. See PI 115.

**RG 273:** *National Security Council, 1947–61.*

Included are policy papers and meeting minutes for the Truman and Eisenhower administrations along with additional documents released through FOIA to the present. There are files relating to the Soviet Union, the spread of communism, and the official national security policy with regard to communism.

**RG 286:** *Agency for International Development.*
There is less than 1 cubic foot in this record group, mostly dating from 1955, before the establishment of AID in 1961. RG 469, Records of the U.S. Foreign Economic Assistance Agencies (see below, in the Suitland Reference Branch) is the primary record group for the predecessor organizations to AID.

**RG 326:** *Atomic Energy Commission (AEC).*
Records from 1947–58 contain substantial national security-related material, principally AEC reports on nuclear weapons, nonproliferation treaties and conferences, and defense programs. AEC records from 1958–75 are stored in the Energy Department Archives (B5).

**RG 353:** *Interdepartmental and Intradepartmental Committees (State Department).*
This is an extremely important RG for peace and security studies because it contains significant information on policy formulation, most of which was done between the army, navy, and State Department during World War II and in the postwar period. The records of the Interdepartmental Advisory Board on Reciprocity of Treaties, 1933–40, deal with economic and political aspects of reciprocity and mutual defense arrangements with American republics in 1940. This RG also contains records of the State-War-Navy Coordinating Committee, 1944–49 (renamed the State-Army-Navy-Air Force Coordinating Committee), which formulated occupation policy and policies for international conferences.

This RG also covers Records of the Committee on Inter-American Economic Development, 1944–45, which was made up of the Commerce and Agriculture Departments, the Foreign Economic Administration, and the Export-Import Bank; the Records of the Latin American Working Group of the Foreign Military Assistance Correlation (Coordination) Committee, 1950 (1948–50); and Records of the Southeast Asia Aid Policy Committee (SEAC), 1950–53.

Also included are materials pertaining to U.S.-Soviet relations, in particular, Records of Interdepartmental and Intradepartmental Committees Maintained by the Executive Secretariat (U.S. Lend-Lease and Surplus Settlement Committee, 1945–46) and the USSR Country Committee, 1946–48, and Records of the Joint U.S.A.-USSR Documentary Publication Project on Russian-American Relations, 1765–1815.

**RG 360:** *Continental and Confederation Congresses and the Constitutional Convention, 1774–96.*
This RG contains material on foreign affairs and the evolution of executive departments dealing with national defense.

*Lot File 54 D 195: State Department, Policy Planning Staff, Numbered Papers, 1947–49.* File contains 63 planning staff papers.

*Lot File 57 D 688: Records Relating to the Use and Control of Atomic Energy, 1944–62.* This collection consolidates records of Combined Policy Committee, International Atomic Energy Agency, Ad Hoc Committee on Atomic Energy, Scientific Intelligence Committee, Office of International Scientific and Technical Affairs, and the United Nations Atomic Energy Commission. The collection also includes country files and covers cooperation, technical assistance, exports and imports of nuclear material, publications, and U.S. position papers.

*Lot File 64 D 21: Records Relating to U.N. Monetary and Financial Conference (Bretton Woods), 1944–50.* These records are from the State Department's Office of International Conferences and relate to the establishment of the IMF and the World Bank. The records relate primarily to the organization and administration of the conference. (The proceedings have been printed separately by GPO.)

*Lot File 64 D 563: State Department, Policy Planning Staff, 1947–53.* These records deal with the State Department's long-range planning; preparation of NSC-68 and NSC-20; memoranda of George Kennan; European Recovery Plan; international control of atomic energy; the situation in Greece, Italy, Russia, China, and the world generally. File includes staff studies, chronological file, geographical file, country and subject files.

*Lot File 67 D 237: State Department, Office of the Director of the Bureau of Intelligence and Research, 1959–66.* This file contains morning briefings, 1959–66.

*Lot File 388: Policy Committee on Arms and Armaments, 1945–49.* This committee was concerned with all questions regarding the formulation of arms policy. Issues include U.S. arms sales, arms sales of communist and third world countries, and the Inter-American Military Cooperation bill.

## CENTER FOR LEGISLATIVE ARCHIVES

(202) 501-5350
Michael L. Gillette, Director

**RG 46:** *United States Senate.*
Included are the files of the Senate Committee on Foreign Relations, which contain hearings, committee papers, and reports. See PIs 23, 48,62 and SL 32; and *Guide to the Records of the U.S. Senate at the National Archives, 1789–1989.*

**RG 128:** *Joint Committees of Congress.*
Pertinent joint committees include the Committee to Investigate Pearl Harbor, 1945–46; the Committee

on the Conduct of the War, 1863–65; and the Committee on Atomic Energy, which contains material on Soviet atomic espionage and weapons testing.

**RG 233:** *United States House of Representatives.*
Contains the records of the House Committee on Foreign Affairs and the House Armed Services Committee. See PIs 11, 70, and 113, and *Guide to the National Archives of the United States.*

**RG 287:** *Publications of the United States Government.*
This is a complete collection of all government documents printed by the Government Printing Office (GPO).

## SUITLAND REFERENCE BRANCH

Washington National Records Center
4205 Suitland Road
Suitland, Maryland

Mail:
Washington, D.C. 20409
(301) 763-7410
John Butler, Director
(Daily shuttle service is available from main archives building.)

**RG 5:** *United States Grain Corporation.*
Its main functions were to regulate grain trade by working in cooperation with the War Trade Board and the American Relief Administration; records offices and missions include those from Paris, Copenhagen, Danzig, Gravosa, Hamburg, Finland, the Baltic States, Poland, the old Austro-Hungarian Empire and Serbia, and Southern Russia.

**RG 61:** *War Industries Board.*
The board was established by the Council of National Defense in 1917 to oversee government orders, price-fixing agreements for certain raw materials; included are records dealing with U.S. contracts with foreign countries.

**RG 153:** *Office of the Judge Advocate General (Army).*
The Judge Advocate General receives the records and proceedings of courts martial, military commissions, and courts of inquiry. Included among the Records of Investigations, 1864–1927, are records relating to President Lincoln's assassination. Records of the International Affairs Division, 1943–57, contain dossiers of war crimes trials held by military commissions in China, the Far East Command, and the European and Mediterranean theaters of operations. There are also reports of investigations of criminal acts by Nazis (German and non-German) in the USSR and by Soviet citizens against other Soviet citizens and persons of other nationalities. Also included are trial records of Nazis that shed light on the Katyn Forest massacre, extermination of Soviet Jews, and participation of Soviet judges in the International Military Tribunal, Far East.

**RG 154:** *War Finance Corporation, 1918–39.*
This corporation was established to support industries essential to the war effort, it was headed by Bernard Baruch and after the armistice assisted in the transition to peace.

**RG 169:** *Foreign Economic Administration.*
Includes records of the Office of Lend-Lease Administration and its predecessors, 1939–44; records of the Board of Economic Warfare and its predecessors, 1940–43; records of the Office of Foreign Rehabilitation Operations, 1942–44; and other records. See PI 29.

**RG 182:** *War Trade Board, 1917–21.*
This board licensed imports and exports and sought to keep strategic goods out of enemy hands. The records of its subsidiary corporation, the Russian Bureau, include documents on contacts of Russian companies with Germany in the 1910s, the Russian budget during World War I, and Russian exports and imports, 1917–19. See PI 100.

**RG 208:** *Office of War Information.*
Records of the Domestic Operations Branch, 1933–46, deal with dissemination of war information within the United States. Records of Overseas Operations Branch, 1941–46, deal with psychological warfare and propaganda efforts. Included are reports on Japanese morale; the Soviet military, 1942–45; the Yalta Conference; the signing of the UN Charter, 1945; and lend-lease to the USSR. See PI 56.

**RG 253:** *Petroleum Administration for War, 1941–46.*
Included is material on the lend-lease of oil goods to the USSR and on Soviet petroleum resources, needs, and production. See PI 31.

**RG 260:** *United States Occupation Headquarters, World War II.*
Included within this RG are records of the Office of Military Government for Germany (U.S.), 1944–52, which contain material on the Berlin Airlift, industrial dismemberment of Germany, and German war reparations; the records of the U.S. Element, Allied Commission for Austria, 1942–54; and the records of the U.S. Civil Administration of the Ryukyu Islands, 1952–54.

**RG 261:** *Former Russian Agencies.*
This RG consists of records of Imperial Russian agencies obtained by the Department of State. Within this RG are records of Russian consulates in the U.S. and Canada, 1862–1922; and records of the Russian Supply Committee, 1914–22, which oversaw purchase of military supplies during World War I.

**RG 331:** *Allied Operational and Occupation Headquarters, World War II.*
This RG contains records from the Supreme Headquarters Allied Expeditionary Forces (SHAEF) 1942–45, and the missions it conducted in Europe, including Russia; records of the Allied Commission/Allied Military Government (Italy), 1943–47; records from General Headquarters Supreme Commander for the Allied Powers (SCAP), 1945–53, which deal with the surrender and occupation of Japan; and records of General Headquarters, Southwest Pacific Area, 1941–49.

**RG 335:** *Office of the Secretary of the Army.*
This RG mostly contains documentation on army administration and logistics following the 1947 military reorganization. It also contains records relevant to U.S.-occupied areas, 1948–52; includes information on the Berlin airlift, Soviet explosion of the atom bomb, and Soviet military strength.

**RG 338:** *United States Army Commands.*
Included are records of U.S. Army Europe, 1942–60, which include British and German military studies relating to World War II; records of U.S. Army Pacific, 1942–52, as well as other army commands. Also included are materials on Nazi criminal acts in the USSR and against Soviet citizens abroad.

**RG 340:** *Office of the Secretary of the Air Force.*
Included are documents on preparing for war against the USSR, 1948–50.

**RG 341:** *Records of Headquarters United States Air Force, 1935–63.*
Included are records of research and development of new air weapons, strategic aircraft, air craft armaments; also includes correspondence, intelligence reports, aerial photos, radar reports, charts, and air attaché reports pertaining to the USSR.

**RG 374:** *Defense Atomic Support Agency (DASA).*
This agency succeeded the Armed Forces Special Weapons Project and the Manhattan Engineer District; it administered Defense Department programs and policies relating to nuclear weapons. Records date from 1943 to 1955. The agency's general records, 1947–55, are almost all classified. The Records of Offices, Divisions, and Branches, 1943–55, contain considerable material on weapons development including collection of atomic weapon effects; the development of radiological defense procedures; records of the Security Division, which consist of counterintelligence investigation and security clearance material; and records of the Test Division, which contain records relating to test operations. Records of the Joint Task Forces, 1946–55, contain records of specific nuclear tests.

**RG 407:** *Adjutant General's Office.*
Includes correspondence, reports, etc., on lend-lease to the USSR; the Berlin blockade, 1948; Russian atomic bomb developments, 1949–54; and U.S.-USSR joint occupation policies after World War II.

**RG 469:** *U.S. Foreign Economic Assistance Agencies, 1948–61.*
These records include the Economic Cooperation Administration, which was established in 1948 to administer the Marshall Plan. In 1951, the ECA was replaced by the Mutual Security Agency (MSA) whose purpose was to provide general welfare by furnishing military, economic, and technical assistance to friendly nations in the interest of peace and security. This organization was followed by the Foreign Operation Administration and the International Cooperation Administration. In 1961, the ICA was replaced by AID (see RG 286, above). Other records in this RG include Technical Cooperation Administration, the Institute for Inter-American Affairs, Office of the Special Representative in Europe (1948–53), and the U.S. Mission to NATO.

*Lot File 60 D 400: Office of U.N. Affairs (Human Rights and Freedom of Information), 1948.* Records relate to State Department meetings held with nongovernmental organizations and government agencies in preparation of the International Covenant and Declaration on Human Rights and the establishment of the U.N. Commission on Human Rights in Geneva.

*Lot File 66 D 428: State Department, Office of Munitions Control, 1951–64.* This office was established in 1946 and dealt with control of international arms traffic, munitions, implements of war, and licensing information.

Note: The collection of Donated Materials (*formerly* RG 200) includes personal papers and manuscripts relating to military service or diplomatic activity.

**MILITARY REFERENCE BRANCH**

(202) 501-5395
Cynthia G. Fox, Chief

**NAVY AND OLD ARMY BRANCH**

(202) 501-5671 (Navy)
(202) 501-5390 (Old Army)

**MODERN MILITARY BRANCH**

(301) 713-7250

*Note:* In general, pre-1940 records are the domain of the Navy and Old Army Branch; the Modern Military Branch oversees post-1940 materials. Certain record groups are maintained jointly by both branches.

**RG 18:** *Army Air Forces, 1907–47.*
Included are World War II planning records.

**RG 38:** *Office of the Chief of Naval Operations.*
This office was responsible for, among other duties, naval strategic planning, training of naval forces, and preparation and readiness. Within the Records of the Chief of Naval Operations (1914–46) are records that concern the military government established in the Dominican Republic, 1916–24. The records of the Deputy Chief of Naval Operations include the Office of Naval Intelligence, containing a great amount of correspondence, files, and reports of naval attachés in foreign countries (1892–1946) dealing with political, economic, social, and diplomatic matters. Also included are records relating to the U.S. Communist Party (1927–30). Among the topics covered in detail are the Russo-Japanese War, the Russian Civil War, and the Russo-Finnish War of 1939–40. This record group also includes records of the Eastern European Section and the Far Eastern Section of the Foreign Intelligence Branch: 1940–52.

**RG 45:** *Naval Records Collection of the Office of Naval Records and Library.*
The voluminous records within this group date between 1691 and 1927 and contain material on diverse naval matters. Included are records of the Office of the Secretary of the Navy, 1776–1913; various squadron reports; the activities of John Paul Jones, 1778–91.

**RG 72:** *Bureau of Aeronautics.*
The bureau was established under the Department of the Navy for development of aircraft, as well as purchasing, constructing, and maintaining aircraft, naval air stations, and fleet air bases. This record group also contains numerous information bulletins from World War II dealing with the allocation of material in the USSR and war relief efforts by Soviet civilians. See PI 26.

**RG 74:** *Bureau of Ordnance, 1818–1946.*
This bureau was responsible for the design, management, and procurement of armaments for the Navy Department.

**RG 77:** *Office of Chief Engineer.*
This RG contains the Harrison-Bundy Files Relating to the Development of the Atomic Bomb, 1942–46. Both were special assistants to Secretary of the Army Stimson. These are part of the Manhattan Engineer District records.

**RG 80:** *General Records of the Department of the Navy.*
Besides general administrative records of the Secretary of the Navy, 1804–1959, are the papers of Frank Knox, 1940–44, James Forrestal, 1940–47, Assistant Navy Secretaries Theodore Roosevelt, 1897–98, and Franklin D. Roosevelt, and minutes of the American Top Policy Group, 1944–47. Also included are naval records on Bolshevik activities in the Soviet Union, 1919–26.

**RG 94:** *Adjutant General's Office, 1780s–1917.*
This very extensive RG contains material dealing with the command, discipline, and administration of the army. Particularly pertinent are reports and other materials from the War of 1812, Mexican War, Civil War, Philippines Insurrection, Spanish-American War, and from U.S. military observers during the Crimean and Russo-Japanese wars. See PI 17.

**RG 107:** *Office of the Secretary of War.*
This RG includes extensive records on organization, administration, and planning, 1798–1947.

**RG 120:** *American Expeditionary Forces (World War I).*
Records of American Expeditionary Force (AEF) General Headquarters, 1917–21, include general staff records on intelligence and operations under General Pershing. Records of the AEF Tactical Units, 1917–19, include records of the 3 corps and 43 divisions that made up the AEF. This RG also contains records of the American Forces in France, 1919–20; records of the American Forces in Germany, 1918–23, which contain intelligence bulletins on political, economic, and social conditions in Germany and dossiers on the Rhineland; records of the American Polish Relief Expedition, 1919–21; records of the AEF, North Russia, 1917–19, which also include the records of the Chief of the American Military Mission to Russia; records of the American Section of the Supreme War Council, 1917–19, which prepared policy recommendations concerning conduct of the war; records of American Military Missions, 1917–19, which consists of correspondence and reports of American officers attached to other allied headquarters; and records of the American Section of the Permanent International Armistice Commission, 1918–20, which dealt with execution of the terms of the armistice.

**RG 165:** *War Department General and Special Staffs.*
The following series contain attaché reports that are of particular military interest, although they also contain political, economic, and social material: Military Intelligence Division Correspondence, 1917–41; English Translations of Foreign Intel-

ligence Documents, 1919–47; War Plans Division Correspondence, 1920–42; German Military Records Relating to World War I; Office of the Chief of Staff, 1942–47; Director of Intelligence, Operations Division, 1942–45; Collection of American and British Conversations (ABC), 1942–47.

**RG 179:** *War Production Board, 1940–47.*
This board was responsible for administration of agencies in cooperation with allies (principally Britain), for controlling scarce and critical material, and for mobilization of industrial resources. Included are extensive materials documenting U.S. lend-lease to the Soviet Union and war production in liberated areas of Europe. See PI 15.

**RG 218:** *United States Joint Chiefs of Staff.*
Included are the records of the United Joint Chiefs of Staff (JCS) and the Combined Chiefs of Staff (CCS), 1942–61, which pertain to the allied coordination of the war effort, 1942–45, and the surrender of German and Japanese forces in World War II. There is also information on Soviet armed forces during and after World War II, the postwar occupation of Austria and Germany, Soviet domination of Eastern Europe, Soviet weapons, and U.S. plans for war in case of Soviet attack. The records of the Joint New Weapons Committee, 1942–46, and of the Munitions Assignment Board are also here.

**RG 226:** *Office of Strategic Services.*
The records of the Research and Analysis Branch, 1941–46, include reports on political, sociological, and economic conditions in various countries, biographic sketches of Italian leaders, and studies of Hitler. The Central Intelligence Division records include intelligence reports on enemy logistics; the Economics Division reports relate to military and economic conditions of Axis powers. There are also reports covering parts of Africa, the Far East, and Latin America. Included also are intelligence, naval, and military reports on Soviet natural resources, nationality problems, and other social, political, military, and economic matters. This record group was expanded dramatically during the last 10 years, and now includes both intelligence and operational records.

**RG 238:** *National Archives Collection of World War II War Crimes.*

**RG 243:** *United States Strategic Bombing Survey.*
This RG contains reports on the effect of Allied bombing on Germany and Japan, 1937–47. See PI 10.

**RG 304:** *Office of Civil and Defense Mobilization, 1947–60.*
This office was responsible for government mobilization efforts, including production, procurement,

stabilization, and transportation. The bulk of the records are from the National Security Resources Board. There are also records from the Defense Production Administration.

**RG 319:** *Records of the Army Staff.*
This RG deals with most aspects of organization, planning, and administration of the army, 1947–60. Particularly relevant subgroups are the records of the following offices: Chief of Staff, 1942–54; Chief of Civil Affairs and Military Government, 1948–54; Assistant Chief of Staff, G-2, Intelligence, 1939–55 (1,163 rolls of microfilm); and Chief of Psychological warfare, 1951–54.

**RG 330:** *Office of the Secretary of Defense.*
Included are vast (but scattered) materials dealing with war planning directed toward the USSR. Subjects discussed include strategic and tactical nuclear weapons; European Defense Community agreements; the Mutual Defense Assistance Program, 1947–54; the Mutual Security Act, 1953; the Soviet wartime and postwar roles; and Soviet-Iranian relations.

**RG 331:** *Allied Operational and Occupation Headquarters, World War II.*
This extremely large record group (17,948 cubic feet of records) concerns the formulation and execution of plans for strategic conduct of the war by Great Britain and the United States, 1938–54. It contains records of the Supreme Headquarters Allied Expeditionary Forces (SHAEF), 1942–45; Subordinate SHAEF Commands, 1943–45; Combined Liquidating Agencies, 1945–47, which dissolved joint or combined commands after July 1945; Allied Force Headquarters (AFHQ), 1942–47, involving activity in North Africa and the Mediterranean, including Italy; Allied Commission/Allied Military Government (Italy), 1943–47; the Allied Screening Commission (Italy), 1944–47; the Allied Military Government, British-U.S. Zone, Free Territory of Trieste, 1945–54; General Headquarters, Supreme Commander for the Allied Powers (SCAP), 1945–52, which oversaw the occupation of Japan; General Headquarters Southwest Pacific Area (SWPA), 1941–49; and the Southeast Asia Command (SEAC), 1943–45.

**RG 333:** *International Military Agencies.*
Records of the Tripartite Naval Commission, 1941–47, contain correspondence, memoranda, and messages among commission members representing the U.S., Great Britain, and the USSR. Also included in this RG are Records of the Headquarters, United Nations Command, 1950–57, which deals with U.N. involvement in Korea. See PI 127.

**RG 334:** *Interservice Agencies.*
This is a very diverse group of records pertaining to interservice agencies established between the army,

navy, and State Department. Particularly relevant are records of the Military Assistance Advisory Groups, 1942–58; records of the U.S. Military Mission to Moscow, 1943–45, which contain documents on the shuttle-bombing of Axis-occupied Europe (Operation Frantic); and records of the National War College, 1943–54, which include indexes relating to strategic politico-military planning, operations, and intelligence, as well as library files on Soviet domestic affairs, military capability, and foreign relations.

**RG 395:** *U.S. Army Overseas Operations and Commands, 1898–1942.*

Included are records from the Spanish-American War and from forces sent to Mexico, the Panama Canal, the Philippines, and Cuba. Also included are records from the China Relief Expedition sent during the Boxer Rebellion, 1900, and the American Expeditionary Forces in Siberia, 1918–20, consisting mostly of war diaries from Vladivostok.

**RG 457:** *National Security Agency/Central Security Office.*

Included are summaries of Japanese diplomatic messages intercepted by the United States and its allies during World War II.

## CAPTURED GERMAN RECORDS STAFF

(202) 501-5383
Robert Wolfe, Director

**RG 242:** *National Archives Collection of Foreign Records Seized, 1941–.*

Extensive series of microfilms of captured Nazi documents and other World War II materials pertaining to Russia are in this group. Pertinent series include Records from the Heere-Archiv, 1679–1947; Miscellaneous Records, 1815–1945; Library of German Microfilms, 1870–1945; Miscellaneous Russian Records, 1870–1947; Records of the All-Union Communist Party, Smolensk District, 1917–41; Records of the National Socialist German Workers' Party, 1915–42; Records of Other Reich Ministries and Offices, 1919–45; Italian Records, 1922–43; Japanese Records, 1928–47; Records of German Air Force Commands, 1932–45; Records of the Soviet Purchasing Commission at Prague, 1936–41; Records of the Reich Commissioner for the Strengthening of Germandom, 1939–45; Records of the Reich Ministry for the Occupied Eastern Territories, 1942–45; and Records Seized by U.S. Military Forces in Korea. RG 242 has a published index and supplement.

4. Accessing NARA holdings can prove difficult for scholars accustomed to the extensive cataloging records and subject indexing offered by libraries. Archives, however, are not libraries and the nature and sheer number of items held by NARA prohibit detailed subject and geographic access to many of the holdings. Access tools vary from record group to record group. Some have their own card indexes that the generating agency prepared when the files were active. Once these files were in the custody of NARA, staff members may have prepared other finding-aids such as acquisition lists, inventories, preliminary inventories (PI), and special lists. Some record groups may have no finding-aids.

The absence of comprehensive finding-aids for each record group combined with the archives' practice of dispersing materials among several administrative divisions and branches makes it mandatory for visiting researchers to discuss their projects with a staff consultant in the Central Reference Division and with consultants in other appropriate divisions. These specialists can explain archival policies in detail and greatly facilitate access to record groups that might otherwise be overlooked. More important, many consultants have acquired a knowledge of the contents of the record groups under their jurisdiction, which only years of close association make possible. Thus consultants are often aware of resources for which no published finding-aid exists or of a particular item or type of document not specifically cited in an inventory.

The single most important printed research aid for all scholars is the NARA *Guide to the National Archives of the United States* (1974), which is available in most academic libraries. In addition to describing each record group, the guide furnishes a brief history of each U.S. government unit; content summaries of record groups; data on the quantity, dates, finding-aids, and format of records; and applicable restrictions. The extensive index should be considered the key to valuable resources on topics relating to peace and international security. Ask in the Central Reading Room for the loose-leaf binder containing annual updates to the guide. Many of the finding-aids for record groups have been published and are available free of charge. For a list of those in print, request a free copy of *Select List of Publications of the National Archives and Records Service.* *Microfilm Resources for Research* lists holdings available for purchase in microfilm. Large portions of the State Department's central file have been microfilmed. These are listed in *Diplomatic Records, A Select Catalog of National Archives Microfilm Publications* and are available for purchase.

In addition to the research and finding-aids cited above, numerous other guides and bibliographies are available. Some of these are *Catalog of National Archives Microfilm Publications* (1974) and its supplements; *The National Archives and Foreign Relations Research* (1974), edited by Milton O. Gustafson; and *List of Record Groups of the National Archives and Records Service* (1976), edited by Annadel Wile. There are also general information leaflets with basic information on how to use the archives. Information on recent NARA accessions appears in *Prologue: The Journal of the National Archives* (quarterly). Also available and particularly useful in identifying consultants is the "National Archive Primary Reference Contact List."

5. Index Terms: Arms Control; Collective Security; Conflict Management and Resolution; Defense Policy, National—History; Development Issues; Diplomacy and Negotiations; Human Rights; Intelligence; International Law; International Organizations; Low Intensity Conflict; Military History; Military Science; Naval Science; Terrorism; War Crimes

See also entries D6, E11, F20, F21, and G10

**National Defense University (Defense Department)—Library    See entry A33**

---

## BI2    National Security Archive.

---

1.a.  2130 H Street, NW, Suite 701
Washington, D.C. 20037
(202) 994-7000
Fax: (202) 994-7005

b.  9:30 A.M.–5:30 P.M. Monday–Friday

c.  The archive is open to the general public. Prior appointment is strongly recommended. Call the Public Service Librarian at (202) 797-0882.

d.  Self-service photocopying service is available.

e.  Thomas Blanton, Executive Director
Malcolm Byrne, Director of Analysis

2.  The archive's databases contain over 115,000 records of released government documents, authority files of individuals and organizations, and Freedom of Information Act (FOIA) requests. Virtually all databases pertain to international security.

3.  The National Security Archive is a unique institution, in which a nongovernmental entity houses a substantial collection of declassified government documents. Originally established as a repository

for material collected by journalists through FOIA requests, the collection now consists of over 1,000 lin. ft. of documents. This nonprofit, nonpartisan organization obtains, catalogs, and makes available primarily declassified government documents relating to international trade, human rights, foreign policies, national defense issues, crises in international relations, multilateral and bilateral negotiations, economic development, access to government information, and many other issues. Examples include State Department cables, presidential national security directives, internal memoranda, telephone logs of government officials, and similar documents. Many of these records are released through FOIA requests and the Mandatory Declassification Review process; others are obtained from government reports, donated record holdings and oral histories, congressional reports and testimony, official court records, and the presidential libraries.

The archive's records are indexed according to document sets that average 17,000 pages in length and cover discrete subject areas. Twelve microfilm document sets have been published. They are: *El Salvador: The Making of U.S. Policy, 1977–1984; The Iran-Contra Affair: The Making of a Scandal, 1983–1988; Iran: The Making of U.S. Policy, 1977–1980; The Cuban Missile Crisis, 1962; The U.S. Intelligence Community, 1947–1989; The Philippines: U.S. Policy during the Marcos Years, 1965–1986; Afghanistan: The Making of U.S. Policy, 1973–1990; South Africa: The Making of U.S. Policy, 1962–1989; Military Uses of Space: The Making of U.S. Policy, 1945–1991; Nuclear Non-Proliferation, 1945–1991; Presidential Directives on National Security from Truman to Clinton;* and *The Berlin Crisis, 1958–1962.* The Archives also publishes a series of documents for the classroom. These include: *The Cuban Missile Crisis, 1962* (1992); *The Iran-Contra Scandal: The Declassified History* (1993); and *South Africa and the United States: The Declassified History* (1994).

4.  The document sets include detailed, cross-referenced indexes and finding-aids generated by a computerized information retrieval system that also identifies unreleased documents or other gaps in the information available to the public. The published document sets are accompanied by finding-aids that average over 1,700 pages and include name indexes, microfiche catalogs, chronologies, glossaries, bibliographies, and introductory essays.

5.  Index Terms: Arms Control; Collective Security; Conflict Management and Resolution; Defense Policy, National—History; Deterrence; Low Intensity Conflict; Regional Conflict; Terrorism

## **BI3**  Naval Historical Center (Navy Department)

1.a.  Washington Navy Yard, Building 57
9th and M Streets, SE
Washington, D.C. 20374
(202) 433-3170 (Archives)
Fax: (202) 433-3172

b.  9:00 A.M.–4:00 P.M. Monday–Friday

c.  Open to the public for on-site use. Some materials are classified. Researchers are requested to give advance notice of their intent to visit the center.

d.  Limited photocopying services are available.

e.  Dean C. Allard, Director of Naval History

2.  The Naval Historical Center is the historical arm of the U.S. Navy. The extensive holdings of the different archive branches are especially relevant to naval science, military science, and national defense. The center's cartographic holdings, oral history collection, and photographic section are described in entries D9, E13, and F23, respectively.

3.  The following branches of the center hold relevant archival materials:

### OPERATIONAL ARCHIVES BRANCH

(202) 433-3170/3224
Bernard F. Cavalcante, Head
Kathy Lloyd, Head of Reference

The Operational Archives Branch was created in 1942 to centralize and organize the basic records documenting the combat activities of naval fleet units. The Operational Archives Branch continues to collect documents on fleet operations as well as official records of the Office of the Chief of Naval Operations and other operational headquarters of the U.S. Navy. The records amount to approximately 10,000 cubic feet (or over 200,000 items), primarily from 1940 to the present. Although most of the recent holdings are classified and restricted, archival materials before 1955 have been declassified and can be used by scholars on the premises. The comprehensive and wide-ranging records of this branch are valuable for perspectives on strategic decision making during and after World War II, as well as for being in-depth sources on all levels of naval activity.

For World War II, the collection *Action and Operational Reports, 1939–1945* (1,298 cubic feet) is of primary usefulness as it contains reports of combat and other engagements throughout the war. It also contains coast guard reports, some training reports, and routine operations during the war. The *Action and Operational Reports, 1946–1973* (declassified up to 1955) contains peacetime deployment reports, reports of Korea and Vietnam, Arctic and Antarctic exploration, and reports on international crises such as Lebanon (1958) and the Cuban Missile Crisis. (There are 175 cubic feet of records up to 1953.)

A second important collection of World War II material is the *War Diaries of Naval Forces, 1941–1945* (748 cubic feet; 384 reels of microfilm). These are day-by-day records of events submitted by all major naval units and commands during the war. The quality of the entries varies considerably, some having sparse accounts, others giving detailed accounts of operations and administration. There are a scattering of diaries from foreign commands and the Marine Corps. There are also war diaries from 1946 and 1950–53, the latter covering the Korean War (59 cubic feet). In Korea, diaries were maintained in combat areas only.

For overall strategic planning of World War II, scholars should consult the checklist *Records of the Strategic Plans Division, Office of the Chief of Naval Operations and Its Predecessor Organizations, 1912–1947.* Holdings of particular note are Lectures and Speeches, 1912–41 (6.5 cubic feet); Miscellaneous Subject File, 1917–47 (15 cubic feet); records relating to the "Are We Ready Study, 1940–41"; records relating to Anglo-American-Dutch Cooperation, 1938–44 (3 cubic feet); Post-War Planning and Sea Frontier Sectors, 1943–47 (11 cubic feet); and Atlantic Sector, 1940–45.

Also of considerable significance are the World War II Command File, 1939–45 (359 cubic feet), and the Post-1946 Command File, 1946–55, which include command histories, manuals, organizational documents, personal manuscripts on various subjects, and other miscellaneous information on navy commands. Other interesting collections include records of the Base Maintenance Division, Office of the Chief of Naval Operations (including histories of overseas bases), 1930–55; records of the Organization, Research, and Policy Division, Office of the Chief of Naval Operations, 1947–49; records of the Top Secret Control Office, Office of the Chief of Naval Operations, 1948–50; records of the Politico-Military Affairs Division, Office of the Chief of Naval Operations, 1944–50; records of the U.S. Atlantic Fleet, 1939–44; records of U.S. Naval Air Station, Bermuda, 1942–45; records of the U.S. 10th Fleet, 1939–47; and records of the Commander, U.S. Naval Forces, Europe, 1938–47 (including material on planning of Operation OVERLORD).

Extensive foreign records held by the Operational Archives deal with World War II. British records include detailed naval staff histories and rare battle summaries of all British naval engagements during the war. Other material found in British records include British War Cabinet Reports on Anti-U-Boat Warfare Committee, 1943–45. These records may be viewed but not copied. There are also the reports of an American liaison officer to the British Navy, September 1939–December 1943.

A large collection of German war records is contained in *Translated Records of the German Navy, Essays by German Officers, and Related Studies, 1922–1945* (98 cubic feet, with checklist); includes a selection on microfilm from the holdings of the War Historical Division of the German Naval Staff. Most of the materials are in the National Archives, but the Operational Archives contains 98 cubic feet of war diaries, essays by German officers on a wide range of topics, British reports and translations from German technical reports, organization charts and directories, minutes of conferences with Hitler, and dossiers of selected German military and civilian personnel. A separate microfilm publication exists for ordering documents from the *War Diary, Operations Division, German Naval Staff, 1939–1945*. Among the documents available are essays by German officers and officials regarding Operation SEA LION and the intensified air war against Great Britain; plans for the invasion of England; reports on the success of Luftwaffe attacks on shipping in the English Channel and on North Atlantic convoys; reminiscences of Admiral Wurmbach describing his experiences as Admiral of Skagerrak, 1943–45; and naval routes used during the German invasion of Norway.

Japanese action and operation reports and war diaries are found in *The Imperial Japanese Navy* (1939–52) collection, which contains 230 microfilm reels of untranslated material and 117 cubic feet of translated material. There are also translations of miscellaneous Japanese records and related studies, histories, and essays.

The archives also has large holdings of office files and personal papers of many 20th-century U.S. naval officers and officials. A partial listing includes papers of: Adm. Daniel E. Barbey, 1943–69 (22 cubic feet); Adm. of the Navy George Dewey (25 feet); Rear Adm. Ernest M. Eller, 1958–70 (58 feet); Adm. Thomas C. Hart, 1897–1945 (1 foot); Adm. Alan G. Kirk, 1937–45 (16 feet); Fleet Adm. Ernest J. King, 1918–55 (85 feet); Fleet Adm. William D. Leahy, 1938–59 (9 feet); Rear Adm. Samuel E. Morison, 1911–69 (50 feet); Fleet Adm. Chester Nimitz, 1901–67 (70 feet), including key dispatches, his command diary, and reports of conferences; Adm. Harold R. Stark, 1916–70 (40 feet); Adm. Richmond K. Turner, 1939–61 (13 feet); Adm. Harry E. Yarnell, 1879–1960 (10 feet); Secretary of the Navy James Forrestal, 1934–51 (2 feet); Secretary of the Navy Frank Knox, 1940–44 (3 feet); and China repository records, 1908–79 (9.5 foot), a collection of personal papers donated by individuals who served in the Far East and with the Yangtze Patrol.

The Operational Archives Branch also maintains an early records collection, 1798–1941 (142 cubic feet), primarily of office correspondence and memoranda, the result of the branch's research in the National Archives and Records Administration (BII) concerning the navy's history. It is particularly rich in biographical information and ships' histories. The biographical file, called the "ZB file" (100 cubic feet), contains entries on 35,000 officers and a few enlisted men. Its chief contents are compiled service records, past offices, and correspondence. There is coverage of 19th-century naval officers and a file of biographies from World War II to the present, which is strongest for the 1930s, 1940s, and 1950s. The "ZC" file (30 cubic feet) has records on 2,000 individual ships. The wars, operations, and expeditions file, the "ZO" file (4 cubic feet), contains folders on the Revolutionary War, the Barbary War, the Quasi-War with France, the War of 1812, the Mexican War, the Civil War, the Spanish-American War, the Boxer Rebellion, the Tampico and Vera Cruz expeditions, and World War I.

## CONTEMPORARY HISTORY BRANCH

(202) 433-3891
Edward J. Marolda, Head

Established in 1987, the Contemporary History Branch focuses on the history of the U.S. Navy in the modern era, with special emphasis on the period since the end of World War II. The professional historians on the staff research and write major narrative volumes and shorter specialized studies on the global operations of the fleet, the navy's interaction with other national security organizations and the defense industry, and the contribution of men and women to the naval service.

Recent publications include *On Course to Desert Storm: The United States Navy and the Persian Gulf* (1992); *Cordon of Steel: The U.S. Navy and the Cuban Missile Crisis* (1993); *Forged in War: The Naval-Industrial Complex and American Submarine Construction, 1940–1961* (1993); *Operation End Sweep: A History of Minesweeping Operations in North Vietnam* (1993); and *"Revolt of the Admirals": The Fight for Naval Aviation, 1945–1950* (1994).

## EARLY HISTORY BRANCH

(202) 433-2364
Michael Crawford, Head

The Early History Branch is responsible for re-searching naval history through World War I. The branch maintains an extensive collection of documents on microfilm gathered from the United States and abroad, relating principally to two ongoing documentary history series: *Naval Documents of the American Revolution* (9 volumes to date) and *The Naval War of 1812: A Documentary History* (2 volumes to date).

## NAVAL AVIATION HISTORY BRANCH

Washington Navy Yard, Building 157
(202) 433-4355/8
Roy Grossnick, Head

This branch maintains aviation command historical records, 1957–present, as well as other documents on naval aviators, air squadrons, and naval air bases. It conducts research on the history of naval aviation since 1911. The branch also manages the Naval Aviation Insignia Program and the archives for the insignia covering World War II to the present.

## SHIPS HISTORIES BRANCH

(202) 433-2585
John Reilly, Head

The Ships Histories Branch handles inquiries concerning navy ships and related subjects. Its staff compiles and maintains research files on ships of the U.S. Navy, 1775–present. It collects the annual historical reports of active navy ships and has charge of their deck logs, 1946–present. The branch researches and publishes the comprehensive *Dictionary of American Naval Fighting Ships*.

4. A list of "Declassified and Unclassified Groups and Collections in the Operational Archives" will be provided on request. There are detailed finding-aids available for most of the individual collections. For the unpublished World War II unit histories, see the Naval Historical Center's *Partial Checklist: World War II Histories and Historical Reports in the U.S. Naval History Division* (1973). The Contemporary History Branch has a list of publications available.

5. Index Terms: Collective Security; Defense Policy, National—History; Military History—Navy; Naval Science; Military Science

See also entries A36, C9, C10, D9, E13, and F23

Navy Department Library    See entry A36

---

## B14    Organization of American States (OAS)—Records Management Center

---

1.a.  Administrative Building, Room G-6
19th Street and Constitution Avenue, NW
Washington, D.C. 20006
(202) 458-3849
Fax: (202) 458-3914

b.  9:30 A.M.–4:30 P.M. Monday–Friday

c.  Open to researchers. An appointment is recommended.

d.  Photocopying services are available.

e.  Beverly Wharton-Lake, Records Management Specialist

2.  The records collection numbers some 40 million documents. It covers such crucial topics as arbitration, diplomacy and negotiations, regional conflict, peacekeeping, human rights and humanitarian issues, international organizations, international law, and economic development and the environment. For a description of the center's Voice Archives see entry E14; for OAS library resources see entries A38, D11, and F24.

3.  This valuable and largely untapped collection consists of the internal staff papers, conference material, and correspondence of the OAS and its predecessor, the Pan American Union. The records, which date back to 1889, are almost entirely open to researchers. Among the few exceptions are 15 boxes of restricted U.S. military records pertaining to 1965 inter-American "peacekeeping" operations in the Dominican Republic. In addition, the Records Management Center administers a locked vault containing the original copies of inter-American treaties, agreements, conventions, and final acts. Also in the vault are many items of physical evidence presented to, or collected by, the OAS relating to inter-American boundary violations (including the 1960s Cuban-Venezuelan dispute).

Following are examples of major collections:

The Alliance for Progress (300 cubic feet; approximately 900,000 letter-size sheets of paper).

Secretariat for Educational Affairs (290 cubic feet; approximately 870,000 letter-size sheets). Documentation dealing with educational trends in Latin America and the Caribbean; operation plans for projects dealing with educational development; inter-American cultural organizations; educational research; cultural heritage; libraries; archives; promotion of cultural values; special education trends and project models; guidance counselling and professional training; inter-American workshops; teacher training; comparative education; Latin American and Caribbean Area Studies and Library Development Programs.

Secretariat for Legal Affairs (342 cubic feet; approximately 1,026,000 letter-size sheets of paper). Provides extensive legal research material dealing with legal conventions, standards, economic integration, assistance, agreements on technical assistance, constitutions of the member countries, statements of the law, declarations, copyright laws, country legislation, Inter-American Juridical Committee, Inter-American Commission on Human Rights, treaties and conventions, and Latin American Free Trade Association, to name a few.

4.   Beverly Wharton-Lake, Records Management Specialist, maintains lists of all records under her jurisdiction, arranged by originating office and date. She will be happy to assist outside researchers.

*Note:* Additional OAS archival materials are administered by the OAS Columbus Memorial Library. See entry A38.

5.   Index Terms: Collective Security; Conflict Resolution and Management: Diplomacy and Negotiations; Development Issues; Environmental Issues, Global; Human Rights; Humanitarian Issues; International Law; International Organizations—Regional; Peacekeeping; Regional Conflict

See also entries A38, D11, E14, F24, and L13

### Organization of American States (OAS)—Columbus Memorial Library   See entry A38

d.   Files may be photocopied for a fee.

e.   Juli Delong, Manager, Information Services
     Bessie Briscoe, Information Specialist

2.   The library maintains a collection of CNS news stories, 1920–present, filed by topic. The principal relevance of the collection lies in human rights and humanitarian issues.

3.   The CNS reports on major news events and covers a wide range of topics worldwide. The news service is particularly concerned with social justice and violent conflict. Recent conflicts that have been well reported by CNS include El Salvador and Nicaragua. The human rights situation in China, especially with regard to the Catholic Church; human rights in Eastern Europe and the former Soviet Union; and international aid organizations are other prominent topics. Vatican positions on many conflicts are extensively reflected in this collection, including topics such as the Balkan conflict, the Gulf War, and Panama. Liberation theology is also a major subject in the collection.

The library also maintains complete files of *Origins,* the weekly documentary service that contains texts, speeches, and other documents. These items reflect USCC and Vatican sources as well as non-Catholic sources. There are also some USCC pamphlets, encyclicals, and pastoral letters, as well as all U.S. diocesan newspapers, which are retained for about one year.

4.   There are subject and biographical indexes and an unpublished thesaurus of key words for files.

5.   Index Terms: Human Rights; Humanitarian Issues; Peace Theory and Research; Religious, Philosophical, and Ethical Concepts of War and Peace; War Crimes

See also entries F28, M55, and N38

---

**BI5**   United States Catholic Conference (USCC)—Catholic News Service (CNS)—Library

---

1.a.   3211 Fourth Street, NE
       Washington, D.C. 20017
       (202) 541-3000

b.   9:00 A.M.–5:00 P.M. Monday–Friday

c.   Open to the public. The library requests that users telephone before visiting.

---

**BI6**   United States Holocaust Research Institute—Archives

---

1.a.   100 Raoul Wallenberg Place, SW
       Washington, D.C. 20024-2150
       (202) 488-0400
       Fax: (202) 479-9726

b.   10:00 A.M.–5:00 P.M. Daily (*Note:* Archival materials must be ordered on Friday for use on weekends.)
     Closed Christmas and Yom Kippur.

c. Open to the public.

d. Photocopying facilities are available, and the archive will make copies of microfilms for a charge.

e. Brewster S. Chamberlin, Director of Archives

2.   The archives holds roughly 1 million pages of paper documents and over 1 million pages of documents on microfilm. All of this material relates to Holocaust studies and is directly pertinent to the study of human rights and humanitarian issues. The United States Holocaust Research Institute is described in entry H72, its library in A45, and its photograph and film collections in F29. Its parent institution, the United States Holocaust Memorial Museum, is discussed in entry C11.

3.   The 2 million documents of the archives are divided into 55 record groups. The focus of the archives is on material from recently opened archives in the former Soviet Union and Eastern Europe. Acquisition policy is currently aimed at acquiring material whose access is difficult or impossible for Western scholars. The three broadest categories of materials are documents (mainly German) captured by the Red Army during World War II and transferred to the Soviet Union; records from German and collaborationist agencies in those countries occupied by the Germans in Eastern Europe and the Soviet Union; and relevant records from Romania and Hungary. The archives is the only facility in the Western Hemisphere with copies of these particular records. Additionally, the archives holds many collections from Holocaust survivors and their families, from scholars, and from concentration camp liberators, among others.

Below are listed the record groups (RG) whose contents are currently cataloged. Each RG is comprised of subcollections and file units (folders). Partial listings of the collections are given to indicate the nature of material within each RG. Microfilm records, unless otherwise indicated, are in 35 mm.

RG 2: *Survivor Testimonies.*
The majority of the collections are individual accounts of people's experiences dealing with concentration camps, ghettos, resistance, liberation, deportation, life in hiding, the killing centers, slave labor, displaced persons, beginning new lives, and the like.

RG 3: *Jewish Communities. 15 subcollections.*
This material includes occupation and administration decrees from the State Jewish Museum in Prague; articles and other documents relating to Rabbi Aladar Deutsch and the Jewish community of Prague; items relating to the Jewish communities of Salonika, Greece; Cyprus; Shanghai; Ostrowiec, Po-

land; Dohla, Transcarpathia; and Gorinchem, Netherlands.

RG 4: *Concentration and Other Camps. 29 subcollections.*
The records in this RG include documents from the State Museum of Majdanek; miscellaneous concentration camp inmate correspondence; Terezín—Memoirs of Leo Holzer, Head of the Fire Brigade in the Vicinity of the Camp; camp log books and administrative records from the Auschwitz Memorial Museum; records relating to the activities of the International Red Cross in Terezín; official SHAEF report on Buchenwald; War Refugee Board report on Auschwitz, November 1944; confession and letter of the Mauthausen commander; records of the Breendonck concentration camp; and blueprints for the construction of Buchenwald.

RG 5: *Ghettos.*
These records include Edith Jacoby letter regarding the Warsaw Ghetto; Carolina Taitz papers relating to the Riga ghetto; Edith David postcard from the Lublin ghetto; and records and photographs relating to the Wisnice ghetto.

RG 6: *War Crimes Investigation and Prosecution. 11 subcollections.*
This material includes records relating to the International Military Tribunal; Report of Henry S. Otto; Seymour Krieger Papers; Office of the U.S. Chief of Counsel records relating to defendant Artur Seyss-Inquart; memo of Telford Taylor, "An Approach to the Prosecution against Axis Criminality: Final Argument for the United States of America on the Indicted Organizations"; records relating to U.S. investigation and prosecution; interrogation of Hitler's secretaries; records relating to investigation and prosecution in Germany; and records relating to war crimes in Sachsenhausen.

RG 7: *Romanies (Gypsies). 10 subcollections.*
Contents of this RG include six essays relating to the persecution of Gypsies and Gypsy children; German newspaper articles concerning treatment of Romany, 1936–84; records relating to the treatment of Gypsies, 1920s–60s; records relating to the Gypsy camp in Frankfurt am Main.

RG 8: *Hadassah Rosensaft Collection. 3 subcollections.*
Contents include general records; Bergen-Belsen—related records; program material from the "Padagogik nach Auschwitz" conference.

RG 9: *Liberation. 10 subcollections.*
Contents include articles concerning the liberation of Landsberg and Hurlach; testimony of Nordhausen liberation by Charles Feinstein; 1981 International Liberators Conference Collection of libera-

tor testimonies; testimony of Ohrdruf liberation; and liberation of Landsberg and other camps.

**RG 10:** *Small Collections. 59 subcollections.*
Contents include Erich Mayer Collection; Leonhard Prager Papers; program booklet and map relating to Reichsparteitage; army platoon reports; Erich and Emil Beamt letters relating to emigration, 1939–42; "Bureaucratic Persecution: Jewish Life in Frankfurt am Main, 1933–1938"; Isabella Leitner Papers; Henry Lasker Papers; the activities of the Ehisatz-Gruppen; Sophie Newman scrapbooks containing Yiddish poetry and articles relating to World War II; records relating to Aryan descent and emigration; articles concerning Palestine, the American Jewish Joint Distribution Committee, and Yad Vashem; and many other files of personal and family papers.

**RG 14:** *Germany. 4 subcollections (on microfilm).*
This RG includes records and case files of Gestapo in Düsseldorf Stapostelle (2 reels); selected records from the Staatsarchiv Leipzig (13 reels); Reichsvereinigung der Juden in Deutschland (2,509 microfiche cards); records of the Landrat des Kreises Briesen (2 reels).

**RG 15:** *Poland. 29 subcollections (on microfilm).*
Contents include Nazi genocide in Poland, 1939–45; documents of the Main Commission for the Investigation of Crimes against the Polish Nation; selected Lodz Gestapo office records from the Regional Commission for the Investigation of Crimes against the Polish Nation (9 reels); records of the Office of the Government Commissar for the Productivity of the Jewish Population in Poland (3 reels); records of the Stadtverwaltung Weichselstadt (1 reel); records of Nazi concentration camps (23 reels); records of the German occupation, 1939–45 (8 reels); records of the Reichsministerium des Innern (3 reels); records of the Institut für Deutsche Ostarbeit (6 reels); records of the Kommandatur der Gendarmerie Lublin (2 reels); records of the Gendarmerie Kreis Hermannsbad (3 reels); records of the der Landrat des Kreises Schrimm (1 reel); records of der Chef der Sicherheitspolizei und SD Umwandererzentralstelle Posen (4 reels); records of the Sicherheitsdienst des Reichführers—SS, SD—Abschnitt Litzmannstadt, SD—Hauptaussenstelle Kalisch (1 reel); Nazi Danzig Proclamation and records of the Waffen SS—SS Standortverwaltung Krakow (1 reel); selected records from the Polish State Archive in Tarnow (11 reels); and records of the Landrat des Kreises Wollstein (1 reel).

**RG 16:** *Nazi Medical Policies and Practices. 2 subcollections.*
Contents of this RG include general records and "The Treatment of Shock from Prolonged Exposure to Cold, Especially in Water," by Leo Alexander, M.D.

**RG 18:** *Latvia. 2 subcollections.*
This material includes general records and selected records from the Latvian Central State Historical Archive (33 reels, 16 mm).

**RG 19:** *Rescue, Refugees, and Displaced Persons. 26 subcollections.*
Material in this RG includes Helen Waren letter concerning displaced persons; Vincent La Vista report on illegal immigration in and through Italy; records relating to the Committee for Refugee Education; records relating to the work of William Ramkey with displaced persons in Allied-occupied Austria; articles, clippings and other materials relating to the UNRRA and displaced persons; affidavit concerning the heroism of Celine Berte Morali; Mann and Mandelbaum family correspondence; the story of Sally and Samuel Bloom; records relating to Joseph Levine and his work at the Regensberg displaced persons camp; Reports of the Detachment F1E2, 2nd ECAR of the 7th U.S. Army in Mannheim, Germany, concerning displaced persons; and articles and U.S. military records relating to displaced persons in postwar Europe.

**RG 20:** *Righteous among Nations. 15 subcollections.*
Contents include "The Story of Dr. Josef Jaksy"; documents relating to Oskar Schindler; records relating to the investigation of Giorgio Perlasca with the United States Holocaust Memorial Council regarding his Righteous status; William and Mies Oudegeest interview; Case of Guy Von Dardel and Sven Hagstromer v. Union of Soviet Socialist Republics; "Testimonies and Evocations Presented to the Leadership of the Yad Vashem Memorial"; and records and photographs relating to the Bata shoe company in Zlín, Czech Republic.

**RG 21:** *Dr. Joseph and Sheila Tenenbaum Collection.*
Numerous subcollections relating to Dr. Tenenbaum's writings and activities as a leader of the American Jewish Anti-Nazi Boycott, among other matters.

**RG 22:** *Russia. 2 subcollections.*
Aside from a general file, this RG contains selected records of the Extraordinary State Commission to Investigate German-Fascist Crimes Committed on the Territory of the USSR from the State Archive of the Russian Federation (26 reels, 16 mm).

**RG 23:** *Resistance. 4 subcollections.*
Contents include White Rose pamphlets; verdict and sentence of Hans Fritz Scholl, Sophia Magdalena Scholl, and Christoph Hermann Probst; and court documents relating to the investigation of the

case of Anna Szenes (Chaṅa Senesh) and the sentence of Gyula Simon.

**RG 24:** *Holocaust in the Arts. 14 subcollections.*
Most of the collections contain poems about the Holocaust, such as "Babi Yar," by Elisaveta Volfson. One collection contains 35 folders of articles and other materials relating to artists, musicians, and writers persecuted during the Holocaust. Also included are records relating to the exhibition of children's art from Terezín held at the University of Oregon Museum of Art, September 1969.

**RG 25:** *Romania. 6 subcollections (on microfilm).*
These files include selected records from the Romanian National Archives (8 reels); selected records of the Romanian Ministry of National Defense (305 reels); selected reels from the Romanian Information Service (54 reels, 16 mm); and selected records from the Romanian Regional National Archives Branches (6 reels).

**RG 27:** *Julius Kühl Collection. 8 subcollections.*
This RG contains correspondence, articles, clippings, miscellaneous reports, Dr. Kühl's autobiographical report, and his Treblinka Report.

**RG 28:** *Restitution and Reparations. 6 subcollections.*
This material includes Austrian Restitution Records from the National Archives and Records Administration (NARA); "Hungarian Gold Train"; United Restitution Organization Records, Los Angeles and Toronto Offices; U.S. case files—Reparations Based on Events in the Netherlands.

**RG 31:** *Ukraine. 7 subcollections (on microfilm).*
Aside from general files there are selected records from the Ukrainian Central State Archive (*formerly* the Archive of the October Revolution) in Kiev; selected records from the Lviv Oblast Archive (1 reel, 16 mm); records from Odessa (4 reels); and records from Czernowitz (37 reels).

**RG 32:** *Jehovah's Witnesses. 12 subcollections.*
This RG is comprised of family and personal papers and one file containing articles from *The Golden Age* and *Yearbook of Jehovah's Witnesses* and other publications relating to the persecution of Jehovah's Witnesses during the Holocaust.

**RG 33:** *Homosexual Victims.*

**RG 34:** *Gaynor Jacobson Collection. 2 subcollections.*
This RG contains personal and professional papers.

**RG 35:** *Jiri Lauscher Collection.*
Numerous subcollections relating to the Terezín (Theresienstaat) ghetto (not yet cataloged), rescue committee, and exiled intellectuals.

**RG 38:** *Cynthia McCabel Collection. 4 subcollections.*

**RG 43:** *France. 2 subcollections.*

This RG contains a general file and an unpublished chapter in the "History of the Deportation of Foreign Jews from France in 1942," by Roswell McClelland.

**RG 44:** *Denmark.*

**RG 48:** *Czechoslovakia (Czech Republic, Slovakia). 4 subcollections (on microfilm).*
This RG contains selected documents from Czech State Archives (1 reel); selected documents from Slovak State Archives (1 reel); and records from the Military Historical Institute, Prague (6 reels, 16 mm).

**RG 49:** *Yugoslavia. 3 subcollections.*
This RG contains records relating to the occupation of Yugoslavia during World War II and records relating to crimes against Serbs, Jews, and other Yugoslav peoples during World War II.

**RG 52:** *Randolph Braham Collection. 3 subcollections.*
This material includes selected microfilmed records from the Hungarian State Archives (180 reels); records relating to the Berend (Belton) case; and records relating to the Jewish communities of Hungary and Romania, the "Final Solution," and the 1946 war crimes trial in Cluj, Romania.

**RG 53:** *Belarus. 6 subcollections (on microfilm).*
These records include the Sara Rosjanki Ross Collection—Selected Records from the Belarus Central State Archive, Minsk and selected records from the following archives: the Minsk Oblast Archive (1 reel, 16 mm); the Grodno Oblast Archive; the Gomel Oblast Archive; and the Mogilev Oblast Archive.

**RG 54:** *Moldova.*
This RG contains selected records from the National Archives of Moldova.

**RG 55:** *Alexander Kulisiewicz Collection.*
This RG contains sound recordings and textual records relating to music from the camps and ghettos.

In addition, the Holocaust Museum houses an oral history archive with approximately 2,500 videotaped and audiotaped oral testimonies by survivors, liberators, rescuers, and other eyewitnesses. More than 400 of the video and audio testimonies were produced by the museum; the rest were obtained from other Holocaust organizations.

The Benjamin and Vladka Meed Registry of Jewish Holocaust Survivors forms another part of the Holocaust archives. The registry currently contains 80,000 files from the American Gathering of Jewish Holocaust Survivors that provide information on the wartime experiences of survivors who came to the United States. This collection of documents is the largest single source of information on survivors in the United States; it also includes some information on relatives who perished. In the future, the archives plans to establish a registry for non-Jewish survivors of the Holocaust.

4.    The archives has a large collection of finding-aids and bibliographic sources. Much of the archival holdings are cataloged on computer as part of an ongoing effort. Many finding-aids issued by the archives from which material was copied are also available. These are in the home languages. There is also a large collection of bibliographies, published and unpublished, from western European institutions, which relate to these records.

5.    Index Terms: Ethnic and Religious Conflict; Human Rights; Humanitarian Issues; International Law; War Crimes

See also entries A45, C11, F29, and H72

**University of Maryland Library—McKeldin Library    See entry A47**

# C

# Museums, Galleries, and Art Collections

**Museums, Galleries, and Art Collections Entry Format (C)**

1.  *General Information*
    a.  address; telephone number(s)
    b.  hours and days of service
    c.  conditions of access
    d.  photocopying services
    e.  name/title of director and heads of relevant divisions

2.  *Size of Holdings Pertaining to Peace and International Security Studies*

3.  *Description of Holdings Pertaining to Peace and International Security Studies*

4.  *Bibliographic Aids Facilitating Use of Collection*

5.  *Library/Archives*

6.  *Index Terms* (relevant subject specialties)

## Introductory Note

The Washington, D.C., area features a number of museums and galleries of potential interest to scholars pursuing international security and peace studies. The army, navy, and marine corps each maintain a museum (C3, C10, and C5, respectively), holding weaponry and other military artifacts relevant to military history. Air Force Art Program (C1), Army Art Collection (C2), Marine Corps Historical Center's Art Collection (C4), and Navy Art Gallery (C9) offer substantial collections of military art. Military artifacts are also held by the Smithsonian Institution's National Air and Space Museum (C6) and National Museum of American History (C8), as well as by the National Firearms Museum (C7). The displays in the recently opened United States Holocaust Memorial Museum (C11) bear, within the scope of this Guide, mainly on human rights issues.

In addition to the institutions with separate entries in section C, the Washington, D.C., area contains smaller, primarily military, museums holding materials relevant to the scope of this Guide, especially on military history.

The Army Center of Military History—Museum Division (Judson E. Bennett, Chief; tel. 703/504-5373) can provide information on those maintained by the army. The following smaller museums and historical sites may be of interest to the users of this Guide:

Clara Barton National Historic Site
5801 Oxford Road
Glen Echo, Md. 20812
(301) 492-6245

Collingwood Library and Museum on Americanism
8301 East Boulevard Drive
Alexandria, Va. 22308
(703) 765-1652

Daughters of the American Revolution Museum
1776 D Street, NW
Washington, D.C. 20006
(202) 879-3254
Fax: (202) 879-3252

Fort Ward Museum and Historical Site
4301 West Braddock Road
Alexandria, Va. 22304
(703) 838-4848

Fort Washington Park
Fort Washington Road
Fort Washington, Md. 20744
(301) 763-4600
Fax: (301) 763-1389

Mail:
1900 Anacostia Drive, SE
Washington, D.C. 20020

Historical Society of the Militia and National Guard—Heritage Gallery
1 Massachusetts Avenue
Washington, D.C. 20001
(202) 789-0031
Fax: (202) 682-9358

Old Guard Museum
Sheridan Avenue, Building 249
Fort Myer, Va. 22211
(703) 696-6670
Fax: (703) 696-2739

National Museum of Health and Medicine
Armed Forces Institute of Pathology, Building 54
6825 16th Street, NW
Washington, D.C. 20306-6000
(202) 576-2348

---

## CI  Air Force Art Program (Air Force Department)

---

1.a.  1690 Air Force Pentagon, Room 4A120
      Washington, D.C. 20330-1690
      (703) 697-6629

b.  8:30 A.M.–4:30 P.M. Monday–Friday

c.  The Pentagon office is not open to the public. Use of the collection by non-air force organizations is limited; researchers must have prior project approval to obtain access to art program files. Selections from the Air Force Art Collection may be seen without appointment along the Pentagon's public tour route.

d.  Photocopying facilities are not available within the art program office.

e.  Robert Limbrick, Art Program Specialist

2.  The collection contains more than 7,500 artworks; its primary relevance is to military science, specifically relating to the air force.

3.  The collection consists of donated artworks by professional artists. Paintings predominate, but holdings also include drawings, sketches, and sculpture. The works are both historical and educational, depicting air force missions, capabilities, personnel, and facilities. The collection is on display in the Pentagon and in air force offices throughout the world.

4.  There is no catalog describing the holdings. The collection is documented in files that contain photos, slides, negatives, transparencies, and narrative descriptions of the individual artworks.

5.  The art program office does not have a library.

6.  Index Terms: Art and War; Military History—Air Force

---

## C2  Army Art Collection (Army Department)

---

1.a.  U.S. Army Center of Military History
      1099 14th Street, NW
      Washington, D.C. 20005-3402
      (202) 504-5396

b.  8:00 A.M.–4:30 P.M. Monday–Friday

c.  Open to the public by appointment. Traveling exhibits are available, on loan, to museums, colleges, and universities in the United States.

d.  Photocopies are available at borrower's cost.

e.  Marylou Gjernes, Army Art Curator

2.  The collection contains 12,000 pieces; its primary relevance is to army military history in the 20th century.

3. The Army Center of Military History (B3) maintains the Army Art Collection for the purpose of encouraging public interest in military history. Comprising some 12,000 pieces of original paintings and drawings, the collection includes artwork depicting U.S. military activities since the American Revolution, with special emphasis placed on the World War II and U.S. involvement in Southeast Asia.

4. Works are arranged alphabetically by artist; a computer index offers access to the paintings and drawings by subject, geographic area, and title. Biographical information about selected artists is available. Descriptions of traveling exhibits are provided upon request. The center publishes a brochure titled *U.S. Army Art Collection.*

5. The collection is part of the Army Center of Military History. For information on the center's archive and library, see B3.

6. Index Terms: Art and War: Military History—Army

See also entry B3

---

## C3 Fort Meade Army Museum (Army Department)

1.a. 4674 Griffin Avenue
Fort Meade, MD 20755
(301) 677-6966

Mailing Address:
ATTN: ANME-OPM
Fort Meade, MD 20755-5094

b. 11:00 A.M.–4:00 P.M. Wednesday–Saturday
1:00 P.M.–4:00 P.M. Sunday

c. Open to the public; free admission.

d. Photocopying facilities available.

e. Robert S. Johnson, Curator

2. The museum holds 3,537 artifacts, approximately one-third of which are displayed in 37 exhibits. The entire collection is relevant to the study of international security, specifically in regard to military science.

3. The collection is divided into two galleries, one covering the history of Fort Meade, which was established in 1917, and the other depicting history of the U.S. 1st Army. The heaviest emphasis in both galleries is on the First and Second World Wars.

The Fort Meade Gallery begins with a display of the 17th-century Patuxtent Forge, located on the future site of the fort. The displays in this gallery most often contain rifles and uniforms from their respective periods. Some of the weaponry presented includes an 18th-century mortar and musket, 19th-century musket and Remington army pistol, a pepperbox pistol, several derringers, two World War I machine guns, a U.S. World War II submachine gun, an AK-47 and M16A1 automatic rifle. There are also military insignia, soldiers' personal equipment, a 1904 cavalry saddle, several models of tanks, signal corps equipment, and numerous photographs. The exhibits are titled "Soldiers on the Patuxtent," "Guarding the Railroad," "The Union Army," "The 92nd Division" (an all African-American division established in 1917, elements of which were trained at Fort Meade), "Camp Meade, 1917–1918," "The Franklin Cantonment" (a signal corps training camp later incorporated into the fort), "Tank School," "Between the Wars," "Don't You Know There's a War On?" "The Armored Cavalry Regiment," "Vietnam," "The 1950s," and "Korea."

The First Army Gallery depicts the history of the 1st Army from 1918, under General "Black Jack" Pershing, to the present. In addition to uniforms and personal equipment of 1st Army soldiers, a number of firearms are displayed; they include a World War I trench shotgun, a 1903 Springfield rifle, a 1918 Browning Automatic Rifle, an M1A1 carbine, and a Thompson submachine gun. Some French, German, and Japanese weaponry and paraphernalia are displayed. These include a World War I French machine gun, a World War I German machine gun along with a bayonet and stick grenade, World War II German and Japanese pistols, two German submachine guns, and a samurai sword. The exhibits are titled "The First Army," "The St. Mihiel Salient," "The Hun," "The Meuse-Argonne Offensive," "Victory," "The Maneuver Years," "The Gathering Storm," "The Normandy Invasion," "Breaking the Atlantic Wall," "St. Lo Breakout," "The German Soldier," "The Ardennes—Battle of the Bulge," "The Final Months," "The Post-War Years," "The First U.S. Army Today."

4. A brochure with a brief description of the collection is available. No catalog exists for the collection but the museum is compiling a computerized inventory of all holdings. This inventory will be accessible through the on-line system of the Army Center for Military History (B3).

5. The museum has a small library of military material, primarily books, journals, and unit histories.

The library contains, for example, yearbooks of the Fort Meade tank school.

The museum also has a photo archive of undetermined size. The archive is separated into eras focusing heavily on the First and Second World Wars. In addition, there is coverage of the interwar years, especially 1930s maneuvers in North Carolina, including tank-training photographs. Holdings are sparser in the post-Vietnam period.

6.  Index Terms: Defense Policy, National—History; Military History—Army; Military Science

See also entry B3

## C4  Marine Corps Historical Center (Navy Department)—Art Collection

1.a. Washington Navy Yard, Building 58
9th and M Streets, SE
Washington, D.C. 20374-0580
(202) 433-3267

b. 10:00 A.M.–4:00 P.M. Monday–Saturday
Noon–5:00 P.M. Sunday

c. Open to the public; free admission.

d. Reproductions of artwork are available at cost.

e. Jack Dyer, Art Curator

2.  The art collection has 5,800 works, whose primary relevance is to military and naval science.

3.  The collection includes paintings, drawings, sketches, sculpture, woodblock and silk screen prints, and cartoons created by marines to document their activities. There are recruiting posters from as early as 1900, salon-quality photographs, and contemporary prints. The bulk of the collection's artwork derives from the marine experience in Vietnam, although there are pieces from Korea, World War II, and World War I. There are also early 19th-century portraits of marines.

4.  The collection is described in *Guide to the Marine Corps Historical Center.*

5.  For information about the museum and archival holdings of the Marine Corps Historical Center see entries B9 and C5.

6.  Index terms: Art and War; Military History—Marine Corps

See also entries B9 and C5

## C5  Marine Corps Museum (Navy Department—Marine Corps Historical Center)

1.a. Washington Navy Yard, Building 58
9th and M Streets, SE
Washington, D.C. 20374-0580
(202) 433-3534
Fax: (202) 433-7265

b. 10:00 A.M.–4:00 P.M. Monday–Saturday
Noon–5:00 P.M. Sundays and Holidays
Closed Christmas and New Year's Day

c. Open to the public; free admission.

d. Visitors may photograph museum artifacts.

e. Charles A. Wood, Chief Curator

2.  The museum consists primarily of 20 large display cases with facing panels on the first floor of the Marine Corps Historical Center. It is immediately relevant to military and naval science.

3.  The museum's exhibits illustrate, through the use of uniforms, weapons, and other military artifacts, a chronological review of the Marine Corps' role in American history. The "time tunnel" exhibit consists of 20 large displays depicting Marine Corps history from the American revolution until the present. Each panel is given a brief description and explanation; the significance of many of the artifacts is noted. Each display case contains uniform items and weaponry corresponding to the period. The weaponry closely reflects technological development and the changing missions of the Marine Corps. Examples of weaponry include a topman's seven-barreled musket; a boarding ax; dismantling and bar shot; a Colt navy revolver; a saber bayonet; a Union Ketchum grenade from the Civil War; a spade bayonet; 1879 and 1884 U.S. issue single-shot cartridge rifles; an 1895 Colt machine gun; a 1918 Browning automatic rifle; a 1921 Thompson submachine gun; and captured weaponry from World War I and II, Vietnam, and other conflicts.

Examples of the displays include "Marines in the Revolution, 1775–1783," which contains a number of portraits with brief biographies; "Marines and the Frigate Navy, 1794–1815"; "The Second War of Independence," containing maps and documents; "Marines in the Far East, 1899–1941," containing a proclamation following the capture of Tientsin, China, by an international force during the Boxer Rebellion; and "Evolution of the Vertical Envelope," containing helicopter models that demonstrate developing tactics. Also on display is the "Marines in Miniature" collection depicting some of the marines' more prominent military maneuvers and battles through the use of figurines. Other items on display include historic flags and marine colors; pieces of early ordnance, such as a Gatling gun and several small cannons; and numerous portraits and photos of Marines with brief descriptions.

The documentary materials are drawn from the center's other components: the Archives, Personal Papers Collection, Oral History Collection, and the Reference Section (see entries B9, D5, and E10).

A number of additional study collections are located at the museum's ordnance and technology storage and exhibit facility, the Marine Corps Air-Ground Museum, at Quantico, Virginia. For information write to Officer-in-Charge, Marine Corps Museum Activities, Building 2014, Marine Corps Combat Development Command, Quantico, Virginia 22134-5001 (703/640-2606, 2607, or 2608).

4.   The Museum publishes a free brochure, *The Marine Corps Museum,* detailing its collections as well as information about hours and parking.

5.   The museum is part of the Marine Corps Historical Center. For information on the center's archives see entries B9, D5, and E10. The center also maintains a historical library of 30,000 titles (see entry B9).

6.   Index Terms: Military History—Marine Corps; Naval Science

See also entries B9, C4, D5, E9, and E10

---

## C6   National Air and Space Museum (NASM) (Smithsonian Institution)

---

1.a.  6th Street and Independence Avenue, SW
Washington, D.C. 20560
(202) 357-2700

Paul E. Garber Preservation, Restoration, and
Storage Facility
3904 Old Silver Hill Road
Suitland, Md. 20746
(301) 238-3480

b.  Summer: 10:00 A.M.–6:30 P.M. Daily
Winter: 10:00 A.M.–5:30 P.M. Daily
Closed Christmas Day

c.  Open to the public; free admission.

d.  Photocopying facilities for photographs as well as textual material available. Use of tripods for photography is prohibited.

e.  Martin Harwit, Director
Tom Crouch, Chairman, Department of Aeronautics
Gregg Herken, Chairman, Department of Space History

2.   The National Air and Space Museum maintains an immense collection of airplanes, jets, rockets, and other material related to aviation and space flight. A sizable portion of the collection pertains directly to peace and security studies. For example, there are over 20 military aircraft on display in the main museum as well as exhibits on World War I and II. In addition, the history and development of aviation is thoroughly presented, which is generally relevant to the development of military technology.

3.   In the main museum, there are several relevant exhibits. The Great War in the Air (Gallery 206), contains the following aircraft: an Albatross D Va, a Fokker D VII, a Pfalz D XII, an R.A.F. FE-8, a Sopwith Snipe, a SPAD XIII, and a Voison Model 8. In the World War II Aviation exhibit (Gallery 205) are displayed a Macchi MC 202 Folgore, a Martin B-26-B "Flak Bait," a Messerschmitt Bf 109G-6 Gustav, a Mitsubishi A6M5 Zero, a North American P-51D Mustang, and a Supermarine Spitfire Mk. VII. The Sea-Air Operations exhibit (Gallery 203) contains a Boeing F4B-4, a Douglas SBD-6 Dauntless, a Douglas A4D-2N (A-4C) Skyhawk, and a Grumann F4F-4 (FM-1) Wildcat. The Jet Aviation (Gallery 106) contains a McDonnell FH-1 Phantom I, and a Messerchmitt Me 262A Schwalbe. The Early Flight exhibit (Gallery 107) contains a Wright 1909 Military Flyer. A Lockheed F-104A Starfighter is displayed in the main hall above the west escalator. Other relevant exhibits are Milestones of Flight (Gallery 100), Air Transportation (Gallery 102), Vertical Flight (Gallery 103), Flight Testing (Gallery 109), Pioneers of Flight (Gallery 208). There are also temporary exhibits. For example, in 1994, Arado-234, a German jet bomber from 1944-45, was on display from the museum's Garber Facility. In the Milestones of Flight Gallery is displayed a full-size replica of the Sputnik I, the first manmade earth satellite, and two nuclear missiles that were outlawed by the Intermediate Nuclear Forces (INF) Treaty, a Soviet SS-20 and U.S. Pershing II. A separate exhibit on the INF Treaty is in the Space Hall, as is a full-size replica of the Soyuz spaceship, linked to an Apollo craft, used in the joint U.S.-USSR Apollo-Soyuz mission.

The Paul E. Garber Facility in Suitland, Maryland, houses the National Air and Space Museum's reserve collection of significant air- and spacecraft. Approximately 160 aircraft, numerous spacecraft, engines, propellers, and other flight-related artifacts are displayed in the buildings that are open to the public. Many of the facility's buildings are used for storage or restoration and are not open to the public. Items of interest include a MiG-15 (Korean War), a Curtiss Jn-4D Jenny (World War I period), a Hawker Hurricane IIC (World War II), Junkers Ju 388L. Currently being restored but available for viewing is Boeing B-29 Superfortress *Enola Gay*. There is also a Soviet Vostok spacecraft and the J-2 engine of a Saturn launch vehicle.

4.    Free brochures describing the museum's exhibits, theaters, educational programs, and special services are available at the information desk on the first floor of the main museum. Free tours at the Paul E. Garber Facility are available, Monday–Friday 10:00 A.M., Saturday and Sunday 10:00 A.M. and 1:00 P.M. Reservations for tours are required and it is advisable to make reservations at least three weeks in advance. For reservations and further information, call (202) 357-1400 (TDD 357-1505). Or write: Scheduling Office, MRC 305, National Air and Space Museum, Smithsonian Institution, Washington, D.C. 20560.

5.    See A32, B10, F18, and F19, respectively for information on the National Air and Space Museum's library, archives, film, and still picture sections. In addition, the Archives Division at the Paul E. Garber Facility (Susan Ewing or Debbie Griggs at 301/238-3480) holds oral histories (over 800 reel-to-reel and cassette tapes) with notables in the field, including interviews with astronauts, as well as recordings of NASA missions, and seminars and symposia at the museum.

6.    Index Terms: Arms Control; Military History—Air Force; Military Science

See also entries A32, B10, F18, and F19

---

## C7    National Firearms Museum (National Rifle Association)

1.a.    11250 Waples Mill Road
Fairfax, Va. 22030
(703) 267-1600

b.    10:00 A.M.–4:00 P.M. Monday–Friday

c.    The museum is open to the public; free admission.

d.    Photocopying facilities are not available. Photographing the collection is permitted.

e.    Douglas Wicklund, Curator

2.    The museum has more than 3,000 firearms on display. The collection is relevant to peace and security studies in terms of the development of military technology.

3.    The museum is located in the National Rifle Association (NRA) headquarters. The collection originated from the NRA's reference collection of donated firearms. The bulk of the collection consists of military rifles and pistols, although there are some sports firearms as well. The display focuses on milestones in the development of firearm technology and ranges from antique matchlocks to current weapons.

4.    A brochure describing the collection is available.

5.    The museum has a library of several thousand highly specialized volumes, 1492–1992, on the development of firearms. The library, open by appointment only to serious scholars working on relevant topics, does not take part in interlibrary loans.

6.    Index Terms: Military History

---

## C8    National Museum of American History (NMAH) (Smithsonian Institution)

1.a.    14th Street and Constitution Avenue, NW
Washington, D.C. 20560
(202) 357-3129 (Information)
(202) 357-1481 (Tour Schedules)

b.    Public Exhibits
10:00 A.M.–5:30 P.M. Daily
Closed Christmas Day.
Extended summer hours determined annually.
Department offices and research collections:
8:45 A.M.–5:15 P.M. Monday–Friday

c.    Exhibit areas are open to the public. Visitors should make prior arrangements to view items not on display or to use research facilities.

d.    Researchers may take photographs of museum holdings, but the Public Affairs Office must approve photographs intended for publication. Reproductions, prints, and color transparencies of many exhibit items are for sale through the Customer Service Division of the Smithsonian Institution's Office of Printing and Photographic Services. Departmental offices can provide photocopying services as needed.

e. Spencer R. Crew, Director
James S. Hutchins, Supervisor, Armed Forces History Division

2.   The museum is devoted to the exhibition, care, and study of artifacts that reflect the experience of the people of the United States. It holds an extremely large and diverse assortment of artifacts related to American military history. It also has a wide assortment of military items from around the world, although principally as a result of U.S. military activity in those regions. The museum collects objects from, or related to, foreign areas only for comparative purposes or to demonstrate the use or influence of foreign technology in U.S. development. No exact count is available for military-related items, but the collection is estimated at over 200,000 items. The collection's principal relevance lies in military and naval history and science.

3.   Most pertinent items are found in the Division of Armed Forces History (202/357-1883), part of the Department of History of Science and Technology, which maintains collections of weapons, uniforms, individual equipment, and models to document the development of armed forces in U.S. history. James S. Hutchins is acting supervisor of the division; Edward Ezell curates firearms collection; Donald Kloster curates nonordnance artifacts (e.g., uniforms, insignia, and heraldry); and Harold Langley curates naval history. At any given time 5 percent or less of the collection is on display.

The museum has the foremost collection of U.S. military uniforms in the world, 1832–present, approaching 3,000 in number. Generally, the uniform holdings are better for the 20th century, with army uniforms predominating. The division also has a great deal of headgear, especially dress uniform hats, and there is a footwear collection that reflects evolution of the manufacture of military footwear from handmade to machine manufactured. In addition, the division holds a particularly strong collection of World War I uniforms from different countries.

The division has numerous illustrations of soldiers, especially American soldiers, in uniform. In addition, it has a very good collection of combat art from World War I, an excellent source of information on uniforms. Examples of uniforms include the following: 17th-century armor chest piece and helmet (Spanish origin); early 19th-century U.S. Army officer's uniform; marine's blouse (ca. 1800–1815);

marine's uniform from the first half of the 19th century; army uniform, forage cap, dress hat from the 1820s; noncommissioned officer's uniform from the period of the Seminole War; U.S. Army uniforms of a major and a private from the Mexican War; and a Confederate and a Yankee private from the Civil War. Examples of foreign uniforms, especially from Europe, are well represented. Of particular note are the division's 19th-century French Zouave uniforms and examples from France, Spain, Denmark, Norway, Sweden, the Netherlands, Belgium, and Britain, mostly between 1870 and World War I. The museum's holdings of military insignia and heraldry is extremely impressive and also reflects the evolution of American forces. These include insignia found on buttons, belt plates, caps, and shoulder patches. This collection is particularly strong for the regimental level and below. Foreign examples include British insignia from World War I and II.

Individual equipment, such as knapsacks, haversacks, and canteens carried by soldiers, is strongly represented from the Civil War on. Collections include a large assortment of canteens going back to the American Revolution; a mess equipment collection dating mainly from the 1870s, when it was standardized; and miscellaneous items such as an entrenching tool from the Revolution, a cartridge box (ca. 1800), and a telescope (ca. 1800). There are also examples of cards, dice, and other nonissue personal possessions. The Belgian and British holdings include complete packs of personal equipment carried in World War I.

The weaponry collection of the division focuses on swords and small arms (e.g., muskets, rifles, and pistols) again with the emphasis on evolution of armed forces. It is one of the largest small arms collection in the area. There is a large and diverse array of U.S. military swords from the 19th century. Examples of swords from the first half of the 19th century include an artillery officer's sword; a militia officer's sword; a general or staff officer's sword; a medical staff officer's sword; a militia artillery sword; a foot artillery sword; and officers' sabers from the militia, infantry, artillery, and cavalry. Other examples include an 1872 cavalry officer's sword; an 1860 light cavalry sword; an 1840 heavy cavalry sword; an 1840 noncommissioned officer's sword. On exhibit are numerous presentation swords. There are Spanish swords from as early as the 16th century. There are also nine Toledo blades given by the Spanish government for the U.S. centennial exhibit.

The changing technology of small arms is thoroughly presented in the firearms exhibit. The displays of the exhibit center around the following aspects of small arms development: arms of colonial America, including early pistols, swords, and muskets; U.S. military weapons, 1795–1840, including pistols, muskets, and a swivel gun used to defend ramparts; breech loading and repeating arms of the Civil War, including an 1860 repeating rifle, a sharpshooter's rifle, several revolvers, and various carbines; the development of the Minie bullet, the first expanding bullet; single-shot and repeating rifles, 1862–89, along with various early examples of breech loading rifles. There is also a display of the infantry machine guns used in U.S. service. These include a Requa-Billinghurst Battery Gun (ca. 1861); an 1862 Gatling gun (scale model); an 1877 Gatling gun; an 1895 MK1 machine gun; a 1904 Colt-Maxim machine gun; a 1909 Bent-Mercie machine rifle; a Lewis MKVI machine gun (ca. 1914); a 1917 Browning water cooled machine gun; a 1940 Browning Automatic Rifle (B.A.R.); an M60 general purpose machine gun (ca. 1960); and a 1965 G.E. M134 minigun. There is also a display of military semiautomatic and automatic rifles, containing: an M16A1; an M1 Garand; an M14; a 1952 Fabrique Nationale rifle; a 1918 BAR; a 1917 St. Etienne rifle; and a 1941 Johnson semiautomatic rifle. Another display depicts the manufacture of the M9 service handgun. This weapon was recently selected to replace the traditional Colt .45 automatic as the U.S. military's standard pistol. The display describes the M9 and shows other pistols tested by the Defense Department.

The scholarly value of the division's firearms collection goes beyond tracing the technological development of small arms; the collection also reflects small arms traffic around the world and how it relates to low-intensity conflict. The museum has acquired examples of arms from conflicts around the world, including the Middle East, Africa, and Southeast Asia. Latin American small arms include locally manufactured weapons from Brazil, Argentina, and other South American nations. Small arms from Cuba, El Salvador, Honduras, and Grenada (and related documentation) that are associated with antigovernment movements in those areas are also on display.

The naval section has numerous artifacts and extensive archival holdings. The division has in its possession many ship models depicting the development of U.S. naval capabilities. Examples of these models include the schooner *Hannah* and the frigates *Raleigh* and *Confederate;* the 1780 privateer *Rattlesnake;* the 1803 brig *Argus;* the brig *Prince of Neufchatel* (War of 1812); the 1813 sloop *Niagara;* and Fulton's 1814 *Steam Battery.* Various shipboard weaponry is on display, including a 12-pounder car-

ronade (ca. 1812). Also on display is the hull of the *Philadelphia,* which was sunk at the Battle of Valcour Island, October 1, 1776, and was raised, with its cannons, in 1935.

Significant naval archives include the Admiral Dewey collection from the Spanish-American War and the Commodore Perry collection on the opening of Japan. There are many naval attaché studies and memoirs of naval enlisted men. Notable holdings include the journal of Frederick Paxton, a British midshipman in the War of 1812; the Howard I. Chapelle Papers with 1,099 reproductions of 17th- to 19th-century ships' plans, mostly from the British Admiralty ship draught collection at the National Maritime Museum, Greenwich, England; the Simon P. Fullinwinder Papers, which document the development of deep-sea mines and the Anglo-American mining of the North Sea during World War I.

Scattered through the collections of other NMAH divisions are artifacts of military significance. The Division of Electricity and Modern Physics, for example, has radio receivers developed for the navy in World War I; vacuum tubes developed for military equipment; Busignie's original "Huff-Duff" (high frequency direction finding) apparatus, which played a role in the battle of the Atlantic during World War II; and a pre-World War I Russian army field telephone and wireless. Included in the Department of Social and Cultural History collection are a complete Mexican rurales uniform and Saltillo blankets, saddles, and spurs.

4. There is no comprehensive published catalog or comprehensive guide to the museum as a whole. The following titles, however, offer visitors excellent introductions to the collections and can alert researchers to certain artifacts that space limitations do not permit mentioning in this Guide: *A Nation of Nations,* edited by Peter Marzio (1976), issued as the bicentennial exhibit catalog; *The National Museum of American History: A Smithsonian Museum,* by Shirley Abbot (New York: Abrams, 1981), and *Guide to Manuscript Collections in the National Museum of History and Technology* (Washington, D.C.: Smithsonian Institution Press, 1978). In lieu of other publications, researchers should turn to the computerized catalogs that the current Smithsonian-wide inventory will generate. Researchers should also not forget the curatorial staff. They possess great expertise and maintain scholarly contacts throughout North America and the rest of the world.

5. Scholars may also wish to consult the museum's library in room 5016 (Rhoda S. Ratner, head librarian; 202/357-2414). Housed here are some

150,000 volumes on American history, the history of science and technology in the United States and elsewhere, numismatics, philately, musical instruments, and other subjects of interest to the museum's exhibits and research staff.

6.   Index Terms: Arms Control—Arms Transfers; Low Intensity Conflict; Military History; Military Science; Naval Science; Terrorism

See also entry D8

## C9   Navy Art Gallery (Navy Department— Naval Historical Center)

1.a.   Washington Navy Yard, Building 67
9th and M Streets, SE
Washington, D.C. 20374
(202) 433-3815

b.   9:00 A.M.–4:00 P.M. Wednesday–Sunday

c.   Open to the public; free admission.

d.   Transparencies will be loaned for duplication purposes.

e.   John Barnett, Curator

2.   The Navy Art Gallery has more than 10,000 works; its primary relevance is to military and naval science.

3.   The Navy Art Gallery's collection grew out of the merger in 1986 of the Combat Art Collection, started during World War II, and the Naval Historical Center's earlier collection. The holdings span the entire history of the U.S. Navy, with more than 500 artists represented. During World War II, the navy sent artists, eight altogether, to combat zones to record battles and the experiences of navy men and women. This became the Combat Art Collection. Since World War II artists have continued to depict navy activity and involvement in conflicts, especially in Korea and Vietnam. Included among the gallery's holdings is the Abbott Collection, part of the Abbott Laboratories World War II Art Program. This collection consists of 300 works by 18 artists and depicts various military medical subjects, amphibious operations, naval aviation, navy submarines, and marines in action.

4.   The gallery has published a number of brochures describing the collection: *Your Navy from the Viewpoint of the Nation's Finest Artists; Navy Art, A Vision of History,* which has brief sketches of the eight artists of the Combat Art Collection and de-

scribes its founding; and *Navy Medical Art of the Abbott Collection.* Full-color prints of some works are available in two sizes; 22x28 inches ($5) and 36x44 inches ($6).

5.   Navy Department Library is described in entry A36, the archival holdings of the Naval Historical Center in entries B13, D9, E13, and F23.

6.   Index Terms: Art and War; Military History— Navy

See also entries A36, B13, D9, E13, and F23

## CIO   Navy Museum (Navy Department— Naval Historical Center)

1.a.   Washington Navy Yard, Building 76
9th and M Streets, SE
Washington, D.C. 20374
(202) 433-4882
Fax: (202) 433-8200

b.   9:00 A.M.–4:00 P.M. Monday–Friday
10:00 A.M.–5:00 P.M. Weekends and Holidays

c.   Open to the public; free admission.

d.   Visitors may photograph museum artifacts.

e.   Oscar P. Fitzgerald, Director

2.   The Navy Museum collects and exhibits works depicting the history of naval sciences in peacetime and in war. Its coverage extends from the American Revolution to recent space age naval activities. Currently there are over 4,000 objects on display. Almost the entire collection is relevant to peace studies and international security.

3.   The collection includes naval weaponry from all periods (e.g., muzzle loaders, World War II ships, and a cruise missile). There is a fully rigged section, the fighting top, of the USS *Constitution* with a replica of its gun deck. There are permanent displays on submarines, American Revolution, Barbary Wars, War of 1812, Civil War, Spanish-American War, World War I and II, Vietnam, British navy, unique ships models, naval electronics, navigation, polar exploration, the Great White Fleet, Commodore Perry and Japan, space, and undersea exploration.
      The Navy Museum Annex in Building 70 contains many unusual artifacts related to undersea warfare. These include human-guided torpedoes, midget submarines, experimental submarines of the 1860s, and a Poseidon missile.

The Willard Park, located just outside the museum, contains over 60 large naval artifacts from the 19th and 20th centuries, including artifacts from the battleship *Maine.*

4. A brochure, *The Navy Museum,* describes the main collection. There is a separate brochure for the museum annex.

5. For information on the Navy Department Library see entry A36; for the Archives, Map Collection, Oral History Collection, and Photographic Section of the Naval Historical Center see entries B13, D9, E13, and F23, respectively.

6. Index Terms: Military History—Navy

See also entries A36, B13, D9, E13, and F23

---

## CII United States Holocaust Memorial Museum

1.a. 100 Raoul Wallenberg Place, SW
Washington, D.C. 20024-2150
(202) 488-2690
Fax: (202) 479-9726

b. 10:00 A.M.–5:30 P.M. Daily

c. Admission is free, although tickets are required for entrance to the Permanent Exhibition.

d. Photography without flashes is permitted; no video cameras are allowed.

e. Jeshajahu Weinberg, Museum Director

2. The museum's 36,000-square-foot Permanent Exhibition consists of a vast array of artifacts, documentary films, photographs, and other items focusing on the Holocaust. The entire museum pertains to issues of genocide, human rights, and humanitarian assistance.

3. The United States Holocaust Memorial Museum is dedicated to presenting the history of the persecution and murder of 6 million Jews and millions of other victims of Nazi tyranny from 1933 to 1945. The Permanent Exhibition, which covers three floors, begins in the early 1930s, on the fourth floor, and moves downward to the aftermath of the Holocaust. The fourth floor display, the Nazi Assault (1933–39), embraces the period when Jews, dissidents, the handicapped, Gypsies, and Jehovah's Witnesses, among other groups, were systematically discriminated against and persecuted in Nazi Germany. This includes portrayals of book burnings in 1933, the impact of the 1935 Nuremberg Laws isolating Jews from German society, and the events of Kristallnacht. The third floor houses the Final Solution (ca. 1940–44) exhibit, presenting the ghettos, the mass murder by mobile killing units, and systematic deportation to Auschwitz, Treblinka, and other death camps. On the second floor, the Aftermath documents rescue and resistance efforts, liberation, the survivors' determination to find haven in Israel, the United States, and elsewhere, and the search for justice. It also presents efforts to reaffirm moral order in the aftermath of the tragedy.

Special exhibits include "Daniel's Story: Remember the Children," designed for ages eight and up, which presents the perspective of a Jewish child growing up in Nazi Germany, and "Assignment Rescue: The Story of Varian Fry," which recounts the efforts of Varian Fry, a New York journalist who also helped refugees escape from France, 1940–41. The museum also includes the American national memorial to the victims of the Holocaust, the Hall of Remembrance, on the second floor. The Wexner Learning Center gives visitors an opportunity for computer-based, self-directed access to texts, maps, videotaped oral history testimony, and music. The Gonda Education Center includes a Resource Center for Educators and three classrooms used for orientation programs, school group visits, and adult workshops.

4. Several brochures are available that list the main features of the exhibits and explain their purpose in terms of the museum's goals.

5. The museum also houses an affiliated United States Holocaust Research Institute (H72), with a library (A45), archives (B16), and oral history (B16), and photographic and film archives (F29).

6. Index Terms: Ethnic and Religious Conflict; Human Rights; Humanitarian Issues; War Crimes

See also entries A45, B16, H72, and F29

# D

# Map Collections

## Introductory Note

The Washington, D.C., map collections related to international political military, economic, and development studies are among the world's best. The Geography and Map Division of the Library of Congress (D4) houses the largest cartographic collection on the North American continent. Copies of U.S. government-produced maps and maps of foreign areas produced by European mapping agencies are often deposited in the National Archives and Records Service (D6), which holds the second-largest cartographic collection in the Washington, D.C., area. Most of the maps produced by the Defense Mapping Agency's Hydrographic/Topographic Center (D1) are classified. Other collections of military maps accessible to scholars, however, are located at the Marine Corps Historical Center (D5), National Museum of American History's Division of Armed Forces History (D8), Naval Historical Center's Operational Archives Branch (D9), and Navy Department Library (D10). The National Geographic Society's collection (D7) is available to scholars and is quite useful. The map collections at George Washington University (D2) and at the University of Maryland at College Park (D12) duplicate to some extent what is in the other collections but have the advantage of being readily available for extended study or ready reference.

For more detail on map collections, the reader should consult the *Scholars' Guide to Washington, D.C., for Cartography and Remote Sensing Imagery* (1987) by Ralph E. Ehrenberg. This section is based on an updated version of relevant information in Ehrenberg's work. In addition, that volume contains (on pp. ix–xiii) an essay by Alan K. Henrikson, "Frameworks for the World," highlighting the role that the use of maps should properly play in the study of international relations.

For more detailed cartographic information on particular world regions, the reader should turn to the geographic volumes in this Scholars' Guide series, listed in the Bibliography. Each of them contains a section on map collections.

## Air Force History Office (Air Force Department)—Photograph Collection   See entry F2

---

### DI   Defense Mapping Agency (DMA) (Defense Department)—Hydrographic/ Topographic Center (HTC)

---

1.a.  4600 Sangamore Road
Bethesda, Maryland 20816-5003
(301) 227-1364 (Public Affairs)
Office of Distribution Services
6101 MacArthur Boulevard
Bethesda, Maryland 20816
(301) 227-2495 (Customer Assistance)

c.  Access restricted to those with security clearance.

d.  Products available to the public through the DMA Office of Distribution Services are described in their Public Sale Catalog.

2.   This center produces up to 3,000 new or revised topographic maps and nautical charts each year, as well as precise position data and cartographic data in digital form for millions of square miles of the earth's surface. Within the scope of the Guide these cartographic materials are relevant to the subjects of military history, planning, and strategy.

3.   The following units of the center are germane to international security studies:

### MAPPING AND CHARTING DEPARTMENT

James Johnson, Head
(202) 222-3220

The Topography Department prepares topographic maps at various scales, including the standard operational topographic map (1:50,000); overlays showing cross-country movements, cover concealment, soil types, and vegetation; terrain elevation data;

and feature analysis data for use in missile and navigation systems. Smaller-scale topographic map series that are available to the public through the Office of Distribution Services include Area Outline Maps (1:20,000,000) showing major areas of the Earth in 27 sheets; Europe (1:2,000,000) showing major regions of Europe, the Mediterranean, and the former Eastern Soviet Union in six sheets; Middle East Briefing Map (1:1,500,000); Africa (1:2,000,000), a set of 36 sheets; Administrative Areas of the USSR (1:8,000,000); former USSR and Adjacent Areas (1:8,000,000); Arabian Peninsula (1:2,250,000); Southeast Asia Briefing Map (1:2,000,000); and United States (1:3,500,000) showing administrative boundaries and major installations of the army, air force, and navy. Unclassified superseded maps published by the Topography Department and its immediate predecessor, the Army Map Service, are found in the collections of the Geography and Map Division of the Library of Congress (D4) and the Cartographic and Architectural Branch of the National Archives and Records Administration (D6, RG 77). The official, unpublished topographic maps prepared by the U.S. Army before World War II are also in the National Archives and Records Administration.

### DIGITAL PRODUCTS DEPARTMENT

Arthur Burnside, Head
(202) 227-2567

This department is responsible for producing port and harbor approach charts, coastal charts, and bottom contour charts of foreign waters. These charts are available for sale to the public from the Office of Distribution Services and several commercial outlets in the Washington, D.C., area. DMA nautical charts are described in *Defense Mapping Agency Catalog of Maps, Charts, and Related Products Part 2—Hydrographic Products,* issued in 10 volumes by geographic area. Complete sets of these hydrographic charts dating from about 1841 are in the Geography and Map Division of the Library of Congress (D6) and the Cartographic and Architectural Branch of the National Archives and Records Administration (D6).

### SCIENTIFIC DATA DEPARTMENT

(301) 227-5518 (Customer Assistance)
Stephen Webb, Hydrographic Desk (301) 227-2051

John Lau, Topographic Desk (301) 227-2311
(301) 227-3220 (Inquiries Section for Library Materials)

The Scientific Data Department collects, catalogs, stores, analyzes, and evaluates cartographic materials of a worldwide nature. The department's Support Division operates and maintains the DMA libraries and performs geographic names research. The department's Analysis and Evaluation Division carries out extensive research on current cartographic and textual documents obtained from foreign and domestic sources. Questions concerning these materials should be directed to the hydrographic and topographic departments or the inquiries section, which will either provide unclassified information directly or refer researchers to appropriate specialists within the department in response to specific questions. In general, information concerning hydrographic data is unclassified whereas topographic data are restricted.

The Map and Chart Library contains the most recent published editions of some 500,000 maps and 30,000 nautical charts, as well as 80,000 books and periodicals, 14,000 magnetic tapes of digital data of terrain elevations, feature analysis, terrain analysis, and catalogs of official charting agencies in foreign countries. Many of the foreign charts in French, German, Japanese, and Spanish have been translated into English. Since about 1951, the superseded maps and charts have been removed from the collection and sent to the Geography and Map Division of the Library of Congress (D4). In 1980, for example, some 400,000 unclassified maps and charts captured during World War II by U.S. military forces were transferred to the Library of Congress.

The Geodetic Library contains some 900,000 geodetic positions worldwide and some textual materials.

The Bathymetric Data Library has unclassified smooth sheets dating from about 1960, navigation logs, survey reports, and special tide studies. Smooth sheets prepared before World War II are in the Cartographic and Architectural Branch of the National Archives (D6); those compiled between World War II and the 1960s are stored at the Washington National Records Center in Suitland, Md. (Reference Service 301/763-7430). Boat sheets have been retained by the United States Oceanographic Office, NSTL Station, Bay St. Louis, Mo. 39522 (601/688-3390). Some 7.5 million soundings of unclassified data have also been digitized.

The Foreign Place Names Library contains some 5 million place names used in support of mapping and charting activities.

The Names Branch carries out research on foreign place names and publishes the U.S. Board on Geographic Names' *Foreign Gazetteer*. These gazetteers contain names for places and features. Each name is further defined by designations indicating the type of place or feature, latitude and longitude, area code, and Universal Transverse Mercator (UTM) grid coordinates. A list of foreign name gazetteers currently available is found in the Defense Department's *Public Sale Catalog*.

4.    Unpublished and published materials are generally restricted to Defense Department personnel and contractors with security clearances, but some information and products are available. Researchers should consult with the Public Affairs Office or the Scientific Data Department described above. The mission and functions of DMA are described in *MC&G . . . A Brief History of U.S. Military Mapmaking and the First Decade of the Defense Mapping Agency* (July 1982). Bibliographic aids are not available on-site to the public.

5.    Index Terms: Military Science; Naval Science

See also entries G7 and K10

**Central Intelligence Agency    See entry K6**

---

### D2    George Washington University Library (GWU)—Gelman Library—Map Collection

1.a.  2130 H Street, NW
Washington, D.C. 20052
(202) 994-6455

b.  8:30 A.M.–Midnight Monday–Friday
10:00 A.M.–Midnight Saturday and Sunday
Special Collections Division
Noon–5:00 P.M. Monday–Friday
These hours are for the fall/spring academic calendar only. Scholars planning to examine the collections at other times should contact the information office for a schedule of the hours.

c.  Open to scholars, but those not affiliated with a Washington Consortium library must present proper identification and register. Interlibrary loan services of maps and rare materials will be considered and evaluated in terms of their physical condition.

d.  Coin-operated photocopiers are located on the first floor and in the basement.

e.  Jack Siggins, University Librarian

2.    The Gelman Library maintains a map library, totaling about 15,600 maps and 100 atlases in sup-

port of the university's major programs in international relations and urban and regional planning. A small number of maps and related works are also found in the Special Collections Division (Francine I. Henderson, Head, 202/994-7549). From the viewpoint of this Guide the relevant cartographic materials fall under the rubrics of military planning and strategy.

3. The Reference Department atlas and map collection (Barbara Maxwell, Government Documents Section, Reference Librarian, 202/994-1354) is located on the main floor of the library. The atlas collection, numbering about 100 volumes, dates from 1890. Census, historical, school, and world atlases predominate.

The map collection consists primarily of maps produced by federal mapping agencies and deposited through the federal government's depository map program. It contains about 15,600 maps, only a few of which were published before 1900. The collection includes the following series relevant to peace and international security studies:

Defense Mapping Agency and its predecessor, the Army Map Service (22 drawers). Worldwide coverage with special emphasis on British Commonwealth countries and World War II strategic areas.

Miscellaneous (6 drawers). Among the most interesting are *Carta General Archipielago Filipino* (Madrid, 1875), overprinted in English by the U.S. War Department's Military Intelligence Division, Adjutant General's Office, to show military telegraph lines, cable lines, and military departments, 1900; a map of the war in Turkey published by the U.S. Army Corps of Engineers, 1897; a series of topographic maps of Central America at 1:250,000 issued by the Geographic Branch, Military Intelligence Division, U.S. Army General Staff, 1933–40 (27 sheets); a series of air navigation maps of South America at 1:500,000 published by the War Department Map Collection, Office of the Chief of Engineers, 1941–42 (32 sheets); and mineral and gas maps (2 drawers).

4. Atlases are listed in the dictionary catalogs in the Reference Department and the Special Collections Division. The Reference Department map collection is not cataloged, but access to the collection, which is generally arranged by authority, series, and title, is furnished by the reference librarian. The Special Collections Division maintains a main catalog, organized by author, title, and subject, and separate catalogs for maps (incomplete), Washington, D.C., and theses.

5. Index Terms: Intelligence; Military History

See also entries A19 and J6

**Interior Department—Geological Survey— Library See entry K21**

---

**D3 International Bank for Reconstruction and Development (World Bank)—Sectoral Library**

---

1.a. 801 19th Street, NW, Room N-145
Washington, D.C. 20433
(202) 473-8670
Fax: (202) 522-3560

b. 8:30 A.M.–5:30 P.M. Monday–Friday

c. The Sectoral Library is closed to the general public, but scholars are occasionally permitted access to examine materials not available in other libraries. Visitors must formally apply for admission at least seven working days before they wish to visit the library. Visitors who are granted permission to visit the library must present a photo ID and proof of affiliation with the organization they are representing.

d. Photocopying facilities are available. Some materials are restricted.

e. Leighton Cumming, Managing Librarian
Christine Windheuser, Map Librarian

2. The Sectoral Library map collection includes 15,000 maps, about 300 atlases, and 125 geographic names gazetteers. Within the scope of this Guide pertinent cartographic materials fall mainly under the rubric of economic development.

3. The map collection consists of printed and photoprocessed maps of some 170 developing countries, many acquired by World Bank staff members during visits to these countries. Coverage is particularly strong for Africa, Brazil, China, Colombia, India, Indonesia, Mexico, Nigeria, Peru, and Venezuela. The maps generally date from 1975.

The atlas collection is comprised of national and thematic atlases (census, climate, economic), many of which were published in third world countries. They date from 1960. Examples include Sahab Geographic and Drafting Institute's *General Atlas of Afghanistan* (Tehran, 1973), with text in English, French, and Persian; Marcel Leroux's *Le Climat de l'Afrique Tropicale* (Paris, 1983); a tourist atlas of China (Beijing, 1984); Instituto Geográfico's *Atlas de Colombia* (Bogota, 1967); Ministère du Plan et du Developpment's *Cartes pour Servir a l'Amenagement du Territoire* (Dakar, Senegal, 1965); and the Census of India's *Census Atlas* (New Delhi, 1964).

4.  An on-line card catalog provides access to the collection.

5.  Index Terms: Development Issues

See also entries A27, G8, F12, and L8

---

## D4 Library of Congress (LC) — Geography and Map Division

---

1.a. James Madison Building, Room B01
     101 Independence Avenue, SE
     (between 1st and 2d Streets)
     Washington, D.C. 20540
     (202) 707-6277 (Maps)

b.  Reading Room:
    8:30 A.M.–5:00 P.M. Monday–Friday

c.  Open to the public; visitors must register. Interlibrary loan service is available on a limited basis.

d.  Photocopying facilities are available. Scholars may also take pictures of maps with their own cameras.

e.  Ralph E. Ehrenberg, Chief
    Ronald E. Grim, Specialist, History of Cartography
    Gary Fitzpatrick, Specialist, Geographic Information Systems

2.  The Geography and Map Division was established as a distinct administrative unit in 1897, but maps, charts, and atlases were housed in the Library of Congress from the time of its establishment in 1800. The division has custody of the largest and most comprehensive cartographic collection in the world. It contains more than 4.2 million maps, 52,000 atlases, 78,000 microforms, 2.2 million aerial and remote sensing images, and 9,000 reference books and pamphlets. About 60,000 cartographic items are added to its permanent collections each year. The collections date from the 14th century to the present and cover virtually every country on earth. Within the scope of this Guide the relevant cartographic materials fall mainly under the rubrics of environmental issues, and military history, planning, and strategy.

3.  The division's resources are organized by format, by area, subject, and date, or by both in several major groupings. Cartographic materials germane to the purposes of this Guide are listed under the headings of Maps and Special Collections.

## MAPS

Series Map Collection is the most relevant for the study of peace and international security issues among the division's general map collections. It consists of approximately 2.1 million individual sheets of large- and medium-scale maps and charts dating from the 18th century. An individual series may range from two maps to several thousand maps. The predominant scales represented are 1:25,000, 1:50,000, 1:100,000, and 1:250,000, although coverage for most countries also includes some town plans at larger scales. Subject coverage is comprehensive. For most countries there are official geologic, land use, mineral, railroad, and topographic map series as well as aeronautical and nautical chart series. Scholars may also find map series relating to forests, flood hazards, military activities, natural resources, population, roads, and weather. For example, this collection contains all editions of printed map series produced by some 40 federal agencies in the United States, including the Defense Mapping Agency (D1) and its predecessor agencies, the Army Map Service, the Aeronautical Chart and Information Center, the Hydrographic Office, the Geological Survey, the National Ocean Service and its predecessors, the Coast and Geodetic Survey and the Lake Survey, and the Soil Conservation Service.

In terms of foreign coverage, most major European official surveying and mapping agencies are represented from the time of their establishment during the first half of the 19th century. Geographical coverage is particularly strong for Europe, Africa, and East Asia in the 20th century, areas that were systematically mapped by competing armies immediately before and during both world wars and between the wars for most colonial possessions.

A major strength of this collection is the nautical chart coverage. Current and retrospective editions of charts from hydrographic bureaus for the following countries are maintained: Argentina, Australia, Canada, Chile, China, Colombia, Cuba, Denmark, Ecuador, El Salvador, Estonia, Finland, France, Germany, Great Britain, Greece, Iceland, India, Italy, Japan, Latvia, Mexico, Netherlands, New Zealand, North Korea, Norway, Peru, Philippines, Poland, Portugal, Russia, South Africa, South Korea, Spain, Sweden, Thailand, Turkey, United States, Uruguay, Venezuela, and Yugoslavia.

Each series is classified and cataloged according to the Library's Classification Class G schedule. The following list, organized according to the G schedule, provides an indication of the number of map series available for specific regions and countries, along with the earliest date and largest scale. The dates and scales provided are those indicated according to the card catalog.

| Call Number | Area | Number in Series | Earliest Date | Largest Scale |
|---|---|---|---|---|
| G3190 | Celestial and Lunar | 30 | 1958 | 1:10,000 |
| G3200 | World | 265 | 1912 | 1:250,000 |
| G3290 | Western Hemisphere | 19 | 1753 | 1:250,000 |
| G3300 | North America | 60 | 1778 | 1:10,000 |
| G3380 | Greenland | 31 | 1932 | 1:2,000 |
| G3400 | Canada | 240 | 1884 | 1:12,500 |
| G3700 | United States | 123 | 1836 | 1:65,500 |
| | Regions and States | 1,175 | 1882 | 1:4,800 |
| | Cities and Towns | 252 | 1872 | 1:1,200 |
| G4410 | Mexico | 130 | 1928 | 1:25,000 |
| G4800 | Central America | 266 | 1871 | 1:1,056 |
| G5200 | South America | 24 | 1895 | 1:250,000 |
| G5250 | Guyana | 14 | 1949 | 1:50,000 |
| G5260 | Surinam | 20 | 1930 | 1:10,000 |
| G5270 | French Guiana | 11 | 1947 | 1:50,000 |
| G5280 | Venezuela | 84 | 1946 | 1:5,000 |
| G5290 | Colombia | 110 | 1936 | 1:2,000 |
| G5300 | Ecuador | 70 | 1928 | 1:2,000 |
| G5310 | Peru | 35 | 1880 | 1:2,000 |
| G5320 | Bolivia | 15 | 1933 | 1:10,000 |
| G5330 | Chile | 70 | 1873 | 1:2,000 |
| G5350 | Argentina | 80 | 1900s | 1:2,500 |
| G5370 | Uruguay | 17 | 1920 | 1:5,000 |
| G6380 | Paraguay | 8 | 1937 | 1:6,200 |
| G5400 | Brazil | 180 | 1899 | 1:10,000 |
| G5620 | Eastern Hemisphere | 26 | 1900 | 1:500,000 |
| G5700 | Europe | 230 | 1844 | 1:10,000 |
| G5740 | Great Britain | 462 | 1830s | 1:1,250 |
| | Counties | 249 | 1752 | 1:2,500 |
| | Cities | 73 | 1728 | 1:2,500 |
| G5830 | France | 208 | 1757 | 1:5,000 |
| | Provinces | 66 | 1879 | 1:2,000 |
| | Cities and Towns | 561 | 1885 | 1:5,000 |
| G6000 | Netherlands | 110 | 1853 | 1:5,000 |
| G6010 | Belgium | 90 | 1840s | 1:10,000 |
| G6020 | Luxembourg | 17 | 1904 | 1:5,000 |
| G6030 | Central Europe | 55 | 1866 | 1:10,000 |
| G6040 | Switzerland | 80 | 1833 | 1:5,000 |
| G6080 | Germany | 80 | 1860s | 1:10,000 |
| G6090 | East Germany | 35 | 1830 | 1:15,000 |
| G6295 | West Germany | 420 | 1791 | 1:5,000 |
| G6480 | Austria | 125 | 1810 | 1:1,000 |
| G6500 | Hungary | 31 | 1869 | 1:10,000 |
| G6510 | Czechoslovakia | 49 | 1910 | 1:15,000 |
| G6520 | Poland | 40 | 1807 | 1:10,000 |
| G6540 | Iberian Peninsula | 27 | 1823 | 1:25,000 |
| G6560 | Spain | 168 | 1875 | 1:500 |
| G6690 | Portugal | 55 | 1862 | 1:1,000 |
| G6700 | Italy | 230 | 1833 | 1:2,000 |
| G6800 | Balkan Peninsula | 13 | 1877 | 1:50,000 |
| G6810 | Greece | 125 | 1909 | 1:2,000 |
| G6830 | Albania | 10 | 1910 | 1:5,000 |
| G6840 | Yugoslavia | 43 | 1861 | 1:25,000 |
| G6880 | Romania | 39 | 1890s | 1:20,000 |
| G6890 | Bulgaria | 18 | 1905 | 1:25,000 |
| G6910 | Scandinavia | 15 | 1920 | 1:250,000 |
| G6920 | Denmark | 78 | 1846 | 1:4,000 |
| G6930 | Iceland | 26 | 1921 | 1:2,000 |
| G6940 | Norway | 160 | 1861 | 1:5,000 |
| G6950 | Sweden | 145 | 1858 | 1:10,000 |
| G6960 | Finland | 85 | 1867 | 1:2,000 |
| G6965 | Eastern Europe | 22 | 1912 | 1:25,000 |
| G7000 | USSR | 185 | 1847 | 1:10,000 |
| G7400 | Asia | 38 | 1894 | 1:500,000 |
| G7420 | Middle East | 133 | 1890 | 1:10,000 |
| G7500 | Israel | 67 | 1880 | 1:2,000 |
| G7520 | Arabian Peninsula | 70 | 1916 | 1:2,000 |
| G7610 | Iraq | 26 | 1918 | 1:7,200 |
| G7620 | Iran | 148 | 1918 | 1:2,000 |
| G7630 | Afghanistan | 5 | 1920s | 1:50,000 |
| G7640 | Pakistan | 16 | 1855 | 1:7,000 |
| G7650 | India | 62 | 1860s | 1:1,000 |
| G7720 | Burma | 26 | 1904 | 1:3,960 |
| G7750 | Sri Lanka | 62 | 1899 | 1:792 |
| G7760 | Nepal | 8 | 1953 | 1:2,000 |
| G7800 | Far East | 15 | 1894 | 1:63,360 |
| G7810 | China | 222 | 1864 | 1:1,200 |
| G7895 | Mongolia | 4 | 1927 | 1:250,000 |
| G7900 | Korea | 59 | 1911 | 1:1,250 |
| G7910 | Taiwan | 36 | 1895 | 1:1,250 |
| G7940 | Hong Kong | 19 | 1928 | 1:600 |
| G7950 | Japan | 130 | 1877 | 1:10,000 |
| | Islands | 60 | 1894 | 1:10,000 |
| | Prefectures | 95 | 1936 | 1:1,200 |
| G8000 | Southeast Asia | 9 | 1941 | 1:250,000 |
| G8005 | Indochina | 44 | 1908 | 1:10,000 |
| G8010 | Kampuchea | 4 | 1940s | 1:20,000 |
| G8015 | Laos | 5 | 1959 | 1:20,000 |
| G8020 | Vietnam | 48 | 1904 | 1:5,000 |
| G8025 | Thailand | 47 | 1897 | 1:4,000 |
| G8030 | Malaysia | 57 | 1928 | 1:3,168 |
| G8040 | Singapore | 8 | 1924 | 1:6,336 |
| G8060 | Philippines | 95 | 1890s | 1:2,000 |
| G8070 | Indonesia | 190 | 1883 | 1:2,000 |
| G8140 | New Guinea | 70 | 1925 | 1:20,000 |
| G8200 | Africa | 75 | 1883 | 1:5,000 |
| G8220 | North Africa | 13 | 1928 | 1:200,000 |
| G8230 | Morocco | 50 | 1899 | 1:5,000 |
| G8240 | Algeria | 42 | 1881 | 1:10,000 |
| G8250 | Tunisia | 36 | 1881 | 1:2,000 |
| G8260 | Libya | 44 | 1914 | 1:2,000 |
| G8300 | Egypt | 136 | 1821 | 1:2,500 |
| G8310 | Sudan | 45 | 1900 | 1:2,500 |
| G8320 | Eastern Africa | 25 | 1904 | 1:25,000 |
| G8330 | Ethiopia | 17 | 1881 | 1:25,000 |
| G8350 | Somalia | 19 | 1908 | 1:25,000 |
| G8410 | Kenya | 34 | 1895 | 1:2,500 |
| G8420 | Uganda | 39 | 1908 | 1:2,500 |
| G8425 | Rwanda-Burundi | 10 | 1925 | 1:25,000 |
| G8440 | Tanzania | 47 | 1894 | 1:2,500 |
| G8450 | Mozambique | 8 | 1896 | 1:20,000 |
| G8460 | Madagascar | 45 | 1899 | 1:1,000 |
| G8500 | South Africa | 60 | 1897 | 1:1,000 |
| G8560 | Zimbabwe | 60 | 1909 | 1:5,000 |
| G8570 | Zambia | 21 | 1933 | 1:5,000 |
| G8580 | Lesotho | 4 | 1950s | 1:2,500 |
| G8590 | Swaziland | 6 | 1932 | 1:2,400 |

| Call Number | Area | Number in Series | Earliest Date | Largest Scale |
|---|---|---|---|---|
| G8600 | Botswana | 26 | 1949 | 1:2,400 |
| G8610 | Malawi | 12 | 1950 | 1:2,500 |
| G8620 | Namibia | 8 | 1900s | 1:50,000 |
| G8630 | Central Africa | 10 | 1894 | 1:20,000 |
| G8640 | Angola | 11 | 1905 | 1:1,000 |
| G8650 | Zaire | 61 | 1910 | 1:2,000 |
| G8660 | Equatorial Guinea | 3 | 1940s | 1:100,000 |
| G8680 | French Equatorial Africa | 20 | 1880s | 1:50,000 |
| G8690 | Gabon | 3 | 1952 | 1:2,000 |
| G8710 | Ubangi-Shari | 3 | 1968 | 1:200,000 |
| G8720 | Chad | 9 | 1951 | 1:2,000 |
| G8730 | Cameroon | 14 | 1920s | 1:5,000 |
| G8735 | West Africa | 34 | 1886 | 1:10,000 |
| G8750 | Dahomy | 9 | 1927 | 1:2,000 |
| G8760 | Togo | 2 | 1902 | 1:200,000 |
| G8770 | Niger | 7 | 1907 | 1:2,000 |
| G8780 | Ivory Coast | 13 | 1895 | 1:2,000 |
| G8800 | Mali | 2 | 1891 | 1:200,000 |
| G8805 | Upper Volta | 2 | 1960s | 1:2,000 |
| G8810 | Senegal | 14 | 1941 | 1:5,000 |
| G8820 | Mauritania | 5 | 1956 | 1:1,000 |
| G8840 | Nigeria | 90 | 1886 | 1:2,400 |
| G8850 | Ghana | 51 | 1907 | 1:1,250 |
| G8860 | Sierra Leone | 21 | 1927 | 1:2,500 |
| G8870 | Gambia | 8 | 1948 | 1:2,500 |
| G8880 | Liberia | 6 | 1956 | 1:2,000 |
| G8890 | Guinea-Bissau | 3 | 1950 | 1:50,000 |
| G8900 | Western Sahara | 4 | 1958 | 1:1,000 |
| G8960 | Australia | 270 | 1848 | 1:1,000 |
| G9080 | New Zealand | 170 | 1900s | 1:7,920 |
| G9095 | Oceans | 9 | 1848 | 1:6M. |
| G9100 | Atlantic Ocean | 2 | 1868 | 1:22M. |
| G9110 | North Atlantic | 20 | 1859 | 1:50,000. |
| G9120 | Bermuda | 3 | 1901 | 1:2,500 |
| G9130 | Azores | 8 | 1940s | 1:2,400 |
| G9140 | Madeira Islands | 3 | 1967 | 1:25,000 |
| G9150 | Canary Islands | 4 | 1954 | 1:12,500 |
| G9160 | Cape Verde Islands | 4 | 1940 | 1:2,000 |
| G9170 | Saint Helena | 9 | 1944 | 1:10,000 |
| G9175 | Falkland Islands | 2 | 1971 | 1:2,500 |
| G9180 | Indian Ocean | 3 | 1942 | 1:2M. |
| G9185 | Mauritius | 5 | 1952 | 1:2,500 |
| G9190 | Reunion | 11 | 1964 | 1:2,000 |
| G9195 | British Indian Ocean Territory | 2 | 1964 | 1:25,000 |
| G9200 | Seychelles | 7 | 1963 | 1:1,250 |
| G9210 | Comoro Islands | 1 | 1958 | 1:50,000 |
| G9230 | Pacific Ocean | 7 | 1942 | 1:2M. |
| G9235 | North Pacific | 9 | 1942 | 1:1M. |
| G9250 | South Pacific | 10 | 1943 | 1:250,000 |
| G9260 | Melanesia | 1 | 1942 | 1:500,000 |
| G9280 | Solomon Islands | 29 | 1942 | 1:4,800 |
| G9285 | New Hebrides | 4 | 1949 | 1:50,000 |
| G9340 | New Caledonia | 9 | 1956 | 1:5,000 |
| G9380 | Fiji | 13 | 1942 | 1:20,000 |
| G9410 | Mariana Islands | 6 | 1921 | 1:20,000 |
| G9415 | Guam | 4 | 1944 | 1:25,000 |
| G9420 | Caroline Islands | 10 | 1921 | 1:12,500 |
| G9460 | Marshall Islands | 3 | 1944 | 1:27,000 |
| G9475 | Gilbert Islands | 5 | 1947 | 1:2,500 |
| G9500 | Polynesia | 11 | 1927 | 1:2,500 |
| G9780 | Arctic Oceans | 10 | 1925 | 1:10,000 |
| G9800 | Antarctica | 26 | 1946 | 1:50,000 |
| G9900 | Theoretical Maps | 4 | 1977 | 1:10,000 |

## SPECIAL COLLECTIONS

The division maintains a number of collections separately because they possess unique intrinsic, artistic, or historical significance. Some of these are described more thoroughly in Annette Melville's *Special Collections in the Library of Congress: A Selective Guide* (Library of Congress, 1980). The major special collections relevant to peace and international security studies are listed below.

Nathaniel Prentiss Banks Collection. Printed and photoprocessed maps relating chiefly to General Banks's Civil War military operations as commander of the Department of the Gulf (22 items).

John Barrett Collection. Printed maps of Latin America and Asia acquired by Barrett, an American diplomat and director of the Pan-American Union, 1894–1920 (85 items). Includes a manuscript map of Manila compiled by Spanish Army engineers, 1894–98.

Andrew H. Benton—Herschel V. Jones Collection. Printed title pages, indexes, introductory materials, time charts, topographic profiles, and fortification plans from various atlases and geographical books, ca. 1700–1915 (ca. 250 items).

Canal Zone Library—Museum Collection. Manuscript, printed, and blueprint maps and photocopies of maps of the Panama Canal collected and maintained by the former Canal Zone Library—Museum, Balboa, Canal Zone, 18th century to 1967 (462 items). There are maps and plans of route surveys, land ownership, harbors, and towns. A number of these maps were prepared by the Panama Railroad Company, the French Compagnie Universelle de Canal Interocéanique de Panama, the U.S. Isthmian Canal Commission, and the U.S. Army Military Survey of Panama. These maps are described in *Subject Catalog of the Special Panama Collection of the Canal Zone Library—Museum* (Boston: G. K. Hall, 1964).

Classified Rare Map Collection. There are also a large number of manuscript maps. The following are relevant for their bearing on the study of diplomacy and negotiations, economic development, the environment, or national and collective security issues: French railroad map of French Guinea, Africa, 1891; map of Chinese immigration in Inner Mongolia, 1908; map of the Defenses of Port Arthur, China, 1905; map of south and east Africa showing H. L. Shantz's agricultural exploration trip, 1919–20; intelligence map issued by G-2, Headquarters, French

Army Morocco, showing tribal areas of North Morocco, 1925; set of statistical maps of Poland, 1930s; German ethnographic map of Romania, 1938; school map showing routes of Alexander the Great, 18th century; water resource and geology map of Saudi Arabia prepared by the U.S. Military Mission, 1944; map of Europe depicting language groups compiled by U.S. Office of War Information, 1943; intelligence map showing categories of main roads in southern France, 1943; plan of military fortifications of Cambrai, France, 17th century; German military panorama of Alsace-Lorraine battlefield found by a French observer, 1918; maps prepared for the Paris Peace Conference, 1921 (3 items); map of the northern frontier of Mexico by Nicolas de Lafora, 1769; reconnaissance map for a central railroad in Nicaragua, compiled by Cpl. J. M. Bankler and Pfc. E. W. Bell, U.S. Marine Corps, 1930; map of a part of Haiti, with coastal soundings, 1780–95; geological map of part of Peru made by Standard Oil of New Jersey; map of central Chile showing timberlands, 1944; and boundary survey maps of the Brazil-Uruguay frontier prepared by Josef Varela y Ulloa, Spanish commissioner following the Treaty of San Ildefonso, 1777 (6 items).

William Faden Collection. A working collection of manuscript and annotated British military maps and plans pertaining to the French and Indian War and the American Revolution, which was assembled by Faden, geographer to the King of England and a noted British map publisher during the late 18th century (101 maps).

Millard Fillmore Collection. Includes printed maps of U.S. cities and states, European countries, and Civil War campaigns collected by President Fillmore (2,247 items). For description, see Richard W. Stephenson's "Millard Fillmore Map Collection" in *The Map Collector* (1980).

Peter Force Collection. Manuscript and printed maps collected by Force concerning chiefly the French and Indian War, and the American Revolution. It includes maps by an American Indian, Thomas Hutchins, William Gerard DeBrahm, Charles Blaskowitz, John Montresor, Nicholas King, Benjamin Henry Latrobe, General John Cadwalader, and others, 1685–1842 (768 maps). Described by Richard W. Stephenson in *Quarterly Journal of the Library of Congress* (1973).

John Hills Collection. Manuscript maps prepared by Hill for Sir Henry Clinton concerning British military operations in New Jersey, 1778–81 (20 maps).

Gen. John L. Hines Collection. Printed and annotated maps concerning American military operations in France during World War I (187 maps).

Jedediah Hotchkiss Collection. Manuscript sketches and maps chiefly of Virginia and West Virginia prepared by Hotchkiss and Albert H. Campbell for Generals Robert E. Lee and T. J. (Stonewall) Jackson during the Civil War (600 items). Described in Clara Egli LeGear's *Hotchkiss Map Collection* (Washington, 1951).

Richard Howe Collection. Manuscript maps and charts of coastal waters of North and South America, the West Indies, and the Philippine Islands that were acquired from the descendants of Adm. Lord Richard Howe, Commander in Chief of the British Fleet in North America during the American Revolution, 1750s–70s (72 maps).

Andrew Jackson Collection. Manuscript maps relating to General Jackson's military operations in the South during the War of 1812 (11 items).

John Johnson Maps and Notebooks. Manuscript maps and survey notebooks pertaining to the Northeastern International Boundary Survey in 1817 (4 items). They were compiled by Johnson, surveyor general of Vermont and U.S. representative for the Northeastern Boundary Survey.

Lewis and Clark Collection. In addition to manuscript maps of the Missouri River basin and the Transmississippi West, the collection contains a manuscript sketch map of the Ojibwa and Sioux boundary line, 1821; a manuscript map of the Illinois and Chicago Rivers relating to the Black Hawk War, 1832; and manuscript maps of Indian cessions in the midwest, 1825–37.

Rochambeau Collection. Manuscript and printed maps and plans of military fortifications and troop positions in North America prepared by French army engineers for Jean Baptiste Donatien de Vimeur, compte de Rochambeau, commander of French forces during the American Revolution, 1777–83 (122 maps and plans).

Ephraim George Squier Collection. Detailed manuscript and printed annotated maps of Honduras, El Salvador, Nicaragua, and Peru relating chiefly to Squier's canal and railway interests, 1850s–1880s (38 maps). Described in John Hébert's "Maps by Ephraim George Squier, Journalist, Scholar, and Diplomat," *Quarterly Journal of the Library of Congress* (January, 1972).

Gilbert Thompson Collection. Includes manuscript landscape sketches drawn by John E. Weyss during his work on the U.S.-Mexican Boundary Survey.

4. The Geography and Map Reading Room maintains a dictionary card catalog to the atlas collections (144 drawers), and author, title, and subject

catalogs provide access to the MARC map collection, 1968–80 (221 drawers).

A general introduction to the division and its resources is Walter W. Ristow's *Geography and Map Division: A Guide to Its Collections and Services* (Washington, D.C.: Library of Congress, 1975). A list of the division's publications is available upon request. It describes almost 70 monographs, exhibit catalogs, checklists, short lists, article reprints, map facsimiles, microforms, and computer tapes available from the division. Information regarding the maps on-line data base is provided in *MARC Formats for Bibliographic Data,* which is available from the Cataloging Distribution Service, Library of Congress, Washington, D.C. 20541.

5. Index Terms: Environmental Issues, Global; Military History; Military Science—Engineering, Logistics, and Support

*Note:* Additional manuscript maps, aerial photographs, survey notes, and related correspondence are found among personal papers and other collections in the Manuscript Division of the Library of Congress (B8). Some are relevant to the scope of this Guide, especially to military history. Of these cartographic materials, approximately 2,000 maps and 1,000 aerial photographs are described in the *Scholars' Guide to Washington, D.C., for Cartography and Remote Sensing Imagery,* by Ralph E. Ehrenberg (Washington, D.C.: Smithsonian Institution Press, 1987), pp. 104–119.

See also entries A29, B8, D4, F14, and F15

---

## D5  Marine Corps Historical Center (Navy Department)—Maps

---

1.a. Washington Navy Yard, Building 58
9th and M Streets, SE
Washington, D.C. 20374-0580
(202) 433-3396 (Personal Papers Collection)
(202) 433-3439 (Archives Section)
Fax: (202) 433-7265

b. 8:00 A.M.–4:30 P.M. Monday–Friday

c. Open to researchers, but scholars must sign in at the Security Section or the Information Desk near the main entrance and obtain a visitor's pass.

d. Photocopying facilities are available.

e. Frederick Graboske, Head, Archives Section
 Amy J. Cantin, Curator, Personal Papers Curator

Charles A. Wood, Chief Curator, Museum

2. The Center serves as an archives and museum for the Marine Corps. In addition to a small map and aerial photography collection, maps and aerial photographs are found scattered throughout the records and papers of the Archives Section and Personal Papers Collection. The museum has a number of printed and manuscript maps on permanent display relating to Marine Corps actions in World War II, Korea, Vietnam, and the Middle East. From the viewpoint of international security and peace studies the relevant cartographic materials concern the fields of military history, planning, and strategy.

3. The principal holdings are as follows:

### MAP COLLECTION

The Map Collection numbers about 2,000 items. It is unclassified and uncataloged, but the materials are generally grouped by names of regions or islands associated with Marine Corps military actions. These include France; Nicaragua, Dominican Republic, and Haiti; Guadalcanal (2 map drawers); Iwo Jima; Okinawa; Marshall Islands; Saipan/Tinian; Guam, Korea (2 map drawers); Peleliu Island; Tarawa; Solomon Islands; Bougainville; New Britain; Philippines; Vietnam; and Marine training camps in California, Hawaii Islands, Samoa, Australia, and New Zealand. Although some of the materials are duplicated in the National Archives and Library of Congress, the collection also includes unique manuscript sketch maps, action overlays from battle reports, printed and manuscript Japanese maps, some 200 to 300 aerial photographic prints and mosaics (some of which are annotated), and air targets. The materials on the Guadalcanal action, for example, contain cadastral plats of local plantations, British and Japanese navigation charts, and aerial photographs that provided the data for compiling the basic 12-sheet topographic map of the battle site.

### ARCHIVES SECTION

The Archives Section serves as the official repository for combat operational reports, plans, after-action reports, and related documents for World War II and later. The section also maintains a few pre-World War II materials. In general, however, pre-World War II Marine Corps records have been transferred to the National Archives and Records Administration (D6, RG 127), and records continue to be transferred on a regular basis. Vietnam-era records (1,500 cubic feet) are housed in the Archives Section; the remaining records (3,500 cubic feet) are stored temporarily in the Washington National Records Center, Suitland, Md. The latter may be recalled to the Archives Section when required for research.

The operation reports and related files are generally organized by Marine Corps unit, activity, or subject, and loosely indexed by accession lists. Cartographic materials are found throughout the files. Some of the more significant materials are listed below:

World War I Collection, 1917–19. Maps and aerial photographs of battle sites, operations, training areas, and military sectors.

Marine Corps Units in Nicaragua, 1927–33. Maps, sketches, intelligence reports, and air mission reports.

1st Provisional Brigade in Haiti, 1933–34. Maps of Santo Domingo, 1919–22.

Marine Corps Air Force Units Historical Reports and Diaries. Reports and histories of ComFleet Air Photographic Group Two, 1940s, and Marine Corps Photographic Squadrons VMD and VMP 154, 254, 354, and 954, 1943–46.

U.S. Marine Corps Geographic Files, 1940–45. Divisional, regimental, and battalion operational plans and action reports contain cartographic data relating to all campaigns in which the Marine Corps participated. For example, the file on Okinawa contains documents on aerial photo support (May–June 1945) and stereographic study, 1st Marine Division photo interpretation reports, and maps and overlays prepared for various battalions of the 1st and 7th Marines.

Marine Corps Aviation History Reference Notes. Photo intelligence and interpretation reports based on aerial photographic reconnaissance sorties carried out by Navy and Marine Corps photo interpretation squadrons, 1943–44 (7 cubic feet).

Terrain Studies, Southwest Pacific, 1942–45. Studies of islands, capes, bays, and peninsulas in the Southwest Pacific area and Japan (115 items).

1st Provisional Brigade, Korea, July–September, 1950. Overlays and plans for Inchon-Seoul, Korea, and Wonson-Hanhung, Manchuria.

## PERSONAL PAPERS COLLECTION

The Personal Papers Collection (PC) contains the papers of some 2,000 marines, many of which include maps and aerial photographs. The following sample is representative of the collection:

PC 72: Robert L. Ghormley Papers contain photostat copies of Admiral Ghormley's 98-page personal log of the Guadalcanal-Tulagi Campaign (August 1–November 13, 1942), which includes many charts and maps.

PC 112: James Roosevelt Papers include a manuscript sketch map of Makin Island prepared from aerial photographs and his typescript operational order for a raid on the island, August 1942.

PC 174: Frank D. Weir Papers contain aerial photographic prints of towns, villages, and airfields in Nicaragua taken about 1927–28 by Marine Observation Squadron Seven (91 prints), related correspondence, and air patrol reports. Weir served as photographic officer for the squadron.

PC 224: Littleton W. T. Waller Jr. Papers contain French situation maps of Verdun and St. Etienne (8 items) and annotated aerial photographic prints of Sivry-Lez (3 items), World War I.

PC 316: Victor J. Croizat Papers consist of maps pertaining to military actions on Guadalcanal, August 18, 1942.

PC 349: Edward W. Snedecker Papers contain a series of aerial photographs of the Chateau-Thierry sector in France dated July 1918 and working maps (some with annotations) used during campaigns on Guadalcanal (1943), Empress Augusta Bay, Bougainville, (1943), and Nanyi-Ri, Korea (1950).

PC 496: Alpha L. Bowser Papers contain maps with overlays relating to the withdrawal from the Chosin Reservoir during the Korean War.

PC 521: Norman C. Bates Papers include aerial photographs of Veracruz and Fort San Juan Ulvoa, taken from a seaplane with the American Expeditionary Forces (AEF), Veracruz, Mexico, 1914.

PC 526: John R. Blandford Papers include various map overlays pertaining to military actions on Guadalcanal and Cape Gloucester during World War II.

4. A brochure, *Guide to the Marine Corps Historical Center* (1986) provides general information on the facility. The Personal Papers Collection is described in a catalog compiled by Charles A. Wood (1974, rev. 1980). The researcher should also consult *An Annotated Bibliography of the United States Marine Corps in the Second World War,* by Michael O'Quinlivan and Jack B. Hilliard (1970).

5. Index Terms: Military History—Marine Corps

See also entries B9, C4, C5, E9, and E10

---

## D6 National Archives and Records Administration (NARA)—Nontextual Archives Division (NNS)—Cartographic and Architectural Branch

---

1.a. 8601 Adelphi Road
College Park, Md. 20740-6001

(301) 713-7040
Fax: (301) 713-6904
Fax-on-demand: (301) 713-6905

b. 8:45 A.M.–5:15 P.M. Monday–Friday
Some evening and Saturday hours by appointment.

c. Open to researchers with a National Archives identification card, obtainable from the Reference Services Division. First-time users should speak with a consultant before beginning work. Some materials are restricted due to national security classifications.

d. Photocopying and microfilming services are available. The Cartographic and Architectural Branch has an oversize photocopier that can accommodate maps up to 36 inches wide and any length.

e. John A. Dwyer, Chief

2.  The National Archives and Records Administration's (NARA) vast holdings of more than 1 million cubic feet of primary source material include more than 2 million maps and 9 million aerial photographs. The map holdings represent the largest collection of manuscript maps in North America. The overall total of maps is surpassed only by the map holdings of the Library of Congress (D4). Within the scope of this Guide relevant cartographic materials fall primarily under the rubrics of military history, planning, and strategy, diplomacy and negotiations, and intelligence; and secondarily under the subjects of economic aid, international trade, international organizations, and war crimes.

Most of the cartographic materials in NARA were originally created or acquired by legislative, judicial, or executive agencies of the federal government in pursuance of their official activities and maintained by them to document these activities or for their informational value. Together with other types of documents, most cartographic materials are organized among some 400 Record Groups (RG), each typically consisting of the documents produced by a government administrative unit at the department, bureau, or agency level. Within a record group, the filing arrangement generally follows the system employed by the government body that generated or acquired the records. In addition, there is a category of Donated Materials (*formerly* RG 200) that consists of documents that are not government records.

3.  The collections of NARA are immense. Because the maps in NARA were at one time closely associated with government agency programs, their scope reflects the activities of the U.S. government. From the viewpoint of the users of this Guide, among the maps dating prior to World War I those relating to U.S. military mapping are of particular interest. Those dated during or after World War I provide more worldwide coverage as a result of the increased role that the United States played in world affairs. Almost one-half of the maps are manuscript or printed maps containing manuscript annotations, making it one of the largest collections of its kind in the world. The aerial photographic collection, numbering more than 9 million photographs, is probably the largest accessible collection of historical aerial photographs in the world. Within the scope of this Guide it provides unique worldwide coverage documenting military activities from 1918 to the 1960s.

## RECORD GROUPS

To facilitate a subject orientation, the following table places relevant RGs (discussed further on in this entry) under major subject headings:
Diplomacy and Alliances: RG 43, RG 46, RG 59, RG 76, RG 256
Economic Aid: RG 169
Intelligence: RG 37, RG 127, RG 165, RG 226, RG 263, RG 289, RG 319, RG 373
International Law: RG 43, RG 46, RG 59, RG 76, RG 238, RG 256
International Organizations: RG 30, RG 43, RG 229
International Trade: RG 59, RG 185, RG 229
Military History, Planning, and Strategy: RG 171, RG 226, RG 242, RG 263, RG 331–332, RG 373, RG 407, RG 456; Army: RG 30, RG 77, RG 92, RG 94, RG 109, RG 117, RG 120, RG 165, RG 200, RG 319, RG 338, RG 393–395; Air Force: RG 18, RG 84, RG 165, RG 243, RG 342; Coast Guard: RG 26; Marine Corps: RG 127; Navy: RG 19, RG 23–24, RG 37–38, RG 45, RG 71, RG 289, RG 313, RG 457
War Crimes: RG 238, RG 373

The following Record Groups (RGs) contain pertinent cartographic materials:
**RG 18:**  *Army Air Force, 1917–47: 6,650 maps.*
Flak and target maps prepared by the Assistant Chief of Air Staff for Intelligence showing towns and areas in Japan, Formosa, Manchuria, China, Indochina, the Philippines, Europe, and North Africa, 1942–44. Climatic weather plotting charts for Italy, France, the Balkans and other parts of the world. Published aeronautical charts, including incomplete series of the World Aeronautical Charts (1:1,000,000), World Pilotage Charts (1:500,000), and World Approach Charts (1:250,000) issued by the Aeronautical Chart Service, 1939–47.
**RG 19:**  *Bureau of Ships, 1820–1910: 100 items.*
Plans of major navy bases in the United States filed among a larger series of ship plans.

**RG 23:** *Coast and Geodetic Survey, 1839–1965: 67,353 maps and drawings.*
Special maps published by the Nautical Division include maps and charts of the southeast during the Civil War. An atlas of the Philippines prepared in 1899 from Jesuit surveys supervised by Jose Algue, S.J., and large-scale topographic maps of the Philippines prepared by the survey, 1913–34.

**RG 24:** *Bureau of Naval Personnel, 1898–1935: 15 maps.*
Manuscript maps relating to naval activities off Cuba during the Spanish American War. Economic and strategic maps of the world produced by the Naval War College, 1905–32.

**RG 26:** *U.S. Coast Guard, 1915–43: 393 maps and charts.*
Manuscript and annotated maps showing harbor and Coast Guard facilities along the North Atlantic Coast. Included are several World War II blackout charts and charts illustrating beach patrol operations in 1943.

**RG 30:** *Bureau of Public Roads, 1920–82: 58,139 maps and 4,900 aerial photographs.*
Maps relating to defense and interstate highways, including maps signed or annotated by Gen. John J. Pershing, Army Chief of Staff, 1922. An incomplete series of aerial photographic prints and negatives documenting the planning and construction of the Inter-American Highway and the Alaska Highway, 1936–59.

**RG 37:** *Hydrographic Office, 1803–1971: 100,000 maps.*
Nautical charts of foreign coastal areas, including World War II emergency reproductions and field charts published hurriedly for wartime use. Aeronautical charts, including World War II Naval Air Combat Intelligence (NACI) charts to help pilots locate airfields and targets in the Pacific.

**RG 38:** *Office of the Chief of Naval Operations, 1884–1955: 280 items.*
Manuscript, printed, and annotated maps collected by naval attachés or prepared by the Office of Naval Intelligence showing naval, transportation, and communication facilities, naval engagements, population, wealth, political boundaries, and trade routes chiefly for Latin America but also China, Japan, France, Germany, the British Empire, and the Middle East. Described in *Preliminary Inventory 85* (1955).

**RG 43:** *U.S. Participation in International Conferences, Commissions, and Expositions, 1890–1947: 1,240 maps.*
Chiefly large-scale manuscript survey maps of the Intercontinental Railway Commission showing cities, towns, and existing and proposed railroad routes in Central America, Colombia, Ecuador, and Peru, 1890–1898. Maps from peace conferences at the end of World War II relating to boundary questions in Eastern Europe, Italy, and France.

**RG 45:** *Naval Records Collection of the Office of Naval Records and Library, 1775–1946: 516 maps.*
Manuscript, printed, and annotated maps, charts, and harbor plans separated from the subject file, relating to naval operations from the Revolutionary War to World War I, including a few maps pertaining to the Siberian intervention, 1920–21. A set of photoprocessed charts relating to the Mediterranean, 1780–1816 (8 items).

**RG 46:** *U.S. Senate, 1800–1966: 1,427 maps.*
Among the miscellaneous manuscript and annotated maps prepared for the Senate by federal agencies, pertinent items relate to international boundaries and battlefields of the Civil War. Maps relating to the Alaskan Boundary Tribunal; the U.S. Nicaragua Ship Canal Commission, 1886; Latin America, 1892–94; and the Venezuela—British Guiana boundary, 1898.

**RG 59:** *General Records of the Department of State, 1844–1974: 3,171 maps.*
Maps of foreign cities annotated to show the locations of American embassies and consulates, 1906–39 (259 maps). Economic maps accompanying consular trade reports, 1943–49 (220 maps). Records of the Office of the Geographer include the correspondence, research reports, and notebooks of Lawrence Martin, 1921–24, and Samuel Whittemore Boggs, 1924–54, most of which pertain to special mapping projects carried out during World War II; thematic maps of Europe, the Middle East, and Asia prepared under the direction of Leo Pasvolsky in preparation for a peace conference following World War II, 1942–45 (1,000 maps); thematic and boundary maps of the world prepared by the Division of Geography and Cartography for the Pauley Reparations Mission, 1939–46 (326 maps); and a report analyzing cartographic and map collecting agencies in Germany, 1946–47.

**RG 71:** *Bureau of Yards and Docks, 1870–1950: 1,000 maps.*
Plans of navy yards, bases, training camps, and other facilities in the United States and abroad are filed among a larger series of architectural plans of navy buildings.

**RG 76:** *Boundary and Claims Commissions and Arbitrations, 1794–1952: 20,241 maps, charts and topographical sketches.*
Cartographic records relating to the international boundaries of the United States contain original treaty, exploratory, and survey maps delimiting the

boundary of the United States with Great Britain, Canada, Spain, Texas, and Mexico (4,000 maps), including the printed edition of John Mitchell's map of the British Colonies that was used by the negotiators for the treaty with Great Britain in 1783, and another copy annotated by Benjamin Franklin. These records are described in PI 170 (1968).

Cartographic records relating to international claims by individuals or groups settled by treaties or other conventions contain manuscript, printed, and annotated maps pertaining to fishing rights in coastal waters of the northeastern United States and Canada, 1854–71. There are also charts of the Straits of Georgia and San Juan de Fuca relating to the sockeye salmon treaty with Canada, 1930, and maps pertaining to various conventions with Mexico regarding Sonora and the Mexican Revolution, 1868–1923.

Cartographic records relating to international arbitrations include maps and charts relating to disputes between the United States and Great Britain concerning fur seals in the Bering Sea and fishing rights in the Atlantic, 1892–1909. Also, manuscript and printed maps submitted as evidence by several Latin American countries concerning boundary disputes with their neighbors where the United States served as arbitrator, some of which were copied from originals in the British Museum, the Archives of the Minister of Foreign Affairs in Paris, the Portuguese Archives in Lisbon, and the Archives of the Indies in Madrid, 1630–1945 (15,000 items). Some aerial photographs record the disputed boundary between Peru and Ecuador, 1945.

**RG 77:** *Office of the Chief of Engineers, 1790–1982: 249,874 maps; 59,000 aerial photographs.*
Manuscript and annotated maps (Headquarters Map File) prepared by the Bureau of Topographical Engineers, 1812–39, the Corps of Topographical Engineers, 1839–63, and other topographical and engineering units pertaining to military surveys of roads and canals, military campaigns, and the administration of army commands and districts (32,500 items). Manuscript maps and plans (Fortification Map File) of U.S. military forts, camps, and reservations, (57,000 items). Manuscript and annotated maps collected or issued by the Military Intelligence Division of the General Staff (War Department Map Collection) cover a wide range of subjects, but the majority of maps pertain to military activities in Mexico and Central America, Cuba, Eastern Europe, Africa, China, Japan, and the Philippines, 1890–1940 (3,000 items). A set of Japanese Imperial Land Survey maps overprinted with English place names, 1925–35. Tactical and Training maps issued by the Engineer Reproduction Plant, 1917–42.

Large-scale topographic map series published by the Army Map Service of most areas of the world, including a number of manuscript and annotated maps transferred from the former Army Map Service Library, 1942–82 (140,000 items). Photographs of photogrammetric and mapmaking equipment used by German mapping units during World War II. Aerial photographic series include views of military fortifications and trenches in France during World War I; and prints of the Inter-American Highway Survey in Central America, 1932.

**RG 84:** *Foreign Service Posts of the Department of State, 1914–44: 12 maps.*
Includes maps of bombed areas of Chungking and roads in China prepared by a U.S. military attaché, 1939–44.

**RG 92:** *Office of the Quartermaster General, 1820–1952: 1,694 maps.*
A series of landform and climatic zone maps prepared by Erwin Raisz and Harry Hoy for the Military Planning Division relating to clothing requirements worldwide, 1943–52. Among textual records there are maps of harbors and military posts in the United States, Alaska, and the Philippine Islands, 1904–5; maps relating to historical sketches of military reservations, 1888–89; maps of U.S. military railroads operated from 1861–66; maps relating to the Quartermaster General's Office of the American Expeditionary Force, 1919–23; and files pertaining to equipment purchased for balloon aerial reconnaissance during the Civil War.

**RG 94:** *Adjutant General's Office, 1780s–1917: 3,121 maps.*
Among the significant series are manuscript and annotated maps used in the preparation of the *Atlas to Accompany the Official Records of the Union and Confederate Armies* (Washington, 1891–95), 1861–95 (1,051 items); manuscript maps prepared by the Military Information Division pertaining to military operations in Africa, Greece, Korea, China, Cuba, Puerto Rico, and the Philippines (1897–1902); and maps prepared during the Mexican Punitive Expedition, 1916.

**RG 109:** *War Department Collection of Confederate Records, 1861–65: 112 maps.*
Manuscript maps and drawings of campaigns and fortifications in the South and border states.

**RG 117:** *American Battle Monuments Commission, 1923–44: 456 maps.*
Manuscript and annotated maps summarizing the military operations of the American Expeditionary Forces in Europe during World War I, many of which later appeared at reduced scales in the 28-volume *Guide to the American Battlefields in Europe in 1927.*

**RG 120:** *American Expeditionary Forces (World War I), 1917–23: 24,000 maps and 4,000 aerial photographs.*

Maps prepared or collected chiefly by the Intelligence (G-2) and Operations (G-3) Sections of the General Staff showing German troop movements and other enemy information, bombing targets, the location and activities of Bolshevist forces, the situation of Allied and German forces on the western front on a daily or weekly basis, 1914–19, and details of troop dispositions on specific dates. Maps prepared or annotated by American armies, corps, and divisions showing the locations and activities of artillery batteries, and troop and unit disposition movements. Maps relating to American military activities in Italy and Siberia, including maps of Russia and Siberia based on a Russian General Staff map. Maps prepared or collected after the war by the Historical Branch of the War Plans Division of the General Staff pertaining to troop operations during the war and the following occupation in Germany. Maps produced by military mapping services in Belgium, 1911–19 (479 items), Great Britain, 1909–19 (1,720 items), France, 1871–1920 (5,742 items), Italy, 1895–1919 (531 items), Austria-Hungary, 1894–1917 (134 items), and Germany, 1848–1920 (3,325 items).

Aerial photographs include a small number of aerial photo mosaics and maps of cities in France, Belgium, Luxembourg, Alsace-Lorraine, and Germany prepared or acquired by AEF Air Intelligence Section and by the French Army Ground Survey Groups, 1917–18. Also, printed aerial views of Giogo dell Stelvio and Spondinig Prad by the Italian 7th Army in 1918, and battle sites in northern France by the German, French, and American air forces.

**RG 127:** *U.S. Marine Corps, 1885–1944: 999 maps.*

Maps and plans of marine corps installations in the United States, 1910–39; manuscript maps prepared by the Marine Intelligence Section of the Headquarters Division of Operations and Training, intelligence sections of individual brigades, and the Mapping Section of the Marine Corps School pertaining to Aruba, the Azores, Barbados, China, Costa Rica, Cuba, Culebra, Curacao, Dominican Republic, El Salvador, Grenada, Guadeloupe, Guatemala, Haiti, Honduras, Ireland, Jamaica, Korea, Martinique, Mexico, Nicaragua, Panama, and Venezuela, 1918–40; and maps relating to the activities of the 4th Marine Brigade in France during World War I. These maps are described in PI 73 (1954). About 100 maps relate to marine corps activities in the South Pacific during World War II.

**RG 165:** *War Department General and Special Staffs, 1904–46: 12,873 maps, 1,100 aerial photographs.*

Maps prepared or collected by the Military Intelligence Division include maps of Cuba, the Philippines, Central America, and Panama; maps relating to the Russo-Japanese War, 1904–5, and the Russian Civil War; maps of Mexico, 1916–22; maps relating to areas of strategic interest throughout the world, 1927–46. Cartographic records of the Army War College and the Command and General Staff Schools contain topographic and strategic maps of Central American countries, including a 70-sheet map of Cuba prepared by the Army of Cuban Pacification, 1906–9, with corrections in 1913; maps relating to World War I, including a set of "Colonel Prices Lecture Maps: Mineral Resources of the German Defense System"; manuscript maps of Revolutionary War battles prepared for the George Washington Bicentennial Atlas; and topographic and strategic maps of Civil War campaigns prepared for use in war games. Color photographs of relief models annotated to show troop locations for specific periods during World War II (11,300 photographs).

Aerial photographic prints relating to combat activities in France and bombing targets in Germany during World War I. Also, French, English, and German publications describing the military use of aerial photographs.

**RG 169:** *Foreign Economic Administration, 1942–45: 2,992 maps.*

Published thematic maps of the world regions and countries relating to transportation, resources, and industry. Maps and plans of terrain intelligence prepared for strategic engineering studies, Securities and Exchange Commission reports, and British Inter Service Information Series reports, chiefly for France, Italy, and East Asia.

**RG 171:** *Office of Civilian Defense, 1941–45: 533 maps.*

Maps of the United States, the 9th Civilian Defense Region (Washington, Oregon, and California), and urban areas annotated to show distribution of civilian defense supplies and facilities, population, target areas, and industrial and military installations.

**RG 185:** *Panama Canal, 1870–1957: 9,844 maps.*

Maps, plans of cities and harbors, survey sheets and profiles compiled by the Compagnie Universelle Canal Interocéanique, 1881–1900 (6,774 items), the Compagnie Nouvelle du Canal du Panama, 1889–99 (730 items), the Nicaragua Canal Commission, 1895–99 (417 items), and the Isthmian Canal Commissions, 1899–1913 (1,284 items). For a further description of these records see PI 153 (1963).

RG 226: *Office of Strategic Services (OSS), 1941–45: 7,500 maps.*

Thematic maps of areas having military significance throughout the world prepared by the Cartographic Section of the OSS (7,500 items). Subjects include military activities, political boundaries, transportation and communications systems, and locations of resources, industries, and population concentrations.

RG 229: *Office of Inter-American Affairs. Maps and correspondence found among the records of the Transportation Department related to the Pan-American Highway survey in Central America and Mexico, and other railroad and highway surveys, 1943–46 (4 lin. ft.).*

Maps accompanying studies of railroads in Bolivia, Columbia, Ecuador, and Mexico, 1942–47. These records are described in PI 7 (1973).

RG 238: *National Archives Collection of World War II War Crimes Records, 1945–48: 50 maps.*

Photostatic copies of maps from the staff evidence analysis records of the Document Control Branch, Office of the Chief Counsel for War Crimes. [*Note:* This collection is administered by the Military Reference Branch of the National Archives and Records Administration, see entry B11.]

RG 242: *National Archives Collections of Foreign Records Seized, 1941–, 1934–45: 22,635 maps; 8,000 aerial photographs.*

Maps prepared or collected by the German Army show German defenses in European countries, troop billeting, propaganda, boundary changes, views of mountain passes in Italy, and topography. Bound volumes of charts, photographs, and descriptive texts issued by the German Navy High Command relating to strategic coastal waters throughout the world, sea ice conditions along the Arctic shores of Siberia and European Russia, and oil tanker routes and facilities in Great Britain (61 volumes). Maps and aerial photographic prints comprising target dossiers prepared by the German Air Force High Command of targets chiefly in France, 1939–40, Great Britain, 1939–43, Italy, 1943–44, and a few for the Balkan Countries, North Africa, the Middle East, and Iceland (22,000 items). Maps seized from Italy showing defense systems. Maps from Japanese forces include a Japanese overprinting of a U.S. Coast and Geodetic Survey map of Washington, D.C., situation maps of China and the Pacific, city plans in China, Japan, and the Southwest Pacific, and charts of the Pacific showing defenses.

RG 243: *U.S. Strategic Bombing Survey, 1944–45: 2,340 aerial photographs.*

Aerial photographic prints of bombing targets (mainly port areas, airfields, and industrial areas) in Japan and Korea taken by the Joint Task Group and the 21st Bomber Command. See PI 10 (1975).

RG 256: *American Commission to Negotiate Peace, 1917–19: 1,178 maps.*

Manuscript, published, and annotated thematic and general maps prepared or collected by the commission's Geography and Cartography Division, the Economic and Statistics Division, and nine regional divisions. These maps, designed specifically to aid in the reestablishment of national boundaries, depict geographical, ethnographic, linguistic, political, economic, topographic, and historical data primarily for Eastern Europe and Africa. See PI 9 (1974).

RG 263: *Central Intelligence Agency, 1947–: about 1,000 maps.*

Published, mostly small-scale maps covering all areas of the world. The focus is mainly on political and economic conditions of individual countries, as well as international boundary lines.

RG 289: *Naval Intelligence Command, 1942–46: 1,000 maps, 20,000 aerial photographs.*

Military Intelligence Photographic Interpretation (MIPI) and Naval Intelligence Photographic Interpretation (NIPI) reports, incorporating aerial photographs and maps in documenting World War II aerial missions in the military theaters of the Pacific, East Asia, Europe, and the Mediterranean. Included are reports on targets, bombing strikes, defenses, shipping, airfield facilities, and port facilities, as well as studies and bulletins on such subjects as the explosives industry, new enemy aircraft, German naval shipbuilding, and prisoner of war camps in Japan and Japanese-occupied territory.

RG 313: *Naval Operating Forces, 1942–45: 725 maps.*

World War II strategic and operational maps of the Pacific Ocean and its islands by the forces under the Commander in Chief, U.S. Pacific Fleet (CINCPAC), and the Commander in Chief, Pacific Ocean areas (CINCPOA). Included are target and flak maps, and submarine war patrol charts.

RG 319: *Army Staff, 1933–51: 12,766 maps.*

Printed maps and overlays of Japan, plans of towns in Hungary, 1951, and map of France, 1933–34, removed from the records of the Assistant Chief of Staff, G-2 (Intelligence). Manuscript and printed maps relating to World War II military theaters in

Europe, the Mediterranean, former Soviet Union, the Far East, and the Pacific, compiled or annotated by the Graphics Art Branch, Center of Military History, for histories of World War II.

RG 331: *Allied Operational and Occupation Headquarters, World War II, 1942–49: 7,000 maps.*

Strategic and operational maps of Europe prepared or annotated by the Supreme Headquarters Allied Expeditionary Forces (SHAEF); of the Mediterranean region by Allied Forces Headquarters (AFHQ); of Australia, New Guinea, and the Philippines by forces of the South West Pacific Area (SWPA); and of Japan by Supreme Commander Allied Powers (SCAP). Includes maps relating to the Normandy invasion and the Allied advance into Germany.

RG 332: *U.S. Theaters of War, World War II, 1941–48: 968 maps.*

Military maps pertaining to the China, Burma, India Theater (CBI), the European Theater of Operations (ETO), and the Africa—Middle East theaters of operations. Included are maps relating to the Normandy invasion, the Maginot Line, and the Allied advance into Germany.

RG 338: *U.S. Army Commands, 1942–56: 100 maps.*

Maps prepared by U.S. Army Commands in World War II and the Korean War, and of U.S. military commands and occupation forces after World War II. Included are maps of U.S. service commands, the Army Forces Pacific (AFPAC), U.S. Army Europe (USAREUR), U.S. Forces Austria (USAF), U.S. Army Caribbean (USARCARIB), Panama Canal Department (PCD), Far East Command (FEC), Army Forces Far East (AFFE), and the 8th Army in Korea (EUSAK).

RG 342: *U.S. Air Force Commands, Activities, and Organizations, 1947–63: 4,458 maps.*

Published aeronautical charts and special maps issued by the Aeronautical Chart and Information Center, a continuation of the series described in RG 18.

RG 373: *Defense Intelligence Agency, 1935–65: 79,000 maps and more than 4.9 million aerial photographs.*

German-flown mapping and combat aerial photographic prints covering much of Europe, including England and western Russia, as well as areas in the Middle East and North Africa, chiefly at scales ranging from 1:20,000 to 1:50,000, 1940–44 (900,000 prints); mapping and reconnaissance photography flown worldwide by U.S. and Allied air forces during World War II, including coverage of major military actions in Europe and North Africa, such as the Normandy beaches on D-Day, many of the Pacific Island campaigns, and unique sites such as the Auschwitz concentration camp in Poland; Dresden, Nagasaki, and Hiroshima bomb damage, and Peenemunde rocket sites in Germany (800,000 photographs); and Japanese-flown aerial photographic negatives of areas in China, eastern Russia, Indochina, the Netherlands East Indies, and the Philippines, ca. 1939–45 (37,000 photographs). Most of these aerial photographs are accompanied by map indexes and overlays showing aerial coverage of individual photographs. (*Note:* Some of the relevant reconnaissance and strike photography by the U.S. Army Air Force during World War II is held by the Photographic Archives of the National Air and Space Museum [NASM, F19]).

RG 393: *U.S. Army Continental Commands, 1821–1920: 3,000 maps.*

Maps of military departments and divisions; and maps and plans of military posts and reservations. See PI 172 (1973).

RG 394: *U.S. Army Continental Commands, 1920–42: 150 maps.*

Cartographic records include maps of Mexico and its border area by the 8th Corps, and photomaps of military reservations and training areas by the 1st and 4th Armies.

RG 395: *U.S. Army Overseas Operations and Commands, 1898–1942: 2,239 maps.*

Topographic and military operation maps of Cuba and Puerto Rico prepared during the Spanish-American War, 1898; of the Philippines during the Philippine Pacification, 1901; of the defenses of Peking and the siege of Pei-Tang during the China Relief Expedition, 1900–1901; and of northern Mexico during Gen. John J. Pershing's Punitive Expedition, 1916. Also a detailed set of 316 manuscript route maps of the Philippines compiled by Spanish troops, 1870–92; reconnaissance and topographic maps of Panama and the Canal Zone, 1916–42; and miscellaneous military maps of the Russo-Japanese War, French forces in Indochina, 1939, Thailand (Siam), and Guam.

RG 407: *Adjutant Generals Office, 1917–45: 2,000 maps.*

Topographic, strategic, tactical, and situation manuscript and annotated maps prepared by U.S. Army and Navy units, 1937–45, relating to World War II military theaters in Europe, the Mediterranean, and the Pacific.

RG 456: *Defense Mapping Agency, 1972–84: 24,000 maps.*

A record set of published topographic map and nautical chart series issued by DMA (see entry D1).

**RG 457**: *National Security Agency/Central Security Service, 1941–45: 3,600 maps.*
Outline charts showing submarine activities and antisubmarine precautions taken during World War II.

## DONATED MATERIALS

National Archives Gift Collection, 1822–1947: 321 maps. Civil War maps of Virginia, Maryland, and Pennsylvania from the Papers of Colonel W. H. Paine, 1861–65; manuscript maps showing troop positions of the 29th Division in Europe during World War I from the papers of Lt. Col. George Stewart Jr.; maps relating to World War II from the papers of M. Henri Michel, Col. Alan P. Sullivan, Col. Kelvin Hunter, and Maj. J. J. Gussak; maps of the Forbes Purchase and the town of St. Marks, Florida, from the papers of J. Edwin White; maps relating to the Northeastern Boundary Treaty between Canada and the United States in 1842 from the papers of Mrs. Paul H. Quigg.

4. Access to the holdings is provided through general guides, inventories (INV), preliminary inventories (PI), unpublished preliminary inventories (NC, NM), and microfilm publications. The basic printed research aid to the general holdings is the *Guide to the National Archives of the United States* (1974), which should be available in most large libraries. A loose leaf *Guide* (1977) is available in the research rooms.

Finding-aids for cartographic materials consist of lists, catalogs, and special indexes maintained by the branch. Most of these exist only in typescript form in the research room; others have been published and are available to users free or at a minimal charge. Photocopies of out-of-print items not protected by copyright may be purchased for a small fee. Although somewhat dated, the best printed description of cartographic holdings in the branch is the *Guide to Cartographic Records in the National Archives* (Washington, D.C.: Government Printing Office, 1971), compiled by Charlotte M. Ashby et al. It serves as a general introduction to cartographic materials acquired prior to July 1, 1966.

See also *Manuscript Charts in the National Archives,* compiled by William J. Heynen for the U.S. Hydrographic Office (Washington, D.C., 1978); *A Guide to Civil War Maps in the National Archives* (Washington, D.C., 1986); and *World War II Records in the Cartographic and Architectural Branch of the National Archives, Reference Information Paper 79,* by Daryl Bottoms (Washington, D.C., 1992).

5. Index Terms: Diplomacy and Negotiations; Intelligence; Military History; Military Science—Engi-neering, Logistics, and Support; Military Science—Strategy and Tactics

See also entries B11, E11, F20, F21, and G10

---

## D7 National Geographic Society (NGS)—Library—Map Collection

1.a. 1146 16th Street, NW
Washington, D.C. 20036
(202) 775-6175
Fax: (202) 429-5731

b. 8:30 A.M.–5:00 P.M. Monday–Friday

c. Open to the public by appointment.

d. Maps published by the society are available at the Explorers Hall sales desk (202/857-7589), located at 17th and M Streets, NW, Washington, D.C.

e. Lynn Kumaraswary, Supervisor
(202) 775-6173

2. The collection includes approximately 135,000 map sheets and 1,000 atlases, mostly of recent origin. The collection has worldwide scope, including political, administrative, physical, and thematic maps; road and street maps; satellite imagery; nautical and aeronautical charts; plastic raised-relief models; pilot guides and sailing directions; gazetteers; and a large variety of atlases. Also included are copies of all *National Geographic Magazine* supplement maps. From the viewpoint of this Guide the relevant cartographic materials fall under the rubrics of economic development, environment, and military planning and strategy.

3. The Library Map Collection contains a wide variety of published U.S. and foreign general reference maps, thematic maps, road maps, and city plans (1,560 titles). It is also a depository library for the U.S. Geological Survey (USGS) (K21) and the Defense Mapping Agency's (D1) Hydrographic/Topographic Center (DMAH/TC). It maintains the most recent published sets of USGS topographic quadrangle maps (1:24,000, 1:62,500), intermediate-scale topographic series (1:100,000), state maps, and maps of the moon and planets; DMAH/TC nautical and aeronautical charts, and some topographic sets; and Canadian topographic maps. The NGS Library also has an extensive collection of plastic raised-relief maps of the United States (85 sheets) prepared by the Army Map Service and the Hubbard Scientific Company at a scale of 1:250,000.

The earliest map is Giuseppe Rosaccio's *Universale Descrittione di Tutto il Mondo* (Venice 1597, revised 1647), a large wall map on display in the Map Reading Room. Most of the maps, however, date from about 1900.

For a geographic distribution of single-sheet general reference and thematic maps, see the regional Scholars' Guides to Washington, D.C., listed in the Bibliography of this volume.

There are two atlas collections. The general atlas collection consists of some 800 recent geographical atlases (individual countries, states, provinces, cities), historical atlases, and thematic atlases (roads, oceanography, population, economic, climatic, physical). A smaller collection of some 50 atlases published before 1900 is maintained in the Rare Book Room.

4. The on-line catalog in the library's map collection provides access to the single-sheet map collection by geographic area and then subject. There is also access to city plans (alphabetical by name of city), historical maps (geographic area), and atlases (author, area, subject, title). The atlas collection is arranged by the Library of Congress classification. The on-line catalog for the book collection (including rare atlases) is located in the Reference Reading Room.

The NGS Library issues subject guides to its services and resources under the title *Research Guides*. Among the guides in this series are "Atlases," "How to Find Maps," "Electronic Maps," and "The Map Collection." A published Visitors Guide to the National Geographic Society Library briefly describes the library.

5. Index Terms: Development Issues; Environmental Issues, Global; Military Science—Strategy and Tactics

---

**D8** National Museum of American History (NMAH) (Smithsonian Institution)—Division of Armed Forces History—Map Collection

---

1.a. 14th Street and Constitution Avenue, N.W.,
    Room 4013
    Washington, D.C. 20560
    (202) 357-2700

b. Generally 10:00 A.M.–5:00 P.M., but hours vary, Monday–Friday

c. Collections are open to serious researchers by appointment only. Collection curators must be contacted well in advance to ensure that the desired research materials are available. Because of security considerations, scholars are required to register at one of the information desks (located at both entrances of the museum); they are then escorted to the appropriate division.

d. Photocopiers are available in most of the collection areas. Interlibrary loans are generally limited to educational institutions for exhibit purposes and must be arranged through the NMAH Office of the Registrar.

e. Harold D. Langley, Curator, U.S. Naval, Marine Corps, and Coast Guard History (202) 357-2249

Donald E. Kloster, Curator, U.S. Army Dress, Insignia, Heraldry, and Graphics (202) 357-1884

2. The Armed Forces History Division contains materials that document the activities of the U.S. Army, Navy, Marine Corps, and Coast Guard. Approximately 1,500 maps and charts, dating from 1777 to the 1970s, are maintained by the division. Within the scope of this Guide the relevant cartographic materials fall under the rubrics of military history, planning, and strategy.

3. The following collections are pertinent to international security studies:

SHAEF War Room Map Collection. Contains some of the maps (some original, some reproduced at a later date) that were in the War Room of the Supreme Headquarters Allied Expeditionary Force (SHAEF) in the École Professionelle, Reims, France, on May 17, 1945. Also, a list of the maps and photographs of the War Room on that date showing the various maps as they were located on the walls.

Pershing Collection. Contains a map of northwestern Europe that was used by Gen. John J. Pershing in the War Room, Allied Headquarters, showing the German and Allied battle lines, July 15—November 11, 1918 (only 6 of these maps were printed). Also, photographs of the Map Room.

Photographic Collection of Relief Models. Set of original color photographs of relief models marked to show American, British, German, and Japanese troop concentrations during military operations in Italy, 1943, and Okinawa, 1945. Some are captioned.

Military History Map Collection. An unarranged collection of approximately 1,400 military maps loosely organized chronologically, with some duplication, 1777–1970s. Significant early maps include a manuscript copy of Tadeusz A. Kosciuszko's situation map of the Saratoga Campaign, 1777, copied from the original in Cracow, ca. 1894; an engraved set of French maps concerning the American Revolution, published in 1807; an engraved map showing the retreat of the French Army from Moscow; a manuscript map of the Battle of South Mountain compiled by the U.S. Army Bureau of Topographical Engineers, September 14, 1862; a wall map of Cuba published by the Adjutant General's Office, Military Information Division, 1897; and two photoprocessed maps of military operations in the vicinity of Manila, compiled by the U.S. Army Signal Corps, 1898.

World War I maps include a set of printed and photoprocessed topographic and intelligence maps with accompanying general or field orders bound by the Historical Section of the General Staff, 2d Division (68 maps); bound order of battle and intelligence maps concerning the 1st Army (ca. 240 maps); a series of printed barrage charts, artillery fire maps, and maps showing deployment of American and German artillery (39 maps); a captured German situation map concerning the St. Mihiel offensive, September 12, 1918; a series of printed maps annotated daily in the Map Room of the 1st Army to show army and divisional boundaries, October–November 1918; and a special series of overprinted maps showing military operations of the Romanian Army during World War I (4 maps).

Significant World War II maps include situation maps prepared by headquarters of the 12th Army Group to accompany G-3 reports, with some reports, August 1944–May 1945 (100 maps); series of 1:250,000 and 1:500,000 U.S. Army Map Service (AMS) and British War Office Geographical Section, General Staff (GSGS) maps, chiefly of Europe with some coverage for Manchuria and Japan, 1942–45 (530 maps); copy of map issued to junior officers for the invasion of Guadalcanal, August 7, 1942; a printed Japanese wall map of the Pacific area; and military maps on cloth of Belgium, Burma, China, Germany, Japan, and Manchuria (16 maps).

Lt. Jonathan W. Sherbourne Collection. Contains a manuscript chart of Annapolis Harbor compiled by Sherbourne, 1818; Spanish manuscript charts of the coasts of South America drawn during the Malaspina Expedition, 1790 (5 charts); and charts of the coasts of Florida and the Carolinas published by Edmund Blunt, 1820–27 (3 charts).

Farragut Collection. Contains a manuscript chart showing the attack on Mobile Bay by Rear Adm. D. G. Farragut, drawn by Robert Weir, 1864.

4.    A card catalog is organized by name of donor and often contains information on date and subject of materials. Not all cartographic materials, however, are listed in the card catalog.

5.    Index Terms: Military History

See also entry c8

---

**D9**   Naval Historical Center (Navy Department)—Operational Archives Branch—Map Collection

---

1.a.  Washington Navy Yard, Building 57
      9th and M Streets, SE
      Washington, D.C. 20374-5060
      (202) 433-3170
      Fax: (202) 433-3172

b.   9:00 A.M.–4:00 P.M. Monday–Friday

c.   Open to serious researchers. It is recommended that researchers call in advance. Some of the post-1955 materials are restricted due to national security classifications. A list of declassified and unclassified records will be furnished on request.

d.   Limited photocopying facilities are available. The branch is unable to reproduce large maps.

e.   Bernard F. Cavalcante, Head

2.    The Operational Archives Branch collects documents relating to the combat and peacetime activities of naval fleet units and to the strategic, policy, and planning programs of naval operational headquarters. Most of the records date from 1939, with heavy emphasis on the World War II era and the Pacific region. The records include a separate collection of some 5,400 maps. There are also related cartographic materials found in documentary series. Within the scope of this Guide, the cartographic materials fall under the rubric of intelligence, naval history, and military logistics.

3.    The map collections, relevant to international security studies, consist of the following series:

Charts of Submarine Sinkings, 1918: 4 maps. Manuscript charts showing the locations and names of ships sunk off the East Coast of the United States by German U-boats.

Daily Situation Charts of Combatant Vessels, 1941–46: 2,600 charts. Plotting charts annotated on a daily basis in the navy's Operations Plotting Room in Washington to show the approximate location of each U.S., allied, and suspected enemy ship and submarine in the Atlantic, October 1941–March 1946 (1,000 charts) and in the Pacific, December 1941–April 1941 (1,600 charts).

Situation Maps of Operations in North Africa, 1942–43: 190 maps. French chart of Casablanca and Fedala, Morocco, annotated to show mine fields, 1944; plotting chart of Atlantic Ocean annotated to show U.S. and Canadian air bases and air routes to Europe and North Africa; and a set of daily situation maps showing military operations in North Africa, November 9, 1942–May 14, 1943.

Detailed Strategic Engineering Study Reports for Italy and Sicily, 1944: 9 volumes. Contains printed topographic maps, aerial photographs, and coastal charts of landing beaches and adjacent areas in Calabria, Campania, Lucania, and Puglia compartimentos in southern Italy and in Sicily prepared by the Intelligence Branch of the U.S. Army's Chief of Engineers (ca. 540 maps).

Maps of the Normandy Invasion and Southern France, 1944: 47 maps. A series of printed and annotated topographic maps and coastal charts of landing beaches and German defenses at Normandy compiled and printed for operation BIGOT, May 20, 1944 (35 maps), and a set of large aerial photographic mosaics, panoramic views, and maps of Utah and Omaha beaches prepared by commander, Task Force 122, for landing boat operations, 1944 (12 items).

Track Charts Pertaining to the Pearl Harbor Attack, December 7, 1941, and the Battle of Midway, June 4–6, 1942: 24 items. Large photoprocessed and printed situation maps. These charts can also be found in the Congressional Hearings, Investigation of the Pearl Harbor Attack.

Strategic Historical Plot Charts, 1941–46: 125 maps. Situation maps of the world or Pacific Ocean area annotated to show the location of U.S. and enemy forces during significant actions from Pearl Harbor through the early occupation of Japan.

Traffic and Decryption Intelligence Charts, 1942: 249 maps. Plotting charts of the Pacific region showing the daily situation of the Japanese Navy as determined by decryption intelligence, January 20–May 1.

Maps of Japanese Naval and Ground Forces in the Pacific, 1942–43: 2 maps. Photoprocessed maps of the Pacific annotated with information copied from a chart prepared by T. Ohmae to show zones of operations of Japanese naval and ground forces.

Maps of U.S. Navy and Air Force Searches in Pacific Region, 1942–45: 13 maps. Colored photographic prints of maps showing air searches.

U.S. Hydrographic Office Charts, 1941–45: 293 charts. Printed nautical charts, chiefly of the Pacific region and the North Sea.

U.S. Hydrographic Office Emergency Nautical Charts, 1943: 27 charts. Emergency printings by the U.S. Hydrographic Office of Australian, Japanese, and German nautical charts of the southwest Pacific.

Maps of Marine Corps Campaigns, 1943: 8 maps. Photoprocessed maps of the Bismarck Archipelago, Bougainville Straits, Guadalcanal, New Britain, Solomon Islands, and Tulagi prepared by M-2 Section, U.S. Marine Corps Headquarters.

Maps of Iwo Jima, 1944: 60 maps. Series of published U.S. Army Map Service topographic quadrangles with aerial photographic maps on the verso (40 maps); printed special air and gunnery target maps at various scales, some measuring 4 x 6 feet (20 maps).

Maps of the Mariana and Marshall Islands, 1943–44: 77 maps. Annotated plotting chart showing the invasion of Guam, June 1944; set of topographic and other maps of Guam, 1944 (20 items); U.S. Marine Corps intelligence study of Marshall Islands, 1943 (24 maps); special air and gunnery target maps of Kwajalein and Saipan (25 maps); and annotated daily situation maps of the Tinian Campaign (8 maps).

Combat Maps of the Caroline Islands, 1944: 56 maps. Printed advanced plotting maps, topographic maps, and special air and gunnery target maps prepared by the 64th U.S. Army Engineer Topographic Battalion for Angaur, Palau, Peleliu, Ulithi, and Yap Islands.

Maps of the Philippine Campaigns, 1944: 36 maps. A manuscript map in Japanese, which accompanied a detailed action report; printed operational maps of the Central Philippines prepared by the U.S. Army, 64th Engineer Topographical Battalion, 1944 (21 maps); and manuscript and photoprocessed charts of the battle of Leyte Gulf showing movements of U.S. and Japanese forces and extent of air searches, October 22–27, 1944 (14 maps).

CINCPAC-CINCPOA Bulletins, 1944: 24 volumes. A set of miscellaneous terrain studies, airfield surveys, air target map bulletins, air information summaries, and target analysis reports with key maps and aerial photographs for the China Coast, Formosa, Kyushu, Leyte, Palau, Tokyo Bay, and other Pacific areas (ca. 500 maps and aerial photographs).

Daily Strategic Plot Charts of Submarines, November 1944–June 1945: 240 items. Plotting charts of the Pacific region annotated in manuscript on a daily basis to show the location of each allied submarine.

Mine Field Charts, 1944–45: 200 maps. Printed charts of Japanese coastal areas and the west Pacific prepared by the U.S. Army, 949th Engineer Aviation Topographic Company showing areas mined by the

U.S. Air Force (43 charts); captured Japanese charts showing the location of Japanese mine fields and underwater obstacles along the south China coast, Manila Bay, and the southwest Pacific, including a mine field laid off the coast by a German auxiliary cruiser (21 maps); and manuscript maps of the Malacca Straits, Sumatra coastal areas, and Aru Bay, Ceylon, showing the location of mine fields planted by Royal Air Force Liberators (7 maps).

Intelligence Reports, Pacific Theater, 1944–45: 2 volumes. Published intelligence studies of the Shang-Hai coastal area prepared by U.S. Naval Group China, 1945 (20 maps), and of the Caroline Islands prepared by the Intelligence Section, U.S. Marine Corps, 1944 (40 maps).

Aerial photographic mosaics and target maps of Okinawa, 1945: ca. 200 maps.

Photo Coverage Report 22, 1946–47: 1 volume. A bound volume of 55 aerial photographic indexes showing the coverage of aerial photographs for the western Pacific region.

Daily Situation Maps of Formosa Straits, 1950: 30 maps. Maps depicting the daily total shipping available along the China Coast, September 4–October.

Daily Situation Maps of the Korean War, 1950–51: 229 maps. Large photographic prints of the map of Korea showing daily troop positions of United Nations and North Korean forces, December 1, 1950–January 24, 1951 (54 maps), daily situation maps of the U.S. Navy WESPAC fleet, September 1, 1950–January 24, 1954 (150 maps), and daily situation maps of the Inchon-Seoul region, September 14–October 10, 1950 (25 maps).

4.   A card index and shelflist provide general access to the map collection and finding-aids are available for most of the record groups. A partial checklist of the unpublished histories has been published under the title *World War II Histories and Historical Reports in the U.S. Naval History Division* (Naval History Division, 1977). General information about the archives is found in *Information for Visitors to the Operational Archives* (1983) and *A History of the Dudley Knox Center for Naval History,* both available on request.

An excellent introduction to naval records in other repositories is *U.S. Naval History Sources in the United States* (U.S. Naval History Division, 1979), compiled by Dean C. Allard, Martha L. Crawley, and Mary W. Edmison. These are available from the Naval Historical Center as long as supplies are available.

5.   Index Terms: Intelligence; Military History—Navy; Military Science—Engineering, Logistics, and Support

See also entries B13, C9, C10, E13, and F23

---

**DIO**   Navy Department Library — Map Collection

---

1.a.  Washington Navy Yard, Building 44
      9th and M Streets, SE
      Washington, D.C. 20374
      (202) 433-4131/2
      Fax: (202) 433-9553

b.   9:00 A.M.–4:00 P.M. Monday–Friday

c.   Open to the public.

d.   Electrostatic copiers are located in the library.

e.   Frances Q. Deel, Director

2.   The Navy Department Library holds a collection of some 1,000 maps and atlases. From the viewpoint of this Guide the relevant cartographic materials fall under the rubric of naval history.

3.   The map collection consists of 28 portfolios of uncataloged manuscript, photoprocessed, and printed maps and charts dating, primarily 1870s–1920s.

These include chiefly British Admiralty charts, French nautical charts (1870s–1980s), Russian nautical charts, and some U.S. hydrographic charts. Some of these charts are annotated, including one of Dover and Calais that has been marked to show enemy submarine tracks and British sound bearings in 1915. A portfolio labeled "Miscellaneous" includes a manuscript U.S. Coast Survey map of Fort Jackson showing bombardment by U.S. Navy gunboats in 1862; manuscript and photoprocessed charts showing the tracks of British cruiser operations in the Pacific and in the vicinity of the Falkland Islands, 1914; and manuscript charts and maps of Cuba prepared for a publication called "Quasi War with France." Another portfolio, "Europe and World War I," contains a manuscript chart showing the war voyages of the USS *Siboney* between the United States and France, April–November 1918; a large manuscript map of the defenses of Heligoland prepared by the Intelligence Section, U.S. Navy Headquarters, London, 1918; maps showing merchant steamship traffic and tonnage in the Mediterranean, 1918; and British Admiralty Coastal Air Charts showing prominent landmarks along the German coast, 1910.

The library also has some 40 reference atlases, including the *English Pilot* (London, 1775), Robert Sayer's *American Military Pocket Atlas* (London, 1776), Rigobert Bonne's world atlas (1783), and the Naval History Division's own facsimile atlas, *The American Revolution 1775–1783: An Atlas of Eighteenth-Century Maps and Charts—Theatres of Operations* (1972). The latter was compiled by W. Bart Greenwood, former director of the Navy Department Library. It consists of a portfolio of 20 maps and charts and an accompanying volume (86 pp.) with an essay by Louis DeVorsey Jr. on surveying and mapping at the time of the American Revolution, a list of the maps, and an index of some 10,000 names of places, features, Indian tribes, and landholders keyed to the maps.

4. The map collection is uncataloged.

5. Index Terms: Military History—Navy

See also entry A36

---

## DII  Organization of American States (OAS)—Columbus Memorial Library—Map Collection

1.a. Constitution Avenue and 19th Street, NW
Washington, D.C. 20006
(202) 458-6037
Fax: (202) 458-3914

b. 9:30 A.M.–4:30 P.M. Monday–Friday

c. Open to the public. Interlibrary loan service is available.

d. Photocopying service is available.

e. Virginia A. Newton, Director

2. The Columbus Memorial Library maintains a map collection of 2,500 maps. Within the scope of this Guide, the collection is relevant for the study of development issues and international politics. The library's book and photograph collections are described in entries A38 and F24, respectively. For the archival and audio holdings of the OAS Records Management Center see entries B14 and E14.

3. The map collection provides the following number of maps for Latin American countries: Argentina (130), Bolivia (56), Brazil (250), Central America (100), Chile (200), Colombia (450), Costa

Rica (50), Cuba (100), Dominican Republic (75), Ecuador (50), El Salvador (50), Guatemala (50), Guyana (50), Haiti (50), Honduras (50), Mexico (300), Nicaragua (75), Panama (100), Paraguay (50), Peru (200), South America (150), Uruguay (75), Venezuela (100), and the West Indies (25). Most of the maps date from 1880 to 1946. The collection includes cadastral maps, city plans, thematic maps, and topographic maps. It is particularly rich in large wall maps and railroad maps. Most of the maps are printed in either Spanish or Portuguese; there are also a few manuscript maps. Particularly noteworthy are a manuscript map in Spanish showing proposed and constructed railroad lines in Bolivia; a large bound volume of agricultural maps of Brazil prepared by the National Society of Agriculture (Rio de Janeiro, 1910); a set of 18 medium-scale maps (1:250,000) of Central America issued by the Geographic Branch, Military Intelligence Division, U.S. Army General Staff, 1933; a manuscript map of Cuba compiled for a Pan-American Union exhibit showing agricultural production, 1943; a Spanish manuscript map displaying the 1824, 1882, and 1900 boundary lines between Guatemala and Mexico, copied by Jorge Contreras, 1900; and a manuscript map of the province of Bocas del Toro, Panama, showing the itinerary of the visit of Belisario Porras, Minister of the Republic of Panama and Costa Rica, 1909.

The general collection of the library (A38) includes a small number of titles relating to cartography (120), geodesy (60), geographic positions (35), and surveying (50). Several thousand maps and plans of towns and cities, international boundaries, and regions are found in works on city and town planning, boundary disputes, and description and travel.

The collections of the Inter-American Specialized Organizations include documentation on the Pan-American Institute of Geography and History (PAIGH), which was established in Mexico City in 1928 to coordinate and promote cartographic, geographic, and historic studies in the Americas (740 titles).

The library's collection of 9,700 information and technical reports issued by the OAS Secretariat includes regional development reports that are often accompanied by maps. A finding-aid to current reports is issued annually under the title *Catalog of OAS Technical Reports and Documents.*

The Library and Records Management Center Archives Collection (B14) includes some boundary maps and surveys relating to border disputes between member nations.

4. The general and special collections are accessed by a public authority/author and subject card catalog. A good introduction to the library is *Guide to the Columbus Memorial Library* (1988), available on request. Also useful is Thomas L. Welch's "Organization of American States and Its Documentation Dissemination," *Revista Interamericana de Bibliografía,* vol. 32 (1982), pp. 200–206.

5. Index Terms: Development Issues; International Politics

See also entries A38, B14, E14, F24, and L13

---

## DI2 University of Maryland—McKeldin Library—Government Documents/Maps Room

---

1.a. McKeldin Library, Second Floor
College Park, Md. 20742-7011
(301) 405-9165

b. 8:00 A.M.–11:00 P.M. Monday–Thursday
8:00 A.M.–6:00 P.M. Friday
10:00 A.M.–6:00 P.M. Saturday
Noon—11:00 P.M. Sunday

c. Open to the public by appointment.

d. Photocopying services are available.

e. F. Joseph McHugh, Acting Head

2. The map collection numbers approximately 100,000 sheets. It consists chiefly of U.S. government depository maps, but also includes several other collections. Within the scope of this Guide the relevant cartographic material falls under the rubrics of military history and intelligence. The book holdings of the University of Maryland at College Park are discussed in entry A47; the National Public Broadcasting Archives in entries E16 and F31.

3. The following collections are germane to peace and international security studies:

UNESCO Collection. Consists chiefly of large geological, soil, and vegetation maps of the world or Europe issued by UNESCO, 1970s–1980s (115 items).

U.S. Depository Maps Collection. This collection consists of map series deposited by federal mapmaking agencies. It includes Army Map Service and the Defense Mapping Agency topographic maps, ca. 1941–present (91 drawers); Hydrographic Office nautical charts, chiefly of Japan during World War II; Air Force Aeronautical Chart and Information Center aeronautical charts, 1940s–1950s (10 drawers); Coast and Geodetic Survey nautical charts, 1904–70 (8 drawers); and Central Intelligence Agency large-scale plans of foreign regions and cities, including Beijing, Guangzhou, Leningrad, Moscow, and Shanghai, 1970s–1980s (3 drawers).

U.S. Office of Strategic Services (OSS) Collection. This unique collection consists of a series of 1,300 printed provisional map editions prepared by the OSS Branch of Research and Analysis and printed by the OSS Reproduction Division during World War II. Some of the maps were compiled by the Board of Economic Warfare, United Nations Division, and the Foreign Economic Administration, Enemy Branch. The series include a wide variety of general and thematic maps covering countries in which hostilities were taking place or that contained strategic resources. Examples of the types of maps that may be found include: population density map of Sardinia (1942), location map of minor nonferrous metal produced in South America (1942), map depicting original vegetation formation in Southern Nigeria (1943), series of maps of Brittany showing terrain, vegetation, roads, beaches, and military objectives (1943), map showing distribution of Japanese in Peru in 1940 (1943), map of the net of precision leveling of Eastern Germany measured and compiled by the trigonometrical division of the Reichsamt für Landesaufnahme in 1941 (1945), map of caves and cave regions of "Greater Germany," (1945), and a series of five maps on Java and Madoera showing major regions of estate products (rubber, cinchona, sugar, tea, coffee, tobacco), population distribution, ethnic groups, Christian missions, elementary education, major native food crops, and telecommunications (1945).

4. The maps are not cataloged, but as they are generally arranged by geographic area, access is not difficult. Some drawers are labeled by source, such as CIA.

5. Index Terms: Intelligence: Military History

See also entries A47, E16, F31, and J13

# E

## Collections of Sound Recordings

### Introductory Note

The most extensive collections of sound recordings concerning international political, military, and economic affairs are located in the Motion Picture, Sound, and Video Branch of the National Archives and Records Administration (E11) and in the Motion Picture, Broadcasting, and Recorded Sound Division of the Library of Congress (E8). Radio broadcasts dealing with the issues of international relations are preserved in Broadcast Pioneers Library (E4), National Public Radio's Information Services and Program Archive (E12), and the University of Maryland's National Public Broadcasting Archives (E16). Air Force History Office (E1), Army Corps of Engineers—Office of History (E3), Coast Guard—Historian's Office (E5), Marine Corps Historical Center (E9), and Naval Historical Center—Operational Archives Branch (E13) offer oral history collections for collective and national security studies. Georgetown University—Lauinger Library—Special Collections (E6) and Senate Historical Office—Oral History Program (E15) do the same for diplomatic affairs.

For more detail on collections of sound recordings, the reader will find useful the *Scholars' Guide to Washington, D.C., for Audio Resources* (1985) by James R. Heintze, as well as the *Scholars' Guide to Washington, D.C., Media Collections* (1994) by Bonnie G. Rowan and Cynthia J. Wood. This section updates the relevant information in these Guides.

## EI  Air Force History Office (Air Force Department) — Oral History Program

1.a.  170 Luke Avenue, Suite 400
Bolling Air Force Base
Washington, D.C. 20332-5113
(202) 767-5764
Fax: (202) 404-7915

b.  9:00 A.M.–5:00 P.M. Monday–Friday

c.  Open to the public. Visitors must have prior visitation clearance, which can be arranged by phone.

d.  Richard P. Hallion, Air Force Historian
William C. Heimdahl, Chief, Historical Services Division

2.  The Office of Air Force History maintains an extensive Oral History Program begun during the 1950s, with recordings and transcripts housed in the Air Force Historical Research Agency, Maxwell Air Force Base, Ala. 36112-6678). The collection, which is relevant to the issues of international military and political relations, and military history, includes some 1,300 interviews. Copies of a number of transcripts are held in Washington, D.C. Although many of the interviews have been conducted by the Office of Air Force History, many have been acquired from numerous other sources.

3.  The range of topics represented is broad and encompasses air force activity dating to the early 1920s. Most of them are pertinent to the study of military history, planning, and strategy. All the campaigns are well represented, as are interviews with individuals responsible for the development of air force weapons systems. The collection includes interviews with former Secretaries of the Air Force, Chiefs of Staff, Major Command Commanders and Commanders in Chief, and Chief Master Sergeants. Examples of interviewees include Gen. Creighton Abrams, Brig. Gen. Cleo M. Bishop, Maj. Gen. Alden R. Crawford, Gen. Dwight D. Eisenhower, Gen. William J. Evans, Gen. Bruce Holloway, Gen. Daniel "Chappie" James, Gen. George C. Kenney, Gen. Curtis LeMay, Gen. Earle E. Partridge, Gen. Horace M. Wade, and Maj. Roland F. Fluck.

Illustrative examples of topics from the European war theaters include a discussion by Maj. Gen. Edward P. Curtis of experiences in France during World War I. Lt. Col. William R. Dunn discusses experiences in World War II: Dunkirk, joining the Royal Air Force in 1940, involvement in the Battle of Britain, and relationships with British colleagues. Maj. Gen. Frederick Anderson discusses the Combined Bomber Offensive (CBO) provision for Royal Air Force participation; British desire to control U.S. air units; Operation CLARION, a joint U.S.-British venture; and many problems that arose between British and U.S. forces due to differences in officer rank. Lt. Gen. Ira C. Eaker discusses operations of the 8th Air Force, stationed in England 1942–45; his account covers a confrontation with Winston Churchill regarding the daylight bombing of Casablanca. An interview with General Jacob Devers is designed to explore military policy in World War II and actions taken in the south of France. Pres. Dwight D. Eisenhower analyzes the use of aerial reconnaissance in the Normandy campaign. Brigadier General Bishop discusses experiences as a prisoner of war in Italy, November 1944–June 1945.

Some interviews include in their coverage the history of air force operations in the Middle East and North Africa, for example, Col. Paul A. Rockwell discusses his experiences as an observer and gunner in the Rif war in Morocco as a member of Sultan's Guard Squadron in 1925. Maj. Gen. Elmer E. Adler reviews his career as senior officer of the North African Mission in World War II, supply and ferrying routes in North Africa, impressions of Field Marshal Montgomery and Field Marshal Rommel, and political aspects of victory of El Alamein. Gen. Leon W. Johnson discusses his World War II experiences with the 8th Air Force, including its support of the North African campaign. Maj. Gen. Lee V. Gossick tells of his North African fighter pilot operations in World War II. Maj. Gen. Albert T. Wilson discusses his experiences as a member of the U.S. Military Mission to North Africa, 1941–42. Gen. James H. Doolittle recounts the story of French military resistance to Allied landings, the North African campaign, and North African Army Air Force operations generally. Gen. Laurence S. Kuter discusses French pilots in North Africa. Lt. Gen. Fred M. Dean reviews the effectiveness of the German air power in North Africa. Maj. Gen. Edward Curtis's career review includes service as assistant executive officer to Gen. Carl A. Spaatz in North Africa. Maj. Gen. John B. Cary and Maj. Gen. John D. Stevenson describe the chief lessons of the Lebanon Crisis of 1958 for the air force.

The collection is also valuable to researchers who seek information not necessarily related to the air force. For example, there are interviews with individuals dealing more generally with military and foreign policy affairs who were associated with presidential administrations, from those of Franklin D. Roosevelt to the present. There are a number of oral history materials representing the other branches of the armed forces, as well as materials dealing with civilians, such as Dean Rusk and Stuart Symington, and congressional matters, and bearing on military and foreign affairs.

4.a. On-site listening equipment is available.

b. Reservations are required.

c. Fees are not charged for listening to recordings.

d. Duplicating permission may be required from the Air Force Historical Research Agency, Maxwell Air Force Airbase, Ala. (205/953-2417).

5. Published guides include Albert F. Simpson Historical Research Center, *U.S. Air Force Oral History Catalog* (Washington, D.C.: Office of Air Force History, Headquarters, USAF, 1982).

6. Index Terms: Defense Policy, National—History; Military History—Air Force; Military Science

*Note:* Recordings in the records of the U.S. Air Force commands, activities, and organizations, 1950–81, are held in the National Archives and Records Administration (E11, RG 342).

See also entries B1 and F2

---

**E2** **American Federation of Labor and Congress of Industrial Organizations (AFL-CIO)—George Meany Memorial Archives (GMMA)—Sound Recording Collection**

---

1.a. 10000 New Hampshire Avenue
Silver Spring, Md. 20903
(301) 431-5451
Fax: (301) 431-0385

b. 9:00 A.M.–4:30 P.M. Monday–Friday

c. Open to the public by appointment.

d. Lynda DeLoach, Archivist

2. The George Meany Memorial Archives serves as the official archives for the American Federation of Labor and Congress of Industrial Organizations and their contents have a direct bearing on the area of conflict resolution and management not only in the domestic, but also the international framework, especially with respect to Latin America, Africa, and Asia. The collection includes some 5,000 audio tapes. GMMA's archival, and film and photograph collections are covered respectively in entries B2, and F3; AFL-CIO's library in A2.

3. The audio tapes document AFL-CIO conventions and radio shows produced by the AFL-CIO or those in which labor representatives participated. There is a considerable coverage of international political and labor issues. Interviews with U.S. and international labor leaders are part of the center's subscription audio series. (See subscription information under point 4.d.) Older interviews are stored in the archives. There is also a small collection of phonograph albums that document convention proceedings, John F. Kennedy's last words to labor, and a few radio shows related to labor, again with significant international coverage.

Other records dealing with international affairs will be opened in the future, such as those of the internationally oriented organizations sponsored by the AFL-CIO's Department of International Affairs (see entry N7): African-American Labor Center (AALC), American Institute for Free Labor Development (AIFLD), Asian-American Free Labor Institute (AAFLI), and Free Trade Union Institute (FTUI).

4.a. Listening equipment is available.

b. Appointments are required.

c. Fees are charged for photocopies, and user fees for commercial use.

d. Duplicating services are available. The patron is responsible for obtaining appropriate permission, if copyright or other restrictions apply. Current interviews with U.S. and international labor leaders are a subscription series produced by the George Meany Center for Labor Studies and distributed to labor organizations.

5. A brochure on the archives' holdings is available free of charge on request.

6. Index Terms: Conflict Management and Resolution—Unofficial and Nongovernmental Approaches; International Organizations—Labor

See also entries A2, B2, F3, and N7

**American University—Bender Library** See entry A4

---

**E3** **Army Corps of Engineers (Army Department)—Office of History—Oral History Collection**

---

1.a. Kingman Building
7701 Telegraph Road
Alexandria, Va. 22315-3865
(703) 355-2543
Fax: (703) 355-8172

b. 8:00 A.M.–4:00 P.M. Monday–Friday.

c. Individuals who want to use the collection should first contact the archivist, Martin K. Gordon (703/355-3559).

d. Paul K. Walker, Chief
William C. Baldwin, Historian/Curator

2. The collection contains materials relevant to the study of military history, as well as the study of economic development and humanitarian relief work. It consists of approximately 200 career interviews of senior engineer officers and civilians and several hundred topical interviews on a wide variety of subjects within the competence of the Corps of Engineers.

3. The interviewees are retired corps officers, civilian employees, and officers' wives, as well as a limited number of active duty officers and civilians. They include former Chiefs of Engineer, officers who served as corps district and division commanders and managers of major corps construction projects, and civilian heads of major headquarters elements. Examples of distinguished interviewees include Gen. Bruce C. Clarke, Lt. Gen. Emerson C. Itschner, Lt. Gen. Arthur G. Trudeau, Lt. Gen. Walter K. Wilson Jr., Maj. Gen. Hugh J. Casey, Maj. Gen. Claude H. Chorpening, Maj. Gen. Roscoe C. Crawford, Maj. Gen. Kenner F. Hertford, Maj. Gen. Charles G. Holle, Maj. Gen. Charles I. McGinnis, Maj. Gen. William E. Potter, Brig. Gen. Miles M. Dawson, Brig. Gen. Roy T. Dodge, Brig. Gen. William M. Glasgow Jr., Brig. Gen. William C. Hall, Brig. Gen. Herbert D. Vogel, Brig. Gen. Orville T. Walsh, Brig. Gen. William W. Wanamaker, and Brig. Gen. Theron D. Weaver.

Topics covered include combat engineering and military construction for all 20th-century wars; overseas military construction; civil works construction and disaster relief; atomic bomb, missile, and space construction programs; the role of the Corps of Engineers in the Panama Canal; and West Point education.

4.a. Contact the Historical Division for information on the availability of sound recording equipment. In most cases, researchers will be provided with transcripts.

b. Prior appointment is recommended.

c. No fees are charged.

d. Duplicating facility is available.

5. A catalog of oral history materials is under preparation. In addition to *Engineer Memoirs: Lieu-*

*tenant General Frederick J. Clarke; Engineer Memoirs: Major General William E. Potter;* and *Engineer Profiles: The District Engineer, Colonel William W. Badger,* several more interviews will be published as part of this series.

6. Index Terms: Arms Production and Acquisition; Environmental Issues, Global; Humanitarian Issues; Military History—Army; Military Science—Engineering, Logistics, and Support

See also entry B4

## E4   Broadcast Pioneers Library (BPL)

1.a. Hornbake Library, University of Maryland
College Park, Md. 20742
(301) 405-9160

b. 10:00 A.M.–6:00 P.M. Monday–Friday

c. The library is open to researchers, writers, students, official organizations, and the public, as well as the broadcasting industry. Appointments are necessary. Those who use the library are encouraged to become members.

d. Mike Mashon, Curator

2. The Broadcast Pioneers Library, established in 1971, holds materials relevant to international affairs and defense policy. Created to preserve and make accessible information about the history of radio broadcasting, the library maintains a core collection of archival material (papers and photographs, as well as sound and visual recordings) relating to radio and, to a lesser extent, television. It also serves as a referral center, directing scholars to broadcast history materials in other libraries.

3. Two of the collections of sound recordings are particularly germane to the scope of this Guide. (1) There are 900 oral histories of broadcast pioneers, primarily those who worked in early radio. Included are commentators on foreign political and military affairs, such as Lowell Thomas. Some of the recordings are available in transcripts. (2) The unique Westinghouse Broadcasting Company Collection (1945–81: 2,300 radio news tapes from the Washington Bureau) contains materials on the political and military aspects of the Cold War era.

4.a. On-site listening equipment available.

b. Reservations are required.

c. No fees for on-site use of tapes.

d. Modest amount of duplication for scholars engaged in specific research, unless special restrictions apply.

5.  The Library has a good collection of catalogs, reference books, and a referral file.

6.  Index Terms: Defense Policy, National—History; Foreign Policy

---

### E5  Coast Guard (Transportation Department)—Historian's Office—Oral History

1.a.  2100 Second Street, SW
Washington, D.C. 20593-0001
(202) 267-2596
Fax: (202) 267-4307

b.  7:00 A.M.–5:30 P.M. Monday–Friday

c.  Open to the public

d.  Robert Browning, Chief Historian

2.  The collection contains oral histories (some with transcripts) and other sound recordings on both audio tapes and video cassettes. The users of this Guide will find material relevant to naval science and military history, as well as humanitarian issues.

3.  Oral histories, covering early biography and career experiences of coast guard vice admirals (3), rear admirals (19), and captains (4), recorded between 1950 and 1981, are available in 113 volumes of transcripts. Interviews (131, on 72 video cassettes) with enlisted men, primarily noncommissioned officers, cover their experiences since the beginning of World War II. There are also some 150 audio tapes recording speeches, lectures, and interviews of Coast Guard admirals.

4.a.  Listening equipment is available.

b.  Appointments are recommended.

c–d.  No fees are charged for duplication, if the patron supplies his own tape or cassette.

5.  For information about the collection contact the historian (202/267-2596). The *Coast Guard Public Affairs Product Guide*, which lists a small selection of videos, is available from the public affairs staff (202/267-1587). A bibliography of coast guard history is available by mail.

6.  Index Terms: Humanitarian Issues; Military History—Coast Guard

See also entry F7

---

### E6  Georgetown University—Lauinger Library—Special Collections—Oral History

1.a.  37th and O Streets, NW
Washington, D.C. 20057-1006
(202) 687-7444

b.  9:00 A.M.–5:00 P.M. Monday–Friday

c.  Open to the public, but the collection does not circulate.

d.  George M. Barringer, Special Collections Librarian

2.  Among other archival materials, the Special Collections Department holds significant collections of sound recordings in the fields of diplomacy and foreign affairs; European and American alliances; national and collective security; peace issues, and war and violence.

3.  The following collections are relevant to peace and international security studies:
Foreign Affairs Oral History Program, cosponsored with Association for Diplomatic Studies. The collection contains almost 1,000 biographical and issues-related interviews with retired senior diplomatic officers. There are interviews by the U.S. Information Agency Alumni Association and the Foreign Service Family History Project, as well as interviews with almost all living women ambassadors. The director of the program is Charles Stuart Kennedy (202/687-4104).
Georgetown University Collection, 1949–72. It holds 1,000 audio recordings of special events at Georgetown, including speeches by such notables as Abba Eban, Eunice Shriver, McGeorge Bundy; and 1,500 audio tapes from "GTU Radio Forum" the university's public affairs radio show. Participants included Richard Nixon, John Kenneth Galbraith, and Eugene J. McCarthy.
Grenada Documents Collection, 1983. Includes photographs and oral history interviews compiled by author Gregory Sandford while writing a book about the American intervention (5 lin. ft.).
Lawrence Suid Collection, 1945–late 1970s. Several hundred taped and transcribed interviews with

producers, writers, directors, and military liaison personnel focusing on the film industry's relations with the military.

Margaret Bearden Papers, 1944–83. An extensive file of tape recordings of lectures concerning various aspects of the Civil War.

McCarthy Historical Project Archive, 1967–70. This is one of the largest record collections of any U.S. political primary campaign during which the issues of peace in Vietnam were particularly conspicuous. Among other resources, it includes a wealth of written and oral history narratives by many participants in the campaign (445 lin. ft.).

4.a. Audiovisual equipment is available.

b. Reservations should be made by phone or letter.

c. Fees are not charged for listening.

d. Materials may be copied; permission must be requested.

5. The collections in this division are described in a richly illustrated catalog *Special Collections at Georgetown* (1989).

6. Index Terms: Defense Policy, National—History; Diplomacy and Negotiations; Military History; Pacifism and Peace Movements

See also entries A20, B6, and F10

and culture of people of African descent. The Oral History Department holds some materials concerning ethnic and religious conflicts, human rights, and war and violence.

3. The following collections contain material relevant to the scope of this Guide:

Lou LuTour Collection, 1963–67. Radio interviews with owners and publishers of black newspapers, some bearing on international relations.

Pacifica Radio Collection, primarily 1960s. Approximately 120 tapes include material concerning human rights in Africa.

Within a separate collection of over 800 oral histories and transcripts there are 35 interviews concerning African-American participation in U.S. military history worldwide.

4.a. Audio equipment is available.

b. Reservations are required.

c. No fees for on-site use of tapes.

d. Modest amount of duplication of transcripts is allowed.

5. A detailed finding-aid is available.

6. Index Terms: Ethnic and Religious Conflict; Human Rights; Military History

See also entries A22 and B7

---

## E7 Howard University—Moorland-Spingarn Research Center—Oral History Department

1.a. Founders Library Building, Room G-2
500 Howard Place, NW
Washington, D.C. 20059
(202) 806-7479 or 806-7480
Fax: (202) 806-6405

b. 9:00 A.M.–1:00 P.M., 2:00–4:30 P.M. Monday–Friday

c. Open to all qualified researchers by appointment. There are restrictions on the use of some transcripts and tapes.

d. Thomas C. Battle, Director
Joellen Elbashir, Curator, Manuscript Division

2. The Moorland-Spingarn Research Center is one of the world's largest and most comprehensive repositories for the documentation of the history

---

## E8 Library of Congress (LC)—Motion Picture, Broadcasting, and Recorded Sound Division—Recorded Sound Reference Center

1.a. James Madison Building, Room 113
Independence Avenue, SE
(between 1st and 2d Streets)
Washington, D.C. 20540-4805
(202) 707-7833

b. 8:30 A.M.–5:00 P.M. Monday–Friday

c. Reference materials are open to the public. Listening facilities are provided for those doing research of a specific nature leading to a publicly available work such as a publication, thesis, radio/film/television production, or public performance.

d. Samuel Brylawski, Reference Librarian
Edwin Matthias, Reference Librarian

2. The collection dates from the 1890s and includes almost 3 million sound recordings. Approximately 1 million are commercial recordings, mostly

music. Three quarters of the collection was recorded in the U.S. and was acquired primarily through gifts, purchases, and transfers from other government agencies. From the viewpoint of international security and peace studies the relevant material falls mainly under the rubrics of diplomacy and foreign affairs, nongovernmental conflict resolution, human rights, humanitarian issues, international organizations, military history, political systems, terrorism, and war and violence.

3. Special collections include music, spoken word recordings, and radio broadcasts. Because of the scope of this Guide this entry focuses on radio broadcasts and other relevant collections of spoken word recordings.

## RADIO BROADCASTS

A. L. Alexander Collection, 1939–53: 41 programs. A. L. Alexander's radio (and later television) programs feature some type of dispute resolution. His programs probably were the first to solve legal problems and offer legal advice to the general public through broadcasting. His "Mediation Board" program settled personal disputes on the air with mediation by a panel of experts. There are hundreds of additional unprocessed items.

American Legion Collection, late 1940s: 82 items. Radio series "This Is Our Day, Decisions Now!" and "This Is Our Duty" with discussion of military recruitment, health, politics, and social problems.

The Armed Forces Radio and Television Service Collection (AFRTS), 1942–present: 300,000 items. AFRTS serves members of the U.S. armed forces with broadcasts in the United States and abroad. This collection includes domestic radio broadcasts and shows, commercial network radio acquired by the AFRTS, and music library discs. The collection has no news broadcasts or AFRTS broadcasts that originated overseas. Access is by record title for the music library and by the name of the radio program for the rest of the collection.

Audio-Scriptions Collection, 1936–45: hundreds of recordings. Speeches, performances, radio programs by members of Congress, Pres. Harry Truman, Harold Ickes, and others. These are indexed in *Radio Broadcasts in the Library of Congress, 1924–1941*; a computerized list; and the Recorded Sound Supplemental card catalog in the Reference Center.

BBC Sound Archive Collection, 1888– mid-1980s: 6,000 items. A selection of the British Broadcasting Corporation's most significant audio recordings, including the voices of every major

political figure of the 20th century. There is a microfiche index.

Columbia Broadcasting System (CBS) Radio Collection, 1957, 1960–67: 700 items. Includes the whole range of programming on network radio including coverage of the Kennedy assassination, Republican national conventions, civil rights marches and debates, the 1964 election campaigns, and a continuous run of CBS programming, May 13–26, 1957.

Central Intelligence Agency (CIA) Collection, 1959–62: 230 items. Speeches by Fidel Castro. There is a finding-aid.

German speeches and broadcasts, 1930–45: 2,500 items. Captured enemy materials include speeches by Nazi officials and foreign radio broadcasts (1939–45) from 20 European countries including exile governments and the United States.

A. F. R. Lawrence Collection, 1920s–1930s: 3,000 items. The collection is primarily speeches from the series "Nation's Forum" and radio broadcasts, 1926–32, on CBS stations. The collection is indexed in *Radio Broadcasts in the Library of Congress, 1924–41* by name of guest and is indexed in the Recorded Sound Supplemental card catalog.

"Meet the Press," 1945–present: over 2,000 recordings. This collection includes, in addition to complete runs of the radio broadcasts, television broadcasts. See entry F14.

National Broadcasting Company Collection (NBC), 1935–70: 175,000 items. This collection includes examples of public affairs, music, interviews, news, and international shortwave broadcasts. Listening copies have been made for 1932–52. There is an impressive card catalog on microfiche compiled by NBC over 40 years. This can be used to locate recordings by particular personalities. There is a title index.

National Press Club Collection, 1952–present: 830 items. Speeches to the press corps in Washington, D.C. by prominent politicians, government officials, and others.

National Public Radio (NPR), 1973–present with five-year delay: over 3,000 items. Cultural programming broadcast on NPR is deposited in the library. News is deposited in the National Archives and Records Administration (E11). There is a microfiche index. See NPR (E12), for more recent recordings.

Office of War Information, 1942–45: 100,000 items. Domestic and foreign radio broadcasts of this pre-Voice of America organization include news, educational reports, and entertainment. Foreign language broadcasts are listed in a card catalog; English broadcasts are in a database by program title. Both are in the reference center.

Raymond Swing, 1944–64: 100s of items. Swing's broadcasts on the Mutual and NBC-blue networks and for the Voice of America. This collection is indexed.

U.S. House of Representatives Floor Proceedings, 1979–85: thousands of items. In 1979, the House began to record its floor proceedings on audiotape and to transmit the signals live to radio systems across the U.S. Videorecordings are described in entry F14. The finding-aid is the *Congressional Record*.

WOR Radio Archive, 1930s–70s: 18,000 items. This is one of the most complete documentations of a radio station's programming: early documentaries, and newscasts from both WOR and the Mutual Broadcasting Network. Voluminous paper files, held by the Manuscript Division (B8), make the recordings far more valuable. The collection came to the library with a computerized file.

*Note:* Smaller radio collections include: Red Cross radio series 1947–53; "Navy Reporter," a variety show sponsored by the U.S. Navy; the commentary of H. V. Kaltenborn; programs from Moral Re-Armament; and Pacifica Radio broadcasts.

## SPECIAL COLLECTIONS OF SOUND RECORDING

Center for the Study of Democratic Institutions, 1963–70: 658 items. Recorded lectures and seminars from the Santa Barbara, Cal., foundation chartered by the Fund for the Republic. Subject matter covered in the programs includes virtually every major social and political issue of the 1960s: nuclear disarmament, containment of the Soviet Union, ecology, inner-city rehabilitation, and capital punishment. Among the hundreds of speakers represented are Aldous Huxley, Michael Harrington, and Paul Tillich.

Compressed Audio Disc, 1890s–1922: 33 hours. This group of recordings is not a collection but rather a convenient way for researchers to listen to the earliest recordings of the spoken word in the library. It includes all surviving pre-1910 spoken word recordings, as well as speeches by politicians, 1908–20. It also includes "Nation's Forum" recordings, 1918–22.

Marine Corps Combat Records, 1943–45: 2,500 recordings. Stories from Guam, Okinawa, Saipan, Iwo Jima, and other locations in the Pacific, consisting in part of interviews with men returning from combat and eyewitness accounts of battles. There is no name access to this collection.

Naval Research Laboratory Collection, 1918, 1943–48: Audio tape recordings of 14 discs. Subjects include interviews, speeches, music performance of the U.S. Navy Band, submarine testing at different speeds (1918), Naval Research Laboratory 20th (1943) and 25th anniversaries (1948), and firing of V-2 rocket at White Sands, New Mexico. Individuals represented include Adm. A. H. VanKueren, Adm. Harold G. Bowen, and E. H. Krause.

Navy Oral History Project, 1951–52: 121 audio tape recordings. The subject is the history of naval radio, which focuses on the years 1898–1934. A number of individuals were interviewed by S. C. Hooper. Topics include signaling by radio, 1911–12; history of nationalization of radio; aviation radio; radio code; wireless companies, 1915; construction of original transpacific and transcontinental navy radio stations, 1916; and introduction of radio into the armed services.

John Toland Collection, early 1970s: 150 recordings. These are interviews with Hitler's intimates and witnesses to key events of the Nazi period, recorded by historian Toland. The collection is indexed.

United Nations 1946–63: 40,000 items. Recordings of the General Assembly and its major committees, all in the original languages. Also rare recordings of speeches by Asian and African leaders. This collection is currently being preserved and indexed.

4.a. There are private listening booths where recordings can be played. This allows a researcher to listen to most of the collection. The earliest recordings of the spoken word are conveniently available on a compressed disc.

b. Appointments are not required, but listening is restricted to those doing research for a publication, thesis, film/television/radio documentary, public performance, or other publicly available work.

c–d. The great majority of the recorded sound holdings have copyright or other restrictions. To obtain a copy, visitors must identify and contact the copyright holder or others who must give permission. The copyright holder will often charge a fee for duplication rights. Information on donor restrictions is available from the staff. When all permissions are received in writing, visitors may order copies from the library. Copies take three to five weeks. Rush service takes five to seven working days and doubles the price.

5. Half the collection is commercial recordings, which are filed by label name and issue number. A large collection of manufacturer's catalogs can be used to help a researcher find commercial recordings. Special collections are listed, indexed, or described in a variety of finding-aids. The largest are Recorded Sound Catalog, a card catalog of primar-

ily music; Recorded Sound Catalog Supplement, a card index of items yet to be cataloged; Rigler and Deutsch Index, a union catalog of 78-rpm recordings in five major U.S. libraries. The listings are by composer/author, performance/radio program, and title.

Since 1984 new sound recordings have been fully cataloged and recently the library has made a commitment to fully catalog many older collections, especially recordings of the spoken word and radio broadcasts. These are included in LOCIS (Library of Congress Information System). LOCIS consists of two subsystems, MUMS and SCORPIO. Since 1978 new sound recordings have also been added to COHM (Copyright Monograph File). Both are accessible on terminals in the reading room. The reference center staff has also created several databases, including the NBC radio index, which they will search for you.

The best source of published information on sound recordings in the library is a combination of *Scholars' Guide to Washington, D.C., for Audio Resources,* by James Heintze (Washington, D.C.: Smithsonian Institution Press, 1985) and *Special Collections in the Library of Congress,* by Annette Melville (Washington, D.C.: Library of Congress, 1980). *Radio Broadcasts in the Library of Congress 1924–41,* by James Smart (Washington, D.C.: Library of Congress, 1981) is a chronological index of the library's radio holdings. It is contained in a database available in the reference center. *Catalog of Copyright Entries* with a "recorded sound" section provides information on sound recordings, 1972–78, but does not necessarily describe what was selected by the library for its collection.

6. Index Terms: Conflict Resolution and Management—Unofficial and Non-Governmental Approaches; Diplomacy and Negotiations; Human Rights; Humanitarian Issues; International Organizations; Low Intensity Conflict; Military History; Political Systems and Ideologies; Terrorism

See also entries A29, B8, D4, F14, and F15

---

## E9 Marine Corps Historical Center (Navy Department)—Marine Band Library

1.a. Marine Barracks
8th and I Streets, SE
Washington, D.C. 20390-5000
(202) 433-4298

b. 8:30 A.M.–4:30 P.M. Monday–Friday

c. The collection is open to researchers by appointment.

d. Michael Ressler, Chief Librarian

2. The collection consists of almost 500 recordings of the Marine Band and Chamber Orchestra. Within the scope of this Guide the relevant holdings of the Marine Band Library fall under the rubric of military music and military history.

3. About 50 recordings, 1955–present, on vinyl records, cassettes, or CDs comprise the recordings for public distribution, copies of which are presented to libraries. Approximately 200 reel-to-reel tapes record transcripted radio programs, 1940–60. Another 200 reel-to-reel tapes comprise the "reference" or "rehearsal" recordings from the same period, maintained primarily for the use of the band director.

The library also holds a photograph collection of the Marine Band with about 1,000 photographs of performances, ceremonies, and individual portraits, 1864–present. In addition there are almost 600 photographs of the band's famous director, John Philip Sousa, and his family.

4.a. Listening equipment is available.

b. An appointment is required.

c. No fees are charged for listening.

d. Duplicating is not permitted.

5. There is a rough hand-written inventory for all the reel-to-reel holdings. A more complete and accurate discography is under preparation.

6. Subject Terms: Military History—Marine Corps

See also entries B9, C4, C5, D5, and E10

---

## E10 Marine Corps Historical Center (Navy Department)—Oral History Collection

1.a. Washington Navy Yard, Building 58
9th and M Streets, SE
Washington, D.C. 20374-0580
(202) 433-3840
Fax: (202) 433-7265

b. 8:30 A.M.–4:30 P.M. Monday–Friday

c. The collection is open to researchers. Some holdings have access restrictions. Researchers and writers doing extensive research should contact the chief historian (202/433-3839). There are five spacious, fully equipped study carrels available for assignment.

 d. Benis M. Frank, Chief Historian
 Richard Long, Head, Oral History Section

2.  The oral history collection in the historical center relates to issues of international security, and military history and planning. It contains over 1,260 hours of tapes transcribed onto over 32,000 edited pages, and more than 6,000 individual interviews relating to Vietnam, which have not been transcribed.

3.  The oral history program was established to obtain personal narratives of the experiences and observations of active duty, reserve, and retired marines. The period covered is 1893 to the present, and is primarily concerned with military service, marine corps history, Spanish American War, World Wars I and II, Korean War, Vietnam War, blacks in the Marine Corps, and the development of marine corps amphibious warfare. The form of the recordings include taped presentations, briefings, debriefings, speeches, and interviews.

 Individuals interviewed include Lt. Gen. Joseph Charles Burger, Lt. Gen. William Henry Buse Jr., Lt. Gen. Francis Patrick Mulcahy, Maj. Gen. Walter Greatsinger Farrell, Maj. Gen. Wood Barbee Kyle, and Brig. Gen. John Carroll Miller. Eight of the last 11 commandants of the marine corps have been interviewed for the program.

 Specific examples of oral histories of those who served in Europe include:

 Robert Blake (b. 1849): His World War I experience encompassed service in Verdun, Belleau Wood, Chateau Thierry, Soissons, Meuse-Argonne.

 Wilburt Scott Brown (1900–1968): His World War I service in France was with the 5th Marines, St. Mihiel, Champagne, Blanc Mont campaigns.

 Clifton Bledsoe Cates (b. 1893): World War I duty in France: Chateau Thierry, Belleau Wood, Argonne Forest campaigns.

 Karl Schmolsmire Day (1896–1973): On duty in France with the Northern Bombing Group.

 Pedro Augusto del Valle (1893–1978): Assistant Naval Attaché, Rome, observer with Italian forces, Italo-Ethiopian War.

 Walter Greatsinger Farrell (b. 1897): World War I service with the U.S. Marine Corps in France.

 Leo David Hermle (1890–1976): World War I service with the 6th Marine Regiment, duty in France: Verdun, St. Mihiel, Meuse-Argonne, and Argonne Forest.

 Richard Bardwell Millin (b. 1892): World War I experience included deployment to France; 45th Co. 3d Battalion, 5th Marines, St. Mihiel Offensive,

Sept. 12–16, 1918; Meuse-Argonne (Champagne) Offensive, Oct. 1–9, 1918 and Nov. 1–14, 1918.

 Francis Patrick Mulcahy (1894–1973): His World War I service included marine air operations in France.

 Don V. Paradis (b. 1896): Assigned to 80th Co., 2d Battalion, 6th Marines, he was deployed to France where he saw combat at Belleau Wood, Soissons, Chateau Thierry, St. Mihiel, Blanc-Mont, Meuse-Argonne.

 Examples of interviewees who discussed Middle East-related experiences and events include Lt. Gen. Joseph Charles Burger, Lt. Gen. Henry William Buse Jr., Maj. Gen. Wood Barbee Kyle, and Brig. Gen. John Carroll Miller (who was Senior Marine Officer with the Commander in Chief, U.S. Naval Forces, European and Mediterranean and the Commander in Chief, Specified Command of the Middle East, at the time of the 1958 Lebanon crisis), all discussing the 1958 marine landing in Lebanon; Lt. Gen. Francis Patrick Mulcahy (military observer with British air units in the Middle East, 1941–42), Gen. Gerald Carthrae Thomas (with the Special Presidential Mission to the Middle East with Capt. James Roosevelt, 1941), and Brig. Gen. Edward Colston Dyer (a naval air observer of British combat operations in the Middle East during World War II). Maj. Gen. Walter Greatsinger Farrell relates his father's experiences with Kitchener's Army in the Sudan on Nile River patrol, and Sgt. Maj. Edgar Richard Huff recounts his experiences at Marine Barracks, Port Lyautey, Morocco as the first African-American marine sergeant major, 1955–57.

 As a specific example bearing on international relations, the collection contains a taped interview with Gen. David Rowan Nimmer who was naval attaché in Moscow, 1934–35. The transcription runs to 117 pages. Nimmer discusses his service as assistant naval attaché, the question of recognition of the Soviet government, and the opening of the U.S. embassy. Another interview with Russian-related material is with Brig. Gen. Lester Dessez, commander of the marine detachment on board the *Helena*, which stood off Vladivostok, April–August 1921. Dessez recounts his experiences ashore.

 One notable group of recordings, consisting of some 27 items, includes interviews (in 1971) with Philip Johnston, who originated the idea of using the Navajo language in coded form for transmitting voice messages in combat situations during World War II. Another issue-oriented set of interviews is with enlisted marine security guards who are assigned to the State Department and provide security to U.S. consulates and embassies. Also in this group are interviews with the marines who were part of the Iranian hostage group.

4.a. Contact the Oral History Section regarding available sound recording equipment.

b. An appointment is recommended.

c. No fees are charged.

5. In addition to a card catalog and indexes to individual transcripts, as well as an index to Vietnam-related tapes, there are published reference sources that provide information about the collection: *Marine Corps Oral History Collection Catalog* (1989) and *Guide to the Marine Corps Historical Center*. Individuals may also want to consult *An Annotated Reading List of United States Marine Corps History* (1971) and *Marine Corps Personal Papers Catalog* (1974).

6. Subject Terms: Military History—Marine Corps; Regional Conflict; Terrorism

See also entries B9, C4, C5, D5, and E9

### National Air and Space Museum (NASM) (Smithsonian Institution) See entry C6

---

### EII National Archives and Records Administration (NARA)—Nontextual Archives Division (NNS)—Motion Picture, Sound, and Video Branch (NNSM)—Sound Recordings

---

1.a. 8601 Adelphi Road
College Park, Md. 20740-6001
(301) 713-7060
Fax: (301) 713-6904
Fax-on-demand: (301) 713-6905

b. 8:45 A.M.–5:00 P.M. Monday–Friday
Some evening and Saturday hours by appointment.

c. Open to researchers with a National Archives identification card, obtainable from the Reference Services Division. First-time users should speak with a consultant before beginning work.

d. John Scroggins, Chief
Les Waffen, Assistant Chief

2. The Motion Picture, Sound, and Video Branch of the National Archives has custody of some 244,549 sound recordings produced by U.S. government agencies, private individuals, and foreign governments. (Motion picture and video holdings of the branch are discussed in entry F20.) The recordings date from the turn of the century to the present and contain material relevant to international security and peace studies, such as press conferences, panel discussions, interviews, speeches, and news broadcasts. Subjects within the scope of this Guide include international relations, economic development, foreign trade and tariffs, human rights and humanitarian issues, immigration, political systems, military history and planning, violence, terrorism, and war crimes.

3. Sound recordings of interest to the users of this Guide are located either in the Record Groups or in the collection of Donated Materials.

### RECORD GROUPS

The records of a single government agency or subdivision are preserved in numbered collections called Record Groups (RG). The Record Group system serves those who are interested in locating media materials produced or acquired by a particular government agency. To facilitate a subject orientation, the following table places relevant RGs (discussed further on in this entry) under major subject headings:
Diplomacy and Alliances: RG 43, RG 46, RG 59, RG 64, RG 208, RG 306
Economic Aid: RG 46, RG 208, RG 220, RG 286, RG 362
Human Rights and Humanitarian Issues: RG 59, RG 208, RG 220
International Organizations: RG 48, RG 208, RG 229
International Trade: RG 16, RG 40, RG 46
Military History, Planning, and Strategy: RG 26, RG 36, RG 46, RG 48, RG 69, RG 165, RG 171, RG 178, RG 188, RG 208, RG 210, RG 311, RG 330; Army: RG 335, RG 338; Air Force: RG 18, RG 243, RG 342, RG 407; Navy and Marine Corps: RG 38
Political Systems and Ideologies: RG 131, RG 242
War Crimes: RG 153, RG 238, RG 242, RG 338
War Propaganda: RG 12, RG 16, RG 36, RG 38, RG 48, RG 60, RG 64, RG 83, RG 107, RG 118, RG 131, RG 165, RG 179, RG 208, RG 226, RG 229, RG 242, RG 262
The following RGs hold relevant sound recordings:
**RG 12:** *Office of Education, 1937–53: 93 items.*
Radio broadcasts of the office including the series "Brave New World," "Americans All—Immigrants All," and "Democracy in Action." Broadcasts on the role of education in wartime and the Voice of Democracy speech contests.
**RG 16:** *Office of the Secretary of Agriculture, 1971–81: 240 items.*
Includes interviews, speeches, press conferences on topics of international trade such as the sale of grain

to the USSR, 1940–50 (210 items). USDA-produced and acquired radio series on farm life and agriculture contains war propaganda materials, such as the radio programs from World War II: "Food Fight for Freedom," "The Farm Labor Challenge for 1944," "Victory Garden Tips," and "Nuts to Hitler."

**RG 18:** *Army Air Forces, 1945: 91 items.*
Radio series "The Fighting AAF," and "Your AAF." General Eisenhower speaks at Orly airport June 18, 1945.

**RG 26:** *U.S. Coast Guard, 1937–39: 10 items.*
Radio broadcasts about coast guard training of merchant seamen; the history and traditions of the coast guard.

**RG 38:** *Office of the Chief of Naval Operations, 1942–45: 195 items.*
Wartime radio series "Meet Your Navy," mainly from the Pacific theater, with eyewitness accounts by Armed Forces Radio Service correspondents. Propaganda recordings, produced by Naval Intelligence, in German, Japanese, and English, include news, anti-Fascist messages, and greetings to their families from German prisoners.

**RG 40:** *Department of Commerce, 1977–82: 210 items.*
Includes interviews and news conferences by officials on such topics of international commerce as China trade agreements, the USSR trade embargo, and auto imports.

**RG 43:** *International Conferences, Commissions, and Expositions, 1947–72: 159 items.*
Recordings of the plenary sessions of the Paris Peace Talks to end the war in Vietnam, 1969–72.

**RG 46:** *U.S. Senate, 1946–83: 458 items.*
Recordings contain materials relevant to international political, economic, and military affairs, such as hearings on defense programs, 1946; Congressional Research Seminars, 1976; interviews with senators and staff on policy making; and committee hearings.

**RG 48:** *Office of the Secretary of the Interior, 1936–52: 800 items.*
Recordings of speeches, discussions, ceremonies, and musical programs from the department's own broadcasts and acquired materials. Pertinent topics related to the department include international wildlife treaties, and American Indian military service. Topics related to other agencies include wartime development of industry, scientific research and atomic energy. Additional recordings include newscasts of war events and the contributions of Allies; Adolph Hitler's Sudeten and Danzig speeches; President Franklin Roosevelt's "Day of Infamy" speech; and discussions of the United Nations and its programs.

**RG 56:** *Department of the Treasury, 1941–61: 1,214 items.*
Radio broadcasts of promotional and informational programs bearing on military history, war propaganda, and international negotiations, for instance, news series "News of the World" and "Army Hour"; recordings of Winston Churchill before Congress, 1943; Harry S Truman reporting on the Potsdam Conference; and Eleanor Roosevelt on her trip to the South Pacific.

**RG 59:** *Department of State, 1938–61: 31,711 items.*
Included are 31,509 Voice of America overseas broadcasts, 1946–52, of informational and news programs covering international, political, economic, and military relations (see also RG 306), as well as speeches by Secretaries of State; a radio drama "And Then Came War" of world history 1918–39; and recorded accounts of imprisonment of Americans in former Czechoslovakia and China.

**RG 60:** *Department of Justice, 1941–63: 598 items.*
Recordings of radio broadcasts of the German Radio Broadcasting Corporation by Herbert J. Burgman, Douglas Chandler, Frederick W. Kaltenbach, and Robert Best, introduced as evidence in the treason trials of these men after World War II.

**RG 64:** *National Archives and Records Administration, 1937–81: 827 items.*
Speeches, interviews, and meetings include Adlai Stevenson, presidents, and others, and often bear on international relations; discussions of captured German documents, foreign relations, and other relevant topics.

**RG 69:** *Works Projects Administration, 1935–41: 418 items.*
Includes special radio programs on national defense, 1941.

**RG 83:** *Bureau of Agricultural Economics, 1939–44: 11 items.*
Filmstrip sound tracks on home front efforts by farmers, rationing, and increased production.

**RG 107:** *Office of the Secretary of War, 1942–43: 37 items.*
Recordings from the series "Orientation Service" and "What Are We Fighting For?" of speeches by war correspondents explaining U.S. and German war aims. Recordings from the "Hour of the Victory Corps" and "Victory Hour" series aimed at high school age youth.

**RG 118:** *U.S. Attorneys and Marshalls, 1944–45: 23 items.*
Radio Tokyo and other Japanese broadcasts during World War II related to the treason trial of "Tokyo Rose."

**RG 131:** *Office of Alien Property, 1930–41: 105 items.*

Recordings of German music and speeches by Adolph Hitler and others used at German-American Bund rallies. Recordings of the actual rallies in New York City.

**RG 153:** *Judge Advocate General (Army), 1969–72: 77 items.*

Recordings of the court martial of Lt. William Calley.

**RG 165:** *War Department General and Special Staffs, 1942–51: 1,293 items.*

Recordings of the Radio Branch of the Bureau of Public Relations, 1942–49; reports from Salerno, Anzio, and other European theater battles; reports from the Pacific including Gen. Jonathan Wainwright's surrender to the Japanese, Gen. Douglas MacArthur's arrival in Melbourne and the Japanese surrender in the Philippines; and press conferences concerning the occupation of Japan and Germany. Axis propaganda broadcasts in German, Japanese, and Chinese. Postwar recordings regarding the Armed Forces Unification Act, opportunities for women, and testimony before the Select Committee on Post-War Military Policy.

**RG 171:** *Office of Civilian Defense, 1939–45: 200 items.*

Radio broadcasts promoting participation in wartime programs. A series on civil defense in England.

**RG 178:** *U.S. Maritime Commission, 1941–45: 127.* Radio broadcasts about the merchant marine and its role in World War II. Dramatizations of the history of the merchant marine.

**RG 179:** *War Production Board, 1942–45: 117 items.*

Radio broadcasts on conservation, increased production, labor-management relations, in the form of dramas, speeches and interviews. Series include "Men, Machines, and Victory," "You Can't Deal with Hitler," and "Deeds Without Words."

**RG 188:** *Office of Price Administration, 1942–47: 202 items.*

Radio broadcasts produced by Office of War Information and the Price Administration on inflation, and rationing.

**RG 208:** *Office of War Information, 1941–46: 1,115 items.*

Broadcasts of news, information, and propaganda aimed at U.S. and foreign audiences: conduct of the war; homefront activities; international events; the surrenders of Italy, Germany, and Japan; the establishment of the United Nations and related world organizations; speeches by world leaders; coverage of international conferences; lend-lease; the Red Cross; and atom bomb tests.

Series broadcast overseas include: "Uncle Sam Speaks," "Voice of Freedom," and "We Fight Back." Domestic broadcasts include: "This Is Our Enemy," "Soldiers of Production," "Two-Thirds of a Nation," "Neighborhood Call," "Hasten the Day," "Victory Front," and "Atomic Bomb Program."

**RG 210:** *War Relocation Authority, 1944–45: 28 items.*

Radio recordings about the relocation program and the accomplishments of Nisei soldiers in World War II.

**RG 220:** *Presidential Committees, Commissions, and Boards, 1968–80: 1,184 items.*

Recordings from conferences including such relevant topics as causes and prevention of violence, and world hunger.

**RG 226:** *Office of Strategic Services, 1942–45: 27 items.*

Recordings and radio broadcasts aimed at German, Japanese, and American audiences: a speech to be broadcast to the Germans if the assassination of Hitler had been successful; American songs in German by Marlene Dietrich; and a Boston radio broadcast to counter Nazi support among black Americans.

**RG 229:** *Office of Inter-American Affairs, 1941–45: 24 items.*

Propaganda and informational broadcasts in Spanish and French about American war efforts and peace aims. Series include "United Nations Speak" and "Americanos Todos."

**RG 233:** *U.S. House of Representatives, 1943–65: 47 items.*

Includes materials bearing on international and military affairs, such as recordings gathered as evidence, and other broadcasts of speeches and hearings.

**RG 238:** *National Archives Collection of World War II War Crimes Records, 1945–48: 16,000 items.*

Recordings of the proceedings of the International Military Tribunal at Nuremberg, Germany. Most of the recordings are testimony of witnesses, listed alphabetically, in the Subsequent Trial Interrogations, held after October 1, 1946.

**RG 242:** *National Archives Collection of Foreign Records Seized, 1925–44: 1,551 items.*

Recordings of speeches by Nazi and Fascist leaders, propaganda materials recorded by the Fascists in Italy, and other recordings gathered as evidence for the war crimes investigators but not used as evidence in the trials.

**RG 243:** *U.S. Strategic Bombing Survey, 1945: 366 items.*

Recordings of interviews with Japanese civilians: effects of American bombing of Japanese cities and an eyewitness account of the bombing of Hiroshima.

**RG 262:** *Foreign Broadcast Intelligence Service, 1940–47: 20,603 items.*
Foreign broadcasts in English, German, Japanese, and other languages. Most are the propaganda broadcasts by Ezra Pound, Frederick W. Kaltenbach, Douglas Chandler, Edward Delaney, Mildred Gillars (known as "Axis Sally"), and "Tokyo Rose." There are speeches by Axis and Allied leaders.

**RG 286:** *Agency for International Development, 1954–73: 375 items.*
Speeches by agency directors and radio broadcasts related to the foreign aid programs. The weekly interview program "Overseas Mission," 1971–73, featuring AID officials, foreign diplomats, and economists.

**RG 306:** *U.S. Information Agency, 1950–present: 11,339 items.*
Recordings made and acquired by the Voice of America and broadcast overseas to provide news coverage of world events in light of U.S. foreign policy. The broadcasts consist of news, entertainment, interviews, and dramas. Holdings include remarks by USIA Director Edward R. Murrow. There is a name index to the Voice of America recordings.

**RG 311:** *Federal Emergency Management Agency, 1951–81: 119 items.*
Recordings of speeches and discussions by agency personnel. Radio materials including warning sirens, public information spots, and information programs.

**RG 330:** *Office of the Secretary of Defense, 1949–85: 1,303.*
Recordings of speeches, briefings, press conferences, most for broadcast, relating to defense policy, foreign policy, military aid, the Korean conflict, and women in the armed forces. Series include "This Is the Story," 1961–62, with anticommunist themes and "Army Hour." Appearances of military leaders on "Meet the Press, "Face the Nation," "Capital Cloakroom," and network news programs.

**RG 335:** *Office of the Secretary of the Army, 1942–74: 613 items.*
Recordings for Armed Forces Day. The 1942–75 radio series "Army Hour" and the 1954 Army-McCarthy Hearings.

**RG 338:** *U.S. Army Commands, 1942–45: 111 items.*
Interviews, in Japanese, with Japanese POW's. Four recordings of testimony on the massacre of U.S. POW's in German camps.

**RG 342:** *U.S. Air Force Commands, Activities, and Organizations, 1950–81: 332 items.*
Radio recordings of series "Stairway to the Stars" and "Our Date with History," which focus on science and technology. Recruitment broadcasts.

**RG 362:** *Agencies for Voluntary Action Programs, 1965–75: 48 items.*
Includes public service announcements and promotional broadcasts about the Peace Corps.

**RG 407:** *Adjutant General's Office, 1917–20s: 26 items.*
Oral histories by army air corps World War I aces, including James H. Doolittle. These were the first syndicated radio series, distributed on discs and called "Chevrolet Chronicles."

## DONATED MATERIALS

These collections were formerly in Record Group (RG) 200. Because they are not government records, they have been removed from the Record Groups and handled separately. The following ones are relevant to military history, international relations, and peace movements:

ABC Radio Collection (ABC), 1943–67: 25,000 recordings. Discs recorded or aired by the ABC Radio News Department: speeches, scheduled news programs, news commentaries, special events, and public affairs programming. Coverage includes international political and military relations with a sampling of news commentaries by Walter Winchell, Drew Pearson, Elmer Davis, and others. National Public Radio Collection (NPR), 1971–80: 4,000 recordings. News programs and commentaries bearing on international relations, primarily the daily newscast "All Things Considered," congressional hearings, presidential speeches, political campaigns, and speeches at the National Press Club. An index on microfiche is available 1971–83. Older non-news NPR programming is at the Library of Congress (E8). See NPR entry (E12), for more recent recordings.

David Goldin Collection (G), 1932–53: 3,200 recordings. Radio broadcasts produced, acquired, or aired by CBS, NBC, Mutual, and Armed Forces Radio Network, and pertinent to military history: speeches, interviews, combat news reels, special events, documentaries, congressional hearings, and entertainment for U.S. troops.

University of Maryland Collection (WTOP), station WJSV/WTOP, 1937–57: 2,500 recordings. Discs of speeches, interviews, and news documentaries with a partial focus on international figures and events.

Milo Ryan Phonoarchive Collection (MR), 1939–45: 2,500 recordings. Speeches, special events, and public affairs programs of World War II era, recorded from broadcasts of KIRO, a CBS affiliate.

John Hickman Collection, 1931–77: 960 recordings. Radio broadcasts produced, acquired, or aired by CBS, NBC, Mutual, Armed Forces Radio Network, and public stations: speeches by presidents beginning with Herbert Hoover; covering in part international and military relations. Includes also news reel recordings of civil rights and anti–Vietnam War demonstrations. This collection is integrated into the general 200 series.

4.a. Listening equipment is available free of charge for on-site use.

b. Equipment and recordings should be reserved in advance.

c–d. The staff can provide copies of recordings in the public domain or those for which researchers have obtained prior permission to duplicate. A price list is available. Researchers may copy items in the public domain using their own equipment.

5. The recorded sound collections are described in a Main Sound Recordings Card Catalog and in an elaborate Name Index. Preservation lists, by Record Group, have many descriptive details. There is a file cabinet of additional finding-aids by subject. Many items also are cataloged on a computerized database. Patrons may request a search.
The primary published source for sound recordings is *Scholars' Guide to Washington, D.C., for Audio Resources,* by James R. Heintze, (Washington, D.C.: Smithsonian Institution Press, 1985).

6. Index Terms: Collective Security; Defense Policy, National—History; Development Issues; Diplomacy and Negotiations; Environmental Issues, Global; Human Rights; Humanitarian Issues; International Organizations; Military History; Military Science—Engineering, Logistics, and Support; Political Systems and Ideologies

See also entries B11, D6, F20, F21, and G10

---

## E12  National Public Radio (NPR)— Information Services and Program Archive

1.a. 635 Massachusetts Avenue, NW
Washington, D.C. 20001
(202) 414-2060
Fax: (202) 414-3329

b. 8:30 A.M.–6:00 P.M. Monday–Friday

c. The library is open to the public by appointment only. It is regarded primarily as a working collection for the NPR staff.

d. Elizabeth Sullivan, Acting Head Librarian

2. National Public Radio, a network of radio stations that produces and distributes programs to member stations, began broadcasting in 1971. All programs produced by NPR are duplicated on reel-to-reel tape and stored in the library.

3. Of interest to the users of this Guide are the news shows bearing on international political and military affairs, including "All Things Considered," "Morning Edition," and "Talk of the Nation," as well as National Press Club addresses and congressional hearings. The last 10 years of programming are housed at NPR. After 10 years, news and information programs are sent to the National Archives and Records Administration (E11). (Music and entertainment programs are sent to the Library of Congress, [E8].)

4.a. On-site listening equipment is available.

b. Prior appointment is required.

c. There are no fees charged to listen to the recordings. A fee is charged to record news programs.

d. Some of the recordings may be duplicated as long as no copyright restrictions exist. Cassettes or transcripts (as of September 1990) are available at cost.

5. A catalog and other finding-aids are available for the collection. The staff recommends that requests be submitted in advance, either in writing or by telephone, thus enabling personnel familiar with the collection to conduct a preliminary search.

6. Index Terms: International Politics

---

## E13  Naval Historical Center (Navy Department)—Operational Archives Branch—Oral History Collection

1.a. Washington Navy Yard, Building 57
9th and M Streets, SE
Washington, D.C. 20374-0571
(202) 433-3170
Fax: (202) 433-3172

b. 9:00 A.M.–4:00 P.M. Monday–Friday

c. The collections are open to the public by appointment. Some materials are classified and restricted.

d. Bernard F. Cavalcante, Head
Gina Akers, Archivist

2. The archives holds a collection of approximately 500 taped oral histories, bearing on international political and military relations; military history, planning, and strategy; and regional conflicts. There are transcripts for three-fourths of the interviews.

3. The primary focus of the interviews includes World War II, the Vietnam conflict, the Persian Gulf War, and navy science and technology. The archives also has some 30 transcripts of oral history biographies of retired naval officers from the Office of Oral History at Columbia University, as well as 15 bound volumes of oral history transcripts from the chaplain corps.

Researchers should also take note of the Navy Oral History Project focusing on 1898–1934 in the Motion Picture, Broadcasting, and Recorded Sound Division of the Library of Congress (E8).

5. The Operational Archives Branch has detailed finding-aids for most of the individual collections.

6. Index Terms: Defense Policy, National—History; Military History—Navy; Naval Science

See also entries A36, B13, C9, C10, D9, and F23

---

### EI4 Organization of American States (OAS)—Records Management Center—Voice Archives

1.a. Administration Building, Room G-6
17th and Constitution Avenue, NW
Washington, D.C. 20006
(202) 458-3849
Fax: (202) 458-3914

b. 9:00 A.M.–5:00 P.M. Monday–Friday

c. Open to researchers by appointment.

d. Beverly Wharton-Lake, Records Management Specialist

2. The OAS Voice Archives, administered by the OAS Records Management Center (B14), contains approximately 151 discs and 48 tape recordings spanning the period 1938–72. Within the scope of this Guide, the collection is relevant to the study of international relations, international organizations, and economic development. For a description of the center's archival holdings see entry B14; for OAS library resources see entries A38, D11, and F24.

3. The collection consists of speeches, statements, and press conferences regarding inter-American issues by prominent political figures. Some of these figures include Guerrero Gutiérrez, Trejos Fernández, Galo Plaza, D. Alberto Hurtado, Lleras Camargo, Antonio Rocha, Castor Jaramillo Arrubla, Bertha Lutz, and Carlos Dávila.

Included are radio transcription recordings of the "America's Town Meeting of the Air" and the Eighth International Conference of American States, both recorded in 1938 by the National Broadcasting Company; recordings of the ceremony commemorating the 40th anniversary of the Inter-American Commission of Women in 1968; meeting of American Chiefs of State in Punta del Este, Uruguay, in 1967; and the meeting of ministers of labor on the Alliance for Progress in 1963.

4.a. The Voice Archives does not have listening equipment.

b. An appointment is recommended.

c. No fees are charged.

d. Researchers may tape some Voice Archives recordings on their own recording equipment.

5. A contents list is available from the records management specialist.

6. Index Terms: Development Issues; Diplomacy and Negotiations; International Organizations—Regional

See also entries A38, B14, D11, F24, and L13

---

### EI5 Senate Historical Office—Oral History Collection

1.a. Office of the Secretary
Senate Historical Office
Hart Senate Office Building, Suite SH-201
Washington, D.C. 20510-7108
(202) 224-6900

b. 9:00 A.M.–5:30 P.M. Monday–Friday

c. Open to the public.

d. Richard A. Baker, Senate Historian
Donald A. Ritchie, Associate Historian

2. The Oral History Program of the Senate Historical Office aims at collecting oral history interviews, particularly with retired members of the senate staff. Almost 200 interviews with 30 individuals are available in transcripts. They cover issues of international

political, economic, and military affairs that are of potential interest to the users of this Guide.

3.   These interviews are both biographical and institutional, including individuals' personal recollections of their careers with the Senate, and discussions of how Congress changed during their tenures.

The project has focused more on staff members than on senators because the latter generally give oral history interviews to universities and historical societies in their home states. The Senate Historical Office encourages such private projects and keeps a record of all resulting transcripts. For its own project, the Historical Office generally concentrates on staff whose service spanned more than two decades and whose experience has included committee work, as well as on individual senators.

Faced with a large pool of prospective interviewees, the Historical Office chose to interview a few representative individuals in depth, rather than to produce a great quantity of short interviews. The typical oral history in this series consists of six to eight interview sessions, each session about an hour and a half in length. Transcripts were produced immediately following each session for the interviewees to review. Interviewees were encouraged to speak fully and candidly, and their transcripts remain closed until specifically opened for research under the terms of a deed of gift.

The Historical Office uses information gained through these oral histories for its own reference work and makes it available to researchers by depositing copies in the Senate Library, the Library of Congress, the National Archives and Records Administration; a microfiche edition is distributed by Scholarly Resources.

4.   Interview transcripts that are open for research may be examined by appointment. Once opened, the interviews become part of the public domain and may be reproduced and cited without additional permission.

5.   Each transcript is individually indexed. A cross-reference index is available to further assist researchers in locating Senate-related material within the oral histories. Only interviews that are open for research have been included in this index, although a few pages within certain transcripts remain closed. In these cases, the transcripts indicate when the restrictions will be lifted.

6.   Index Terms: Defense Policy, National—History; Development Issues; Diplomacy and Negotiations

See also entry K35

United States Catholic Conference (USCC)—
Catholic News Service/Catholic
Communication Campaign   See entry F28

United States Holocaust Research Institute—
Archives   See entry B16

## E16   University of Maryland—National Public Broadcasting Archives—Audio Tapes

1.a.  Hornbake Library, 4th Floor
      College Park, Md. 20742-7011
      (301) 405-9255

b.   9:00 A.M.–5:00 P.M. Monday–Friday

c.   Open to researchers by appointment.

d.   Thomas Connors, Archivist

2.   The archives was established at the University of Maryland at College Park in June 1990. Its objective is to collect and maintain historical records, manuscripts, kinescopes, audio and video tapes, films, and personal papers dealing with the development of public broadcasting in the United States. Topics relevant to international security and peace studies include international relations, regional conflict, human rights, and peace movements. Book collections at the University of Maryland libraries are discussed in entry A47; map and video tape collections in entries D12 and F31, respectively.

3.   The following audio tape collections are particularly germane to the purposes of this Guide:

National Association of Educational Broadcasters (NAEB)—National Educational Radio, 1951–71, 6,500 audio tapes from the precursor to National Public Radio, including programs on international and military affairs, such as the series "News in the Twentieth Century."

Pacifica Radio, 1980s–, 30 cartons of newscuts, reflecting the peace movement's views, especially on El Salvador and Nicaragua.

WAMU-FM, 1960–, approximately 1,200 audio tapes, including programs on U.S. national security interests with respect to Cuba, Grenada, and Iran.

4.a.  Audiovisual equipment is available.

b.   Because most tapes are not in user format, researchers should call at least 10 days ahead so that a tape conversion can be arranged.

c.   Fees are charged if tape conversion is required.

d. Permission from the original producers is required for copying.

5. "Mediagraphies" (media bibliographies) are prepared to assist users in locating materials on popular topics, such as "U.S. foreign policy." Copies are available for examination at the service desk. Parts of the collection are listed on VICTOR, the university's on-line catalog, which can be accessed on-site or via Internet and can be searched under terms such as *terrorism*.

6. Index Terms: Defense Policy, National—History; International Politics; Pacifism and Peace Movements; Terrorism

*Note:* For other public broadcasting materials see National Archives and Records Administration (entry EII) and Library of Congress (entry E8). For other holdings of the University of Maryland libraries see entries A47, D12, and F31.

---

**EI7** Voice of America (VOA) (United States Information Agency)—Audio Services

---

1.a. William J. Cohen Building, Room 3166
330 Independence Avenue, SW
Washington, D.C. 20547
(202) 619-1344

b. 7:00 A.M.–8:00 P.M. Monday–Friday
9:00 A.M.–5:00 P.M. Saturday
9:00 A.M.–4:00 P.M. Sunday

c. Individuals must contact Joseph O'Connell, Public Affairs Office of VOA (202/619-2538), stating specific requests. A 1948 law prohibits domestic dissemination of VOA productions less than 12 years old, but materials are available for on-site listening and research.

d. Roblyn A. B. Hymes, Audio Services Supervisor

2. The Voice of America is the official international broadcasting service of the U.S. government, operating as part of the U.S. Information Agency (USIA). The VOA first went on the air in February 1942 as the radio component of the U.S. Office of War Information. After 1945 it became part of the State Department, and in 1953 it was one of the elements making up the newly created U.S. Information Agency (USIA). Like all activities of the USIA, the VOA broadcasts have a significant bearing on international political and military relations.

3. Audio Services, holding, among others, approximately 75,000 reel-to-reel and cassette tapes, is basically a working collection for the use of the broadcasters and programmers in the English and foreign language departments at VOA. Each day Audio Services receives a large number of off-the-air tapes of noncommercial and network news and public information programs bearing on international relations (e.g., "All Things Considered," "The Today Show," "MacNeil/Lehrer Report," "WGMS at Noon"). These tapes are recorded by accession numbers in the daily log book and are generally held for a period of one to three months. Important segments are taken from these recordings and maintained in a permanent archive collection that was established in 1942.

Of particular interest to users of this Guide are the recordings of presidential speeches and news conferences; news items concerning senators, major diplomats, and other prominent persons; other important current events; speeches by foreign dignitaries visiting the United States; State Department briefings; and VOA features on major policy matters. Tapes that are made on-site by the staff of VOA and maintained in Audio Services include a number of 10-minute special reports with "actualities" collected for potential use in broadcasts for programs such as "Classical Calendar" and "People in the News."

4.a. On-site listening equipment is available.

b. Reservations are required.

c. Fees are not charged to listen to recordings.

d. Duplicate copies of tapes can be made if arranged in advance and if permitted by law or by contractual agreement.

5. Descriptive control of Audio Services' holdings was accomplished through a system of log books and catalog cards, including daily sheets of Recordings Received in the Program Documentation Unit (January 1962–December 1984), recording log books, personality log books, and index cards. Since July 1984 recordings in Audio Services have been indexed using a data retrieval format that provides access via the principal speaker and selected subject headings. This system supersedes the manual indexes described above.

6. Index Terms: International Politics

See also entry K41

**Woodrow Wilson International Center for Scholars  See entry H76**

# F

# Film Collections
## (Still Photographs and Motion Pictures)

## Film Collections (Still Photographs and Motion Pictures) Entry Format (F)

1. *General Information*
   a. address; telephone number(s)
   b. hours of service
   c. conditions of access
   d. name/title of director and key staff members

2. *Size of Holdings Pertaining to Peace and International Security Studies*

3. *Description of Holdings Pertaining to Peace and International Security Studies*

4. *Facilities for Study and Use*
   a. availability of audiovisual equipment
   b. reservation requirements
   c. fees charged
   d. duplication facilities

5. *Bibliographic Aids Facilitating Use of Collection*

6. *Index Terms* (relevant subject specialties)

### Introductory Note

The Washington, D.C., area contains remarkable still photograph and motion picture resources con-

cerning international military and political affairs, as well as international development issues. The richest collections, covering all of these areas, are those in the Library of Congress (F14 and F15) and in the National Archives and Records Administration (F20 and F21). Substantial holdings of international political and military television news can be also found in the University of Maryland—National Public Broadcasting Archives—Video Tapes (F31). Rich collections of military still photographs are held by Air Force History Office (F2), Coast Guard—Historian's Office (F7), Defense Department—Still Media Records Center (F8), National Air and Space Museum (NASM)—Archives Division—Photographic Archives (F19), and Naval Historical Center—Photographic Section (F23). Substantial still photograph and motion picture collections concerning international development issues are held by Agency for International Development (AID)—Photo Collection/Audiovisual Services (F1), Inter-American Development Bank (IDB)—Audiovisual Department (F11), International Bank for Reconstruction and Development (World Bank)—Photo Library/Film Unit (F12), and Peace Corps Photograph Collection (F25). Major photograph, film collections, or both, in the area of humanitarian issues and concerns, are held by American Red

Cross (ARC)—Photographic Service (F5), United Nations Information Centre—Library—Film Collection (F27), United States Catholic Conference (USCC)—Catholic News Service/Catholic Communication Campaign (F28), United States Holocaust Research Institute—Photography Department/Film Department (F29), and World Health Organization (WHO)—Regional Office for the Americas—Photograph Collection (F32).

For more detail on still photographs and motion pictures, the reader may wish to consult Shirley L. Green, *Pictorial Resources in the Washington, D.C., Area* (Washington, D.C.: Library of Congress, 1976) and two volumes in this series, *Scholars' Guide to Washington, D.C., Film and Video Collections* (1980), by Bonnie G. Rowan, and *Scholars' Guide to Washington, D.C., Media Collections* (1994), by Bonnie G. Rowan and Cynthia J. Wood. This section updates information from these Guides that is relevant to international security and peace studies.

---

## FI Agency for International Development (AID) (International Development Cooperation Agency)—Photo Collection/Audiovisual Services

---

1.a. Office of External Affairs
State Department Building, Room 4889
320 21st Street, NW
Washington, D.C. 20523-0056
(202) 647-4330
Fax: (202) 647-3945

b. 8:30 A.M.–3:30 P.M. Monday–Friday

c. Open to researchers, by appointment. Call ahead for clearance.

d. Donna Woolf, Deputy Chief (202/647-4309)
Clyde McNair, Photographer
Patricia Adams, Audiovisual Services

2. The collection contains approximately 10,000 photographs and 20,000 slides, as well as 1,000 video tapes. The subject coverage includes AID-sponsored development projects, activities of AID field personnel, and general scenes of people and living conditions. From the viewpoint of peace and international security studies the audiovisual material falls within the areas of economic development, the environment, and humanitarian issues.

3. The photograph collection, ca. 1970–present, occupies 10 filing cabinets. One part is arranged by world regions and subdivided by countries. The other part is arranged by subjects, such as agriculture, disaster assistance, energy, environment, food/nutrition, forestry, health/sanitation, malaria, pollution, rural development, and women in development projects. In addition, there are 46 binders of slides arranged by country.

The video collection consists of three parts. (1) Master tapes include about 230 fully edited tapes: some from late 1940s–early 1950s (depicting, for instance, Marshall Plan activities, Europe in ruins, General [later President] Eisenhower), some from 1960s–70s, most from 1980–present. (2) Raw footage contains 409 unedited tapes. (3) Off-air footage (almost 300 tapes) was taken from TV news, news shows, and similar programs that pertained to AID activities or personnel.

4.a. Audiovisual equipment is available.

b. Prior reservations are recommended.

c. There are no fees for viewing or copying.

d. Patrons are asked to supply their own tapes for copying. Off-air footage is limited to viewing due to copyright restrictions.

5. A computerized cataloging system for photographs and slides is under preparation. A computerized catalog for the video tape collection is already in place, enabling retrievals by country and subject. There is also a "shot-description" catalog giving a shot by shot description from every tape. Researchers can obtain assistance with searches in the collection.

6. Index Terms: Development Issues; Environmental Issues, Global; Humanitarian Issues

See also entries A1, G2, G3, and K1

---

## F2 Air Force History Office (Air Force Department)—Photograph Collection

---

1.a. 170 Luke Avenue, Suite 400
Bolling Air Force Base
Washington, D.C. 20332-5113
(202) 767-5764
Fax: (202) 404-7915

b. 9:00 A.M.–5:00 P.M. Monday–Friday

c. Open to the public. Visitors must have prior visitation clearance, which can be arranged by phone.

d. Richard P. Hallion, Air Force Historian
William C. Heimdahl, Chief, Historical Services Division

2. The Office of Air Force History possesses microfilm copies of archival materials in the U.S. Air Force Historical Research Center (Maxwell Air Force Base, Ala. 36112-6678), which number some 500,000 documents relating to the history of U.S. military aviation from the time of the Civil War. Within the scope of this Guide the photographic material of interest falls under the rubrics of military history, planning, and strategy.

3. About one-half of the office's holdings consist of unit histories with supporting aerial photographs, maps, and charts prepared and assembled by field historians serving with commands, air forces, wings, groups, and squadrons. Of particular note are the unit histories for the 1st Mapping Group (later the 1st Photographic Charting Group) that charted and mapped parts of the United States, Alaska, Canada, Africa, the Middle East, India, and Central and South America (1941–43); the 2d Photographic Reconnaissance and Mapping Group, which trained other crews and units for photographic reconnaissance and mapping, 1942–43; the 3d Photographic Reconnaissance and Mapping Group, which provided photographic intelligence in Tunisia, Sicily, and Italy, and mapped areas in France and the Balkans, 1942–45; the 4th Photographic Reconnaissance and Mapping Group, which was active in New Caledonia, Guadalcanal, Morotai, Mindanao, and Borneo, 1942–45; the 5th Photographic Reconnaissance and Mapping Group, which mapped coastal areas of Southern France, 1944; the 6th Reconnaissance and Mapping Group, which engaged in mapping activities in Luzon and Mindanao and photographed Japanese strategic areas in New Guinea, the Bismarcks, Formosa, China, and Kyushu, 1943–46; and the 7th Photographic and Reconnaissance Group, which provided mapping support for allied troops in France, the Low Countries, and Germany, 1943–45.
Also of interest are the records of the Air Photographic and Charting Service and the Army Air Force Charting Service, which form part of the Major Global Services of the Army Air Force and United States Air Force Collection, 1935– (838 lin. ft.) and the records of the Aeronautical Chart Service, located in the Zone of Interior Commands and Organization Collection, 1926– (3392 lin. ft.). The historical records of the Aerospace Cartographic and Geodetic Service, which was established in 1954, are maintained by the Office of Air Force History (Forbes Air Force Base, Kans. 66620).

In addition, personal papers may include collections pertinent to military photography. For instance, the papers of Joseph L. Albright, Chief of the Photographic Records and Services Division, Aeronautical Chart and Information Center, contain manuals, catalogs, memoranda, regulations, and personnel rosters, 1919–43. The papers of Gen. Charles P. Cahill include material on British aerial photography during World War II.

4. Photocopying service is available.

5. A microfilm catalog provides access to the microfilm collection by subject and country. Published guides include *Air Force Historical Archives Document Classification Guide* (1971). Also useful is *Air Force Combat Units of World War II*, edited by Maurer Maurer (1983), which provides a chronological listing of the activities of each unit.

6. Index Terms: Military History—Air Force

See also entries B1, E1, and K3

---

**F3** American Federation of Labor and Congress of Industrial Organizations (AFL-CIO) — George Meany Memorial Archives (GMMA) — Photograph and Film Collection

---

1.a. 10000 New Hampshire Avenue
Silver Spring, Md. 20903
(301) 431-5451
Fax: (301) 431-0385

b. 9:00 A.M.–4:30 P.M. Monday–Friday

c. Open to the public by appointment.

d. Lynda DeLoach, Archivist

2. The collection at the archives contains approximately 60,000 still images and over 500 film titles that depict trade union activities. Though primarily domestic in coverage, the collection reflects U.S. trade union activities abroad, as well as international labor issues. The archives serves as the official repository for the AFL-CIO. For information about GMMA's archival and audio collections see entries B2 and E2; for AFL-CIO's library, see entry A2.

3. Photograph collection. Covering late 19th century to 1981, and approximately 60,000 images, this is the most heavily used resource in the archives. Images include depictions of international labor activities, as well as involvement with international labor

organizations. Approximately half of the images were produced by AFL-CIO. Others are from a variety of sources including news photos from Associated Press (AP), United Press International (UPI), Black Star, and other press bureaus.

Frank Alexander Negative Collection. With over 18,000 photographic assignments, this collection documents major labor events (international as well as domestic) and personalities of the times, mid-1940s to mid-1980s.

Film collection. Over 500 titles, primarily 16mm; most films have been retired from the AFL-CIO Education Department Film Library. Most are acquired, but a few were produced by AFL-CIO. They include coverage of international labor and political affairs.

Video collection. The collection, 1980s–present, includes approximately 200 videos, most of which were produced by the Labor Institute of Public Affairs (LIPA); a few are network television interviews with labor leaders. Coverage of international labor and political affairs is included.

Other records dealing with international affairs will be opened in the future, such as those of the internationally oriented organizations sponsored by the AFL-CIO's Department of International Affairs (see entry N7): African-American Labor Center (AALC), American Institute for Free Labor Development (AIFLD), Asian-American Free Labor Institute (AAFLI), and Free Trade Union Institute (FTUI).

4.a. Screening facilities are available for most formats.

b. Appointments are required.

c. Fees are charged for photocopying, and user fees for commercial use.

d. Duplication services are available. The patron is responsible for obtaining the appropriate permissions, if copyright or other restrictions apply.

5. A brochure describing the archives' holdings is available.

6. Index Terms: Conflict Management and Resolution—Unofficial and Nongovernmental Approaches; International Organizations—Labor

See also entries A2, B2, E2, and N7

---

## F4 American Red Cross (ARC)—Frank Stanton Television Production Center

1.a. 5816 Seminary Road
Falls Church, Va. 22041

(703) 379-8160
Fax: (703) 820-1533

b. 8:30 A.M.–5:00 P.M. Monday–Friday

c. Requests to use the collection are considered on a case by case basis. Those who wish to use this collection must submit scripts and other detailed information about the intended use of materials.

d. Craig Reinertson, Manager

2. This is the national audiovisual production center for the American Red Cross. It maintains a collection of 500 films, 1930s–present, and 800 videos, 1970–present. Within the scope of this Guide the collection is relevant to humanitarian issues and certain aspects of warfare.

3. The Production Center holds a wide variety of films and videotapes about the Red Cross and events with which the Red Cross is often asked to assist. Refugees, food parcels, celebrity fund appeals, and natural disasters are among the subjects in the collection. There are many films from the 1940s and 1950s and there is a remarkable film about Vietnam produced in Saigon in 1966. A number of films were produced by Red Cross organizations in Europe and East Asia. Also included are public service announcements and other short Red Cross productions from 1950 to the present.

4.a. Viewing equipment is available.

b. Prior permission to use the collection is required.

c–d. Duplication of materials is considered on a case by case basis. Current, completed productions may be borrowed from local Red Cross chapters or purchased from the Supply Division (800/969-8890).

5. Staff can inform users about the nature and location of specific items.

6. Index Terms: Human Rights; Humanitarian Issues; Military History

See also entries F5 and N9

---

## F5 American Red Cross (ARC)— Photographic Service

1.a. 431 18th Street, NW
Washington, D.C. 20006
(202) 639-3563
Fax: (202) 639-3792

b. 9:00 A.M.–Noon and 2:00 P.M.–4:00 P.M. Monday–Friday

c. Open by appointment to scholars, journalists, and media representatives.

d. Elizabeth Hooks, Photographic Librarian

2. The collection consists of 300,000 black-and-white photographs and color transparencies, mainly from World War II to the present, with fewer earlier images dating as far back as the Civil War. Within the scope of this Guide the relevant materials fall under the headings of human rights, humanitarian issues, and military history.

3. The collection depicts the widely varied aspects of the Red Cross's mission to serve the public. Subjects pertinent to peace and international security studies include relief efforts, disasters, service to military members and their families, blood services, and health services. Illustrative examples cover Red Cross nursing and relief activities during the Spanish-American War and Mexican Revolution, Red Cross disaster-relief activities in the aftermath of several 20th-century Central and South American earthquakes (including the Mexican reconstruction after the 1985 earthquake), and Red Cross involvement in the 1962–63 U.S.-Cuban "prisoner exchange."

4.a. Special equipment is not needed to view the photographs.

b. Scholars should call (202) 639-3563 in order to make an appointment to use the collection.

c. There are no research fees.

d. The charge for photocopying and one-time use for an 8″ × 10″ black-and-white glossy print is $15. The images may be used for news, educational, and editorial purposes only. They may not be used for trade or advertisements.

5. Photographs are arranged in well-labeled file drawers, for example, "Historical—WWII—France—Hospital Trains." There is also a historical file (arranged chronologically) and an international services file (arranged by country).

6. Index Terms: Human Rights; Humanitarian Issues; Military History

See also entries F4 and N9

**American University—Bender Library** See entry A4

# F6 Center for Defense Information (CDI)— Film Collection

1.a. 1500 Massachusetts Avenue, NW
Washington, D.C. 20005
(202) 862-0700
Fax: (202) 862-0780

b. 9:00 A.M.–5:00 P.M. Monday–Friday

c. Open to the public by appointment.

e. Daniel Sagalyn, Associate Producer

2. The CDI conducts research on U.S. defense- and weapons-policy issues, attempting to present an alternative view to that of the Pentagon. Its audiovisual collection consists of more than 2,000 videos of stock footage, 1910–present, and more than 200 videos of "America's Defense Monitor" programs, 1986–present. Arms production; military spending, planning, and strategy; and warfare are the collection subjects relevant to this Guide.

3. CDI's Stock Footage Library covers such topics as U.S. defense and foreign policy. Subjects include weapons systems, Operations Desert Storm and Desert Shield (Persian Gulf War), Operation Just Cause (Panama), Defense Department, World War I, World War II, and the Korean and Vietnam Wars. Many items in this collection have been acquired from the Defense Department (K10) or the National Archives and Records Administration's Motion Picture, Sound and Video Branch (F20).
   The series "America's Defense Monitor," exploring defense and foreign policy issues, is produced by CDI and airs on public television. Specific topics include the Pentagon, military spending, nuclear testing, covert action, and U.S. forces in Asia and the Persian Gulf.

4.a. Viewing equipment is available.

b. Appointments are required.

c–d. Materials from stock footage library may be reproduced for a fee. Tapes of "America's Defense Monitor" are available for $25 per tape.

5. A descriptive list of "America's Defense Monitor" programs is available by mail.

6. Index Terms: Arms Production and Acquisition; Defense Policy, National—U.S. Strategic Interests; Military History; Military Science—Strategy and Tactics

See also entry H11

## F7 Coast Guard (Transportation Department)—Historian's Office—Photograph Collection

1.a. 2100 2d Street, SW
Washington, D.C. 20593-0001
(202) 267-2596
Fax: (202) 267-4307

b. 7:00 A.M.–5:30 P.M. Monday–Friday

c. Open to the public.

d. Robert Browning, Chief Historian

2. The collection holds more than 1 million images, 1850s–present, with the post-World War II period represented most strongly. The users of this Guide will find material relevant to military history, planning, and strategy, as well as humanitarian issues.

3. The bulk of the collection is divided into seven major categories: cutters, stations, small craft, aviation, personnel, lighthouses, and lightships. The rest is divided into several hundred subjects, many dealing with emergency relief and humanitarian concerns, such as search and rescue at sea, life saving, disasters, and floods.

4.a. Audiovisual equipment is available.

b. Call in advance to reserve equipment.

c–d. Fees are charged for photocopying only.

5. The *Coast Guard Public Affairs Product Guide,* which lists a small selection of still images and videos, is available from the public affairs staff (202/267-1587). A bibliography of Coast Guard history is available by mail.

6. Index Terms: Humanitarian Issues; Military History—Coast Guard

See also entry E5

## F8 Defense Department—Still Media Records Center (SMRC)

1.a. Anacostia Naval Station, Building 168
Washington, D.C. 20374-5080
(202) 433-2166

b. 7:00 A.M.–4:00 P.M. Monday–Friday

c. Open to the public. Appointments are suggested and should be made at least one day before arrival.

d. James Sage, Head, Records Management

2. The Still Media Records Center (SMRC) is the central repository for photographs of all branches of the Defense Department. It is operated by a contractor, under the supervision of the navy. The collection encompasses 150,000 images, 1982–present. Within the scope of this Guide the collection falls under the rubrics of military history, planning, and strategy.

3. The photographs depict Defense Department, air force, army, marine corps and navy personnel and installations, troop movements, equipment, planes, ships, bases, and construction.

Images prior to 1982 are held by the National Archives and Records Administration's Still Picture Branch (F21, major collections exist in RG 18, RG 80, RG 111, RG 127, RG 342, and RG 428), except for air force photographs before 1954, which are held by the National Air and Space Museum (F19).

4.a. Audiovisual equipment is not necessary.

b. Appointments should be made in advance to view photographs on-site.

c. Minimal fees are charged for photocopies and staff research time.

d. Defense Department permission is not required to obtain materials, except if they will be used in advertising. The SMRC maintains a file of 35mm color slides of 10,000 of the most frequently requested images for off-the-shelf sales.

5. The collections are organized by military service. Geographic, military, and subject indexes are available.

6. Index Terms: Military History

See also entries A33, D1, and G7

## F9 European Union—Delegation of the European Commission—Press and Public Affairs Office—Exhibits and Audiovisuals

1.a. 2100 M Street, NW, 7th Floor
Washington, D.C. 20037
(202) 862-9541
Fax: (202) 429-1766

b. 9:00 A.M.–5:30 P.M. Monday–Friday

c. Requests to use the collection are considered on a case by case basis.

d. Sandra Auman, Audiovisual Producer/ Coordinator

2. The collection consists of several hundred mostly black-and-white photographs, 1940s–present, and 300 slides; a stock footage library of approximately 500 tapes, mid-1980s–present; and more than 20 edited videos that may be borrowed. The audiovisual materials are relevant to the subjects of alliance systems, international organizations, and economic development.

3. The photographs and slides focus on European Union Council meetings, officials, events, and headquarters buildings as well as industry sectors. Logos and maps are also available.

Stock footage library documents political events and aspects of European life. Topics include European Summit meetings; state visits; Trans-European networks and communications; East and Central Europe transportation, infrastructure, financial organizations; environment; and European monetary union. There is also a small collection of archival films from the 1970s.

The edited videos cover topics that include recession and unemployment, German unification, aspects of 1992 Single Market, and research and technological development. "Europe World Partner" features archival footage and special effects graphics.

4.a–b. Direct access normally granted to producers; other researchers are accommodated by mail through loan of materials.

c. Fees are not charged.

d. Duplications are made for producers from stock footage under some circumstances.

5. Descriptive list of the videos and shots-lists of the stock footage are available.

6. Index Terms: Collective Security—Regional Alliance Systems; International Economics—Integration; International Organizations—Regional

See also entry A13 and L2

## Fort George G. Meade Army Museum (Army Department) See entry C3

## George Mason University—Fenwick Library See entry A18

## George Washington University—Gelman Library See entry A19

---

## FIO Georgetown University—Lauinger Library—Special Collections—Photographs and Films

1.a. 37th and O Streets, NW
Washington, D.C. 20057-1006
(202) 687-7444

b. 9:00 A.M.–5:00 P.M. Monday–Friday

c. Open to the public, but the collection does not circulate.

d. George M. Barringer, Special Collections Librarian

2. Among other archival materials, the Special Collections Department holds significant photograph collections pertaining to diplomacy, international relations, and military history, planning, and strategy. Many of the manuscript or personal papers collections contain small photograph collections. There is also a film and video collection pertinent to defense and peace issues.

3. The following collections contain material relevant to international security and peace studies:

### PHOTOGRAPHS

Ernest Larue Jones Collection, 1863–1917: 1,500 items relating to early American aviation, including military.

Richard Crane Papers, 1915–38. Photographs taken during Crane's diplomatic career assignments around the world. There are many images of diplomatic events and places, especially in the Czech Republic and Slovakia.

Cornelius Van H. Engert Papers, 1917–65. This U.S. diplomat's personal papers contain a significant number of international photographs, including a historical record of his time as U.S. Ambassador to Afghanistan.

Thomas Murray Wilson Papers, 1899–1942: 3,500 items. These images reflect Wilson's assignments and travels in Asia, Africa, and Europe as well as other countries where he served as a diplomatic officer.

Gene Basset Collection, 1960–80: 2,000 items. American political figures, including those in military and diplomatic affairs, from the Kennedy administration through the Carter administration.

Journalists' Papers, Georgetown has significant personal papers collections covering foreign affairs from journalists Roscoe Drummond, Michael Amrine, Frank Reynolds, and André Visson, including some photographs and tape recordings, as well as materials from William R. Downs and Riley Hughes.

Editorial Cartoon Collections: late 1800s–present. Nearly 200 original editorial cartoons relating to national and international issues.

## FILMS

McCarthy Historical Project Archive, 1967–70 (445 lin. ft.). This is one of the largest records collections of any U.S. political primary campaign, during which international relations and peace issues were particularly conspicuous. It includes stills; four hundred reels of uncut footage, some of it by the documentarist Emile de Antonio; and 600,000 feet of two-inch videotape of political commercials.

Department of Defense Film Collection: contains hundreds of scripts submitted to the Defense Department between 1948 and 1960, bearing mainly on military history and propaganda.

4.a. Audiovisual equipment is available.

b. Reservations should be made by phone or letter.

c. Fees are not charged for viewing.

d. Materials may be copied, with permission.

5. The collections in this division are described in a richly illustrated catalog, *Special Collections at Georgetown* (1989).

6. Index Terms: Diplomacy and Negotiations; International Politics; Military History; Pacifism and Peace Movements

See also entries A20, B6, E6, and J7

---

**FII** Inter-American Development Bank (IDB)—Audiovisual Department

---

1.a. 1300 New York Avenue, NW
Washington, D.C. 20577
(202) 623-1357
Fax: (202) 623-3096

b. 9:00 A.M.–5:30 P.M. Monday–Friday

c. Open to the public by appointment. Use of the collection is subject to review by the Office of External Relations.

d. Luis M. Galvan, Photo Librarian

2. The IDB Photo Library has a collection of some 150,000 photographs, 1960–present, dealing with Latin American socioeconomic, agricultural, and technical development projects funded by the IDB. From the viewpoint of this Guide the main area of interest is economic development.

3. Specific subjects include industry, energy, agriculture, health, education, and infrastructure. Photographs also depict IDB events and staff.

4.a. Audiovisual equipment is not required.

b. Appointments are necessary.

c. Prints, slides, and captions are supplied without charge.

d. Materials may not be used for advertising purposes.

6. Index Terms: Development Issues—Aid and Investment

See also entries A24 and L7

---

**FI2** International Bank for Reconstruction and Development (World Bank)—Photo Library/Film Unit

---

1.a. 1818 H Street, NW
Washington, D.C. 20433
(202) 473-1789
Fax: (202) 676-0578

b. 9:00 A.M.–5:30 P.M. Monday–Friday

c. Open to researchers by appointment.

d. Maggie Sheen, Public Affairs Adviser (202) 473-1789
Francis Dobbs, Head, Film Unit (202) 473-2126

2. The World Bank Photo Library maintains a collection of approximately 10,000 black-and-white prints and somewhat fewer color slides. The Film Unit has a collection of approximately 100 video tapes. Both collections deal with bank-funded economic development projects worldwide. Within the scope of this Guide these holdings fall under the area of economic development.

3. The photograph collection in the Photo Library consists of scenes of highway and dam construction, rural development, and family planning activities in some 70 developing countries. Major subject areas are agriculture, industry, social services, and trans-

portation. The video collection in the Film Unit documents the same type of development projects; it also provides information on the structure and functions of the World Bank and the International Finance Corporation.

4.a–b. Appointments are required to view the collections.

c–d. Print copies of black-and-white photographs are provided without charge for nonadvertising purposes, but must be properly acknowledged. The video tapes may be borrowed under certain conditions.

5. A computerized catalog for the Photo Library is under preparation. A list of the video tapes is available from the Film Unit.

6. Index Terms: Development Issues—Aid and Investment

See also entries A27, D3, G8, and L8

## FI3 International Labor Organization (ILO) (United Nations)—Washington Branch Office Library—Photograph Collection

1.a. 1828 L Street, NW, Suite 801
Washington, D.C. 20036
(202) 653-7652

b. 9:00 A.M.–4:30 P.M. Monday–Friday

c. Open to the public by appointment.

d. Jean Decker Mathews, Technical Information Officer

2. The collection consists of some 3,000 black-and-white prints. Within the scope of this Guide it concerns areas of conflict resolution, human rights and humanitarian issues, and economic development.

3. The photographs relate to workers and working conditions worldwide. The collection is arranged by topic. Topics include cooperatives, employment, ILO conferences and projects, living conditions, labor conditions, production, social security, trade unions, vocational training, welfare facilities, and women workers. Within most topic files a researcher may find coverage for all major world regions. Contents of the total collection date from 1919 to the present.

4.a. Audiovisual equipment is not necessary.

b. Appointments are required.

c. No fees are charged.

d. Duplicating services are provided on a selective basis. Proper credit must be given to the ILO when the items are published.

5. Three drawers contain folders of photographs arranged alphabetically by subject. There is no catalog or index.

6. Index Terms: Conflict Resolution and Management—Unofficial and Non-Governmental Approaches; International Organizations—Labor; International Organizations—United Nations

*Note:* The prints have been drawn from the much larger photo library at the ILO headquarters in Geneva, Switzerland. The *ILO Photo Library: Catalogue* (Geneva, 1973) describes the content and arrangement of the collection, and provides instructions on how researchers may order prints from Geneva.

See also entries A25 and L10

## FI4 Library of Congress (LC)—Motion Picture, Broadcasting, and Recorded Sound Division—Motion Picture and Television Reading Room

1.a. James Madison Building, Room 336
Independence Avenue, SE
(between 1st and 2d Streets)
Washington, D.C. 20540-4805
(202) 707-8572

b. 8:30 A.M.–5:00 P.M. Monday–Friday

c. The reading room is open to the public. The viewing facilities, however, are limited to those doing research leading to a publicly available work, such as a publication, thesis, or film/television production.

d. David Francis, Chief
Patrick J. Sheehan, Head, Documentation and Reference Section
Rosemary Hanes, Reference Librarian
Madeline Matz, Reference Librarian

2. The Motion Picture, Broadcasting, and Recorded Sound Division of the Library of Congress (LC) is responsible for the acquisition, cataloging, preservation, and service of the motion picture and television collections, including items on film, video-

tape, and videodisc. Television and film collections number over 250,000 titles. Annual acquisitions are the result of copyright deposit, purchase, gift, and exchange. From the viewpoint of peace and international security studies the relevant material falls under the rubrics of diplomacy, foreign affairs, military history, terrorism, war, and violence. For a discussion of LC's collections of recorded sound see entry E8.

3. Within the scope of this Guide the following motion picture and television collections are pertinent:

Actualities, 1894–1912: about 1,300 with an additional 60 re-creations of events. These brief films are the precursors of newsreels and television news. Many items include subjects of military history and affairs, such as the Spanish-American War. There are also numbers of international policy items featuring Presidents William McKinley and Theodore Roosevelt. The collection is described and indexed in Kemp R. Niver's *Early Motion Pictures, the Paper Print Collection in the Library of Congress.*

Copyright Deposits Collection, 1942–present: 100,000 titles. Newsreels in the copyright deposits include "Movietone News" with a few issues 1942–59 and almost continuous runs 1960–63; "News of the Day" with a few issues 1941–56 and a continuous run 1957–67; "Paramount News" with some issues 1942–57; and "Universal Newsreels" with scattered issues 1941–45, no issues for 1955–56, and continuous runs for the remaining years 1946–67. (*Note:* A researcher on American newsreels [1929–67] should also check the relevant holdings at the National Archives and Records Administration, see entry F20.) Television news, with a six- to eight-month lag, includes "ABC Evening News" beginning 1977; some "Nightline" beginning 1987; nearly all CBS news programs beginning 1975 and "60 Minutes" from 1968. There are growing collections of NBC news and deposits of Vanderbilt Television News Archives master tapes.

Embassy of South Vietnam Collection, 1950s–60s: 527 reels. Documentaries and newsreels, bearing on military history, terrorism, and low intensity conflict, which had been at the embassy until the fall of South Vietnam in April 1975. A limited number of reference prints are available, and the collection is described in a study guide and in the subject files.

German Newsreels and Films, 1919–46: 3,000 titles. After World War II this group of German films was confiscated by the U.S. government and transferred to LC. A 1963 agreement with the German government gave the copyrights back to the original owners but allowed the library screening privileges and the permanent custody of the prints. The collec-

tion contains over 1,000 newsreels, including extensive runs of "Die Deutsche Wochenschau" (1934–45). The numerous educational and documentary shorts, all in the original language, are also of relevance to the users of this Guide because of their political and war propaganda content. Reference prints are available for most of the newsreels, and 60 percent of the shorts. There is a card index.

Italian Newsreels and Films, 1930–43: 500 titles. This group of Italian films was confiscated by the U.S. government after World War II and transferred to LC. In 1963 the copyrights were returned to the original owners; the library maintained screening rights and permanent custody of the prints. The collection includes documentary, newsreel, education, and propaganda films, all with Italian soundtracks. Reference prints are available for most of the 275 "Istituto Luce" newsreels (1938–43) and 100 "Luce" shorts (1930–43). There are fact sheets for most of the newsreels. The collection is listed, title by title, in a card index.

Japanese Newsreels and Films, 1933–45: 1,400 titles. These films were confiscated after World War II and transferred to LC. In 1962 the copyrights were returned to the original owners; the library maintained screening rights and permanent custody of the prints. Newsreels include "Asahi News" (1935–39), "Yomiuri News" (1936–40), and "Nippon News" (1940–45). Of interest to the users of this Guide are also 700 educational and documentary shorts that have political and war propaganda content. Reference prints are available for many titles. The collection is in Japanese, but English translations of headlines for "Asahi News" and English summaries for "Nippon News" are available in the reading room.

"Meet the Press" Collection, 1949–present: 2,000 titles. Lawrence Spivak and the National Broadcasting Company (NBC) donated a large collection of "Meet the Press" materials. Most of the paper materials are in the Lawrence Spivak Papers in the Manuscript Division (B8); photographs and cartoons are in the Prints and Photographs Division (F15); and the audiotapes are held by the Recorded Sound Section (E8). There are reference prints for many of the telecasts, and a published guide to all of the library's "Meet the Press" materials is available.

National Broadcasting Corporation (NBC) Collection, 1948–77: 18,000 programs. This collection from the early decades of television was mostly produced by NBC and is either kinescopes of live broadcasts or productions on film. International affairs includes documentaries and coverage of special events. Most of the collection is made up of negative film and is not yet accessible to researchers.

National Educational Television (NET) Collection, 1955–69: 10,000 programs. The early decades of noncommercial television, bearing in large part on international affairs, are documented in this three-part collection. The earliest acquisition was 550 titles of educational and instructional programming from 1965–67. These titles are in the Film and Television Card Catalog, and reference prints are generally available. The next acquisition was 1,019 titles, mostly instructional and intended for broadcast to schools and universities. The third part is the 8,000-title collection formerly known as the Public Television Archives. This collection includes both U.S. and international series. There is only a title list for the second and third parts of the collection and no reference copies because it is mostly on negative filmstock.

U.S. House of Representatives Floor Proceedings, 1979–present: more than 4,000 items. On January 15, 1979 the House began limited coverage of floor proceedings; regular coverage, including international and military affairs, began in 1983. These are recorded by the House Recording Unit and sent to the Library of Congress and National Archives and Records Administration (entry F20, RG 233) quarterly. This collection of floor proceedings is accessible only by using the *Congressional Record*.

U.S. Senate Floor Proceedings, 1986–present: more than 7,000 items. On June 2, 1986 the Senate began limited television coverage of Senate floor proceedings; regular coverage began in October, 1989. Video copies are deposited in the Library of Congress and the National Archives and Records Administration (entry F20, RG 46) quarterly. The material includes a wide coverage of international and military affairs. To locate items, it is necessary to use TV logs, which are located in the National Archives and Records Administration (entry F20, RG 46) and the *Congressional Record* on microfiche.

Miscellaneous Television Collections. The library does off-air recording of Public Broadcasting System (PBS) productions and others, often covering international and military affairs, and adds them to the division's collections. The library also has master video recordings from the Vanderbilt Television News Archive.

See also the National Public Broadcasting Archives at the University of Maryland at College Park, entry F31

4.a. Film and video machines with headphones are available for individual research.

b. Viewing equipment must be reserved in advance, usually at least one week.

c. No fees are charged for equipment use.

d. Duplication services are available for film footage not under copyright or other restriction.

5. The Film and Television Catalog, although not entirely dependable, has an entry, by title, for each non-nitrate motion picture and television production received before 1986. It is the best finding-aid available. Entry cards for motion pictures may include release date, production company, director, a synopsis, credits and notes on the availability of a reference print, and preprint materials. Entries for television materials are by series title and by episode title. Some of the television holdings are also indexed by "content descriptors," 41 categories of genre and subject descriptors.

Study guides have been prepared by the staff, including "Discovery and Exploration Footage in the Library of Congress," "Films and Videos about World War I," "Labor-related Films in the Library of Congress," "U.S. Naval Academy Collection of Soviet and Russian Television in the Library of Congress," and "Vietnam on Film and Television: Documentaries in the Library of Congress."

The Special Collections Card Index is arranged by collection and has an entry for each motion picture in those collections.

The Nonfilm Card Catalog contains information on non-motion picture materials within the division. This catalog is arranged by title of the related motion picture; some entries list available stills, reviews, publicity materials, and other documentation.

Some of the holdings of the Motion Picture, Broadcasting, and Recorded Sound Division are included in the electronic finding-aids, LOCIS (Library of Congress Information System, within subsystems MUMS and SCORPIO) and COHM (Copyright History Monograph file). The systems are different from each other and complex, but learnable. Both are accessible on terminals in the reading room.

A useful printed catalog is *Three Decades of Television: A Catalog of Television Programs Acquired by the Library of Congress, 1949–1979*, by Sarah Rouse and Katharine Loughney (Washington, D.C.: Library of Congress, 1989), which describes 14,000 television programs in the Library of Congress and uses 41 content descriptors in its subject index. A helpful source that lists items that may not be in LC's collection is *Catalog of Copyright Entries Cumulative Series, Motion Pictures*. Consisting of five volumes in 1988, the *Catalog* listed over 135,000 motion pictures registered since the beginning of the motion picture industry through 1969.

6. Index Terms: Diplomacy and Negotiations; Foreign Policy; Low Intensity Conflict; Military History; Terrorism

See also entries A29, B8, D4, E8, and FI5

---

## FI5 Library of Congress (LC)—Prints and Photographs Division

---

1.a. James Madison Building, Room 337
Independence Avenue, SE
(between 1st and 2d Streets)
Washington, D.C. 20540
(202) 707-5836 (Division Office)
(202) 707-6394 (Reference)

b. 8:30 A.M.–5:00 P.M. Monday–Friday

c. Open to the public but photo-identification and registration are required. In 1988 the division ceased to provide access, in most instances, to unprocessed (closed) collections.

d. Stephen E. Ostrow, Chief
Bernard F. Reilly, Head, Curatorial Section (202) 707-8685
Mary Ison, Head, Reference Section (202) 707-8867

2. The Prints and Photographs Division cares for and makes available more than 15 million prints, photographs, and drawings with emphasis on architecture, design, and engineering; documentary photographs; fine prints; master photographs; popular and applied graphic arts; and posters. The photograph collection contains 11 million images and goes back to 1846. From the viewpoint of peace and international security studies the relevant material falls under the rubrics of diplomacy and international relations; human rights and humanitarian issues; immigration and colonization; political systems; military history, planning, and strategy; war and violence.

3. Photograph collections pertinent to the scope of this Guide are described under Aerial Photography Collections, Newsphoto Collections, and Special Collections.

### AERIAL PHOTOGRAPHY COLLECTIONS

These collections are relevant mainly to military history, planning, and strategy.
Ira Clarence Eaker Collection. Includes aerial photographs of oil refineries in Austria,

Czechoslovakia, Germany, Hungary, Italy, Poland, Romania, and Yugoslavia, 1944 (ca. 200 items); aerial photographs of bombing attacks on airfields, bridges, convoys, and rail yards, and other targets by the 8th and 9th Air Forces in France and Germany, some during the German Ardennes offensive, 1944–45 (ca. 750 prints); aerial photographs of bomb damage in cities and other areas in Burma, China, Formosa, Japan, Singapore, and Thailand, 1945 (142 prints; 2 maps); aerial photographic views of atomic bomb tests and photographs of the equipment and activities of Task Unit 1.52, Air Photo Unit, 58th Wing, U.S. Army Air Force, which recorded the atomic bomb tests over Bikini Atoll. (Lots 10407, 10410–13).

German Aerial Photographic Collection. Contains three separate collections of German aerial photographs of areas in Finland, France, and Italy, 1914–18, originally collected by the Air Division of the German War Ministry or the Rehse Archives in Munich (ca. 200 prints). Also, a teaching set of aerial photographs and maps produced by the Reichsluftfahrtministerium for photo-interpretation instruction, 1943 (3 folders). (Lots 3146, 3638, 3656, 4641).

German Materials Confiscated by U.S. Military Intelligence Authorities Collection. Includes a set of photographs of pictorial propaganda maps relating to the Nazi repatriation of Germans from southern and southeastern Europe, ca. 1939 (40 items); German aerial photographic mosaics of Poland and Yugoslavia, 1943 (111 prints); and German aerial photographs of French towns and areas in Austria and northern Italy during World War I. (Lots 2674, 2838, 2893, 3679).

Greenough Collection. Contains aerial photographs of communication lines and trenches in France, some captioned, prepared by the French Army's Section de Photo Aérienne, 1915, and of Forts Domaumont and Fleury, and others, 1916 (ca. 75). (Lot 4028).

John J. Pershing Collection. Includes a series of 14 albums relating to World War I combat activities, which contain many aerial photographs; large aerial photographic prints, aerial print mosaics, and aerial prints overprinted with intelligence and map information showing U.S. military installations, battlefields, and towns in France, 1918–19 (56 prints); an album of aerial photographs of Washington, D.C., taken from an observation balloon, 1919 (17 prints); and an album showing the facilities and work of the 29th Topographic Engineers (26 prints). (Lots 7707, 7712, 7715, 7729).

Polish Aerial Photograph Collection. Consists of composite German aerial photographs of Poland showing canals, rivers, roads, and towns, ca. 1943 (100 prints). (Lot 2893).

Carl A. Spaatz Collection. Contains aerial views of bombing attacks by the 8th Air Force in Germany, 1943–44 (153 prints); aerial photographs of D-Day landing craft, Berlin, and other areas taken by the Royal Air Force 106 Photoreconnaissance Group and the U.S. Army Air Force 7th Photo Group, 1944 (56 prints); aerial views of urban areas and bombing targets in Japan, 1945 (150 prints); an album of captioned aerial photographs documenting the Allied invasion of Europe, 1944 (1 volume); annotated strike and reconnaissance aerial photography, some relating to the Normandy invasion on June 6, 1944 (50 prints); and a photographic history of the 9th Air Force Tactical Operations during the German offensive in the Ardennes, which contains about 100 aerial photographs, 1944–45. (Lots 6116–19, 7587).

Nathan Farragut Twining Collection. Consists of aerial photographic prints documenting the reconnaissance and bombing operations of the U.S. Strategic Air Forces in Europe and the U.S. 15th Air Force in southeastern Europe, 1944–45 (22 volumes); aerial photographs of Japanese cities and a photo album recording the activities of the Air Photo Unit of the 58th Wing of the Army Air Force "Operations Crossroads," which filmed the testing of the atomic bomb, 1946 (2 volumes).

U.S. Air Force Collections. Includes aerial photographs of islands, shorelines, and landing fields in Costa Rica, Guatemala, Honduras, and Salvador, ca. 1932–45 (74 prints); aerial photographs of the bombing of the U.S. battleship *Alabama*, 1921 (20 prints); aerial photographs of the ruined parts of Nagoya and Tokyo, Japan, following U.S. bombing raids, 1939–45 (11 prints); photographs of photo reconnaissance equipment and photointerpreters during World War II (18 prints); and aerial views of the bombing of the Gilbert Islands and Ploesti, Romania, 1943. (Lots 838, 852, 2373–75, 2399, 3541, 3894, 7735, 9779).

U.S. Army Collection. Contains aerial photographic prints of the Japanese occupied Aleutian Islands and the invasion of Sicily, 1943. Also, aerial photographs, interfiled among 4,500 captioned photographs prepared by the Photographic Branch of the U.S. Army's Persian Gulf Command, showing ports, railroads, and roads in Iran, ca. 1950. (Lots 803, 805).

U.S. Defense Department Collection. Contains aerial photographs of ballistic missile sites in Cuba, 1962 (14 copy photographs) and aerial photographs of airfields and seaplane landings in the Hawaiian Islands, ca. 1933 (62 prints). (Lot 6372).

## NEWSPHOTO COLLECTIONS

These collections are relevant mainly to the areas of diplomacy and international relations, and to the study of political systems.

German news photo compilations: "Grossdeutschland im Weltgeschehen," 1939–42: 1,325 photos. Annual compilations of the events of the German war effort. "Im Kampf und das Dritte Reich," 1936–42: 23 volumes. The Nazi Party in Bavaria. Reichsministerium . . . , 1937: 272 items. All are on microfilm.

*Look Magazine* Collection, 1940s–71: 5 million items. The photo archives of *Look Magazine*, 1937–71. The collection documents political developments in the world in the middle of the 20th century. Access is limited to citations from the magazine itself although the collection holds many photos not published in *Look*. Unprocessed.

*New York World-Telegram and Sun Collection,* 1920–60s: 1.25 million items. The complete picture files of a series of New York newspapers. There are enormous numbers of subjects relevant to international relations and military events and policy. This collection will soon be fully cataloged.

*U.S. News and World Report:* (85 drawers) 1953–86. Contact sheets of photos taken for the publication. They are arranged by month, and each contact sheet is labeled. There is an elaborate card catalog by subject. Negatives are available for this entire collection.

## SPECIAL COLLECTIONS

These collections include materials relevant to military history, immigration and colonization, and the study of political systems. Abdul-Hamid II Collection, late 1800s: 2250 items. Photos of Turkey collected to show Turkey as a modern European state. The photos include formal views of military activities and facilities.

American Colonization Society Collection, 1823–1912: 550 photos and prints. Portraits of the founders and promoters of the society that encouraged a return to Africa.

American National Red Cross Collection, early 1900s: 62,000 photos. Work of the Red Cross services before, during, and after World War I with refugees, U.S. military personnel, and medical facilities in Europe and Asia. Most of the collection is unprocessed.

Civil War Photograph Collection, 1861–65: 10,000 negatives. Photos by Matthew Brady, but most by his staff of photographers, and others to document the conflict. Most portraits and images of troops, facilities, and landmarks are of the Union armies and navy. There are a few Confederate studio and field portraits. Some of these are in the Civil War File in the reading room. Also available on microfilm. A Civil War Card Catalog is available in the reading room.

Office of War Information (OWI), 1940–50. The library holds part of the photo collection of OWI, which served publication, exhibit, and filmstrip programs. World War II from the U.S. viewpoint and the U.S. way of life are the focus of the collection but there are some foreign subjects. OWI photos are also at the National Archives and Records Administration (F21, RG 208).

PH Series or Photograph Series, 1842–present (*formerly* Master Photographs Collection): 5,000 items. These photographs illustrate and document significant aspects of the development of the art of photography. Beginning with callotypes by Henry Fox Talbot and others, the images include daguerreotypes and examples of the wet-plate era. There is considerable photo coverage of the Civil War and the Crimean War. Although most photographs in the library are described in groups, this growing body of photographs, chosen for aesthetic or historical reasons, is individually cataloged.

William "Billy" Mitchell Collection, 1888–1946: 4,800 items. Documentation of early aviation and the U.S. Army career of Gen. Billy Mitchell including tours in the Philippines, Alaska, China, Korea, and Manchuria. Early in his army career he was a signal corps photographer.

See also entry F4

*Note:* There are hundreds of smaller collections, some described in *Guide to the Special Collections of Prints and Photographs in the Library of Congress,* by Paul Vanderbilt (Washington, D.C.: Library of Congress, 1955), as well as others that can be located in the division catalog or the shelflist in the reading room. Some of these collections include photos relevant to the scope of this Guide, such as eyewitness drawings by Civil War newspapermen, the Crimean War, 47 Hermann Goering albums, and photo albums of the Third Reich.

**OTHER MATERIALS**

Among the division's holdings are over 110,000 prints dating from the 1400s, and including woodcuts, engravings, etchings, lithographs, and other print media by artists throughout the world. Of special interest to the users of this Guide are the many war and propaganda posters.

4.a. Massive numbers of images are in the reading room and many others are viewable on microfilm and videodisc. Additional items can be ordered from the stacks.

b. Appointments may be required. Researchers are requested to call in advance of visit.

c–d. Patrons may make photocopies of most items or use their own still or video camera to make reference copies of the unrestricted parts of the collection. Copies may also be ordered through the library's Photocopying Services.

5. Card indexes, videodiscs, and the books cited above will guide researchers to the images they seek. There also are many reference books and published books of photographs in the reading room and a large collection of photo exhibit catalogs from around the world. The staff can guide the users to the appropriate finding-aids.

6. Index Terms: Diplomacy and Negotiations; Humanitarian Issues; International Politics; Military History; Military Science—Strategy and Tactics

See also entries A29, B8, D4, and F14

**Marine Corps Historical Center (Navy Department)—Marine Band Library   See entry E9**

---

**FI6**   Martin Luther King Memorial Library (District of Columbia Public Library)— Washingtoniana Division

---

1.a. 901 G Street, NW
Washington, D.C. 20001
(202) 727-1111 Recorded Information
(202) 727-1213

b. 9:00 A.M.–9:00 P.M. Monday–Thursday
9:00 A.M.–5:30 P.M. Friday, Saturday
1:00 P.M.–5:00 P.M. Sunday
Hours may vary in the summer.

c. To be eligible for a library card, a person must live, work, or own property in D.C. or reside in one of the member regions of the Metropolitan Council of Governments: Montgomery or Prince George's counties in Maryland; the cities of Arlington, Alexandria, or Falls Church, or the counties of Fairfax, Loudon, or Prince William in Virginia.

There is free, short-term parking in the basement of the library. Enter on 10th Street, between G and H Streets.

d. Roxanna Deane, *Division Chief*
Matthew Gilmore, *Reference Librarian*
Mary C. Ternes, *Photo Librarian*

2.   The Washingtoniana Division holds the *Washington Star* Collection, which includes the photo library of the *Washington Star* that ceased publication in 1981. The photo library reflects all the various topics covered in the newspaper that bear on fields germane to peace and international security studies, in particular diplomacy and international relations, conflict resolution, alliance systems, economic development, ethnic and religious conflict, human rights, humanitarian issues, international organizations, peacekeeping, regional conflict, war, and violence.

3.   The collection holds over 1 million images, 1960s–81, with a few older photographs. The images relate to international, as well as national and Washington, D.C., news. In addition the collection contains some 13 million clippings, 1940s–81, with a few dating back to the 1920s. This is the only newspaper morgue available to researchers in Washington.

4.a. Researchers may examine photographs in the research room.

b.   Reservations are normally not necessary.

c–d. Items in the public domain may be copied by researchers. Coin-operated photocopying machines are available.

5.   Photographs and clippings are arranged by subject and personal name.

6.   Index Terms: Collective Security: Diplomacy and Negotiations; Development Issues; Ethnic and Religious Conflict; Human Rights; Humanitarian Issues; International Organizations; Military History; Peacekeeping; Regional Conflict

## FI7   Media Research Center (MRC)

1.a. 113 South West Street
Alexandria, Va. 22314
(703) 683-9733
Fax: (703) 683-9736

b.   9:00 A.M.–5:00 P.M. Monday–Friday

c.   The video and newsletter collections are open to the public. Appointments are necessary.

d.   Brent Baker, *Editor*
Tim Graham, *Associate Editor*

2.   The mission of the Media Research Center (MRC) is to document liberal bias in the news media. However, the collection, which includes over 5,000 videotapes of network news (1987–present), provides a substantial coverage of international affairs and defense policies and is, therefore, valuable for researchers in international security and peace studies.

3.   The programs, taped off-air from CBS, ABC, NBC, CNN, and PBS's "MacNeil-Lehrer Newshour," include all evening news broadcasts; most morning news shows; news magazines such as "60 Minutes," "Primetime Live," and "Real Life"; and overnight news shows such as "Nightline" and "Night Watch."

4.a. Audiovisual equipment is available.

b.   Reservations are required.

c.   Fees are not charged for viewing.

d.   Materials may be copied, with permission.

5.   MRC has compiled a database of summaries of newscasts. Researchers may apply to use this database. MRC also publishes *Media Watch* (1987–present), a monthly newsletter of media analysis, and *Notable Quotables* (1988–present), a "biweekly compilation of quotes . . . from the liberal media."

6.   Index Terms: Collective Security; Defense Policy, National; Foreign Policy; Military History

## FI8   National Air and Space Museum (NASM) (Smithsonian Institution)—Archives Division—Film Archives

1.a. 6th Street and Independence Avenue, SW, Room 3103-C
Washington, D.C. 20560
(202) 357-4721
Fax: (202) 786-2835

b.   10:00 A.M.–4:00 P.M. Monday–Friday

c.   Open to adults. Appointments must be made at least a day in advance.

d.   Mark Taylor, *Film Archivist*

2.   The collection consists of 700,000 feet of motion picture and video tape, 1908–present, documenting the history of aviation and space exploration. Relevant material falls mainly under the rubrics of military history, planning, and strategy.

Photographic archives are described in entry FI9, the museum's general archives in BIO, library holdings in entry A32, and museum artifacts in entry C6.

3. The collection includes a complete set of "The Air Force Story," a 33-chapter history. This series is the best single source of film clips concerning the air force prior to 1962. There are many other World War II air force documentaries.

The aeronautics collections of historical materials have been donated by government agencies, aerospace manufacturers, trade and professional associations, and individuals. The astronautics and astronomy collection consists primarily of films produced by NASA. The emphasis of the collection is on the 1950s and 1960s, particularly U.S. manned space flight program. Of particular interest from the viewpoint of international cooperation in space is the material on the Apollo-Soyuz test project.

4.a. Viewing equipment is available.

b. Appointments should be made at least one day before the planned visit.

c–d. In addition to the photocopier shared by the Archives Division and the NASM Branch Library, videoprinters are attached to each videodisc player in the reading room. The videoprints, black-and-white thermal prints much like small photocopies, are 20 cents each, although the archive usually does not charge researchers for fewer than five prints. Normal photocopies are 15 cents.

5. There is a computer database that is indexed by title (abstract and key word descriptors), producer, running time, and date.

6. Index Terms: Military History—Air Force

See also entries A32, BIO, C6, and FI9

---

## FI9  National Air and Space Museum (NASM) (Smithsonian Institution)—Archives Division—Photographic Archives

1.a. 6th Street and Independence Avenue, SW, Room 3100
Washington, D.C. 20560
(202) 357-3133
Fax: (202) 786-2835

b. 10:00 A.M.–4:00 P.M. Monday–Friday

c. Open to adults. Appointments at least a day in advance are required; a week in advance is recommended.

d. Melissa Keiser, Chief Photo Archivist

2. Total holdings are between 1.5 and 1.7 million images, 1850–present, covering aerospace history and technological achievements; this includes prints, negatives, and transparencies in a variety of formats. The bulk of the collections are black-and-white, with color accounting for no more than 5 percent of the total number of images. Relevant material falls mainly under the rubrics of military history, planning, and strategy. The museum's film archives are described in entry FI8, general archives in BIO, library holdings in entry A32, and museum artifacts in entry C6.

3. The majority of the collections concern aviation, both in the United States and abroad, including the Wright Brothers, military aviation, aviation manufacturers, and the collections of several aviation photographers.

Of particular interest to the users of this Guide is the U.S. Air Force Pre-1954 Official Still Photography Collection. This collection of approximately 145,000 images (5,300 in color) is administered for the U.S. Air Force by the NASM Archives Division. The collection, which covers the history of the U.S. Air Force (USAF) and its predecessors (U.S. Army Air Corps and U.S. Army Air Forces) prior to 1954, consists of photographs collected by the air force as a representative record. Post-1982 material is still maintained by the Defense Department's Still Media Records Center (F8); the material covering 1955 to 1981 has been deposited in the Still Picture Branch of the National Archives and Records Administration (F21, RG 342).

The photographic prints in the collection have been rehoused into document boxes, retaining their original USAF arrangement. Almost all photographs retain their original USAF captions, which vary in length from a single phrase to several paragraphs. The collection is divided into five series that are roughly chronological in nature: Pre-1940 (81 boxes), World War II (204 boxes), Pre-1954 Domestic (231 boxes), Pre-1954 Non-Domestic (5 boxes), and Korean War (62 boxes). Each series has its own system of organization, but all are essentially arranged alphabetically according to topic. The whole of the collection has been reproduced on two analog laser videodiscs and a detailed USAF subject heading finding-aid is currently available.

The Pre-1940 and Pre-1954 Domestic series, combined for convenience in the collection finding-aid, consist of photographs taken in the United States. Subjects covered include foreign and domestic aircraft; bombing tests (including nuclear weapons testing); photographic, electronic, and other equipment; training; fields and installations; personnel; operations; and organizations within the air force. Also included is a large section relating to the American Expeditionary Force (AEF) in France in World War I. The following may be of particular interest to readers of this Guide: a group of 120 maps and charts showing noteworthy flight routes, 1920s–30s; maps prepared under the direction of Col. William Mitchell showing spheres of influence and radii of airplane action in Asia and the Atlantic, 1920s–30s; and maps of air defenses used during lectures at the Army War College by Gen. H. H. Arnold and other officers, 1936–38.

The World War II series (approximately 50,000 photographs) includes aircraft, crews, fields and installations, reconnaissance, bombing, prisons and prisoners, captured material, and strafing and combat. This series includes some reconnaissance and strike photography, but not all the aerial photography taken by the U.S. Army Air Force during World War II. Researchers seeking aerial photographs taken at specific times, places, or during specific raids should contact the Cartographic and Architectural Branch of the National Archives and Records Administration (D6, RG 373), which has a much larger collection of World War II aerial photography.

The Pre-1954 Non-Domestic series is relatively small (approximately 2,000 photographs) and consists of post-World War II activities overseas. It is arranged alphabetically by country and topic and includes subjects such as the Berlin Airlift ("Operation Vittles") and the occupation of Japan. The Korean War series covers USAF activities during the Korean War and includes aircraft, bombing, crews, fields and installations, operations, photography (by type), prisons and prisoners, strafing and combat, training, transportation, troops and paratroops, and conferences.

4.a. Viewing equipment is available.

b. Appointments should be made at least one day before the planned visit; appointments of one week in advance are recommended.

c–d. In addition to the photocopier shared by the Archives Division and the NASM Branch Library, videoprinters are attached to each videodisc player in the reading room. The videoprints, black-and-white thermal prints much like small photocopies, are available for a small fee, as are normal photocopies. Copy photographs may be ordered through the Smithsonian Institution Office of Printing and Photographic Services (202/357-1487).

5.   The databases constructed for use by the Photo Archives are generally collection-specific. The technical files and collections are generally arranged alphabetically by topics as are the various indexes that help the researcher in assessing the different collections. The archives also publishes various summaries of its holdings and facilities.

In addition, there are seven analog videodiscs that describe portions of the holdings. Scholars should contact the Archives Division for current information on purchasing copies of the videodiscs.

6.   Index Terms: Military History—Air Force

See also entries A32, B10, C6, and F18

---

**F20   National Archives and Records Administration (NARA)—Nontextual Archives Division (NNS)—Motion Picture, Sound, and Video Branch (NNSM)—Film and Video Collection**

1.a. 8601 Adelphi Road
   College Park, Md. 20740-6001
   (301) 713-7060
   Fax (301) 713-6904
   Fax-on-demand: (301) 713-6905

b. 8:45 A.M.–5:00 P.M. Monday–Friday
   Some evening and Saturday hours by appointment.

c. Open to researchers with a National Archives identification card, obtainable from the Reference Services Division. First-time users should speak with a consultant before beginning work.

d. John Scroggins, Chief
   Les Waffen, Assistant Chief

2.   The National Archives' Motion Picture, Sound, and Video Branch holds some 80 million feet of film, 250,000 reels of film, and 45,000 video recordings that have been produced by a variety of U.S. government agencies, private individuals, and foreign governments. (The sound recordings held by the branch are discussed in entry E11.) The collection, 1894–1990s, contains a wealth of material for students of peace and international security issues, including newsreels, documentaries, and propaganda films. Subjects within the scope of this Guide include arms control, international relations, diplomacy and negotiations, international organizations, economic development, international trade, ethnic and reli-

gious conflict, human rights and humanitarian issues, political systems, peace movements, military history and planning, violence, terrorism, and war crimes.

3.   Films and video recordings, pertinent to peace and international security studies, are located either in the Record Groups (RG) or in the collection of Donated Materials.

## RECORD GROUPS

The records of a single government agency or subdivision are preserved in numbered collections called Record Groups (RG). The Record Group system serves those who are interested in locating media materials produced or acquired by a particular government agency. To facilitate a subject orientation, the following table places relevant RGs (discussed further on in this entry) under major subject headings:

Arms Control: RG 46, RG 330
Diplomacy and Alliances: RG 18, RG 24, RG 46, RG 59, RG 64, RG 80, RG 111, RG 210, RG 226, RG 233, RG 306, RG 330
Economic Aid: RG 46, RG 59, RG 233, RG 286, RG 306, RG 326, RG 362
Ethnic and Religious Conflict: RG 59, RG 242
Human Rights and Humanitarian Issues: RG 24, RG 59, RG 208
International Organizations: RG 24, RG 59
International Trade: RG 46, RG 233, RG 306
Military History, Planning, and Strategy: RG 26, RG 46, RG 59, RG 171, RG 178, RG 208, RG 226, RG 233, RG 235, RG 242, RG 304, RG 306, RG 311, RG 330; Army: RG 77, RG 107, RG 111, RG 338; Air Force: RG 18, RG 243, RG 342; Navy and Marine Corps: RG 24, RG 80, RG 127, RG 428
Political Systems and Ideologies: RG 238, RG 242, RG 306
Terrorism: RG 18, RG 226, RG 233
War Crimes: RG 18, RG 111, RG 153, RG 238, RG 338, RG 342
War Propaganda: RG 24, RG 56, RG 179, RG 188, RG 208, RG 242, RG 263, RG 342
The following RGs hold relevant films and tapes:
**RG 18:** *Army Air Forces, 1912-49: 6,132 items.*
World War II training films illustrating the coordination of the various operational units of the American 8th Army Air Force and the combined efforts of these units in preparing and completing a bombing mission; instructional films on flight, gunnery, and maintenance. Air Transport Command briefing films consisting of aerial and ground views of terrain, flight routes, and landing facilities in the South

and North Atlantic, Europe, India, China, the Caribbean, South America, Africa, the Pacific, and the British Isles.

Outtakes from "Thunderbolts," a 1946 William Wyler production documenting activities of the 12th Army Air Force in Europe, June 1944–April 1945. Combat footage made in all theaters of operation in World War II concerning activities of the USAAF and containing camera records on all other aspects of the war, including such things as land and sea battles; amphibious operations; civilian and military leaders of the Allied Powers attending conferences and visiting troops; war correspondents; Red Cross activities; native peoples and their customs and participation in the war; captured enemy spies and saboteurs; Allied and Axis prisoners of war and POW camps; internee camps; concentration camps; Axis atrocities; V-E and V-J Days; the occupation of Germany and Japan; the A-bomb blast over Nagasaki; and damage to Nagasaki and Hiroshima. Color footage shot by the army air force during the closing months of the war in France and Germany, March-June, 1945.

**RG 24:** *Bureau of Naval Personnel, 1917-27, 101 reels.*
Films of naval air activities during World War I in the Atlantic and at the Key West Naval Station, including submarine patrol, convoy escort, rescue operations, and ground operations; submarine maneuvers; marine training; torpedo manufacturing and firing; and mine laying in the North Sea from a base in England. Films of Liberty Loan drives, parades, ceremonies, and armistice celebrations in New York City, Washington, D.C., Pittsburgh, and London; films of President Wilson's first visit to Europe following the armistice, including the welcoming procession in the streets of Brest; war damage to Rheims, Ostend, and other areas of France and Belgium; German prisoners of war, captured German armament, and a U-boat. Films of World War I era leaders aboard U.S. Navy vessels.

Films of rescue operations by lighter-than-air craft, a demonstration of aerial mapping techniques at Miami, Fla.; post-World War I navy training in seamanship; dirigibles; airplanes aboard ships; navy yards and bases; the Naval Academy and the Great Lakes Naval Training Station. Films of the rescue of personnel from grounded and burning ships; and U.S., Italian, British, and Turkish navy ships in harbors, at sea, and on maneuvers.

1920-21: 5 items. News coverage and navy films of League of Nations, Red Cross, and U.S. Navy activities relating to the removal of Armenian and Greek refugees from Turkey to Greece, ca. 1921.

**RG 26:** *U.S. Coast Guard, 1918-55: 84 items.*
Films, 1918-38 and 1945-55, about activities during World War II, including dock and harbor patrol, ship inspection, investigations of ship sinkings, firefighting, weather observation, beach patrol, and a film showing FBI agents posing with German spies captured by the coast guard. Films of the coast guard overseas during World War II: amphibious operations, transportation of troops and materiel, rescue at sea, submarine patrol, and convoy escort.

**RG 46:** *U.S. Senate, 1986–present: over 7,000 items.*
On June 2, 1986, the Senate began limited television coverage of Senate floor proceedings; regular coverage began in October 1989. Video copies, including coverage of international relations and military affairs, are deposited in the Library of Congress (F14) and the National Archives quarterly. To locate desired material, use the *Congressional Record* on microfiche and the TV logs located in the reference room.

**RG 56:** *Department of the Treasury, 1941–78: 307 items.*
Incentive films and advertising spots used in connection with bond drives primarily during World War II but also the Korean War and the Vietnam War.

**RG 59:** *Department of State, 1911–68: 47 items.*
Films on foreign policy and history: the Panama Canal in 1911; Nazi infiltration in South America; Office of Strategic Services films about the invasions of Italy in 1944; the Foreign Liquidation Commission and surplus property programs in Italy in 1946; a United Nations film on students; Marshall Plan, Point 4, and other aid to Italy, France, Great Britain, Mexico, and Ecuador. United Nations films on the U.S. delegation, Abu Simel, Latin America, and the Indian Ocean.

1917–66: 160 items. News coverage of British Foreign Secretary Arthur J. Balfour's visit to Washington, D.C., 1917. Films of activities aboard the Swedish Red Cross ship *Gripsholm* in New York harbor as it prepared to repatriate Japanese citizens and deliver packages to U.S. prisoners of war in Japan, 1943.

Newsreels produced by the Office of War Information: reporting on World War II activities at home and in the combat theaters; covering a visit to the United States by Madame Chiang Kai-shek, 1943; and reenacting the sinking of the freighter *Delia B* by a German submarine and the sinking of the submarine by a B-24. News film of international events, 1945–51: the Japanese peace treaty conference held in San Francisco, 1951; the plight of Arab refugees from Israel in the Gaza Strip and Jerusalem, 1950; refugees from East Berlin, 1951; the Korean War;

and youth activities in East and West Germany, 1950–51. Televised speeches, interviews, and discussions, 1950–65, relating to U.S. foreign policy and world conditions.

**RG 64:** *National Archives and Records Administration, 1947–68: 19 items.*
"And That's the Way It Was, T.V. News 1947–1968," a series of 19 programs that were shown at the archives and then donated to the collection. Events include the Cuban missile crisis, the Bay of Pigs, the U-2 incident, the Nixon-Khrushchev debate, as well as many others.

**RG 77:** *Office of the Chief of Engineers, 1940–63: 102 items.*
Footage (16mm, color) of military construction. Color footage of the Trinity test of the atomic bomb on July 16, 1945.

**RG 80:** *Department of the Navy, 1798–1965: 1,083 items.*
World War II training films: naval aviation, ships, submarines, airplanes, training of personnel; kamikaze attacks; the battles of Midway and the Marianas; invasions of the Solomon Islands, Eniwetok, Saipan, and Guam; preparations for the invasions of the Ryukyus and Okinawa; and bombing raids over Japan. Captured enemy films relating to naval activities during World War II.

1938–45: unknown number. British and U.S. films of the Atlantic Conference between President Roosevelt and Prime Minister Churchill aboard the USS *Augusta*, 1941. "March of Time" issues about the U.S. Navy and Japan.

**RG 107:** *Office of the Secretary of War, 1941–45: 191 items.*
Films from the Bureau of Public Relations documenting U.S. military activities in all theaters of operation during World War II and activities of the Allied military governments in Europe and in the Far East. Some captured German films for the same period.

**RG 111:** *Office of the Chief Signal Officer, 1909–64: 22,436 items.*
Pre-World War I films about flight; the Panama Canal, 1910–14; and the Mexican Punitive Expedition, 1916. World War I films of American Expeditionary Forces in France; homefront activities, such as mobilization, training, and industrial production; U.S. Navy activities, submarine warfare, and convoys carrying troops overseas; British, French, Russian, and Italian participation in the war; the war in the Near East; peace celebrations in Paris and in the United States; and Pres. Woodrow Wilson in France and at the signing of the Treaty of Versailles.

World War II films of the conflict, including the Allies and the Axis Powers and their conduct of the war in all theaters; the Italian invasion of Ethiopia, 1935; the Spanish Civil War, 1937; the Japanese invasion of China, 1937; U.S. homefront activities and war production; mobilization and training; the roles of women, African Americans, and Nisei in the war effort; the atom bomb; the end of the war; the Cairo, Teheran, Yalta, Quebec, and San Francisco conferences; Allied military governments in Germany and Japan; postwar problems in Europe and Asia; and war crimes trials in Germany and Japan. Films relating to the Korean action and covering all aspects of the conflict and the peace negotiations.

**RG 127:** *U.S. Marine Corps, World War I–Vietnam: 2,934 items.*
Twenty-one edited World War II training films and films of combat in the South Pacific. Marine Corps Stock Film Library: unedited footage shot by the marine corps during wars from World War I to Vietnam and in the Caribbean.

**RG 153:** *Judge Advocate General (Army), 1940s–71: 7 items.*
Evidence used in the court martial of Lt. William Calley, including a film showing Viet Cong atrocities.

**RG 171:** *Office of Civilian Defense, 1941–45: 57 reels.*
Films used in training civilian defense workers.

**RG 178:** *U.S. Maritime Commission, 1924–45: 75 reels.*
Films depicting the history of the merchant marine from Revolutionary times through World War II; rescue work; and convoy duties in all theaters of operation during World War II. Films of shipbuilding; the manufacture of World War II trains, B-24 bombers, and tanks.

**RG 179:** *War Production Board, 1940–44: 15 reels.*
Films to stimulate war production; films of Allied and Axis military and political leaders.

**RG 188:** *Office of Price Administration, 1943–46: 15 reels.*
Films to enlist the cooperation of the public with rationing and price controls during World War II.

**RG 208:** *Office of War Information (OWI), 1941–45: 661 reels.*
Informational, propaganda, and documentary films covering all phases of homefront activities, including farming, industry, housing, education, manpower needs, the roles of women and African Americans in the war effort, resettlement of refugees, and Japanese relocation. Films urging citizen support for the war effort on the homefront. Films on lend-lease activities; all aspects of the war, from training of the armed forces to the fighting fronts in all theaters; Allied peoples, customs, and contributions to the war

effort; and Axis Powers and their conduct of the war, military strength, and ambitions.

"United News," a weekly newsreel sponsored by the OWI, covers aspects of the war, the homefront, and world political events. One series runs from mid-1942 to mid-1946; another from D-Day to VE-Day. Other newsreels include Free French newsreels, 1945; Russian News, made in Russia, 1942–45; and "War Pictorial News," produced in England, 1943.

**RG 210:** *War Relocation Authority (WRA), 1942–43: 7 items.*
Films about the activities of the WRA, life in relocation camps, and the training and combat record of Nisei (second-generation Japanese-American) soldiers in World War II.

**RG 226:** *Office of Strategic Services (OSS), 1937–45: 600 items.*
Films produced or acquired by the OSS include an assessment of Axis industrial, mineral, and agricultural resources; sociological portraits of the Japanese people; military equipment, explosives, sabotage, and training of OSS agents and commando units; operations in the Balkans; the Allied invasion of North Africa; the rescue of U.S. POW's in Romania; diplomatic and military missions to the Communist Chinese in Yenan, with footage of Mao Tse-tung and Chou En-lai; Yugoslav and Italian partisan activities; the training of Polish agents and Chinese Nationalist troops; films on the geography and wartime action in the China-Burma-India theater.

**RG 233:** *U.S. House of Representatives, 1953–present: 4,691 items.*
Videotapes of floor proceedings of the U.S. House of Representatives, bearing on a wide range of international and military affairs. Recorded by the House Recording Unit and sent to the National Archives and the Library of Congress (F14) quarterly. Videotapes of the past 60 days are available from the House Recording Unit.

1969–72: 16 items. Newscasts, newsreels, and documentary films gathered as evidence of the activities of those in opposition to government policies, including the Black Panther Party.

**RG 235:** *Department of Health, Education, and Welfare, 1963–73: 72 items.*
Films and public service announcements, including those on mobilizing hospitals for nuclear and other disasters.

**RG 238:** *National Archives Collection of World War II War Crimes Records, 1921–45: 76 items.*
Films used as evidence at the war crimes trials of Axis leaders before the International Military Tribunal, Nuremberg, 1945–46, and before the International Military Tribunal for the Far East, Tokyo,

1946–48. The collection consists of German films documenting the Nazi rise to power and triumphs in Europe, 1921–44; the political and industrial activities of the Krupp family and company officials, 1930–40; and the Nazi Supreme Court trial of the July 10, 1944 conspirators against Adolf Hitler. Films of concentration camps taken by U.S. and Russian forces as they advanced through Germany, 1945.

**RG 242:** *National Archives Collection of Foreign Records Seized, 1941–51: about 2,000 items.*
German documentaries covering World War I land and sea battles. Leni Riefenstahl's "Triumph of the Will" made at the 1934 Nazi Party rally at Nuremberg. A feature film that was used in anti-Semitic indoctrination, "The Jew Suss." The personal film collection of Eva Braun, ca. 1939–40. German films on the history of the Nazi Party in Germany, many aspects of World War II on all fronts, materiel manufacture and weapons development, German culture, and the training of Hitler Youth and political leaders for administrative posts in occupied countries. Italian documentaries covering World War II on several fronts, including the Ethiopian and Greek invasions and the North African campaign. Japanese documentaries, 1932–44, relating to the invasion of China and many aspects of the war in the Pacific.

Russian educational films, documentaries, and feature films. Films on the fall of Berlin at the end of World War II; the meeting of Russian and Western Allied troops at the Elbe; Hungary; the socialization of several republics of the Soviet Union; Soviet cooperation with other Communist countries; and North Korea, 1950. Also several anti-American dramas and North Korean films about the campaign against the Vietminh in Indochina. Chinese Communist anti-Nationalist propaganda films made during the post-World War II period. U.S. films relating to civilian victims of war, 1942, and to the escape of U.S. prisoners of war from the Island of Palawan in the Philippines.

1937–50: about 500 items. Newsreels, 1937–44, produced by Germany: "U.F.A. Newsreels," "Die Deutsche Wochenschau," "German News," and "German-Portuguese News." Those produced by Italy: "Italian News" and "Giornale di Guerra." Those produced by Japan: "Nippon News," "Yomiuri News," "Toa News," and "Asahi News." 1944 French newsreels. 1947–50 Russian newsreels from the series "Novosti Dnia," captured in North Korea in 1951. See Library of Congress (F14) for similar newsreels.

**RG 243:** *U.S. Strategic Bombing Survey, 1944: 11 items.*
Captured German films relating to U.S. incendiary bombs and bombing methods and to German war industries.

**RG 263:** *Central Intelligence Agency, 1952: 3 items.*
Films produced in China and Korea alleging U.S. use of germ warfare during the Korean War.

**RG 286:** *Agency for International Development, 1955–70s: 317 items.*
Films of the International Cooperation Administration and Agency for International Development, highlighting U.S. assistance to India, Libya, Ecuador, Indochina, Sudan, Ethiopia, Paraguay, Thailand, Indonesia, and Afghanistan. Topics include education, agriculture, and medicine. Films chronicle U.S. military assistance programs and cooperation in RIO, NATO, and SEATO.

**RG 304:** *Office of Civil Defense and Mobilization, 1952–61: 66 items.*
Films of the Federal Civil Defense Administration: nuclear bomb explosions, civil defense exercises and plans, and slow-motion footage of the 1955 Nevada atomic bomb tests.

**RG 306:** *U.S. Information Agency (USIA), 1942–86: 16,376 items.*
Documentaries produced or acquired by the agency for distribution abroad. Coverage of U.S. foreign relations: treaties, the Marshall Plan and reconstruction in Europe, visits of foreign heads of state to the United States, cultural exchange, international trade, and the Berlin airlift. Many instructional films that were used in technical assistance programs on such subjects as farming, child care, training of nurses and teachers, medicine, apprentice training, civilian defense, and industry.

1945–present: "World Net," a daily feed of news via satellite, beginning April 22, 1985. This two-hour news and information package includes 30 minutes of hard news, features, and cultural programs. Landmark telecasts include international satellite links for journalists, scientists, and educators. "Welt im Film," a German-language newsreel that was produced jointly by the British and U.S. military governments and shown in the British and U.S. zones of Germany, Austria, Vienna, and Berlin, 1945–52. The newsreels were part of the de-Nazification efforts.

There is a USIA film title card file but cataloging of the films, television, and sound recordings has just begun. "World Net" is indexed and there are USIA distribution catalogs.

**RG 311:** *Federal Emergency Management Agency, 1956–70: 99 items.*

Films, television programs, television spots: civil defense, the dangers of nuclear war, radiation, and fallout. Many programs focus on survival after a nuclear attack, including a television series "Ten for Survival."

**RG 326:** *Atomic Energy Commission (AEC), 1964: 255 items.*

Films about AEC's contribution to the peaceful uses of atomic energy. Seventy-nine films produced by the atomic energy agencies of the USSR, France, Italy, India, and Canada and shown at the Third International Conference on Peaceful Uses of Atomic Energy, Geneva, 1964.

**RG 330:** *Office of the Secretary of Defense (DOD), 1961–85: 598 items.*

DOD kinescopes of excerpts from television newscasts, August 20, 1965–August 20, 1970, which dealt with the Vietnam War and other stories of interest to the DOD such as arms limitation and foreign relations. The excerpts were taped off-air for internal use. Some typed daily summaries are available. This is a rare early collection of network news.

**RG 338:** *U.S. Army Commands, 1942–45: 51 items.*

Rolls of assembled footage of the Malmedy line during the Battle of the Bulge, as well as footage of the liberation of POW camps in relation to the War Crimes investigations into the Malmedy massacre and other atrocities against U.S. POWs.

**RG 342:** *U.S. Air Force Commands, Activities, and Organizations, 1900–1973: 4,179 items.*

History of Flight: Films made or collected by the air force on the history of the development of flight; and on the development of airplanes, gliders, balloons, dirigibles, autogiros, helicopters, rockets, jets, satellites, parachutes dating from the 1930s, ballistic cameras, and radar.

Noncombat Films: Films reflecting noncombat activities of the air force and its predecessors, 1920s to 1964, including the Berlin Airlift; women in the air force; training and maneuvers; the opening of the Air Force Academy, 1955; A-bomb tests in the Pacific and elsewhere; and research and development work in the fields of guided missiles, remote-control weapons, and supersonic flight.

Wartime Films: World War I films illustrating the activities of the army air service in France. World War II films concerning the army air forces: women in the AAF; combat footage of World War II; Dachau concentration camp; Axis concentration, prisoner-of-war camps, and atrocities; Allied bombing missions over Europe and Africa and in the Pa-

cific area; the defense of Britain and Moscow; "China Crisis," the 14th Air Force in China, 1944; "Wings for This Man," the Tuskegee airmen; the effects of bombing raids on Japan, including the atomic bombing of Hiroshima and Nagasaki; the surrender of Germany and Japan; and Allied occupation of Japan. Films on aerial aspects of the Korean action, combat, and truce-signing ceremonies. "News Review" series, 1956–61. Footage of the Tactical Air Command, Strategic Air Command, and the Aerospace Defense Command during the Cuban missile crisis, 1962.

Captured German films depicting the war in Poland and covering research and development of planes, gliders, helicopters, jets, rockets, and ballistic missiles, 1912–44. Captured Japanese films relating to preparations for the Pearl Harbor attack and World War II combat. A Russian film of the 1949 May Day celebration.

Stock Footage: Unedited footage, 1909–60s: the USAF Thunderbirds and their audiences in the U.S., Europe, and Latin America, 1958–67; footage from Bien Hoa Air Force Base, Vietnam, 1963–70, including activities and personnel on the base, in the air, in surrounding villages; visits by U.S. and South Vietnamese officials; footage of psychological warfare activities, 1971–73; turnover of aircraft to the Vietnamese Air Force; and much footage listed in a card file arranged by aircraft but otherwise uncataloged.

1952–64: 415 items. News Releases on Film: Korean combat, signing of the Korean truce, guided missile research, development of the X-15, construction of the DEW line, training of Chinese Nationalist Air Force, and U.S. Air Force activities in Vietnam.

**RG 362:** *Agencies for Voluntary Action Programs, 1961–71: 144 items.*

Films created, commissioned, or acquired by Peace Corps and other voluntary action programs: programs in action, conditions in other countries, and orientation to prepare volunteers for their assignments.

**RG 428:** *Department of the Navy, 1941–65: 12,347 items.*

This navy stock film collection is primarily silent, unedited footage. This collection includes comprehensive photographic coverage of World War II, the Korean conflict, and peacetime: naval and aerial operations, amphibious landings, cruises, launchings, sea rescues, submarines, experimental equipment, aircraft in flight, flight deck operations, the Allied occupation of Japan, returning prisoners of war, and military leaders. There are acquired newsreel clips and captured films.

## DONATED MATERIALS

These collections were formerly in Record Group (RG) 200. Because they are not government records, they have been removed from the Record Groups and handled separately. The following collections of documentaries, newsreels, and television programs are relevant to military history, international relations, international organizations, religious and ethical aspects of war and peace, and peace movements:

Films from foreign sources. Pictures of German air raids on London; the Russo-Finnish War; Dutch troops in exile and the liberation of Greece; a collection of German newsreels covering the early stages of the war.

League of Nations Collection, 1920–46: 56 reels. This collection consists of films of the first and last meetings of the league; of meetings and activities concerning such problems as the Greco-Bulgar incident, 1925, the Sino-Japanese conflict, 1932, and the Italo-Ethiopian conflict, 1936; of health and disarmament conferences; and of league delegates and officials.

"March of Time" (MT). This collection of edited documentaries consists of two major parts: the classic "March of Time," 1939–51: 205 releases, and "March of Time" for television, 1950s: 64 programs, both addressing international affairs, as well as U.S. domestic issues. There are also 15,000 reels of unedited footage.

National Council of Churches (NC), 1970–72: 26 reels. Discussions and interviews with writers, theologians, scientists, and public leaders about peace, violence, racism, justice, and other issues that affect the morality of public life.

Television Newscasts, April 1, 1974–present. The National Archives holds licenses to record the evening network news from ABC and NBC. The collection includes ABC evening news, daily except Sunday, from April 11, 1977, and NBC evening news, daily, from July 19, 1976. CBS has deposited their evening, morning, and midday news, daily, from April 1, 1974. The "Robert MacNeil Report" and the "MacNeil-Lehrer Report" were deposited from 1976 to 1983.

Television News Specials, April 1, 1974–present. CBS news specials from April 1, 1974–present and selected specials from ABC and NBC from 1976–present, often dealing with international relations. Microfiche copies of the transcripts of "Face the Nation" are available.

Universal Newsreel Collection (UN), 1929–67. The most-viewed news collection in the National Archives, consisting of twice-a-week releases and 866 hours of outtakes. A fire at the National Archives destroyed 75 percent of the outtakes from the 1930s and 1940s and most of the releases from August 1941 to March 1944.

"Washington Debates of the Seventies" (AEI), 1970–73: 40 reels. Filmed recordings of televised discussions and seminars relating to public affairs, including U.S. policy in the Middle East; the role of Congress in foreign policy, defense, civil disobedience, Vietnam; and the "Nixon Doctrine." Sponsored by the American Enterprise Institute.

World War I films, 1917–19. Films made behind German lines by Jacob Berkowitz and 1915 Durburough War Films; the "Official War Review" series on land and air battles, maneuvers, and training; "The Great War," a documentary on World War I, produced in 1956 by NBC; and a large quantity of footage collected by CBS from sources all over the world in producing the documentary "World War I."

World War II films, 1940–45. Films produced by Warner Brothers, Paramount Pictures, and Columbia Pictures about, and under the technical supervision of, the armed services, and several films distributed by the War Activities Committee of the Motion Picture Industry.

Other newsreel collections, 1919–67. Holdings include chiefly unbroken series of "Paramount News" (PN), 1941–57; "Movietone News" (MN), 1957–63; and "News of the Day" (ND), 1963–67. Newsreels produced by Movietone, Pathe, Fox, International, Paramount, and Telenews include selected news items, such as the Big Four at the Paris Peace Conference, 1919; events leading to and occurring during World War II. There are also documentaries compiled from newsreels, including the 26-part Thames Television "World at War" and NBC's "Twisted Cross."

4.a. Viewing equipment is provided for on-site use; researchers are required to operate all equipment themselves after staff members have provided initial instruction.

b. Researchers are encouraged to reserve films and equipment before their visit.

c. Viewing facilities are provided free of charge.

d. Researchers may use their own equipment in the media research room to make sound and video copies of items in the public domain or for which permission to duplicate has been obtained. The staff can loan copies to approved private vendors who will copy them for a fee.

5. Researchers will find motion picture and video recordings held here to be easily accessible through the card catalog and several card files, all of which

permit reliable subject searching. Useful guidance is also provided by Bonnie G. Rowan's entries on the National Archives in *Footage 89: North American Film and Video Sources* and *Footage 91: North American Film and Video Sources,* both edited by Richard Prelinger and published in New York by Prelinger Associates in 1989 and 1991, respectively.

6.   Index Terms: Arms Control; Diplomacy and Negotiations; Development Issues; Ethnic and Religious Conflict; Human Rights; Humanitarian Issues; International Organizations; Low Intensity Conflict; Military History; Pacifism and Peace Movements; Political Systems and Ideologies; Terrorism; War Crimes

See also entries B11, D6, E11, F21, F22, and G10

---

**F21**   National Archives and Records Administration (NARA)—Nontextual Archives Division (NNS)—Still Picture Branch (NNSP)

---

1.a.   8601 Adelphi Road
College Park, Md. 20740-6001
(301) 713-6625
Fax: (301) 713-6904

b.   8:45 A.M.–5:00 P.M. Monday–Friday
Some evening and Saturday hours by appointment.

c.   Open to researchers with a National Archives identification card, obtainable from the Reference Services Division. First-time users should speak with a consultant before beginning work.

d.   Elizabeth Hill, Chief
Frederick Pernell, Assistant Chief for Reference

2.   The National Archives' Still Picture Branch has custody of an estimated 7 million photographs taken by U.S. government agencies, private individuals, and foreign governments. Included are photographs of persons, places, events, and works of art that illustrate social, cultural, diplomatic, military, naval, political, and economic history throughout the world. The collection covers a large number of subjects within the scope of this Guide: international relations, diplomacy and negotiations, international organizations, economic development, international trade, human/civil rights, humanitarian issues, refugees, political systems, regional conflict, military affairs, military art, violence, war, and war crimes.

3.   Still picture collections pertinent to peace and international security studies are located either in the Record Groups (RG) or in the collection of Donated Materials.

## RECORD GROUPS

The records of a single government agency or subdivision are preserved in numbered collections called Record Groups (RG). The Record Group system serves those who are interested in locating media materials produced or acquired by a particular government agency. To facilitate subject orientation, the following table groups relevant RGs (discussed further on in this entry) under major subject headings:
Art and War: RG 117
Diplomacy and Alliances: RG 59, RG 306
Economic Aid: RG 59, RG 115, RG 268, RG 286, RG 306, RG 490
Human Rights: RG 47, RG 208
Humanitarian Issues: RG 4, RG 26, RG 90, RG 112, RG 210, RG 260, RG 331, RG 395
International Organizations: RG 59, RG 208, RG 306
International Trade: RG 364
Military History, Planning, and Strategy: RG 26, RG 49, RG 59, RG 74, RG 168, RG 171, RG 210, RG 226, RG 331; Army: RG 77, RG 94, RG 111, RG 117, RG 156, RG 165, RG 319, RG 391, RG 393–395, RG 407; Air Force: RG 18, RG 120, RG 243, RG 341–342; Navy and Marine Corps: RG 19, RG 24, RG 38, RG 52, RG 71–72, RG 80, RG 127, RG 181, RG 428
Political Systems and Ideologies: RG 238, RG 242
War Crimes: RG 131, RG 153, RG 165, RG 208, RG 238–239, RG 260
War Propaganda: RG 4, RG 44–45, RG 53, RG 56, RG 59, RG 86, RG 120, RG 131, RG 179, RG 188, RG 208, RG 226, RG 242, RG 407
The following RGs hold relevant photographs:
**RG 4:**   *U.S. Food Administration, 1917–20: 5,812 items.*
Photos with a focus on food conservation during World War I: sugar production, canning, wartime destruction, refugees, and Herbert Hoover.
**RG 18:**   *Army Air Forces, 1903–64: 118,700 items.*
Lantern slides of early aviation 1903–27; U.S. and foreign aircraft; balloons and airships; aerials, aircraft in Germany and France in World War I; and aerials of urban and rural areas and natural disasters.
**RG 19:**   *Bureau of Ships, 1776–1966: 450,000 items.*
Photos and illustrations of the history of the U.S. Navy including navy vessels, construction, shipyards, sailors, and officers; steam engineering; dam-

age to ships; French and German navies; ship launchings including nuclear submarines.

**RG 24:** *Bureau of Naval Personnel, 1777–1944: 11,400 items.*

Portraits and photos of navy officers, enlisted men, and some families, 1904–38; navy chaplains; Spanish ships during the Spanish-American War; training facilities; and recruiting posters and slides from World War II.

**RG 26:** *U.S. Coast Guard, 1855–1974: 52,627 items.*

The general file of photos: enforcement of customs and navigation laws, protection of life and property at sea, and maintenance of aids to navigation, ships, crews, the Coast Guard Academy, participation in World War II and the Vietnam conflict, and aid to Cuban refugees in the 1960s.

**RG 38:** *Office of the Chief of Naval Operations, 1891–1946: 18,389 items.*

Photos to 1920 include armor tests; sailors in training; coastal defenses in the U.S. and Chile; Italian ports, landmarks, and aerial bombing tests; Mexico; Haiti; construction of the *Kaiser Wilhelm II.* Aircraft design and construction, 1914–43, is documented in manufacturers' photos. There are 1935 photos of Japanese defenses in the Marshall, Caroline, and Mariana islands. World War II photos include portraits of Allied military and political leaders, civilian and military personnel at the Navy Department, antimine and torpedo devices, mine warfare tests, and the training and history of advance base naval units.

**RG 44:** *Office of Government Reports, 1939–45: 4,000 items.*

World War II posters from federal agencies, foreign information services, and war relief associations. "Newsmaps" with U.S. military action, 1942–45.

**RG 45:** *Office of Naval Records and Library, 1914–18: 783 items.*

World War I posters, both U.S. and foreign, promoting enlistment, conservation, productivity, and the Red Cross.

**RG 47:** *Social Security Administration, 1936–70: 72,788 items.*

Includes post-1950 photos bearing on welfare and human rights in the USSR, Sweden, Finland, Scotland, and Germany.

**RG 49:** *Bureau of Land Management, 1814–1946: 721 items.*

Includes the War Relocation Centers for Japanese-Americans at Manzanar and Tule Lake, Calif.

**RG 52:** *Bureau of Medicine and Surgery, 1900–1970: 1,434 items.*

World War I illustrations of gas warfare and first-aid, and photos of navy hospitals. World War II pho-tos of casualties and U.S. Navy hospitals in Normandy, France, and southern England. Korean War photos of navy hospitals, dispensaries, hospital ships, evacuation, battlefield surgery, and personnel.

**RG 53:** *Bureau of the Public Debt, 1917–46: 524 items.*

Drawings, paintings, and posters for war bond drives.

**RG 56:** *Department of the Treasury, 1804–1907: 900 items.*

Portraits of Civil War generals and officials. War and savings bond promotions.

**RG 59:** *Department of State, 1774–1956: 13,100 items.*

Portraits of presidents, vice-presidents, State Department officials, and colonial and early U.S. statesmen. Posters of World War I bond drives. Photos of World War II enemy aliens, war surplus, and lend-lease, UNESCO, 1945–51. 126 photos of war and conflict in Indonesia, 1943–47.

**RG 70:** *Bureau of Mines, 1910–78: 97,453 items.*

An album documenting the World War I research by the Chemical Warfare Service including gases, gas masks, production of gases, and anticontamination methods.

**RG 71:** *Bureau of Yards and Docks, 1876–1944: 178,895 items.*

Photos of U.S. naval yards, docks, air stations, submarine bases, and training bases. Pictures of World War I yeomen and World War II naval construction battalions known as Seabees.

**RG 72:** *Bureau of Aeronautics, 1918–54: 100,950 items.*

Photos showing construction and testing of dirigibles, balloons, airplanes, and parachutes. Training materials for aviators and aerial photographers. Photo documentation of designs and tests of aircraft manufactured for the U.S. Navy.

**RG 74:** *Bureau of Ordnance, 1863–1946: 11,465 items.*

Photos of U.S. and foreign ordnance and testing of armaments, 1863–1922. Photos of the Allied fleet at Scapa Flow, Scotland; mine laying; and documentation of damage to naval ordnance and ships during Operation Crossroads, Bikini, 1946.

**RG 77:** *Office of the Chief of Engineers, 1783–1948: 115,600 items.*

Photos of Corps of Engineers surveys, waterways, and fortifications. Photos of the World War I occupation of Vladivostok, Siberia; U.S. troops in China during the Boxer Rebellion; and destruction and injuries in Hiroshima and Nagasaki, Japan, 1945.

**RG 80:** *Department of the Navy, 1798–1958: 785,600 items.*

Portraits of Secretaries of the Navy from 1798 and naval officers. Photos of ships, yards, docks, training, personnel, tests, wartime naval operations, and other aspects of naval history. Photos of early naval aviation; and the Japanese surrender ceremonies aboard the USS *Missouri* in 1945. For later photos see RG 428.

RG 86: *Women's Bureau, 1892–1945: 3,625 items.*
Includes photos of women at work during World War I and II.

RG 90: *Public Health Service, 1862–1985: 10,573.*
Civil War era illustrations and photos of hospitals and wounded. Photos of Public Health Service personnel and their work in developing countries, and the treatment of malaria, yellow fever, and other communicable diseases. 1906 photos of Panama, Costa Rica, Nicaragua, Honduras, and Guatemala. Posters teaching about communicable diseases.

RG 92: *Office of the Quartermaster General, 1776–1938: 20,355 items.*
Revolutionary War portraits and illustrations of uniforms. Photos of U.S. Army forts, uniforms, flags, insignia, horse and mule tack, vehicles, and food service operations. Panoramas of national cemeteries, 1881–1907; U.S. cemeteries in France, England, Belgium, and Scotland; and memorials to Confederate Civil War dead in Maryland and Illinois. Photos of disaster relief in Koblenz, Germany, 1920.

RG 94: *Adjutant General's Office, 1780–1917: 1,981 items.*
Prints showing Union and Confederate fortifications in Georgia, South Carolina, Tennessee, and Virginia; and military recruitment posters, 1908–16. Photos of the Spanish-American War and the Philippine Insurrection, 1898–1900; the Mexican Punitive Expedition, 1916.

RG 111: *Office of the Chief Signal Officer, 1754–1981: 1,038,800 items.*
Prints and photos of war and related subjects from the French and Indian War, the Revolutionary War, the War of 1812, the Mexican War, the Civil War, the Indian wars, the Spanish-American War, the Philippine Insurrection, the China Relief Expedition, the Mexican Punitive Expedition, World War I, World War II, the Korean War, and the Vietnam War. Civil War photos, many by Matthew Brady. Photos of the Sino-Japanese War, the Boxer Rebellion, and the Japanese capture of Tsingtao, China, 1914.

RG 112: *Office of the Surgeon General (Army), 1799, 1918–24, 1942–49: 2,770 items.*
World War I photos on medical treatment. World War II-era photos of the work of the Typhus Commission in Europe and Africa; and photos of the Army Medical Corps in Europe, wounded soldiers and civilians.

RG 115: *Bureau of Reclamation, 1899–1958: 50,268 items.*
Photos of irrigation projects under construction in the United States and foreign countries.

RG 117: *American Battle Monuments Commission, 1923–37: 3,317 items.*
World War I cemeteries and memorials in Europe and the United States; battlefields in France and Belgium; and dedication ceremonies, 1937.

RG 120: *American Expeditionary Forces, 1915–23: 5,123 items.*
Photos, drawings, and maps from the Army Air Service in France. Photos of training programs, U.S.-occupied areas of France and Belgium, and the effects of Allied bombing. Recruitment and propaganda posters.

RG 127: *U.S. Marine Corps, 1775–1981: 216,000 items.*
The general photographic files of the marine corps: images of the Revolutionary War, the Civil War, World War I, World War II, the Korean War, and the Vietnam War; photos of officers and enlisted personnel, uniforms, bands, aircraft, ordnance, vehicles, camps, wounded, and training; presidential portraits and ceremonies; activities in Santo Domingo, 1923, China, 1927–29, and aviation, 1931–37.

RG 131: *Office of Alien Property, 1910–43: 44,813 items.*
Includes Nazi propaganda photos of Adolph Hitler and other Nazis, Hitler Youth, rallies, military parades, and the German American Bund.

RG 153: *Judge Advocate General (Army), 1912–46: 798 items.*
Photos of Buchenwald concentration camp, World War II destruction, Pre-World War II Germany, German and Nazi atrocities, war crime trials, and looted property.

RG 156: *Office of the Chief of Ordnance, 1860–1967: 64,983 items.*
Early photos of arsenals in Virginia, and Pennsylvania and German armaments. World War I photos of weapons, vehicles, mobile machine guns, quickfire cannons, chemical plants, and munitions plants. Pre-World War II photos of small arms, bombs, antiaircraft equipment, armor plate, and aerial ordnance research. World War II posters and broadsides.

RG 165: *War Department General and Special Staffs, 1860–1947: 95,780 items.*
Civil War-era photos of Union and Confederate fortifications, troops, camps, barracks, hospitals, battlefields, gunboats, ships, railroads, and portraits of generals, other officers, groups of soldiers, and civilians. Photos of General Sherman's march through Georgia, Tennessee, and South Carolina. Photos of military

personnel, frontier forts and conflict with the Modoc of California. Photos of the Spanish-American War: troops, weapons, fortifications, ships, battles, Cuba, Puerto Rico, and the Philippines. Photos of the Philippine Insurrection: troops, fortifications, and insurgents. Photos of China Relief Expedition: U.S. and foreign troops in China during the Boxer Rebellion. Photos of the Mexican Punitive Expedition: Mexican Army maneuvers, villages, transportation, and U.S. troops in Veracruz, Mexico. Photos of the Russo-Japanese War, and armies in China, Morocco, and Czechoslovakia.

World War I photos from the Committee on Public Information of life on the homefront: war industries, bond drives, volunteers, war relief, women's suffrage, and the flu epidemic of 1918. Photos of U.S. military camps, troops, battlefields; and European subjects including military action in Belgium, France and the Balkans, and military activities of the Germans, Italians, British, Rumanians, and Russians.

World War II-era photos of Japanese atrocities in the Philippines; German, Japanese, and Russian military equipment; and general military activities.

1898–1905: Magazine illustrations of the Spanish-American War; news photos of U.S. troops during the Mexican Punitive Expedition; and a Colliers publication on the Russo-Japanese War; World War I newsphoto coverage in the *New York Herald Tribune* and the *New York Times*.

**RG 168:** *National Guard Bureau, 1898–1935: 609 items.*

Photos of national guard units, their insignias, and their work.

**RG 171:** *Office of Civilian Defense, 1930–45: 4,376 items.*

Visual material relating to camouflage; World War II civil defense programs including communication, air raid drills, uniforms, and personnel; civil defense in other countries; poison gas and decontamination; and plans for blackouts and bomb shelters.

**RG 179:** *War Production Board, 1942–45: 1,602.*

Posters used to encourage increased production of steel, guns, ammunition, aircraft, ships, and uniforms.

**RG 181:** *Naval Districts and Shore Establishments, 1891–1963: 3,854 items.*

Photos of ships, shipyards, ship repair and construction in Washington, New York, and Philadelphia. Photos of airplanes, and airships.

**RG 188:** *Office of Price Administration, 1941–47: 1,896 items.*

Posters, photos, and slides to explain and encourage compliance with rationing and price control.

**RG 208:** *Office of War Information (OWI), 1939–51: 206,100 items.*

The OWI master negative file covers World War II combat and the homefront, U.S., Allied and Axis subjects, and political and diplomatic events, 1939–45. Subjects include prisoners of war, refugees, displaced persons, war bond drives, wartime destruction, concentration camps, the atomic bomb blasts, surrender ceremonies, and victory celebrations. Photos of politicians, royalty, and scientists; and photos of those in international organizations such as the United Nations. Photos printed in OWI magazines *USA, Photo Review,* and *Victory;* and photos from OWI's Negro Press Section. A variety of cartoons, sketches, and mock-ups promoting the war effort.

**RG 210:** *War Relocation Authority (WRA), 1942–46: 15,200 items.*

Photos documenting the evacuation, confinement, and relocation of Japanese- Americans by the WRA and the U.S. Army; the assembly centers; and the facilities and residents of relocations centers at Colorado River, Gila River, Granada, Heart Mountain, Tule Lake, Minidoka, Manzanar, Topaz, and Rohwer. Photos of the Fort Ontario Emergency Refugee Shelter for Europeans in Oswego, N.Y.

**RG 226:** *Office of Strategic Services (OSS), 1919–45: 2,989 items.*

Photos taken by the OSS: facilities in London, England, and Scotland; aftermath of the Allied victory in Algeria and Tunisia; preparation for the Normandy invasion; and bomb damage in London and Cherbourg, France. Photos from OSS bases in Kunming, China, and Kandy, Ceylon. Military operations in Burma and Thailand. Materials from an exhibit on propaganda.

**RG 238:** *National Archives Collection of World War II War Crimes Records, 1940–48: 5,355 items.*

An album dedicated to Dr. Hans Frank, the German governor general of occupied Poland, with civil and military buildings, rallies, parades, ceremonies of Nazis in Poland. Thirty-five still frames of a German film taken in a Nazi concentration camp. Photos of the International Military Tribunal and U.S. military tribunals at Nuremberg and the International Miliary Tribunal for the Far East, Tokyo.

**RG 239:** *American Commission for the Protection and Salvage of Artistic and Historic Monuments in War Areas, 1943–46: 19,950 items.*

Photos of World War II combat damage and vandalism in Europe, North Africa, Palestine, the Philippines, Burma, China, and the Netherlands East Indies.

**RG 242:** *National Archives Collection of Foreign Records Seized, 1913–45: 350,000 items.*

Official photographs of the National Socialist (Nazi) Party by Heinrich Hoffman: Adolph Hitler, Axis leaders, Nazi officials, construction of the Führerhaus, ceremonies, rallies, Hitler Youth, and life in Germany. Photos of Munich, 1919, and the Spanish Civil War. Photos of the invasions of the Soviet Union and other countries to be used as propaganda; photos from the trial of those accused of an attempted assassination of Adolph Hitler; and photos of Luftwaffe pilots and German servicemen. Personal photo collections of Foreign Minister Joachim von Ribbentrop, Gen. Erwin Rommel, and Eva Braun. Filmstrips on Germany, the news of the week, 1938–41, Hitler Youth, and German history. Magazine illustration on Germany, Nazi leaders, the war, and the history of Russia. An album of World War I-era German photos.

**RG 243:** *U.S. Strategic Bombing Survey, 1944–47: 12,660 items.*

Photos of bomb damage: Operation Strangle; Noball, a German rocket site; industries, utilities, transportation, and social services in Germany, France, and Belgium, 1944–45; incendiary bombing of Japan; and the atomic bomb damage in Hiroshima and Nagasaki.

**RG 260:** *U.S. Occupation Headquarters, World War II. 1945–72: 145,800 items.*

Photos of the Public Relations Office, Office of Military Government for Germany: personnel and conferences, restitution, ruins, refugees, displaced persons, CARE and other relief programs, and the Berlin airlift. Photos of the U.S. Civil Administration of the Ryukyu Islands: personnel and programs, and life in the Ryukyu Islands. Photo documentation of damage to the Italian Benedictine Monte Cassino abbey and German monuments, cities, archives, libraries, and castles. The Linz Collection of photos documenting the artwork plundered by the Axis, collected by Hermann Goring, and recovered at the Wiesbaden Central Collecting Point. Photos from the Einsatzstab Reichleiter Rosenberg of Nazi documentation of art looted from France; Polish and Russian art; and art from synagogues.

**RG 268:** *Philippine War Damage Commission, 1945–50: 1,100 items.*

Photos of damage and rebuilding of government buildings in 33 provinces of the Philippines.

**RG 286:** *Agency for International Development, 1948–67: 31,00 items.*

Photos to document aid programs: recovery programs in Europe under the Marshall Plan; assistance programs in the areas of agriculture, land reclama-

tion, education, medicine, and technology; and military assistance. Assistance to Austria, Germany, Portugal, the Netherlands, Sweden, and Turkey.

**RG 306:** *U.S. Information Agency (USIA). 1900–78: 939,000 items.*

A master file that served press, publication, and exhibit needs with images of the United States, foreign relations and aid programs, military activities, and visits of foreign dignitaries to the United States. Materials to promote and document: the aid program to Latin America, called the Alliance for Progress, 1961–69; and civic action programs in Vietnam. Great amount of coverage of U.S. presidents, Roosevelt to Nixon, and vice-presidents. Photos of U.S. dignitaries, especially overseas. Photos of U.S. involvement in World War II, the Korean War, and the Vietnam War. Photos of activities of international organizations: United Nations, North Atlantic Treat Organization (NATO), and the South East Asian Treaty Organization (SEATO).

1900–1950: 211,000 items. The *New York Times* Paris Bureau file of photos include worldwide coverage of political and cultural events: World War I, Paris riots of 1934, the Saar plebiscite, the Russo-Finnish War, the Sino-Japanese War, World War II, and postwar occupations, treaties, peace conferences, the United Nations, labor strife, and economic conditions.

The collection is open for viewing and duplication "12 years after the initial dissemination of the material abroad, or in the case of such material not disseminated abroad, 12 years after the preparation of the material." The photo collection is served by several elaborate card catalogs.

**RG 319:** *Army Staff, 1931–66: 16,780 items.*

Photos of U.S. Army operations, World War II through the Vietnam War: personnel, camps, NATO exercises, atomic bomb tests, prisoners of war and war criminals, military and civilian casualties and refugees, and postwar Japan.

**RG 331:** *Allied Operational and Occupation Headquarters, World War II, 1937–45: 4,704 items.*

Photographic prints of paintings by Japanese artists illustrating events from the Sino-Japanese War to World War II, and photos of Japanese leaders, 1939. Photos of the invasion and occupation of Europe by the Allied Expeditionary Forces including refugees, displaced persons, prison camps, military trials, war damage to cities, food rationing, Allied officials, and officials of occupied and liberated countries.

**RG 341:** *Headquarters U.S. Air Force, 1954–66: 8,300 photographs.*

**RG 342:** *U.S. Air Force Commands, Activities, and Organizations, 1945–81. 148,600 photographs.*

RG 364: *Office of the U.S. Trade Representative, 1969, 1978: 54 items.*
Photos of the Kennedy Round Trade Agreement and the Tokyo Round Trade Talks.

RG 391: *U.S. Regular Army Mobile Units, 1821–1942, 1850–1950: 1,650 items.*
Photos of the American West, 1866–79: American Indians, pueblos, Fort Wingate, N.M. Photos of the Philippines: Emilio Aguinaldo and other insurgents. Photos of officers and enlisted personnel of U.S. Cavalry units in the United States, China, and Japan.

RG 393 AND RG 394: *U.S. Army Continental Commands, 1821–1920, 1920–42; 1917–18, 1925–38: 920 items.*
Photos of training at Fort Jackson, S.C. Photos related to military readiness in the 1930s; and training camps.

RG 395: *U.S. Army Overseas Operations and Commands, 1900–1919: 800 items.*
Photos of the American Expeditionary Forces in Siberia: diplomats, Bolshevik prisoners, refugees, and military personnel of Allies. Photos of the Philippines: insurgents including Emilio Aguinaldo, and U.S. military.

RG 407: *Adjutant General's Office, 1917–46: 10,088 items.*
World War I photos of the personnel of the Paris office of the American Expeditionary Forces, and of military attachés in France; the Moroccan War; and recruitment posters for Citizen Military Training camps. World War II photos: chemical warfare, airplanes and air fields, aerials of the Philippines, and scrapbooks of materials on individual units.

RG 428: *Department of the Navy, 1956–81: 341,800 items.*
For earlier photos see RG 80. This massive collection of photos, formerly at the Naval Photographic Center, covers all aspects of naval activities including aircraft, ships, ordnance, training, bases, the U.S. and foreign geographical locations, naval operations during the Vietnam War, officers, and enlisted personnel.

RG 490: *Peace Corps, 1961–: 135,000 black-and-white photographs, 35,000 color slides.*
Coverage concentrates predominantly on the living and working conditions of Peace Corps volunteers around the world from the organization's inception to mid-1980s.

## DONATED MATERIALS

These collections were formerly in Record Group (RG) 200. Because they are not government records, they have been removed from the Record Groups and handled separately. The following photograph collections are relevant to peace and international security studies:

Stewart Collection (GS), 1917–19: 2,000 items. Photos documenting the 29th Division, American Expeditionary Force.

Tracy Collection (WT), 1918: 320 items. Photos of military activities in northwestern France including Gen. John Pershing and Georges Clemenceau.

Miscellaneous Collections (M), 1785–1967: 1,362 items. Photos of most presidents, Abraham Lincoln through Lyndon Johnson, military activities from the Civil War through World War II, American Indians, and World War I posters.

4.a. Researchers may examine prints and negatives in the research room. When handling photographic records, researchers are required to wear gloves provided by the staff.

b. Reservations are normally not necessary.

c–d. Items in the public domain may be copied by researchers using their own photographic equipment or by staff for a fee. Coin-operated photocopying machines are available for copying captions.

5. In addition to providing a series of finding-aids, the division maintains a card file of its holdings. Researchers should also consult Barbara Lewis Burger's detailed *Guide to the Holdings of the Still Picture Branch of the National Archives* (1990).

6. Index Terms: Art and War; Diplomacy and Negotiations; Development Issues; Human Rights; Humanitarian Issues; International Organizations; International Trade; Low Intensity Conflict; Military History; Political Systems and Ideologies; Regional Conflict; War Crimes

See also entries B11, D6, E11, F20, F22, and G10

---

## F22 National Audiovisual Center (NAC) (National Archives and Records Administration)

---

1.a. 8700 Edgeworth Drive
Capital Heights, Md. 20743-3701
(301) 763-1896 (Reference)
(800) 683-1300 (Orders)
Fax: (301) 763-6025

b. 8:00 A.M.–4:30 P.M. Monday–Friday

c. Open to the public.

d. George H. Ziener, Director

2. The National Audiovisual Center (NAC) serves as the central source of information on federal audiovisual and other multimedia materials and provides distribution services for these materials through sale and rental programs. The collection on the premises encompasses 9,000 titles, 1970s–present (with a few older materials), on videotape, film, slide/tape kits, videodiscs, floppy disk, and CD-ROM. There is a considerable coverage of military and foreign affairs, alliance systems, human rights, international organizations, and political systems.

3. A large history collection covers classic government documentaries and many military and aviation history subjects. In addition, there are other groups of titles focusing on World War II, communism, democracy, international relations, and NATO, with some dating back to the 1930s.

Recent legislation has made many of the films produced by and for the U.S. Information Agency (USIA) (K41) available to the public through the center. For decades, these films were restricted from being shown in the United States. Many are classics of the filmmaker's art. A documentary, "Why We Fight," Frank Capra's award-winning World War II series, is now considered to be a propaganda classic.

Most of the films and videotapes are recent productions. For older materials, see National Archives and Records Administration, Motion Pictures, Sound, and Video Branch (F20).

NAC can provide information on the location of other audiovisual collections within the government.

4.a. All films for which there are preview prints may be viewed at the center.

b. Those wishing to view films at the center should contact the Reference Section to ask if prints are available. Preview prints are available by mail only to educational institutions.

c–d. Frequently, the easiest and fastest way to obtain a copy of a government film or video is to purchase it from NAC.

5. The *Media Resource Catalog,* a descriptive catalog of 600 of the most popular NAC titles with extensive cross-indexing, is available by mail. For other smaller collections, specific catalogs and brochures such as the *Documentary Film Classics* and *World War II* are also available by mail.

The NAC Staff has access to the Defense Audio-Visual Information System (DAVIS) file and can search it for scholars who have specific questions and needs. At the time this Guide was being prepared, NAC was in the process of implementing an on-line bulletin board service (BBS) to provide public access to its catalog of holdings.

The *Annual Audiovisual Report* is published by NAC. All federal government agencies must report information on their audiovisual activities for inclusion in this report.

6. Index Terms: Collective Security; Diplomacy and Negotiations; Human Rights; International Organizations; Political Systems and Ideologies

See also entries B11 and F20

---

## F23 Naval Historical Center (Navy Department)—Photographic Section

1.a. Washington Navy Yard, Building 44
9th and M Streets, SE
Washington, D.C. 20374-5060
(202) 433-2765
Fax: (202) 433-3172

b. 9:00 A.M.–4:00 P.M. Monday–Friday

c. The collections are open to the public by appointment. Researchers may use study facilities in the Photographic Section for on-site research. The Photographic Section does not lend its file prints for research or exhibits.

d. Charles Haberlein Jr., Head

2. The Photographic Section of the Naval Historical Center maintains an extensive collection of pictorial files on all aspects of naval history of the United States prior to 1920. Materials depicting post-1920 events supplement naval pictorial collections at the National Archives and Records Administration (F21) and at the Still Media Records Center of the Defense Department (F8). The collection of images (photographs, paintings, prints) numbers approximately 250,000 pieces. Within the scope of this Guide most of the visual materials fall under the subject areas of military history, planning, and strategy.

3. The collection focuses on the U.S. Navy during the entire span of its history. It contains everything from rare photos of the last sailing vessels and Civil War ironclads to current day missile cruisers and carriers. Emphasis is on pre-1950 subjects without, however, neglecting the more recent times. Except for central Eurasia (including Russia), south Asia and sub-Saharan Africa, naval activities in other world regions also receive substantial coverage, particularly western Europe. Many items, of course, depict U.S. vessels in foreign waters or U.S. personnel

in foreign lands, but a considerable number of pictures show foreign vessels and personages.

This applies particularly to Great Britain, and to a lesser extent to Scandinavian countries. A major collection of British photos is the British Naval Intelligence Collection, which offers rare glimpses of the Royal Navy prior to World War II. Among these are views of various marine facilities and naval activities throughout the country. Other pictures in the collection show the U.S. naval headquarters in Sweden during World War I, mine sweeping near North Cape Harbor, Norway, and numerous Dutch, Danish, Norwegian, Swedish, and Finnish ships. Photos of weapons, uniforms, clothing, battles, and harbors are also available.

A considerable number of pictures show vessels and naval personnel of France and south European countries. The photographs include at least 800 scenes from France, 500 from Italy, 100 from Spain, almost 100 from Malta, and about 50 from Portugal. French ships are depicted on approximately 1,500 photographs, Italian on 500, Spanish on 300, and Portuguese on 30. Two hundred photos of personnel and naval planes stem from France and the countries of southern Europe. Other photos depict weapons, uniforms, and clothing. Sources of the pictures range from the British Naval Chronicle in the early 19th century to personal photographs taken by naval officers while on duty in the mid-20th century.

There are groups of several hundred photos apiece on the German navy, 1870s–1945, and the Austro-Hungarian navy. Besides naval vessels, arranged alphabetically under country, merchant ships are illustrated in an alphabetical file regardless of country. A few Bulgarian, Greek, Polish, and Romanian ships are covered; so are incidents like the *Graf Spee* episode. A researcher can also find photos of seacoasts, ports, and battles in the central European area.

The Middle East portion of the collection reflects the subject strengths of the overall collection and offers selected coverage of the World War II invasion of North Africa and the invasion of Europe launched from North Africa; several ports in the Ottoman Empire, Egypt, and Arabia; Turkey in the early 1920s; and Turkey's War of Independence. There are also several photographs of 19th-century naval paintings, engravings, and illustrations of locations in North Africa, such as Algiers, Tripoli, and Alexandria. Other photos show French naval vessels at Algiers, 1861–1920; various scenes in Egypt, Constantinople, Jerusalem, Damascus, 19th century; the meeting between FDR and Ibn Saud, 1945; Egyptian

air fields, 1956; the U.S. Marine landing in Lebanon, 1958; and the "Nimbus Star" operation to clear the Suez Canal, 1974. A small but growing collection of photographs depict the Turkish, Israeli, Iranian, and Saudi Arabian navies.

Photographs of east Asian naval ships and installations focus on the 1900–1940 period. There are a modest number of photos of other years. Although the file on the Korean War is rather weak, fairly good files exist on the following actions and campaigns of World War II: Pearl Harbor attack, Midway, Guadalcanal, Central Solomons, and Leyte Gulf.

The collection includes several thousand items from southeast Asia. Several hundred photos are from the Philippines, covering the early 1900s and showing a variety of naval scenes. Also to be found are 600 to 700 photos from Vietnam, showing military operations and installations. The other countries of the region are less well represented, although there are some interesting items from Indonesia in the 1920s.

The core of the collection for Latin America consists of photographs of naval vessels, mid-19th century–present. The 19th-century holdings are particularly impressive and include—in addition to Latin American ships dating back to the 1860s—photographs of 19th-century naval paintings, engravings, and illustrations. Mexican War materials (illustrations, war art, photos of participating U.S. officers) and Spanish-American War photographs are well represented. There is also coverage of early 20th-century U.S. naval interventions in the Caribbean basin, the Cuban missile crisis, and 20th-century Latin American naval vessels, officers, crews, and operations.

4.a. Viewing equipment is not necessary.

b. Researchers are requested to call in advance for appointment.

c–d. Prints of most unrestricted views can be purchased. Researchers may also copy unrestricted items in the collection using their own equipment.

5. Thanks to automated files, accessing the collection is relatively easy. Items have been indexed by persons, places, events, ships, and weapons. A free brochure describing the Photographic Section is available on request.

6. Index Terms: Military History—Navy; Naval Science

See also entries A36, B13, C10, D9, and E13

## F24 Organization of American States (OAS)—Columbus Memorial Library—Photograph Collection

1.a. Constitution Avenue and 19th Street, NW
Washington, D.C. 20006
(202) 458-6095
Fax: (202) 458-3914

b. 9:30 A.M.–4:30 P.M. Monday–Friday

c. Open to researchers.

d. Miguel Rodriguez, Archivist

2. The collection consists of some 40,000 black-and-white prints and is growing at a rate of approximately 100 prints per month. Within the scope of this Guide the collection is relevant to the study of international relations, economic development, human rights, and international organizations. The library's book and map collections are described in entries A38 and D11, respectively. For the archival and audio holdings of the OAS Records Management Center see entries B14 and E14, respectively.

3. The main collection of the OAS photo archives is organized by country, with each country file subdivided into categories. The following categories are pertinent to peace and international security studies: agriculture, cities and towns, education, history, industry, minerals, native activities, native types, natural history, politics, public welfare, topography, and transportation. The photographs date from the very early 20th century to the present. Unfortunately, precise dates for many of the early prints are not recorded.

Germane to the study of international organizations is a 3,500-print, alphabetically arranged, portrait collection of Latin American political and cultural figures, and a Pan-American conferences file held by the photo archives.

4.a. Viewing equipment is not necessary.

b. An appointment is recommended.

c. Prints are reproduced by the OAS Graphic Services Unit for a fee.

d. For researchers outside of Washington, D.C., the archivist will supply photocopies of available prints on specific topics; reproductions of desired prints may then be ordered by mail.

5. A contents list is available from the archivist.

6. Index Terms: Collective Security; Diplomacy and Negotiations; Development Issues; Environ-mental Issues, Global; Human Rights; Humanitarian Issues; International Economics—Integration; International Organizations—Regional

*Note:* The OAS Columbus Memorial Library (A38) has within its rare book collection a portrait album of delegates to the First Inter-American Conference, 1889–90.

See also entries B14, D11, E14, and L13

## F25 Peace Corps Photograph Collection

1.a. Office of Creative Services
1990 K Street, NW, 8th Floor
Washington, D.C. 20526
(202) 606-3373
Fax: (202) 606-3110

b. 8:00 A.M.–5:00 P.M. Monday–Friday

c. Open to researchers. Appointment recommended.

d. Michael Sassani, Multimedia Specialist

2. The collection contains some 3,000 color slides and 6,000 black-and-white photographs. Photographs older than 10 years, and most negatives after a shorter period of time, are regularly transferred to the National Archives and Records Administration (F25, RG 490). Within the purview of this Guide the photographic collection is relevant to the areas of economic development, human rights, and humanitarian issues.

3. The photographic coverage concentrates predominantly on the living and working conditions of Peace Corps volunteers around the world. The world regions represented are Europe, Commonwealth of Independent States (the former Soviet Union), Africa, East Asia, and Latin America. Activities include agriculture, forestry, small enterprise development, health, nutrition, environmental management, rural development, youth development, and English language teaching.

4.a. Viewing equipment is available.

b. Appointments are recommended.

c. Fees are charged for special search services.

d. Because most negatives are at the National Archives and Records Administration's Still Picture Branch (F21, RG 490), reproductions are normally arranged through the archives (202/501-5452).

5. Holdings are arranged by country.

6. Index Terms: Development Issues; Human Rights; Humanitarian Issues

*Note:* A video collection is located in the Peace Corps Library (A40).

See also entry K33

---

## F26   Public Interest Video

---

1.a. 4707 Overbrook Road
Bethesda, Md. 20816
(301) 656-7244
Fax: (301) 656-0327

b. 9:00 A.M.–5:00 P.M. Monday–Friday

c. Open to researchers by appointment.

d. Arlen Slobodow, Director

2. Public Interest Video produces public affairs programs for nonprofit organizations and PBS. Although this is primarily a production house, the organization maintains a stock footage library that is available for noncommercial use. The collection consists of approximately 1,000 videotapes, including completed programs and outtakes, 1979–present. Within the scope of this Guide the video materials fall under the rubrics of arms control, conflict resolution, economic development and the environment, human rights, and peace movements.

3. Topics relevant to peace and international security studies include nuclear power and arms control, poverty, and environmental issues. Of particular note is the footage of political rallies in Washington, D.C., especially disarmament, antinuclear, and labor rallies, including the Solidarity rally. There is also extensive coverage of environmental damage, some within international scope: smokestack pollution, logging, toxic sites, and groundwater contamination.

4.a. Viewing equipment is available.

b. Appointments are required.

c–d. Borrowing, viewing, and purchasing tapes are negotiable. Search and use fees may be required in some circumstances, particularly if the intended use is for cable or broadcast television.

5. Descriptions of programs are available.

6. Index Terms: Arms Control; Conflict Resolution and Management; Development Issues; Envi-

ronmental Issues, Global; Human Rights; Humanitarian Issues; Pacifism and Peace Movements

---

## F27   United Nations—Information Center—Library—Film Collection

---

1.a. 1775 K Street, NW
Washington, D.C. 20006
(202) 331-8670
Fax: (202) 289-4267

b. 9:00 A.M.–1:00 P.M. Monday–Friday

c. Open to the public for on-site use. Telephone inquiries accepted until 5:00 P.M.

d. Jeanne Dixon, Film Librarian

2. This collection, relevant mainly for the study of international organizations, consists of 125 film titles, 1960s–present. Older works are on film; productions since 1988 are available on VHS. The book holdings of the library of the United Nations Information Centre are described in entry A44.

3. Of major interest for peace and international security studies are the film and video productions on the following: economic concerns (aid for developing countries, world economy, rural development and agriculture, technology, new world information and communications order); human settlements (city planning, urban problems, cultural heritage); natural resources and the environment (conservation, energy, modern technology, natural disasters, oceans, pollution, water); political affairs (apartheid, decolonization, disarmament, Namibia, Palestine, peacekeeping); social issues (children and youth, crime prevention and penal reform, health and welfare, human rights and refugees, narcotics, population, status of women); and the United Nations (United Nations history, United Nations organization, men and women in field work for the United Nations).

4.a. Viewing equipment is not available.

b. To borrow films, call for reservation.

c. There is no fee for borrowing films.

d. Copies of films can be ordered from Public Information, Dissemination Division, Room S-805A, United Nations, New York, N.Y. 10017 (212/963-6982/6939/6953; fax 212/963-6869).

5. *United Nations Film and Video Catalogue* (1992) is available on request.

6. Index Terms: Development Issues; Environmental Issues, Global; Human Rights; Humanitarian Issues; International Organizations—United Nations; Peacekeeping

*Note:* The United Nations Photo Library in New York (Photo Library, Room S-8050, United Nations, New York, N.Y. 10017, 212/963-6927) contains over 180,000 photographs, with about 4,000 new images added yearly. A laser disc project is in process. The League of Nations photographic collection is part of the United Nations Library in Geneva, Switzerland. There is also a League of Nations film collection at the National Archives and Records Administration (F20, Donated Materials).

The United Nations Visual Materials Library in New York (Department of Public Information, Room S-805N, United Nations, New York, N.Y. 10017, 212/963-7318 or 212/963-1562; fax 212/963-0765) is the depository of 35mm and 16mm archival footage from 1945, and video footage since 1985.

See also entries A44 and H69

---

## F28 United States Catholic Conference (USCC)—Catholic News Service (CNS)—Catholic Communication Campaign

1.a. 3211 4th Street, NE
  Washington, D.C. 20017
  (202) 541-3000

 b. 9:00 A.M.–5:00 P.M. Monday–Friday

 c. Open to researchers by appointment.

 d. Richard Dau, Secretary for Communications

2. The extensive collections at the U.S. Catholic Conference include 150,000 photograph images, 1950s–present (with a few earlier photographs), in the Catholic News Service and approximately 250 video documentaries in the Catholic Communication Campaign. Relevant parts of these holdings pertain to the subjects of economic development, human rights and humanitarian issues, and ethnic conflict.

3. The following materials are relevant to peace and international security studies:

### CATHOLIC NEWS SERVICE PHOTO RESEARCH

Sarah Davis, Photo Researcher
(202) 541-3252

The images depict worldwide economic help by the Catholic Church, especially in Latin America and eastern Europe. Specific subjects include assistance to poor and homeless, Third World countries and personalities, and a small number of images of missionary activities.

### CATHOLIC COMMUNICATION CAMPAIGN

Patricia Ryan Garcia, Manager, Operations
(202) 541-3404
Fax: (202) 541-3129

Many documentaries were produced by the conference and were broadcast on time donated by commercial networks. Topics include cultural and political revolution in China, history of immigration, and the church's international involvement with labor and social justice. Of special note is the 1986 documentary "Witness to Apartheid," which includes footage shot before the government ban on press coverage of racial disturbances.

4.a. Screening and listening facilities are available.

 b. Appointments are required.

 c–d. Items may be borrowed or purchased and some may be duplicated. Many conference video productions can be purchased from the Office for Publications and Promotion (800/235-8722).

5. A descriptive catalog of the video productions is available by mail. For specific holdings of the photographs and their subject arrangement call Sarah Davis (202/541-3252).

6. Subject Terms: Ethnic and Religious Conflict; Human Rights; Humanitarian Issues; Religious, Philosophical, and Ethical Concepts of War and Peace

*Note:* The Archive of the USCC (Guy Wilson, Archivist, 202/541-3193) holds recordings of sermons (with transcripts) by Archbishop Oscar Romero of El Salvador delivered in the 1970s and bearing on the subjects of social justice and human rights.

See also entries B15, M55, and N38

---

## F29 United States Holocaust Research Institute—Photography Department/Film Department

1.a. 100 Raoul Wallenberg Place, SW
  Washington, D.C. 20024-2150

(202) 488-0400
Fax: (202) 479-9726

b. 10:00 A.M.–5:30 P.M. Daily
Closed Christmas and Yom Kippur.

c. Open to researchers and the public.

d. Genya Markon, Head, Photography Department
Peter Martz, Head, Film Department

2. The collections consist of more than 40,000 photographs and negatives, 1930s–48, and over 200 hours of archival film, 1920s–48. From the viewpoint of peace and international security studies the audiovisual materials fall under the rubrics of human rights, ethnic and religious conflict, and war crimes. The research institute is discussed in entry H72, its library in A45, and archives in B16. For the U.S. Holocaust Memorial Museum see entry C11.

3. The photographs depict the Holocaust, pre-World War II Jewish life, and post-World War II liberation. The collection has been gathered from over 250 different sources and continues to grow.

The archival film records the Holocaust, pre-World War II Jewish life, and post-World War II liberation. Rare footage includes material from the archives of the former German Democratic Republic and home movies. There is also an extensive collection of documentaries and feature films related to the Holocaust. The museum produced 3 films and approximately 70 videos for inclusion in exhibits. There is textual documentation for some of the film collection.

6. Index Terms: Ethnic and Religious Conflict; Human Rights; Humanitarian Issues; War Crimes

See also entries A45, B16, C11, and H72

---

### F30 United States Institute of Peace (USIP)—Photograph and Film Collection

1.a. 1550 M Street, NW
Washington, D.C. 20005
(202) 457-1700
Fax: (202) 429-6063

b. 9:00 A.M.–5:00 P.M. Monday–Friday

c. Open to the public by appointment only.

d. Richard H. Solomon, President

2. The audiovisual holdings of the institute are related to peace, international security, and the broadly defined topic of international conflict management.

3. Two divisions of the institute hold significant audiovisual collections:

### LIBRARY PROGRAM

Margarita S. Studemeister, Director
(202) 457-1700

The holdings include about 200 videos on nuclear winter and other topics. Many have been acquired from PBS.

### EDUCATION AND TRAINING

(202) 429-3840

The office holds two video series that were broadcast on public television, 1987–92: "Breaking the Mold: History of U.S.-Soviet Cold War Relations, 1945–1989," which contains significant archival footage, and "Face to Face," concerning U.S.-Soviet summitry.

4.a–b. Researchers may call the Education and Training Department (202/429-3845) for an appointment to screen the video programs at the institute.

c–d. Videos are distributed independently of the institute: "Breaking the Mold" by Encyclopedia Britannica (800/554-9862; fax 312/347-7903) and "Face to Face" by SCETV (800/553-7752).

5. Information on the photos of peace treaty signings is available from the Administrative Office (202/429-3800).

6. Index Terms: Conflict Management and Resolution; Diplomacy and Negotiations; Peacekeeping

See also entries A46 and H73

---

### F31 University of Maryland—National Public Broadcasting Archives—Video Tapes

1.a. Hornbake Library, Ground Floor
College Park, Md. 20742-7011
(301) 405-9255

b. 9:00 A.M.–5:00 P.M. Monday–Friday

c. Open to researchers by appointment.

d. Thomas Connors, Archivist

2. The archives was established at the University of Maryland in June 1990. Its objective is to collect and maintain historical records, manuscripts, kinescopes, audio and video tapes, films, and personal papers dealing with the development of public broadcasting in the United States. Topics relevant to peace and international security studies include international relations, regional conflict, terrorism, human rights, and peace movements. Book collections in the University of Maryland libraries are discussed in entry A47; map and audio tape collections in D12 and E16, respectively.

3. The following video tape collections are particularly germane to the purposes of this Guide:

Corporation for Public Broadcasting, 1968–present: over 1,000 titles and growing. All were funded in part by the Corporation for Public Broadcasting, such as the series "Capitol Journal," bearing on U.S. foreign policy and military affairs.

Maryland Public Television (MPT) Video Archives, 1961–present: 1,500 videotapes. The goal is to collect copies of all programs produced by MPT, including international news.

Tribune Broadcasting, 1986: 414 videotapes of the Iran-Contra Congressional Hearings in their entirety.

4.a. Audiovisual equipment is available.

b. Because most tapes are not in user format, researchers should call at least 10 days ahead so that a tape conversion can be arranged.

c. Fees are charged if tape conversion is required.

d. Permission from the original producers is required for copying.

5. "Mediagraphies" (media bibliographies) are prepared to assist users in locating materials on popular topics such as U.S. foreign policy. Copies are available for examination at the service desk. Parts of the collection are listed on VICTOR, the university's on-line catalog, which can be accessed on-site or via Internet and can be searched under terms such as *terrorism.*

6. Index Terms: Diplomacy and Negotiations; Human Rights; Humanitarian Issues; Low Intensity Conflict: Military History; Pacifism and Peace Movements; Regional Conflict; Terrorism

*Note:* For other public broadcasting materials see National Archives and Records Administration (E11, Donated Materials) and Library of Congress (E8 and F14). For other holdings of the University of Maryland libraries see entries A47, D12, and E16; for the university entry see J13.

---

**F32** World Health Organization (WHO) (United Nations)—Regional Office for the Americas—Photograph Collection

---

1.a. 525 23d Street, NW
Washington, D.C. 20037
(202) 861-3200

b. 9:00 A.M.–5:00 P.M. Monday–Friday

c. Open to the public by appointment.

d. Dan Epstein, Public Information Officer

2. The collection consists of approximately 6,000 black-and-white prints and 4,000 color slides. The color slides are computer-cataloged by subject and country. Within the scope of this Guide the photographic holdings are pertinent to economic development, human rights and humanitarian issues, as well as international organizations.

3. The majority of the photographs relate to Latin American public health services in the fields of nutrition, contagious diseases, maternal and child care, nursing, dental health, and sanitation. Additional subjects include inter-American health conferences and the effects of natural disasters, disease, and starvation on the peoples of Latin America. Coverage dates generally from the 1950s to the present.

4.a. Viewing equipment is available.

b. Appointments are required.

c–d. There is no duplication service. Prints might be loaned to researchers for outside commercial duplication, although the staff is reluctant to loan its prints to individuals who are not affiliated with a press service or publishing firm.

5. The collection is arranged by medically related subject, and therein by country.

6. Index Terms: Development Issues—Health; Humanitarian Issues; International Organizations—United Nations

See also entry L17

# G

# Data Banks

## Data Banks Entry Format (G)

1. *General Information*
  a. address; telephone number(s)
  b. hours of service
  c. conditions of access (including fees charged for information retrieval)
  d. name/title of director and key staff members

2. *Description of Data Files* (hard-data and bibliographic reference)

3. *Bibliographic Aids Facilitating Use of Storage Media*

4. *Index Terms* (relevant subject specialties)

## Introductory Note

A large number of Washington-area libraries, government agencies, academic institutions, and research organizations maintain their own series subscriptions to a wide variety of data banks that can be accessed throughout the United States and, in some cases, throughout the world. The listings included here are primarily of those database systems that were developed or prepared in Washington and contain significant resource material of potential interest to scholars concerned with peace and international security studies. Due to the nature of the medium, the vast majority of the collections listed below deal, not surprisingly, with scientific or economic data. As machine-readable data storage is a burgeoning field, users of this Guide should not consider the data banks described in this section to be the sole source in Washington of machine-readable data for peace and international security studies.

---

## G1 ACCESS

---

1.a. 1511 K Street, NW, Suite 643
    Washington, D.C. 20005-1401
    (202) 783-6050
    Fax: (202) 783-4767

  b. 9:00 A.M.–5:00 P.M. Monday–Friday

  c. Available to the public. There is an annual subscription fee of $49 for individuals and $59 for organizations. Database searches are charged individually.

  d. Mary E. Lord, Executive Director
    Bruce Seymore II, Director of Information Services

2.  Established in 1985, ACCESS is a clearinghouse for information on international security, peace, and world affairs. It provides an inquiry and speaker referral service using a database of over 2,400 organizations in 105 countries. It will produce lists of scholars, specialists, and organizations on any issue related to international affairs. It will also do customized searches by topic, geographic region, focus area of organization, or other feature.

In addition to the inquiry and referral service, ACCESS publishes a single-page briefing paper, *Resource Brief,* 10 times a year, and a 4- to 6-page newsletter, *Security Spectrum,* twice a year. It also publishes directories and special guides. These include *Search for Security: The ACCESS Guide to Foundations in Peace, Security, and International Relations; The ACCESS Guide to Ethnic Conflicts in Europe and the Former Soviet Union;* and *The ACCESS Guide to International Affairs Internships in the Washington, D.C., Area.*

3.  ACCESS publishes the *International Affairs Directory of Organizations: The ACCESS Resource Guide,* a guide to organizations, specialists, and resources in the field of international security, peace, and foreign policy. It has information on 865 organizations in over 81 countries. The staff will also assist in developing searches.

4.  Index Terms: Arms Control; Collective Security; Conflict Resolution and Management; Defense Policy, National; Deterrence; Ethnic and Religious Conflict; Peace Theory and Research; Peacekeeping

---

**G2  Agency for International Development (AID) (International Development Cooperation Agency) — Development Information Center (DIC)**

---

1.a.  Center for Development Information and
       Evaluation
       1601 North Kent Street
       Rosslyn, Va. 22209
       (703) 875-4973
       Fax: (703) 875-5269

Mail:
CDIE/DI Room 209, SA-18
Agency for International Development
Washington, D.C. 20523-1802

b.  10:00 A.M.–4:00 P.M. Monday–Friday

c.  The data bank is primarily for the use of AID project designers, field project managers, and con-

tract researchers, but terminals may be used by private scholars engaged in development research. Use is on-site only.

d.  John E. Butsch, Coordinator

2.  AID's Development Information Office holds computerized technical and financial data on some 8,000 AID development projects initiated since 1974 and 70,000 associated project and technical reports. These data are germane to the scope of this Guide in terms of economic development and humanitarian assistance.

Data have been abstracted from AID project reports, feasibility studies, end-of-tour reports, project evaluations, and contract research studies. Each project is indexed by 20 to 40 project-subcomponent descriptors. Actual documentation listed in the data banks can be also found in the AID Development Information Center (AI) on microfiche or (in some cases) hardcopy.

4.  Index terms: Development Issues; Humanitarian Issues

See also entries AI, G3, and KI

---

**G3  Agency for International Development (AID) (International Development Cooperation Agency) — Economic and Social Data Bank**

---

1.a.  Center for Development Information and
       Evaluation
       1601 North Kent Street
       Rosslyn, Va. 22209
       (703) 812-9770
       Fax: (703) 812-9779

Mail:
CDIE/DI Room 209, SA-18
Agency for International Development
Washington, D.C. 20523-1802

b.  8:45 A.M.–5:30 P.M. Monday–Friday

c.  The data bank is for the use of AID personnel. Private scholars cannot use the Economic and Social Division's terminals, but the staff may conduct data searches on specific topics for researchers if time permits.

d.  David Moore, Project Manager

2.  AID's Economic and Social Data Bank draws on databases in the International Bank for Reconstruction and Development (World Bank) (G8), In-

ternational Monetary Fund (IMF) (G9); Agriculture Department (G4 and G5), and Census Bureau (G6), and other U.S. government agencies; the United Nations and Organization for Economic Cooperation and Development (A39).

Included are major social indicators (e.g., population, birth and death rates, life expectancy, literacy) and economic indicators (e.g., national accounts, central government expenditures, international trade [by commodity and trading partners], agricultural and food production) for many developing countries. Time series date back 30 years in many categories. The data bank also contains AID-generated Latin American statistics (population figures, loans and grants from the United States and international organizations, military expenditures, import/export figures), 1946–present.

4.   Index terms: Development Issues; International Economics

See also entries A1, G2, and K1

## G4   Agriculture Department (USDA)— Economic Research Service—Agriculture and Trade Analysis Division

1.a.  1301 New York Ave, NW
Washington, D.C. 20005-4788
(202) 219-0705
Fax: (202) 219-0368

b.  8:30 A.M.–5:00 P.M., Monday–Friday

c.  The database is maintained primarily for internal use. Numerous statistical bulletins and electronic data products are available for purchase, on diskette and CD-ROM. To obtain a list of current bulletins and data products, call 1 (800) 999-6799 or (301) 725-7937 and request copies of *Reports* and *ERS-NASS Electronic Data Products.*

d.  C. Charles Overton, Manager, Information Resources

2.   Economic Research Service provides a vast amount of data on worldwide agriculture including labor, land use, crop and livestock production, food consumption and many other issues. Data files directly relevant to the focus of this Guide cover a wide variety of indicators related to trade and international agriculture. Relevant data sets include PL480 and Other Concessional U.S. Exports (this set contains information by commodity and country for agricultural exports under the Food for Peace and

other food-aid programs); USSR Agricultural Trade, 1986–89; U.S.-USSR Bilateral Trade; USSR Trade Compendium; Asia/Near East Agricultural Trade; U.S. Trade, 1978–87; U.S./Pacific Rim Agricultural Trade; World Agricultural Trade Flows; East European Agriculture; Agricultural Statistics of the European Community, 1960–85; and World Agriculture: Trends and Indicators. There are approximately 40 data sets dealing with trade and international agriculture.

4.   Index terms: Development Issues—Agriculture; Humanitarian Issues; International Economics

See also entries A31, G5, and K2

## G5   Agriculture Department (USDA)— Foreign Agricultural Service—Trade and Economic Information Division

1.a.  14th Street and Independence Avenue, SW
Washington, D.C. 20250
(202) 720-3935 (Foreign Agricultural Service)
(202) 720-1294 (Trade and Economic Information Division)
Fax: (202) 720-7729

b.  8:30 A.M.–5:00 P.M. Monday–Friday

c.  Not open to the public.

d.  Dewain H. Rahe, Director, Trade and Economic Information Division

2.   The Foreign Agricultural Service makes the Foreign Production, Supply, and Distribution of Agricultural Commodities database available through the National Technical Information Service (NTIS) (K29, Appendix III) and the National Trade Data Bank (G6, Economics and Statistics Administration). These data consist principally of bulk commodity information by country for approximately 200 commodities. The Foreign Agricultural Service maintains information for internal use drawn from a variety of sources, for example, the United Nations, International Monetary Fund (IMF) (L11), Food and Agricultural Organization (FAO) (L3), and agricultural attaché information from the State Department. Selective hard copies of these data may be furnished on a cost basis in response to questions posed by telephone.

4.   Index terms: Development Issues—Agriculture; International Economics

See also entries A31, G4, and K2

**American Psychological Association (APA)**
See entry M8

**Citizens Democracy Corps (CDC)** **See entry**
M21

---

## G6 Commerce Department Data Bases

1.a. Main Commerce Building
14th Street and Constitution Avenue, NW
Washington, D.C. 20230
(202) 482-2000

2. Databases relevant to peace and international security studies are located in several bureaus, divisions, and subunits of the Commerce Department. The availability of tapes or hard copy for use or purchase varies from office to office.

### CENSUS BUREAU

The Center for International Research of the Census Bureau, located in Washington Plaza II, 8905 Presidential Parkway, Upper Marlboro, Md. 20772 (mail: Washington, D.C. 20233-3700), produces the International Data Base (IDB), which is a computerized data bank containing statistical tables of demographic and socioeconomic data for all countries of the world. The IDB contains demographic, economic, and social data from 1950 to the present pertaining to 227 countries. Sources of data are the U.S. Census Bureau, national statistical offices; United Nations and its specialized agencies (International Labor Organization [L10]; United Nations Educational, Scientific and Cultural Organization [UNESCO]; World Health Organization [L17]); International Bank for Reconstruction and Development (World Bank) (L8); International Monetary Fund (L11); and the Organization for Economic Cooperation and Development (A39). Where applicable, demographic data have been projected to the year 2050. Categories of data pertaining to peace and international security studies include population (urban/rural, age, sex); vital rates (infant mortality, life tables); fertility and child survivorship; migration; ethnic, religious, and language groups.

Products of the database are printed reports and machine-readable files (microcomputer disks). Scholars may call Peter Johnson, Chief, Information Resources Branch (301/763-4811) for information pertaining to the IDB.

### ECONOMIC ANALYSIS BUREAU (BEA)

BEA plays a crucial role in measuring and analyzing U.S. commercial activity by maintaining an accounting framework designed to facilitate modern economic analysis. BEA data are available in several forms: printed reports; diskette; the Economic Bulletin Board (EBB), a PC-based electronic bulletin board; and EBB/FAX, which transmits government press releases and information files. For information on access to EBB, call (202) 482-1986 (8:30 A.M.–4:30 P.M.). The phone number to receive EBB/FAX transmissions is 1 (900) 786-2329; further information is available by writing U.S. Department of Commerce, Economics and Statistics Administration, Office of Business Analysis/H4885, Washington, D.C. 20230.

BEA information on international economics covers international transactions accounts (balance of payments) and direct investment estimates. The international transactions accounts include merchandise trade, trade in services, the current account balance, and capital transactions. The direct investment estimates cover estimates of U.S. direct investment abroad and foreign direct investment in the United States, income and other flows associated with these investments, and other aspects of the operations of multinational enterprises. Examples of BEA data include *BEA Reports: International Reports* (approximately 13 a year, available as publications, EBB, EBB/FAX); *U.S. Merchandise Trade Data* (publication, diskette); *Foreign Direct Investment in the United States: Operations of U.S. Affiliates of Foreign Companies* (publication, diskette); *U.S. Direct Investment Abroad: 1989 Benchmark Survey, Final Results* (publication, diskette); *U.S. Direct Investment Abroad: Operations of U.S. Parent Companies and Their Foreign Affiliates* (publication, diskette).

For information contact Howard Murad, Chief, Merchandise Trade Branch (202/606-9577). Complete information on data provided by BEA is published in *User's Guide to BEA Information,* available from Public Information Office, Bureau of Economic Analysis, U.S. Department of Commerce, Washington, D.C. 20230.

### ECONOMICS AND STATISTICS ADMINISTRATION

The Office of Business Analysis in the Economics and Statistics Administration (202/482-1405) maintains the National Trade Data Bank (NTDB) (202/482-1986; fax: 202/482-2164), which compiles international trade and economic data from numerous U.S. government agencies and departments and makes them available on CD-ROM for subscribers. Current subscription rates are $360 per year for 12 two-disc issues or $35 per issue. The information is oriented toward developing U.S. foreign trade.

Altogether the NTDB draws information from 18 government sources. Relevant departments and agencies include the following: Board of Governors of the Federal Reserve; Central Intelligence Agency, including data from *Handbook of Economic Statistics* and *The World Factbook;* Export-Import Bank of the United States; State Department, including information from *Background Notes, Key Officers of Foreign Service Posts, Resource Guide to Doing Business in Central and Eastern Europe,* and *Country Reports on Economic Policy and Trade Practices;* U.S. International Trade Commission, including data from *Trade between the U.S. and Non-Market Economy Countries;* Agriculture Department—Foreign Agricultural Service (see G5 for description); and Commerce Department—aside from extensive information from the divisions listed above, data are collected from the Bureau of Export Administration's *Export Licensing Information.*

## INTERNATIONAL TRADE ADMINISTRATION (ITA)

The ITA's Office of Trade and Economic Analysis, Jonathan C. Menes, Director (202/482-5145), maintains a database containing extensive trade information arranged by country. This database contains perhaps the most extensive computerized East-West trade information in the D.C. area. The ITA's reference room is open to the public. The Export Promotion Services Group of the U.S. and Foreign Commercial Service sells two computer tapes: The Export Mailing List and the Trade Opportunities Program. The group will also do custom searches and sell printouts of specific export data.

4.   Index terms: Defense Policy, National; Development Issues—Population policy; International Economics—International Trade

**Cooperative Housing Foundation (CHF)**   See entry N17

---

## G7   Defense Technical Information Center (DTIC) (Defense Department)

1.a.   Cameron Station, Building 5
Alexandria, Va. 22304-6145

(703) 274-7633 (Documentation Information)
Fax: (703) 274-9307

b.   7:30 A.M.–4:00 P.M. Monday–Friday

c.   DTIC services are available to U.S. government organizations and their contractors.

d.   Kurt Molhom, Administrator

2.   DTIC is a computerized repository of more than 2 million classified and unclassified research reports produced or funded by the Defense Department (DOD). Virtually all formal research results from DOD-funded projects are deposited here. The strength of the collection is in the physical sciences, technology, and engineering as they relate to national defense and military matters. An undetermined number of studies relative to international security, national defense, military science, and other issues pertinent to the scope of this Guide are within the database.

3.   The bibliographic database is accessible online; full reports are available in hardcopy or on microfiche. Unclassified, unlimited reports in the database may be purchased through the National Technical Information Service (NTIS) (K29, Appendix III), which announces the DTIC reports released to it through the publication *Government Reports, Announcements, and Indexes.*

4.   Index Terms: Defense Policy, National; Military Science

See also entries A33, D1, and K10

**Education Department—National Center for Education Statistics (NCES)**   See entry K11

**Energy Department (DOE)—Energy Information Administration (EIA)**   See entry K12

**Forum for Intercultural Communication**   See entry N23

---

## G8   International Bank for Reconstruction and Development (World Bank)— International Economics Department

1.a.   1818 H Street, NW
Washington, D.C. 20433
(202) 473-3830
Fax: (202) 477-0966

b. 9:00 A.M.–5:30 P.M. Monday–Friday

c. The World Bank maintains a variety of data systems for internal use. Copies of magnetic tapes are exchanged with U.S. government agencies and other international organizations and will be made available to private users (universities, research centers, individual scholars) upon request, at a reasonable charge. Data are also now available on diskette in a compressed format for easy handling and retrieval.

d. Masood Ahmed, Director, International Economics Department

Henry Burt, Chief, Systems Division

2. The World Bank's International Economics Department stores a broad spectrum of statistical data in machine-readable format. Information relevant to peace and international security studies deals primarily with international economic affairs. Data systems of particular interest are:

*Socio-Economic Data Bank,* containing time series on a wide range of macrolevel social and economic indicators by country. Examples of statistical categories include current GNP per capita, population, foreign trade, origin and use of resources, determinants of population growth, labor force, income and poverty, production, and core international transactions. These data also appear in published form and on diskette in the World Bank's *World Tables, Social Indicators of Development, World Bank Atlas,* and *World Development Report.*

*External-Debt (or Debtor-Reporting) Data System,* containing, by country, data on public borrowing, external indebtedness, debt restructuring, principal repayments, balance of payments, and related issues. This information is largely data published in the bank's *World Debt Tables,* available on diskette.

*Capital Markets Data System,* containing data on transactions in international capital markets, primarily western Europe, Japan, and the United States (data that appear in the bank's quarterly publication *Borrowing in International Capital Markets*).

*Commodities and Commodity Prices Data Systems,* comprising time series of data published in the annual *Commodity Trade and Price Trends.*

3. World Bank print and electronic publications are available through the World Bank Book Store, 701 18th Street, NW, Washington, D.C. 20433 (202/473-2941). The booklet *International Economic Analysis and Statistics, Including Data on Diskette* contains information on data covered by different publications and which data are available on diskette. It is available by contacting the International Economics Division of the bank.

4. Index terms: Development Issues; Humanitarian Issues; International Economics—International Finance

See also entries A27, D3, F12, and L8

**International Foundation for Electoral Systems (IFES) See entry N29**

---

## G9 International Monetary Fund (IMF)— Statistics Department

---

1.a. 700 19th Street, NW
Washington, D.C. 20431
(202) 623-6180
Fax: (202) 623-6278

b. 9:00 A.M.–5:30 P.M. Monday–Friday

c. The International Monetary Fund (IMF) maintains data from its four statistical publications in machine-readable form. Copies of magnetic tapes are made available by subscription. Each subscription covers 12 monthly tapes; the corresponding IMF book publication, which serves as a guide to the contents of the tape; and documentation and instructions on how to use the data and programs contained on tape.

d. John McLenaghan, Director, Statistics Department (data inquiries 202/623-6180)

Frank Maranto, Chief, Systems Production Division (technical inquiries 202/623-7510)

2. Information relevant to peace and international security studies deals primarily with international economic affairs. The four statistical publications in machine-readable form are:

*International Financial Statistics* tape subscriptions contain some 26,000 time series, including all series appearing in the IMF's *International Finance Statistics* country pages and world tables (except daily exchange rate series), international liquidity series for all fund member countries, and 14 major series on countries' relationships with the IMF. On a higher-density tape, annual entries cover 1948–present; quarterly and monthly entries start in 1957. These data are also available on CD-ROM.

*Direction of Trade* tape subscriptions contain approximately 62,000 country and area time series reported in the IMF's *Direction of Trade* country pages. Data cover imports and destinations of exports for each country. On the higher-density tape, annual entries begin with the year 1948; quarterly entries start with 1967; monthly entries start with 1963.

*Balance of Payments* tape subscriptions consist of over 63,000 time series balance-of-payment components and aggregates covering more than 140 countries. Of these series, some 35,000 correspond to data in the IMF's *Balance of Payment Yearbook,* with annual data beginning in 1965 or later. The remaining time series are long-term data series often extending back to the mid-1950s.

*Government Finance Statistics* tape subscriptions contain approximately 46,000 time series as reported in the IMF's *Government Finance Statistics Yearbook.* Included are data on revenues, expenditures, grants, lending, financing debt, and social security funds. Monthly tapes reflect updates and revisions; in some cases, they provide historical data beyond those reported in the *Yearbook.*

4. Index terms: Development Issues; Humanitarian Issues; International Economics—International Finance

See also entries A27 and L11

## Justice Department—National Institute of Justice (NIJ)   See entry K23

## Labor Department—Bureau of Labor Statistics   See entry K24

---

## GIO   National Archives and Records Administration (NARA)—Center for Electronic Records (NNX)

---

1.a.  8601 Adelphi Road
College Park, Md. 20740-6001
(301) 713-6645
Fax: (301) 713-6911

b.  8:45 A.M.–5:00 P.M. Monday–Friday
Contact reference services for access to records at times when research complex is open nights and weekends.

c.  Open to the public; fees are charged for documentation and computer processing. Duplication services include copying to nine-track open reel magnetic tape, 3480-class tape cartridge, electrostatic (paper) copying, and microfiche. A fee schedule and quotes are available upon request.

d.  Kenneth Thibodeau, Director
Thomas E. Brown, Chief, Archival Services Branch

Fynnette Eaton, Chief, Technical Services Branch
Margaret O. Adams, Assistant Chief, Archival Services Branch

2.  The Center for Electronic Records is the organization within the National Archives and Records Administration (B11) that appraises, collects, preserves, and provides access to federal records in a format designed for computer processing. The center maintains electronic records with continuing value created by Congress, the courts, the Executive Office of the President, numerous presidential commissions, and nearly 100 bureaus, departments, and other components of executive branch agencies and their contractors. Approximately 7,000 data files (from a total of 16,000 at the center) are currently included in the database. The following record groups (RG) include machine-readable data pertinent to peace and international security studies.

RG 29:  *Bureau of the Census.*
Exports Data Bank, Annual, 1964–92; Imports Data Bank, Annual, 1964–92; contains annual U.S. export and import data by commodity and by country of origin or destination.

RG 210:  *War Relocation Authority.*
This RG contains evacuee summary data from 1942.

RG 218:  *U.S. Joint Chiefs of Staff.*
Machine-readable data within this RG include combat activities file, October 1965–December 1970; combat naval gunfire support file, March 1966–January 1973; mine warfare activities file, May 1972–January 1973; naval surveillance activities file, February 1966–December 1972; combat air summary, January 1962–August 1973; situation report army file, May 1966–March 1973; Southeast Asia database, January 1970–June 1975.

RG 286:  *Agency for International Development.*
This RG contains the documents and projects in the Development System Database (DIS), 1950–89, relating to developmental assistance, as well as the Demographic and Health Surveys Program databases compiled in the 1980s, with demographic and health information on the developing countries of Africa, Asia, and Latin America.

RG 306:  *United States Information Agency.*
International public opinion surveys taken on behalf of the USIA. The data are from over 1,100 USIA-sponsored surveys that have been transferred to the National Archives. They generally date from 1974 through the 1980s.

RG 330:  *Office of the Secretary of Defense.*
Within this RG are the "American Soldier in World War II" series, 1942–45, which contains 138 public

opinion surveys of U.S. soldiers; Cambodian incidents file, 1970–74; enemy base area file, July 1966–
June 1971; foreign military sales, case report, 1948–
86; master item detail, 1949–86; hamlet evaluation
system, 1967–74; herbicide files, 1965–70; international military balance of payments, fiscal years
1960–86; military prime contract file, 1960s–1970s;
Southeast Asia friendly forces file, 1966–72; Southeast Asia province summary file, 1966–73; territorial forces activity reporting system, 1972–73;
Vietcong initiated incidents file, 1963–71.

RG 335: *Secretary of the Army.*
This RG contains data on the U.S. Army and Joint
Services Environmental Support Group (ESG) dealing with army nuclear testing (1945–62) personnel
review as of October 1987. It also contains battalion
tracking study for the agent orange study, 1983–86,
and the Vietnam experience study (restricted).

RG 338: *U.S. Army Commands.*
This RG contains combat operations loss and expenditure data, such as ammunition expenditure
data, from Vietnam, 1968–79.

RG 349: *Joint Commands.*
Relevant data sets in this RG include ground operations reporting system, 1967–72; integrated tactical
data file, which contains combat incident data
1969–70; national police infrastructure analysis in
Vietnam, which contains a master file and information from the hamlet evaluation system, 1971–73;
people's self-defense force management information
system, February–August 1972; and territorial
forces evaluation systems, 1968–70.

RG 373: *Defense Intelligence Agency.*
This RG contains an index to the microfiche of the
captured Grenada documents, October 1983.

RG 389: *Office of the Provost Marshal General,
1941–.*
This RG contains data on U.S. military prisoners of
war returned alive from the European and Pacific
theaters in World War II.

RG 407: *Army Adjutant General's Office.*
This RG contains data from the Casualty Information System, 1961–81, and Korean conflict casualties, 1950–53.

3.	The center produces informational handouts
for heavily used record series or data files in its custody. Also available are "Information about Electronic Records in the National Archives for Prospective Researchers" and "Title List: A Preliminary and
Partial Listing of the Data Files in the National
Archives and Records Administration," which lists
titles and current processing status of a portion of
the data files in the center's custody. The "Title List"
is continuously updated and revised.

4.	Index Terms: Defense Policy, National; Devel-
opment Issues; International Economics; Low Intensity Conflict; Military History; Military Science;
Terrorism

See also entries B11, D6, E11, F20, and F21

**National Security Archive   See entry B12**

**Peace Links (*formerly* Women against Nuclear
War)   See entry M45**

**Refugee Policy Group   See entry H66**

# Organizations

# H

## Research Centers and Information Offices

### Introductory Note

Some of the nation's leading research centers have their headquarters or branch offices in Washington, D.C., and many of these institutions are actively involved in research on peace and international security. American Enterprise Institute for Public Policy Research (AEI) (H3), Brookings Institution (H8), Carnegie Endowment for International Peace (H9), Center for Strategic and International Studies (CSIS) (H18), Ethics and Public Policy Center (H28), United States Holocaust Memorial Research Institute (H72), United States Institute of Peace (USIP) (H73), and Woodrow Wilson International Center for Scholars (WWICS) (H76) are among the best known.

In approaching the entries in this section, scholars should be cautioned that, as with U.S. government agencies, programs and personnel in the research centers may undergo frequent changes. Many research centers introduce new research programs on the basis of current interests or availability of funds. Personnel brought into a research institution for a specific research program may leave after the conclusion of the project. Also, a specific program may disappear from the activities of one organization only to reappear with another at a later date.

Research Centers that are administered by universities are described under their parental institutions in section J and listed in Index IV.

For research centers dealing with specific geographic areas or individual countries see the geographic volumes in this Scholars' Guides series, listed in the Bibliography.

It is important to note that Washington, D.C., boasts a wide variety of consulting firms that may from time to time pursue topics relevant to international security and peace studies. In general, such private companies are excluded from this Guide because much if not all of the information gathered remains the exclusive property of the client and is unavailable to researchers. For locating additional research centers of potential interest, scholars may contact the Commerce Department (K7), which monitors foreign contracts obtained by U.S. firms. It may also be fruitful to consult the lists prepared by various government agencies, particularly the State Department (K37), the U.S. Information Agency (K41), and the Defense Department (K10), for contracts awarded by U.S. government agencies for work on international development, economic, political, and military issues.

---

### HI  American Academy of Diplomacy

1. 1726 M Street, NW, Suite 800
   Washington, D.C. 20036
   (202) 223-0510
   Fax: (202) 833-2369

2. L. Bruce Laingen, President
   Lawrence S. Eagleburger, Chairman

3. The academy was established in 1983 as a way for former diplomats to cooperate to promote the highest standards in American diplomacy. The academy's concern is with the foreign policy process. Its objectives are to foster high standards of qualification and performance in the conduct of foreign policy; increase public understanding of diplomacy's contribution to U.S. national security; study and disseminate findings on the conduct and content of U.S. foreign policy; and encourage stronger U.S. diplomatic representation abroad.

4. The academy has conducted a series of seminars on the tasks confronting U.S. diplomacy in the post-cold war period. In conjunction with the Nitze School of Advanced International Studies of Johns Hopkins University, it engaged in a study on improving multilateral negotiations. It also has joined in an annual "West/West" conference of senior former policy officials of NATO on problems facing the alliance following the cold war. The academy has established an award, granted periodically, to recognize exemplary performance of diplomatic duties.

5. The academy's resources are not available for use by outside researchers.

7. Index Terms: Collective Security; Conflict Resolution and Management; Diplomacy and Negotiations

---

### H2  American Defense Institute

1. 1055 North Fairfax Street, Suite 200
   Alexandria, Va. 22314
   (703) 519-7000
   Fax: (703) 519-8627

2. Eugene B. McDaniel, President

3. The American Defense Institute (ADI) was founded in 1983 to promote a strong national defense with a special emphasis on the development of future American leaders. The ADI sponsors several public affairs activities. These include Fellowship in National Security Studies; Internship in National Defense Studies; Outstanding Leadership Award; the Pride in America program to promote appreciation of citizenship in a free society; Military Voter Program; POW Awareness Program. The institute has a speakers bureau, which focuses on communicating about freedom to young Americans.

4. The institute conducts a National Security Leadership Seminar Series, held on Capitol Hill, which gives congressional interns and staff members opportunities to hear experts debate topical national security issues.

5. ADI has a collection of information more than an operational library. This collection consists of files dating back about eight or nine years on geopolitical questions and weapons systems. It also has back issues of the Pentagon's *Early Bird* (from 1990), *Defense News,* and *Defense Weekly,* as well as congressional and government reports on issues such as base closings and women in combat. The best contact for getting information is John Isaf (703/519-7000). Mr. Isaf can act as a clearinghouse for information, put scholars in touch with the appropriate analyst or adjunct scholar, and authorize scholars' use of ADI's resources.

6. The institute publishes the *ADI Newsletter*. It also publishes a regular series of briefing papers entitled *ADI Briefing,* prepared by ADI Fellows, Adjunct Scholars, and staff members, and the *ADI Security Review,* which is a collection of articles commenting on U.S. national security policy. The institute has also published two books about ADI president and founder, Capt. "Red" McDaniel's ex-

periences as a POW in Vietnam and with his family following his return: *Scars and Stripes* (1975) and *After the Hero's Welcome* (1991).

7.   Index Terms: Defense Policy, National—U.S. Strategic Interests

---

## H3   American Enterprise Institute for Public Policy Research (AEI)

---

1.   1150 17th Street, NW
Washington, D.C. 20036
(202) 862-5800
Fax: (202) 862-7178

2.   Paul F. Oreffice, Chair
Christopher C. DeMuth, President
Jeane Kirkpatrick, Director of Foreign Policy and Defense Studies

3.   AEI sponsors original research on government policy in the areas of social and political studies, foreign and defense policy, and economic policy. The foreign and defense policy studies program examines threats to international security in Asia, the Middle East, Eastern Europe, and the former Soviet Union. Among the numerous topics that institute scholars pursue are Russian foreign policy; transition to democracy in developing countries; U.S.-Asian relations; China; Germany; Japan; Korea; arms control; foreign aid; human rights; U.S. defense capabilities; use of U.S. military forces in humanitarian missions abroad; and the role of international organizations in the post-cold war world. Issues on which the economic policy program of the institute focuses include energy policy; environmental policy; GATT; international finance; NAFTA; and trade policy. A scholar directory is available.

4.   AEI conducts numerous conferences throughout the year including the Annual Policy Conference each December. Conferences are by invitation only.

5.   AEI's library contains 5,000 volumes and 200 periodicals focusing on economics, foreign policy, and political science. The library is not generally open to outside researchers, but exceptions may be made. To request permission to use the library, contact the librarian, Yvonne Caldwell (202/862-7181). Hours of operation are 8:30 A.M.–4:30 P.M. Monday–Friday.

6.   AEI publishes a bimonthly magazine called *The American Enterprise*, as well as a monthly newsletter. Books published by the institute on international trade and economics include *Agricultural Policy and U.S.-Taiwan Trade*, by D. Gale Johnson and Chiming Hou (1993); *Capital Markets and Trade*, edited by Claude E. Barfield and Mark Perlman (1992); *Monetary Policy for Volatile Global Economy*, edited by William S. Haraf and Thomas D. Willett (1990). Books on foreign and defense policy studies include *The Chinese and Their Future: Beijing, Taipei, and Hong Kong*, edited by Zhiling Lin and Thomas W. Robinson (1993); *Democracy and Development in East Asia: Taiwan, South Korea, and the Philippines*, edited by Thomas W. Robinson (1990); *The Japanese Question, Power and Purpose in a New Era*, by Kenneth B. Pyle (1992); *Constitution Makers on Constitution Making*, edited by Robert A. Goldwin and Art Kaufman (1988); *Exporting Democracy, Fulfilling America's Destiny*, by Joshua Muravchik (1991); *Foreign Policy and the Constitution*, edited Robert A. Goldwin and Robert A. Licht (1990); *The Future of Germany and the Atlantic Alliance*, by Constantine C. Menges (1991); *The Hidden Hand, Gorbachev and the Collapse of East Germany*, by Jeffrey Gedmin (1992).

7.   Index Terms: Arms Control; Defense Policy, National; Development Issues; Environmental Issues; Foreign Policy; Human Rights—Theory and Research; Humanitarian Issues—Research Organization; International Economics—International Trade; International Organizations; International Politics; Military Spending; Political Systems and Ideologies; Regional Conflict

---

## H4   American Security Council

---

1.   1155 15th Street, NW, Suite 1101
Washington, D.C. 20005
(202) 296-9500
Fax: (202) 296-9547

2.   John M. Fisher, Chair and CEO
Gregg Hilton, Executive Director

3.   The American Security Council (ASC) is an advocacy organization that has lobbied since 1955 for the modernization and expansion of U.S. national defense forces. Activities include dissemination of "Legislative Alerts," on a wide range of issues; nationwide petition campaigns; congressional testimony; and media outreach. Current projects include lifting the arms embargo on the Bosnian Muslims; U.S. financial support of Russia; and developing a new national security strategy.

5.   The ASC Foundation's Sol Feinstone Research Library is located at its Congressional Conference Center in Boston, Va., rather than in its Washington office. The library's holdings consist of diverse writings focusing on national security and foreign policy (including a substantial collection of military officers' personal papers dating back to World War II). The library is open to researchers 9:00 A.M.–5:00 P.M. Monday–Friday.

6.   Since 1970, ASC has published the *National Security Voting Index,* which measures lawmakers' votes on national security issues, at the conclusion of each Congress.

7.   Index Terms: Defense Policy, National—U.S. Strategic Interests

## Army Center of Military History (Army Department)   See Entry B3

## Army Corps of Engineers (Army Department)—Office of History   See Entry B4

---

## H5   Aspen Institute

---

1.   1333 New Hampshire, NW
Washington, D.C. 22036
(202) 736-5800
Fax: (202) 986-1913

2.   David T. McLaughin, Chairman and CEO
Fred Starr, President
Christopher Makin, Vice-President, Policy Programs

3.   The Aspen Institute convenes seminars and conferences that bring together leaders from business, government, the nonprofit sector, academia, and the media in order to further their ability to address issues facing the national and international community. It is headquartered in Aspen, Colo., where the conferences were started in 1949, but is an international organization with offices in Europe and a conference center in Wye, Md. Through the seminar and conference process the institute seeks to reinforce enduring values of civilization that underlie democratic societies and traditions. Institute activities are divided into seminar programs, which focus on enhancing the perspective and judgment of participants through broad reflection, and policy programs, which seek to provide relevance in dealing with major policy issues.

A number of specific programs (with director's name in parenthesis) are relevant to peace and international studies. The Aspen Strategy Group (Jan Lodal) focuses on the challenges and opportunities of the post-cold war world. Major topics have been arms control and the proliferation of weapons of mass destruction, as well as long-term U.S. strategy, especially in the context of Japanese economic power. The Congressional International Program (Dick Clark) seeks to promote foreign policy leadership in Congress through meetings with leading scholars and experts and high-level international world leaders. It has focused on four areas: the former Soviet Union, Eastern Europe, Indochina, and Southern Africa. Another project will be added: multilateral diplomacy and cooperative security— focusing on the United Nations, major transformations in the world economy, and the international environment and sustainable development. The Pew Global Stewardship Initiative (Susan Sechler) addresses problems associated with rapid population growth, the unsustainable consumption of resources, and the deterioration of the natural environment.

4.   The institute does not host conferences in the Washington area, but does host conferences on the Eastern Shore of Maryland, as well as in Aspen, Colo.

6.   The institute publishes the *Aspen Quarterly.* In addition, each program publishes results of its conferences and seminars. For example, the Congressional International Program has reports on the following 1993 conferences: Russia, Ukraine, and the U.S. Response; U.S. Relations with Central and Eastern Europe; and The U.S.-Vietnam Dialogue.

7.   Index Terms: Development Issues—International Development Policy; Environmental Issues, Global—Sustainable Development; Foreign Policy; International Economics; Political Systems and Ideologies; Proliferation

---

## H6   Atlantic Council of the United States

---

1.   1616 H Street, NW
Washington, D.C. 20006
(202) 347-9353
Fax: (202) 737-5163

2.   Andrew J. Goodpaster, Cochair
Rozanne L. Ridgway, Cochair
David C. Acheson, President

3. The Atlantic Council of the United States is a bipartisan public policy center that addresses the advancement of U.S. interests around the globe. The council seeks to identify challenges and opportunities, illuminate choices, and foster informed public debate about U.S. foreign, security, and international economic policies alone and in their interrelationships. The council's programs focus on examining new relationships within Europe, and between Europe and North America; assessing new relationships among the Pacific nations, including North America, and their relationships with Europe; addressing the transformation of the former Soviet Union; examining U.S. security requirements; shaping an agenda for the 21st century; and fostering in the next leadership generation an understanding of America's global position. These programs are integrated into roundtables, discussions, briefings, dialogues, conferences, and publications.

4. Participation in Atlantic Council meetings is by invitation.

5. The Atlantic Council no longer has a library.

6. The council publishes bulletins and special reports on numerous issues; examples of titles include *Russia and Ukraine: Political and Economic Update,* by James A. Duran (December 1992); *Franco-German Relations in Post-Cold War Europe,* by Edwina S. Campbell with Jack M. Seymour Jr. (July 1992); *The Western European Union,* by Marten H. A. van Heuven (April 1992); *Nuclear Weapons Dismantlement: An Opportunity to Advance the Goals of Non-Proliferation,* by Lawrence Scheinman and David A. V. Fischer (February 1992). In addition, the council publishes occasional papers. Titles include *Assuring the Nuclear Non-Proliferation Safeguards System,* by Lawrence Scheinman (May 1992); *Tighter Limits on Nuclear Arms: Issues and Opportunities for a New Era,* by Andrew J. Goodpaster (May 1992); *CSCE: The Diplomacy of Europe Whole and Free,* by James E. Goodby (July 1991). Policy papers published by the council include *United States and China Relations at a Crossroads,* Barber B. Conable Jr. and John C. Whitehead, co-chairs, David M. Lampton and Alfred D. Wilhelm, co-rapporteurs (February 1993); *Energy Technology Cooperation for Sustainable Economic Development,* John E. Gray, chair, Donald L. Guertin, rapporteur (September 1992).

7. Index Terms: Collective Security—NATO; Defense Policy, National—U.S. Strategic Interests; Foreign Policy

## H7 British American Security Information Council (BASIC)

1. 1900 L Street, NW, Suite 401
   Washington, D.C. 20036
   (202) 785-1266
   Fax: (202) 387-6298

2. Daniel Plesch, Director
   Natalie J. Goldring, Deputy Director

3. BASIC is an independent research organization that analyzes international security issues. Its primary function is to enhance the flow of information relevant to defense policy across the Atlantic; in particular, it works to promote public awareness of defense, disarmament, military strategy, and nuclear policy issues. BASIC focuses on four issue areas: nuclear weapons, the international arms trade, European security, and democratic accountability for defense and foreign policy. Research on nuclear issues has focused on U.S.-U.K. nuclear cooperation, nonproliferation, a nuclear test ban, NATO nuclear policy, the safety of U.K. nuclear weapons, and French nuclear policy. In regard to European security, BASIC's research has dealt with the Conference on Security and Cooperation in Europe, the future role of NATO, the war in Yugoslavia, and security around the Mediterranean. BASIC actively disseminates information worldwide regarding prospects for restraining the arms trade. Research focuses on regional arms races, transparency issues, and policy options for controlling arms transfers.

5. BASIC's library is more an ad hoc collection of their own publications, press work released about those publications, and resources from its international contacts than a standard library. The resources from international contacts range from government reports to UN and NATO releases. Researchers wishing to use these materials are encouraged to call in advance.

6. BASIC publishes a newsletter, *BASIC Reports,* every six to eight weeks. BASIC also publishes research reports and analytical papers, which include *The 1995 NPT Conference: The Second Session of the Preparatory Committee* (1994); *Extraordinary Circumstances? Arming Human Rights Abusers* (1994); *From Deterrence to Denuking: Les Aspin and New Thinking on Nuclear Weapons* (1993); *Ukraine and Nuclear Weapons* (1993).

7. Index Terms: Arms Control; Collective Security—NATO; Defense Policy, National; Military Science—Strategy and Tactics; Proliferation

---

## H8 Brookings Institution

1. 1775 Massachusetts Avenue, NW
   Washington, D.C. 20036-2188
   (202) 797-6000
   Fax: (202) 797-6004

2. Bruce K. MacLaury, President

3. Brookings is a private institution devoted to nonpartisan and independent public policy research. Its major research programs focus on economics and foreign policy although research is conducted in other areas as well. The components of the Economic Studies Program include a project on international economics and a major research center on international macroeconomics, trade, and finance. Some relevant studies currently being conducted relate to the following: Southeast Asian and Latin American economic growth through the export of manufactured products; integrating the world economy; the Network for Empirical Research in International Macroeconomics; the role of redistributive policies in integrating the world economy; and saving and investment in the global economy.

The Foreign Policy Studies program is subdivided into international security studies, regional studies, and the international political economy. International security topics include arms control and cooperative warning, control of chemical and biological weapons, cooperative security and control of proliferation, and the formulation of nuclear strategy, among others. Regional studies are conducted on the former Soviet Union, Europe, China, Japan, the Middle East, Africa, and Latin America. Particular issues include development of democracy in the Arab world; reform in the Russian defense industry; relations of unified Germany; post-cold war American-Russian relations; how to create markets democratically in Eastern Europe; Japan's changing relations with the world; U.S. relations with China; and the Yugoslav civil war. Studies within the international political economy program include the World Bank; strategic trade policy in the semiconductor industry; systemic reform in Europe; assessing the impact of NAFTA; politics of employment during market transition; economic reform and the integration of the Eastern Bloc into the world economy; and transforming communist economies. The foreign policy program is also conducting a study on global sustainable development as part of a research consortium.

Brookings sponsors fellowships and guest appointments. These include predoctoral fellowships; Federal Executive Fellowships; a Visiting Scholar Program, open to a limited number of scholars; and a Guest Scholar Program.

4. The institution's Center for Public Policy Education conducts a number of programs, forums, and conferences. It hosts approximately 50 conferences a year for senior corporate executives and government officials who share the goal of improving communication among leaders in business and government. Topics are mostly domestic, but there is an international program, held globally in different cities and with an expected two-day seminar in Washington, D.C., on trade and investment issues and the environment in the Middle East. Topics of conferences for senior government officials include U.S. defense and national policy making. Brookings also hosts National Issues Forums, a series of one-day forums consisting of government officials, private analysts and scholars, professionals, reporters, and the general public; and Washington Issue Seminars, which bring together senior executives from government and business to explore single issues in depth.

5. The Brookings library contains 80,000 volumes and receives 700 periodicals primarily focused on research areas of the institution. There is also a vertical file, government documents, and selected United Nations documents. On-site use of the library is restricted to Brookings staff and is accessible to the public only through interlibrary loan. For information call (202) 797-6240, 8:30 A.M.–5:00 P.M. Monday–Friday.

Brooking's Social Science Computation Center (202/797-6180) possesses some 30 databases, including a file of International Monetary Fund financial data. The facility (Vax computers 8650 and 785) may be used by outside researchers who are affiliated with a nonprofit or government organization.

6. Brookings publishes books based on its research and conferences as well as relevant books from outside authors. The institution also publishes a quarterly magazine, *The Brookings Review,* and a journal, *Brookings Papers on Economic Activities.* A catalog of Brookings publications may be obtained through the following numbers: (202) 797-6258 or toll-free 1 (800) 275-1447; fax: (202) 797-6004; e-mail: BIBOOKS@brook.edu.

7. Index Terms: Arms Control; Defense Policy, National; Environmental Issues, Global—Sustainable Development; Foreign Policy; International Economics—Integration

---

## H9 Carnegie Endowment for International Peace

---

1. 2400 N Street, NW, Suite 700
Washington, D.C. 20037
(202) 862-7900
Fax: (202) 862-2610

2. Morton I. Abramowitz, President

3. The Carnegie Endowment for International Peace is a private operating (not a grant-making) foundation that conducts its own programs of research, discussion, and education in international relations and U.S. foreign policy. The Carnegie Endowment currently supports associates engaged in research in the following relevant areas: the future of multilateral institutions; Middle East arms control; immigration; international and national security law; and nuclear nonproliferation. Carnegie Endowment programs include National Commission on America and the New World; Project on Self-determination; Immigration Policy Project; Study Group on Nuclear Weapons and the Security of Korea; Nuclear Non-Proliferation Project; Middle East Arms Control Project; Study Group on Indo-American Relations; Cyprus Study Group; Emerging Issues in U.S.-Asian Relations; Study Group on Russia and Commonwealth Affairs.

4. The Carnegie Endowment sponsors a number of forums. These include Face-to-Face, by-invitation-only, off-the-record, informal dinner discussions of U.S. foreign policy professionals and international leaders; Foreign Policy Press Breakfast Meetings, for-the-record sessions between foreign policy newsmakers and the media; the Western Hemisphere Forum, off-the-record monthly meetings of Latin American and Caribbean ambassadors to the United States and the Organization of American States; Mid-Atlantic Club, informal monthly luncheon sessions jointly sponsored by the Carnegie Endowment and the Delegation of the European Union; India Roundtable, informal discussions on significant developments in India and Indo-American relations; Emerging Issues in U.S.-Asian Relations, luncheon series to discuss changes in the region, cosponsored by the Carnegie Endowment and the Center for Asian Pacific Affairs; Inter-American Roundtable Breakfast Meetings, attended by media members, congressional staff, specialists, which meets regularly to discuss current issues and problems; South Africa Forum, cosponsored with Aspen Institute; Women's Foreign Policy Group, a nonpartisan group of women in media, government, and the private sector, with informal monthly sessions on current issues facing U.S. foreign policy.

5. See entry A6.

6. The Carnegie Endowment publishes *Foreign Policy* magazine. Other publications include *The Control of the Middle East Arms Race* (1991) and *Self-Determination in the New World Order* (1992).

7. Index Terms: Arms Control; Ethnic and Religious Conflict; Foreign Policy; Proliferation; Regional Conflict

---

## H10 Cato Institute

---

1. 1000 Massachusetts Ave., NW
Washington, D.C. 20001
(202) 842-0200
Fax: (202) 841-3490

2. Edward H. Crane, President

3. The Cato Institute was founded in 1977 to develop and promote public policy options consistent with limited government, free markets, and individual liberty. Cato focuses its "market liberalism" philosophy on 10 major areas of research: Fiscal Policy; Energy; Regulation; Entitlements/ Health Care; Foreign Affairs; Global Economic Liberty; Constitution; Education; Environment; and Monetary Policy.

4. Cato sponsors conferences in Washington, D.C., and abroad throughout the year. Past conference topics have included democratization; hemispheric free-trade zones; and health care reform.

5. Cato's library is open to outside researchers 9:00 A.M.–5:00 P.M. Monday–Friday, by appointment only. Contact Gregory Taylor for an appointment.

6. Cato publishes *Cato Policy Report,* a bimonthly memo on its activities, and two magazines, the *Cato Journal* and *Regulation.* The Policy Analysis and Policy Briefing series is the most useful series of reports Cato publishes. It also publishes titles such as *Patient Power* (1992), *Market Liberalism*

(1993), and *Sound and Fury: The Science and Politics of Global Warming* (1992).

7. Index Terms: Foreign Policy; Transnationalism

## HII  Center for Defense Information (CDI)

1. 1500 Massachusetts Avenue, NW
Washington, D.C. 20005
(202) 862-0700
Fax: (202) 862-0708

2. Eugene J. Carroll Jr., Director

3. CDI conducts research on U.S. defense policy and seeks to provide up-to-date information on a wide range of military spending and policies, and weapons systems. The center was founded in 1972 and is directed by retired military officers. The center draws on an advisory council of 90 retired senior officers around the country. The staff is made up of permanent researchers and special consultants. CDI offers approximately 12 internships per year.

5. The center's 2,500-volume library contains Defense Department documents, post-1960 congressional committee hearing records, periodicals, and vertical file materials, all bearing on military and foreign affairs matters. Included in the vertical file materials are defense-related newspaper clippings that date back to the 1970s. The library is open to researchers, 9:00 A.M.–5:00 P.M. Monday–Friday for on-site use. For a description of CDI's Stock Footage Library see entry F6.

6. The CDI publishes a monthly newsletter, *The Defense Monitor.* It also produces a weekly half-hour program, *America's Defense Monitor,* for broadcast on PBS and nationwide cable television, and *Questions of the Week,* a public radio series on defense and foreign policy.

7. Index Terms: Arms Control; Arms Production and Acquisition; Defense Policy, National—U.S. Strategic Interests; Military Spending

## HI2  Center for Democracy

1. 1101 15th Street, Suite 505
Washington, D.C. 20005
(202) 429-9141
Fax: (202) 293-1768

2. Allen Weinstein, President and CEO

3. The Center for Democracy is a nonpartisan organization that seeks to promote and strengthen the democratic process worldwide. The center is based in Washington, D.C., but maintains offices also in Moscow; Strasbourg, France; and San Jose, Costa Rica. It seeks to help establish and strengthen democratic institutions, encourage dialogue in conflict situations, and facilitate and support the accomplishment of long-range objectives in democracies at various stages of development. In addition to informal contacts within the U.S. government, the center maintains working relationships with international leaders, especially in Latin America, Eastern/Central Europe, and the successor nations of the former Soviet Union.

The center maintains an active Latin American/Caribbean legislative development program, which has worked with the national legislatures of Bolivia, Chile, Costa Rica, Guatemala, Haiti, Nicaragua, Panama, and Paraguay. In Europe, in cooperation with the Council of Europe, the center has organized a series of conferences and dialogues to assist emerging democracies of Central and Eastern Europe and the republics of the former Soviet Union. In Moscow, the center cofounded the International Commission for Promoting Legal Reform in Russia as part of its activity in assisting reform of the Russian legal system. It has also cosponsored conferences and meetings on such topics as the environment and the role of intelligence agencies in democracies. The center has monitored elections in El Salvador, the Philippines, the Bahamas, Panama, Nicaragua, Honduras, Costa Rica, Poland, and Guatemala.

4. The center hosts conferences in various cities around the world on topics such as the transition to democracy.

6. Conference proceedings include *Courts of Ultimate Appeal: The Constitutional and Supreme Courts of the New Democracies of Central/Eastern Europe and the Former Soviet Union* (1993); *The Environmental Crisis in Central and Eastern Europe, and the Former Soviet Union: Strategies and Solutions* (1993); *The Role of Women and the Transition to Democracy in Central and Eastern Europe* (1992); *The Proper Role of an Intelligence Agency in a Democracy* (1992); and *The Status of Human Rights Under the Helsinki Accords: An Agenda for the Future* (1990).

7. Index Terms: Human Rights—Monitoring Organizations; Political Systems and Ideologies

## HI3   Center for International Policy

1.   1755 Massachusetts Avenue, NW
     Washington, D.C. 20036
     (202) 232-3317
     Fax: (202) 232-3440

2.   Robert E. White, President
     James R. Morrell, Research Director

3.   The Center for International Policy was founded to promote U.S. policy in the third world that is focused on human rights and long-term U.S. interests. The center has been active in Central America, attempting to promote negotiated settlements in Nicaragua, El Salvador, Panama, and Haiti. The center has also been active in informing Congress on human rights laws. Other areas of interest include South Africa, Cuba, and the Arias peace process in Latin America.

7.   Index Terms: Human Rights—Monitoring Organization; Regional Conflict

## HI4   Center for National Policy (CNP)

1.   1 Massachusetts Avenue, NW, Suite 333
     Washington, D.C. 20001
     (202) 682-1800
     Fax: (202) 682-1818

2.   Maureen S. Steinbruner, President

3.   CNP is a research organization that seeks to develop new approaches and creative solutions to critical national issues through debate and analysis and through serving as a forum for the exchange of ideas. Many of the issues that the center addresses are in the realm of U.S. foreign or defense policy, international economics, or international security. CNP solicits policy ideas from a range of sources, including elected officials, academic experts, and interest groups. Relevant issues include post-Soviet ethnic and religious differences and U.S. competitiveness.

4.   CNP hosts a number of public forums. "Squaretable" discussions feature politicians, media figures, policy makers and analysts, and interest group representatives who evaluate and debate current issues. The invitation-only monthly Newsmaker luncheons host important actors in the policy making process. CNP also holds off-the-record policy forums.

5.   CNP does not have a library or a reading room.

6.   CNP has published a number of books, such as *Democrats and the American Idea* (1992); *Exploring Cambodia* (1991). Policy papers include *A New Look at the U.S.-Vietnam Relationship: Report of a CNP Study Group* (1993); *Building for Peace: U.S. Foreign Policy for the Next Decade; Keeping America Safe: Studies in Military Policy; Rethinking Defense and Conventional Forces; Toward a Safer World: A New Proposal for Nuclear Arms Control* (1988).

7.   Index Terms: Arms Control; Defense Policy, National

## HI5   Center for National Security Studies (CNSS)

1.   122 Maryland Avenue, NE
     Washington, D.C. 20002
     (202) 544-1681
     Fax: (202) 546-0738

2.   Kate Martin, Director

3.   CNSS, sponsored by the American Civil Liberties Union and the Fund for Peace, monitors the activities of U.S. intelligence agencies and national security institutions and works to safeguard civil liberties and constitutional procedures in the face of government claims of national security. The center's activities fall into several related areas. A large part of the center's work focuses on research and public education through policy reports, books, and an annually updated litigation manual to assist lawyers in using the Freedom of Information Act (FOIA). The center engages in litigation, both to secure individual rights and as part of its overall strategy challenging abuses by the government. It has two staff lawyers who work with volunteers from private law firms. It also works toward coalition building with other organizations and groups. Lobbying and government relations are other areas of center work. It shares its expertise with congressional committees and parts of the Executive Branch on pending national security legislation that affects civil liberties.
     The center undertakes special projects relating to national security and civil liberties. Current projects include Ending the Cold War at Home; National Security and Civil Liberties; Access to Government Information; Free Trade in Ideas; Rights of Government Employees; and Constitutional Government and Military Intervention.

4.   The center hosts a yearly seminar on Freedom of Information Act and its ramifications.

5. The center has a small library that contains congressional hearings, reports, and books on national security and civil liberties; access is by appointment.

6. The center publishes a newsletter, *First Principles,* quarterly; an index to the newsletter is available. Books published by the center include *Litigation Under the Federal Freedom of Information Act and Privacy Act,* edited by Allan Robert Adler, updated yearly; *Using the Freedom of Information Act: A Step by Step Guide,* by Allan Robert Adler (1990); *Salvadorans in the United States: The Case for Extended Voluntary Departure* (1983); *Former Secrets: Government Records Made Available through the Freedom of Information Act,* by Evan Hendricks (1982). Center reports include *Covert Operations and the Democratic Process: The Implications of the Iran/Contra Affair* (1991), by Alex Whiting and Morton H. Halperin; and *Ending the Cold War at Home: A Public Policy Report,* by the American Civil Liberties Union (1991).

7. Index Terms: Defense Policy, National; Foreign Policy; Human Rights—Theory and Research; Intelligence

---

## HI6 Center for Naval Analysis (CNA)

1. 4401 Ford Avenue
   Alexandria, VA 22302-0268
   (703) 824-2000
   Fax: (703) 824-2949

2. Robert J. Murray, President

3. The CNA is an independent, federally funded research and development center and works almost exclusively on contract for the Department of Defense. Chief topics of its research include air warfare, antisubmarine warfare, fleet air defense, naval communications, submarine warfare, and tactical development and evaluation.

4. The center hosts an annual conference as well as a National Security Seminar series.

5. The center has a library of 15,000 titles, 450 subscriptions, and over 200,000 technical reports. The library is not open to the public without appointment. A written need-to-know and active security clearance are required in most instances. The library accepts interlibrary loan requests.

6. Although the majority of CNA's work is classified, the center has an extensive number of publica-

tions approved for public release. These fall into the following categories: *Research Contributions,* which are methodological or descriptive documentation; *Research Memoranda,* which generally are interim findings of major research projects; *CNA Professional Papers,* which may be written independently by CNA authors; *CNA Reports,* which represent the CNA's views on major issues; *CNA Information Manuals;* and miscellaneous publications, such as seminar or symposia papers, occasional papers, or briefing papers. Indexes of publicly released material are available. Contact: Supervisor, Document Distribution (703/824-2107).

7. Index Terms: Defense Policy, National; Deterrence; Military Science—Strategy and Tactics; Naval Science

---

## HI7 Center for Security Policy

1. 1250 24th Street, NW, Suite 875
   Washington, D.C. 20037
   (202) 466-0515
   Fax: (202) 466-0518

2. Frank J. Gaffney Jr., President

3. The Center for Security Policy is an advocacy organization focusing on current foreign policy and defense issues and supporting a strong national defense and an engaged U.S. foreign policy. It attempts to serve as a "policy information network," commenting on important international issues affecting U.S. security in timely fashion through an advisory board of experienced policy makers. Quite frequently, the center seeks to influence near term decisions by dissemination of information and analysis through radio, television, and print media as well as fax transmissions. The center sponsored a Working Group on Technology Policy that examined U.S. ability to compete technologically. It has also established a Strategic Defense Project to promote continued development of the Strategic Defense Initiative. A University Internship Program accommodates eight students per semester. Each year a Keeper of the Flame award is presented to an individual whose work exemplifies the ideals of freedom, democracy, and U.S. economic strength.

4. The center hosts a roundtable discussion series on current issues.

6. The center frequently publishes decision briefs, which respond to current issues. Occasionally the center prepares white papers of greater length.

7. Index terms: Defense Policy, National—U.S. Strategic Interests; Foreign policy

## HI8 Center for Strategic and International Studies (CSIS)

1. 1800 K Street, NW, Suite 400
Washington, D.C. 20006
(202) 887-0200
Fax: (202) 775-3199

2. David M. Abshire, President
William J. Taylor Jr., Vice-President for International Security
John N. Yochelson, Vice-President for International Business and Economics

3. CSIS conducts policy-oriented research on international affairs. The center's programs (with director's name in parenthesis) on international security are Energy and National Security (G. Henry M. Schuler), International Business and Economics (John N. Yochelson), International Communications (Diana L. Dougan), International Economics and Social Development (David A. Wendt), Political-Military Affairs (David A. Blackwell), and Science and Technology (Irwin M. Pikus). The center's programs on regional studies are African Studies (Helen Kitchen), Asian Studies (Gerrit Gong), Americas Program (George A. Fauriol), European Studies (Robert E. Hunter), Middle East Studies (Robert G. Neumann), Russian and Eurasian Studies (Stephen R. Sestanovich), and Pacific Forum/CSIS (Honolulu, Amos A. Jordan).

4. CSIS hosts numerous meetings and conferences every year on a wide range of international issues.

5. The CSIS library is described in A9.

6. CSIS publishes an international studies review, *Washington Quarterly,* as well as several series of papers. The Washington Paper Series has been published, jointly with Praeger Publishers, for over 20 years. Recent titles have included *When Businesses Cross Borders: Strategic Alliances and Their Alternatives,* by Harvey S. James and Murray Weidenbaum (February 1993); *Cruise Missile Proliferation in the 1990s,* by W. Seth Carus (1992); *Hungarian Foreign Policy: The Experience of a New Democracy,* by Joseph C. Kun (1993); and *The Future of Biological Weapons,* by Barend ter Haar (1991).

The Significant Issues Series covers a wide range of topics. Titles include *Conflict Resolution and Democratization in Panama: Implications for U.S.*

*Policy,* Eva Loser, editor (1992); *The Chemical Weapons Convention: Implementation Issues,* Brad Roberts, editor (1992); and *The Atlantic Alliance Transformed,* by David M. Abshire, Richard R. Burt, and R. James Woolsey (1992).

CSIS Panel Reports cover meetings on current issues held by the center. Titles include *Reassessing U.S. Strategic Forces: An Interim Report,* report of CSIS Congressional Study Group on Future Strategic Systems (1990) and *Conventional Combat Priorities: An Approach for the New Strategic Era* (1990).

The regional and international studies programs publish the following series: Policy Papers on the Americas, Post-Soviet Prospects, CSIS Africa Notes, Pacific Forum Publications and International Communication Reports. Brief and informal papers are put out by various center programs as *CSIS Reports.*

The center also copublishes books with various publishing houses; titles include *Chemical Disarmament and U.S. Security,* edited by Brad Roberts (1992) and *Desert Storm: The Gulf War and What We Learned,* by Michael J. Mazarr, Don M. Snider, and James A. Blackwell Jr. (1993).

7. Index Terms: Arms Control; Conflict Management and Resolution; Defense Policy, National; Development Issues—International Development Policy; Energy; Foreign Policy; Intelligence; International Economics; Low Intensity Conflict; Military Science; Naval Science; Political Systems and Ideologies; Proliferation; Regional Conflict; Terrorism

## HI9 Center of Concern

1. 3700 13th Street, NE
Washington, D.C. 20017
(202) 635-2757
Fax: (202) 832-9494

2. James E. Hug, Executive Director

3. Center of Concern is a research, education, and advocacy organization addressing questions of international justice and peace. Its work is based on Roman Catholic social thought, and it seeks to promote people's participation, accountability, and human rights (including economic rights) with the overall goal of systemic and institutional change toward a more just world. It works through local coalitions and national and international networks.

Center of Concern undertakes a number of projects. It monitors U.N. conferences, actively participates in their preparation, and works to shape their agenda and outcomes. The center also focuses on the global situation of women; it initiated the Alternative to Women in Development Project, a coalition effort with other Washington-based groups seeking to alter the development process. The center also sponsors the Coalition for Peace in the Horn of Africa program, which undertakes advocacy and education; the center also does research on hunger and humanitarian intervention in the region. The Global Economic Justice Project focuses on the social impact of third world debt and proposes reform of global economic and financial institutions.

5.    The Center's library consists of 300 to 400 books on faith and justice theory, and a periodical collection. Its periodicals range from ones dealing with faith and justice to more standard ones like *U.S. News and World Report*. The library is open from 9:00 A.M. to 5:00 P.M. Monday–Friday. Researchers should call in advance.

6.    The center publishes a newsletter, *Center Focus*. The center has also published numerous reports; these include *Continuing the Dialogue on Debt*, by Jo Marie Griesgraber; *The Role of International Solidarity in the Latin American Church's Struggle for Justice*, by Jo Marie Griesgraber; *Dialogue on Debt: Alternative Analysis and Solutions*, by George Ann Potter; *Catholic Feminist Committed to Justice and Peace*, by Maria Riley; *Eco-Theology*, by Phil Lands; *Forests Are Not Forever: A Liturgical Resource Handbook on the Environment*, by Edna Orteza; *Struggle for Sudan's Soul*, by John Prendergast; *Similar Structures, Devastating Results: Hunger and Unemployment in the U.S. and Africa*, by John Prendergast; and *Peace, Development, and People in the Horn of Africa*, by John Prendergast.

7.    Index Terms: Developmental Issues—International Development Policy; Environmental Issues, Global—Sustainable Development; Human Rights—Theory and Research; Humanitarian Issues—Research Organization; Pacifism and Peace Movements; Religious, Philosophical and Ethical Concepts of War and Peace

---

## H20   Churches' Center for Theology and Public Policy

---

1.    4500 Massachusetts Avenue, NW
      Washington, D.C. 20016-5690
      (202) 885-8648

2.    James A. Nash, Executive Director

3.    The Churches' Center for Theology and Public Policy is an ecumenical research center focusing on the link between theological-ethical reflection and Christian action on issues of peace and justice. The center concentrates on public policy making issues where peace and justice are seriously threatened and where churches acting together can help shape the future. A prime area of concern of the center is peacemaking and disarmament. The center serves as a consultation resource for public and private agencies. The center also has a visiting scholars program of a semester's or year's duration.

4.    The center sponsors a number of forums, conferences, and lectures. Center Associates meet several times a year for papers and discussion. Large-scale conferences are planned occasionally, such as the Public Policy Conference for Religious Leaders, which was cosponsored with the Brookings Institution. There is also the Cynthia Wedel Lecture, which honors the founder of the center.

5.    The center does not have a library, but it does have about a bookshelf full of its own publications, which researchers are welcome to come in and use.

6.    The center publishes the semiannual *Theology and Public Policy*. The center has also published the Shalom Papers, its own series of monographs examining current issues. A list of publications is available on request.

7.    Index Terms: Disarmament; Pacifism and Peace Movements; Peace Theory and Research; Religious, Philosophical and Ethical Concepts of War and Peace

---

## H21   Committee for Economic Development (CED)

---

1.    2000 L Street, NW, Suite 700
      Washington, D.C. 20036
      (202) 296-5860
      Fax: (202) 223-0776

2.    Sol Hurwitz, President
      Van Doorn Ooms, Senior Vice-President and Director of Research

3.    The CED is a business-related research and educational organization with headquarters in New York City. Composed of some 250 trustees (mostly board chairs, and university and corporation presidents) and a research support staff (including five researchers in Washington), CED issues policy state-

ments and recommendations on public policy issues, especially domestic and international economic policy. Topics in international economics studied by CED have included U.S. trade policy, third world economic growth, U.S.-Japan trade, and transnational corporations and developing countries.

5.  CED does not have a library that outside researchers can use.

6.  CED has published an extensive series of reports on its policy research. A publications catalog is available.

7.  Index Terms: Development Issues—International Development Policy; International Economics—International Trade

**Congressional Research Service (CRS)  See entry K9**

---

## H22  Council for a Livable World

---

1.  110 Maryland Avenue, NE
    Washington, D.C. 20002
    (202) 543-4100
    Fax: (202) 543-6297

2.  John Isaacs, President

3.  The Council for a Livable World was founded in 1962 by physicists and other scientists to promote nuclear arms control and disarmament. The council has provided the Senate with technical and scientific information about arms control, strategic weapons, and military budget issues. The council continues to advocate deep reduction in weapons of mass destruction (i.e., biological and chemical weapons). The council currently focuses on ending the proliferation of weapons (including arms sales to foreign governments), promoting a nonmilitary economy, and strengthening international peacekeeping. Most of the council's activities are through the Council for a Livable World Education Fund, which finances research and dissemination of information on arms control and waste of resource due to military buildups. The council operates a political action committee that contributes to campaigns of congressmen who favor arms control.

4.  The council holds information meetings for Congress and other government agencies from time to time.

5.  Council for a Livable World does not have a library, but it does keep a collection of its own fact sheets, newsletters, and briefing books. Researchers are welcome to use these materials in-house.

6.  The council publishes a monthly newsletter. It also publishes fact sheets on specific issues of arms control and weapons systems, as well as booklets such as *The Military Industrial Complex* (1993). A publications list is available.

7.  Index Terms: Arms Control; Disarmament; Military Spending; Peacekeeping; Proliferation

---

## H23  Council for Social and Economic Studies

---

1.  1133 13th Street, NW
    Washington, D.C. 20005
    (202) 371-2700
    Fax: (202) 371-1523

2.  Roger Pearson, Executive Director

3.  The Council for Social and Economic Studies is an educational organization that prepares and disseminates economic, social, and political analyses, both domestic and international.

5.  The council has a library of approximately 12,000 books and manuscripts. Unfortunately, it does not have a librarian so its resources are too unorganized for anyone unfamiliar with the collection to use. Scholars who wish to attempt to use the council's resources must contact Executive Director, Roger Pearson, for permission.

6.  The council publishes *Journal of Social, Political, and Economic Studies* quarterly and the journal *Space Power,* which covers aerospace research. It also publishes a monograph series, currently about 22 in number, most recently, *Nations at the Crossroads,* by Diana Pikcunas (1993).

7.  Index Terms: International Economics

---

## H24  Council on Hemispheric Affairs (COHA)

---

1.  724 9th Street, NW, Suite 401
    Washington, D.C. 20001
    (202) 393-3322
    Fax: (202) 393-3423

2.  Larry Birns, President

3.   COHA seeks to promote the common interests of the hemisphere, raise the visibility and the importance of the inter-American relationship, and encourage the formulation of rational U.S. policy toward Latin America and Canada. COHA monitors inter-American political, economic, diplomatic, and military relations, and works to promote democratic ideals, human rights, and freedom of thought and person. It monitors Canadian-Latin American relations as well. The organization disseminates its research through media releases, reports to foreign policy organizations throughout the United States, and in petitions to the State Department, the Inter-American Commission Human Rights, and other agencies on behalf of Latin American victims of human rights violations. It offers approximately 30 internships a semester. Interns are expected to write opinion pieces for major newspapers and represent the council on radio and television public affairs programs.

5.   A reference file on patterns of human rights violations in each country in Latin America (containing case histories of persecuted religious leaders and political dissidents, by country) is open to researchers. Also open to researchers is a vertical file with holdings on relevant topics such as poverty and development, and material on each nation's political, economic, and diplomatic profile. A clippings file of U.S. and Latin American newspaper and periodical articles is also available. On an availability basis, COHA offers research facilities to scholars working on themes of interest to it and also welcomes the onsite participation of scholars on sabbatical leave.

6.   COHA publishes *Washington Report on the Hemisphere* (biweekly), as well as two annual reports: *Survey of Press Freedom in Latin America* and *Human Rights Report.*

7.   Index Terms: Human Rights—Monitoring Organization; Political Systems and Ideology

---

## H25   Defense Budget Project

1.   777 North Capitol Street, NE, Suite 710
Washington, DC 20002
(202) 408-1517
Fax: (202) 408-1526

2.   Andrew Krepinevich, Director

3.   The Defense Budget Project is an independent research organization committed to fostering a coherent U.S. national security policy that reflects a realistic assessment of available fiscal resources and national needs over the long term. The project analyzes national security policies and defense budgets and seeks to inform policymakers, defense analysts, the media, and others. The project issues an annual analysis of the president's defense budget. The project also undertakes specialized research on topical defense issues as well as tailored research to customer needs. Project staff are available for briefings and presentations to diverse organizations. Research and policy analysis are available in the following areas: U.S. defense budget trends and processes; military policy and strategy; funding projections for weapons programs; costing of U.S. military force structure; state and regional defense spending forecasts; defense industrial labor force impacts; defense industry transition strategies; globalization of the defense industry; weapon systems/contractor profiles; federal defense economic adjustment programs; the role of defense budgets in civil-military relations; and legislative proposals on defense matters.

4.   The project sponsors an annual educational conference in April and hosts briefings and discussion groups from time to time.

5.   Staff members of the project have their own independent source libraries.

6.   The project has published over 500 studies, reports, and briefing papers. This includes two annual studies: *The President's Defense Budget Request* and *Potential Impact of Defense Spending Reductions on the Defense Industrial Labor Force by State.* Other publications include *Globalization of Arms Production: Defense Markets in Transition* (1993) and *The Bottom-Up Review: An Assessment* (1994). The project also disseminates fact sheets and media advisories on related topics.

7.   Index Terms: Arms Production and Acquisition; Defense Conversion; Defense Policy, National—U.S. Strategic Interests; Military Science—Strategy and Tactics; Military Spending

**Defense Department—Office of the Secretary—Historian's Office   See entry K10**

---

## H26   Economic Policy Institute (EPI)

1.   1730 Rhode Island Avenue, NW
Suite 200
Washington, D.C. 20036

(202) 775-8810
Fax: (202) 775-0819

2. Gerald McEntee, Chair
Jeff Faux, President

3. EPI is a research and education organization that seeks to redefine economic strategy for the United States. In addition to many domestic economic issues, the institute focuses on trade policies, defense conversion, U.S. and third world debt, NAFTA, comparative international economic performance, especially regarding U.S. competitiveness, standards of living, and foreign trade.

4. The institute holds several conferences per year and numerous seminars.

5. EPI has a small library that outside researchers may use. Its 300 volumes focus on economic issues, social security, and foreign affairs. Scholars who wish to use the library must call for an appointment (Yi Ngan, librarian). Hours of operation are 9:00 A.M.–5:00 P.M. Monday–Friday.

6. EPI publishes a monthly journal. It also publishes policy studies and briefing papers; titles include *Japanese Auto Transplants and the U.S. Automobile Industry,* by Candace Howes (1993); *Economic Nationalism and the Future of American Politics,* by Ruy A. Teixeira and Guy Molyneux (1993); *Converting the Cold War Economy: Investing in Industries, Workers, and Communities,* by Ann Markusen and Catherine Hill (1992); and *Industrial Policy in Developing Countries: Reconsidering the Real Source of Export-Led Growth,* by Stephen Smith (1991).

7. Index Terms: Defense Conversion; International Economics—International Trade

---

## H27 Economic Strategy Institute (ESI)

1. 1100 Connecticut Avenue, NW
Suite 1300
Washington, D.C. 20036
(202) 728-0993
Fax: (202) 728-0998

2. Clyde V. Prestowitz, President

3. ESI is a research and advocacy institute concerned with maintaining the U.S. leading economic position. Its work focuses on the links between domestic and international economic policies, technological prowess, and global security issues. Specific issues have been NAFTA, closing the U.S. trade gap

with Japan, and the prospects for the Uruguay round of GATT. ESI acts as the national secretariat for the United States Member Committee of the Pacific Basin Economic Council, which seeks to foster a favorable international business environment.

4. ESI hosts conferences and seminars throughout the year.

5. ESI does have a library, but it is extremely small. Scholars looking for resources dealing with international economics are encouraged to use other libraries.

6. ESI publishes a quarterly newsletter, *News and Notes.* Books published by the institute include *Beyond Capitalism: The Japanese Model of Market Economics,* by Eisuke Sakakibara (1993); *Closing the Trade Gap with Japan,* by Clyde V. Prestowitz (1993); *World Trade at the Crossroads: The Uruguay Round, GATT, and Beyond,* edited by Robert W. Jerome (1992); and *The New North American Order: A Win-Win Strategy for U.S.-Mexican Trade,* by Clyde V. Prestowitz and Robert B. Cohen (1991). The institute also publishes special reports on relevant topics.

7. Index Terms: International Economics—International Trade

---

## H28 Ethics and Public Policy Center

1. 1015 15th Street, NW, Suite 900
Washington, D.C. 20005
(202) 682-1200
Fax: (202) 408-0632

2. George Weigel, President

3. The Ethics and Pubic Policy Center's aim is to strengthen the connection between the Judeo-Christian moral tradition and the public debate over domestic and foreign policy issues. It affirms the political relevance of the Western ethical imperatives—respect for the dignity of every person, individual freedom and responsibility, justice, the rule of law, and limited government. The center explicitly examines moral values in addressing contemporary issues, analyzes the moral reasoning and public policy positions of organized religions, strives to broaden public debate on the ordering of society and its relationship to the rest of the world, and seeks to foster a wiser moral and political debate across ideological barricades.

The five main areas of research and publication are religion and society; foreign policy; law and society; education and society; and business and society.

The religion and society program works with Protestant, Catholic, Jewish, and Orthodox scholars and religious leaders to create a more thoughtful encounter between religiously grounded moral values and the U.S. public policy agenda. Its three major studies are *Evangelical Studies, Catholic Studies,* and *Orthodox Studies.* The foreign policy program addresses a broad range of issues relating to U.S. political, economic, military, and human rights responsibilities in the world. Its primary publication is *American Purpose,* a quarterly commentary on the peace, freedom, and security debate. The law and society program assesses trends in those areas of law that affect the culture-forming institutions of society, such as schools and religious institutions. Examining the role of educational institutions in teaching facts, ideas, and values is the role of the education and society program. Business and society evaluates the problems and achievements of corporations. A domestic issues newsletter, *The American Character,* began quarterly publication in 1992 and addresses issues of American identity and the renewal of citizenship.

4. The center conducts several one- and two-day conferences each year. Topics have included Peace and Revolution: American Pacifism Today; Glasnost and Religion; Evangelicals, Politics, and the Religious New Right; and The Middle East: Prospects for Peace and Security.

5. The center does not have a library open to outside researchers.

6. The center publishes several newsletters, and a quarterly, *American Purpose.* It has published more than 60 books. Titles include *Amsterdam to Nairobi: The World Council of Churches and the Third World* (1985); *Arming the Dragon: U.S. Security Ties with the People's Republic of China* (1988); *Candle in the Wind: Religion in the Soviet Union* (1990); *The Price of Prophecy: Orthodox Churches on Peace, Freedom, and Security* (1993); and *Building the Free Society: Democracy, Capitalism, and Catholic Social Teaching* (1993). A center publications catalog is available upon request.

7. Index Terms: Collective Security; Peace Theory and Research; Religious, Philosophical and Ethical Concepts of War and Peace

## H29 Freedom House — Washington Office

1. 1319 18th Street, NW
Washington, D.C. 20036

(202) 296-5101
Fax: (202) 296-5078

2. Charles Brown, Director
Frank Calzon, Washington Representative

3. Freedom House, based in New York City, monitors the United Nations and is especially concerned with human rights.

6. The organization compiles and publishes an annual report rating the degree of democracy in countries around the world.

7. Index Terms: Human Rights—Monitoring Organization; Political Systems and Ideologies

## H30 Friends Committee on National Legislation (FCNL)

1. 245 Second Street, NE
Washington, D.C. 20002-5795
(202) 547-6000
Fax: (202) 547-6019

2. Joseph Volk, Executive Secretary

3. FCNL was founded in 1943 by the Religious Society of Friends (Quakers) in response to the effect of military policy on American life. In addition to supporting the rights of conscientious objectors the committee is concerned with issues of peace and social justice. These issues include disarmament, international economic justice, and human rights. FCNL advocates particular legislative initiatives, conducts educational campaigns, and produces informative background materials.

5. Outside scholars are generally not permitted to use FCNL's library. However, researchers who want to use a particular document the committee has may be permitted to use the library. To receive a copy of FCNL's document list, phone (202) 547-6000.

6. The committee publishes a monthly newsletter and a quarterly, *Indian Report.*

7. Index Terms: Disarmament; Human Rights; Pacifism and Peace Movements

## H31 Friends of the Earth

1. 1025 Vermont Avenue, NW, Third Floor
Washington, DC 20005
(202) 783-7400
Fax: (202) 783-0444

2. Jane Perkins, President
   Janet Brown, Chair

3. Friends of the Earth is an environmental organization engaged in domestic and international work. Its international activities promote equitable solutions to environmental problems that are global or regional in scope. It designs campaigns aimed at achieving greater public accountability by national and international institutions. Friends of the Earth is active in such areas as free trade problems; reforming the International Monetary Fund; challenging environmentally destructive lending policies of multilateral banks; preserving the ozone layer; protecting Ecuador's Yasuni National Park from oil developers; protecting Brazil's rainforests; and reporting on Russia's nuclear power plants.

5. The Friends of the Earth library is only open to staff members.

6. Friends of the Earth publishes a journal, *Friends of the Earth* (formerly *Not Man Apart*). Other publications include *The Living Ocean: Understanding and Protecting Marine Biodiversity* (1991); *Facing Reality: A Citizen's Guide to the Future of the U.S. Nuclear Weapons Complex* (1992); *New Items: World Bank* (1992); *Know More Toxics: Will Companies Give Citizens around the World the Right-to-Know?* (1992); *The Earth Budget: Making Our Tax Dollars Work for the Environment* (1993); *Crude Awakenings: The Oil Mess in America* (1994).

7. Index Terms: Development Issues; Environmental Issues, Global; International Economics—International Finance; International Economics—International Trade

## H32  George C. Marshall Institute

1. 1730 M Street, NW, Suite 502
   Washington, D.C. 20036
   (202) 296-9655
   Fax: (202) 296-9714

2. Robert Jastrow, President
   Jeffrey Salmon, Executive Director

3. The George C. Marshall Institute conducts technical assessments in scientific fields that have an impact on public policy. Because science and technology have an important influence on public policy and even purely scientific appraisals are often politicized, the institute seeks to provide policymakers with rigorous, clearly written and unbiased analysis.

The institute is directed by senior scientists of international renown. Marshall Institute scientists examine technical issues underlying political decisions in environmental science, national defense, the U.S. space program and technology policy.

4. The institute sponsors the Washington Roundtable on Science and Public Policy, which brings together members of the scientific, policy making, business, and media communities for informal discussions of current topics in science and public policy.

5. The George C. Marshall Institute does not have a library.

6. Publications of the institute include *Global Warming Update, Recent Scientific Findings* (1992); *Two Environmental Issues* (1992); *U.S. Responses to the Emerging Ballistic Missile Threat* (1991); *Defending against Ballistic Missile Attacks* (1990); *The Concept of Defensive Deterrence: Strategic and Technical Dimensions of Missile Defense* (1988); *Issues in Strategic Defense: Security Requirements for the* 1990s (1988).

7. Index Terms: Arms Control—Ballistic Missile Defense; Defense Policy, National; Development Issues; Environmental Issues, Global; Military Science

## H33  Greenpeace USA—National Office

1. 1436 U Street, NW
   Washington, D.C. 20009
   (202) 462-1177
   Fax: (202) 462-4507

2. Barbra Dudley, Executive Director

3. Greenpeace, an international environmental organization active in protecting endangered species, was founded in 1971 to protest proposed nuclear weapons testing in Alaska; in 1987 it began a campaign against dumping radioactive waste at sea (which since has been banned) and launched a campaign for nuclear-free seas. Major concerns of Greenpeace USA focus on research and advocacy about nuclear issues. These concerns include nuclear disarmament, including an end to development, testing, and production of nuclear weapons; elimination of nuclear weapons at sea, the Nuclear Free Seas Campaign; ending U.S. nuclear deployments in Europe; and safe disposal of nuclear weapons material and radioactive waste in general. It also advocates

that nuclear proliferation measures should start with U.S. policy. It further advocates U.S. leadership in the movement away from use of force in solving international disputes; bolstering international peacemaking and conflict resolution institutions; reducing the level of arms sales; curtailment of U.S. military relations such as training, exercises, deployments; and expanding the legal protection of noncombatants.

5.  Greenpeace does not maintain a library that outside researchers may use.

6.  Greenpeace publishes a quarterly, *Greenpeace Magazine*. It also publishes the *Neptune Papers* series in conjunction with its Nuclear Free Seas campaign. It includes: *The Nuclear Arms Race at Sea,* by William M. Arkin (October 1987); *Nuclear Warships and Naval Nuclear Weapons: A Complete Inventory,* by Joshua Handler and William M. Arkin (May 1988); *Naval Accidents 1945–1988,* by William M. Arkin and Joshua Handler (June 1989); *Naval Safety 1989, The Year of the Accident,* by Joshua Handler, Amy Wickenheiser, and William M. Arkin (April 1990); *Nuclear Warships and Naval Nuclear Weapons 1990: A Complete Inventory,* by Joshua Handler and William M. Arkin (September 1990); *U.S. Naval Nuclear Weapons in Sweden,* by Hans M. Kristensen, William M. Arkin and Joshua Handler (September 1990). Other reports include: *Modern Warfare and the Environment: A Case Study of the Gulf War,* by William M. Arkin, Damian Durrant, and Marianne Cherni (May 1991); *Naval Nuclear Propulsion after the Cold War,* by Hans M Kristensen (September 1992); *Russian Navy Nuclear Submarine Safety, Construction, Defense Conversion, Decommissioning, and Nuclear Waste Disposal Problems (A Trip Report),* by Joshua Handler (February 1993); *U.S. Navy Warships in Irish Ports, 1980–1990, Their Nuclear Weapons and Naval Operations,* by Hans M. Kristensen (October 1990).

7.  Index Terms: Arms Control—Arms Transfers; Defense Policy, National; Disarmament; Environmental Issues, Global; Proliferation

**Center for Advanced Study in the Health Sciences (FIC)   See entry K19**

---

## H34   Henry L. Stimson Center

---

1.  21 Dupont Circle, NW, Fifth Floor
    Washington, D.C. 20036

(202) 223-5956
Fax: (202) 785-9034

2.  Michael Krepon, President
    Barry M. Blechman, Chair

3.  The Henry L. Stimson Center is devoted to public policy research focusing on difficult national and international security issues where policy, technology, and politics intersect. Institute projects assess the sources and consequences of international conflict, as well as the tools needed to build national security and international peace. They deal with regional security (peacekeeping, preventive diplomacy, and confidence-building measures), U.S. foreign and defense policies, arms control measures and their verification, and other building blocks of international security.

Current projects (with director's name in parenthesis) are United Nations Peacekeeping (William J. Durch); Confidence-Building Measures for Regions of Tension (Steven A. Wolfe); Arms Control in the Middle East (Michael Krepon); Roles and Missions of the U.S. Armed Services in the Twenty-First Century (Barry M. Blechman); Verification of Multilateral Arms Control Agreements (Amy E. Smithson); U.S. Arms Control and Disarmament Agency (Amy E. Smithson); International Center for Support of Chemical Weapons Convention (Michael Krepon); Impact of Declining Defense Expenditures (Steven M. Irwin); Multilateral Arms Transfer Guidelines for the Middle East (Pamela L. Reed); Confidence Building Measures for the Korean Peninsula (Matthew C.J. Rudolph); U.S. Interests in the Future of Multilateral Export Control Policy (John H. Henshaw); Conventional Weapons Proliferation (William J. Durch); Politics of the Arms Control Treaty Ratification (Michael Krepon); and Naval Arms Control (William J. Durch).

4.  The center sponsors and cosponsors conferences. Conference reports are available.

5.  The center's collection contains about 3,000 volumes focusing on arms control, foreign policy, international relations, peacekeeping issues, structure of forces, proliferation, and their own publications. The Stimson Center is currently in the process of putting its library catalog on-line. Until this transition is completed the center's collection is available to outside researchers on a case-by-case basis only. Scholars wishing to use the library should contact Erica Warner.

6.  The center publishes a series of occasional papers; titles include *Confidence Building in South Asia: Two Views from New Delhi; Does the Arms*

*Control Agency Have a Future?; Combatting Chemical Weapons Proliferation: The Use of Sanctions and Assurances.* Reports published by the center include *Implications of Strategic Defense Deployment for U.S.-Russian Relations; Key West Revisited: Roles and Missions of the United States Armed Forces in the Twenty-first Century; The U.S. Experience in CoCom: Lessons for Contemporary Proliferation Control Regimes.* Books published by the center are available through St. Martin's Press; titles include *Naval Arms Control: A Strategic Assessment* (1992); *Open Skies, Arms Control, and Cooperative Security* (1989).

7.   Index Terms: Arms Control—Arms Transfers; Conflict Management and Resolution; Defense Policy, National—U.S. Strategic Interests; Deterrence; International Organizations; Military Science—Strategy and Tactics; Peacekeeping; Regional Conflict

## H35   Heritage Foundation

1.   214 Massachusetts Avenue, NE
Washington, D.C. 20002
(202) 546-4400
Fax: (202) 546-8328

2.   Edwin J. Feulner, President
Kim R. Holmes, Director, Foreign Policy and Defense Studies

3.   The Heritage Foundation is a research organization that seeks to promote responsible conservatism through various programs. In addition to research and analysis, the Heritage Foundation sponsors lectures and debates, communications and publications, and promotes cooperation among conservative scholars and research organizations worldwide. It deals with a wide range of domestic and foreign policy issues. A current focus of research activities relating to foreign policy and defense studies is postcommunist transition in Russia and Eastern Europe. The E. L. Wiegand Fellows program has brought Russian reformers to the United States. Other areas of research include strategic missile defense; conventional force structuring; expansion of free trade. The Asian Studies Center seeks to improve U.S. understanding of Asia. The Mexico Project of the Center for Hemispheric Affairs seeks to highlight the importance of U.S.-Mexican relations. The Center for Economic Growth proposes

market-oriented solutions to the problems of slow or stagnant growth in the third world, Eastern Europe, and other areas.

4.   The Heritage Foundation hosts many lectures, debates, seminars, and meetings annually.

5.   The foundation maintains a library of some 1,000 volumes and 150 periodicals, the bulk of which is devoted to foreign affairs. Outside researchers need special permission to consult the collection.

6.   The Heritage Foundation publishes a quarterly journal, *Policy Review.* It also publishes books, such as *A Safe and Prosperous America: A U.S. Foreign and Defense Policy Blueprint.* The series *Critical Issues* has included security issues such as *SDI at the Turning Point: Readying Strategic Defenses for the 1990s and Beyond.* Other serial publications include *The Heritage Lectures; Executive Memoranda; Backgrounder; Issue Updates;* and *Heritage Talking Points.* Foreign policy and defense studies, reports, and monographs include *Expanding the U.N. Security Council: A Recipe for More Somalias, More Gridlock, and Less Democracy* (1993); *The New World Disorder* (1992); *Toward U.S.-Russian Strategic Defense: Ban the ABM Treaty Now* (1992); and *A Plan for Preserving America's Military Strength* (1992), among many others.

7.   Index Terms: Arms Control—Ballistic Missile Defense; Defense Policy, National—U.S. Strategic Interests; Deterrence; Development Issues—International Development Policy; Political Systems and Ideology; Regional Conflict

## H36   High Frontier

1.   2800 Shirlington Road, Suite 405-A
Arlington, Va. 22206
(703) 671-4111
Fax: (703) 931-6432

2.   Daniel O. Graham, Director

3.   High Frontier is a nonpartisan educational and research institute founded to advocate support of the Strategic Defense Initiative (SDI). It is associated with the Space Transportation Association. High Frontier produces a variety of books, films, and reports on SDI and sponsors a nationwide speakers bureau.

4.   High Frontier hosts seminars on SDI.

5.   High Frontier does not have a library for out-side researchers to use.

6.   The institute publishes a monthly newsletter, *The Shield,* and a quarterly, *Journal of Practical Applications in Space.*

7.   Index Terms: Arms Control—Ballistic Missile Defense; Defense Policy, National—U.S. Strategic Interests; Deterrence; Military Science—Strategy and Tactics

---

# H37   Historical Evaluation and Research Organization (HERO)

1.a.  11614 Helmont Drive
      Oakton, Va. 22124
      (703) 648-2520

2.   Charles Hawkins, President

3.   HERO supports the military analytical and operations research community through historical research and analysis. One of its stated goals is to change people's perspectives: to get people to look at defense issues in light of historical evidence. Specifically, HERO uses data from military history to develop combat models and defense operation strategies. It also uses military history as a basis for developing analytical studies of defense policy issues. For example, currently HERO is researching what U.S. military purpose and strategies should be by looking at how past events shaped U.S. defense strategies and goals.

5.   HERO's library has an extensive collection of volumes on military history, strategy, and operations. Its most important asset is the Weiner collection of military law books. The library has interlibrary loan status with the Library of Congress (A29) and the Pentagon Library (A41). Scholars interested in using the library's resources should call to make an appointment.

6.   HERO offers a catalog of over 200 publications (both its own and those published by the former Data Memory Systems. Scholars interested in obtaining a catalog or a specific report should phone (703) 648-2520.

7.   Index Terms: Defense Policy—U.S. Strategic Interests; Military History; Military Science—Strategy and Tactics

---

# H38   Hudson Institute

1.   1015 18th Street, NW, Suite 200
     Washington, D.C. 20036
     (202) 223-7770
     Fax: (202) 223-8537

2.   Leslie Lenkowsky, President
     William E. Odom, Director, Washington Office

3.   The Hudson Institute is a public policy research organization headquartered in Indianapolis with an office in Washington, D.C. The institute has a strong focus on national security and foreign affairs and conducts research in international economic issues and the environment. In the area of Eastern Europe and the former Soviet Union, the current research program centers on postcommunist transition in Eastern Europe and the former Soviet Union. The institute managed the overall direction of the Hungarian International Blue Ribbon Commission, which provided policy advice to the Hungarian government. The institute's Baltic Economic Commission is conducting a study of private sector development in Estonia, Latvia, and Lithuania. Another research project centers on military conversion in the former Soviet Union. Other projects include postreunification Germany; regional stability in the third world; the post-cold war security environment in East Asia; prospects and implications for the reunification of Korea; South Korea's involvement in the Asia-Pacific Economic Cooperation group. The institute's economic program examines international economic issues, especially free trade. The institute's Center for Global Food Issues researches sustainable development and other environmental issues.

4.   The institute hosts a yearly policy forum.

5.   The institute's library is located at its headquarters in Indianapolis. If scholars wish to use resources from the library, they may call Indianapolis (317/545-1000) and the institute will send the materials to the Washington office.

6.   Publications resulting from institute research include *The Rise and Fall of Gorbachev* (1992); *Trial after Triumph: East Asia after the Cold War* (1992).

7.   Index Terms: Collective Security—Regional Alliance Systems; Defense Conversion; Defense Policy, National; Deterrence; Environmental Issues, Global—Sustainable Development; International Economics—International Trade; International

Politics; Political Systems and Ideologies; Regional
Conflict

---

## H39  Institute for Defense Analysis (IDA)

1. 1801 N. Beauregard Street
Alexandria, Va 22311-1772
(703) 845-2000

2. Larry D. Welch, President

3. IDA is a research institute that provides analysis to the Defense Department on a wide array of national security issues. Over 200 research tasks are being pursued at any one time by the institute, about three-quarters of which involve assessments of advanced technologies.

There are five primary areas of the institute's research. Technology Assessment examines science and technology thrusts; strategic defense and its derivatives; technologies for improved conventional defense; materials; the software environment; and export control. Systems Evaluation examines strategic systems (B-1B aircraft and a future strategic submarine); tactical systems (surface-to-air missile systems); and command, control, and communications. Force and Strategy Assessments examines force assessments (net assessment of new weapons technologies and nonstrategic nuclear forces); defense strategy and policy (arms control verification analysis); methodology development, and command and communication modeling improvements. Resource and Support Analyses examines defense program projections; costs of force structures and policies; reconstitution studies; effectiveness of acquisition initiatives; defense aircraft manufacturers; computer-aided acquisition and logistic support; industrial mobilization studies; and military manpower issues. The last primary area focuses on high performance computing and communications.

Other IDA research areas are modeling and simulation; test; evaluation; and space systems and concepts.

4. The institute sponsors a series of colloquia.

5. For security reasons, the institute's library is closed to outside researchers.

7. Index Terms: Arms Control—Ballistic Missile Defense; Arms Production and Acquisition; Defense Policy, National—U.S. Strategic Interests; Deterrence; Military Science—Engineering, Logistics, and Support; Military Science—Strategy and Tactics; Military Spending

---

## H40  Institute for Foreign Policy Analysis

1. 1725 DeSales Street, NW, Suite 402
Washington, D.C. 20036
(202) 463-7942
Fax: (202) 785-2785

2. Robert L. Pfaltzgraff, President
Jacqueline K. Davis, Executive Vice-President

3. The Institute for Foreign Policy Analysis is a nonpartisan research organization based in Cambridge, Mass. It conducts research on a variety of foreign policy and national security issues ranging from proliferation of weapons of mass destruction to ethnic conflict. Beyond a small staff of specialists, the institute draws on the expertise of scholars, scientists, journalists, and members of the business community. It also seeks to strengthen education on foreign policy, to train policy analysts, and to award fellowships and research appointments to graduate students.

5. Due to lack of space, the institute's library is only open to its in-house researchers.

6. The institute publishes reports of policy analysis; examples for 1993 include *Pacific Partners: Canada and the United States* and *Security Perspectives and Defense Priorities in Northeast Asia.* The following monographs were published in 1993: *Aircraft Carriers and the Role of Naval Power in the Twenty-first Century; Leadership in a Transnational World: The Challenge of Keeping the Peace;* and *The Interagency Process: Engaging America's Full National Security Capabilities.* The following conference reports were issued in 1993: *Allied Peacekeeping and Conflict Management: Tailoring Military Means to Political Ends; The South Pacific: Emerging Security Issues and U.S. Policy; Transatlantic Relations in the 1990s: The Emergence of a New Security Architecture;* and *Preventing Instability in Post-Cold War Europe: The Institutional Responses of NATO, the WEU, the EU, the CSCE, and the UN.*

7. Index Terms: Defense Policy, National; Foreign Policy

---

## H41  Institute for International Economics (IIE)

1. 11 Dupont Circle, NW, Suite 620
Washington, D.C. 20036

(202) 328-9000
Fax: (202) 328-5432

2.   C. Fred Bergsten, Director

3.   IIE is a private, nonpartisan research institute with a focus primarily on trade policy and related topics in international economic affairs. It is composed of approximately 35 full-time and visiting fellows whose work is oriented toward policy making. Areas of research include supply and demand of investment funds around the world; regional economic integration, trading, and currency blocs; the United States and Japan in the 1990s; national security and the world economy; globalization of industry; protectionism and its costs; aggressive trade policies; managing the world economy; equilibrium exchange rates; the new Europe in the world economy; international monetary policy making in the United States, Germany, and Japan.

5.   IIE's library is closed to the public, but most of its collection consists of its own publications, which may be purchased by scholars. A publications listing is available upon request.

6.   The institute publishes *International Economic Insights,* a bimonthly journal on related issues. The institute has published over 80 books covering money and finance, trade and competitiveness, debt and development, energy and environment, Eastern Europe and the former Soviet Union, Asia, and Latin America. Recent titles include *Who's Bashing Whom? Trade Conflict in High Technology Industries* (1992); *North American Free Trade: Issues, Recommendations, Results* (revised, 1992); *Pacific Dynamism and the International Economic System* (1993); *Foreign Direct Investment in the United States* (1992); and *American Trade Politics* (1991).

7.   Index Terms: International Economics—Integration; International Economics—International Finance; International Economics—International Trade

---

## H42   Institute for Policy Studies (IPS)

1.   1601 Connecticut Avenue, NW, 5th Floor
Washington, D.C. 20009
(202) 234-9382
Fax: (202) 387-7915

2.   Michael Shuman, Director

3.   IPS is an independent research center on U.S. domestic and international policy problems. The institute seeks to serve as a catalyst for political debate and is concerned with a wide range of foreign policy issues confronting the United States. These include, among others, arms control and disarmament, U.S.-Latin American relations, U.S. drug control policies and the international drug economy, defense policy and military budgets, NAFTA, the international debt crisis, human rights, activities of global corporations, post-cold war foreign policies, and the environment. The institute also sponsors the Project on Demilitarization and Democracy, which is concerned with making third world demilitarization a priority of U.S. foreign policy; the Global Economic Integration Project; and a study on Hiroshima. The institute has a speakers bureau and an intern program.

5.   IPS has a small book room, which will be of little use to scholars.

6.   IPS publishes *Global Communities,* a quarterly report. Other publications include *Conditions of Peace: An Inquiry* (1991); *The Debt Boomerang* (1992); *Economics of Militarization* (1992); *Paradigms Lost* (1991); and *Trading Freedom* (1992).

7.   Index Terms: Arms Control; Defense Policy, National; Development Issues—Agriculture; Development Issues—International Development Policy; Disarmament; Environmental Issues, Global; Human Rights—Theory and Research; Pacifism and Peace Movements; Peace Theory and Research

---

## H43   Institute for the Research on Small Arms in International Security (IRSAIS)

1.   424 South Washington Street
Alexandria, Va. 22314-3630
(703) 549-7353
Fax: (703) 549-7354

2.   Virginia Ezell, President

3.   IRSAIS is an independent, nonpartisan research and educational organization focusing on the implications of international small arms transfers. It seeks to increase understanding on the policy level and to develop databases covering new developments in small arms and international transfers. The institute promotes discussion of issues ranging from application of latest developments in infantry weapons to current and future military and paramilitary tactics. The institute has a country by country database of small caliber weapons inventories. In addition to extracting data from official government sources,

IRSAIS has developed a network of industry, government, academic, and defense journalism contacts. It is in the process of developing a database on development and production of small caliber weapons. The institute accepts applications for a limited number of unpaid internships.

4.   IRSAIS's future plans include symposia and seminars on related issues.

5.   IRSAIS maintains a reference library relating to defense policy, military tactics and strategy, arms transfers, and research and development. It is available to researchers.

6.   The institute publishes a quarterly newsletter.

7.   Index Terms: Arms Control—Arms Transfers; Low Intensity Conflict; Military Science—Strategy and Tactics

6.   The IRD publishes the newsletter *Faith and Freedom* four times a year. It also publishes frequent briefing papers and denominational bulletins. Titles include *Episcopal Action; United Methodist Action; Partnership Briefing; Executive Briefing; Mainstream; Reading the World: An Integrated Reference Guide to International Affairs; The Soviet Union on the Brink; Sowing Confusion among the Flock: Church Leaders and Anti-Gulf War Reasoning; The World Economy after the Cold War: A Symposium;* and *Other Voices: Economic Alternatives in Latin America.*

7.   Index Terms: Developmental Issues—Agriculture; Human Rights—Monitoring Organizations; Humanitarian Issues—Relief Organizations; Pacifism and Peace Movements; Religious, Philosophical and Ethical Concepts of War and Peace

## H44   Institute on Religion and Democracy (IRD)

1.   1331 H Street, NW, Suite 900
Washington, D.C. 20005-4706
(202) 393-3200
Fax: (202) 638-4948

2.   Diane L. Knippers, President

3.   IRD explores the relationship between Christianity and democratic social development, studies how the institutional church engages in public witness about international affairs, provides information in support of responsible Christian mission work in the world, and supports people and groups around the world who are persecuted for their religious beliefs. The institute maintains relations with Christians and prodemocracy advocates in the Commonwealth of Independent States (CIS), Eastern Europe, Latin America, South Africa, the Middle East, and elsewhere. The institute's Christian Resource and Study Center monitors and collects information on Christian and humanitarian missions working in the CIS. The IRD grants an annual religious freedom award. It seeks to foster healthy church-state relations in emerging democracies in Eastern Europe.

4.   The IRD holds conferences to inform U.S. Christians on critical international issues.

5.   The organization maintains a research collection of books and files, which it will make available to outside researchers.

## H45   Inter-American Dialogue

1.   1211 Connecticut Avenue, NW, Suite 510
Washington, D.C. 20036
(202) 822-9002
Fax: (202) 822-9553

2.   Peter Hakim, President
Javier Perez de Cuellar, Cochair
Peter D. Bell, Cochair

3.   Inter-American Dialogue is composed of 100 members who are policymakers, business and financial leaders, heads of nongovernmental organizations, and intellectuals from the United States and Latin America. It serves as a forum for the policymaking community, focusing on inter-American economic and political relations. Research on democratic change, human rights, and conflict resolution are the focus of the Program on Democracy and Peace. A major project of the Dialogue centers on collective defense of democracy. The Program on Hemispheric Integration is concerned with economic issues, specifically free trade and problems of inequality and poverty.

5.   Inter-American Dialogue maintains a library of its own publications and a small conference room that researchers may use by appointment.

6.   Proceedings of the plenary meetings are published as *Report of the Inter-American Dialogue.* The 1992 volume is entitled *Convergence and Community: The Americas in 1993.*

7.  Index Terms: Conflict Management and Resolution; Development Issues—International Development Policy; Human Rights; International Economics—Integration

## H46  International Center

1.  731 8th Street, NE
    Washington, D.C. 20003
    (202) 547-3800
    Fax: (202) 546-4784

2.  William H. Sullivan, Chair of the Board
    Lindsay Mattison, Executive Director

3.  The International Center conducts research programs, sponsors overseas travel, and hosts foreign visitors in order to promote understanding of the impact of U.S. policies abroad. Its work relates to Africa, Asia, Latin America, and Russia and the Commonwealth of Independent States.

The center maintains regional commissions on Russia and on Asia. The Commission on U.S.-Asian Relations focuses on the democratic process in Taiwan and the civil war and democratic movements in Burma. It maintains institutional exchanges with the China Association for International Friendly Contact in Beijing and the Institute for International Relations in Hanoi. The commission also staffs the United States-Vietnam Trade Council. The Commission on U.S.-Russian Relations is working to coordinate the parliamentary initiative to assist Russian legislators in their transition to democracy. The center's commissions on Africa and Latin America are currently inactive. In the past the Commission on U.S.-Latin American Relations has worked on military reform, human rights, and conflict resolution throughout the region, and normalization of relations with Cuba. The Commission on U.S.-African Relations was active in issues regarding U.S. foreign policy in Africa.

Concerning the center's New Forests Project see entry N28.

5.  On library resources see entry N28.

6.  The center publishes occasional papers on relevant issues. It recently published *Russian Government Today.*

7.  Index Terms: Conflict Management and Resolution; Development Issues—Agriculture; Development Issues—International Development Policy; Foreign Policy; Human Rights; Political Systems and Ideologies; Transnationalism

See also entry N28

## H47  International Economic Studies Institute (IESI)

1.  1064 Papermill Court, NW
    Washington, D.C. 20007
    (202) 338-7234

2.  Timothy W. Stanley, President

3.  IESI carries on research relative to a number of intersecting issues within the broad contexts of international economics, national security, and global development. IESI collaborates with larger nonprofit organizations such as the Atlantic Council of the United States (H6) and the United Nations Association (National Capital Area). Issues on which IESI has worked include defense industrial base and mobilization problems; hostile takeovers and U.S. international competitiveness; international security and defense economics; integrating security and economics in East-West and U.S.-Russian relations; raw materials and foreign policy; technology transfer and economic development; and trade and development in the Pacific Basin.

5.  IESI does not have a library open to outside researchers.

6.  The institute's publications include *To Unite Our Strength: Enhancing the United Nations Peace and Security System,* by T. Stanley, T. Lee, and R. Pagenhardt (1992); *Mobilizing U.S. Industry: A Vanishing Option for National Security?* by J. Ellison, J. Frumkin, and T. Stanley (1988); *The Rise of the Phoenix: The United States in a Restructured World Economy,* by J. Behrman (1987); *The Forgotten Deficit: America's Addiction to Foreign Capital,* by T. Stanley, R. Danielian, and S. Rosenblatt (1982); and *U.S. Foreign Economic Strategy for the Eighties,* by T. Stanley, R. Danielian, and S. Rosenblatt (1982).

7.  Index Terms: Defense Policy, National; International Economics; Military Spending

## H48  International Food Policy Research Institute (IFPRI)

1.  1200 17th Street, NW
    Washington, D.C. 20036-3006
    (202) 862-5600
    Fax: (202) 467-4439

2.  Per Pinstrup-Andersen, Director General

3.   IFPRI identifies and analyzes alternative national and international strategies and policies for meeting world food needs with particular emphasis on low-income countries and on the poorer groups in those countries. Although its research effort is geared to the precise objective of contributing to the reduction of hunger and malnutrition, the wide-ranging factors involved require analysis of underlying processes extending beyond a narrowly defined food sector. The institute's research program reflects worldwide interaction with policymakers, administrators, and others concerned with national and international food and agricultural policy. As a constituent of the Consultative Group on International Agricultural Research, IFPRI receives support for its integrated program of research from a number of government, multilateral organizations, foundations, and other sources.

4.   IFPRI sponsors policy seminars and meetings.

5.   The IFPRI library is open to researchers for on-site use, 9:00 A.M.–5:00 P.M. Monday–Friday; interlibrary loan is available.

6.   IFPRI publishes a newsletter three times a year on its activities. It also publishes numerous working papers, reports, policy briefs, occasional papers, and books on all areas of food policy. Relevant titles include *Contingency Planning for Famines and Other Acute Food Shortages: A Brief Review* (1983); *The GATT, Agriculture and Developing Countries* (1990); *The Role of the World Bank in Agricultural Development in the 1990s* (1990); and *Japan and Third World Agricultural Development* (1989).

7.   Index Terms: Development Issues—Agriculture

Lawyers associated with the institute are active in many postcommunist countries in Eastern Europe and the former Soviet Union. The institute offers fellowships and training courses to foreign law students and officials from around the world.

4.   ILI sponsors annual conferences on relevant issues. During the academic year it presents a luncheon speaker series.

5.   The institute continues to work in cooperation and association with Georgetown University. It has traditionally made use of the latter's Law Center library (202/662-9140), which houses a collection of nearly 250,000 volumes. The Division of International Law holds approximately 3,000 volumes and 100 periodical titles. The library is open to outside researchers for on-site use with permission of the librarian.

6.   The institute publishes a newsletter. It also publishes numerous works on international legal, economic, and financial issues. Titles include *International Transactions and Claims Involving Government Parties: Case Law of the Iran-United States Claims Tribunal* (1991); *Judicial Enforcement of International Debt Obligations* (1987); *The Legal Environment for Foreign Direct Investment* (revised, 1984); *International Judicial Assistance* (volumes 1–2: 1985, volumes 3–6: 1990); *Gulf War Claims Reporter* (1991); *Chinese Foreign Economic Law: Analysis and Commentary* (1989); and *Economic and Political Incentives to Petroleum Exploration: Developments in the Asia-Pacific Region* (1990).

7.   Index Terms: Development Issues—Infrastructure; International Economics—International Finance; International Law

## H49   International Law Institute (ILI)

1.   1615 New Hampshire Avenue, NW
Washington, D.C. 20009
(202) 483-3036
Fax: (202) 483-3029

2.   Stewart Kerr, Executive Director

3.   ILI, formerly affiliated with Georgetown University, is an independent organization that seeks, through research and training programs, to find solutions to legal, economic, and financial problems of the international community. Its staff researches a wide array of legal issues in developing countries.

## H50   International Security Council (ISC)

1.   2000 L Street, NW, Suite 506
Washington, D.C. 20036
(202) 828-0802
Fax: (202) 429-2563

2.   Joseph Churba, President

3.   ISC is a nonpartisan public policy institution composed of former statesmen, senior military officers, diplomats, government officials, political scientists, economists, and historians. The ISC sponsors conferences and conducts studies with a focus on geopolitics, emphasizing in particular the impor-

tance of Eurasia and military power in international politics. ISC's current concern is the effect that the collapse of Soviet power will have on world politics. ISC's concern focuses on the U.S.-European relationship and the role of Germany in Europe, economic and political reform in the former Soviet Union, and the future of the Eurasian rimlands among other problems.

4. The ISC sponsors conferences on related issues. Examples include "Economic Reform and Defense in Russia: The Interplay" and "C.I.S. and Nuclear Weapons: Liabilities and Risks"; "Proliferation and Strategic Defense."

5. ISC does not have a library.

6. The ISC publishes *Global Affairs,* a quarterly policy journal that focuses on strategy and geopolitics.

7. Index Terms: Defense Policy, National; International Politics

---

### H51 ISAR (*formerly* Institute for Soviet-American Relations)

1. 1601 Connecticut Avenue, NW, Suite 301
Washington, D.C. 20009
(202) 387-3034
Fax: (202) 667-3291

2. Eliza K. Klose, Executive Director

3. ISAR promotes citizen diplomacy and bilateral and multilateral cooperative activities on a grassroots level, which can serve as the basis for solutions to problems of the former Soviet Union. Through publications, environmental partnership programs, and clearinghouse activities, ISAR collects and distributes information about joint efforts that address areas of critical need and encourage personal initiative and democratic approaches. The focus of its activities is on reducing poverty and economic inequity underlying ethnic unrest and on practical projects in such areas as environmental protection, alternative energy, sustainable economics, and agriculture. ISAR is also engaged in numerous environmental projects throughout the former Soviet Union.

5. ISAR has a small library (about four bookshelves) of books and periodicals on foreign policy, the environment, peace and security issues, and the former Soviet Union. Researchers may access this material 9:00 A.M.–5:00 P.M. Monday–Friday.

6. ISAR publishes the quarterly *Surviving Together.* Other ISAR publications include *1990 Handbook of Organizations Involved in Soviet-American Relations; Proceedings of the Joint US-USSR NGO Conference on the Environment; The State of the Environment in the Russian Federation for 1991; The State of Public Health in the Russian Federation for 1991.*

7. Index Terms: Development Issues; Environmental Issues, Global—Sustainable Development; Ethnic and Religious Conflict; Transnationalism

---

### H52 Logistics Management Institute

1. 2000 Corporate Ridge
McLean, Va. 22102
(703) 917-9800
Fax: (703) 917-7597

2. William G. T. Tuttle Jr., President

3. Logistics Management Institute is a federally funded research organization that provides recommendations for improvements of logistics management to government (and some other nonprofit) agencies, principally the Defense Department. The institute's research program covers supply and maintenance, transportation, mathematical modeling, standards systems for defense logistics, distribution and health systems logistics, installations and economic adjustment, energy and environment, acquisition, weapons support, operational logistics, force management, international programs (interoperability and standardization with coalition partners), and information sciences.

5. The institute's one-room library contains materials on specific logistics problems, as well as miscellaneous government documents pertaining to defense. Outside researchers are occasionally given permission to use the library (9:00 A.M.–4:00 P.M. Monday–Friday). Contact librarian, Nancy Eichelman Handy (703/917-7249) for permission.

6. The institute's work is provided to sponsors as reports, which are generally available through the Defense Technical Information Center (G7) or the National Technical Information Service (K29 and Appendix III). These reports cover virtually all areas of logistics. Past subjects have included prospects for the U.S. industrial base; spares requirements; NASA's Space Station Freedom; information resources management; electronic commerce and electronic data interchange; relationships with overseas

trading partners; government contracting and procurement practices; and logistic performance of U.S. forces during international crises.

7.  Index Terms: Arms Production and Acquisition; Environmental Issues, Global; Military Spending; Military Science—Engineering, Logistics and Support

**Marine Corps Historical Center (Navy Department)   See entry B9**

---

**H53   National Academy of Sciences (NAS)—Committee on Human Rights**

---

1.  2101 Constitution Avenue, NW
    Washington, D.C. 20418
    (202) 334-3043
    Fax: (202) 334-2225

2.  Torsten Wiesel, Chair

3.  The Committee on Human Rights (CHR), which assists scientists around the world who are victims of human rights abuse, is part of the National Research Council complex made up of the National Academy of Sciences, National Academy of Engineering, and the Institute of Medicine. CHR is drawn from all members of the academy complex, and more than 1,500 members actively participate in CHR's work. Since its inception in 1976, the committee has taken action in numerous cases in behalf of scientific colleagues in 63 countries.

CHR's work is based on the U.N. Declaration of Human Rights: freedom from torture and arbitrary detention; the right to a fair and public hearing by an independent and impartial tribunal; and the right to freedom of speech, conscience, and religion. The committee's activities include private inquiries and appeals to governments; communications with prisoners and their families; and workshops, conferences, and symposia. On occasion, the committee also carries out missions of inquiry and issues public statements, reports and other documents. It works to improve conditions where scientists are held as political prisoners, lends support to scientists' families, works to locate detained scientists, and tries to seek justice for victims of murder.

4.  CHR holds occasional symposia, such as the one on science and human rights held in 1993.

5.  CHR does not have a library of its own, but the National Academy of Science (M36) maintains a library of 30,000 volumes.

6.  CHR has published *Science and Human Rights,* edited by Carol Corillon (1988). It also publishes delegation reports; these include *Scientists and Human Rights in Syria* (1993); *Scientists and Human Rights in Guatemala* (1992); *Scientists and Human Rights in Somalia* (1988); and *Scientists and Human Rights in Chile* (1985).

7.  Index Terms: Human Rights—Science and Human Rights

See also entry M36

---

**H54   National Commission for Economic Conversion and Disarmament**

---

1.  1828 Jefferson Place, NW
    Washington, D.C. 20036
    (202) 728-0815
    Fax: (202) 728-0826

2.  Seymour Melman, Chair
    Gregory Bischak, Executive Director

3.  The National Commission for Economic Conversion and Disarmament is a nonpartisan research and public education organization whose purpose is to inform the public on the need and the means for an orderly transfer of military resources to civilian use. It advocates a comprehensive program of economic conversion including replacing the stimulus of military spending.

5.  The commission's library consists of books and periodicals that focus on conversion and defense spending. Due to space restraints, the library may only be used by in-house researchers.

6.  The commission publishes *The New Economy,* a quarterly journal. It also publishes briefing papers; titles include *Military Base Closures in the 1990s: Lessons for Redevelopment* (1993); *Successful Conversion Experiences* (1992); *Economic Conversion and International Inspection: Alternatives to Arms Exports and Militarism* (1991); *Arms Control Versus Disarmament* (1991).

7.  Index Terms: Defense Conversion; Military Spending; Pacifism and Peace Movements

## H55 National Defense Council Foundation (NDCF)

1. 1220 King Street, Suite 230
   Alexandria, Va 22314
   (703) 836-3443
   Fax: (703) 836-5402

2. F. Andy Messing Jr., Executive Director
   Dan Burton, Chair

3. NDCF is a research, education, and charitable organization whose focus is on low intensity conflict, international drug trade, and some specific environmental and energy issues as they relate to national defense. Since 1978 the council has conducted field research on social, political, economic, and military conditions in 27 areas of conflict, to some of which it took members of Congress. It produces policy-oriented reports, studies, and briefings based on this research. In addition, NDCF focuses on humanitarian relief to augment its research efforts. Since 1984 it has conducted 25 relief missions delivering over 134 tons of relief material into conflict areas.

4. NDCF regularly conducts seminars and briefings on related issues.

5. NDCF has a library open to researchers by appointment.

6. The NDCF publishes issue alerts on various topics such as the security implications of NAFTA in terms of drug trade, environment, and terrorism. Examples from August 1993 include *NAFTA and the Environment: Defense and Security Implications; Security Implications of NAFTA I: Narcotics;* and *Security Implications of NAFTA II: Terrorism.*

7. Index Terms: Humanitarian Issues—Relief Organizations; Low Intensity Conflict

## H56 National Institute for Public Policy

1. 3031 Javier Road, Suite 300
   Fairfax, Va. 22031-4662
   (703) 698-0563
   Fax: (703) 698-0566

2. Colin S. Gray, Chair
   Keith B. Payne, President

3. The National Institute for Public Policy promotes public education on international issues. The areas of international relations and national security affairs include geopolitics; U.S. defense policy analy-

sis; arms control, with a special emphasis on verification; regional political and military developments; weapons proliferation and export controls; space policy; low-intensity conflict. The institute sponsors a nationwide series of training seminars for high school teachers.

5. The institute maintains a small library of several hundred volumes for use by its staff members. The books and periodicals that make up the collection focus mostly on nontechnical aspects of national security (i.e. arms control and strategy).

7. Index Terms: Arms Control; Defense Policy, National—U.S. Strategic Interests; Deterrence; Low Intensity Conflict; Military Science—Strategy and Tactics; Regional Conflict; Terrorism

## H57 National Interreligious Service Board for Conscientious Objectors (NISBCO)

1. 1612 K Street, NW, Suite 1400
   Washington, D.C. 20006-2802
   (202) 293-3220
   Fax: (202) 293-3218

2. Rev. L. William Yolton, Executive Director

3. NISBCO counsels individuals and families about conscientious objection and participation in war. NISBCO is an association of religious bodies that joins to protect, defend, and extend the rights of conscientious objectors. It provides information about military service and the draft that is competently researched through professional relationships with government and private agencies. It provides assistance to other agencies in preparing literature. NISBCO also serves as a resource center for information on the peace witness of religious bodies in the United States; it assists scholars in their work by providing documentation on conscription and other issues of conscience, and maintaining copies of government and independently produced materials. NISBCO works directly with Congress on issues that affect conscientious objectors and informs the public about changes that are being considered in draft laws and regulations.

5. NISBCO maintains archives in cooperation with the Swarthmore College Peace Collection. NISBCO updated the CPS Directory, listing all the people who served in World War II alternative service with current information.

6. NISBCO publishes *The Reporter for Conscience Sake,* a newsletter. Other publications in-

clude *Draft Counselors Manual* (revised, 1991); *Conscientious Objection Information Packet* (updated frequently); and *Words of Conscience* (1983).

7.   Index Terms: Pacifism and Peace Movements; Peace Theory and Research; Religious, Philosophical and Ethical Concepts of War and Peace

---

## H58   National Strategy Information Center (NSIC)

---

1.   1730 Rhode Island Avenue, NW, Suite 500
Washington, D.C. 20036
(202) 429-0129
Fax: (202) 659-5429

2.   Roy Godson, President

3.   NSIC is a nonpartisan public policy center that promotes education about international security issues, advocates innovation in military and security affairs, and promotes democracy. Its areas of interest are intelligence, national security, international organized crime, terrorism, and ethnic and religious conflict. The following programs are conducted by the center: National Security Education—the development of curricula for national security studies; Consortium for the Study of Intelligence—academics from universities and research centers analyze the role of intelligence in a democratic state; Global Ungovernability—multiyear research project examining effects of ungovernability on U.S. interests at home and abroad; European and American Cooperation—cooperation with European public policy institutions, largely through annual meetings and conferences on such issues as military and the environment; and Media Relations—a resource center for information on national security issues.

4.   NSIC sponsors colloquia on teaching and academic research in intelligence under its Consortium for the Study of Intelligence program. This includes the Working Group on Intelligence Reform, which seeks to address the evolving post-cold war security environment.

5.   NSIC's library consists of a large bookcase of their own publications, which researchers are welcome to use.

6.   The Consortium for the Study of Intelligence has produced the following works: *Intelligence Requirements for the 1990s* (1989); *Bibliography on Soviet Intelligence and Security Services* (1985); *Resource Reports on Intelligence for Teaching Faculty* (revised, 1992); *Comparing Foreign Intelligence: The US, the USSR, the UK, and the Third World* (1988); and *Intelligence Requirements: The 1980s* (7 volumes, 1988).

7.   Index Terms: Defense Policy—U.S. Strategic Interests; Intelligence; Low Intensity Conflict; Political Systems and Ideology; Terrorism

**Naval Historical Center (Navy Department)**
See entry B13

---

## H59   Nuclear Control Institute (NCI)

---

1.   1000 Connecticut Avenue, NW, Suite 804
Washington, D.C. 20036
(202) 822-8444
Fax: (202) 452-0892

2.   Paul L. Levanthal, President

3.   NCI is a research and policy institute specializing in nuclear proliferation issues. NCI monitors nuclear policies worldwide and pursues strategies to halt the spread and reverse the growth of nuclear armaments. The chief issue for NCI is the elimination of weapons-usable nuclear material from civilian nuclear power and research programs.

5.   NCI's library is only for in-house use.

6.   The institute has published a number of books based on conferences and task forces. They include *Averting a Latin American Arms Race: New Prospects and Challenges for Argentine-Brazilian Nuclear Cooperation* (1991); *The Tritium Factor: Tritium's Arms Reduction Potential* (1988); *Preventing Nuclear Terrorism: The Report and Task Force on Prevention of Nuclear Terrorism* (1987); *Nuclear Terrorism: Defining the Threat* (1986); *The Plutonium Business* (1984).

7.   Index Terms: Arms Control—Arms Transfers; Proliferation; Terrorism

**Office of Air Force History (Air Force Department)**   See entry B1

---

## H60   Overseas Development Council (ODC)

---

1.   1875 Connecticut Avenue, NW, Suite 1012
Washington, D.C. 20009

(202) 234-8701
Fax: (202) 745-0067

2.   John W. Sewell, President
Catherine Gwin, Executive Vice-President

3.   ODC is an independent research and policy analysis organization sponsoring programs that focus on U.S. relations with developing countries. The policy areas with which the ODC is concerned are U.S. foreign policy and developing countries in the post-cold war world; international finance and easing the debt crisis; international trade; development strategies and cooperation; and the environment and development.

4.   ODC sponsors conferences, seminars, and workshops on international issues related to development; transnational dialogues and other discussions bringing together participants from developing and developed countries; media briefings; and workshops for private voluntary organizations.

5.   ODC's library contains about 3,000 volumes on issues such as population, environment, development, and democratization. It also has a collection of standard periodicals, including *Congressional Quarterly*, the *Economist*, and the *National Journal*; a collection of publications from various think tanks and research institutes; and a collection of its own publications. Use of the library is on a permission-only basis (contact librarian, Zena Mansour), but interlibrary loan is available.

6.   The ODC produces a number of serial publications. *U.S.-Third World Policy Perspectives* focuses on single issues in U.S.-developing country relations; titles include *Premise and Promise: Free Trade in the Americas; Poverty, Natural Resources, and Public Policy in Central America* (1992); *After the Wars: Reconstruction in Afghanistan, Indochina, Central America, Southern Africa, and the Horn of Africa* (1990). Policy Essays is a monograph series with titles such as *Encouraging Democracy: What Role for Conditioned Aid?* (1992) and *Pressing for Peace: Can Aid Induce Reform?* (1992). Policy Focus is a briefing paper series providing background information and analysis; topics include international finance and investment, international trade, U.S. foreign assistance, environment and population, and regional issues around the world. The council also publishes the *Alternative International Affairs Budget* and *Washington Economic Watch*, a digest.

7.   Index Terms: Development Issues—International Development Policy; Environmental Issues, Global; International Economics—International Trade

## H61   Peace Action

1.   1819 H Street, NW, Suite 640
Washington, D.C. 20006-3606
(202) 862-9740
Fax: (202) 862-9762

2.   Monica Green, Executive Director

3.   Peace Action is an advocacy group in favor of the redistribution of resources from military spending to human and environmental needs. It supports redirecting the U.S. economy toward domestic investment. Activities include coalition building on the national and local level; public education through community forums; organizing for economic conversion by holding congressional and press briefings with the National Commission on Economic Conversion; distributing publications; and lobbying Congress. The Peace Action Education Fund (*formerly* the SANE/FREEZE Education Fund) through its Disarmament Campaign seeks to educate the public and policymakers about nuclear testing, nuclear proliferation, and the international trade in conventional arms. Activities include the Grassroots Arms Transfer Network; mass media contact; and tracking U.S. arms exports.

5.   Approximately five bookcases of books from the 1970s and 1980s on arms control issues make up Peace Action's library. Scholars are welcome to stop by anytime and use these resources.

6.   Peace Action publishes a quarterly newsletter, *Peace Action;* a fact sheet and briefing paper series; and a monthly packet for activists, *The Grassroots Organizer.*

7.   Index Terms: Arms Control—Arms Transfers; Defense Conversion; Disarmament; Pacifism and Peace Movements; Peace Theory and Research

## H62   Population Reference Bureau (PRB)

1.   1875 Connecticut Avenue, NW, Suite 520
Washington, D.C. 20009-5728
(202) 483-1100
Fax: (202) 328-3937

2.   Peter Donaldson, President

3.   PRB is a scientific and educational organization that gathers, interprets, and disseminates information about national and international population issues.

5.  A 15,000-volume research library is open to the public 9:00 A.M.–4:30 P.M. Monday–Friday.

6.  PRB publishes a monthly newsletter, *Population Today* and *Population Bulletins* (usually 40–50 pages); other titles include *America's Minorities—The Demographics of Diversity,* by William P. O'Hare (1992); *Population, Resources, and Environment: An Uncertain Future,* by Robert Repetto (1991); *The Middle East Population Puzzle,* by Abdel R. Omran and Farzaneh Roudi (1993); *Europe's Second Demographic Transition,* by Dirk J. van der Kaa (1987). PRB also publishes Population Data Sheets, providing current population-related statistics, such as *World Environment Data Sheet* and *World Population Data Sheets* (in English, French, and Spanish). International Program Publications are intended to assist policymakers in developing country accessible information, for example, *Family Planning Success Stories* (1994); *Africa: Demographic and Health Surveys Chartbook* (1992); and *The UN Long-Range Population Projections and What They Tell Us* (1993).

7.  Index Terms: Development Issues—Population Policy; Environmental Issues, Global

## H63  Progressive Policy Institute (PPI)

1.  518 C Street, NE
    Washington, D.C. 20002
    (202) 547-0001
    Fax: (202) 544-5014

2.  Will Marshal, President
    Seymour Martin Lipset, Senior Scholar

3.  PPI is a research group affiliated with the centrist Democratic Leadership Council. PPI was established "to adapt America's progressive tradition of individual liberty, equal opportunity and civic enterprise to the challenges of the post-industrial era." Most of its activities center on domestic issues. Part of its current agenda focuses on post-cold war U.S. global leadership and defense policy.

4.  The institute conducts seminars and public forums.

5.  The institute does not have a library.

6.  PPI publishes backgrounders, policy reports, and longer political studies. Relevant policy reports include "War Powers in a New Security Era: Restor-

ing the Constitutional Balance" (1990) and "An American Foreign Policy for Democracy" (1991).

7.  Index Terms: Defense Policy, National—U.S. Strategic Interests

## H64  Project on Government Oversight

1.  2025 I Street, NW, Suite 1117
    Washington, D.C. 20006-1903
    (202) 466-5539
    Fax: (202) 466-5596

2.  Danielle Brian, Director

3.  The Project on Government Oversight is a nonpartisan group that investigates and exposes examples of systemic waste and fraud in government spending. It was started as the Project on Military Procurement. It has worked on the "black" budget, secrecy, the military budget, and exposed problems with numerous weapons systems. These include the Bradley Fighting Vehicle, the Sergeant York DIVAD Air Defense Gun, and the M1 Tank.

6.  Project publications include *More Bucks for Less Bang: How the Pentagon Buys Ineffective Weapons* (1983); *The Pentagon Underground* (1985); *The Pentagonists* (1989); *Defense Procurement Papers* (1988); *The Army's M1 Tank: Has It Lived Up to Expectations?* (1990); *High Tech Weapons in Desert Storm: Hype or Reality?* (1991); *James Baker: A Broken Ethics Problem?* (1992); *Informed Sources* (Spring and Summer, 1992); *The Superconducting Collider's Super Excess* (1993); *Children's Ears and Antibiotics: Gold Mine for Pharmaceutical Companies, Land Mine for Children* (1994).

7.  Index Terms: Arms Production and Acquisition; Defense Conversion; Military Spending

**Radio Free Europe/Radio Liberty—Research Institute   See entry K34**

## H65  Rand Corporation—Washington Office (RAND)

1.  2100 M Street, NW
    Washington, D.C. 20037-1270
    (202) 296-5000
    Fax: (202) 296-7960

2. Lloyd N. Morrisett, Chair
   James A. Thomson, President and Chief Executive Officer
   David S. C. Chu, Director, Washington Research Department

3. RAND is a private research corporation chartered to "promote scientific, educational, and charitable purposes, all for the public welfare and security of the United States." Although there is a domestic branch of RAND research, it has a strong focus on international security issues on an extremely broad range of subjects. Its headquarters is in Santa Monica, Calif. The major portion of its research support comes from government agencies, principally the Defense Department. Three divisions within the corporation conduct most of the national security studies. These are Project AIR FORCE, sponsored by the U.S. Air Force; the National Defense Research Institute, sponsored by the Secretary of Defense; and the Arroyo Center, sponsored by the Department of the Army.

5. The Washington office library—which contains several thousand volumes, mostly in the social sciences—is closed to non-RAND personnel. Nonclassified materials may be obtained through the library's interlibrary loan service.

6. RAND publishes more than 250 books, reports, and professional papers in any given year. Bibliographies of RAND publications are available on many topics, including Africa, arms control, Asia, China, civil defense, Europe, international trade, Latin America, logistics, Middle East, military manpower, military strategy and tactics, NATO, nuclear research, operations research methods, Strategic Defense Initiative, terrorism, U.S. foreign relations, and the USSR.

7. Index Terms: Arms Control; Defense Policy, National; Deterrence; International Economics—International Trade; International Politics; Military Science—Strategy and Tactics; Naval Science; Regional Conflict; Terrorism

---

## H66 Refugee Policy Group (RPG)

1. 1424 16th Street, NW, Suite 401
   Washington, D.C. 20036
   (202) 387-3015
   Fax: (202) 667-5034

2. Dennis Gallagher, Executive Director

3. RPG seeks to improve international and domestic programs for refugees and to promote recognition and understanding of refugee problems in broad social, political, and economic contexts. RPG tries to foster links between refugee issues and peace, security, development assistance, human rights, and health. Four areas of special attention are East-West relations and their impact on refugees; refugees and human rights; internally displaced refugees; and development and refugees. RPG undertakes policy studies on a number of issues. These include problems of mass exodus, such as asylum, safe haven, protection, early warning, and emergency response, and a North American-European dialogue on refugees. Other policy areas are refugee health, special refugee populations, refugee assistance in developing countries (these include Southeast Asia, Afghanistan, Central America, and Africa), and refugee resettlement in industrialized countries.

4. RPG regularly holds conferences, briefings, and seminars on many of the issues in which it is involved.

5. RPG houses a large collection of data and documents on refugees and serves as an important database for scholars, researchers, and experts in the field.

6. *RPG Review,* a newsletter, is published periodically. RPG publishes about 10 major reports a year. Titles include *Refugees and Human Rights: A Research and Policy Agenda* (1989); *Improving International Response to Humanitarian Situations* (1990); *If the War in Nicaragua Ends: Where Will the Contras Go?* (1988); *Afghanistan: Trends and Prospects for Refugee Repatriation* (1992).

7. Index Terms: Human Rights—Theory and Research; Humanitarian Issues—Research Organization; Refugees

---

## H67 Resources for the Future (RFF)

1. 1616 P Street, NW
   Washington, D.C. 20036
   (202) 328-5000
   Fax: (202) 939-3460

2. Robert W. Fri, President

3. RFF provides impartial and independent research and policy analysis about natural resources and the environment. RFF has more than 50 resident scholars engaged directly in research and policy

analysis. The institute also sponsors a number of grants, fellowships, and internships. The Energy and Natural Resources Division of RFF focuses on energy policy and the management of renewable resources, both regionally and globally. It explores world oil markets and energy security; the relationship between energy and the environment; and improved management practices in agriculture, water, and forestry. It pursues research on outer space as an economic resource. There is also a division on environmental quality and a center for risk management.

4.   RFF hosts a series of Wednesday noon seminars during the academic year for RFF researchers and invited scholars and policymakers. RFF holds conferences and colloquia on resource and environmental issues and arranges policy briefings for members of Congress, business leaders, the media, and others.

5.   RFF's library contains 7,600 volumes on economics, natural resources, and energy, as well as various periodicals on similar issues. Librarian, Chris Clotworthy, will make appointments and orient those scholars who wish to use the library, which is open 9:00 A.M.–5:00 P.M. Monday–Friday.

6.   RFF publishes *Resources,* a quarterly series of discussion papers. It also has published over 100 books and reports through the Johns Hopkins University Press.

7.   Index Terms: Energy; Environmental Issues, Global—Sustainable Development

**Senate Historical Office   See entry K35**

**Smithsonian Institution   See entry K36**

**State Department—Office of the Historian
See entry K37**

---

# H68   Union of Concerned Scientists (UCS)

1.   1616 P Street, NW, Suite 310
Washington, D.C. 20036
(202) 332-0900
Fax: (202) 332-0905

2.   Howard Ris, Executive Director
Alden Meyer, Legislative Director

3.   UCS, an association of scientists with 75,000 members nationwide, is based in Cambridge, Mass., with an office in Washington, D.C. It focuses on global problems. Relevant programs of the UCS are:

center on environmental and resource problems, arms control, nuclear proliferation, multilateral security, and peacekeeping.

5.   UCS's library contains about 500 volumes and a vast number of periodicals focusing on the public policy aspect of issues such as energy, arms control, and the environment. The library is open by appointment, 9:00 A.M.–5:00 P.M. Monday–Friday. Contact librarian, Louise Farr, to make an appointment.

6.   UCS publishes the quarterly journal *Nucleus.* It also publishes books, reports, briefing papers, and information brochures. Titles include *Beyond Safeguards; Nonproliferation and the National Interest: America's Response to the Spread of Nuclear Weapons;* and *Missing the Target: SDI in the 1990s.* For publications information contact the publications department in Cambridge, Mass. (617/547-5552).

7.   Index Terms: Arms Control; Collective Security; Environmental Issues, Global; Peacekeeping; Proliferation

---

# H69   United Nations—Information Center

1.   1775 K Street, NW
Washington, D.C. 20006
(202) 331-8670
Fax: (202) 289-4267

2.   Michael Stopford, Director
Joan Hills, Deputy Director/Information Officer

3.   The center provides services reflective of the main functions of the UN Department of Public Information. These include the use of press, radio, television, films, and exhibits for the dissemination of information. The Information Center's primary goal is to establish direct contacts with representatives of the local press and information media, Congress, the administration, educational institutions, and government and nongovernmental organizations, and to cooperate with them in providing a greater understanding of the aims and functions of the UN.
The center plays an important role in the observance of special UN occasions, such as UN Day and Human Rights Day, as well as publicity for ongoing UN programs.

5.   The center's library is described in A44.

6. The United Nations issues numerous series of publications; a catalog is available.

7. Index Terms: International Organizations—United Nations; Peacekeeping

See also entries A44 and F27

## H70 U.S.-CREST (Center for Research and Education on Strategy and Technology)

1. 1840 Wilson Boulevard, Suite 204
Arlington, Va. 22201
(703) 243-6908
Fax: (703) 243-7175

2. Jean-Francois Delpech, President
Kate Holder, Executive Director

3. U.S.-CREST seeks to promote public understanding of the interactions between defense, international relations, and science and technology particularly in reference to transatlantic relations. It maintains close ties with the Centre d'Étude des Relations entre Technologies et Stratégies of France's École Polytechnique. Its research focuses on the following areas: cooperative strategies among U.S. allies in high-technology defenses; international space cooperation; proliferation of weapons of mass destruction; and European military interventions in Africa. The center has launched an exchange program to increase the French academic presence in Washington, D.C.

5. U.S.-Crest maintains a small library consisting mostly of current periodicals, newspapers, United Nations publications, reports of international nonprofit agencies or public policy institutes in Washington, D.C., and U.S.-CREST's own publications. All resources deal with defense and international policy. The library is accessible by appointment 9:00 A.M.–5:00 P.M. Monday–Friday.

6. The center publishes a newsletter. Reports include *Strategy and Technology: an American Bibliography* (revised, 1994); *The Modernization of Short-Range Nuclear Weapons in Europe* (1989); *U.S. Perspectives on the CFE Negotiations* (1990); *Wargaming and Simulation in U.S.* (1991); *The Use of Space Assets During the Gulf War* (1991); *Technical and Strategic Implications of Nuclear Thermic Propulsion* (1992); *Cooperative Strategies: High Technology Security Cooperation, A Transatlantic Industrial Perspective* (1991); *Partners in Space: International Cooperation in Space, Strategies for the*

*New Century* (1993); *The Changing Franco-American Security Relationship* (1993); and *Disconsolate Empires: French, British and Belgian Military Involvement in Post-Colonial, Sub-Saharan Africa* (1994). The organization also publishes a European Viewpoint Series of occasional papers.

7. Index Terms: Arms Control; Military Science—Strategy and Tactics; Proliferation

## H71 United States Global Strategy Council (USGSC)

1. 1800 K Street, NW, Suite 1102
Washington, D.C. 20006
(202) 466-6029
Fax: (202) 331-0109

2. Ray S. Cline, Chair

3. USGSC is a nonpartisan research organization dedicated to the improvement of strategic planning and decision making by the Executive Branch and the Congress of the United States. The council helps to define a coherent and long-term national strategy for the United States in its national, regional, and global contexts.

Areas of research include military affairs; strategic intelligence; science, technology, and natural resources; as well as other topics.

6. USGSC has published several books and reports on relevant topics.

7. Index Terms: Defense Policy, National—U.S. Strategic Interests; Military Science—Strategy and Tactics

## H72 United States Holocaust Research Institute

1. 100 Raoul Wallenberg Place, SW
Washington, D.C. 20024-2150
(202) 488-6115
Fax: (202) 479-9726

2. Michael Berenbaum, Director
Wesley A. Fisher, Deputy Director

3. The United States Holocaust Research Institute is the scholarly division of the United States Holocaust Memorial Museum. The institute contains seven departments: academic programs; library (see

entry A45); archive (B16); photo archive (F29); oral history (B16); film and video (F29); and the Benjamin and Vladka Meed Registry of Jewish Holocaust Survivors. The chief areas of research are historiography and documentation of the Holocaust; ethics and the Holocaust; comparative genocide studies; and the impact of the Holocaust on contemporary society and culture.

In addition to research projects of the staff and fellows, the institute collaborates with other organizations and universities to increase and disseminate knowledge of the Holocaust. The institute annually appoints a distinguished scholar as the J. B. and Maurice Shapiro Senior Scholar-in-Residence. The Pearl Resnick Post-Doctoral Fellowship Program provides $40,000 for one academic year to scholars who have received a Ph.D. or equivalent degree and are no more than 40 years of age. For more information contact Dr. Wesley A. Fisher, Deputy Director, Research Institute, United States Holocaust Memorial Museum, 100 Raoul Wallenberg Place, SW, Washington, D.C. 20024-2150 (fax 202/479-9726). Other short- and long-term research fellowships are planned, along with support for dissertation research; fellowships in medical ethics are being developed with Medical Advisory Committee of the New York Academy of Medicine.

4. The institute holds conferences on a regular basis. The Holocaust: An International Scholars' Conference on the Known, the Unknown, the Disputed, and the Reexamined was conducted in December 1993 to mark the institute's opening. Another conference, Commemoration of the 50th Anniversary of the Deportation of Hungarian Jewry, was held in May 1994. Weekly programs of seminars and lectures are planned.

5. For information on the institute's library see A45.

6. The institute's publication program currently focuses on a monograph and documentation series, a memoir series, and an occasional papers series. In addition to original scholarly work, the institute will publish reprints of important works on the Holocaust and genocide not generally available. Recent publications include *The World Must Know,* by Michael Berenbaum (April 1993); *Anatomy of the Auschwitz Deathcamp: An Anthology,* by Yisrael Gutman (June 1994); and *Atlas of the Holocaust* (in CD-ROM format). The institute also publishes a journal, *Holocaust and Genocide Studies,* three times a year.

7. Index Terms: Ethnic and Religious Conflict; Human Rights—Theory and Research; International Law; Refugees; War Crimes

See also entries A45, B16, C11, and F29

## United States Information Agency (USIA)— Office of Research See entry K41

---

# H73 United States Institute of Peace (USIP)

---

1. 1550 M Street, Suite 700
   Washington, D.C. 20005-1708
   (202) 457-1700
   Fax: (202) 429-6063

2. Chester Crocker, Chair
   Richard Solomon, President

3. USIP is an independent and nonpartisan federal institution, created by an act of Congress in October 1984, that promotes international peace and the resolution of international conflict without violence. Its activities are aimed at education, training, research, and public information. USIP maintains grant and fellowship programs, undertakes special initiatives, engages in its own research, and supports a program of education. It also awards the Spark M. Matsunaga Medal of Peace to individuals who have made outstanding contributions to peace.

USIP annually makes a wide selection of grants to a variety of nonprofit institutions, including schools and universities, which examine underlying causes of conflict and ways to resolve them. The institute accepts unsolicited grant proposals, but also solicits proposals on special issues it considers high priority. The institute's categories for administering grants include international conflict resolution and conflict management training; arms control; East-West relations; international organizations and international law; rule of law, human rights, and democracy; regional and national conflicts and regional security; religion, ethics, and nonviolence; secondary education; higher education; public education; and library and information services. The institute also maintains the Jennings Randolph Fellowship Program, which supports outstanding individuals from a range of professional backgrounds. Resident fellows include men and women from different countries, cultures, and generations, working on projects concerned with the sources of conflict, lessons of successful and unsuccessful efforts to manage violent conflict around the world, and the dynamics of international negotiation. The program also supports Peace Scholars, who are doctoral students working on dissertations related to international conflict.

In order to augment its fellowship programs USIP also maintains in-house research and study programs that bring together experienced practitioners and academic scholars in conferences, study and working groups, and workshops. Examples of these include Conference on the Origins of the Cold War; Conference on Conflict Resolution; and a study group on The Future Prospects for Conflict or Peace in Central and Eastern Europe. Other in-house research focuses on Middle Eastern peacemaking and conflict resolution, and on religion, ethics, and human rights.

Examples of special initiatives sponsored by the institute include Peacemaking in the Middle East and Persian Gulf, which organized a symposium and study groups on regional arms control and peacemaking among Arabs and Israelis, and the ongoing Rule of Law project, which focuses heavily on emerging polities in the former Soviet republics and Eastern Europe as well as in Africa. The Rule of Law project produced a 300-page commentary on the draft of the Russian constitution, directories of American resources and initiatives for advancement of the rule of law, and various country reports.

4.    In addition to conferences and seminars that USIP hosts throughout the year, there is an annual conference, the topic of which varies from year to year.

5.    USIP's library is described in entries A46 and F30.

6.    USIP has issued publications from all of its programs. Examples of books include *Democracy's Dawn, A Directory of American Initiatives on Constitutionalism, Democracy, and the Rule of Law in Central and Eastern Europe*, by A. E. Dick Howard (1990); *Approaches to Peace, An Intellectual Map*, edited by W. Scott Thompson and Kenneth M. Jensen with Richard N. Smith and Kimber M. Schraub (1991); *Soviet-American Conflict Resolution in the Third World*, edited by Mark N. Katz (1991); *Negotiating Across Cultures*, by Raymond Cohen (1991); *Ukraine, The Legacy of Intolerance*, by David Little (1991); *Origins of the Cold War: The Novikov, Kennan, and Roberts 'Long Telegrams' of 1946* (1991). Special reports published by the institute include *Relief, Reconstruction, and Reconciliation—Views of Prominent Somalis* (November 1992); *The OAS and Democratic Development*, by Francisco Villagran de Leon (September 1992); *Two Views of Collective Security*, by Richard Gardner and Joseph Lorenz (July 1992); *Three Views on the Issue of Humanitarian Intervention*, by David Scheffer, Richard Gardner, and Ger-

ald Helman (July 1992); *Strengthening Peacekeeping: New Challenges and Proposals*, by Maj. Gen. (Ret.) Indar Jit Rikhye (June 1992); *Afghanistan and Post-Soviet Central Asia* (July 1992); *Interim Report of the Study Group on Regional Arms Control Arrangements and Issues in the Post-War Middle East* (April 1991); *Making Peace Among Arabs and Israelis: Lessons from the Fifty Years of Negotiating Experience* (October 1991). The institute also publishes *Peacewatch* (formerly the *United States Institute of Peace Journal*) bimonthly.

7.    Index Terms: Arms Control; Collective Security; Conflict Management and Resolution; Defense Policy, National; Deterrence; Development Issues; Diplomacy and Negotiation; Disarmament; Environmental Issues, Global; Ethnic and Religious Conflict; Foreign Policy; Human Rights—Theory and Research; International Economics; International Law; International Organizations; Peace Theory and Research; Peacekeeping; Political Systems and Ideologies; Regional Conflict

See also entries A46 and F30

---

# H74    Urban Institute

1.    2100 M Street, NW
Washington, D.C. 20037
(202) 833-7200
Fax: (202) 223-3043

2.    William Gorham, President
Raymond J. Struyk, Director, International Activities Center

3.    The Urban Institute is a nonprofit policy and research organization that investigates the social and economic problems confronting the nation, and the government policies and public and private programs designed to alleviate them. The International Activities Center extends the institute's expertise on domestic policy to help solve similar problems in developing countries. The center's mission is to assist the governments of developing countries in defining their needs, organizing resources to meet those needs, and implementing revised policies. To this end, staff researchers investigate the problems of such countries and then send field teams to work with local private and public organizations in coordinating change. Three primary issues for the center are housing and housing finance; urban development and management; and health and population. For example, in Kingston, Jamaica staff members

have been working with private and public organizations in the largest urban development project ever funded by the Agency for International Development (KI): "Redeveloping Old Kingston."

5.  The library provides information support to the research staff at the Urban Institute. The library's collections contain material deemed essential to the work of the institute and mirror the broad, multidisciplinary arenas of public policy. These collections include over 31,000 volumes, 770 periodical titles, over 5,500 reels of microfilm, and a growing collection of CD-ROMs. The library is particularly strong in materials from federal agencies, such as the Census Bureau and the Labor Statistics Bureau. However, the main thrust of the library's collections is domestic policy.

6.  Three times a year the Publications Office disseminates *Policy and Research Report,* which summarizes key research findings and explores their policy implications. The *Reporter's Sourcebook,* updated annually, provides the media with a guide to the institute's areas of expertise and the researchers who specialize in them. Other published research papers include *Guidelines for Creating a Housing Finance Strategy in a Developing Country* (1987); *Public-Private Partnership in Water Supply and Sanitation in African Urban Development* (1987); and *Housing Finance in LDCs: India's National Housing Bank as a Model?* (1992).

7.  Index Terms: Development Issues—Infrastructure; Transnationalism

## H75 Washington Peace Center (WPC)

1.  2111 Florida Avenue, NW
    Washington, D.C. 20008
    (202) 234-2000
    Fax: (202) 265-5233

3.  WPC serves as a resource center for local organizations and groups active in issues of peace and justice, both locally and internationally. Its primary focus is on racism, economic justice, and violence. WPC publishes the *Washington Peace Letter* and organizes demonstrations and direct actions. Past activities of the organization have included involvement in Haiti solidarity week, Gulf War antiwar demonstrations, and a 1992 yearlong recognition of the legacy of Columbus.

4.  WPC hosts several meetings and public information events per month.

5.  WPC maintains a small library containing books and a clippings file on relevant topics.

6.  WPC's chief activity is the publication of *Washington Peace Letter,* a monthly compilation of information regarding peace issues and activities in the Washington, D.C., area. It also publishes the *Media Guide for Activists* and *Washington Peace and Justice Directory,* both annually. A monthly guide to events is also available.

7.  Index Terms: Pacifism and Peace Movements

## H76 Woodrow Wilson International Center for Scholars (WWICS)

1.  1000 Jefferson Drive, SW
    Washington, D.C. 20560
    (202) 357-2429
    Fax: (202) 357-4439

2.  Charles Blitzer, Director
    Samuel F. Wells Jr., Deputy Director
    Robert Litwak, Director, Division of International Studies

3.  WWICS was created by Congress in 1968 as the nation's official living memorial to its 28th president. As a national institution with international interests, the center seeks to encourage the creative use of the unique human, archival, and institutional resources in the nation's capital for studies illuminating our understanding of the past and present.

Through its residential fellowship program of advanced research, the center seeks to commemorate the scholarly depth and the public concerns of Woodrow Wilson. The center welcomes outstanding project proposals representing diverse scholarly interests and approaches from individuals throughout the world. It has no permanent or tenured fellows. Its fellowships are normally awarded for periods of an academic year (nine months), although a few shorter time slots are also available.

Scholars working on projects concerned with peace and international security are normally associated with the Division of International Studies, one of the center's seven geographical or thematic programs. (The other six are Asian; East and West European; Historical, Cultural, and Literary Studies; Kennan Institute for Advanced Russian Studies; Latin American; and United States). The Division of International Studies superseded in 1989 the earlier International Security Studies Program, originally established in 1977.

In 1993–94 WWICS scholars pursued the following topics while affiliated with the Division of International Studies: Amatzia Baram (Iraq of the Ba'th 1968–93: domestic strife and regional conflict); Elizabeth Cobbs (the Peace Corps and the international response to decolonization); Anthony H. Cordesman (strategic analysis of the political, military, and arms control lessons of the Gulf War, and the crisis in Iraq); Robert Hansen (the effectiveness of European security institutions in managing ethnic conflicts); Roberta B. Miller (the road to apartheid: social science and the Afrikaner ascendancy, 1903–48); Sari A. Nusseibeh (rights, freedom, and self-determination: the Palestinian case); and Mitchell Reiss (negotiating nuclear status).

4. The center's activities include frequent colloquia, conferences, and workshops designed to foster intellectual exchange among the participants. Scheduled events are announced in the center's monthly calendar.

For the Division of International Studies a central focus of activity has been its project on nuclear nonproliferation challenges in the 1990s. A major international conference in December 1992 provided an opportunity not only to analyze the failings of the nonproliferation regime but also to suggest means to reform the regime and improve national policies before the Nonproliferation Treaty (NPT) Review Conference in 1995. An important complement to the conference was the creation of a Working Group on Nuclear Nonproliferation at the center to provide a forum in which new ideas and approaches can be discussed, as well as to expose Washington policy practitioners to non-American viewpoints.

Another central concern of the division, like the International Security Studies Program that preceded it, is the study of the formulation of U.S. foreign and defense policy. Several seminars sponsored by the division in 1993–94 focused on the special challenges posed by the end of the cold war for U.S. policymakers. Regional security issues affecting the Middle East and South Africa were addressed in a series of meetings involving current and former fellows. Walter Reich, a physician and a senior scholar affiliated with the division, coordinates a project on health, science, and public policy. In July 1993 he directed a major international conference, Trauma and Atrocity in the Former Yugoslavia: The Psychiatric Consequences of Ethnic Conflict. In addition, the division played a principal role coordinating centerwide activities on the theme of ethnicity. These included clusters of guest scholars in the summers of 1993 and 1994 and a series of workshops, involving several center programs, that are exploring the global phenomenon of ethnic conflict in comparative perspective.

A final core activity of the Division of International Studies has been the multiyear Cold War International History Project (CWIHP), established in 1991 and coordinated by James G. Hershberg (202/357-2967). Primarily through publications, meetings, and fellowships, the project seeks to improve scholarly and public understandings of the cold war's history on the basis of new evidence emerging from the archives of the erstwhile communist bloc. In January 1993 CWIHP sponsored in Moscow a major international conference on New Soviet Evidence on Cold War History. Future plans call for conferences on the 1968 Soviet invasion of Czechoslovakia and on Germany and the cold war, 1945–1962.

Starting in 1984 the center has offered a weekly half-hour FM radio program entitled "Dialogue," which is built around the center's fellows and guest scholars, as well as drawing upon meeting and conference participants. Directed by George Liston Seay "Dialogue" is heard across the United States on 160 radio stations through the NPR Satellite Service and the National Association for College Broadcasters Network (U-NET). For names of stations call (202) 287-3000 ext. 325. "Dialogue" is available also on Internet via the Internet Multicasting Service; for further information, send email to info@radio.com or phone (202) 628-2044. Copies of programs can be obtained on cassettes by calling 1-800-747-7444. For a list of all "Dialogue" programs call (202) 287-3000 ext. 325.

In 1993–94, programs of interest to scholars in peace and international security studies included "Leashing the Whirlwind: Nuclear Proliferation in the 1990s" with Mitchell Reiss (March 1993); "From Plowshares to Swords: Global Ethnic Conflict" with Donald L. Horowitz and others (April 1993); "New World Orders: 1919 and 1991" with Michael Burns (June 1993); "Security and the Single Superpower" with Jeanne J. Kirkpatrick and others (July 1993); "Peacekeeping in Cambodia" with Kate Frieson (December 1993); "The Mideast Peace: After the Handshake" with Amatzia Baram (December 1993); "The Third World and the New World Order" with James Clad (January 1994); and "Before the Fall: American Policymakers and the End of the Cold War" with Robert Hutchings (March 1994).

5. WWICS has a library containing approximately 16,000 volumes of basic reference works, particularly bibliographies, indexes, abstracts, dictionaries, encyclopedias, general histories and treatises, and basic document collections. Emphasis is

on the social sciences and humanities, and on the geographic and thematic areas covered by the center's programs. In addition, the library maintains a collection of some 10,000 volumes for the Kennan Institute, covering Russia and the other countries of Central Eurasia. The library subscribes to and maintains the back files of about 240 scholarly journals and periodicals. As a part of a National Presidential Memorial the library has special access to the collections of the Library of Congress and other federal government libraries. The reference librarian is Linda L. Warden (202/357-3157).

6. Although publication of the projects completed by the center fellows and guest scholars usually remain their responsibility, the center sponsors publications of papers prepared for the conferences held at the center. Most such volumes are published by the Woodrow Wilson Center Press in copublishing arrangements with the Johns Hopkins University Press or the Cambridge University Press. In recent years the Woodrow Wilson Center Press issued the following conference volumes relevant to peace and international security studies: *Origins of Terrorism: Psychologies, Ideologies, Theologies, States of Mind* (1990), edited by Walter Reich; *The Helsinki Process and the Future of Europe* (1990), edited by Samuel F. Wells Jr.; *The United States and the Pacific Basin: Changing Economic and Security Relationships* (1991), edited by Mary B. Bullock and Robert S. Litwak; *Reappraising the Munich Pact: Continental Perspectives* (1992), edited by Maya Latynski; *Dismantling Communism: Common Causes and Regional Variations* (1992), edited by Gilbert Rozman and others; and *Constitution Making in Eastern Europe* (1993), edited by A. E. Dick Howard. The press also published *Ethnopolitics and Transition to Democracy: The Collapse of the USSR and Latvia* (1994), by Rasma Karklins.

The center's programs publish several series of short papers, which are distributed free of charge to interested parties upon request. The former International Security Studies Program issued more than 80 working papers from 1978 to 1989. The Cold War International History Project began to publish working papers in 1991, including "Archival Research on the Cold War Era: A Report from Budapest, Prague and Warsaw," by P. J. Simmons (1992). CWIHP also has issued an occasional bulletin since 1992.

The *Wilson Quarterly* (cir. 75,000), published four times per year by the center, carries occasional articles on subjects within the scope of this Guide, especially ethnic and religious conflicts, such as

"The Rise of Europe's Little Nations" (winter 1994), and "The Idiocy of Race" (spring 1994).

The center sponsors the preparation and publication of the Scholars' Guides to Washington, D.C. Edited by Zdeněk V. David, and available from the Johns Hopkins University Press, 701 West 40th Street, Suite 704, Baltimore, Md. 21211, (800/537-JHUP), the Guides survey the collections, institutions, and organizations pertinent to the study of the following geographic areas: Africa; Central and Eastern Europe; East Asia; Latin America and the Caribbean; the Middle East; Northwest Europe; Russia, central Eurasia, and the Baltics; South Asia; Southeast Asia; and Southwest Europe. Separate Guides cover film and video collections, audio resources, cartographic resources, and media collections in the Washington, D.C., area. The *Annual Report* and a bulletin, the *Woodrow Wilson Center Report* (published five times per year), are sent to former fellows and other friends of the Wilson Center.

7. Index Terms: Arms Control; Deterrence; Ethnic and Religious Conflict; Proliferation; Regional Conflict; Terrorism

---

## H77 World Jurist Association (WJA) (American Bar Association)

1. 1000 Connecticut Avenue, NW, Suite 202
Washington, D.C. 20036
(202) 466-5428
Fax: (202) 452-8540

2. Raoul I. Goco, President
Margaret M. Henneberry, Executive Vice-President

3. The WJA, a special committee of the American Bar Association, serves as an independent organization that aims at strengthening the world's legal institutions, such as the International Court of Justice. Members are drawn from four constituent professional affiliates: the World Association of Law Professors, the World Association of Law Students, and the World Association of Judges. WJA has members in over 100 countries worldwide. The association sponsors special sections on human rights, intellectual property, international legal education and law, and computer technology. It also engages in research on investment disputes, human rights, refugee rights, and other international issues.

4. The WJA sponsors World Law Day and the biennial World Law Conferences held in varying locations around the world.

5. The WJA does not have a library.

6. Publications include *The World Jurist,* a bimonthly newsletter; *Law/Technology,* a quarterly; and *Law and Judicial Systems of Nations.* The *Publications Directory* lists other publications of the association.

7. Index Terms: Human Rights—and International Law; International Law; Refugees

## H78 World Priorities

1. 3013 Dumbarton Avenue, NW
Washington, D.C. 20007
(202) 965-1661

2. Ruth Leger Sivard, President

3. World Priorities is a research and public education organization that collects and analyzes information on social policy issues of global importance. Its main focus is the publication of the annual *World Military and Social Expenditures,* started in 1974. This publication offers a range of indices on current military and social problems worldwide.

6. In addition to *World Military and Social Expenditures,* World Priorities has published *World Energy Survey* (1979) and *Women . . . a World Survey* (1985).

7. Index Terms: Arms Control; Defense Policy, National; Development Issues; Military Spending

## H79 World Resource Institute (WRI)

1. 1709 New York Avenue, NW, Suite 700
Washington, D.C. 20006
(202) 638-6300
Fax: (202) 638-0036

2. Jonathan Lash, President

3. WRI engages in policy research and technical assistance in order to assist governments, the private sector, and development organizations address problems of economic growth while maintaining environmental integrity. WRI works to broaden public understanding through generating accurate infor-

mation on global resources and environmental conditions. In developing countries, WRI provides technical support to government and nongovernmental organizations. It has a network of advisers, collaborators, fellows, and cooperating institutions in more than 50 countries. WRI maintains programs in policy research in the following areas: biological resources and institutions; economics and population; climate, energy and pollution; technology and the environment; and resource and environmental information.

The institute's Center for International Development and Environment provides technical support and policy advice to developing countries through four main programs: natural resource management strategies; natural resource information management; community planning and nongovernmental organization support; and sectoral resource policy and planning. The WRI has also launched the 2050 Project with the Brookings Institution (H8) and the Santa Fe Institute to examine sustainable development.

4. WRI holds briefings, seminars, and conferences.

5. The library of the Center for International Development and the Environment includes a collection of specialized United Nations conference documents relating to environmental issues. The library is open to researchers by appointment.

6. The institute publishes a newsletter, *NGO Networker.* It also publishes other books, reports, and papers on a wide range of environmental issues.

7. Index Terms: Development Issues—Technical Assistance; Environmental Issues, Global; Transnationalism

## H80 Worldwatch Institute

1. 1776 Massachusetts Avenue, NW
Washington, D.C. 20036-1904
(202) 452-1999
Fax: (202) 296-7365

2. Orville L. Freeman, Chair
Lester R. Brown, President

3. Worldwatch Institute is a research and public education organization focusing on global environmental issues. The institute researches environmental problems in an integrative fashion and seeks to collect information and statistics on a broad range

of issues. It focuses heavily on development issues such as energy, biodiversity, food, agriculture, and population. Diverse topics with which it is concerned include global deforestation; women's reproductive health, as well as environmental health risks in general; sustainable development; nuclear waste; safeguarding oceans; environmental effects of the arms race; peacekeeping; the state of the U.S. nuclear arsenal; and transportation.

6. Worldwatch publishes *World Watch,* a bimonthly magazine. It also publishes the annuals, *State of the World* and *Vital Signs,* a compendium of economic and environmental trends. Worldwatch also has issued *Worldwatch Papers* on a wide range of topics. Approximately 100 of these papers are still in print; a publications list is available. In addition, the institute publishes an environmental alert series of books on specific environmental topics; 1994 issues include *Full House,* a world population study, and *Power Sense,* an analysis of present and future world energy.

7. Index Terms: Developmental Issues—Agriculture, Population; Energy; Environmental Issues, Global; Peacekeeping; Proliferation

# J

## Academic Programs and Departments

### Introductory Note

The Washington, D.C., area offers a wide range of scholastic opportunities for both undergraduate and graduate studies. Four universities maintain substantial programs or research centers in peace theory and research, and conflict management and resolution: American University (J1), George Mason University (J5), Nitze School of Advanced International Studies (J11), and University of Maryland at College Park (J13). All 12 of the surveyed institutions provide opportunities for the study of international security, but 5 stand out with substantial programs and research centers in that field: American University (J1), George Washington University (J6), Georgetown University (J7), Nitze School of Advanced International Studies (J11), and University of Maryland at College Park (J13). Law schools of the following universities offer courses in international law or joint degrees with departments of politics in international relations: American (J1), Catholic (J2), George Washington (J6), Georgetown (J7), and Howard (J8).

Several Washington-area universities have established research centers that complement their academic programs, for instance, the Institute for Conflict Analysis and Resolution (ICAR) at George Mason University (J5), and Johns Hopkins Foreign Policy Institute (FPI) at Nitze School of Advanced International Studies (J11). Such centers are described in this section under the relevant universities and are also listed under the relevant universities in Index IV.

For academic departments and programs dealing with specific geographic areas or individual countries, see the geographic volumes in this Scholars' Guides series, which are listed in the Bibliography.

## JI   American University (AU)

1.   School of International Service (SIS)
4400 Massachusetts Avenue, NW
Washington, DC 20016
(202) 885-1600
Fax: (202) 885-2494

Washington College of Law (WCL)
International Legal Studies Program
4400 Massachusetts Avenue, NW
Washington, D.C. 20016-8087
202-885-2612
Fax: (202) 885-8084

2.   Louis W. Goodman, Dean, SIS
Robert K. Goldman, Acting Director, Graduate
International Legal Studies WCL

3.   AU awards undergraduate and graduate degrees in international affairs through the School of International Service. The B.A. in international studies is based on an interdisciplinary curriculum involving coursework in international relations, comparative foreign policy analysis, regional international systems, international development, international communications, and international economics.

At the graduate level SIS grants M.A. degrees in international development, international communications, and international affairs; and an M.S. degree in development management. Students in these programs may concentrate in areas such as international law, international business, public administration, economic development, comparative and regional studies, or international politics.

In partnership with Ritsumeikan University's Graduate School of International Affairs in Kyoto, Japan, SIS offers a dual master's degree program in international affairs. This program allows students who are fluent in English and Japanese to complete their degree in two years, taking the first at SIS and the second at Ritsumeikan.

SIS also has a Ph.D. program in international affairs and a joint J.D./M.A. program with the Washington College of Law (WCL) in law and international affairs. The joint degree program offers students the political, historical, and economic background necessary to practice international law. For more information on graduate programs contact the School of International Service graduate office (202/885-1690).

WCL offers a one-year Master of Laws (LL.M.) degree for attorneys from both the United States and abroad. Participants in the LL.M. program special-

ize in one of the following areas: international trade and banking, international organizations, international environmental law, or international protection of human rights. To learn more about the program, write to Prof. Robert K. Goldman, Acting Director of Graduate International Legal Studies, Washington College of Law, American University.

4.   SIS offers a concentration in peace and conflict resolution studies at the undergraduate and graduate levels (Abdul Said, Director, 202/885-1632). The Peace and Conflict Resolution Program combines peace theory with nonviolent conflict resolution methodologies to create a curriculum geared to prepare students to participate creatively in building a peaceful society. Examples of courses include Peace Paradigms, Holocaust and Modern Man, World Human Needs and International Planning, and Global Politics as Cultural Activity.

SIS also offers, at the undergraduate level, a Washington semester in peace and conflict resolution.

WCL maintains a program of student externships in federal and nongovernmental organizations that deal with international law; it also operates an international human rights law clinic. Participants handle international and domestic human rights cases. At the Inter-American Commission on Human Rights students represent people asserting violations of basic human rights. On the domestic level, students represent refugees seeking political asylum in the United States.

5.   For graduate students, SIS offers conferences and weekly forums on various international issues related to international development, international communication, and foreign policy. More specifically, the Peace and Conflict Resolution Studies Program sponsors lectures and seminars on current global conflicts, as well as training sessions with groups such as Children's Creative Response to Conflict. The International Law Society at WCL sponsors speakers and symposia on current international law issues and coordinates student participation in the Jessup International Moot Court Competition.

6.   For a description of AU's Bender Library, see entry A4. The Alvina Reckman Myers Law Library (John Heywood, Reference Librarian, 202/885-2689), along with its 300,000-volume collection, houses a European Community depository and the Baxter Collection in International Law.

7.   The *American University Journal of International Law and Policy* focuses on private, public, and comparative international law in an attempt to keep scholars, students, and professionals abreast of current issues and trends in international law. For

subscription information contact the journal staff (202/885-2696).

8. Index Terms: Collective Security—Academic Course Offerings; Defense Policy, National—Academic Course Offerings; Conflict Management and Resolution—Academic Course Offerings; Conflict Management and Resolution—Theoretical Approaches; Conflict Management and Resolution—Unofficial and Nongovernmental Approaches; Development Issues—Academic Course Offerings; Foreign Policy—Academic Course Offerings; International Law—Academic Course Offerings; Peace Theory and Research—Academic Course Offerings

## J2   Catholic University of America (CUA)

1. Arts and Sciences
109 McMann Hall
Washington, D.C. 20064
(202) 319-5115
Fax: (202) 319-4463

2. Antanas Suziedelis, Dean

3. Catholic University offers an undergraduate minor in peace and world order studies that enables students to explore the moral, philosophical, and religious concepts of justice, peace, and world order. For information concerning the Peace and World Studies Program contact James R. Price in the Religion and Religious Education Department (202/319-5700).

On the graduate level CUA awards an M.A. in international political economics, which focuses on aspects of international finance and politics, and an M.A. in international affairs at the Pentagon, which focuses on international politics and security issues. For more information on either degree contact James O'Leary, chair of the Department of Politics (202/319-5128).

4. Catholic University's Columbus School of Law houses the Comparative and International Law Institute (Professor Rett R. Ludwikowski, director, 202/319-5140), which offers a J.D. in comparative and international law. Students pursuing this degree may concentrate in international trade, international organizations, or human rights. In addition to this program, the institute conducts research and sponsors colloquia on topics relating to international law.

CUA's School of Philosophy sponsors the Center for Research in Values and Philosophy. The center invites scholars from around the world to partici-

pate in seminars and colloquia on issues such as values, democracy, and culture. The result of these meetings is the publication of works such as *Culture, Human Rights and Peace in Central America* and *Democracy, Culture, and Values.* Interested scholars should contact George McClain, emeritus professor in the School of Philosophy (202/314-5259).

5. For colloquia and seminars see the Comparative and International Law Institute and the Center for Research in Values and Philosophy described in point 4.

6. For a description of Catholic University's Mullen Library, see entry A7. CUA's Robert J. White Law Library (202/319-5155; Stephen G. Margeton, Director) is located at 620 Michigan Avenue, NE, Room 102, Washington, D.C. 20064.

7. Brochures and catalogs listing course offerings can be obtained on request by writing to either the Undergraduate Office of Admissions or the Graduate Office of Admissions and Financial Aid, Catholic University of America, Washington, D.C. 20064. Concerning the publications of the Center for Research in Values and Philosophy see point 4.

8. Index Terms: Collective Security—Academic Course Offerings; Defense Policy, National—Academic Course Offerings; Foreign Policy—Academic Course Offerings; International Economics—Academic Course Offerings; International Law—Academic Course Offerings; International Organizations—Academic Course Offerings; Peace Theory and Research—Academic Course Offerings; Religious, Philosophical, and Ethical Concepts of War and Peace—Academic Course Offerings

## J3   Christian College Coalition—American Studies Program (ASP)

1. 327 Eighth Street, NE
Washington, D.C. 20002-6158
(202) 546-3086
Fax: (202) 546-8913

2. Jerry S. Herbert, Director

3. The Christian College Coalition, an association of Christian colleges and universities, brings students to study in Washington through its American Studies Program. ASP maintains a study unit on international policy issues affecting the United States. Among other issues, the studies program examines U.S. relations to Russia and Eastern Europe, and the

social, economic, political, and human rights problems of transition. Other issues concern foreign aid, the U.S. response to world hunger, refugee policies, the International Monetary Fund (IMF) Treaty, the Gulf War, and the role of the military in humanitarian efforts in Somalia and the former Yugoslavia. ASP runs four-month internships placing students in government offices and agencies.

7.   ASP publishes *Washington Notes,* a newsletter.

8.   Index terms: Foreign Policy—Academic Course Offerings; Human Rights—Academic Course Offerings; Humanitarian Issues—Academic Course Offerings

---

## J4   Consortium of Universities of the Washington Metropolitan Area

---

1.   1 Dupont Circle, NW, Suite 200
Washington, D.C. 20036
(202) 331-8080
Fax: (202) 332-7925

2.   Interested students are advised to contact the appropriate administrators in member universities for information on peace studies and international security resources and classes.

3.   Twelve academic institutions in the Washington area—American University, Catholic University, Gallaudet College, George Mason University, George Washington University, Georgetown University, Howard University, Marymount University, Mount Vernon College, Trinity College, University of Maryland, and University of the District of Columbia—are associated in a consortium through which they coordinate the use of their respective programs. Degree candidates in approved programs at these institutions may register for coursework at a consortium member institution and systematically transfer credits to the home institution. Faculty and students are assured access to library resources at all member institutions. The practical result of this cooperative effort is that the resources of all institutions are pooled to enhance the programs offered by each institution independently.

5.   Washington Research Library Consortium, 901 Commerce Drive, Upper Marlboro, Md. 20772 (301/390-2000) grew out of the work of the Library Council of the Consortium of Universities of the Washington Metropolitan Area. It began operating in 1990, and its mission is to enhance and expand the existing library and information resources and ser-

vices of its member universities through (1) establishing a common database of library information accessible to the participants; (2) planning and implementing a cooperative collection development program; (3) planning and implementing a delivery and telecommunications program; (4) planning and implementing a program of preservation and conservation of informational materials; (5) planning and implementing a depository program to store infrequently used research materials under appropriate environmental conditions; (6) constructing a facility to accommodate these programs. As of May 1994 the library consortium consists of only American University, Catholic University, Gallaudet University, George Mason University, George Washington University, Marymount University, and the University of the District of Columbia.

7.   Index Terms: Collective Security—Academic Course Offerings; Defense Policy, National—Academic Course Offerings; Peace Theory and Research—Academic Course Offerings

---

## J5   George Mason University (GMU)

---

1.   Department of Public and International Affairs
4400 University Drive
Fairfax, Va. 22030
(703) 993-1400
Fax: (703) 993-1399

2.   Louise White, Chair, Department of Public and International Affairs

3.   GMU offers an undergraduate program leading to a B.A. in international studies. The courses in this program focus on international relations, economics, history, and sociology.
   On the graduate level, GMU makes available an international management concentration in its Master of Public Administration program. Contact the department's coordinator for graduate affairs, Marianne Marsolais (703/993-1411) for information.
   The George Mason School of Law (3401 North Fairfax Drive, Arlington, Va. 22201-4498) offers a specialized program in international business law. The international business transactions track prepares students for practice in the changing global business community, as well as providing them with a well-rounded legal education. Courses in international law, international tax, European Union law, and international trade law and regulation form the core of the program. The program's coordinator,

Jagdeep S. Bhandari (703/993-8044), will answer prospective students' questions.

4. GMU also maintains the Institute for Conflict Analysis and Resolution (ICAR), which offers M.S. and Ph.D. degree programs in conflict analysis and resolution. The courses in these programs explore sociology, anthropology, and conflict resolution theory in order to give students a greater understanding of the causes of current conflicts and better equip them to develop workable solutions to these conflicts. For information on either the M.S. or Ph.D. program contact Chris Mitchell, ICAR director (703/993-1300).

ICAR also publishes a newsletter to keep students and professionals of dispute resolution abreast of current trends and issues.

5. In its outreach program, GMU's Institute for Conflict Analysis and Resolution seeks to promote knowledge of conflict resolution through lectures, conferences, workshops, and special briefings.

6. GMU library is described in entry A18. In addition, located within GMU's Center for European Union Studies (703/993-8200) is the European Documentation Center. This collection of European Union Documents provides scholars access to primary sources on the union. GMU's law library houses a collection of more than 260,000 volumes focusing on business, economic theory, history, tax, patent law, and international law. The law library has an on-line catalog (XLibris) and an automated circulation system, as well as access to ALADIN, LEXIS, and WESTLAW. Interlibrary loan is available.

8. Index Terms: Conflict Management and Resolution—Academic Course Offerings; Conflict Management and Resolution—Theoretical Approaches; Conflict Management and Resolution—Unofficial and Nongovernmental Approaches; Foreign Policy—Academic Course Offerings; Peace Theory and Research—Academic Course Offerings

*Note:* Two national associations currently housed in the GMU are the Consortium on Peace Research, Education, and Development (COPRED) (entry M24) and the National Conference on Peacemaking and Conflict Resolution (NCPCR) (entry M39).

## J6  George Washington University (GWU)

1. Elliot School of International Affairs
Stuart Hall, Room 101
2013 G Street, NW

Washington, D.C. 20052
(202) 994-6240
Fax: (202) 994-0335

2. James Miller, Acting Dean

3. The Elliot School offers B.A. and M.A. programs in international affairs. The programs are multidisciplinary and emphasize both domestic and foreign governmental policy. Course offerings draw heavily on the various academic departments of the university. At the undergraduate level the program tends to be broader based, but students can concentrate on regional area issues. The graduate program attempts to increase the student's level of competence in a world region or discipline. Concentrations at the graduate level are offered in Latin American studies, European studies, Russian and East European studies, East Asian studies, security policy studies, international development studies, and science, technology and public policy studies. The Elliott School cooperates with the National Law Center (202/994-7230) in offering a program of study leading to a joint M.A.-J.D. degree. It also cooperates with the School of Business and Public Management (202/994-7538) in offering a program of study leading to a joint M.A. and M.B.A.

George Washington's National Law Center (202/994-7230) offers a Master of Laws (LL.M.) and a J.D. degree. Students in the LL.M. program may specialize in International and Comparative Law. Coursework for this degree includes classes such as international commercial law, law of human rights, international organizations, and international law of air and space. On the J.D. level, the Law Center also offers a substantial number of courses in international and comparative law. Unlike the LL.M. program, there is no specific J.D. program in international law. For information concerning the International and Comparative Law Program or international law courses in general contact the director, Thomas Buergenthal (202/994-7002).

4. The Elliott School maintains several research centers. The Institute for European, Russian, and Eurasian Studies (202/994-6340) provides a program of specialized graduate study and research focusing on economic, geographic, historical, and literary issues. This institute's director is James Millar (202/994-6342). Institute faculty also administer and teach three geographically based graduate programs: European Studies, Russian and East European Studies, and East Asian Studies. The Center for International Science and Technology Policy (202/994-7292) has become a locus for research and

the exchange of information and ideas. The center also offers courses for M.A. and Ph.D. students of science and public policy. The Space Policy Institute (202/994-7292) research includes the issues of interactions of civilian space activities with international security space programs. Contact the director, Jon Logsdon, for information.

5.    The Institute for European, Russian, and Eurasian Studies sponsors scholarly conferences, seminars, colloquia, and public lectures. The Center for International Science and Technology Policy organizes several seminar series and dinner discussion series dealing with science in the international realm. The Space Policy Institute also hosts seminars, meetings, and lectures on space policy, such as its dinner discussion series on international space issues held in conjunction with the Association of Space Explorers.

6.    George Washington University Gelman Library is described in entries A19 and D2; the Information Center for the Former Soviet Union, Eastern Europe, and East Asia in entry A19. National Law Center's Burns Law Library (202/994-6648; Scott Pagel, librarian) is located at 716 20th Street, NW, Washington, D.C. 20052.

7.    Annual reports for both the Center for International Science and Technology Policy and the Space Policy Institute, detailing their current and pending research, may be obtained from the joint office of the two research centers (202/992-7292). Scholars at the center and institute regularly publish articles and books relating to their research.

8.    Index Terms: Collective Security—Academic Course Offerings; Defense Policy, National—Academic Course Offerings; Foreign Policy—Academic Course Offerings; International Economics—Academic Course Offerings; International Law—Academic Course Offerings

---

## J7  Georgetown University

1.    Edmund A. Walsh School of Foreign Service
Intercultural Center
37 and O Streets, NW
Washington, D.C. 20057
(202) 687-5696
Fax: (202) 687-1431

2.    Peter Krough, Dean, School of Foreign Service

3.    Georgetown University offers B.S. and M.S. degree programs in foreign service. At the undergraduate level the School of Foreign Service offers a structured program of study in the social sciences, languages, and humanities. Students may pursue a B.S. that concentrates on history and diplomacy, international politics, international economics, regional and comparative studies, or humanities and international affairs. In spring 1993 Georgetown instituted an undergraduate certificate in justice and peace studies (JPS). To get a JPS certificate, students must complete an introductory course in peace and justice; four electives, one of which must include a community service component; and a research project. Elective offerings includes classes such as revolution and society, European diplomacy since 1914, ethical issues of international relations, theology and social justice, and power and justice in the international system.

The M.S.F.S. (M.S. in foreign service) program offers professional education entailing training in the social sciences, languages, and humanities. Within the M.S.F.S. program qualified students may concentrate on international business diplomacy through the Karl F. Landegger program. Besides an M.S. in foreign service, students may also obtain a joint M.S./M.A. degree in foreign service and economics or history.

The Walsh School of Foreign Service offers a Fellows in Foreign Service program for international professionals from the public and private sectors. This program entails one year of advanced study in international affairs and foreign policy decision making. For information contact the Dean's Office of the Master of Science in Foreign Service program (202/687-5763).

The Georgetown University Law Center (600 New Jersey Avenue, NW, Washington D.C. 20001; 202/662-9010) has extensive programs for scholars of international law. Its joint degree (M.S. or Ph.D.) in Foreign Service and Law (Richard Diamond, Codirector) combines legal theory with problem-solving techniques to create a broader and deeper understanding of the world's legal, political, economic, and sociocultural processes. Joint degree coursework includes courses in international trade, development and business diplomacy, international law, and security studies. To offer financial assistance to students pursuing a joint J.D./M.S.F.S. degree, the Law Center offers a J.D./M.S.F.S. Ford Foundation Fellowship Program in Public International Law. This fellowship provides stipends for students to conduct research under a full-time faculty member. Similarly, a Ford Foundation Summer Internship Program provides stipends to students who have internships with institutions dealing with public international law issues.

The Law Center also has an International Summer Program in Florence, Italy, in conjunction with the European University Institute. Professors from the Law Center and other major universities seek to prepare students for an increasingly integrated world. For information about any of the Law Center's international programs, contact Mary Bilodeau Jackson at (202) 662-9319.

4. Beyond its teaching programs the School of Foreign Service sponsors two research centers focusing on international issues. These institutes—Institute for the Study of Diplomacy (202/687-6279) and Karl Landegger Program in International Business Diplomacy (202/687-5854)—host seminars and lectures, conduct policy research, and issue publications concerning their specific areas of expertise.

Opportunities to explore international relations exist outside the School of Foreign Service in the university's School of Business through the Center for International Business Education and Research (CIBER) (202/687-6993). The center arranges seminars, lecture series, and workshops throughout the year focusing on issues such as global markets, international competition, and world resource management.

Georgetown University also sponsors the Center for Peace Studies (202/337-1040) and the Center for Intercultural Education and Development (202/298-0200). The Center for Peace Studies, directed by Richard McSorley, coordinates peace studies on the university campus, maintains contact with peace groups worldwide, and engages in occasional publications. The Center for Intercultural Education and Development (CIED), directed by Julio Giulietti, coordinates and focuses the university's intellectual and human resources on international migration issues and sponsors local and international programs geared to assisting migrating peoples and inner city youth. The CIED is oriented toward immigration issues involving mainly the Caribbean and Central America, but East Central Europe has also become an area of concern since 1990. The CIED is located at the Car Barn, 3d Floor, 3520 Prospect Street, NW, Washington, D.C.

5. The School of Foreign Service offers a seminar and lecture series in international affairs. The Master's of Foreign Service Director's Seminar focuses on the policy-planning environment in foreign affairs. The International Business and Diplomacy Conference and Seminar Series bring members of the corporate, government, and communications worlds to speak. The Samuel D. Berger Memorial Lecture reflects on current problems in diplomacy; the Oscar Iden Lecture focuses on more general trends in diplomacy. Other lecture series include the Landegger Distinguished Lecture Series, which deals with international business-government relations, and the Institute for the Study of Diplomacy's lecture series, which features senior diplomats discussing current problems in diplomacy and strategic policy.

The CIED focuses intellectual resources on international migration issues through policy dialogues, lectures, and conferences on relevant migration and refugee issues. Concerning the meetings arranged by CIBER, see point 4.

6. Georgetown University's Lauinger Library is described in A20. The School of Foreign Service maintains a separate George C. McGhee Library (202/687-5676) consisting of some 500 volumes mainly on Turkish affairs.

7. World Beat, the media production arm of the School of Foreign Service, produces foreign affairs programming for the education community and for public and cable television. These programs focus on international strategic, economic, and political issues. World Beat has produced several prime-time PBS documentaries, as well as coproducing the Great Decisions series with the Foreign Policy Association, which is carried by over 125 public television stations. Peter F. Krogh, Dean of the School of Foreign Service, anchors this series.

The Center for International Business Education and Research publishes a newsletter, *CIBER News*.

8. Index Terms: Development Issues—Academic Course Offerings; Foreign Policy—Academic Course Offerings; Humanitarian Issues—Academic Course Offerings; International Economics—Academic Course Offerings; International Law—Academic Course Offerings; Peace Theory and Research—Academic Course Offerings

## J8 Howard University

1. School of Business and Public Administration
   2600 6th St, NW
   Washington, D.C. 20059
   (202) 806-1500
   Fax: (202) 797-6393

2. Lawrence A. Johnson, Dean

3. Although Howard University has no formal undergraduate degree program in international studies, an undergraduate concentration in interna-

tional business is offered by the School of Business and Public Administration.

Howard University's Law School (Henry Ramsey, Dean; 2900 Van Ness Street, NW, Washington, D.C. 20008; 202/806-8008) offers a Master of Comparative Jurisprudence (M.C.J.) to lawyers from countries outside the United States. The aim of the M.C.J. program is to allow lawyers to compare and contrast the U.S. legal system to those of their home countries. The M.C.J. program hopes to encourage discussion within the international legal community about the best techniques for achieving justice. For J.D. students, Howard offers a number of courses focusing on various aspects of international law. Typical courses include international human rights, contemporary developments in human rights, international business law, international economic law, and comparative law.

5. The M.C.J. program sponsors lectures on international issues throughout the year. Recent lectures include talks by the legal adviser to the State Department, by members of Congress on NAFTA, and by justices of the International Court of Justice.

Howard University's International Law Society enables students to sponsor discussions and in-house lectures on international legal issues.

6. Howard University's Founders Library is described in entry A22. The university's Law Library (202/806-8045; Warren Rosmarin, Director) is located at 2900 Van Ness Street, NW, Washington, D.C. 20008.

7. Index Terms: International Economics—Academic Course Offerings; International Law—Academic Course Offerings

**Inter-American Defense College** See entry L6

**International Monetary Fund (IMF)** See entry L11

---

## J9  Marymount University

1. 2807 North Glebe Road
   Arlington, Va. 22207-4299
   (703) 522-5600
   Fax: (703) 284-1685

2. Robert Sigethy, Dean, School of Business Administration

3. Marymount University's School of Business Administration offers a B.A. in international business. Coursework for this major includes international business, international economics, international finance, and international relations. The school also offers graduate courses in international business in its M.B.A. programs. Course offerings include global markets, international finance, global business management, and global operations strategy. The School of Arts and Sciences also offers courses in international relations, although it does not offer an official international studies degree program.

5. The university's Emerson G. Reinsch Library (Lynn Scott Cochrane, Director; 703/284-1533), holding a collection of more than 120,000 volumes and 1,100 journal titles, is open to the public. The library also has CD-ROM databases and participates in interlibrary loan.

7. Index Terms: Foreign Policy—Academic Course Offerings; International Economics—Academic Course Offerings

---

## J10  Mount Vernon College

1. Department of Political Science
   2100 Foxhall Road, NW
   Washington, D.C. 20007
   (202) 625-4575
   Fax: (202) 337-0259

2. Hanita Blumfield, Chair

3. Mount Vernon College offers an undergraduate program leading to a B.A. in international studies. The coursework in the international studies program includes cultural anthropology, developmental economics, history, ethnic pluralism, comparative politics, international relations, and foreign policy.

6. The college's Eckles Library (Lucy S. Cocke, Director; 202/625-4588), holding some 60,000 titles, is not open to the public, but it does engage in interlibrary loans.

8. Index Terms: Foreign Policy—Academic Course Offerings; International Economics—Academic Course Offerings

**Defense Department—National Defense University (NDU)** See entry K10

## JII Nitze School of Advanced International Studies (SAIS) (Johns Hopkins University)

1.  1740 Massachusetts Avenue, NW
    Washington, D.C. 20036
    (202) 663-5600
    Fax: (202) 663-5656

2.  Paul D. Wolfowitz, Dean

3.  The Nitze School of Advanced International Studies, a graduate division of Johns Hopkins University, offers M.A. and Ph.D. programs in international studies. Courses are grouped within three functional fields, international economics, international relations, and social change and development; and eight regional studies, Africa, American foreign policy, Asia, Canada, Europe, Latin America and the Caribbean, Middle East studies, and Russian area and East European studies. Of special interest to the users of this Guide are the strategic studies, and international law and institutions and conflict management programs, both included in the functional field of international relations. Agreements with the Wharton School and with Institut Européen d'Administration des Affaires (INSEAD), Fontainebleau, France, allow students to obtain a joint M.A./ M.B.A. in international relations and business management. Other joint degrees include dual master's degrees in health sciences and international relations (in cooperation with the School of Hygiene and Public Health of Johns Hopkins University) or a joint degree in law and international relations (in cooperation with Stanford University Law School).

SAIS also provides several special education opportunities. For midcareer professionals, SAIS offers a one-year program leading to the Master's of International Public Policy. To encourage and facilitate international study and internships for regular graduate students, SAIS operates centers for study in Bologna, Italy, and Nanjing, the People's Republic of China.

4.  The Johns Hopkins Foreign Policy Institute (FPI) (Andrew J. Bacevich, Executive Director; 202/663–5886), established in 1980, is the main branch of SAIS conducting research on contemporary foreign policy dilemmas. In conjunction with its research, FPI invites scholars, journalists, diplomats, and foreign policymakers to roundtables, seminars, and lectures on issues such as security policy and international energy policy.

Under the umbrella of the FPI exist the International Energy and Environment Program, and the Media and Foreign Policy Program. The International Energy and Environment Program sponsors teaching and research on energy policy analysis, international energy security, and the interface between energy use and the environment. The Media and Foreign Policy program holds a series of seminars on various aspects of international reporting, and sponsors conferences on the role of the media in foreign policy.

5.  In addition to the meetings arranged by the Foreign Policy Institute and its components, SAIS also sponsors a variety of other conferences and lectures, including an annual Christian A. Herter Lecture Series on a selected topic in world affairs and several annual forums in which corporate executives, government officials, and scholars discuss the overseas operations of U.S. business.

6.  For a description of the SAIS library, see entry A37.

7.  The FPI publishes the student-edited and student-managed *SAIS Review,* as well as the *SAIS Energy Reports, FPI Policy Briefs,* and *FPI Case Studies.* The International Energy and Environment Program publishes periodic Energy Papers and books reporting on research.

8.  Index Terms: Collective Security—Academic Course Offerings; Conflict Management and Resolution—Academic Course Offerings; Defense Policy, National—Academic Course Offerings; Foreign Policy—Academic Course Offerings; Intelligence—Academic Course Offerings; International Economics—Academic Course Offerings; International Law—Academic Course Offerings; International Organizations—Academic Course Offerings; Military History—Academic Course Offerings; Military Science—Academic Course Offerings

**State Department—Foreign Service Institute    See entry K37**

## JI2 Trinity College

1.  History Department
    125 Michigan Avenue, NE
    Washington, D.C. 20017
    (202) 939-5221
    Fax: (202) 939-5134

2.  Susan Farnsworth, Director, International Studies

3. Trinity College offers an undergraduate program leading to a B.A. in international studies. The program is interdisciplinary, with courses in economics, comparative politics, international relations, history, language, anthropology, geography, and statistics. Within the program, students may concentrate in international relations, international business, or area studies.

6. Trinity College Library (Karen S. Leider, Librarian; 202/939-5176), holding about 170,000 volumes, is not open to the public, but it participates in interlibrary loan.

8. Index Terms: Foreign Policy—Academic Course Offerings; International Economics—Academic Course Offerings

---

## JI3 University of Maryland at College Park

1. Department of Government and Politics
LeFrak Hall
College Park, Md. 20742
(301) 405-4160
Fax: (301) 314-9690

2. Jonathan Wilkenfeld, Chair

3. Although the University of Maryland does not offer a formal program in international studies, it does offer a variety of opportunities to specialize in international issues. The Office of International Affairs (Marcus Franda, Director; 301/504-4772) distributes a directory of international programs on campus. Undergraduate students pursuing a B.A. in government and politics may concentrate on international affairs. The coursework for this concentration includes international relations, comparative politics, economics, and resource management.

On the graduate level, students pursuing an M.A. or Ph.D. degree in the Department of Government and Politics specialize in international relations, international law, international security, and international political economy. M.A. students may narrow their specializations to focus specifically on national security issues, international political economy, or may create their own international concentration. The Department of Government and Politics houses the Russian Littoral Project, which contains material on Russia, Eastern Europe, and the newly independent states of Eurasia. The Department also houses the Harrison Program on the Future Global Agenda (Dennis C. Pirages, Director). The Harrison

Program focuses on environmental, demographic, and technological change and its policy impact.

The School of Public Affairs (SPA), a professional graduate school teaching public policy and management, has a strong international orientation. SPA offers a two-year Master of Public Management degree and a selective doctoral program. The school offers a core specialization in international security and economic policy. This specialization examines the changing role of military force, the growing role of international institutions, and evolving U.S. security relationships with Europe and Japan. Economic Policy concentration focuses on global trade competition and the policy choices that affect U.S. trade, investment, and competitiveness. The environmental policy specialization, in addition to domestic environmental issues, focuses on problems of global warming and other international issues.

The Department of Agriculture and Resource Economics (301/405-1291) offers a B.A. in international agriculture, with courses in food and agriculture policy, international economics, global environmental issues, and world hunger. Similarly, the department has M.S. and Ph.D. programs with concentrations in resource management and international development. Embodied in these degree programs is the opportunity to do policy-oriented research on the economic aspects of agriculture.

The Department of Business and Public Policy (301/405-6330) offers a concentration in international issues.

4. The University of Maryland houses several research centers focusing on international affairs. Undergraduate students may participate in the computerized International Communication and Negotiation Simulations (ICONS) Project (Jonathan Wilkenfeld, Director; 301/405-4172), in which they assume the roles of foreign policymakers and negotiate through teleconference on behalf of the nations they represent. For graduate students, ICONS provides the opportunity to create scenarios, use simulation as a teaching tool, and monitor the computer-assisted negotiations.

The Center for International Development and Conflict Management (CIDCM), established in 1981 (Edy Kaufman, Director; 301/314-7703), conducts research on the management and resolution of protracted conflicts in the world. CIDCM concentrates on three dimensions of conflict: between the individual and the state; between and among groups and the state; and between and among nations and states. This focus is combined with a focus on international development through CIDCM's three endowed chairs: The Baha'i Chair for World Peace; the

Anwar Sadat Chair for Population, Development, and Peace; and the Kahlil Gibran Chair on Values and Peace. The research and programs these chairs coordinate are interdisciplinary, with a primary focus on the influence of values (cultural and religious), population, and economics in causing conflict.

The Center for International and Security Studies at Maryland (CISSM), established in 1987 (I. M. Destler, Director; 301/405-7601), provides conferences, guest lectures, and special seminars on a broad range of international issues. CISSM follows a broad research agenda, with priority on three general areas: building cooperative security, managing complex interdependence, and reforming the foreign policy-making process. Ongoing research projects (Ivo Daalder, Research Director; 301/405-7577) currently include Project on Rethinking Arms Control; Project on U.S.-Japan Relations, Project on a New U.S.-European Dialogue; Program on International Policy Attitudes; Managing Nuclear Proliferation in South Asia; U.S. Nuclear Weapons Policy in a New World; Nuclear History Project (a multinational program involving U.S., British, German, and French scholars); and Project on Arms Control in Europe. For policy professionals, CISSM sponsors the Maryland Seminar on the Foreign Policy Process. The seminar is a five-month program providing intensive academic training and practical exposure to the impact of U.S. policy making on international and economic questions. Participants are drawn from around the world. CISSM also has an active Fellows Program that invites U.S. scholars and policymakers, as well as researchers from many countries, including Ukraine, China, Finland, Switzerland, Argentina, and Germany. CISSM also houses Women in International Security (WIIS) (see entry M57).

The university's collaborative research center on international issues is the Center for the Study of Post-Communist Societies (CSPCS) (Bartolomiej Kaminski, Director; 301/405-4126). Established in May 1990, CSPCS operates in conjunction with the Budapest Economic University, Hungary, and the University of Cluj, Romania. This triumvirate studies the business and public policy activities that link the U.S. and East European leaderships in joint efforts to solve some of the problems in the transition to democracy.

The Center for International Business Education and Research (CIBER), Lee Preston, Director (301/405-2136), works to bolster teaching, research, and outreach activities related to international business on campus. Areas of interest include international institutions and relationships, languages, foreign environments and cultures as well as business operations and strategies.

5. The Baha'i Chair, the Anwar Sadat Chair, and the Kahlil Gibran Chair of the Center for International Development and Conflict Management sponsor conferences, seminars, and public lectures on various aspects of peace studies. CISSM also arranges conferences, guest lectures, and special seminars.

6. The University of Maryland's McKeldin Library is described in entries A47, D12, E16, and F31. CISSM has an archive of selected historical materials in international security affairs. The Center for International Development and Conflict Management maintains the Conflict and Peace Data Bank (COPDAB) and is developing the Global Event Data System (GLOBAL or GEDS) to update COPDAB and provide analytic data for research on conflict management. The Russian Littoral Project houses an archive of materials (primarily clippings) on Russia, Eastern Europe, and the states of the former Soviet Union.

8. Index Terms: Arms Control—Academic Course Offerings; Defense Policy, National—Academic Course Offerings; Development Issues—Academic Course Offerings; Environmental Issues, Global—Academic Course Offerings; Ethnic and Religious Conflict—Academic Course Offerings; Foreign Policy—Academic Course Offerings; Humanitarian Issues—Academic Course Offerings; International Economics—Academic Course Offerings; Peace Theory and Research—Academic Course Offerings; Proliferation—Academic Course Offerings

*Note:* The Committee on the Political Economy of the Good Society (PEGS) (entry M23) is a national association currently housed on University of Maryland's College Park Campus.

---

## J14 University of the District of Columbia (UDC)

---

1. Department of Political Science
   4200 Connecticut Avenue, NW
   Building 48, Room 6400
   Washington, D.C. 20008
   (202) 274-7074

2. Krishan D. Mathur, Chair

3. No formal international studies program has been established at UDC, but a variety of courses are offered in international politics, economics, and history by the Department of Political Science.

The District of Columbia School of Law (DCSL) (719 13th Street, NW, Washington, D.C. 20005; 202/727-5232) received provisional accreditation from the American Bar Association on February 12, 1991. As of yet, there is no formal international law program at DCSL. But second- and third-year students may take international law as an elective. For more information contact Prof. James C. Gray Jr. (202/727-5234).

6. UDC's library (Albertine C. Johnson, reference librarian, 202/282-3067), holding 507,000 volumes, 2,500 current subscriptions, and 18,500 media materials, is open to the public and participates in interlibrary loan.

8. Index Terms: Foreign Policy—Academic Course Offerings; International Economics—Academic Course Offerings; International Law—Academic Course Offerings

# K

# United States Government Agencies

## United States Government Agencies Entry Format (K)

1. *General Information*
   a. address; telephone number(s)
   b. conditions of access
   c. name/title of director and heads of relevant divisions

2. *Agency Function, Programs, and Research Activities* (including in-house research, contract research, research grants, employment of outside consultants, and international-exchange programs)

3. *Agency Libraries and Reference Facilities*

4. *Internal Agency Records* (unpublished materials and aids, indexes, vertical files, etc.)

5. *Publications*
   a. published research products
   b. research bibliographies

*Note:* In the case of large, structurally complex agencies, each relevant division or bureau is described separately, following the description of the organization as a whole, and cross-referenced in the text and in indexes.

## Introductory Note

The student of contemporary international affairs will find enormous resources of information in the agencies and departments of the U.S. government in the Washington, D.C., area. Many government personnel are willing, within the constraints imposed by work schedules and security restrictions, to discuss research projects with visiting scholars, provide them with information and materials, and direct them to appropriate organizations or persons having expertise on the subject being researched. In addition many government agencies and departments, subject to certain restrictions, allow private scholars to examine their libraries, reference collections, data banks, and other facilities, which contain records and documents not generally available elsewhere.

In obtaining access to those internal records and documents that are not publicly available, either from the agencies or departments generating the materials or from the National Archives and Records Administration (B11), researchers may find it advantageous to familiarize themselves with Freedom of Information Act procedures. The Freedom of Information Act (Public Law 89-487 of 1966, as amended by Public Laws 93-502 of 1974 and 94-409 of 1976) provides that any citizen has the right of access to, and can obtain copies of, any document, file, or other record in the possession of any federal agency or department, with specified exceptions (including certain personnel records and classified documents whose classification can be justified as essential to national security).

Most government agencies have a Freedom of Information office or officer available to process requests for internal agency documents. When contacting these offices, whether in writing or by telephone, researchers should cite the Freedom of Information Act and should make their request as detailed and specific as possible. Researchers are not required to explain or justify their request. Denials of request may be appealed to the director of the agency. Such appeals are often successful and rejected appeals may by challenged through court litigation. By law, agencies have 10 working days in which to respond to an initial Freedom of Information Act request and 20 days in which to respond to an appeal. Researchers should note that agencies are permitted to charge rather substantial fees for document searches and photocopying of released documents. Information on such fees should be requested when filing the initial request. In most cases researchers are permitted to examine released records in person at the agency.

Several organizations in Washington can assist researchers in using (and litigating) the Freedom of Information Act procedures. They include the Freedom of Information Clearinghouse, P.O. Box 19367 (2000 P Street, NW, Suite 700), Washington, D.C. 20036 (202/833-3000), which is a project of Ralph Nader's Center for the Study of Responsive Law, and the Project on National Security and Civil Liberties, 122 Maryland Avenue, NE, Washington, D.C. 20002 (202/544-5380), an organization sponsored by the American Civil Liberties Union and the Center for National Security Studies (H15). These organizations distribute free guides to Freedom of Information Act procedures. Another useful source of information is *Access Reports Reference File,* a biweekly newsletter published by Harry Hammond Publishing, 1624 Dogwood Lane, Lynchburg, Va. 24503 (804/384-5334), that reports on the latest developments in the Freedom of Information field.

Researchers should be aware that bureaucratically inspired reorganizations of government offices are frequent; indeed, various agencies within the national intelligence community regularly reorganize their internal structures in order to disguise their functional activities and confuse foreign observers. Elections also often lead to major administrative disruptions within the federal bureaucracy. As a result many of the names and telephone numbers listed in the entries below are subject to probable change and must be considered temporary. Researchers would be well advised to obtain the latest telephone numbers for various offices by consulting the most current edition of each government department's telephone directory. Some are updated quarterly. Most are available for purchase from the Government Printing Office (see Appendix III). Other useful tools are Carroll Publishing Company's *Federal Executive Directory,* updated bimonthly, and Monitor Publishing Company's *Federal Yellow Book,* updated quarterly (see Appendix I). Subscription fees cited for periodical publications listed in this section are subject to change. The frequency of publication for some titles may change; others may cease completely due to federal budget cuts.

## KI   Agency for International Development (AID) (International Development Cooperation Agency)—Regional Bureaus

1.a.  State Department Building
320 21st Street, NW
Washington, D.C. 20523
(202) 647-1850 (Public Inquiries)
Fax: (202) 647-8321; (703) 875-1498

b. Not open to the public. Visitors are admitted by appointment.

2.   In cooperation with the State Department, AID directs the foreign economic and humanitarian assistance programs of the United States. Development assistance—largely in the form of grants and technical training services—focuses on population and health, broad-based economic growth, environment, and democracy. Aside from development aid, AID also administers economic support funds that are intended to stem economic and political disruption, and to help friendly governments in dealing with threats to their security.

The vast bulk of AID's research is produced under contract and research grant by universities and research centers. The Bureau for Global Programs, Field Support and Research; the Bureau for Policy and Program Coordination; and the regional bureaus each contract for research and periodically engage academic specialists as consultants in the fields listed above.

3.   For AID library resources and databases see entries A1, G2, and G3; for AID Photo Collection/Audiovisual Services see entry F1.

4. The internal records and unpublished reports in the files of AID bureaus and offices are periodically turned over to the agency's Information Support Services Division for transfer to storage facilities in the Washington National Records Center (Suitland, Md.) where they will eventually be made available to researchers by the National Archives and Records Service. The AID Records Management staff (202/736-4748) and the originating agency offices maintain shelflist-indexes of retired documents. Researchers may be able to gain access to these shelflists by contacting the AID Freedom of Information Office in the Bureau for Legislative and Public Affairs.

AID's Freedom of Information Office (202/ 647-1850) is most cooperative in helping outside researchers gain access to classified AID documents. The staff works aggressively for public disclosure of records in declassification-review decisions within the agency. An estimated 95 percent of materials requested under FOIA are released to the researcher. Released materials may be inspected by the researcher in the staff's office.

A large number of agency research studies (published and unpublished, classified and unclassified), program reports, and project files are available in the AID Development Information Center (entry AI).

5.a.–b. Summaries of agency-sponsored research studies are published in the quarterly *A.I.D. Research and Development Abstracts,* which contains information on how to purchase a full paper or microfiche copy of any study listed therein. A multivolume series, Research Literature for Development, provides similar abstracts, by subject, of cumulative AID-sponsored research produced since 1962. AID-funded research projects are listed in a semiannual index, Current Technical Service Contracts and Grants. Copies of these publications can be obtained from the AID Development Information Center's (AI) reference desk (703/875-4818).

Copies of the agency's annual budget presentation and program review to Congress, Fiscal Year Submission to the Congress (including a volume on Latin American programs), can be obtained from the Office of Public Inquiries (202/647-1850), which also distributes *Development Digest,* an annual of excerpts, summaries, and reprints of current materials on social and economic development. *Front Lines,* an internal agency newsletter, is available monthly from the Multimedia Communications Office (202/647-4330).

Other publications are described below, under their originating office.

## REGIONAL BUREAUS

AID regional bureaus—Bureau for Africa (202/647-9232), Bureau for Asia and the Near East (202/647-8298), Bureau for Europe and the Newly Independent States (202/647-9119), Bureau for Latin America and the Caribbean (202/647-8246)—are a primary source of region-specific information on U.S. aid programs, the operations of USAID field missions, current economic conditions, and development activities in their regions of responsibility. They can provide researchers with unclassified agency materials, including "working documents," "program evaluation studies," and Development Assistance Program (DAP) field reports from USAID missions surveying development activities and general conditions in their host countries. Desk officers within the regional bureaus can also place researchers in contact with the appropriate sectoral specialists within the agency.

## BUREAU FOR HUMANITARIAN RESPONSE

M. Douglas Stafford, Assistant Administrator
(202) 647-0220
Fax: (202) 647-0218

### Office of Private and Voluntary Cooperation
Louis C. Stamberg, Director
(703) 351-0221

This office supports private and nongovernmental organizations working in AID missions abroad by educating and training volunteers, and by providing funding. AID field programs generally focus on increasing productivity and self-sufficiency in developing countries.

### Office of Food for Peace
1515 Wilson Blvd.
Arlington, Va. 22209

H. Robert Kramer, Director
(703) 351-0106

Mail:
State Department Building
Washington, D.C. 20523

The office administers U.S. food aid programs, under funding from the Agriculture Department. Food aid is supplied both on a bilateral, government-to-government basis, and through U.S. voluntary assistance organizations (CARE, Catholic Relief Services, Seventh-day Adventists, etc.). Programs include preschool feeding, school lunch programs, food-for-work programs (food as payment to unskilled laborers on development projects), and disaster relief.

**Office of U.S. Foreign Disaster Assistance**
Nan Borton, Director
(202) 647-8924

This office coordinates public and private relief efforts during natural and man-made disasters that occur throughout the world. The office prepares an annual report, *Foreign Disaster Assistance Relief*. A duty officer is on call 24 hours a day.

## BUREAU FOR GLOBAL PROGRAMS, FIELD SUPPORT AND RESEARCH

Sally Shelton, Assistant Administrator
(202) 647-1827

This functional bureau provides technical expertise and support to USAID field missions throughout the world. Its offices are structured in accordance with the sectors of development assistance in which the agency is active. Each office designs, coordinates, and manages AID contract-research studies in its sector of specialization.

**Office of Agriculture**
Rosslyn Plaza Center
1601 N. Kent Street
Arlington, Va. 22209

Harvey Hortik, Director
(703) 875-4300

The office is concerned with agricultural economics, soil and water management, food crop production, livestock production (including animal husbandry, disease, and range management), and commercial development of fisheries (both inland and coastal) in poor regions.

**Office of Health and Nutrition**
Robert Wrin, Director
(703) 875-4600

This office is interested in malnutrition levels, food fortification, vitamin deficiencies and their alleviation, and food technology, particularly the development of weaning foods. It is also concerned with environmental sanitation, water-supply systems, and other health-related development projects.

**Office of Economic and Institutional Development**
Russ Anderson, Acting Director
(703) 875-4502

This office studies components of integrated rural-development programs, such as agricultural production, financial markets, rural credit facilities, income generation, social services, transportation, health care, education, and nongovernmental forms of local participation.

**Office of Population**
Elizabeth Maguire, Acting Director
(703) 875-4402

*Family Planning Services Division*
Virginia Sewell, Chief
(703) 875-4721

The division assists AID missions in the design and development of family planning projects; public awareness educational programs; training programs for community health leaders, health administrators, physicians, nurses, midwives, et al.; and clinic development programs. Researchers may obtain current demographic data from Jeffrey Spieler, Research Division Chief (703/875-1510).

**Office of Environment and Urban Programs**
Peter M. Kimm, Director
(202) 663-2530

The office supports a program of research and technical assistance in urban development on a worldwide basis. It emphasizes the application of new tools for analyzing urban issues and investment strategies, and assists in strengthening urban investment strategies and financial management policies and practices. Substantively, the office is interested in city planning, urban finance and tax revenue programs, credit facilities, employment, regional village patterns and migration trends, and the development of agricultural marketing centers and commercial and public enterprises.

## OFFICE OF WOMEN IN DEVELOPMENT

Katherine M. Blakeslee, Acting Director
(703) 875-4668

In recognition of the significant role that women play in developing countries, Congress requires that U.S. bilateral aid be administered to give particular attention to programs that tend to integrate women into the economies of their countries. To that end, research has centered around women's contribution to their households and communities.

## CENTER FOR DEVELOPMENT INFORMATION AND EVALUATION

Rosslyn Plaza Center
1601 North Kent Street
Rosslyn, Va. 22209

John R. Eriksson, Director
(703) 875-4314

Mail: State Department Building
Washington, D.C. 20523

The center constitutes a "memory bank" for AID missions and project designers. It administers the AID Development Information Center (A1), and the computerized Development Information System (G2) and the Economic and Social Data Bank (G3) for AID project materials. The center can assist researchers in identifying and obtaining project papers (feasibility studies, evaluations, etc.), AID contract research studies, and development assistance data, by country or development activity. It produces the quarterly A.I.D. Research and Development Abstracts and the Research Literature for Development series. It also plans to prepare a series of project histories summarizing and evaluating the performance of individual AID field missions, as well as a series of information packages analyzing AID development programs by subject area (with bibliographies).

6. Index Terms: Development Issues—Aid and Investment; Development Issues—Agriculture; Development Issues—Education; Development Issues—Health; Development Issues—Infrastructure; Development Issues—International Development; Development Issues—Population Policy; Development Issues—Technical Assistance; Humanitarian Issues

See also entries A1, G2, and G3

---

## K2   Agriculture Department (USDA)

1.a. 14th Street and Independence Avenue, SW
   Washington, D.C. 20250
   (202) 720-4623 (Public Affairs)
   (202) 720-8164 (Freedom of Information)

b. Open to the public. Appointments recommended.

2. USDA participates in U.S. food aid, commodity sales, and agricultural development programs in developing countries. Several of its divisions collect information and conduct research on agricultural conditions in developing countries. Virtually all research is produced in-house.

3. See National Agricultural Library, entry A31; for USDA's databases, see entries G4 and G5.

4. There is no centralized USDA records management facility. The internal records of each departmental subunit remain in that unit's files until they ultimately reach the National Archives and Records Administration (B11).

5. USDA publications are described below with their respective offices.

### ECONOMIC RESEARCH SERVICE (ERS)

1301 New York Avenue, NW
Washington, D.C. 20005-4788

Katherine Reichelderfer, Acting Administrator
(202) 219-0300

ERS monitors economic activity, makes short-term forecasts of key indicators, and develops long-range projections of U.S. and world agricultural production. Its analysts study demand for land and water resources, food products, and other agricultural commodities, and forecast potential consequences of policy alternatives. ERS releases its information through research monographs, situation and outlook periodicals, staff reports, professional and trade journals, radio and television, newspapers, and direct computer access, as well as an annual "outlook" conference in Washington, D.C.

**Agricultural and Rural Economy Division**
Kenneth L. Deavers, Director
(202) 219-0530

*National Economy and History Branch*
Thomas F. Hady, Chief
Ralf Monaco, Agriculture and Rural History, Acting Chief
(202) 219-0782

This branch is primarily concerned with the history of U.S. agriculture. Its research pertains to such topics as the role of machines, grains, and animals within their U.S. context. Material on international agricultural issues focuses on U.S. food aid and foreign agricultural development programs since World War II. Researchers may use extensive biographical files housed here.

### AGRICULTURE AND TRADE ANALYSIS DIVISION

Bob H. Robinson, Director
(202) 219-0700

*Trade and Development Analysis*
Barry Krissoff, Acting Chief
(202) 219-0680

This branch's primary responsibility is to analyze developing countries' demand for U.S. agricultural products, as well as their competitiveness with the United States in world markets. It investigates prices, costs of production, agricultural and trade policies, monetary conditions, institutions, technological change, and political development. The branch collaborates in publication of the quarterly *Outlook for United States Agricultural Exports;* the monthly *Foreign Agricultural Trade of the United States;* and *World Agricultural Outlook and Situation,* published three times a year. Working in conjunction with this department are three region-specific branches—Africa and Middle East (202/219-0630); Asia and Pacific Rim (202/219-0610); and Europe (202/219-0620).

See also entry G4

## RESOURCES AND TECHNOLOGY DIVISION

**Land and Global Resources**
Betsey Kuhn, Director
(202) 219-0409

This branch focuses its research on the status of the world's land-based resources. Also, it investigates how U.S. and world agricultural production affect the global demand for production resources.

## NATIONAL AGRICULTURAL STATISTICS SERVICE

14th Street and Independence Avenue, SW
Washington, D.C. 20250
(202) 720-2707

**International Programs Office**
Larry A. Sivers, Director
(202) 720-4505

The office provides technical assistance and training for establishing agricultural data systems in foreign countries, particularly in the developing world. The work is done on a reimbursable basis, usually in coordination with the Agency for International Development (KI).

## AGRICULTURAL STABILIZATION AND CONSERVATION SERVICE

Bruce Weber, Acting Administrator
(202) 720-3467

**Financial Management Division**
John J. Sikora, Chief, International Control Staff
(703) 305-1409

This division is responsible for guaranteeing the credit sale of U.S. commodities abroad. In conjunction with this responsibility, the staff oversees the direction of food aid to developing countries. Working under the auspices of the Food for Peace Act of 1966, staff members direct the supply of commodities to

combat hunger and malnutrition, and to encourage economic development in developing nations. The division also encourages U.S. financial institutions to provide financing to developing countries.

## FOREIGN AGRICULTURAL SERVICE (FAS)

Richard B. Schroeter, Acting Administrator
(202) 720-3935

**Information Division**
Geraldine Schumacher, Director
(202) 720-7115

Information on FAS publications is available from the Information Division, Foreign Agricultural Service, U.S. Department of Agriculture, Room 5918, South Building, Washington, D.C. 20250-1000, (202/720-9330). FAS circulars covering commodity data and export marketing information are published periodically and are available by subscription. *AgExporter* (formerly *Foreign Agriculture*) is a monthly magazine featuring articles on agricultural trade, also available by subscription from FAS. A series of brochures and fact sheets offers exporters information about trade issues and FAS services to help tap overseas markets. *International Agricultural Statistical Profiles* provides compilations of agricultural trade activity by country or commodity (call 202/382-9509). *Buyer Alert* is a free overseas product publicity service using high-speed telecommunications to promote U.S. food and agricultural products to interested overseas buyers (call 202/475-3421). Daily, weekly, and monthly reports of foreign trade opportunities are available electronically (call 202/475-3422). For more information on the Trade and Economic Information Division see entry G4.

Foreign proposals concerning agricultural product standards are often sent to the Foreign Agricultural Service. FAS publishes these notifications in *Export Briefs,* a weekly newsletter of trade leads and market information. It is available for $75 per year. To subscribe, contact the High Value Products Division, Foreign Agricultural Service, U.S. Department of Agriculture, Room 4945, South Building, Washington, D.C. 20250-1000, (202/720-3416).

**Foreign Agricultural Affairs**
Mattie Sharpless, Assistant Administrator
(202) 720-6138

FAS, the export promotion agency for the Department of Agriculture, has a network of agricultural counselors, attachés, and trade officers stationed overseas. They are supported by a backup team of analysts, marketing specialists, economist negotiators, and related specialists in Washington, D.C. For information on trade activities at overseas posts, contact the appropriate regional desk officer: East Asia and the Pacific, 202/720-2690; EC European area, 202/720-2144; and non-EC European area, 202/720-3080; Near East, South Asia, and Africa, 202/720-7053; Western Hemisphere, 202/720-3221.

### International Trade Policy
Richard B. Schroeter, Assistant Administrator
(202) 720-6887

Within FAS, the International Trade Policy (ITP) section plays a crucial role in the formulation and coordination of U.S. policies aimed at maintaining, regaining, and improving sales of U.S. agricultural products to foreign markets. ITP's regional teams deal with specific agricultural policy problems between the United States and countries in their area of specialization. ITP also maintains information about major tariff and nontariff barriers in those countries.

### Trade and Economic Analysis Division
Dewain H. Rahe, Director
(202) 720-1294

This division gathers, analyzes, and disseminates statistical information on foreign crop and livestock production. The group uses advanced satellite, meteorological, database, and communications technologies to assess agricultural crop conditions in major grain and oilseed growing regions of the world. It also develops, maintains, and analyzes trade, international, financial, and macroeconomic data and information to support expansion of U.S. agricultural exports. The division issues a weekly report of key U.S. agricultural export sales. Data on specific commodities, agricultural statistics for many countries, and U.S. bilateral trade statistics are available.

See also entry G4

### Commodity and Marketing Programs
Philip L. Mackie, Assistant Administrator
(202) 720-4761

Agricultural economists in this unit analyze world agricultural commodities from the standpoints of production, trade, competition, marketing, prices, etc. The unit is organized by divisions for individual commodity groups, such as Dairy, Livestock and Poultry Division (202/720-8031), Forest Products Division (202/720-8138), Horticultural and Tropical Products Division (202/720-6590), and To-

bacco, Cotton and Seeds Division (202/720-9516). The focus of each division is worldwide, so there are staff members who can provide information specific to almost any country in the world.

### Export Credits
Glenn D. Whiteman, Deputy Assistant Administrator
(202) 720-4274

Constance Delaplane, Public Law 480 Operations Division, Director
(202) 720-3664

The division's major emphasis is on combating hunger and malnutrition, and encouraging economic development by carrying out assigned foreign assistance activities. One way this is done is by directing the sales of surplus commodities. Another is by granting low-interest long-term credit to recipients of U.S. farm commodities. The Public Law 480 Operations Division also cooperates with AID (K1) to improve the long-range economic conditions of developing countries by donating agricultural commodities. The Commodity Credit Corporation Operations Division (202/720-6211) directs the Export Credit Guarantee and the Intermediate Export Credit Guarantee programs. These programs encourage the development of overseas markets by providing guarantees on private financing of U.S. exports to foreign markets. Through this system the foreign buyer gets resources it needs immediately, but may make payments over a 3- to 10-year period.

### INTERNATIONAL COOPERATION AND DEVELOPMENT (ICD)

Lynnett Wagner, Acting Deputy Administrator

All of USDA's policies and programs pertaining to international agricultural development and cooperation are planned, coordinated, and evaluated by this office. ICD focuses on providing technical assistance and training in agriculture to other countries, particularly in the developing world, as well as conducting research and other programs of mutual interest to the United States and other nations. ICD is also responsible for coordinating representation of U.S. agricultural interests in international organizations. Much of this work is done on a reimbursable basis, with funding from the Agency for International Development (K1), the Food and Agricultural Organization (FAO) (L13), governments of other countries, and other organizations.

### International Organizations Division
David P. Winkelmann, Acting Director

(202) 690-1801

Fax: (202) 690-2488

This unit establishes and maintains liaisons between the USDA and international organizations concerned with food and agriculture. In addition to the FAO, international relations advisers work closely with the Organization for Economic Cooperation and Development (A39), the International Bank for Reconstruction and Development (L8), and the Inter-American Institute for Cooperation on Agriculture, among others.

### Research and Scientific Exchanges Division
Valdis E. Mezainis, Director

(202) 690-4872

This division helps scientists from the Agriculture Department, university community, and elsewhere seek new technological knowledge beneficial to the United States and cooperating countries. This is accomplished by providing support for international collaborative research and exchange programs in agriculture and forestry. The division has ongoing bilateral activities with many less-developed countries.

### Food Industries Division
Frank A. Fender, Director

(202) 690-1339

This division's technical assistance, professional development, and trade and investment enhancement programs focus on the nonfarm industries related to the food and fiber system—fertilizer, feed, seed, equipment, and agricultural chemicals; food processing, packaging, wholesaling and retailing; and the product processing and distribution businesses such as wood, cotton, and flax. In cooperation with other USDA agencies, the U.S. university community, trade associations, and agribusinesses, the division arranges programs in the above subjects for public and private sector persons and organizations from less-developed and middle-income countries. The division also arranges agricultural training programs in the United States for foreign nationals.

### Development Resources Division
Arlene Mitchell, Director

(202) 690-1924

A synopsis of technical assistance projects and activities in progress during 1993 included social and water conservation; agricultural cooperatives, information management, rural roads, nutrition, and private enterprise development; forestry and small farm improvement; plant inspection; fumigation/ certification and phytosanitary clearance; agricultural statistics; marketing and transportation; ag-

ricultural trade and development; and technical advisory services on natural resources management, food security, and plant quarantine/treatment.

The division also carries out technical assistance activities, which are available across geographical regions. Some of these activities are disaster assistance and preparedness, soil management, forestry, and pest management. Training activities include short courses conducted in the United States on a variety of subjects; courses developed specifically for delivery in other countries (often in a language other than English); and consultancies to assess training needs or to address management improvement needs.

## MARKETING AND INSPECTION SERVICES

### Animal and Plant Health Inspection Service
Federal Building #1

6505 Belcrest Road

Hyattsville, Md. 20782

Lonnie King, Associate Administrator

(202) 720-3668

*International Services*

Alex Thiermann, Director

(202) 720-7593

The service was established to administer regulatory and control programs to protect and improve animal and plant health. Staff members in the International Services branch have carried out cooperative plant pest programs with several foreign countries. In addition, inspectors work in developing countries to supervise preclearance of agricultural materials for entry into the United States.

*International Programs*

John C. Prucha, Deputy Administrator

(202) 720-3473

The division works to improve and expand the transportation of U.S. agricultural products to world markets and to ensure the quality of agricultural products coming from world markets into the United States. Programs of interest include studies of grain shipments from U.S. ports; international agreements with developing countries' food purchasing agencies to establish bilateral transportation groups; and occasional seminars conducted on the transportation and handling of fresh fruits and vegetables.

## FOREST SERVICE

### International Forestry Staff
201 14th Street, SW

Washington, D.C.

Jeff M. Sirmon, Deputy Chief
(202) 205-1650

Mail: USDA P.O. Box 96090
Washington, D.C. 20090

Two major programs have been of interest to specialists in developing countries in the early 1990s: the Forestry Support Program provided technical support for AID (K1) projects abroad; the Disasters Assistance Support Program provided help through AID to countries in times of natural disasters and sponsored hazard preparedness training.

## SOIL CONSERVATION SERVICE

### International Conservation Division
South Agriculture Building, Room 4241
14th Street and Independence Avenue, SW
Washington, D.C. 20250

Mail:
Soil Conservation Service
P.O. Box 2890
Washington, D.C. 20013

Jerome S. Hammond, Director
(202) 720-2218

The division is responsible for carrying out the projects of the Soil Conservation Service (SCS) abroad. These projects resemble SCS's domestic projects in that they focus on planning, developing, and carrying out programs that accelerate the conservation, development, and utilization of natural resources.

## AGRICULTURAL RESEARCH SERVICE

BARC-West, Building 005
Beltsville, Md. 20705

### International Programs
Richard S. Soper, Assistant Administrator
(301) 504-5605

The International Activities Office participates in planning, coordinating, and evaluating overseas research programs that focus on animal and plant protection; conservation and improvement of soil, water, and air; processing and distribution of agricultural products; and improving human nutrition. Research is conducted at eight overseas laboratories as well as at the headquarters in Beltsville, Md. Specific current subjects of interest are rangeland weeds, southeastern pasture and crop weeds, and fire ants.

6. Index Terms: Development Issues—Agriculture; Environmental Issues, Global

See also entries A31, G4 and G5

## K3 Air Force Department (AFD)

1.a. The Pentagon
Washington, D.C. 20330-1000
(703) 697-1128 (Information)

b. The Pentagon is closed to anyone without appropriate security clearance; an appointment is required.

2. Most research is conducted in-house. The Media Relations Division in the Office of Public Affairs (703/695-5554) deals with contracts.

3. See entry B1 for a description of the Office of Air Force History collections. For a description of the History Office's Oral History Program, see entry E1, and for its Photographic Collection see F2. Entry C1 discusses the Air Force Art and Museum Branch.

4. Internal records are maintained in several locations prior to their transfer to the National Archives and Records Administration (B11). Researchers should contact the Resource Library (703/697-6701) of the Directorate of Public Affairs for assistance in locating desired records. Persons wishing to gain access to restricted items will find information pertinent to their needs under this entry's discussion of the Office of the Secretary of the Air Force, Directorate of Information Management.

5. Publications are described with the issuing bodies presented below.

## OFFICE OF THE SECRETARY OF THE AIR FORCE

### Directorate of Public Affairs

*Media Plans/Operations Division*
Lt. Col. Cathy Roeder, Director
(703) 695-0640

This division is involved in issues affecting the U.S. Air Force from strategy and tactics to logistics, contracts, and personnel. The various teams in this division are concerned with current issues only. Historical questions should be directed to the Office of Air Force History (B1).

*Directorate of Information Management*
Col. Edward A. Pardini, Director
(703) 697-4191

Researchers wishing to gain access to air force records through FOIA procedures should begin their request by writing to Headquarters, U.S. Air Force, DADF, Pentagon, Washington, D.C. 20330-5025.

Correspondence should describe specific items wanted and specify that the Freedom of Information Act is involved. A response is usually sent within 10 days. For further information researchers may call (703) 695-4992. The headquarters office issues *AF Regulation 12-30, Air Force Freedom of Information Act Program,* specifying established procedures.

## OFFICE OF THE CHIEF OF STAFF

Deputy Chief of Staff (Plans and Operations)
Lt. Gen. Buster C. Glosson
(703) 697-9991

Mail:
1630 Air Force Pentagon
Washington, D.C. 20330-1630

The desk officers in this unit assist in formulating U.S. Air Force policies on politico-military issues of concern to the air force. The division also investigates political and military issues as they bear on air force involvement in specific areas of the world. It does not routinely assist outside researchers.

### Air Force Intelligence Support Agency
Col. Michael J. Sterling, Commander
(703) 806-5406

The analysts in the assessments division (703/695-0006) monitor current events and maintain technical data (on aircraft, airfields, etc.) on topics of interest to the U.S. Air Force.

*Office of Air Force History*
The agency also maintains a historical research office (Richard P. Hallion, Historian, Building 5681, Bolling Air Force Base, 170 Luke Ave., Washington, D.C. 20332-5113; 202/767-5764).

**See entry B1.**

6.  Index Terms: Collective Security; Defense Policy, National; Intelligence; Military Science

See also entries B1, C1, E1, and F2

---

# K4  Arms Control and Disarmament Agency (ACDA)

---

1.a.  U.S. Department of State
    320 21st Street, NW
    Washington, D.C. 20451
    (202) 647-8677 (Public Information)
    (202) 647-3582 (Freedom of Information)

b.  Access to the State Department building is restricted. Researchers should make an appointment prior to visiting ACDA offices.

c.  John D. Holum, Director

2.  The U.S. Arms Control and Disarmament Agency was established in 1961 to assist the president, the secretary of state, and Congress in developing, negotiating, and implementing international arms control agreements. ACDA's missions include direct responsibility for specific negotiations, the analysis of intelligence information concerning compliance with negotiated arms control agreements, coordination of research for arms control and disarmament policy formulation, and the dissemination and coordination of public information concerning arms and disarmament.

In support of these activities, the agency monitors, among other tasks, weapons buildups and the flow of arms trade in developing countries. ACDA's specialists conduct research and studies in arms transfers, multilateral hemispheric arms control treaties, and regional nuclear nonproliferation. They will confer with private researchers and can refer them to specialists in the State Department and Defense Department.

ACDA's "external research program" has occasionally funded contract-research studies on arms control in developing countries, weapons transfers, and relationships between domestic economies and levels of national military spending. Individuals seeking to do business with the agency or obtain information on research contracts may contact the Contracts Division (202/235-3288). Outside research projects funded by ACDA are announced in the *Commerce Business Daily.*

ACDA grants Hubert H. Humphrey Fellowships in arms control and disarmament to advanced graduate students for research, as well as William C. Foster Fellowships to visiting scholars to work in ACDA.

3.  The Arms Control and Disarmament Agency Library and Technical Reference Center (A5) is located in room 5840 and is open to researchers by appointment from 9:00 A.M. to 4:30 P.M. Monday–Friday. The collection contains a complete set of agency publications, unclassified contract research reports, and a small number of titles pertaining to NATO arms trade, nuclear proliferation, and related subjects. Further information may be obtained from ACDA's librarian, Diane Ferguson (202/647-5969).

4.  ACDA's internal records and classified research reports are maintained by the Personnel and General Services Division within the Office of Administration (202/647-8666). Access to these documents is possible only through Freedom of Information Act

procedures. Researchers may contact the ACDA FOIA office (202/647-3596) or State Department FOIA (202/647-6070). Charles Oleszycki is ACDA's Freedom of Information officer.

5.a. Two important ACDA publications appear annually: *Arms Control Impact Statements* and *World Military Expenditures and Arms Transfers*. These and the ACDA Annual Report are available from the Office of Public Information (202/647-8677) and the Government Printing Office (see Appendix III).

b. Bibliographies of the agency's other publications include *ACDA External Research Reports* and *Official Publications of the United States Arms Control and Disarmament Agency*. The agency also publishes *ACDA Publications List* and *Current Articles of Interest* on a monthly basis. The Office of Public Information (800/581-ACDA or 202/647-8677) will provide information about these and other ACDA publications. ACDA's electronic bulletin board is accessible 24 hours a day (202/736-4436).

6. Index Terms: Arms Control; Deterrence; Disarmament; Proliferation

See also entry A5

---

## K5   Army Department

1.a. The Pentagon
Washington, D.C. 20310
(703) 545-6700 (Public Information)
(703) 697-1180 (Freedom of Information Act)
Fax: (703) 614-5520

b. The Pentagon is closed to anyone without appropriate security clearance; an appointment is required.

2. Most research is conducted in-house. Contract procurement policies and procedures are the responsibility of the deputy assistant secretary for procurement, Office of the Assistant Secretary of the Army (Procurement Policy), Room 2E661, The Pentagon, Washington, D.C. 20310 (703/697-9982).

3. See entry A41 for a description of the Pentagon Library. Other army libraries are listed in the introduction to section A; archival materials are described in entries B3, B4, and E3. For information concerning army museums see the introduction to section C, and entries C2 and C3.

4. Recent army records are held in the Office Systems Management Branch, Headquarters, USAISC, Ft. Huachuca, Ariz. 85613-5000. Older records have been transferred to the National Archives and Records Administration (B11).

5. The department sponsors the monthly publication of *Soldiers Magazine* (703/487-0050).

## OFFICE OF THE SECRETARY

**Public Communications Division**
Col. Steven F. Rausch, Chief
(703) 697-2564

The branch will accept initial research and will redirect scholars to the appropriate unit. It does not maintain or distribute materials germane to Army policies or general activities.

## OFFICE OF THE CHIEF OF STAFF

Deputy Chief of Staff for Operations and Plans
Lt. Gen. P. E. Blackwell
(703) 695-2904

**Strategy, Plans, and Policy**

*Politico-Military Division*
Kenneth Fess, Chief
(703) 695-2283

Desk officers in the regional branches of this unit prepare memoranda and position papers (some unclassified) that contribute to the formulation of army policy on the full range of issues affecting U.S. security interests throughout the world. The staff is willing to answer questions.

Deputy Chief of Staff for Intelligence
Lt. Gen. I. C. Owens
(703) 695-3033

*Foreign Intelligence*
Col. J. L. Solomon, Director
(703) 697-3398

The staff monitors global developments, and prepares information papers and army contributions to national intelligence estimates. Security and classification considerations may, however, prevent a substantive response to public inquiries.

**Army Center of Military History**   See entry B3.

**Army Corps of Engineers Office of History**   See entries B4 and E3.

6. Index Terms: Collective Security; Defense Policy, National; Intelligence; Military Science

See also entries A41, B3, B4, C2, C3, and E3

---

## K6  Central Intelligence Agency (CIA)

1.a. Langley, Virginia
(703) 482-1100 (Information)
(703) 482-7676 (Public Affairs)

Mail:
Washington, D.C. 20505

b. Closed to the public. Security clearance is required for entry. Tours for large groups from academic, business, or other private organizations can be arranged through the Public Affairs Office.

2. The CIA is responsible for the collection of foreign intelligence, for conducting counterintelligence abroad, and for research and development of technical collection systems. Regional specialists in the Directorate of Intelligence monitor and analyze world affairs and produce finished intelligence reports for policy makers. They are not regularly accessible to private researchers. The main contact-point within the CIA for outside researchers is the Center for the Study of Intelligence (703/351-2689).

The CIA occasionally funds contract research, primarily for technical studies and for research on aspects of methodology and model-building. The agency also utilizes foreign-area specialists as outside consultants for regional studies and has a program for staff sabbaticals to universities and vice versa.

3. The CIA Library (Reference, 703/482-7701; Interlibrary Loan, 703/482-2419) is accessible only to those nonagency personnel who have the necessary security clearance and the prior approval of the agency. Outside researchers may borrow unclassified library holdings through interlibrary loans. The library's unclassified holdings are accessible through the OCLC bibliographic database available in most academic and public libraries. Because of restrictions on library access, an evaluation of CIA holdings is impossible at this time.

The CIA map and remote sensing collections consist of national classified materials and are not accessible to private researchers.

4. The internal records of the CIA are classified and are available only to researchers who petition for the release of specific records through Freedom of Information Act procedures. Researchers should direct FOIA inquiries to the Information and Privacy Coor-

dinator (703/351-2083). The history staff of the CIA, located in the Center for the Study of Intelligence, has an important advisory role in this process. The staff, headed by Kenneth McDonald (703/351-2689), is responsible for assisting other official historians with security clearances (e.g., at the State Department). The staff cannot make any of its records or analyses available to outside researchers, but can sometimes be helpful in directing inquiries elsewhere.

Many of the documents that the agency has released are cited in the *Declassified Documents Quarterly Catalog* published by Research Publications, 12 Lunar Drive, Woodbridge, Conn. 06525 (203/397-2600). There is no central collection of CIA documents released through FOIA, but see the private National Security Archive (B12).

Declassified, noncurrent maps of the Office of Strategic Services (OSS), the predecessor of the CIA, have been transferred to the National Archives and Records Administration (B11). Currently, these maps are the only significant materials in the CIA record group at the National Archives. The Military Archives Division–Modern Military Branch (B11) has assembled a collection of copies of declassified CIA documents found in the branch's post–World War II military records.

5. The Central Intelligence Agency produces a number of unclassified publications, including a semiannual *World Factbook* (containing regional maps showing current political, economic, and population data for each country), a bimonthly *Chiefs of State and Cabinet Members of Foreign Governments*, the *International Handbook of Economic Statistics,* and other publications.

A number of sources in the Washington, D.C., area sell unclassified CIA publications. The National Technical Information Service (NTIS) (703/487-4650) offers all unclassified maps produced by the CIA, selected atlases and databases, and individual documents that have appeared since 1972 (see Appendix III). NTIS also offers full or tailored subscriptions to documents that have been published since February 1, 1979, regardless of subject or geographic focus. Publications available from NTIS are cited in *CIA Maps and Publications Available to the Public,* a catalog that is free from the public affairs staff.

The Library of Congress Photocopying Service, Washington, D.C. 20540 (202/707-5543) can provide earlier CIA publications in hardcopy or microfilm for a fee; photocopies of out-of-stock selected CIA maps may also be obtained through the service. Researchers and institutions can subscribe to all available CIA publications by writing the Document Expediting Project (DOCEX), Exchange and Gifts Division, Library of Congress, Washington, D.C. 20540 (202/707-9526). DOCEX staff will supply prospective subscribers with a list of titles issued during the past two years that are still in print. Currently CIA publications available through the DOCEX are received by the Library of Congress (A29), American University (A4), George Mason University (A18), Georgetown University (A20), and the University of Maryland (A47). The unclassified published CIA maps and atlases received through DOCEX are found in the Library of Congress (D4), George Mason University (A18), and the University of Maryland (D12). A limited number of maps, atlases, and books produced by the agency may be obtained at Government Printing Office bookstores (see Appendix III).

6.   Index Terms: Intelligence; International Law

---

## K7   Commerce Department

1.a.   14th Street and Constitution Avenue, NW
       Washington, D.C. 20230
       (202) 482-4115 (Freedom of Information)
       (202) 482-5151 (Office of Public Affairs)

*Note:* Branches are scattered throughout the metropolitan area.

b.   Not open to the public.

2.   Among its many functions, the department offers assistance and information to help increase exports and prevent unfair trade competition. It provides social and economic statistics and analysis for business and government, as well as research and support for the increased use of scientific engineering and technological development. The department grants patents and registers trademarks. It also seeks to improve understanding of the earth's physical environment and oceanic life.

3.   Commerce Department libraries are described in entries A8 and A10.

4.   The Management and Information Systems Division of the Commerce Department oversees internal records prior to their eventual transfer to the National Archives and Records Administration (B11). Inventories of retired office files are maintained by each subunit of the department. Researchers interested in consulting department records should contact Robert E. Shute, department records management officer (202/377-1300), who can direct them to appropriate record management offices and provide assistance in obtaining retired documents.

5.   Publications are described within their respective agencies below.

### INTERNATIONAL TRADE ADMINISTRATION (ITA)

Herbert Clark Hoover Building
14th Street and Constitution Avenue, NW
Washington, D.C. 20230
(202) 377-3808 (Public Affairs)

ITA strives to promote world commerce while strengthening the international trade and investment position of the United States. It is the responsibility of the under secretary to coordinate agency involvement in the areas of trade administration and development, as well as international economic policy and programs. ITA sponsors overseas commercial exhibitions of U.S. products, collects and publishes commercial and marketing information on each country in the world, and encourages formation of export trading companies.

ITA's Trade Information Center (800/872-8723) is the Commerce Department's central point of contact on many export related issues. It serves as a clearinghouse for 19 federal agencies that administer international trade and export promotion programs and publishes a booklet, *Export Programs: A Business Directory of U.S. Government Resources.* The Business Information Center for Newly Independent States (BISNIS, 202/482-4655; fax 202/482-8723) provides a single source on commercial relations with the countries of the former Soviet Union. The Eastern Europe Business Information Center (EEBIC, 202/482-2645, fax: 202/482-4473) provides similar information relating to Eastern Europe. The principal publication of the International Trade Administration is the biweekly magazine *Business America.*

Of related interest is the National Library of International Trade (A26), maintained by the International Trade Commission (ITC) (K22).

### Deputy Assistant Secretary for International Operations
Charles A. Ford, Deputy Assistant Secretary
(202) 482-0300

The officers under the deputy assistant secretary in this division work with their counterparts around the world to keep abreast of trade and investment issues, and maintain in-depth commercial and economic information on individual countries and regions. They produce detailed research surveys and studies of foreign markets, many of which may be purchased from the National Technical Information

Service (see Appendix III). Among these are *Overseas Business Reports* and *Foreign Economic Trends and Their Implications for the United States.*

### U.S. and Foreign Commercial Service (US&FCS)
Lauri Fitz-Pegado, Assistant Secretary and General Director
(202) 377-5777

US&FCS strives to help new exporters enter the overseas market and experienced ones penetrate additional, more resistant arenas. As a part of this endeavor US&FCS maintains 120 posts in the 66 countries that are the principal trading partners of the United States. Staff members overseas include commercial officers who provide political and credit risk analysis; advice on market entry strategy; sources of financing; and major project identification, tracking, and assistance. Questions about international initiatives can be directed to the Office of Information Systems (202/482-5291). The US&FCS publishes *Commerce Business Daily.*

### Export Promotion Services
Janet Barnes, Deputy Assistant Secretary
(202) 482-6220

The office focuses on export promotion. It assists U.S. companies marketing their products and services abroad by developing market research, facilitating contacts with local companies, supporting local promotion efforts, and coordinating the presence of U.S. firms in international trade shows, particularly for those firms that are new to exporting or new to a particular market.

### Assistant Secretary for Import Administration
Susan Esserman, Assistant Secretary
(202) 482-1780

The units in this division study comparative prices in home markets to investigate unfair trade practices of foreign manufacturers. They investigate whether a foreign company receives preferential treatment in its home market and whether dumping or less than fair-value pricing occurs in order to drive competitors out of a market. Based on their findings, staff members determine the rate of duty that the United States should levy against certain products. Many of the files in these offices are available for public scrutiny.

### Assistant Secretary for Trade Development
Raymond E. Vickery, Jr., Assistant Secretary
(202) 482-1461

This division gathers, analyzes, and disseminates information on international trade and investment policies pertaining to U.S. industrial sectors. It also promotes increased participation by U.S. industry in international markets and manages an integrated Trade Development Program that includes policy development, industrial analysis, and promotion. The Office of Trade and Economic Analysis (202/482-5146) can provide scholars with current analysis of international economic trade trends.

### Assistant Secretary for International Economic Policy
Charles F. Meissner, Assistant Secretary-Designate
(202) 482-3022

This division serves as the department's primary source of information and analysis on U.S. industrial sectors, trade, and foreign investment. Within the branch, the offices of the five deputy assistant secretaries—Africa, Near East, and South Asia (202/482-4925); East Asia and the Pacific (202/482-5251); Europe (202/482-5638); Japan (202/482-4527); and Western Hemisphere (202/482-5324)—provide information on U.S. economic involvement in their jurisdictions.

See also entries A10 and G6

### CENSUS BUREAU
Federal Office Building 3
Silver Hill and Suitland Roads
Suitland, Md. 20746

Mail:
Department of Commerce
Washington, D.C. 20233
(301) 763-4040 (Public Information Office)
(301) 763-2758 (Freedom of Information)

The Bureau of the Census compiles current statistics on U.S. foreign trade, including data on imports, exports, and shipping. The Census Bureau Library is described in entry A8. The statistical results of the bureau's censuses are available to the public though printed reports, computer tape, CD-ROMs, and microfiche. A list of the bureau's publications is available from the Publications Services Division (301/763-4100).

### Foreign Trade Division (FTD)
Juanita H. Noone, Administrative Officer
(301) 763-7682

FTD compiles data on the quantity and value of U.S. exports and imports by commodity and by either country of destination or origin. These data appear in several publications: *U.S. Exports: Schedule B, Commodity by Country* (annual); *Schedule E, Com-*

*modity by Country* (monthly); *U.S. General Imports; Highlights of U.S. Exports and Import Trade; U.S. Waterborne Exports and General Imports;* and *U.S. Airborne Exports.*

The division's Trade Data Services Branch (Haydn R. Mearkle, Chief, 301/763-5333) sells U.S. foreign trade data on computer tapes and in microform. The Commodity Analysis Branch (301/763-5333) provides reference information on U.S. bilateral trade for the latest five-year period.

### Associate Director for Demographic Programs
Center for International Research (CIR)
Washington Plaza II
8905 Presidential Parkway
Upper Marlboro, Md. 20772

Judith Banister, Chief
(301) 763-2870

CIR is the result of a merger of the former Foreign Demographic Analysis Division with the International Demographic Data Center. It conducts studies on global demographic, manpower, and economic questions. Staff members monitor major population trends and can provide researchers with growth-rate projections and population estimates for foreign countries. The Local Area Data Branch (301/763-4016) within the CIR plots population densities graphically on maps and in machine-readable format. The center maintains within its Population and Health Studies Branch (301/763-4232) international and national statistical yearbooks and specialized population reports, which may be made available to the public. It is occasionally possible for researchers to consult with members of this branch.

The Information Resources Branch (Peter D. Johnson, Chief, 301/763-4811) stores data on microform and can supply researchers with hardcopy demographic statistics for foreign countries (often in considerably greater depth than those produced in the unit's publications) dating back to the mid-1950s.

See also entry G6

CIR also provides training and consultation services to representatives of foreign governments who are responsible for demographic and statistical surveys in their own countries. Training is conducted both in the United States and at foreign locations. The program is aimed predominantly at developing countries and is administered by the Training Staff (Richard Storm, Chief, 301/763-2860). An annual training program booklet is available on request.

See also G6

## BUREAU OF ECONOMIC ANALYSIS (BEA)
1441 L Street, NW
Washington, D.C. 20230
(202) 606-9900 (Public Information)

The Bureau of Economic Analysis measures and analyzes U.S. economic activity, producing quantitative studies of the production, distribution, and use of the country's output. Among these studies are balance-of-payments accounts that detail U.S. transactions with foreign countries. The accounts contain estimates of merchandise exports and imports, travel and transportation services, foreign aid, direct investment, and other private and official capital flows. The bureau also produces estimates of the international investment position of the United States. The monthly *Survey of Current Business* (202/606-9683) publishes data and research on domestic and international economic activity. The bureau's Research Resources Center (202/606-9644), located in room 1115, houses a collection of bureau publications and staff papers. Its hours are 9:00 A.M. to 4:00 P.M. Monday–Friday; interlibrary loan service is available. BEA information is available online through the electronic bulletin board (EBB) (for information call 202/482-1986) or by fax through EBB/FAX (to receive EBB/FAX call 900/786-2329). A free user's guide to BEA information is available through the Public Information Office.

### Balance of Payments Division
Christopher L. Bach, Chief
(202) 606-9545

The Balance of Payments Division prepares current statistics and analyses of the balance of international payments and investment transactions between the United States and foreign countries. Global regional totals are published quarterly in *Survey of Current Business.* For specific questions on the following topics use the accompanying numbers: current-account estimates (202/606-9577); merchandise trade (202/606-3384); capital-account transactions (202/606-9579); government transactions (202/606-9574).

### International Investment Division
Betty L. Barker, Chief
(202) 606-9805

The division collects, maintains, and interprets data on U.S. direct investment abroad and foreign direct investment in the United States. The primary data consist of confidential quarterly reports from U.S. corporations, as well as from the U.S. branches of foreign-owned companies. The division publishes aggregated annual statistics (with foreign investment figures broken down by country or subregion) in the bureau's *Survey of Current Business*. In addition, the division's Direct Investment Abroad Branch (Patricia C. Walker, Chief, 202/606-9889) has produced a "benchmark census," *U.S. Direct Investment Abroad,* 1966–77 (published in 1981) and 1978–82 (published in 1985).

The division staff can provide researchers with aggregate data on U.S. private investments abroad, by country and industry, back to the late 1940s. Records pertaining to individual companies are confidential. The raw statistical data gathered by the division are transferred to computer tapes for storage. Private researchers may gain limited access to the tapes on a commercial basis. Contact the division's Data Retrieval and Analysis Branch (Smith W. Allnutt, Chief, 202/606-9803) for further information. For specific questions on the following topics, use the accompanying numbers: foreign direct investment in the United States (202/606-9804); operations of U.S. affiliates of foreign companies (202/606-9893); establishment-level data on foreign direct investment in the United States (202/606-9898); U.S. direct investment abroad (202/606-9867); operations of U.S. parent companies and their foreign affiliates (202/606-9867); international services (202/606-9804).

See also G6

## NATIONAL INSTITUTE OF STANDARDS AND TECHNOLOGY (*formerly* National Bureau of Standards)

Quince Orchard and Clopper Roads
Gaithersburg, Md. 20899
(301) 975-3058 (Information)
(301) 975-2393 (Freedom of Information)

Arati Prabhakar, Director
(301) 975-2300

The institute serves as the U.S. national science and engineering laboratory for measurement technology and standards research. Its responsibilities encompass assisting U.S. companies in adopting new technologies and scientific advances and increasing their international competitiveness. The Office of International and Academic Affairs (George A. Sinnot, Director, 301/975-3089) assists visiting foreign scientists. Questions regarding specific bilateral and multilateral programs with foreign countries should be directed to this office. The institute's Research Information Center (Patricia W. Berger, Chief, 301/975-2784) has limited resources from and about foreign countries, con-

sisting largely of technological and scientific journals and reference works. This library facility is open from 8:30 A.M. to 5:00 P.M. Monday–Friday.

See also G6

## NATIONAL OCEANIC AND ATMOSPHERIC ADMINISTRATION (NOAA)

Washington Science Center, Building 5
6010 Executive Boulevard
Rockville, Md. 20852
(301) 413-0900 (Information)
(301) 413-0610, (Freedom of Information)

The mission of NOAA is to explore, map, and chart the global ocean and its living resources; to manage, use, and conserve those resources; to describe, monitor, and predict conditions in the atmospheric, ocean, and solar environments; to issue warnings against impending destructive natural events; to develop beneficial methods of environmental modification; and to assess the consequences of inadvertent environmental modification over time. NOAA library services are described in entries A10 and G6.

**Oceanic and Atmospheric Research Office**
Ned A. Ostenso, Assistant Administrator
(301) 713-2458

This office investigates the oceans, the atmosphere, and sun-earth relationships vital to an understanding of the environment.

**International Activities Office**
Barbara S. Moore, Chief
(301) 713-2469

This office serves as the organizational focal point in the United States for the International Oceanographic Commission, the World Meteorological Organization, and interested parties to various bilateral agreements. Staff members can direct researchers to the units within NOAA that undertake climatological, meteorological, oceanographic, and marine resources data-gathering germane to specific global regions.

**National Marine Fisheries Service**
Metro One Building
1335 East-West Highway
Silver Spring, Md. 20910

Rolland A. Schmitten, Assistant Administrator
(301) 713-2239

*Office of International Affairs*
Henry R. Beasley, Director
(301) 713-2272

When the State Department acts to develop international fishing agreements, this office supports those efforts by providing technical backup on issues. Staff members collect data, prepare policy and position papers, and offer advice pertinent to U.S. agreements with foreign governments. The International Organizations and Agreements Division (301/713-2276) assists the State Department in negotiating and implementing bilateral and multilateral fisheries agreements. The Foreign Fisheries Analysis Team of the International Science, Development, and Foreign Fisheries Analysis Division (301/713-2288) collects, synthesizes, and analyzes information from fisheries around the world, including reports prepared by U.S. missions abroad. The resultant holdings contain fishery information on topics such as joint country ventures and where particular stocks of fish are found. Files are organized by country and broken down into more than 30 different subjects. Maps and photographs are also included. Although available for public use, the files must be examined in the office. The division's International Science Team acts as the focal point for the NMFS senior scientist with respect to international science issues involving living marine resources.

### National Ocean Service

W. Stanley Wilson, Assistant Administrator
(202) 713-3074

*Coast and Geodetic Services*
Silver Spring Metro Center
1315 East-West Highway
Silver Spring, MD 20910
Rear Adm. James A. Yeager, Acting Director
(301) 713-3163

The main responsibility of this office is the charting and mapping of U.S. waters and airspace. Cartographic coverage of foreign waters is handled by the Defense Mapping Agency (D1). The National Geodetic Survey Division (301/713-3222) and the National Charting Division (301/713-2700) serve as repositories for aeronautical charts of various global regions from foreign sources. Researchers may examine the collections by prior arrangement.

### Office of Ocean Resources and Assessments

Charles N. Ehler, Director
(301) 713-2989

The division administers a database on oil pollution in international and domestic waters as part of its program to provide alternatives to ocean dumping. The Strategic Assessments Branch (Daniel Basta,

Chief, 301/713-3000) has prepared the *Strategic Assessment Atlas* (1985), which includes coverage of the shoreline features, marine life, and economic characteristics of the world's oceans.

### National Weather Service

1325 East-West Highway
Silver Spring, Md. 20910

Elbert W. Friday Jr., Assistant Administrator
(301) 713-0689
Fax: (301) 713-0610

The National Weather Service attempts to forecast weather conditions in the United States by making worldwide meteorological observations and predictions, and constructing models of global conditions. Multilateral cooperation is coordinated through the International Activities Division (301/713-0645). Within the National Meteorological Center, the Agricultural Weather Section (202/720-7917) of the Climate Analysis Center prepares a weekly weather and crop bulletin that covers many less-developed countries. Sizable collections of daily weather maps from other countries are held in NOAA's Library and Information Services Division (301/713-2600).

### National Environmental Satellite, Data, and Information Service

Federal Office Building 4
Suitland Road and Silver Hill Road
Suitland, Md. 20233

Robert S. Winokur, Assistant Administrator
(301) 763-7190
Fax: (301) 763-4011

The National Environmental Satellite, Data, and Information Service operates the U.S. civil operational weather and land satellites, and provides data products for countries throughout the world through the World Meteorological Organization, direct readout from these satellites, or both. The data products are used by countries to enhance meteorological and hydrological research, land-use planning, and crop and forest monitoring. Within the Office of International and Interagency Affairs (301/763-4586), regional specialists can be contacted concerning the current data, projects, or research germane to particular geographic regions.

See also G6

### PATENT AND TRADEMARK OFFICE (PTO)

Crystal Park
Arlington, Va. 22202

Mail:
Commissioner of Patents and Trademarks
Washington, D.C. 20231
(703) 305-8341 (Office of Public Affairs)

The PTO examines applications for patents, as well as for federal registration of trademarks, service marks, certification marks, and collective membership marks. The *Official Gazette* and *Trademark Official Gazette* are published weekly. The *Official Gazette* contains a brief description of each patent issued that week. The *Trademark Official Gazette* contains a facsimile of each mark "published for opposition" by interested members of the public.

**Legislation and International Affairs Office (OLIA)**
Michael K. Kirk, Deputy Commissioner
(703) 305-9300

This office drafts and comments on legislation involving U.S. trademarks, patent law, and copyright regulations. It offers expertise in the negotiation of conventions pertaining to intellectual property worldwide. Staff members in the legislative and international intellectual property division (703/305-9300) can provide information pertaining to particular countries' intellectual property laws.

**International Patent Documentation Office**
J. Russell Goudeau, Director
(703) 305-6532

The office collects published materials on foreign patent and trademark laws and regulations. Staff can offer reference information relating to any country's patent laws.

**Scientific and Technical Information Center**
Barrington Balthrop, Supervisor, Foreign Patents Services
(703) 308-0810
Fax: (703) 308-0989

This library facility is open to the public, 8:45 A.M.–4:45 P.M. Monday–Friday, and has interlibrary loan and photocopying services. The holdings include 196,000 volumes, 1,500 current periodicals, and 20 million foreign patents in numerical arrangement.

**NATIONAL TELECOMMUNICATIONS AND INFORMATION ADMINISTRATION (NTIA)**

Herbert Clark Hoover Building
14th and Constitution Ave, NW
Washington, D.C. 20230
(202) 482-1816 (Freedom of Information)

Clarence L. Irving, Assistant Secretary
(202) 482-1840

One of the main functions of NTIA is to prescribe policies for managing domestic television and radio; it also prescribes some foreign communication policy. Specifically, the Office of International Affairs (202/482-1304) develops and presents U.S. plans concerning international communication policy. Through international communication conferences, it also coordinates U.S. telecommunications and information policy with that of other nations.

6.   Index Terms: Development Issues; Environmental Issues, Global; International Economics—International Trade

See also entries A8, A10, G6, and K29

---

# K8   Congress

1.a.  The Capitol
Washington, D.C. 20510
(202) 224-3121

b.  The Senate and House of Representatives galleries, as well as most committee hearings, are open to the public. Visitors should call on their senators or congressmen to obtain gallery passes for the respective chambers; seating at hearings is available on a first come first served basis.

2.   Both houses of Congress are normally in session throughout the year, with periodic recesses intervening. Congressional committees and subcommittees seldom adhere to a formal fixed schedule in holding meetings and hearings. Those committees and subcommittees with jurisdiction over international matters are listed below. Committee staff members are usually willing to confer with private researchers. Announcements of forthcoming committee activities—including locations and subject matter—appear in the "Daily Digest" section of the *Congressional Record*. In addition, the *Washington Post* publishes each morning a schedule of that day's congressional activities.

The Congressional Research Service (entry K9) serves as the principal research arm of Congress. International affairs specialists in its Foreign Affairs and National Defense Division can provide information on recent or forthcoming congressional activities pertaining to international affairs.

3.   The Library of Congress is discussed in entry A29, House of Representatives Library in A21, Sen-

ate Library in A42, and Senate Historical Office in K35.

5. Congressional proceedings are published in the *Congressional Record,* issued daily when Congress is in session. A permanent bound edition of the *Record* is also published. University Microfilms International (Ann Arbor, Mich.) publishes the *Congressional Record* in microfiche, with histories of bills and resolutions, and a daily digest. Each house also publishes a journal at the end of each session. Other publications of interest are the Senate Foreign Relations Committee's occasional compilation on legislation on foreign relations; House and Senate hearings on foreign aid authorization (titles vary); foreign aid appropriations (titles vary); Department of State appropriations; and the series of *Required Reports to Congress in the Foreign Affairs Field.* Transcripts of hearings, special reports, and other documents produced by the various committees and subcommittees of Congress are available from the committees. Some of these publications may be purchased from the Superintendent of Documents, U.S. Government Printing Office (GPO) (see Appendix III). Several—although not all—committees maintain mailing lists, and scholars or researchers may request to have their names included on these lists. The GPO also occasionally prepares subject bibliographies of congressional publications on foreign affairs, U.S. intelligence activities, and other topics. Lists of these bibliographies, and the bibliographies themselves, are available without charge.

The committees listed below have the jurisdictional and functional responsibilities indicated. This is a selective list and only the more important committees, from the viewpoint of international scholars, appear in it. No attempt has been made to name the various subcommittees that have more specific spheres of responsibility. A variety of activities of the committees are worthy of the researcher's attention. They hold meetings at least once a month, which are generally open to the public; they convene hearings annually, which are open to the public in most cases. Hearings especially produce a wealth of oral and written testimony, which can be of considerable value to international affairs specialists.

## STANDING COMMITTEES OF THE SENATE

### Foreign Relations Committee
Dirksen Senate Office Building (SOB), Room 450

Jesse Helms, Chair
(202) 224-4651

Specializing in matters relating to all U.S. treaties and agreements with foreign countries, this committee deals with international issues through its subcommittees: International Operations (Olympia Snowe, chair, 202/224-5344); Western Hemisphere and the Peace Corps (Paul Coverdell, Christopher Dodd, chair, 202/224-3643); and International Economic Policy, Export and Trade Promotion (Fred Thompson, chair, 202/224-4944).

### Appropriations Committee
The Capitol, Room S-128

Mark Hatfield, Chair
(202) 224-3471

This important committee has jurisdiction over funding of all government programs. Of particular interest to the international affairs scholar are the subcommittees on defense (Ted Stevens, chair, 202/224-3004) and foreign operations (Mitch McConnell, chair, 202/224-2541).

### Armed Services Committee
Russell SOB, Room 228

Strom Thurmond, Chair
(202) 224-3871

This committee has jurisdiction over matters relating to the national military establishment such as research and development, multilateral operations, and arms control. Subcommittees include Seapower (William S. Cohen, chair, 202/224-2523); Airland Forces (John Warner, chair, 202/224-2023); Readiness (John McCain, chair, 202/224-2235); Strategic Forces (Trent Lott, chair, 202/224-6253); and Acquisition and Technology (Robert C. Smith, chair, 202/224-2841).

### Banking, Housing, and Urban Affairs Committee
Dirksen SOB, Room 534

Alfonse D'Amato, Chair
(202) 224-7391

Of special interest are the activities of the Subcommittee on International Finance (Christopher S. Bond, chair, 202/224-5721) relating to international economic affairs and their effect on U.S. monetary policy, credit and financial institutions, economic growth, and urban affairs.

### Finance Committee
Dirksen SOB, Room 205

Bob Packwood, Chair
(202) 224-4515

This committee has jurisdiction over revenue and tax matters. The Subcommittee on International Trade (Charles E. Grassley, chair, 202/224-3744) is concerned with international issues such as customs, tariffs, and import quotas.

### Commerce, Science, and Transportation Committee
Dirksen SOB, Room 508

Larry Pressler, Chair
(202) 224-5115

This committee is concerned with foreign commerce, science, transportation, communication, and transfer of technology to developing countries.

### Judiciary Committee
Dirksen SOB, Room 224

Orrin Hatch, Chair
(202) 224-5225

Responsibilities of this committee include refugees, escapees, immigration and naturalization, intellectual property rights, and espionage.

## STANDING COMMITTEES OF THE HOUSE OF REPRESENTATIVES

### Committee on Appropriations
The Capitol, Room H-218

Robert L. Livingston, Chair
(202) 225-2771

*Subcommittee on Defense*
The Capitol, Room H-144
C.W. Bill Young, Chair
(202) 225-2847

*Subcommittee on Foreign Operations, Export Financing, and Related Programs*
The Capitol, Room H-307
Sonny Callahan, Chair
(202) 225-2041

### Committee on National Security
Rayburn HOB, Room 2120

Floyd D. Spence, Chair
(202) 225-4151

### Committee on Banking, Finance, and Urban Affairs
Rayburn HOB, Room 2129

Jim Leach, Chair
(202) 225-7502

*Subcommittee on Domestic and International Monetary Policy*
Rayburn HOB, Room B304
Michael N. Castle, Chair
(202) 225-5931

### Committee on Commerce
Rayburn HOB, Room 2125

Thomas J. Bliley, Chair
(202) 225-2927

### Committee on International Relations
Rayburn HOB, Room 2170

Benjamin A. Gilman, Chair
(202) 225-5021

*Subcommittee on International Economic Policy and Trade*
Rayburn HOB, Room 2234
Toby Roth, Chair
(202) 225-5665

*Subcommittee on International Operations and Human Rights*
Rayburn HOB, Room 2353
Christopher R. Smith, Chair
(202) 225-3765

### Committee on the Judiciary
Rayburn HOB, Room 2138

Henry J. Hyde, Chair
(202) 225-3951

*Subcommittee on Immigration and Claims*
Rayburn HOB, Room B-370B
Lamar Smith, Chair
(202) 225-5727

### Committee on Science
Rayburn HOB, Room 2320

Robert S. Walker, Chair
(202) 225-6371

### Committee on Ways and Means
Longworth HOB, Room 1102

Bill Archer, Chair
(202) 225-3625

## JOINT COMMITTEES OF CONGRESS

### Joint Economic Committee
Dirksen SOB, Room G-01

Sen. Connie Mack, Chair
Rep. H. James Saxton, Vice-Chair
(202) 224-5171

*Note:* Various select and special committees of the House and Senate—notably the House's Permanent Select Committee on Intelligence (202/225-4121) and the Senate's Select Committee on Intelligence (202/224-1700)—focus on subjects with an international slant. Lists of standing and select committee members of both houses are available on request. There are also numerous joint commissions and groups that gather information and generally provide a supporting role in congressional activities. Particularly relevant are the Commission on Security and Cooperation in Europe (Christopher H. Smith and Steny Hoyer, cochairs, 202/225-1901), which monitors compliance with the Helsinki Accords, especially regarding human rights; and the Arms Control and Foreign Policy Caucus (M12).

See also the selected list of congressional publications in the Government Printing Office's subject bibliography for foreign affairs (see Appendix III). The *Official Congressional Directory,* published annually by the GPO, and the annual *Congressional Staff Directory* (publisher varies) provide details on committee members and staffs.

6.   Index Terms: Arms Control; Development Issues; Foreign Policy; Human Rights; Intelligence; International Economics; International Law; International Organizations; Military Spending; Regional Conflict; Terrorism

See also entries A29, A21, A42, K9, and K35

## K9   Congressional Research Service (CRS)

1.a.   Library of Congress
James Madison Building
Independence Avenue, SE, between 1st and 2nd Streets
Washington, D.C. 20540
(202) 707-5775

b.   Not open to the public.

c.   Joseph E. Ross, Director

2.   The CRS provides reference, research, and policy analysis to members of Congress and congressional committees. Specialists in the Foreign Affairs and National Defense Division prepare research reports, background studies, and other materials on foreign policy issues of current concern in Congress.

Their reference and research services are not available to the public.

3.   See Library of Congress, entry A29.

4.   CRS research products are considered to be the property of the congressional member or committee that requested them. They are normally available to private researchers only from the office of a member or committee of Congress. Periodically, CRS research studies are read into the *Congressional Record* or published in a congressional committee report.

5.   CRS Issue Briefs review major policy topics, summarize the pertinent legislative history, and provide bibliographies for further reading. They are distributed only to members of Congress. For copies of these publications, researchers should contact the office of one of their congressional representatives. CRS also publishes a bimonthly journal, *The CRS Review.* Researchers may subscribe to it through the Government Printing Office (see Appendix III). In addition, the CRS indexes recent periodical articles on public policy issues (including foreign affairs, by country) from some 3,000 U.S. and foreign journals. This "Bibliographic Citation" file is accessible to researchers in machine-readable format through the Library of Congress' SCORPIO automated database (A29).

### FOREIGN AFFAIRS AND NATIONAL DEFENSE

Charlotte P. Peece, Chief
(202) 707-5064

This division is the best starting point for scholars in international relations looking for research help from CRS. Although specialists only provide research at the request of a member of Congress, they are generally willing to answer a few queries over the phone. John Collins (202/707-7618) is the specialist for international affairs, especially issues relating to national defense. For international security policy questions contact Stanley Sloan (202/707-1011). Analysts also tackle humanitarian issues. Larry Knolls is the analyst for U.S. foreign assistance questions (202/707-5064) and Lois McHugh (202/707-5064) handles refugee research. Research pertaining to international economics is done jointly with the economics division. The specialist who handles the foreign affairs division's end is Ray Hern (202/707-7629).

6.   Index Terms: Defense Policy, National; Development Issues; Foreign Policy; International Economics; Regional Conflict

See also entries A29 and K8

## KIO  Defense Department (DOD)

1.a.  The Pentagon
Washington, D.C. 20301
(703) 697-9312 (Public Affairs)
(703) 697-1180 (Freedom of Information)
Fax: (703) 695-1149 (Public Affairs)

b.  The Pentagon is closed to anyone without appropriate security clearance; an appointment is required.

2.  DOD is responsible for providing forces to protect the security of the United States. The major elements of these forces are the army (K5), navy (including the Marine Corps) (K30), and air force (K3), each forming a department within DOD. Other relevant sections of the department include the Office of the Secretary of Defense, the Chairman of the Joint Chiefs of Staff and the Joint Staff, and several defense agencies. DOD is an enormous and complex department, and a complete listing of all departments and subunits is beyond the scope of this Guide.

Global events are constantly monitored and reviewed by staff specialists, who compile their findings in the form of in-house reports. Some additional research is conducted in the private sector on a contractual basis. Much country-specific information is classified. Researchers may petition for release of reports through the Freedom of Information Act (703/697-1180).

3.  Library and reference facilities are described with the agency units presented below.

4.  Each major subunit of DOD controls its own internal records until they are retired to the jurisdiction of the National Archives (B11). DOD's Directorate for Defense Information, Research, and Distribution Office (703/693-2528) can refer researchers to individual records-control facilities within the department.

A Directorate for Freedom of Information and Security Review (William M. McDonald, Director, 202/697-4325) in the Office of the Assistant Secretary of Defense for Public Affairs processes FOIA requests for the records of the Office of the Secretary of Defense and the Joint Chiefs of Staff; it can direct researchers to appropriate FOIA officers in other DOD subunits, agencies, and services.

5.  There are a few Defense Department publications of primary interest to scholars of international studies. Researchers will find statistical and financial data regarding U.S. military sales and assistance in *Foreign Military Assistance Facts,* issued annually by the Defense Security Assistance Agency, as well as in the *Annual Report to Congress* submitted by the Office of the Secretary. DOD-generated data on other countries' armed forces and U.S. military assistance also appear in the State Department's *Background Notes.* The DOD-funded *Area Handbook* series, which is prepared by the Federal Research Division of the Library of Congress, is available through the government printing office bookstore, see Appendix III.

The Defense Technical Information Center (G7), which is closed to anyone without a security clearance, maintains classified and unclassified reports produced by DOD and its contract researchers. Unclassified research reports are available through the National Technical Information Service (see Appendix III).

### OFFICE OF THE SECRETARY OF DEFENSE (OSD)

(703) 695-5261

This office is of primary interest because the Secretary of Defense, in addition to exercising overall direction and control of the department, is responsible for developing and promulgating policies in support of national security objectives. The OSD also provides the focal point for departmental participation in the U.S. security community and other government activities.

### Public Affairs
Directorate for Public Communication

Harold Heilsnis, Director
(703) 697-5737

Researchers who wish to contact DOD offices or personnel should begin with a telephone call or letter to the Public Affairs Office. Staff members can provide general information about DOD, give major policy pronouncements, and identify divisions and individuals who are able to further assist the researcher. The office provides unclassified information about defense policy, programs, and activities.

### American Forces Information Service (AFIS)

*Current News Analysis and Research Services*
Herbert J. Coleman, Chief
(703) 695-2884

In order to access materials housed in this department researchers must write to the chief outlining the precise nature and purpose of their inquiry. Once on-site, they will find 4 to 5 million unindexed documents dating back to the early 1950s, 300 magazines, 60 current newspapers, and studies on international affairs generated by between 200 and 300 think tanks. Many items pertain to security issues at home and abroad, and are organized first by subject (often country or person) then in chronological order. The division publishes *Current News,* a compilation of newspaper and magazine articles dealing with national and international security affairs, and *Friday Review of Defense Literature,* which presents summaries and reviews of relevant books and studies emerging from publishing houses and think tanks.

## Administration and Management

*Office of the Historian*
Alfred Goldberg, OSD Historian
(703) 697-4216

The OSD Historian's Office prepares historical studies of the Department of Defense. It maintains a small archive of retired DOD documents and a reference file of unclassified materials (legislative records, DOD publications, press clippings, etc.) relating to the structural evolution of the department, its subagencies, and related military services. The office may be visited by outside researchers with an appointment. The staff can provide a variety of reference- and research-assistance services.

The Historian's Office is preparing for publication several historical studies, including a multivolume history of the Office of the Secretary of Defense. Two volumes covering the years 1940–53 are already in print; three additional volumes covering the years 1953–65 are due out soon.

## OFFICE OF THE UNDER SECRETARY, POLICY

Walter B. Slocombe, Under Secretary
(703) 697-5136

### International Security Policy
Ashton B. Carter, Assistant Secretary
(703) 695-0942
Fax: (703) 693-9146

The Cooperative Threat Reduction (703/697-0030) and the Counter Proliferation Policy (703/697-6963) divisions monitor global conditions and formulate U.S. arms control policy in reference to them. The Cooperative Threat Reduction division is charged, specifically, with creating policies for verifying arms reductions. Some of the Counter Proliferation Policy division's specific duties include developing policies concerning multilateral arms control negotiations and European security.

Forces Policy (703/695-5553) divisions formulate strategy, forces, and operational policies for U.S. nu-

clear forces and for space—advanced technology policy.

### International Security Affairs (ISA)
Joseph S. Nye Jr., Assistant Secretary
(703) 695-4351

Regional desk officers are the researcher's best contact-point in DOD. They monitor political-military and economic affairs in specific regions of the world and draft policy papers for the Secretary of Defense on issues such as U.S. military assistance and arms sales. The regional offices are Asian and Pacific Affairs (703/695-4175), European and NATO Affairs (703/697-7207), Inter-American Affairs (703/697-5884), and Middle East and African Affairs (703/697-1355). Staff members will confer with researchers and provide them with access to unclassified U.S. military assistance advisory program (MAAP) data.

Virtually all of the internal policy papers of the regional offices remain classified. ISA's external research program, however, contracts defense studies through private research centers. Unclassified contract-research studies may be made available to researchers.

The best contact-point for researchers interested in DOD's policy pertaining to human rights is the Foreign Civil Military Affairs division (703/693-2046).

### Special Operations and Low-Intensity Conflict (SO/LIC)
H. Allen Holmes, Assistant Secretary
(703) 693-2895

This office exercises overall supervision (including oversight of policy and resources) of all Special Operation (SO) and Low-intensity Conflict (LIC) activities within DOD. SO/LIC also develops and coordinates DOD implementation of drug control policy and the DOD counter-drug mission. It also directs DOD policy with respect to humanitarian assistance, refugees, and disaster relief.

### Strategy, Requirements, and Resources
Edward L. Warner III, Assistant Secretary
(703) 697-7728

This division develops U.S. defense strategy and national force requirements and assists in identification of capabilities required to underwrite the defense strategy. It issues the Defense Planning Guide (DPG) and ensures DPG priorities are implemented by the military departments and defense agencies. It issues the Contingency Planning Guidance, reviews contingency plans, and develops DOD policy on peace operations.

## DEFENSE INTELLIGENCE AGENCY (DIA)

James R. Clapper Jr., Director
(703) 695-7353

DIA coordinates the foreign military intelligence-gathering activities of the U.S. armed forces' three intelligence services: the Army's Deputy Chief of Staff for Intelligence, the Office of Naval Intelligence, and the Air Force Intelligence Agency. DIA monitors daily military developments throughout the world, including international tensions, political interventions, and arms purchases. Defense attachés from U.S. embassies, representing the three services provide DIA analysts with information on the world's armed forces, including their military capabilities, number of personnel, order of battle, deployments, equipment, and political roles, as well as biographic data on leading members of the officer corps. Attaché reports remain classified.

Occasionally, scholars are allowed to discuss unclassified topics with DIA experts. Interested scholars should begin by calling the Academic Liaison Staff (202/373-4525). The library (202/373-3836) is closed to outside researchers, but unclassified materials may be obtained through standard interlibrary loan procedures.

DOD is the major repository for the intelligence and mapping aerial photography film taken by the army, navy, and air force. Although the majority of the collection is classified, a fairly large amount of unclassified imagery dating back to World War II has been turned over to the National Archives (B11). Scholars desiring aerial photography of a foreign area should begin their search at the Cartographic and Architectural Branch of NARA, particularly for earlier date coverage. In some instances, if the film has been declassified and is no longer required for official business, DIA will release it to NARA to satisfy a researcher's request. Because of the sensitivity of this collection, no public list of the film coverage is available. An important book, based in part on this collection and written by a former employee of the agency, is Roy M. Stanley's *World War II Photo Intelligence* (New York: Charles Scribner's Sons, 1981).

The DIA Historical Program (Deane J. Allen, Historian, 202/373-4934) was formulated to identify, collect, preserve, and record information of historical significance concerning the agency and its relationship to defense intelligence matters.

## NATIONAL SECURITY AGENCY/CENTRAL SECURITY SERVICE (NSA/CSS)

Fort George G. Meade, Md. 20755-6000
(301) 688-6524 (Public Affairs)

One of the big three of the U.S. intelligence community (along with CIA and DIA), NSA/CSS is an intelligence gathering unit of the Defense Department that conducts technical communications surveillance worldwide. It is far more secretive than other U.S. intelligence agencies, to the point that the agency's very existence was not officially acknowledged until recently. NSA still supplies a minuscule amount of information about itself. The library is considered a strictly internal research facility. Scholars may, however, be able to access unclassified library holdings through standard interlibrary loan procedures. For a discussion of the National Security Archive see entry B12.

## DEFENSE SECURITY ASSISTANCE AGENCY (DSAA)

Thomas Rhame, Director
(703) 604-6604
Fax: (703) 604-6544

**Operations Directorate**
Edward Ross, Director
(703) 604-6640

The two regional divisions in the directorate (Europe/Pacific, 703/604-6609 and Middle East/Africa/Americas, 703/604-6623) administer DSAA operations in their respective areas of the world. Although primarily involved in foreign military sales, DSAA oversees DOD's International Military Education Training program (IMET) and aids foreign governments in military construction projects. Statistical and financial data relating to U.S. military assistance programs and arms sales are regularly published in *Foreign Military Sales and Military Assistance Facts,* an unclassified DOD publication that provides annual and cumulative statistics on a country-by-country, and in some cases, region-by-region basis. Researchers may receive copies of this publication by contacting the Management Division (703/604-6635).

## JOINT CHIEFS OF STAFF (JCS)

Office of the Chairman
(703) 697-9121

**Joint History Office**
David A. Armstrong, Director
(703) 695-2114

The JCS Historical Division prepares JCS histories and special background studies. A majority of its products are classified, although most volumes dealing with the JCS up to the 1950s have been declassified and released to the National Archives and Records Administration (entry B11). In addition to providing reference assistance on the history of the Joint Chiefs of Staff, the staff can assist researchers in identifying and locating JCS documents.

**Strategic Plans and Policy Directorate**
Lt. Gen. Barry R. McCaffrey, USA, Director
(703) 695-5618

*International Negotiations*
Maj. Gen. David W. McIlvoy, USAF, Deputy Director
(703) 695-5903

The Conventional/Missile Defense Arms Control (703/695-6011), Nuclear Arms Control (703/695-9148), and Weapons Technology Control (703/695-6626) divisions prepare policy papers for the Joint Chiefs of Staff concerning reduction of the world's conventional and nuclear arms. The work done here is classified.

*Politico-Military Affairs*
Rear Adm. Frank L. Bowman, USN, Deputy Director
(703) 697-8591

The regional divisions (Asia/Pacific, 703/695-8134; European, 703/614-9420; Middle East/Africa, 703/614-9405; Western Hemisphere, 703/697-5449) prepare policy papers and estimates for the Joint Chiefs of Staff relating to U.S. security interests, security assistance, and military relations with countries throughout the world. Its products are all classified.

**Office of the Secretary of the Joint Chiefs of Staff**
(703) 697-2700

*Documents Division*
Edmund F. McBride, Chief
(703) 695-5363

The Documents Division is responsible for maintaining the official records of the Joint Chiefs of Staff. After 20 years, many JCS documents and internal records are declassified and transferred to the National Archives and Records Administration (B11). In some cases the division also processes Freedom of Information Act requests involving JCS material.

**NATIONAL DEFENSE UNIVERSITY (NDU)**

Fort Lesley J. McNair
4th and P Streets, SW, Bldg. 62
Washington, D.C. 20319-6000

(202) 287-9406 (Office of Chief of Staff)
Lt. Gen. Ervin J. Rokke, USAF, President

The NDU is a senior-level, joint educational institution operating under the direction of the Joint Chiefs of Staff. The Office of the President, the University Directorates, the Industrial College of the Armed Forces (ICAF), the National War College (NWC), and the Armed Forces Staff College (AFSC) are the major components of NDU.

**National War College (NWC)**
Gerald P. Stadler, Commandant
(202) 475-1776

The National War College is the only senior-service college in the military educational system that is dedicated to the study of national security policy formulation and the planning and implementation of national strategy. It offers a 10-month program on national security formulation to 160 specially selected midcareer civil servants and military officers. The core curriculum includes seminars on global issues, regional politics, military strategy, and military issues. Students may also take as an elective yearlong courses on U.S. national security issues in different regions of the world (e.g., Latin America, the Middle East).

Most lectures and seminars are presented by government and academic specialists invited by the college. Annual region-specific course guides and syllabuses may be obtained from the National War College Chief of Staff (202/475-0859) or from the directors of the various regional studies programs. Interested outsiders are permitted to attend selected lectures and seminars.

**Industrial College of the Armed Forces (ICAF)**
(202) 475-1832
Ambassador Robert W. Farrand, International Affairs Adviser
(202) 475-1750

The ICAF is the only senior-service college in the military educational system dedicated to the study of management of resources for national security.

**National Defense University Library**
Sarah Michaels, Director
(202) 287-9111
(202) 287-9460 (Reference Desk)

The library is open primarily to the faculty, staff, and students of the National Defense University. With prior permission, outside researchers may gain access to the library from 7:00 A.M.–5:30 P.M. Monday–Friday. Visitors must sign in at the entrance. The collection consists largely of current imprints in

English on history, economics, politics, and international relations. Included are studies by the Brookings Institution (H8), Rand Corporation (H65), and some classified government reports. The library also participates in interlibrary loan and the OCLC database. For more information on the National Defense University library see entry A33.

**Research Directorate**
Frederick Kiley, Director of Research
(202) 475-0948

The Research Directorate provides one-year fellowships without stipend to government and military personnel who wish to conduct independent research on national security policy formulation, military strategy, and civil-military affairs. Proposals from individuals not employed by the government are also considered. Researchers receive study space, typing services, and (sometimes) assistance in publishing research carried out while at the directorate.

A list of NDU publications for sale is available upon request.

6.   Index Terms: Arms Control; Collective Security; Defense Policy, National; Deterrence; Humanitarian Issues; Intelligence; Low Intensity Conflict; Military History; Military Science; Naval Science; Peacekeeping; Proliferation; Terrorism

See also entries D1, F8, G7, K3, K5, and K30

---

## KII   Education Department

1.a.   400 Maryland Avenue, SW
Washington, D.C. 20202
(202) 401-1576 (Public Information)
(202) 708-9263 (Freedom of Information)

b.   Open to the public.

2.   This department is the cabinet-level agency that administers, coordinates, and establishes policy for most federal assistance to education. A number of its programs were, however, transferred to the U.S. Information Agency (K41) in the mid-1980s.

3.   The department's Education Research Library is described in entry A11.

5.   A list of publications of the Education Department is available upon request.

**OFFICE OF COMMUNICATIONS AND PUBLIC AFFAIRS**

Kay Kahler, Director
(202) 401-3026

The Editorial Policy Division (202/401-3550) can supply a complete listing of titles issued by the agency. For Freedom of Information Act requests telephone (202) 708-9263.

**CENTER FOR INTERNATIONAL EDUCATION (CIE)**

470 L'Enfant Plaza East, SW
Washington, D.C. 20202

Mail:
Federal Office Bldg. 6
400 Maryland Ave, SW
Washington, D.C. 20202
(202) 732-6065

Richard D. Scarfo, Director

The center is responsible for administering foreign language and area studies scholarships. An international studies specialist (Ralph Hines, 202/732-6067) assists in answering questions concerning international education issues. A senior international visitors program specialist (Karen Wenk 202/708-8815) is part of a staff that plans itineraries and provides educational counseling for visiting foreign educators who are not on U.S. government grants. The staff also arranges appointments for individual foreign educators who wish to consult with specialists working for the Education Department. The Center for International Education is divided into two branches.

**Advanced Training and Research Branch**
John Paul, Chief
(202) 732-6067

Launched after Sputnik and originally designed to encourage the study of less commonly known languages, this branch now allocates funds to institutions of higher education, consortia, and academic libraries so that they may establish, strengthen, and operate national resource centers that focus on a single region of the world or on specific global topics. These centers in turn provide instruction in the languages of their area of expertise, as well as in other disciplines, and conduct research in their specialty or area of responsibility. Most of these programs concentrate on the developing countries, Eastern Europe, and Russia and the other successor states of the former Soviet Union.

Additional grants offered by the Advanced Training and Research Branch include the Foreign Language and Area Studies (FLAS) Fellowship Program, which offers academic year and summer awards for graduate students in foreign language studies, area studies, and international studies. The Undergraduate International Studies and Foreign Language Program awards are granted to an institution of higher education or a combination of such bodies to plan, develop, and carry out a comprehensive undertaking designed to strengthen and improve undergraduate instruction in international studies and foreign languages. The Doctoral Dissertation Research Abroad Grant provides assistance for graduate students engaged within a foreign country in full-time Ph.D. dissertation research pertaining to modern language and area studies. The Faculty Research Abroad Program is designed to assist colleges and universities in strengthening their foreign language and area studies instruction by enabling faculty members to obtain relevant expertise through research outside the United States.

**International Studies Branch**
Ralph Hines, Chief
(202) 732-6066

This branch offers the Business and International Education Program, which is designed to provide matching grants to colleges and universities. The object is to foster links between colleges and universities and components of the U.S. business community that are engaged in international economic activity. For example, in the past universities have received grants to create information centers that generate information for the public on business conditions in particular regions of the world, or to conduct seminars on business conditions in other countries.

The Group Projects Abroad Program provides opportunities for U.S. colleges and universities, state departments of education, private nonprofit instructional organizations, or various combinations of these to conduct joint projects overseas. The Special Bilateral Projects/Seminars Abroad Program enables U.S. high school teachers and administrators, supervisors and curriculum directors of school districts, local and state education agencies, and university faculty to participate in short-term seminars overseas on topics that focus on history, culture, and language of participating foreign countries.

**NATIONAL CENTER FOR EDUCATION STATISTICS (NCES)**

555 New Jersey Avenue, NW, Room 400
Washington, D.C. 20208-1405
Fax: (202) 219-1736

Emerson Elliot, Commissioner
(202) 219-1828

The NCES gathers, analyzes, and disseminates data on U.S. and foreign education programs. Researchers should contact the Indicators and Reports Branch (202/219-2252) for information relating to any country other than the United States.

6.    Index Terms: Development Issues—Education; Transnationalism

See also entry A11

---

## KI2    Energy Department (DOE)

1.a.  Forrestal Building
       1000 Independence Avenue, SW
       Washington, D.C. 20585
       (202) 586-6827 (Public Information)
       (202) 586-5955 (Freedom of Information)
       Fax: 586-5049

b. DOE is open to the public; researchers should make appointments. Some files and documents in offices listed below are classified. Scholars should direct questions regarding Freedom of Information Act procedures to P. J. Paradise (202/586-5955), Chief, Freedom of Information and Privacy Acts.

2.    The department was established in 1977 to coordinate and administer energy research, analysis, and planning for the federal government. DOE oversees programs in energy production, use, conservation, and other areas relating to nuclear weapons. The department is involved in defense-related projects that include verification of international arms control agreements and regulation of sensitive technological transfers.

3.    The Energy Department Library is described in entry A12, and the Energy Department Archives is described in entry B5.

4.    DOE does not maintain a central records management division; each office retains its own files. Many technical reports, journals, and a sampling of department publications are located in the Freedom of Information Reading Room (202/586-3284). Regardless of whether items are classified, researchers should contact the Freedom of Information and Privacy Activities Division (202/586-5955) when trying to locate agency materials.

5.    Publications are described with the issuing bodies described below.

## ENERGY INFORMATION ADMINISTRATION (EIA)

Jay E. Hakes, Administrator
(202) 586-1441

The EIA, the primary data-gathering element in DOE, is responsible for all data collection and data processing.

### Energy Markets and Contingency Information Division

Arthur T. Andersen, Director
(202) 586-1441

*International Statistics Branch*
Louis D. De Mouy, Chief
(202) 586-6557

The branch maintains an extensive and growing collection of foreign language publications on virtually all aspects of energy throughout the world, including government statistics and energy accounts, the reports of power companies and commissions, and development corporation reports. This specialized collection, which may be one of the most comprehensive in existence, is filed by country and energy commodity. It may be consulted by private researchers.

The branch supplies international energy data (production, consumption, capacity, trade, etc.) to other DOE units and prepares energy-statistics surveys of foreign countries (including one on Brazil).

### Energy Demand and Integration Division

*International Economic and Integrated Forecasting Branch*
Gerald E. Peabody, Chief
(202) 586-1142

The branch is involved in econometric forecasting and modeling. Its computer files include United Nations data on world energy consumption (1950–87) and DOE nuclear facility profiles, both broken down by country. Computer printouts will be supplied to researchers upon request.

*National Energy Information Center (NEIC)*
Sandra R. Wilkins, Branch Chief
(202) 586-1185

As part of its mission, the NEIC provides energy information and referral assistance to federal, state, and local governments, the academic community, business and industrial organizations, and the general public. NEIC publishes *Commercial Nuclear Power: Prospects for the U.S. and the World* (an-

nual), the *International Energy Annual, International Energy Outlook* (annual), *International Oil and Gas Exploration and Development Activities* (quarterly), *International Petroleum Annual* (containing data on oil production, trade, consumption, and prices, by country), and *Monthly Energy Review* with international statistics based on published CIA data. To order publications call (202) 586-1174 or write to National Energy Information Center, Energy Information Administration, U.S. Department of Energy, IF-048 Forrestal Building, Washington, D.C. 20585.

## ASSISTANT SECRETARY FOR POLICY, PLANNING, AND PROGRAM EVALUATION

### Office of International Affairs
1000 Independence Avenue, SW
Washington, D.C. 20585

Richard Williamson, Deputy Assistant Secretary
(202) 586-5493

This office monitors global energy supplies. Concerned with assuring adequate resources for U.S. needs, it coordinates relevant multinational programs and consults with foreign governments and international organizations on matters affecting the availability of energy resources.

### International Energy Organization and Policy Development Division
Robert S. Price, Jr., Director
(202) 586-6383

The office is responsible for ensuring that U.S. international energy policies and programs conform to national goals, legislation, and treaty obligations. To this end, the division coordinates U.S. participation in multilateral and bilateral organizations.

### International Research and Development Policy Office
Harold Jaffe, Director
(202) 586-6770

International cooperative energy research and development activities with foreign countries are conducted by this office. Jointly with the National Science Foundation (K27), the office conducts a research project examining the collaboration of countries on energy-related scientific and technological issues. The office is also concerned with questions relating to fossil energy. Scientific and technical reports resulting from these activities can be requested through this office.

**Non-Proliferation and National Security Office**

John G. Keliher, Director

(202) 586-0645

This office is primarily concerned with nonproliferation issues, such as giving technical and analytical support for monitoring nonproliferation treaties and intelligence support for dealing with nuclear weapons and materials. It works with other security agencies (such as the FBI, NSC, ACDA, and DOD) on counter-terrorism policy.

6. Index Terms: Energy; Intelligence; Proliferation; Terrorism

See also entries A12 and B5

---

## K13   Environmental Protection Agency (EPA)

---

1.a. Waterside Mall West Tower
401 M Street, SW
Washington, D.C. 20460
(202) 260-2080 (Public Information)
(202) 260-4048 (Freedom of Information/Privacy Act)

b. Open to the public. Appointments are recommended.

c. Carol Browner, Administrator
(202) 260-4700

2. The EPA is responsible for executing federal laws protecting the environment. Established in 1970, with the merger of 15 components from 5 executive departments and independent agencies into 1 autonomous entity, its mission is to control and abate pollution in the areas of air, water, solid waste, pesticides, radiation, and toxic substances. The telephone number of the Contracts Management Division is (513) 366-2002. The Freedom of Information Office can be reached at (202) 260-4048.

**ASSISTANT ADMINISTRATOR FOR INTERNATIONAL ACTIVITIES**

Alan Hecht, Assistant Administrator
(202) 260-4870

Jamison Koehler, Acting Director International Cooperation Division
(202) 260-4875

International activities of EPA administered by this office are designed to promote cooperation in the investigation and alleviation of long-range environmental pollutants. While pursuing this goal, the agency maintains contact and exchanges information with scientists and policymakers from other countries and international organizations. One of the main international organizations the EPA works with is the United Nations Environment Programme (UNEP) (202/289-8456). The EPA, along with U.S. business and industry and nongovernmental organizations, engages in policy and program activities with UNEP in support of environmental-developmental policies and activities.

The EPA's International Activities Office coordinates various other U.S. bilateral environmental programs and agreements. The developing countries staff (202/260-0797) in this office maintains a collection of information on international environmental conditions (including reports from EPA's counterparts worldwide), national environmental legislation, and materials from the World Health Organization and international conferences. The files, which are arranged by country, will be made available to private researchers.

3. The EPA Headquarters Library (202/260-5922) houses 12,000 books; 800 current journals, abstracts, indexes, newsletters, and newspapers; 21,000 hardcopy documents and technical reports; and 300,000 documents on microfiche. Subject areas include water pollution, water quality, water supply, air pollution, noise abatement, radiation, hazardous wastes, solid waste management, resource recovery, pesticides, chemistry, and toxicology. The library is open from 10:00 A.M.–2:00 P.M. Monday–Friday. Photocopy machines and microform reader-printers are available to patrons for photocopying up to 25 pages of literature not covered by copyright. The library has computer access to CAS On-line, Dialog, National Groundwater Information Center Database, National Library of Medicine database, NewsNet, and NEXIS.

The EPA Law Library (202/260-5919) contains approximately 7,000 volumes. The focus of the collection is federal law, with emphasis on environmental legislation. Computer search services are JURIS and LEXIS. The Law Library is open 8:00 A.M.–5:00 P.M. Monday–Friday. Copying privileges are extended to agency employees only.

The Chemical Library (202/260-3944) is open 8:30 A.M.–4:30 P.M. Monday–Friday. Most of its 5,000 books, 300 serial titles, and 3,000 reports cover projects supported by the Office of Toxic Substances (OTS) and the Office of Pesticide Programs (OPP) and related to international developments in chemical substance control and regulation. There is a microfiche file of 130,000 articles. Collection coverage includes toxicology, chemistry, cancer, genetics, teratology, biotechnology, and ecological effects of commercial and industrial chemicals. The library has computer access to BRS, CAS On-line, CIS, Dialog, Global, National Library of Medicine, Orbit, and Super Handbook.

5.　A monthly publication on EPA overseas activities, *Summaries of Foreign Government Environment Reports,* is distributed by the National Technical Information Service (NTIS) (K29 and Appendix III) as is the two-volume *EPA Cumulative Bibliography, 1970–1975.* Other publications include the annual *EPA Research Program Guide,* which lists all EPA-funded projects; the bimonthly *EPA Journal,* available from the Government Printing Office (see Appendix III) by subscription; and the *Monthly Accession List,* which is compiled for internal use. For information concerning EPA publications contact the EPA Public Information Center (202/260-2080).

6.　Index Terms: Environmental Issues, Global; International Law; International Organizations

---

## KI4　Export-Import Bank of the United States (Eximbank)

---

1.a.　811 Vermont Avenue, NW
　　　Washington, D.C. 20571
　　　(202) 566-8990 (Information)
　　　(202) 566-8910 (Freedom of Information)
　　　Fax: (202) 566-7524

　b.　Open to the public. Internal records restricted.

　c.　Kenneth D. Brody, President and Chair
(202) 566-8144

2.　Eximbank extends loans and credit to foreign borrowers to assist them in financing purchases of U.S. goods and services. Country loan officers and international economists in the international lending division (202/566-5038) maintain loan project files and prepare country and regional studies of credit worthiness and economic conditions. Loan records and country assessments are confidential, but staff members will discuss general questions with scholars.

　In addition, the bank's policy and planning staff prepares research studies—from a global rather than a regional perspective—on international economic developments that may have an impact on Eximbank and its programs. Research areas include

methodologies for country analysis and review of bank programs, export financing patterns and programs in the United States and other industrialized nations, trends in individual industries and commodities worldwide, international and domestic capital market development, and fluctuations in interest rates, prices, and other economic indicators. These studies are confidential. A bibliography is maintained.

3.　The Export-Import Bank Library is discussed in entry A14.

4.　Virtually all of the bank's loan project files, research reports, and other internal records are privileged and confidential. Researchers may gain access to them only through Freedom of Information Act processes. (To date, such efforts have been largely unsuccessful.) For Freedom of Information/Privacy Act requests phone (202) 566-8910.

　Most of Eximbank's internal records, from its inception in 1934 to the present, are under the jurisdiction of the Administration Division (202/566-8111). Records for 1934–67 are being microfiched, after which the originals will be transferred to the National Archives (B11). A computerized index is being developed for records relating to the bank's active loan projects. Contact Carlista D. Robinson, Manager of Records and Communications (202/566-8313), for further information.

5.　Bank publications include an annual report; a semiannual *Report to the U.S. Congress on Export Credit Competition and the Export-Import Bank of the United States;* and a quarterly newsletter, *Eximbank Record.* Copies are available from the Public Affairs Office (202/566-8990).

6.　Index Terms: Development Issues; International Economics—International Finance; International Economics—International Trade

See also entry A14

**Federal Emergency Management Agency Library　See entry A15**

---

## KI5　Federal Reserve System (FRS)

---

1.a.　20th Street and Constitution Avenue, NW
　　　Washington, D.C. 20551
　　　(202) 452-3204 (Public Information)
　　　(202) 452-3684 (Freedom of Information)
　　　Fax: (202) 452-3819

b. Appointments are necessary. Tours are available.

c. Alan Greenspan, Chairman

2.   The Federal Reserve System is the central bank of the United States. Its International Finance Division (202/452-3614) monitors international economic matters—including foreign exchange operations, changes in the structure of U.S. international transactions, and economic and financial development abroad—that may affect U.S. monetary policy. Staff economists in the division's seven sections compile data (largely from other U.S. government sources and foreign central banks) and prepare policy analyses and research reports, some of which are distributed to the public (see point 5 below) and some of which are for internal use only (see point 4 below).

   The International Development Section (202/452-3308) has specialists who focus on economic/financial problems and policies in the developing countries. The section is probably the internationalist's best contact-point within the division, although other sections may periodically focus on economic affairs from a global perspective. The International Banking Section (202/452-3533) monitors the foreign activities of U.S. banks and analyzes international banking flows and their impact on money and credit markets. The U.S. International Transactions Section (202/452-3426) deals with international trade and capital movements and their influence on the U.S. economy. The Financial Markets Section (202/452-3712) analyzes the behavior of exchange markets and international money and capital markets. The World Payments and Economic Activity Section (202/452-3308) examines economic trends and policies in the industrial nations (primarily the Group of Ten). The International Trade and Financial Studies Section (202/452-3796) conducts long-range theoretical research on international economic problems. The Quantitative Studies Section (202/452-3796) has responsibility for the development and maintenance of econometric models of the interdependence of the U.S. economy and foreign economies.

   The Division of International Finance employs private economists in various consulting roles. Scholars are frequently invited to lead or participate in staff seminars.

3.   The Research Library of the Board of Governors of the Federal Reserve System is discussed in entry A16.

4.   Division of International Finance research reports, briefing papers, and other internal studies are filed in the division's Information Center, which is closed to private researchers. Copies of these and all other Federal Reserve System internal records are also filed in the system's Records Section. Access to unpublished reports and other internal records, many of which are confidential, is possible only through Freedom of Information Act processes. The board's Freedom of Information office may be reached at (202) 452-3684.

5.   Some Division of International Finance reports and briefing papers are periodically selected for outside circulation and are made available as International Finance Discussion Papers. A bibliography and copies of individual papers may be obtained from the division. To be placed on the mailing list, call (202) 452-3245.

   Statistical releases and articles by division staff members occasionally appear in the Federal Reserve System's monthly *Federal Reserve Bulletin.*

6.   Index Terms: Development Issues; International Economics—International Finance; International Economics—International Trade

See also entry A16

---

## KI6   Foreign Broadcast Information Service (FBIS)

1.a. P.O. Box 2604
     Washington, D.C. 20013
     (202) 338-7835 or 6735

   b. FBIS and Joint Publications Research Service (JPRS) publications are available for subscription.

   c. Robert Schreiner, Director

2.   The FBIS monitors overseas media and publishes translations to government agencies and contractors. These translations (and transcripts) are published Monday–Friday in eight geographically arranged volumes: Central Eurasia, China, East Asia, East Europe, Latin America, Near East and South Asia, Sub-Saharan Africa, and Western Europe.

   JPRS publishes reports on less time-sensitive information from foreign publications. These publications contain political, military, economic, environmental, technological, and sociological news and commentary. Of special interest to the users of this Guide might be the JPRS topical report series on proliferation and terrorism.

4.   Back issues of FBIS's *Daily Report* and JPRS's publications are kept in the Library of Congress, Mi-

croform Reading Room (A29). The Reading Room has *Daily Reports* dating back to 1941 and JPRS publications back to the 1950s. FBIS and JPRS publications are also on file for public reference at many Federal Depository Libraries.

A commercially produced *Index to the FBIS Daily Report* is published monthly with annual compilations by News Bank/Readex, 58 Pine Street, New Canaan, Conn. 06840 (800/243-7694). A monthly index (with annual cumulations) to JPRS translations is available from University Microfilm International, 300 North Zeeb Road, Ann Arbor, Michigan 48106 (313/761-4700). Called UMI TRANSDEX Index, it has keyword, name, and bibliographic listing sections. Neither index is an FBIS-sponsored publication.

5. FBIS *Daily Report* and JPRS publications are available free of charge to U.S. government offices. The National Technical Information Service (see Appendix III) provides subscriptions to *Daily Reports* and JPRS publications to the public.

6. Index Terms: Ethnic and Religious Conflict; Low Intensity Conflict; Proliferation; Refugees; Regional Conflict; Terrorism

---

### KI7 Foreign Claims Settlement Commission of the United States

---

1.a. Bicentennial Building
600 E St, NW, Room 6002
Washington, D.C. 20579
(202) 616-6975
Fax: (202) 616-6993

b. Open to the public.

2. The Foreign Claims Settlement Commission of the United States adjudicates claims by U.S. nationals against foreign governments in cases arising from major foreign nationalizations involving numerous U.S. claimants. Claims involving a single U.S. claimant in a foreign country (e.g. an expropriated corporation) remain under the jurisdiction of the State Department. The claims the commission deals with take basically two forms: presettlement adjudication and postsettlement adjudication. For example, title VII of the 1949 International Claims Settlement Act, enacted in December 1980, established the Vietnam Claims Program as a presettlement adjudication. Under this program 192 awards, for a total of more than $99 million were entered in favor of individuals and corporations whose prop-

erty was expropriated by the Vietnamese Communist regime, which took power in South Vietnam in 1975. No payments on the awards will be made until a lump sum claims settlement agreement is negotiated with Vietnam. An example of a postsettlement adjudication was the Second Czechoslovakia Claims Program, completed in 1985.

3. A small library (202/616-6975) contains bound volumes of the commission's claims decisions since 1950. Included is material relating to Panama, Cuba, Czech Republic, Slovakia, Yugoslavia, and several other European countries, as well as China and Vietnam.

5. The commission publishes an annual report to Congress.

6. Index Terms: International Law

**Government Printing Office (GPO)** See entries in Appendixes I and III

---

### KI8 General Accounting Office (GAO)

---

1.a. 441 G Street, NW
Washington, D.C. 20548
(202) 512-3000
Fax: (202) 512-5505

b. GAO personnel will meet with researchers by appointment.

c. Charles A. Bowsher, Comptroller General
Frank C. Conahan, Assistant Comptroller General, National Security and International Affairs Division

2. The GAO is an independent, nonpolitical congressional agency that has oversight of government spending. The National Security and International Affairs Division (NSIAD) (202/512-2800; fax 202/512-7686) seeks to improve management and accountability of national security, space, and international affairs programs. It has audit jurisdiction over the Departments of Defense and State and the National Aeronautics and Space Administration. NSIAD contains six subdivisions. National Security Analysis (Richard A. Davis, Jess T. Ford, 202/512-3504) is engaged in analyzing threat assessment, force structuring, and cost-effectiveness. Military Operations and Capabilities Issues (Mark E. Gebicke, Norman J. Rabkin, 202/512-5140) assesses operations and capabilities of DOD's forces, weapons systems, and support mechanisms as to

whether they fulfill objectives. Acquisition Policy, Technology, and Competitiveness Issues (David E. Cooper, James F. Wiggins, 202/512-4587) assesses effectiveness of defense-related acquisition policies and programs. Systems Development and Production Issues (Louis J. Rodrigues, Brad Hathaway, Thomas J. Schulz, 202/512-4841) examines individual systems and the budgeting process in the context of the need to modernize under reduced budget constraints. Defense Management and NASA Issues (Donna M. Heivlin, David R. Warren, 202/512-8412) assesses the efficiency of recent management initiatives. International Affairs Issues (Joseph E. Kelley, Harold J. Johnson, Benjamin Nelson, 202/512-4128) assesses how agencies and programs address U.S. policy requirements regarding arms control, nonproliferation, economic cooperation, disaster relief, international military agreements and commitments, and peacekeeping.

3. The GAO Information Services Center has two libraries that are open to the public for on-site use. The Technical Library (Room 7016, 202/512-5180; fax 202/512-3373) and the Law Library (Room 7056, 202/512-2585) together contain approximately 140,000 items. It is a general research collection and does not contain many GAO reports. Library hours are 9:00 A.M.–4:00 P.M. Monday–Friday; Ellen Swain is Manager of Research Services. Interlibrary loan is available to other libraries.

4. In general, the GAO publishes all findings that are nonclassified. Internal records are not accessible to outside researchers. As a congressional agency, the GAO is exempt from the Freedom of Information Act.

5. The GAO publishes roughly 900 reports a year. A monthly list of reports is available. Contact the Document Handling Facility (202/512-6000; fax 202/258-4066) for orders and information.

6. Index Terms: Arms Control; Defense Conversion; Defense Policy, National; Military Spending; Peacekeeping; Proliferation

---

# K19   Health and Human Services Department (HHS)

---

1.a.  200 Independence Avenue, SW
      Washington, D.C. 20201
      (202) 690-7850 (Public Affairs)
      (202) 690-7453 (Freedom of Information/
      Privacy Act)

b. Open to the public. Identification must be presented.

2. HHS strives to protect and advance the well-being and quality of life of residents of the United States. In carrying out its mission, the department engages in many international activities.

3. The National Library of Medicine is described in entry A35.

4. In order to obtain substantive information from certain HHS units, scholars may find it necessary to use Freedom of Information Act procedures (202/690-7453). Selected internal records and publications are described below with their respective bureaus.

5. Publications are discussed under individual units described below.

## PUBLIC HEALTH SERVICE (PHS)

Philip R. Lee, Assistant Secretary for Health
(202) 690-7694

### International and Refugee Health Office
5600 Fishers Lane
Rockville, MS 20857

Linda A. Vogel, Director
(301) 443-1774
Fax: (301) 443-6288

This agency is a policy and program coordination office for international programs of the Public Health Service. The office has oversight responsibility for a number of bilateral agreements for cooperation in the health field (primarily health sciences, but also including aspects of public health and health policy) with other countries. It also provides official liaison on technical matters for the U.S. government with the World Health Organization (L17). The agency maintains a close working relationship with other multilateral agencies (e.g., UNICEF) and cooperates with the Agency for International Development (K1) on health policy issues and the conduct of selected activities in developing countries. An on-site library can be a source of limited information on international health issues.

### National Institutes of Health
9000 Rockville Pike
Bethesda, Md. 20892

Harold E. Varmus, Director
(301) 496-2433

*John E. Fogarty International Center for Advanced Study in the Health Sciences (FIC)*
Philip E. Schambra, Director
(301) 496-1415

The FIC was established within the NIH in 1968 to promote international cooperation in the biomedical sciences and to serve as the organizational focus for NIH international activities. FIC fosters research partnerships between U.S. scientists and foreign counterparts through research and training awards, fellowships, scientist exchange programs, and international agreements.

*Note:* For a discussion of NIH's National Library of Medicine see entry A35.

## SOCIAL SECURITY ADMINISTRATION

### Research and Statistics Office
4301 Connecticut Avenue, NW, Suite 200
Washington, D.C. 20008

Peter Wheeler, Director
(202) 282-7200

The Office of Research and Statistics conducts research pertaining to Social Security and related legislative systems abroad, and prepares the biennial report *Social Security Programs Throughout the World.* The staff also produced a bibliography, *Five Decades of International Social Security Research* (HHS, 1991), which lists Social Security Administration studies written between 1937 and 1990. It covers most countries and is organized by country and subject matter. In addition, comparative international studies prepared by the staff appear in the quarterly *Social Security Bulletin* and in special reports.

Open 9:30 A.M.–5:00 P.M. Monday–Friday, the International Reference Room is available to researchers by appointment (202/282-7270). The room contains a collection of monographs and serials that address such topics as health insurance, economic indicators, social legislation and social policy, and the impact of taxation systems of foreign countries on standards of living overseas. Holdings include publications and fact sheets from the Organization for Economic Cooperation and Development (A39), International Labor Office (L10), International Social Security Association, World Health Organization (L17), and the International Bank for Reconstruction and Development (World Bank) (L8). Vertical files are maintained on a country-by-country basis. There is no interlibrary loan system; photocopying facilities are available.

6. Index Terms: Development Issues—Health

See also entry A35

## K20 Housing and Urban Development (HUD)

1.a. 451 7th Street, SW
Washington, D.C. 20410
(202) 708-0980 (Public Affairs)
(202) 708-3054 (Freedom of Information)

b. Open to the public.

2. HUD was established in 1965 to assist the president in the coordination of programs pertaining to housing and the development of urban, suburban, and metropolitan areas. In addition to domestic issues in these areas, HUD is involved in cooperative programs and projects with foreign countries and international organizations.

### ASSISTANT SECRETARY FOR POLICY DEVELOPMENT AND RESEARCH

Michael A. Stegman, Assistant Secretary
(202) 708-1600

#### Office of Policy Development

*International Affairs*
John M. Geraghty, Senior International Affairs Specialist
(202) 708-0770

The International Affairs Department serves as the central coordinating point within HUD for all matters relating to participation in international activities and exchanges. The primary functions of the office are to administer exchange programs in urban policy and research studies with foreign governments and international organizations and to assist HUD officials participating in these international meetings. The mandates of the office are found in congressional legislation (Section 604 of the Housing Act of 1957, as amended) and in White House and State Department directives requiring HUD support for foreign policy reasons.

The urban policy and research studies that the office receives from the developing countries are usually sent to the Agency for International Development (K1).

3. The HUD Library, located in room 8141 (202/708-2370), contains a modest number of works—almost exclusively post-1960 imprints—on

international housing issues such as city growth, urban planning and development, urban finance, economic planning, and building construction. Included are sporadic government reports on housing, slum eradication, and social welfare, along with some housing censuses and reports from national housing and mortgage banks. The library is open 8:30 A.M.–5:15 P.M. Monday–Friday.

5. Because of cutbacks in funding, some publications (e.g., *HUD International Country Reports* and *HUD International Review*) are now defunct. Also terminated was the automated Foreign Information Retrieval System, which offered bibliographic references on the subjects of housing and urban affairs.

6. Index Terms: Development Issues—Infrastructure; Transnationalism

---

## K21 Interior Department

---

1.a. 1849 C Street, NW
Washington, D.C. 20240
(202) 208-3171 (Public Information)
(202) 208-5342 (Freedom of Information/ Privacy Act)

b. Open to the public

2. The Interior Department administers over 500 million acres of federally owned land and is responsible for formulating and implementing conservation policies that protect the natural resources under its jurisdiction. It is also involved in international data gathering and research exchanges. Studies of domestic and foreign issues are usually conducted within the agency, but nongovernment researchers are sometimes employed on a contract basis.

3. Interior Department's Natural Resources Library (Victoria A. Nozero, project manager, 202/208-5815) is open to the public, for on-site use 7:45 A.M.–5:00 P.M. Monday–Friday. Interlibrary loan and photocopying services are available. The library's holdings of more than 900,000 volumes focus on environment and ecology, government documents, land use, mines and mineral resources, and parks.

4–5. Internal records and publications are described with their respective offices.

### TERRITORIAL AND INTERNATIONAL AFFAIRS

Kathryn C. Washburn, International Affairs Director
(202) 208-3101

This office formulates policies related to international programs and bilateral cooperative efforts with other countries.

### BUREAU OF MINES

810 7th Street, NW
Washington, D.C. 20241

Herman Enzer, Acting Director
(202) 501-9300

A research and fact-finding body, the bureau is responsible for ensuring sufficient national mineral supplies for security and other reasons. Two of its publications are the three-volume *Minerals Yearbook* and the quinquennial *Mineral Facts and Problems*. Further information is available from the bureau's Publication Division (202/501-9551).

### International Minerals Division

George J. Coakley, Chief
(202) 501-9660

The division collects information concerning mineral production, importation, exportation, and consumption in most countries of the world. It produces *Area Reports International,* which constitutes volume three of the *Minerals Yearbook.* The division's regional branches (Africa and the Middle East, 202/501-9685; Asia and the Pacific, 202/501-9698; Europe and USSR, 202/501-9668; Latin America and Canada, 202/501-9676) have area specialists willing to speak with researchers.

### MINERALS MANAGEMENT SERVICE (MMS)

Room 4212, Main Interior Building
1849 C Street, NW
Washington, DC 20240

Tom Fry, Director
(202) 208-3983 (Public Affairs)

### Office of International Activities and Marine Minerals

Carolita U. Kallaur, Program Director
(703) 787-1300

The office acts as a focal point for all international activities in MMS and also carries out a program of hard mineral resource investigations, the latter mainly by means of cooperative arrangements with coastal states. Scholars may call this office to inquire about projects underway, as well as training programs that are being developed.

## GEOLOGICAL SURVEY (USGS)

### Geological Survey National Center
12201 Sunrise Valley Drive
Reston, Va. 22092

Gordon P. Eaton, Director
(703) 648-4460 (Public Affairs)

The USGS maintains relations with international geological, hydrological, and cartographic services and arranges for participation of U.S. scientists in international conferences and meetings.

### National Mapping Division

*Earth Science Information Center*
John T. Wood, Branch Chief
(703) 648-5915

Scholars may call the center for information pertaining to USGS publications. Included among a substantial list of titles is the annual *Publications of the U.S. Geological Survey,* which represents a cumulation of monthly new publications lists. Examples of entries in new publications include oceanography, geological surveys, economic geology, petrology, and sedimentary petrology.

### Geologic Division
International Geology Office

A. Thomas Ovenshine, Chief
(703) 648-6047

Scholars may call this office to inquire about projects currently underway. The deputy chiefs are Asian and Pacific Geology, Jack Medlin, 703/648-6062; European Geology, Richard Krushensky, 703/648-6060; International Polar Programs, Bruce Molnia, 703/648-4120; Latin American Geology, Jean Weaver, 703/648-6012; Middle Eastern and African Geology, 703/648-6055; and Soviet Affairs, Paul Hearn, 703/648-6287.

### Water Resources Division
Philip Cohen, Chief
(703) 648-5215
Robert M. Hirsch, Assistant Chief, Research and External Coordination
(703) 648-5041
Ann Lenox, International Water Resources
(703) 648-5053

The assistant chief hydrologist is responsible for coordinating water resource information exchange programs with foreign countries. The office organizes international training courses, such as Tech-

niques of Hydraulic Investigations. The International Water Resource Specialist works with individuals from abroad who are involved in developing water resources.

### Library
Barbara A. Chappell, Chief Librarian
(703) 648-4302/3
Fax: (703) 648-6373

Holdings include 790,000 volumes and 9,500 current serial titles. The collection focuses on earth sciences, environment and ecology, geology, mineralogy, and water resources development. A special collection includes 325,000 geoscience maps. The library is open 7:30 A.M.–4:15 P.M. Monday–Friday. Interlibrary loan and photocopying facilities are available.

## FISH AND WILDLIFE AND PARKS

1849 C Street, NW
Washington, D.C. 20240

Molly H. Beattie, Director
(202) 208-4717

### International Affairs Office
4401 North Fairfax Drive, Room 860
Arlington, Va. 22203

Lawrence N. Mason, Chief
(703) 358-1763

This office is in charge of implementing the Convention on Nature Protection and Wildlife Preservation in the Western Hemisphere. Since 1985 it has sought to meet the need for training international biologists through workshops, seminars, and graduate studies in natural resources conservation, with an emphasis on establishing a few high-quality, comprehensive training programs. Staff members also coordinate U.S. cooperation with other countries in identifying, protecting, and restoring endangered species of fish, wildlife, and plants through the Endangered and Threatened Species List.

6.   Index Terms: Development Issues; Environmental Issues, Global; Transnationalism

---

## K22   International Trade Commission (ITC)

---

1.a.  500 E Street, SW
      Washington, D.C. 20436

(202) 252-1819 (Public Information)
(202) 205-1802 (Freedom of Information)
Fax: (202) 205-2798

b. Open to the public.

2. The ITC monitors the impact of imports on U.S. domestic agriculture and industry. The ITC advises the president and Congress on tariff and trade issues, assists in drafting trade legislation, comments on proposals from other government agencies, and conducts research on tariffs, international trade, and commercial policy.

## OFFICE OF OPERATIONS

Roger A. Rogowsky, Director
(202) 205-2230

This agency and its several subunits (e.g., Applied Economics Division, 202/205-3245) compile economic data and forecast changes in trade trends as they relate to exports to the United States. Files, which are broken down by country, are accessible to outside researchers.

**Industries Office**
Vern L. Simpson, Director
(202) 205-3296

Staff analysts in this office and its various subdivisions monitor international flows of individual commodities. Much of the raw statistical data studied by ITC analysts comes from the Commerce Department's (K7) Bureau of the Census, but ITC economists evaluate these data differently to produce distinct information. A large part of ITC research is based on specific commodities and their countries of origin. The international trade analyst (William Cunningham (202/205-3334) can provide researchers with tallies on specific commodities by country.

3. For a description of the ITC's National Library of International Trade, see entry A26.

4. The Office of the Secretary (202/205-2000) maintains control of retired internal records. Researchers should direct inquiries to the Freedom of Information Office (202/205-1802).

5. A monthly calendar of ITC hearings and investigations is available outside the secretary's office (202/205-1807). There is a "Factual Highlight Bulletin" that will help researchers ascertain the status of particular cases under consideration. The Office of the Secretary is also the proper location for obtaining reports resulting from specific investigations.

The ITC's *Quarterly Report on East-West Trade* is an invaluable, up-to-date, compilation of trade-related statistics; the report is organized by country or region.

The commission's annual report, *Operation of the Trade Agreement Program,* contains data on U.S. bilateral trade by country and commodity, changes in foreign investment policies, and recent developments in regional economic groupings. Copies may be obtained from the Office of the Secretary (202/205-1807).

6. Index Terms: Environmental Issue, Global; International Economics—International Trade; International Law

See also entry A26

---

# K23 Justice Department

1.a. 10th Street and Constitution Avenue
Washington, D.C. 20530
(202) 514-2007 (Public Information)
(202) 514-3642
Fax: (202) 514-4371

b. Some departmental agencies, such as the FBI, are closed to the public. Researchers should contact each office for its respective policy on accessibility.

2. Justice Department divisions with international activities are described following point 5.

3. The Justice Department Library (Dee Sampson, Library Director, 202/514-2133) is open 9:00 A.M.–5:30 P.M. Monday–Friday. It contains approximately 150,000 volumes of legal and general reference works and is accessible by special permission. Interlibrary loan service (202/514-3695) is available.

4. Questions related to the department's restricted internal records are answered by the Freedom of Information Office (202/514-3642).

5. Publications are described below with the appropriate issuing agency.

## CRIMINAL DIVISION

10th Street and Constitution Avenue, NW
Washington, D.C. 20530

Jo Ann Harris, Assistant Attorney General
(202) 514-2601

## Internal Security Section
John L. Martin, Chief
(202) 514-1187

The section has exclusive prosecutorial responsibility for criminal statutes regarding espionage, sabotage, neutrality, and atomic energy. It also administers and enforces the Foreign Agents Registration Act of 1938 and related statutes. This act requires that individuals representing foreign principals—including foreign governments, industry associations, firms, and political organizations—file regular reports on their activities in the United States. These reports are available for public inspection and constitute an excellent source of information on foreign efforts to influence U.S. policy (especially in economic areas such as trade policy). A publication of the Criminal Division entitled *The Foreign Agents Registration Act of 1938 as Amended: The Rules and Regulations Prescribed by the Attorney General* provides source material of potential interest to scholars of international relations. Of interest to scholars pursuing the question of who represents whom is the annual *Report of the Attorney General to the Congress of the United States on the Administration of the Foreign Agents Registration Act.* Issued since 1950, the text lists all registrants of record at any time during the calendar year, the identity of the foreign principal(s), and a description of the activities in which the agent engaged. Many of those listed and described are located within the Washington, D.C., area. Inquiries pertaining to the act may be addressed to the Registration Unit of the Internal Security Section, Department of Justice, Washington, D.C. 20530. Registration statements, dissemination reports, and copies of political propaganda filed under section 4(a) of the Registration Act are available for public examination at the Public Office of the Registration Section on workdays, 10:00 A.M.–4:00 P.M. The Public Office is located at 1400 New York Avenue, Room 7120, Washington, D.C. 20530. Copies of registration statements and dissemination reports are available for a fee of 10¢ per page. Also on file at the Public Office are over 800 case studies of foreign espionage agents now residing in the United States. These, too, are open to researchers.

Other branches of the Criminal Division with multinational responsibility include the International Affairs Office (202/514-0000), which handles judicial assistance and extradition matters, the Terrorism and Violent Crimes Section, which prosecutes domestic and international terrorism cases, and the General Litigation and Legal Advice Section (202/514-1026), which deals with criminal matters related to immigration.

## FEDERAL BUREAU OF INVESTIGATION (FBI)

J. Edgar Hoover Building
9th Street and Pennsylvania Avenue, NW
Washington, D.C. 20535

Louis Freeh, Director
(202) 324-3000 (Information)

The FBI is the principal investigative arm of the U.S. Department of Justice. It has a wide range of responsibilities in the criminal, civil, and security fields (including espionage, sabotage, and other domestic security matters). FBI internal records are classified, but information from past FBI investigations may be made available through Freedom of Information procedures. Requests should be sent to the director of the FBI. The Public Affairs Office (202/324-5354) can provide basic information and assistance.

## IMMIGRATION AND NATURALIZATION SERVICE (INS)

425 I Street, NW
Washington, D.C. 20001

Mail:
INS, Washington, D.C. 20536

Doris Meissner, Commissioner
(202) 514-4316 (Public Information)
Fax: (202) 514-3296

The International Affairs and Outreach Department (202/633-1100) coordinates cooperation between the Washington headquarters and INS's Bangkok, Rome, and Mexico City offices. Together these offices attempt to facilitate the entry of legal immigrants into the United States. The Refugee Division and the Asylum Division review requests by refugees and asylum seekers to enter the United States.

The Statistics Staff (202/376-3008) of the INS monitors immigration and nonimmigrant visits to the United States from abroad. A detailed set of figures, prepared quarterly, includes the country of origin, age, sex, and occupation for immigrants and nonimmigrants. The branch's library contains useful historical literature and statistical data. Cumulative statistical tables with information on past and present immigration and nonimmigrant visitors to the United States are reproduced in the INS *Annual Report and Statistical Yearbook*. Copies are available from the Statistical Branch. For a fee the Statistical Analysis Branch can supply researchers with a computer printout of immigration statistics available from the most recent quarterly compilation. Requests for these data must be submitted in writing.

## DRUG ENFORCEMENT ADMINISTRATION (DEA)

Lincoln Place West
700 Army Navy Drive
Arlington, Va 22202

Mail:
DEA, Washington, D.C. 20537

Thomas A. Constantine, Administrator
(202) 307-8000

DEA was created on July 1, 1973, by the merger of four drug enforcement agencies: the Bureau of Narcotics and Dangerous Drugs, the Office of Drug Abuse Law Enforcement, the Office of National Narcotics Intelligence, and those drug investigative and intelligence activities previously performed by the U.S. Customs Service.

DEA is charged with enforcing the provisions of Title II of the Comprehensive Drug Abuse Prevention and Control Act of 1970, commonly known as the Controlled Substances Act. A survey, *Drugs of Abuse,* is issued annually.

### Operations Division

*Office of International Operating Programs*
Matthew J. Maher, Director
(202) 307-4233

The regional sections (Central American/Caribbean, 202/307-4263; European/Mid-East, 202/307-4252; Far East, 202/307-4256; South American, 202/307-4268) are involved in data analysis. They receive information on narcotics production and trafficking from DEA field agents and local law enforcement agencies in their specific regions. Their files are classified and access to restricted materials may be obtained only through the Freedom of Information Office (202/514-3642).

## NATIONAL INSTITUTE OF JUSTICE (NIJ)

**National Criminal Justice Research Service (NCJRS)**
Indiana Building
633 Indiana Ave., NW
Washington, DC 20530

Jeremy Travis, Director
(202) 307-2942

Established in 1972, NCJRS is a rapidly growing international clearinghouse of information about law enforcement and criminal justice. Staff members are able to provide researchers with reference and referral services, as well as on-line data searches. The reference collection comprises some 100,000 U.S. and foreign law-related documents, which NCJRS can provide on interlibrary loan.

The Reference Service's data bank contains domestic and foreign documentation on a variety of law enforcement issues. For each foreign language document, an English language abstract is prepared; important documents receive extended summaries of three to four pages. The data bank is accessible on-site or through DIALOG.

## INTERNATIONAL CRIMINAL POLICE ORGANIZATION (INTERPOL)—UNITED STATES NATIONAL CENTRAL BUREAU (USNCB)

Bicentennial Building
Washington, D.C. 20530

Mail:
10th St and Constitution Ave., NW
Washington, D.C. 20530

Shelley Altenstadter, Chief
(202) 272-8383

Interpol is an association of 169 countries dedicated to promoting mutual assistance among law enforcement authorities in the prevention and suppression of international crime. Interpol does not have its own police force, thus it has no powers of arrest. Rather, it serves as a means of communication for the police forces of its member countries. U.S. participation in Interpol began in 1938 by congressional authorization. Since then, USNCB has operated through cooperative efforts on the federal, state, and local levels, as well as on the international level. Programs such as the State Liaison Program and the Canadian Interface Project illustrate the cooperative efforts USNCB relies on to battle international crime.

6. Index Terms: Intelligence; International Law; Low Intensity Conflict; Terrorism

---

## K24 Labor Department

---

1.a. 200 Constitution Avenue, NW
Washington, D.C. 20210
(202) 219-7316 (Public Information)
(202) 219-8188 (Freedom of Information)
Fax: (202) 219-7312

b. Department offices are open to the public.

2. The functions of the Bureau of International Labor Affairs and Bureau of Labor Statistics are outlined below.

3. The Labor Department Library is described in entry A28; the National Labor Relations Board Library is described in entry A34.

4. Many internal records on U.S. bilateral labor relations are classified and are available only through Freedom of Information Act processes. Miriam Miller (202/219-8188) is the department's Freedom of Information officer.

5. Publications, with the appropriate issuing agency, are described below.

## BUREAU OF INTERNATIONAL LABOR AFFAIRS

Joaquin Otero, Deputy Under Secretary
(202) 219-6043

### Foreign Relations Office
John Ferch, Director
(202) 219-7631

Regional specialists and development cooperation specialists in the Office of Foreign Relations are the Labor Department's primary experts on U.S. labor relations and trade union relations with other countries. They serve as the department's contact-point with labor attachés in U.S. embassies throughout the world and are responsible for liaison with private U.S. labor organizations involved in other countries' labor development. They are accessible to private researchers and will make available unclassified labor-attaché reports.

### International Economic Affairs Office
Jorge Perez-Lopez, Director
(202) 219-7597

Members of this office participate on interagency teams involved in global economic issues and the negotiation of bilateral agreements. Staff attend meetings of the Trade Policy Staff Committee and other interagency groups chaired by the Office of U.S. Trade Representative and remain in close contact with the State Department (K37) and Commerce Department (K7).

### Foreign Economic Research Division
Gregory K. Schoepfle, Director
(202) 219-7610

Trade and labor economists in the Office of Foreign Economic Research analyze the impact of U.S. foreign trade, foreign investment, and tariff policies on the U.S. domestic labor force. Their research studies have included evaluations of the effects that U.S. investments and technology transfer in other regions of the world have on wages and employment in the United States. Much of the unit's research is performed under contract by academic institutions and private scholars. Lists of research reports and copies of reports will be made available to researchers on request.

## LABOR STATISTICS BUREAU

### Foreign Labor Statistics and Trade Division
Arthur Neef, Chief
(202) 606-5654

The Division of Foreign Labor Statistics and Trade collects data and conducts research on foreign labor conditions such as employment and wage levels, labor force, costs, benefits, and productivity. Although its primary focus is on the advanced industrial nations, the unit receives government publications containing industrial and labor statistics from some developing countries. Current holdings are available to the public; older materials are sent to the Labor Department Library (A28). Division staff members will confer with researchers.

The division publishes foreign labor figures in the Bureau of Labor Statistics' monthly *Labor Review* and annual *Handbook of Labor Statistics*.

### International Prices Division
Katrina Reut, Assistant Commissioner
(202) 606-7100

This unit measures and analyzes price trends for U.S. imports and exports, by commodity.

6. Index Terms: Development Issues; International Economics

See also entries A28 and A34

## National Archives and Records Administration (NARA)  See entry B11

---

## K25  National Aeronautics and Space Administration (NASA)

---

1.a. 600 Independence Avenue, SW
Washington, D.C. 20546

(202) 358-0000

Fax: (202) 358-2810

b. Open to the public; appointments are recommended.

c. Daniel Goldin, Administrator

2.   NASA supports very little outside research on subjects other than aeronautical and space research and development. It has contracted a few studies concerning such subjects as U.S.-Soviet cooperation in space. In-house research is limited to subjects not in the social sciences.

### DEFENSE AFFAIRS DIVISION

Conrad Forsythe, Director

(202) 358-0330

NASA has a small office, roughly six professional staff, on Defense Department (K10) affairs. Its purpose is to maintain liaison with DOD to coordinate programs and avoid duplication. It also represents NASA's interests in regard to arms control treaties so that any NASA prerogatives, for example, inspection requirements, are maintained.

### INTERNATIONAL RELATIONS DIVISION

Peter G. Smith, Director

(202) 358-1639

Fax: (202) 358-3029

NASA's interaction with other nations is conducted by this division. It coordinates and directs NASA's activities in connection with a variety of international cooperative agreements on development of space technology. NASA has entered into over 1,200 agreements with 135 countries. Space Station Freedom is the largest science and technology project ever undertaken on a cooperative basis. The nine countries of the European Space Agency, Japan, and Canada are the other participating nations. Another project utilizing international cooperation is the Cassini mission to Saturn and its moon Titan. In December 1993, Russia and the United States agreed on a three-phase program of human space flight that will involve the U.S. space shuttle and the Russian Mir space station. There will be eventual participation by Russia in the international cooperative space station program.

3.   The NASA headquarters library contains extensive material on all aspects of the history and development of space flight, including cooperative efforts with other countries. It also contains extensive literature on the development of the Soviet space program. The librarian is Mary E. Anderson (202/358-0168).

4.   NASA headquarters has no central file of internal records and documents. Each NASA unit retires its own records to the National Archives and Records Administration (B11) at its own pace. For more information regarding internal documents, researchers should contact Lee D. Saegesser, NASA archivist (202/358-0386).

5.   NASA has an extensive publications program. NASA publications are regularly listed in *Scientific and Technical Aerospace Reports,* published semimonthly by the GPO (see Appendix III). NASA also furnishes a publications catalog. Information may be obtained through the NASA publication office, Kevin Durham, director (202/453-1287).

6.   Index Terms: Arms Control

---

## K26   National Endowment for the Humanities (NEH)

---

1.a.   1100 Pennsylvania Avenue, NW
Washington, D.C. 20506
(202) 606-8400 (Public Information)
(202) 606-8322 (Freedom of Information)

b. Open to the public.

c. Sheldon Hackney, Chairman
(202) 606-8310

2.   The NEH provides postdoctoral fellowships and grants for research in all disciplines in the humanities, including diplomatic and military history; languages; linguistics; literature; jurisprudence; philosophy; archeology; comparative religion; the history, criticism, theory, and practice of the arts; and "those aspects of the social sciences which have humanistic content and apply humanistic methods."

The Division of Fellowships (202/606-8466) provides stipends to individual scholars and teachers.

The Division of Research Grants (202/606-8494) provides support to group projects and research centers and for projects relating to the preparation of research tools and the editing of humanistic texts.

3.   The NEH Library (Enayet Rahim, Librarian, 202/606-8244) houses a reference collection of about 7,000 volumes and 500 periodical titles intended to meet the informational needs of NEH staff. The collection contains NEH annual reports, copies of other NEH publications, and all NEH-

funded publications. The library is open 8:30 A.M.–5:30 P.M. Monday–Friday. Interlibrary loan and photocopying services are available.

5. The annual booklet entitled *Overview of Endowment Programs* is a useful resource. It lists and describes the activities of the divisions of the NEH (including Research Programs, Fellowships and Seminars, Education Programs, Preservation/Access Programs, State Programs, and Public Programs) and provides information about application procedures and deadlines. The annual report contains particulars about the endowment and its programs and lists all grant recipients and the amounts awarded for each year. The bimonthly journal *Humanities* has articles on NEH-funded projects, bibliographies, and other features of potential interest to scholars. *Humanities* is sold through the Government Printing Office (see Appendix III). Other publications of the NEH are available free upon request.

6. Index Terms: Diplomacy and Negotiations; Military History

---

## K27 National Science Foundation (NSF)

1.a. 4201 Wilson Boulevard
Arlington, Va 22230
(703) 306-1234 Public Information
(703) 306-1070 Freedom of Information

b. Open to the public.

2. NSF provides grants and fellowships for research, primarily but not exclusively in the fields of physical science and technology.

### DIRECTORATE FOR SOCIAL, BEHAVIORAL, AND ECONOMIC SCIENCES

Cora B. Marrett, Assistant Director
(703) 306-1700

This agency supports some foreign-area research (dissertation level and postdoctoral) in economics, political science, sociology, demography, economic and social geography, and the history and philosophy of science.

**International Programs Division**
Marcel Bardon, Director
(703) 306-1710

The division's Office of International Science and Technology Issues (Pierre Perrolle, Coordinator,

703/306-1711) constitutes a useful initial contact-point for scholars with inquiries relating to NSF research-funding activities. The Division of International Programs coordinates a variety of cooperative NSF bilateral research and exchange programs linking scientific researchers in the United States and abroad. Scholars with inquiries about programs in a specific geographic region should begin their information search with the appropriate regional division (Africa, Near East, and South Asia, 703/306-1707; Americas, 703/306-1706; East Asia and Pacific, 703/306-1704; Eastern Europe, 703/306-1703; Japan, 703/306-1701; and Western Europe, 703/306-1702). This division also administers a Scientists and Engineers in Economic Development (SEED) program that provides grants to U.S. development specialists working or teaching in developing nations.

### GRADUATE EDUCATION AND RESEARCH DEVELOPMENT DIVISION

Terence L. Porter, Director
(703) 306-1630

The division administers two internationally oriented postdoctoral programs. The NATO program offers grants to engineers, physical scientists, and social scientists who have had a Ph.D. for five years or less to study in any of the NATO countries or cooperative partner countries of Eastern Europe. Applicants must be U.S. citizens, permanent residents, or nationals. For more information about the grant itself or the application process contact the NATO program assistant (703/306-1696).

3. The National Science Foundation Library is open 8:30 A.M.–5:00 P.M. Monday–Friday. Interlibrary loan and photocopying facilities are available. This small reference collection of approximately 16,000 volumes and 500 periodicals includes general works and current research in the fields of environmental, biological, and social sciences, national and international science policy, and the history and philosophy of science.

5. An NSF *Guide to Programs,* a monthly NSF bulletin, and the organization's annual report are available from the Publications Office (703/306-1130). Brochures describing the specific programs of individual divisions may be obtained by contacting the respective divisions.

6. Index Terms: Development Issues—Education; Political Systems and Ideologies; Transnationalism

## K28 National Security Council (NSC)

1.a. Old Executive Office Building
  17th Street and Pennsylvania Avenue, NW
  Washington, D.C. 20506
  (202) 456-2947 (Public Affairs)

  b. No public access.

2. NSC staff members—including the council's specialists in global issues and multinational affairs (202/395-3393)—do not regularly make themselves available to private researchers, although individual exceptions might be made. The NSC has, in the past, occasionally engaged private academic specialists as consultants.

4. Access to most National Security Council internal documents is possible, if at all, only through Freedom of Information Act processes. The Information Disclosure Directorate (202/395-3103) administers FOIA matters for the council. The NSC periodically provides the Civil Reference Branch (202/501-5395) of the National Archives (B11) with an updated computer printout of those policy papers, intelligence directives, and other internal records that have been wholly or partially declassified by NSC. Copies of many of these declassified NSC records, which date from 1947 to present, are available in the Civil Reference Branch, although no formal NSC record group has been established. The Civil Reference Branch also has a complete index to NSC numbered policy papers 1–177 (1947–53) and 5401–6028 (1954–60), which is a useful source of information for the preparation of FOIA requests. Contact Milton Gustafson, Chief, Civil Reference Branch (202/501-5395) for further information.

6. Index Terms: Defense Policy, National; Intelligence

See also entry B11

## K29 National Technical Information Service (NTIS) (Commerce Department)

1.a. Sills Building
  5285 Port Royal Road
  Springfield, Va. 22161
  (703) 487-4650 (Information)
  (703) 487-4929 (Bibliographic HELP Desk)

  b. Open 7:45 A.M.–6:00 P.M. Monday–Friday.

  c. Joseph F. Caponio, Director

2. NTIS collects and distributes to the public, research reports and analyses prepared, sponsored, or funded by U.S. government agencies and foreign sources. Currently, over 200 U.S. government agencies and 15 foreign sources contribute to the NTIS collection. NTIS's Office of International Affairs (Forbes Building, 8001 Forbes Place, Springfield, Va. 22161, 703/487-4822) maintains a network of foreign cooperating agencies, government and private, which represent NTIS abroad. These cooperating agencies contribute about 30 percent of NTIS's collection each year. S. Dickson Tenney, Foreign Affairs Officer (703/487-4825), is in charge of this network.

4. At present NTIS offers almost 2 million titles for sale. Helpful aids for locating specific publications include the biweekly *Government Reports Announcements and Index* (with annual index), containing summaries of recently acquired research titles, and *Published Search Master Catalog*, a subject index to more than 3,000 NTIS-published bibliographies and others produced by previous computer searches. NTIS's bibliographic database may be accessed through several on-line services such as DIALOG, CISTI (Canada), ESA/IRS (Italy), or NERAC. The database is also available on CD-ROM. To help researchers search material on-line or manually, NTIS publishes *NTIS Subject Category Descriptions*. To acquire this guide call (703) 487-4650. A descriptive brochure, *NTIS Catalog of Products and Services* (annual), is also available without charge.

5. Most NTIS publications are scientific and technical, but there are also Department of Commerce (K7) foreign market airgrams and international market share reports; Foreign Broadcast Information Service (K16) and Joint Publications Research Service reports; unclassified reports from Defense Technical Information Center (G7) relating to national and international defense; Environmental Protection Agency (K13) foreign environmental reports; and research on international energy matters and military sciences. In addition, the NTIS collection includes State Department cables and airgrams on foreign political, economic, social, cultural, and military affairs (to be indexed by country and subject). Items can be purchased in hardcopy or microform.

6. Index Terms: Development Issues; Intelligence

See also Appendixes I and III

## **K30**  Navy Department

1.a.  The Pentagon
Washington, D.C. 20350
(703) 695-0911 (Public Information)
(202) 697-1459 (Freedom of Information)

b.  The Pentagon is closed to anyone without appropriate security clearance; an appointment is required.

2.  Most research is conducted in-house.

3.  For a description of navy library collections see entries A30 and A36; for archival collections see entries B9 and B13.

4.  Internal records procedures are described in the entry for the Defense Department (K10). See also reference to the Freedom of Information Office (202/614-2817) further on in this entry.

5.  For the description of publications see entries on the Marine Corps Historical Center (B9) and the Naval Historical Center (B13).

### VICE CHIEF OF NAVAL OPERATIONS

Assistant Vice Chief of Naval Operations
Freedom of Information Office
Gwendolyn R. Aitken, Chief
(703) 614-2817

Scholars may contact the Freedom of Information Officer for details about how to process an FOIA request within the Navy Department.

### PLANS, POLICY, AND OPERATIONS

**Operations, Plans, Politico-Military Affairs**
Rear Adm. W. F. Doran, Director
(703) 695-2453

Regional desk officers monitor political and military developments throughout the world and prepare policy papers on events and issues that pertain to the U.S. Navy's role in national and international defense programs.

### NAVAL INTELLIGENCE

Rear Adm. Edward D. Sheafer, Jr., Director
(703) 695-0124

Desk officers in units such as Foreign Counterintelligence (202/433-8800) and the Intelligence Community (703/614-0426) maintain data on other countries' naval affairs and their effects on U.S. naval activities. The resulting reports are usually classified.

**Naval Historical Center    See entry B13.**

**Marine Corps Historical Center    See entry B9.**

6.  Index Terms: Defense Policy, National; Intelligence; Military Science; Naval Science

See also entries A30, A36, B9, B13, C4, C5, C9, and C10

## **K31**  Office of Management and Budget (OMB)

1.a.  Old Executive Office Building
17th Street and Pennsylvania Avenue, NW
Washington, D.C. 20503
(202) 395-3000
Fax: (202) 395-3746

b.  Access is restricted, although consultation by phone is possible.

c.  Alice M. Rivlin, Director

2.  OMB reviews and clears all agency budgetary requests and legislation submitted by the administration to Congress. Its National Security and International Affairs section (Gordon Adams, Director, 202/395-4567) not only oversees State and Defense Departments budgets but also examines specific positions taken by the administration on particular national security questions. It also makes policy recommendations within the budget process.

6.  Index Terms: Defense Policy, National; Military Spending

## **K32**  Overseas Private Investment Corporation (OPIC) (International Development Cooperation Agency)

1.a.  1100 New York Ave, NW, 12th Floor
Washington, D.C. 20527
(202) 336-8400 (Public Information)

b.  Open to the public. Appointment recommended.

2.   OPIC's purpose is to promote economic growth in developing countries by encouraging private investment. The agency encourages investment by providing discounted insurance policies to U.S. multinational corporations to protect them against the political risks of expropriation, inconvertibility of foreign currency holdings, and damage from war, revolution, or insurrection. It also protects U.S. lending institutions by guaranteeing payment of principal and interest on loans made to private investors. In addition, OPIC offers investment information and counseling, and shares in the costs of finding, developing, and financing investment projects overseas.

Specialists in OPIC's Insurance Department (Caribbean/Central America/South America Region, 202/336-8582; Europe/Communist/Post-Communist States Region, 202/336-8587; Africa/Middle East/Asia Region, 202/336-8574) and Finance Department (Africa/Middle East/Asia Region, 202/336-8491; Central/Eastern Europe Region, 202/336-8474; Latin America Region, 202/336-8492; Russia/Newly Independent States Region, 202/336-8494) monitor global business conditions and investment environments. Periodically they travel to their regions of expertise to identify new investment projects and assist U.S. investors. They will confer with researchers.

3.   OPIC's library (202/336-8559) has diverse holdings relating to international business and investment. Included are reports from private U.S. corporations with investments in developing countries, publications of U.S. government agencies (departments of State, Commerce, Treasury, Agriculture), confidential World Bank (L8)/International Monetary Fund (L11) country and project assessments, an alphabetically arranged vertical file of miscellaneous foreign country data, and legislation pertaining to OPIC. There are also separate volumes of records relating to OPIC involvement in overseas investment disputes and settlements. The library maintains a card index to facilitate researchers' use of these holdings. The library is open 8:45 A.M.–5:00 P.M. Monday–Friday. An appointment is recommended.

4.   The corporation's internal records—which include claims settlement files as well as information submitted by private U.S. companies in developing nations (their agreements with host governments, business and project forecasts, etc.)—are considered confidential and are inaccessible to private researchers except via Freedom of Information Act processes. Sheila Creal (202/336-8636) is OPIC's Freedom of Information officer.

5.   OPIC publishes an annual report. It also issues quarterly reports featuring information on countries and regions of investor interest.

6.   Index Terms: Development Issues—Aid and Investment

---

## K33   Peace Corps

1.a.   1990 K Street, NW
Washington, D.C. 20526
(202) 606-3010 (Press Office)
(202) 606-3261 (Freedom of Information)
Fax: (202) 606-3110

b.   Open to the public. Appointment recommended.

2.   Peace Corps programs overseas are administered through the Office of International Operations (Jack Hogan, Associate Director, 202/606-9454). Within this office, country desk officers in the Africa Region (Sandra Robinson, Director, 202/606-3180), Asia and Pacific Region (Margaret Goodman, Director, 202/606-1005), Eurasia and Middle East Region (Fred O'Regan, Director, 202/606-3835), and Inter-America Region (Victor Johnson, Director, 202/606-3337) provide liaisons between field volunteers and the Washington, D.C., headquarters. These officers can provide information on past and present Peace Corps programs (frequently having served as field volunteers themselves). They are accessible to researchers.

The Inspector General (202/606-3320) and the Planning, Policy, and Analysis Staff (202/606-3650) prepare assessments of Peace Corps programs and projects.

3.   The Peace Corps Library is discussed in entry A40. For a description of the Peace Corps Photograph collection see entry F25.

4.   The Peace Corps miscellaneous program documents, country reports, and all program evaluations are available in the Peace Corps Library (202/606-3307). The Freedom of Information Act officer in the Records Management Branch (Tom Pierce, 202/606-3261) is a good source of information on retired records.

5.   An irregularly issued *Training Forum* contains background and country-training information for Peace Corps volunteers. Copies may be obtained through the Office of Training and Program Support (202/606-3086). For volunteers in the field, the Peace Corps publishes the *Peace Corps Times,*

which attempts to keep volunteers in touch with one another and the Washington office.

6. Index Terms: Development Issues—Infrastructure; Development Issues—Technical Assistance; Humanitarian Issues—Relief Organization

See also entry A40, F25, and M41

---

## K34  Radio Free Europe/Radio Liberty (RFE/RL)

1.a. 1201 Connecticut Avenue, NW
Washington, D.C. 20036
(202) 457-6900
Fax: (202) 457-6992

c. Oleh Zwadiuk, Director, News Office
(202) 457-6953

2. As of mid-1994, Radio Free Europe/Radio Liberty broadcasts 829 hours a week of unbiased news, commentary, and analysis to Eastern Europe, Russia, and the newly independent states. To supplement its political broadcasts, RFE/RL offers reports on literature, the arts, history, and religion. Programs such as an interview with Mikhail Gorbachev on the anniversary of the August coup, an election debate between Czech and Slovak leaders, and "Studio Bulgaria," which allows listeners to put telephone questions to guests, are typical of RFE/RL.

Unlike Voice of America broadcasts, which focus mainly on U.S. issues, RFE/RL broadcasts focus mainly on the issues of importance in its broadcast region. RFE broadcasts are conducted in Bulgarian, Czech and Slovak, Hungarian, Polish, Romanian, Latvian, Lithuanian, and Estonian. RL broadcasts are conducted in Armenian, Azerbaijan, Belorussian, Georgian, Kazakh, Kyrgyz, Dari and Pashto (Radio Free Afghanistan), Russian, Tajik, Tatar-Bashkir, Turkmen, Ukrainian, and Uzbek.

3. The research and archival collections of the former Research Institute of RFE/RL, located in Munich, Germany, have been largely transferred to the Open Media Research Institute in Prague, Czech Republic (P.O. Box 268, Kaprova 12, 11001 Prague 1).

4. Radio Free Europe/Radio Liberty began in 1951. Copies of past recordings and transcripts were kept primarily at the former Research Institute.

5. Transcripts are made free of charge, but the staff does not have a great deal of time to fill such requests.

6. Index Terms: Foreign Policy; International Politics

---

## K35  Senate Historical Office

1.a. Office of the Secretary
Senate Historical Office
Hart Senate Office Building, Suite SH-201
Washington, D.C. 20510-7108
(202) 224-6900

b. 9:00 A.M.–5:30 P.M. Monday–Friday
Open to the public.

c. Richard A. Baker, Senate Historian
Donald A. Ritchie, Associate Historian

2. This office provides bibliographic and research assistance to historians, political scientists, and other scholars, serves as a clearinghouse for Senate-related research activities, and aids researchers in locating and gaining access to Senate documents.

3. Special collections held by the office include a photo archive of well over 30,000 Senate-related photographs. The photo collection includes likenesses of the more than 1,800 senators who have served since 1789. An oral history project is underway to tape record interviews with retired senior Senate staff members; see entry E15.

5. This office is responsible for editing the Executive Sessions of the Senate Foreign Relations Committee (Historical Series), which reprints the verbatim transcripts of confidential committee sessions from the late 1940s to the 1960s. Volumes still in print are available free from the Senate Foreign Relations Committee or may be used at the National Archives. For information about the Senate as an institution, a useful reference tool compiled with the assistance of this office is Robert C. Byrd's *Senate, 1789–1989,* 4 volumes (GPO, 1988–94). Volume one provides a chronological account of the Senate's history; volume two offers a survey of major topics associated with the Senate's institutional growth; volume three includes approximately 50 classic Senate speeches, delivered between 1830 and 1993; and volume four is a compendium of Senate historical statistics. Another valuable reference tool is *Guide to Research Collections of Former United States Senators, 1789–1982* (1983) and its supplements. The guide encompasses the entire membership of the Senate from 1789 to the present and provides information on the scope, location, and accessibility of the many collections of senators' private papers, oral

histories, portraits, photographs, and memorabilia held in libraries and archives throughout the United States. Also to be published by the Historical Office in the next year or two is a bibliography compiling writings done by and about former U.S. Senators.

6.   Index Terms: Foreign Policy; International Law; Military History

See also entry E15

## **K36**   Smithsonian Institution

1.a.   Smithsonian Institution
1000 Jefferson Drive, SW
Washington, D.C. 20560
(202) 357-2700 (Public Information)
Fax: (202) 786-2515

b.   The main administrative building and the numerous museums, galleries, and other Smithsonian facilities in the Washington, D.C., area are open to the public; some administrative offices and research areas are accessible only by appointment. The Smithsonian offers a recorded message service, Dial-A-Museum (202/357-2020), describing current events and exhibits of interest.

c.   I. Michael Heyman, Secretary

2.   The Smithsonian Institution was created by an act of Congress in 1846, 20 years after Englishman James Smithson bequested his property to the United States "to found . . . an establishment for the increase and diffusion of knowledge among men." Today the Smithsonian is one of the world's great scientific, cultural, and educational bodies. It administers a number of national collections, museums, and art galleries; conducts scientific and scholarly research; maintaining libraries, laboratories, and archives; and runs several educational and public service programs. The research projects supported by the institution are many and varied, being conducted both in and out of house. The principal relevance of the institution to the users of this Guide lies in the areas of economic development, global environmental issues, military history, and transnationalism. Most of the activities and collections that pertain to international studies are described at appropriate points elsewhere in this Guide. See A32, B10, C6, C8, D8, F18, and F19.

### OFFICE OF FELLOWSHIPS AND GRANTS

955 L'Enfant Plaza, Suite 7000
Washington, D.C. 20560

Roberta Rubinoff, Director
(202) 287-3271

The Smithsonian Institution encourages access to its collection, staff, and resources by visiting scholars and scientists through in-residence appointments for research and study. These appointments are supported by grants, internships, and predoctoral and postdoctoral fellowship programs that enable scholars to work with Smithsonian resources. For more information consult *Smithsonian Opportunities for Research and Study in History, Art, Science,* available through the fellowships office.

### SMITHSONIAN ASSOCIATES PROGRAMS

Smithsonian Institution
Washington, D.C. 20560

Mara Mayor, Director
(202) 357-2696

Various categories of membership, including resident associate, national associate, and contributing member, are available. Members are entitled to participate in numerous special Smithsonian educational and cultural programs, including culturally oriented educational tours of foreign countries (202/357-4090).

### OFFICE OF INTERNATIONAL RELATIONS (OIR)

S. Dillon Ripley Center
1100 Jefferson Drive, SW, Suite 3123
Washington, D.C. 20560

Francine Berkowitz, Director
(202) 357-4795

The OIR provides technical assistance and diplomatic support for Smithsonian programs abroad. It facilitates the international exchange of museum objects and staff and serves as the channel of communication between the Smithsonian, foreign institutions, and government agencies. The office administers two grant programs: the International Exchange Program, which provides support for Smithsonian divisions seeking to establish long-term cooperative relationships with foreign institutions, and the Smithsonian Foreign Currency Program, which provides research grants in countries where the United States has excess currency (e.g., India). Leonard Hirsch (202/357-4795), the Smithsonian's International Liaison, is a good primary contact for scholars seeking information about potential grants. The office also coordinates the Smithsonian's USIA-authorized visitor exchange program, through which foreign scholars may obtain U.S. visa documentation to conduct research.

Beyond the administration of grant programs, the office sponsors conferences, lectures, publications, meetings, and exhibitions on various international topics. It also maintains a database on the range of Smithsonian international activities for Smithsonian officials and staff planning work abroad.

3. The Smithsonian Institution Libraries (Barbara J. Smith, Director, 202/357-2240) include several decentralized research and reference collections located in the museums and laboratories corresponding to the subject of their holdings. The central library is housed in the National Museum of Natural History, Constitution Ave. at 10th Street, NW, Washington, D.C. 20560. For a description of the National Air and Space Museum Library see entries A32, F18, and F19.

4. The Smithsonian Institution Archives are described in entry B10.

5. *Smithsonian* magazine contains news of the institution and its activities, as well as articles of general interest.

The Smithsonian Institution Press (955 L'Enfant Plaza, Suite 7100, Washington, D.C. 20560; Daniel Goodwin, acting director, 202/287-3738) publishes in numerous fields, including global environment and military history. The institution's annual report, *Smithsonian Year,* is available from the press. Until 1987, the press was the publisher of the Woodrow Wilson Center's series of Scholars' Guides (see entry H76); all Guides are now available from Johns Hopkins University Press, 701 West 40th Street, Suite 275, Baltimore, Md. 21211; tel. 1 (800) 537-5487.

6. Index Terms: Transnationalism

See also entries A32, B10, C6, C8, D8, F18, and F19

---

## K37 State Department

1.a. 2201 C Street, NW
  Washington, D.C. 20520
  (202) 647-6575 (Public Information Service)
  (202) 647-8484 (Freedom of Information Act requests)

b. The building is not open to the public. Appointments should be made with department personnel to ensure admittance.

2. All State Department offices (described below) monitor international conditions, conduct research,

and prepare foreign policy papers. Personnel are usually willing to talk with researchers, within the limits imposed by security regulations.

3. The State Department Library is described in entry A43.

4. State Department internal classified records (dispatches, telegrams, and other message-communications between Washington and the department's diplomatic posts overseas, inter- and intraoffice memoranda, research studies, policy papers, etc.) are filed in the Bureau of Administration's Office of Information Services (described below), which eventually forwards them to the National Archives, Civil Reference Branch (B11). There they may become accessible to private researchers on a gradual basis determined by the latest year for which the State Department's official Foreign Relations of the United States documentary series has been published. Currently, most records are open at the National Archives through 1954 (access to post-1954 records is possible only via Freedom of Information Act processes). A computerized index exists for all internal records processed by the Office of Information Services since July 1973.

Within the Office of Freedom of Information, Privacy, and Classification Review, a Freedom of Information staff (202/647-8484) receives FOIA declassification-review requests for restricted State Department records and coordinates the subsequent records-search and review process with the department's geographic bureaus. Of the nearly 700,000 pages of documents reviewed in 1988, approximately 500,000 pages were released to the public. Researchers may examine documents that have been released to them in the unit's public-access reading room. The staff (Frank M. Machak, Director) cooperates with researchers throughout the review process and can be of assistance in appealing release-denials.

5.a. State Department publications include the weekly *Department of State Dispatch* (containing statements, addresses, and excerpts from news conferences of the president, secretary of state, and other officials; State Department press releases; texts of treaties and international agreements; articles on international affairs; and lists of congressional documents relating to foreign policy); a background notes series of general-information fact-sheets, by country (updated biannually); *Gist,* a series of one-page reference aids on current international issues; and a monthly *Department of State Newsletter.* Useful directories include the regularly updated *Biographic Register of State Department Officials* (classified since 1974); a trimestral *Key Officers of Foreign Service Posts—Guide for Business Representatives* (formerly *Foreign Service List*); the quarterly *Diplomatic List and Employees of Diplomatic Missions* (names and addresses of foreign diplomatic personnel in Washington); an annual *Foreign Consular Officers in the United States;* and periodically revised *Lists of Visits of Presidents of the United States to Foreign Countries, 1789–1982*, and *Lists of Visits of Foreign Chiefs of State and Heads of Governments, 1789–1982.*

In addition, the department issues many special public releases, including discussion papers, policy statements, speeches, addresses, news conferences, and other selected documents. A valuable reference work is *Atlas of the United States Foreign Relations* (1985). To be placed on the department's mailing list, contact the Bureau of Public Affairs' Office of Plans and Management (202/647-6575). Other department publications are discussed below under their originating office.

b. Bibliographies include *Major Publications of the Department of State: An Annotated Bibliography* (revised edition, 1977).

## BUREAU OF INTERNATIONAL ORGANIZATION AFFAIRS

Douglas J. Bennet, Jr., Assistant Secretary
(202) 647-9600

This bureau coordinates U.S. participation in the United Nations. Selected staff members in the bureaus's various offices monitor the activities of foreign delegations, and the repercussions of U.S. policy positions within the UN General Assembly and Security Council and in the many specialized UN commissions and conferences (CEPAL, UNCTAD, etc.). Offices of interest to scholars include Office of International Development Assistance (202/647-1269), Office of Technical Specialized Agencies (202/647-2330), Office of UN Political Affairs (202/647-2392), and the Office of Research and Reference (202/647-7993).

### Global Issues

Melinda Kimble, Deputy Assistant Secretary
(202) 647-9604

This unit oversees U.S. involvement in international organizations focused on social and environmental issues. The Office of Democracy, Human Rights, and Social Affairs (202/647-6878) monitors U.S. multilateral efforts to bring democracy to burgeoning nations. The Office of Economic and Environmental Affairs (202/647-2506) formulates policy regarding the preservation of the global environment. Creating and implementing agricultural and economic development policy is the Office of International Development Assistance (202/647-1269).

### Peacekeeping and International Organization Management

George F. Ward, Jr, Acting Deputy Assistant Secretary
(202) 647-9602

This division monitors U.S. participation in international organizations involved in peacekeeping efforts. The individual offices review multilateral programs to see if U.S. involvement in them is consistent with U.S. policy on peace. Units such as the Office of International Conferences (202/647-6875) and the UN System Administration (202/647-6424) may be of particular help in locating information on U.S. multilateral peacekeeping operations.

*Office of Peacekeeping and Humanitarian Operations*
John Brims, Director
(202) 736-7732

This branch of the Peacekeeping and International Organization Management division is responsible for managing U.S. policy with regard to UN peace and security operations, humanitarian relief operations, enforcement of economic sanctions, and electoral assistance. Essentially, this means crafting appropriate Security Council resolutions, evaluating the performance of missions, and helping coordinate the delivery of humanitarian aid.

## BUREAU OF INTELLIGENCE AND RESEARCH

Tobi T. Gati, Assistant Secretary
(202) 647-9176

The principal research arm of the State Department, this office prepares some 8,000 to 12,000 research reports each year, ranging from 1-page current intelligence spot analyses to 20–30 page research memoranda. Its primary clientele are high-level officers and the various regional bureaus. Research subject areas encompass the full range of Latin American policy issues and are primarily short- to midterm in scope. Virtually all the office's work is classified.

### Office of Research

Kenneth Roberts, Director
(202) 736-9060

This office, which serves as the State Department's primary contact-point with private scholars, manages the department's contract-research program and arranges for the use of outside consultants. It also periodically invites selected regional experts to participate with State Department and other government officials in conferences, colloquia, roundtable discussions, and ambassadorial briefings. Staff members do not engage in research activities of their own, but they can provide researchers with copies of unclassified State Department in-house and contract-research studies and research bibliographies.

### Office of the Geographer
William B. Wood, Geographer and Director
(202) 647-2021

This unit monitors international politico-geographic patterns; it issues two series of unclassified publications: *International Boundary Studies* (irregular) and *Geographic Notes,* issued each time a significant change in international sovereignty occurs—such as the emergence of a new state, name-change of a country, or modification of major civil divisions within a country. A periodically updated general reference booklet, *Status of the World's Nations,* last appeared in 1989.

### Office of Politico-Military Analysis and Warning
Charles J. Jefferson, Director
(202) 647-8869

This office conducts research (some relating to Latin America) on international arms sales, national military production and military capabilities, nuclear capabilities, and potential international military confrontations.

### Office of Strategic Forces and Proliferation Affairs
Gary D. Dietrich, Director
(202) 647-8216

The research interests of this office include nuclear nonproliferation, nuclear technological advances, and the strategic aspects of space.

### Office of Terrorism and Narcotics Analysis
Judy Bird, Director
(202) 647-6812

Analysts in this office provide guidance to overseas missions on matters concerning terrorism and narcotics. Much of the work is classified, but analysts are willing to communicate with scholars. Outside scholars are occasionally invited to conferences sponsored by the office.

### Deputy Assistant Secretary for Analysis
Phyllis Oakley, Deputy Assistant Secretary
(202) 647-9633

The unit houses the various geographic regional offices. Each office is further divided into departments focusing on specific sections of that region. The analysts in these subregional departments are the best contact for researchers looking for country-specific information.

## BUREAU OF ECONOMIC AND BUSINESS AFFAIRS
Daniel K. Tarullo, Assistant Secretary
(202) 647-7971

The functionally structured bureau has primary responsibility within the State Department for the formulation and implementation of U.S. foreign economic policy. It monitors the economic policies of foreign countries, coordinates regional economic policies of the United States with other U.S. government agencies, conducts bilateral and multilateral negotiations on economic matters, and represents the United States at international conferences. Scholars engaged in research on technical economic topics may find the most knowledgeable State Department expertise within this bureau rather than within the regional bureaus.

### Office of Economic Sanctions Policy
Robert Deutsch, Director
(202) 647-5673

Dealing with U.S. export control and embargo policies toward countries currently sanctioned by the United States, the office maintains liaison with the Treasury (K40) and Commerce (K7) departments on U.S. and international embargoes and foreign policy export controls.

### Office of Global Energy
Glen Rase, Director
(202) 647-2875

The office formulates energy policy, represents the United States at international conferences, and conducts negotiations with producers of oil and gas.

### Office of International Commodities
Wesley Scholz, Director
(202) 647-2744

This is the lead office for negotiations of deep seabed mining provisions of the UN Law of the Sea Convention. It is involved in the negotiation of multilateral commodities agreements. The agency's focus centers on strategic materials (rubber, tine, bauxite, iron ore, oil), tropical timber, and the transactions of the National Defense Stockpile Center.

## International Finance and Development

*Office of Development Finance*
Louis Warren, Director
(202) 647-9426

This office is concerned primarily with the development of U.S. financial and economic policy vis-à-vis developing nations and the international and regional organizations relating to them. It is the focal point within the department for matters concerning development assistance, development banks, and export financing.

*Office of Monetary Affairs*
G. Paul Balabanis, Director
(202) 647-9498

This office is interested in global monetary conditions, financial loans, balance-of-payment problems, debt policies, rescheduling policies, and the collection of debts and claims. It has primary responsibility for State Department relations with the International Monetary Fund (LII) and maintains liaison with the Treasury Department (K40).

## Trade and Commercial Affairs

*Office of Bilateral Trade Affairs*
James Derham, Director
(202) 647-4017

This office, which has divisions for developing and developed countries, designs and administers policies and programs relating to bilateral international trade.

*Office of Multilateral Trade Affairs*
William Craft, Director
(202) 647-3696

The office develops and administers policies and programs relating to multilateral trade issues. Its activities include matters relating to GATT and the Uruguay Round, antidumping and countervailing duty cases, government procurement, and the operation of the textile quota program.

*Office of Agricultural Trade, Policy, and Programs*
Thomas Robinson, Director
(202) 647-3090

The agency handles questions relating to agricultural exports and coordinates U.S. food-aid programs with the Agriculture Department (K2).

## BUREAU OF POLITICO-MILITARY AFFAIRS

Robert L. Gallucci, Assistant Secretary
(202) 647-9022

The bureau provides policy guidance and general direction within the State Department on issues that affect U.S. security policies, military assistance, and arms control matters. In addition, the bureau maintains liaison with the Defense Department (K10) and other federal agencies on a wide range of political-military affairs. Its primary focus is functional rather than geographic. Most records and documents of the bureau are classified.

### Chemical Weapons and Non-Proliferation Division
Robert Einhorn, Deputy Assistant Secretary
(202) 647-8699

The primary focus of this division is nuclear nonproliferation. Analysts identify countries of proliferation concern and follow their actions with respect to the attainment of nuclear weapons. Once these countries have been identified and tracked, analysts recommend policy to ambassadors and country desk officers. Although country desk officers are regional experts, they often lack the technical expertise needed to make comprehensive nonproliferation policies. Thus, this department provides the link between regional concerns and technical-strategic concerns.

*Nuclear Risk Reduction Center*
Colonel Harold Kowalski, Staff Director
(202) 647-0025

The center maintains two communications centers to expedite verification that countries are complying with arms control agreements. The first communication center is with Russia and three other former Soviet Republics (Kazakistan, Ukraine, and Belarus) to verify their compliance with various arms reduction treaties. The second communication center is online 24 hours with most European countries to ensure their compliance with the Conventional Forces in Europe Treaty.

## BUREAU OF DEMOCRACY, HUMAN RIGHTS, AND LABOR

John H. F. Shattuck, Assistant Secretary
(202) 647-2126

This bureau monitors human rights conditions in foreign nations as reported by U.S. embassies abroad and prepares policy recommendations concerning U.S. military and economic development assistance programs. It also coordinates the preparation of annual (since 1976) State Department unclassified reports to Congress on the human rights situation in countries receiving U.S. military or economic aid. Human Rights Regional Officers maintain close contact with private organizations and individuals interested in international human rights issues.

## BUREAU FOR INTERNATIONAL NARCOTICS MATTERS

Robert S. Gelbard, Assistant Secretary
(202) 647-9822

This bureau works with foreign governments to stem the flow of narcotics into the United States. It cooperates also with the White House Office of National Drug Control Policy, the departments of Defense (K10), Justice (K23), Health and Human Services (K19), and Treasury (K40), as well as the immigration service and the coast guard. The bureau has provided monetary and technical assistance to help eradicate the international drug problem. Much of the work is classified.

### Office of Program Management
John Nix, Director
(202) 647-9090

*Americas/Caribbean Division*
Dianne Graham, Chief
(202) 647-7097

*Andean/South American Division*
Michael Ranneberger, Chief
(202) 647-8727

*Asia/Africa Division*
Douglas Rasmussen, Chief
(202) 647-5092

The regional divisions within this office are responsible for setting goals and maintaining programs within their respective countries. Within each division there are desk officers for individual areas. In the Americas/Caribbean Division there are desks for Mexico, Central America, and the Caribbean. In the Andean/South American Division there are desks covering Andean Region, Bolivia, Peru/Ecuador, and Southern Cone. In the Asia/Africa Division there are desks for Africa, Southeast Asia, and Southwest Asia.

## BUREAU OF OCEANS, INTERNATIONAL ENVIRONMENTAL AND SCIENTIFIC AFFAIRS

Elinor G. Constable, Assistant Secretary
(202) 647-1554

This functional bureau focuses on foreign policy questions relating to oceans, fisheries, environmental, health, space and energy technology issues. It represents the United States in international negotia-

tions and conferences and directs the State Department's overseas Science and Technology Counselor/Attaché Program.

### Environmental Policy Office
Day Mount, Director
(202) 647-9266

This office is concerned with a broad range of global environmental issues, including natural resource depletion, land and sea pollution, endangered species, and weather modification.

### Marine Conservation Office
Larry L. Snead, Director
(202) 647-2335

The office monitors U.S. bilateral fishing disputes. It represents the United States in the International Fisheries Commission and negotiates bilateral and multilateral fishing agreements.

### Ocean Affairs Office
R. Tucker Scully, Director
(202) 647-3262

This office is concerned with oceans law and policy, maritime marine science, marine pollution, whales, and Arctic and Antarctic resources and affairs. This office represents the United States in international oceans forums.

### Science, Technology, and Health Office
Edward Malloy, Director
(202) 647-2841

This office is concerned with international space activities, including the space station, remote sensing policy, and space cooperation. It handles large multilateral cooperation in science and technology including Organization for Economic Cooperation and Development (A39) and NATO committees. This office monitors technological trends and the status of international health programs, with a particular focus on less-developed nations.

## BUREAU OF POPULATION, REFUGEES, AND MIGRATION

Brunson McKinley, Deputy Assistant Secretary
(202) 647-5822

### Office of Refugee Assistance for Europe, the Near East, and South Asia
Michael J. Metrinko, Director
(202) 663-1034

**Office of Refugee Assistance for Africa, Southeast Asia, and the Americas**
Margaret J. McKelvey, Director
(202) 663-1027

The bureau is responsible for the operation of U.S. refugee programs overseas, carried out in cooperation with other governments, private and international organizations, and other U.S. government agencies. These programs include relief and repatriation of refugees and the selection, processing, and training of refugees to be admitted into the United States. Within the bureau there are regional offices with specialists who develop refugee policy unique to their respective regions.

## BUREAU OF LEGISLATIVE AFFAIRS

Wendy R. Sherman, Assistant Secretary
(202) 647-4204

Staff members of this bureau seek the opinion of Congress on major foreign policy issues, explain U.S. foreign policy initiatives, and arrange formal and informal meetings, briefings, and appearances before committees. The bureau is actively involved in drafting and monitoring legislation affecting foreign policy. Joel Davis (202/647-9037) is the legislative management officer for narcotics and counter-terrorism. Carl Raether (202/647-2135) is the legislative management officer for foreign assistance, arms, sales, and security assistance. Susan Jacobs (202/647-9036) is the legislative management officer for consular affairs and refugee programs. Susan Kakesako (202/647-8732) is the legislative management officer for human rights and humanitarian affairs.

## OFFICE OF THE LEGAL ADVISER

Conrad K. Harper, Legal Adviser
(202) 647-9598

Staff lawyers in the Office of the Assistant Legal Adviser for International Claims and Investment Disputes (202/647-7810) and Private International Law (202/653-9851) provide researchers with information on U.S. involvement in global legal issues. The Assistant Legal Adviser for Ocean, Environment, and Scientific Affairs (202/647-1370) handles questions involving maritime and fisheries boundaries. The Assistant Legal Adviser for Politico-Military Affairs (202/647-7838) works on legal aspects of U.S. arms sales around the world. Scholars may make arrangements to use the law library of the Office of the Legal Adviser (202/647-1146).

Publications of the Office of the Legal Adviser include the annual *Digest of United States Practice in International Law,* containing policy statements of the official U.S. position on every major question of international law, including human rights and law of the sea. The office also publishes *Treaties in Force,* an annual list of all U.S. international agreements in force on January 1 of the year of publication. Full texts of U.S. treaties and international agreements are found in the 13-volume *Treaties and Other International Agreements of the United States of America, 1776–1949,* and *Annual United States Treaties and Other International Agreements* (1950–present), which includes a subject and country index.

## BUREAU OF PUBLIC AFFAIRS

(202) 647-6607

**Office of the Historian**
U.S. Department of State
Room 3100, SA-1
Washington, D.C. 20522-0103

William Z. Slany, Historian
(202) 663-1123
Glenn LaFantasie, Deputy Historian and General Editor
(202) 663-1133
David H. Herschler, Declassification Coordinator
(202) 663-1145
Reference Inquiries
(202) 663-1126

The primary activity of the Office of the Historian is the preparation of the State Department's *Foreign Relations of the United States* documentary series. This office also produces the series *American Foreign Policy: Current Documents.* The office's other principal activity is the preparation of a variety of narrative historical studies, some of which are released to the public domain or even published.

The office, which has expert knowledge of the documentary holdings of the department, maintains close contact with the information management staff of the State Department, the National Archives and Records Administration (B11), and the presidential libraries throughout the United States. Staff members are excellent sources of information on past and present records-filing systems of the State Department and the location, content, and accessibility of U.S. and foreign diplomatic records and source materials.

The Office of the Historian also maintains up-to-date records of basic data relating to foreign visits of the president and the secretary of state; official visits by heads of state to the United States; names of the principal officers of the State Department; and the names of the chiefs of U.S. missions. This list has been published most recently as *Principal Officers of the Department of State and United States Chiefs of Mission, 1778–1990*. These publications can be purchased from the GPO (see Appendix III).

## FOREIGN SERVICE INSTITUTE

Lawrence P. Taylor, Director
1400 Key Boulevard
Arlington, Va. 22204-1500
(703) 302-6703

**School of Area Studies**
Richard Jackson, Dean
(703) 302-6858

The State Department's Foreign Service Institute provides language and area training programs for U.S. government personnel. Included within the six-month general program of studies are regional seminar programs covering history, politics, economics, society, and culture; general policy issues; and special problems (e.g., economic development, delayed industrialization, migration and urbanization, and the role of women). Most courses are taught in part by guest lecturers from the academic community. Interested outsiders may receive permission to attend lectures. A general bibliography and syllabus for Latin American studies are available, as are individual course syllabuses.

Several specialized Foreign Service Institute programs may be of particular interest, including Executive Seminar in National and International Affairs, a 10-month orientation to contemporary trends in domestic and foreign issues for senior officials of U.S. government agencies; Foreign Affairs Interdepartmental Seminar, providing midlevel officials with two weeks of training on major policy issues as perceived by various government agencies; a Post-Professional Development Program, providing scholarly books, articles, lectures, seminars, and discussions for foreign-service officers abroad; and training programs focusing on international narcotics control and terrorism.

## REGIONAL BUREAUS

There are six regional bureaus within the State Department—Inter-American Affairs, Near Eastern Affairs, South Asian Affairs, European and Canadian Affairs, East Asian and Pacific Affairs, and African Affairs. The assistant secretaries for these bureaus are responsible for advising the secretary on matters concerning countries within their jurisdiction, for coordinating policy recommendations re-

lating to their region, and for guiding the diplomatic operations in their area. For more specific information on individual regions, consult the region-specific Scholars' Guides.

6.   Index Terms: Arms Control; Collective Security; Defense Policy, National; Development Issues; Diplomacy and Negotiations; Energy; Environmental Issues; Foreign Policy; Human Rights; Humanitarian Issues; Intelligence; International Economics; International Organizations; Low Intensity Conflict; Peacekeeping; Proliferation; Refugees; Regional Conflict; Terrorism

See also entries A43 and M6

---

## K38   Trade and Development Agency (TDA) (International Development Cooperation Agency)

---

1.a.  Rosslyn Plaza East
     1621 N. Kent Street
     Rosslyn, Va. 22209

Mail:
SA-16 Room 309
Washington, D.C. 20523-1602
(703) 875-4357

b.   The agency is open to the public. Appointments are strongly recommended.

c.   J. Joseph Grandmaison, Director

2.   The TDA provides funding for U.S. firms to carry out feasibility studies, consultation, and other planning services related to major projects in developing countries. By providing assistance in project planning, the agency promotes economic development and simultaneously helps U.S. firms get involved in projects that offer significant export opportunities. Because of U.S. legal restrictions, TDA is currently unable to fund certain activities in some countries.

TDA funds planning services for public sector projects, which are to be wholly owned by foreign governments, and for private sector projects in which a U.S. investor plans to take an equity position.

In situations where neither a feasibility study nor consultation is appropriate, TDA may provide funding for training, technical seminars, or orientation visits to the United States.

3. TDA has a small library specializing in international business and investment. Its collection of reports and its vertical files include materials dealing with developing nations. Clearance from a regional officer is required for the use of the library, which is open 9:00 A.M. to 5:30 P.M. Monday–Friday.

4. TDA's internal files are maintained in the relevant offices or in the TDA library. The files (with a few exceptions) are accessible to researchers after clearance has been obtained from a TDA staff member.

5. TDA has no major publications, but lists of current projects are usually available from the relevant offices.

6. Index Terms: Development Issues—Infrastructure; Development Issues—Technical Assistance

See also entries K1 and K32

## K39   Transportation Department (DOT)

1.a.  400 7th Street, SW
Washington, D.C. 20590
(202) 366-5580 (Public Information)
Fax: (202) 366-5583
(202) 366-4542 (Freedom of Information)
Fax: (202) 366-7152

b. Open to all federal contractors and employees with U.S. government identification, as well as the media. Other interested persons should make an appointment and present identification.

2. International activities of the Transportation Department are described below.

3. The Transportation Department Library (Richard K. Pemberton, Director) is located in Nassif Building, Room 2200, 400 7th Street, SW, Washington, D.C. 20590; 202/366-0746. The library is open 9:00 A.M.–4:00 P.M. Monday–Friday; interlibrary loan and photocopying facilities are available. Its holdings of 370,000 volumes and 2,000 periodical subscriptions, focus on the coast guard; highways and bridges; and air, marine, and mass transit transportation.

4. Internal records are discussed below with the offices in which they are housed.

5. Most DOT publications are available for examination in the Transportation Department Library, Room 2200D, 400 7th St. SW, Washington, D.C. 20590. The Office of the Secretary of Transporta-

tion provides the document distribution system with two essential services: a computerized mailing list operation and a centralized distribution and warehousing facility. The mailing list unit (Department of Transportation, Distribution Requirements Section, Room 2311, 400 7th Street, SW, Washington, D.C. 20590) serves those who want recurrent publications. The Property Utilization Section (Department of Transportation, 7200, 400 7th St. SW, Washington, D.C. 20590) operates the warehousing facility and will send up to nine copies of any free publication on request.

The Government Printing Office (see Appendix III) and the National Technical Information Service (see K29 and Appendix III) sell DOT publications. At the Federal Aviation Administration, Washington Office, the public can acquire a wide variety of documents. Contact the office at FAA Headquarters, Public Inquiry Center, APA-430, 800 Independence Avenue, SW, Washington, D.C. 20591 (202/267-3484). Publication lists are available on request.

**ASSISTANT SECRETARY FOR AVIATION AND INTERNATIONAL AFFAIRS**

Raymond G. Romero, Assistant Secretary
(202) 366-8822

**Office of International Transportation and Trade**
Arnold Levine, Director
(202) 366-4368

This office is responsible for a wide range of international transportation and trade policy and program issues in such areas as reimbursable technical assistance to developing countries, science and technology cooperation with developed countries, international maritime and land transport, maritime support programs, international standards development and harmonization, facilitation of trade and transport documentation and procedures, and transport-related trade promotion.

**Office of International Aviation (OIA)**
Paul L. Gretch, Director
(202) 366-2423

The OIA is responsible for formulating, coordinating, and executing U.S. international aviation policy and for administering the economic regulatory functions related to foreign air transportation. OIA originates aviation negotiation positions with respect to foreign countries; coordinates negotiating policy, strategy, and positions with the State Department (K37), other government agencies, and U.S. air carrier industry; and conducts or participates in those negotiations. OIA also receives formal and informal complaints from U.S. carriers experiencing difficulties in foreign markets and intervenes to resolve those problems.

On the regulatory side, OIA receives, processes, and makes or recommends disposition of all U.S. and foreign air carrier requests for economic authority to operate between the United States and foreign points. It also determines the disposition of all tariff filings by U.S. and foreign airlines. The office administers (and is responsible for reviewing and revising as needed) some 20 parts of Title 14 of the Code of Federal Regulations.

## FEDERAL AVIATION ADMINISTRATION (FAA)

800 Independence Avenue, SW
Washington, D.C. 20591
(202) 267-3484 (Public Information)
(202) 267-3490 (Freedom of Information)

### Office of International Aviation
Joan W. Bauerlein, Director
(202) 267-3213

The FAA's Office of International Aviation (AIA) develops and promotes U.S./FAA policy on technical safety issues, manages technical assistance and cooperative efforts with other civil aviation authorities, and serves as a point of contact for U.S. aviation industry and citizens interested in the operational and technical aspects of international civil aviation information, policy, and programs. AIA has various records of agreements and background information on civil aviation in other countries, and serves as the executive secretariat for the Interagency Group on International Aviation (IGIA), which develops and coordinates technical policy for the United States to present at the International Civil Aviation Organization. For further information on types of records or other information holdings in AIA, contact Craig Lindsay, International Analyst (202/267-8176). For information concerning the International Civil Aviation Organization and the IGIA process, contact Roberta C. Proffitt, IGIA Principal Officer (202/267-8146).

## MARITIME ADMINISTRATION

400 7th Street, SW
Washington, D.C. 20590
(202) 366-5812 (Public Information)
(202) 366-5746 (Freedom of Information)

### Office of Trade Analysis and Insurance
Edmond J. Fitzgerald, Director
(202) 366-2400

This office compiles statistical data—from private U.S. commercial shippers' reports and other sources—on U.S. ocean-borne trade with other countries and on other countries' merchant shipping, by country. Data are available to researchers in hardcopy or computer files. The office produces several annual publications that contain international data, including *Merchant Fleets of the World; Foreign Flag Vessels Owned by U.S. Parent Companies; United States Oceanborne Foreign Trade;* and *U.S. Vessels Inventory.*

### Office of International Activities
James A. Treichel, Director
(202) 366-5773

This office is responsible for supporting U.S.-flag shipping in its operations abroad. The office manages the Maritime Administration's efforts to remove foreign restrictions on U.S.-flag carriers' access to cargo and their operating freedom. It also acts in a similar manner in support of the U.S. shipbuilding industry.

6.    Index Terms: International Economics—International Trade; International Organizations; Transnationalism

---

# K40    Treasury Department

1.a.  15th Street and Pennsylvania Avenue, NW
      Washington, D.C. 20220
      (202) 622-2960 (Public Information)
      (202) 622-2427 (Freedom of Information/ Privacy Act)
      Fax: (202) 622-0073

   b.  Open to the public by appointment.

2.    The Department of the Treasury formulates and recommends economic, financial, tax, and fiscal policies. Treasury representatives located in U.S. embassies abroad are financial advisers to the U.S. diplomatic missions.

3.    Treasury Department Library, located in room 5030 (Michael Conklin, Director; 202/622-0990) is open to researchers with restrictions, by appointment, 9:00 A.M.–5:30 P.M. Monday–Friday. Interlibrary loan and photocopying services are available. The library's holdings of some 80,000

volumes, 400,000 microfiche, and 7,300 reels of microfilm focus on economics, finance, law, and treasury history.

4.   Retired Treasury Department internal records are controlled by the Office of Administration's Information Resources Management Branch (202/622-1599). Access to most of these documents is through Freedom of Information Act procedures.

5.   Internal Revenue Service publications revised annually include *Tax Guide for U.S. Citizens Abroad* (Publication No. 54), *Foreign Tax Credit for U.S. Citizens and Resident Aliens* (Publication No. 514), *Tax Information for U.S. Government Civilian Employees Stationed Abroad* (Publication No. 516), and *Tax Information for American Scholars in the U.S. and Abroad* (Publication No. 520). For information call (202) 622-2150.

A *Selected List of Treasury Publications* is periodically updated and can be acquired free from the Office of Public Affairs (Robert Levine, International Affairs Specialist, 202/622-2960). Publications of interest include the monthly *Treasury Bulletin,* which contains international financial statistics on receipts and expenditures, public debt, and capital movements between the U.S. and foreign countries; *Foreign Credit by the United States Government: Status of Active Foreign Credits of the United States Government and of International Organizations* (semiannual), which records debts owed to the U.S. government and various international organizations; *Annual Report of the National Advisory Council on International Monetary Policies;* and *Annual Report of the Secretary of the Treasury on the State of the Finances* (with a separate statistical appendix).

## OFFICE OF INTERNATIONAL AFFAIRS

Jeffrey R. Shafer, Assistant Secretary
(202) 622-0060

A primary duty of this office is to formulate and implement policies dealing with international monetary, financial, commercial, energy, and trade programs. Issues it monitors include the balance of payments, gold outflow, international monetary and foreign exchange problems and accords, the Bretton-Woods Agreement, the operation of the International Monetary Fund (L11), and the workings of the International Bank for Reconstruction and Development (World Bank) (L8).

### International Development, Debt, and Environment Policy

Susan B. Levine, Deputy Assistant Secretary
(202) 622-0659

The office is responsible for advising the assistant secretary for international affairs in the formulation and execution of policies dealing with the financial, commercial, monetary, energy, and trade policies and programs of developing nations.

### Office of Multilateral Development Banks

Joseph Eichenberger, Director
(202) 622-1810

This division monitors the operation of the various multilateral banks worldwide (e.g., International Bank for Reconstruction and Development [L8]) and contributes to the formation of U.S. policy toward them.

### Office of Developing Nations

James H. Fall III, Deputy Assistant Secretary
(202) 622-0667

Each staff analyst monitors the monetary and fiscal conditions of a particular country. These specialists are the primary contact-points within the Treasury Department for information on developing nations' debt levels with the United States, balance-of-payments conditions, and general monetary conditions. Their data sources include individual countries' banking reports and reports of U.S. financial attachés. Most of the office's internal products, which consist primarily of operational policy papers, are for internal use only, but staff members will confer with private scholars. Bruce Juba is director of the Office of Latin America and Caribbean Nations (202/622-1282); Edwin Barber is the director of the Office of African Nations and Paris Club (202/622-1730); and Meg Lundsager is the director of the Office of Asia and Near Eastern Nations (202/622-0359).

### International Monetary and Financial Policy

Timothy F. Geithner, Deputy Assistant Secretary
(202) 622-0656

Members of this office study financial, trade, investment, banking, and security issues. Analysts prepare briefing papers on issues pertinent to their country of expertise from broad global and topical perspectives on banking and monetary issues. Most reports are classified.

### Trade and Investment Policy

William E. Barreda, Deputy Assistant Secretary
(202) 622-0168

The office monitors bilateral and multilateral trade discussions. Staff members regularly prepare reports on foreign investment regulations, rules, and policies to determine their impact on U.S. investments abroad. Most of the resulting policy papers are for internal use only, but staff members are permitted to confer with researchers.

## OFFICE OF ECONOMIC POLICY

Alicia Munnell, Assistant Secretary
(202) 622-2200

Economic analysts in this office prepare forecasts of U.S. trade and current account balances for Treasury Department officials to use in formulating economic policy. They conduct research and analysis of international trade, monetary, and energy issues. The analysts also monitor the flow of banking and corporate capital to and from the United States, as well as the extent of portfolio investment by foreign nationals in the United States and by Americans abroad.

## INTERNAL REVENUE SERVICE (IRS)

1111 Constitution Avenue, NW
Washington, D.C. 20224
(202) 622-5164 (Freedom of Information/Privacy Act)

**Office of Assistant Commissioner (International)**
Regina M. Deanehan, Assistant Commissioner
(202) 874-1900

*Office of Tax Administration Advisory Services (TAAS)*
Socorro Velazquez, Director
(202) 874-1330

In providing technical advisory assistance, IRS/TAAS offers several services to foreign governments. Through the INTAX (International Tax Administration training series) managerial seminars are conducted worldwide in English and in various foreign languages. TAAS sponsors an International Visitors Program for foreign government tax and finance officers visiting the United States, as well as individually designed programs in the United States for top-level foreign tax officials who are enabled to observe IRS upper-management procedures. Since 1963, TAAS has also been engaged in an overseas advisory assistance program involving tax surveys and short- and long-term on-site assistance activities in every major geographical region in the world.

## COMMITTEE ON FOREIGN INVESTMENT IN THE UNITED STATES (CFIUS)

Don Crafts, Chairman
(202) 622-1860

The advisory committee, although housed at the Treasury Department, is an interagency committee composed of members drawn from Treasury, Defense (K10), and State (K37). Its purpose is to investigate foreign investment in the United States and to determine whether it is detrimental to the national economy.

## UNITED STATES CUSTOMS SERVICE

**Office of International Affairs**
Douglas M. Browning, Assistant Commissioner
(202) 927-0400

The Office of International Affairs oversees the Customs Service's training programs. Working in conjunction with other Custom Service departments, federal departments and agencies, and foreign governments, the office develops policies, training programs, and protocol for customs officers stationed at home and abroad.

**Office of International Operations**
David H. Harrell, Director
(202) 927-1490

This office works with AID (K1), the State Department (K37), the Defense Department (K10), and foreign governments to develop programs for improving foreign countries' customs assessments. Current examples of such programs are in Saudi Arabia, Trinidad and Tobago, and Costa Rica.

**Office of International Policy**
Jerrald Worley, Director
(202) 927-0440

Similar to the Office of International Operations, this office works in conjunction with foreign governments to improve customs operations. Rather than trying to improve individual countries' assessments, this office attempts to obtain simpler, more efficient international customs procedures. Although most agreements are achieved on a bilateral level with U.S. trade partners, multilateral agreements are also sought through the Customs Cooperation Council and the Cabinet Committee to Combat Terrorism.

Index Terms: Development Issues; Energy; International Economics

**United States Holocaust Memorial Museum** **See entry C11**

## K41 United States Information Agency (USIA)

1.a.  301 4th Street, SW
Washington, D.C. 20547
(202) 619-4355 (Information)
(202) 619-5499 (Freedom of Information)
Fax: (202) 554-0072

b.  The agency is open to the public. Appointments are recommended.

c.  Joseph D. Duffey, Director

2.  USIA, an independent organization within the executive branch, is responsible for the U.S. government's overseas information and cultural activities. These range from the Fulbright Program to the USIA Television and Film Service. To carry out its mission the agency uses international cultural and academic exchanges, media products, and a network of computerized news files in several languages. It conducts direct broadcasts worldwide via its radio network (Voice of America) and television service (WORLD-NET). USIA has a close working relationship with the State Department (K37), the National Security Council (K28), and the Defense Department (K10). It provides foreign public opinion analysis on international issues, as well as daily summaries of foreign media treatment of U.S. actions and policies. The agency occasionally hires outside consultants.

3.  USIA Library, some 50,000 volumes strong, contains the USIA Historical Collection. The repository is closed to the public. For interlibrary loan information contact Karen S. Mitchell, Chief of Collection Development (202/619-6925; fax 202/619-6190). For a description of Voice of America's Music and Tape Libraries, see entry E17.

4.  USIA is required to have its overseas program materials available for public inspection at its Washington, D.C., headquarters. Reference reels of Voice of America and WORLDNET programs are available from the USIA Tape Library, William J. Cohen Building, Room 2231, 330 Independence Avenue, SW, Washington, D.C. 20547; Roblyn Hymes, Librarian (202/619-1344) (see entry E17). Scholars may only examine the material on-site. Note-taking is permitted. Special permission is required to photocopy material acquired from foreign sources.

5.  A number of pamphlets and brochures describing academic exchange programs, cultural centers, and Voice of America broadcasting services are available free from the Publications Division (202/619-4257).

### REGIONAL OFFICES

(202) 619-4860

The key contact units of USIA, these offices oversee the agency's programs in specific regions of the world and serve as the coordinating points between USIA field offices and the agency's Washington-based elements (described below). Regional affairs officers are accessible and willing to discuss USIA activities in their respective areas of responsibility: Robert LaGamma (African Affairs, Director, 202/619-4894); Don Hamilton (American Republics Affairs, Director, 202/619-4860); George Beasley (East Asian and Pacific Affairs, Director, 202/619-4829); John P. Harrod (West European and Canadian Affairs, Director, 202/619-4563); Anne M. Sigmund (East European and Newly Independent States Affairs, Director, 202/619-4563); Kent Obee (North African, Near Eastern and South Asian Affairs, Director, 202/619-4520).

### BUREAU OF POLICY AND PROGRAMS

(202) 619-6048

**Washington Foreign Press Center**
National Press Building, Suite 898
529 14th Street, NW
Washington, D.C. 20045
Fax: (202) 724-0007

Jacob Gillespie, Director
(202) 724-0032

The Foreign Press Center in Washington, D.C., assists foreign journalists, both resident correspondents and visitors, by giving press conferences and policy briefings by U.S. officials and outside experts, conducting thematic tours, and providing general assistance. The center makes available commercial wire service and database outlets, and electronic links to press briefings at the White House, State Department, Defense Department, and elsewhere. The center compiles a regularly updated directory of foreign correspondents on assignment in the United States. This useful research tool is available to scholars upon request.

### PRESS AND PUBLICATIONS SERVICE

**Publications Division**
Lewis Luchs, Chief
(202) 619-4265

The division produces special thematic pamphlets and special publications. A standard set of pamphlets deals with topics such as democracy and market economies. It also produces, upon request, pamphlets for other government agencies, U.S. embassies abroad, or domestic representatives of foreign USIA posts. These pamphlets can be published in almost any language.

### Press Division
Terrence Kneebone, Chief
(202) 619-4136

The Press Division produces a daily *Wireless File,* which is distributed through U.S. embassies, consulates general, and USIA centers to host-country media and individuals worldwide. This fully computerized press service, produced in English, Arabic, French, Russian, and Spanish, features White House press briefings, addresses by U.S. leaders, and background stories pertaining to U.S. domestic and foreign policies. Back copies of the *Wireless File* are contained in a computerized database known as Public Diplomacy Query.

### OFFICE OF RESEARCH AND MEDIA REACTION
Anne Pincus, Director
(202) 619-4965
Fax: (202) 619-6977

Staff members design and analyze public opinion and audience surveys conducted by commercial polling organizations throughout the world. Regional branches (American Republics, 202/619-5104; East Asia and Pacific, 202/619-4987; Europe, 202/619-5136; Near East, South Asia, and Africa, 202/619-4994; Russia, Ukraine, and Commonwealth, 202/619-5130) produce public opinion surveys of foreign attitudes toward current domestic and international issues, and publish country studies and multiyear trend comparisons going back almost 30 years. Each branch also produces information media and programs (periodicals, films, radio broadcasts, etc.) on foreign audiences, by region and country. The Media Reaction Branch of the office produces two daily summaries of media reaction commentaries from around the world on issues of interest to U.S. policymakers.

The Office of Research and Media Reaction disseminates its research reports to some 30 depository libraries in the United States, including the Library of Congress (A29).

### VOICE OF AMERICA (VOA)
Wilbur J. Cohen Building
330 Independence Avenue, SW
Washington, D.C. 20547
(202) 619-2538

### Regional Divisions
The divisions (VOA Europe, 202/619-2167; Africa, 202/619-3657; American Republics, 202/619-2960; Central Asia, 202/619-3921; East Asia and Pacific, 202/619-1405; Eurasia, 202/619-3422; North Africa, Near East, and South Asia, 202/619-0331; North Europe, 202/619-2000; and South Europe, 202/619-2200) produce Voice of America shortwave, medium-wave, and satellite radio broadcasts. VOA broadcasts in 46 languages for overseas audiences and to approximately 1,100 affiliate stations worldwide. Its programming includes world and regional news, reports from field correspondents, analysis, features, music, and editorials. The regional divisions also supply tapes of newscasts and commentaries to radio stations overseas through USIA field offices. The staff of each division is partially composed of emigrants with long experience in radio broadcasting in their former home countries. Divisions periodically contract private specialists to prepare feature reports on specialized scientific and cultural topics.

Radio and T.V. Martí (Radio: 202/401-7013, TV: 202/501-7210) serve as VOA's regional divisions for Cuba. Their broadcasts accord with all VOA standards of objectivity, accuracy, balance, and diversity.

### Current Affairs Division
Fred Cooper, Chief
(202) 619-2938

The staff of the Current Affairs Division keeps abreast of international events on a 24-hour-per-day basis.

See also entry E17

### OFFICE OF WORLDNET TELEVISION AND FILM SERVICE
Patrick Henry Building
601 D Street, NW, Room 5000
Washington, D.C. 20547

Charles W. Fox III, Director
(202) 501-7806

The service is responsible for planning, organizing, and directing the agency's television and film activities. WORLDNET is an interactive, state-of-the-art television network inaugurated in November 1983 to link Washington, D.C., via satellite with all U.S. embassies and overseas posts. Daily broadcasts are made possible through agreements signed by USIA/TV and broadcasting services in host countries. Broadcasts, which are conducted in English, Spanish, French, Arabic, Serbian, Ukrainian, Russian, and several other languages, include news, public affairs, and feature programming.

Since April 1985, these broadcasts have been offered through a public feed to television stations abroad, where they are most often carried on cable networks. Regional components of WORLDNET (ARNET, for the American Republics region; AFNET for Africa; EURONET for Europe; NEANET for the Near East and South Asia; and EANET for East Asia and the Pacific) broadcast on a 24-hour basis.

Title/synopsis records on the WORLDNET (AFNET, ARNET, EANET, EURONET, NEANET) and many other WORLDNET productions are maintained in computer files currently accommodating key word and program number searches. Subject matter indexing of these records is underway. Address inquiries to Eugenia Nigro, Public Affairs Specialist at WORLDNET (202/501-8274).

## BUREAU OF EDUCATIONAL AND CULTURAL AFFAIRS

John P. Loiello, Associate Director
(202) 619-4597

### Office of Cultural Centers and Resources
William LaSalle, Acting Director
(202) 619-4866

This office provides policy direction, program support, professional guidance, and materials to USIA libraries, cultural centers, and binational centers overseas.

### Library Programs Division
Jeanette Kidd, Reference Branch Chief
(202) 619-4887

The library is not open to the public, but it offers interlibrary loan service (8:15 A.M.–5:00 P.M. Monday–Friday). Its holdings of 50,000 volumes include USIA's Historical Collection. The division provides services and support to USIA posts and agency program offices abroad, including library training, technology, and the services of regional library officers.

### Office of Academic Programs
Thomas E. E. Spooner, Acting Director
(202) 619-6409

*Academic Exchange Programs Division*
Barry Ballow, Chief
(202) 619-4360

The division, in conjunction with private cooperating agencies, Fulbright commissions, and USIA posts abroad, administers most of the Fulbright programs. The Fulbright program is designed to "increase mutual understanding between the people of the United States and the people of other countries."

Each year approximately 4,800 grants are awarded to U.S. and foreign scholars around the world. Grants are available through several programs: the U.S. Scholar Program; the Fulbright Student Program; the Visiting Scholar Program and the Scholar-in-Residence Program; the Fulbright Teacher Exchange Program; the University Affiliations Program; and the Hubert H. Humphrey North-South Fellowship Program for midlevel professionals from the developing world. Grants are generally for study periods of one semester, one year, or two years; the application process begins at least one year before the academic year of the grant. Interested lecturers and researchers should contact Council for International Exchange of Scholars (202/686-7871); graduate students should contact the Institute of International Education (212/984-5314); and professionals should contact the Special Programs Unit of USIA (202/619-5434). Some Fulbright funds are administered by the Department of Education (K11), rather than USIA. These funds are awarded to U.S. individuals or institutions for research and training focusing on non-Western languages and world area studies. For more information call the Center for International Education (202/708-7283).

*Advising, Teaching, and Specialized Program Division*
Judith Siegal, Chief
(202) 619-5434

The division conducts programs and provides services to strengthen overseas educational advising centers and to improve the quality of the exchange experience for foreign students in the United States. It administers the Hubert H. Humphrey North-South Fellowship Program, which awards grants to midcareer professionals from the developing world for a year of study and practical experience in the United States. It also administers the University Affiliations Grant Program, which provides seed money for the initiation and expansion of institutional relationships between U.S. and foreign academic institutions.

*Office of Citizen Exchange*
Robert Schiffer, Director
(202) 619-5348

The office awards grants to U.S. nonprofit institutions for cooperative projects designed to support linkages between U.S. and foreign institutions worldwide. The projects aim to promote mutual understanding through exchanges in such areas as public administration, rule of law, business management, media, the environment, and parliamentary exchanges. The office administers a number of special initiatives for Russia and the Newly Independent States. Youth exchange programs are also administered by this office.

*Office of International Visitors*
Lula Rodriguez, Director
(202) 619-5217

Each year USIA invites approximately 5,000 foreign leaders in such fields as government, labor, mass media, science, and education to the United States to participate in the International Visitor Program. About half come to the United States at their own or their government's expense; others remaining are fully or partially funded by the agency. Selection of candidates is made by the USIA and U.S. embassy personnel abroad. Further information may be obtained from the Grant Programs Division (202/619-5239).

6.   Index Terms: Political Systems and Ideologies; Transnationalism

See also entry E17

## United States Institute of Peace   See entry H73

---

## K42   United States Trade Representative

---

1.a.  Winder Building
      600 17th Street, NW
      Washington, D.C. 20506
      (202) 395-3350 (Public Affairs)
      Fax: (202) 395-3911

b.  Open 9:00 A.M.–5:00 P.M. Monday–Friday; appointments are necessary.

c.  Michael Kantor, U.S. Trade Representative

2.   The office of the U.S. Trade Representative began in 1963 as the Office of the Special Representative for Trade Negotiations. Today, the U.S. trade representative is a cabinet-level position (the trade representative holds the rank of ambassador) within the Executive Office. The Office of the Trade Representative is small for a federal office, having only 150 staff members. This is an advantage for scholars because it makes finding the right person to talk to fairly easy.

The trade representative is responsible for developing U.S. international trade policy, coordinating the implementation of that policy, advising the president on that policy, and negotiating international trade agreements. For example, the representative serves as U.S. liaison to meetings on the General Agreement on Tariffs and Trade (GATT), negotiations of the Organization for Economic Cooperation and Development, negotiations in the United Nations conference on Trade and Development, and other bilateral and multilateral negotiations on trade. The representative is also the vice-chair of the Overseas Private Investment Corporation (K32), an ex-officio member of the Export-Import Bank of the United States (K14), and a member of the National Advisory Committee on International Monetary and Financial Policies.

Within the office of the trade representative there are negotiators for each region of the world, as well as for general topics such as agriculture. Scholars with questions about U.S. trade policy toward a particular country or region should contact the appropriate negotiator: Robert Cassidy, Asia and the Pacific; Charles E. Roh, Jr., Canada and Mexico; Peter Allgeier, Europe and the Mediterranean; Ira Wolf, Japan and China; and Carmen Suro-Bredie, Latin American, the Caribbean and Africa.

3.   The Trade Representative's Office maintains a small reading room that scholars may access. The first step in using the reading room is contacting Dianne Wildmann in Public Affairs. She approves use of the room and can put scholars in contact with negotiators. Housed in the reading room are documents (such as the NAFTA agreement), testimony, press releases published by the Trade Representative's Office, and reference books on trade. Correspondence between U.S. and foreign negotiators is not available in the reading room until negotiations are completed and the material has been released by the Trade Representative's Office. Scholars looking for information on older trade agreements may wish to check the National Archives (B11); the reading room carries mostly current material.

5.   The Trade Representative's Office publishes two major reports along with its press releases. The *Annual Federal Trade Estimates Report* (301 Report), which focuses on foreign trade barriers and agreements, is released on March 31 each year. The *Intellectual Property Issues* (Special 301), which focuses on current trends in international intellectual property law, is released on April 30.

6.   Index Terms: Diplomacy and Negotiations; International Economics—International Trade

## Woodrow Wilson International Center for Scholars (WWICS)   See entry H76

# L

# International Government Organizations

## Introductory Note

The presence of international organizations—especially the International Bank for Reconstruction and
Development (World Bank) (L8) and its affiliates in
Washington, D.C., and the International Monetary
Fund (IMF) (L11)—yield valuable resources for
scholars, particularly in fields of international development, and international economic, humanitarian,
and political affairs. The personnel of the international organizations described in this section may
provide useful information and materials within the
limits imposed by their schedules and official
regulations.

In addition to the organizations listed in section L,
Washington, D.C., is the home of more than 150 foreign embassies that can provide general information
on current developments and may assist scholars by
putting them in contact with organizations and individuals in their respective countries that have information and data otherwise difficult to obtain in the
United States. The embassies also sponsor lectures
and special events, and disseminate newsletters,
pamphlets, statistics, and posters projecting the historical, political, and development programs in their
countries. For a list, addresses, and professional personnel of the foreign embassies in Washington,
D.C., see the *Diplomatic List*, published quarterly
by the State Department (K37).

A dependable source of information on the Organization for Economic Cooperation and Develop-

ment (A39) is its Publications and Information Center, located at 2001 L Street, NW, Suite 700, Washington, D.C. 20036, (202) 785-6323.

## L1 African Development Bank Group— North American Representative Office

1.a. 2001 Pennsylvania Avenue, NW, Suite 350
Washington, D.C. 20006
(202) 429-5160
Fax: (202) 659-4704

b. Not open to the public.

c. Daouda Toure, Principal Economist

2. Established in Abidian, Ivory Coast, in 1963, the African Development Bank Group is composed of the African Development Bank (ADB), the African Development Fund (ADF), and the Nigerian Trust Fund (NTF). The bank is a membership organization composed of 51 African nations and 34 non-African nations whose objective is to contribute to the economic development and social progress of regional (African) members. It tries to mobilize the resources at its disposal to finance unilateral and multilateral investment projects, promote international dialogue and understanding on development issues, promote investment in Africa, and provide the technical assistance needed to study and prepare development projects. The ADB acquires its funding from capital subscriptions by member countries and from borrowing on the international market. The bank uses its funds to finance projects and programs that focus on the development of agriculture, public utilities, transportation and communication, industry, and social sectors. The bank also provides loans and technical assistance to regional nations. Although the bank is an independent entity from the International Bank for Reconstruction and Development (World Bank) (L8), it cofinances some programs with the World Bank.

The North American Representative Office is charged with initiating, developing, and maintaining contacts between each bank and the international financial and investment community, and with government agencies and nongovernmental organizations (NGOs) in North America.

4. Most internal records and documents are housed at the Ivory Coast headquarters, though general reports are available from the North American Office in Washington. Reports are translated into French and English and may be obtained by calling (202) 429-5160.

5. The African Development Bank Group publishes an annual report, which gives an in-depth look at the group's programs, projects, lending, and finances. The annual report also includes Financial Statements and Reports of the External Auditors for the ADB, ADF, and NTF.

6. Index Terms: Development Issues—Aid and Investment; International Economics—International Finance

## L2 European Union—Delegation of the European Commission

1.a. 2100 M Street, NW, Suite 707
Washington, D.C. 20037
(202) 862-9500

c. Andreas A. M. van Agt, Ambassador

2. Established in 1952 the European Union (EU) (*formerly* the European Community) seeks to achieve the economic and political integration of Europe. The delegation has been representing the EU in Washington since 1954. The delegation functions as the EU's diplomatic mission in the United States (although it lacks the visa-granting and culture marketing aspects of a regular embassy). The delegation and its resources are an outstanding source of information on the official activities of the EU, its internal policies and external agreements.

3. For a description of the European Union Information Service see A13. For more information on the European Union's exhibits and audiovisual collection see entry F9. A list of libraries in the United States that house collections of official EU documents is available upon request.

5. News releases on EU matters are issued free of charge about 50 times a year in the series *European Union News*, restricted to the press, and in *Euromemo*. The delegation also publishes *Europe* magazine, which offers information on the single market, provides interviews with European political, government, and business leaders, and focuses on culture and sports in Europe. *Europe* is available by subscription. EU publications can be purchased by writing UNIPUB, 4611 Assembly Drive, Lanham, Md. 20706-4391, or by calling (301) 459-7666.

6. Index Terms: Collective Security—Regional Alliance Systems; International Economics—Integration; International Organizations—Regional

See also entries A13 and F9

## L3 Food and Agriculture Organization (FAO) (United Nations)—Liaison Office for North America

1.a. 1001 22d Street, NW, Suite 300
Washington, D.C. 20437
(202) 653-2402 (Library)
Fax: (202) 653-5760

b. 8:30 A.M.–5:00 P.M. Monday–Friday

c. Dennis Brydges, Executive Officer
James T. Hill, Officer-in-Charge

2. The FAO is an autonomous specialized agency of the United Nations, which is composed of 169 member nations. FAO is pledged to improve the production and distribution of food and agriculture products in all parts of the world. In cooperation with the UN Development Program (L14), the International Fund for Agriculture Development, the International Bank for Reconstruction and Development (World Bank) (L8), and regional banks and funds, the FAO designs and supports a wide range of projects, including technical and scientific assistance to a variety of agricultural, fisheries, and forestry programs around the world.

3. For a description of the Liaison Office for North America's library, see entry A17.

5. FAO's extensive publications program emphasizes food, nutrition, fisheries, forestry, and agriculture. Copies of FAO publications are available from UNIPUB, 4611-F Assembly Drive, Lanham, Md. 20706 (800/274-4888).

6. Index Terms: Development Issues—Agriculture; International Organizations—United Nations

See also entry A17

## L4 Inter-American Commercial Arbitration Commission (IACAC)

1.a. 19th and Constitution Avenue, NW, Room 211
Washington, D.C. 20006
(202) 458-3249
Fax: (202) 828-0157

b. Open to the public.

c. Charles R. Norberg, Director General

2. IACAC is a quasi-governmental international body that promotes arbitration and conciliation of international commercial disputes in the Western Hemisphere. The commission is composed of delegates from National Sections in Latin American countries, Canada, and the United States. The National Sections consist of representatives of chambers of commerce and other commercial or legal groups in each member nation. When called upon to assist in the settlement of an international commercial dispute, IACAC provides advice and consultation; when necessary, it works through its appropriate National Sections to appoint arbitrators and establish arbitration rules and procedures.

The commission meets biennially at an Inter-American Conference on Commercial Arbitration, held at varying sites throughout the hemisphere. It also sponsors seminars in the United States and Latin America on an ad hoc basis and maintains an Academy of International Arbitration in Mexico City.

4. The director general's collection of documents and research materials on Latin American arbitration laws is open to researchers, but arbitration case files remain confidential.

5. A quarterly newsletter, *Inter-American Arbitration,* is disseminated.

6. Index Terms: Diplomacy and Negotiations; International Economics—International Trade; International Organizations—Regional

## L5 Inter-American Defense Board

1.a. 2600 16th Street, NW
Washington, D.C. 20441
(202) 939-6600
Fax: (202) 939-6620

b. Not open to the public, but visitors will be received by appointment.

c. Maj. Gen. James R. Harding USA, Chair

2. The Inter-American Defense Board is an autonomous, multinational military organization funded through the Organization of American States (L13). Its staff of delegates—high-level armed forces officers from member countries—prepares hemispheric defense plans, develops procedures for the standardization of inter-American military organizations and operations, and produces studies on strategic and military affairs. A Council of Delegates meets biweekly at closed general assemblies. The Inter-American Defense Board also operates the Inter-American Defense College (A23 and L6).

3.   A small reference library is maintained for staff use. It contains a growing collection of official military documents, transcripts of military conferences, and the proceedings of Inter-American Defense Board delegate assemblies. The collection is excellent for research on selected aspects of military affairs.

4–5.  The staff of officer-delegates produces a variety of research publications, all classified. They include "Strategic Defense Plans," "Guerrilla and Counterguerrilla Warfare," "Contribution of the Armed Forces in Economic-Social Development of Countries." These, along with the board's internal documents and working papers, are maintained in the board's Conferences and Documents Section. Although all such resources are "for official use only," there are indications that outside scholars working on research projects of particular interest to the board might be provided with at least limited access. Inquiries should be directed to the Secretary, Inter-American Defense Board.

6.   Index Terms: Collective Security—Regional Alliance Systems; Military Science

## L6   Inter-American Defense College

1.a.  Fort Lesley J. McNair, Building 52
      Washington, D.C. 20319-6100
      (202) 646-1337

b.  Not open to the public, but visitors will be received by appointment.

c.  Maj. Gen. James R. Harding USA, Director

2.   The Inter-American Defense College is an international military institute for advanced studies operated by the Inter-American Defense Board. The student body consists of military officers (usually with a rank equivalent to colonel or lieutenant colonel) and civilian government officials selected by the various American republics for a nine-month period of instruction at the college. The curriculum emphasizes international politics, economics, the social sciences, and military affairs—with periods of study devoted to theoretical considerations, the global situation, and inter-American affairs. The faculty consists of a small number of nonteaching advisers and guest speakers.

3.   The Inter-American Defense College Library is discussed in entry A23.

4.   During the course of study, students prepare individual research papers on selected geopolitical,

economic, sociopsychological, and military topics. These papers are filed in the Inter-American Defense College Library. Currently restricted to internal use, they could reveal valuable insights into the philosophies of influential members of various officer corps, many of whom have gone on to assume positions of importance in their national governments.

6.   Index Terms: Collective Security—Regional Alliance Systems; International Politics; Military History; Military Science

See also entry A23

## L7   Inter-American Development Bank (IDB)

1.a.  1300 New York Avenue, NW
      Washington, D.C. 20577
      (202) 623-1000
      Fax: (202) 623-3096

b. Bank offices are open to visitors by appointment.

c. Enrique V. Iglesias, President

2.   The Inter-American Development Bank is an international financial institution representing 46 member nations, whose stated function is "to foster social and economic development of the regional developing member countries, individually and collectively." Bank operations are centered around three groups of lending sectors, the social, productive, and physical infrastructure sectors, and technical cooperation to promote institutional strengthening and regional economic integrations. The bank conducts in-house research on socioeconomic and financial conditions in Latin America within three divisions: the Office of Chief Economist, the Integration and Regional Programs Department, and the Social Programs and Sustainable Development Department. The bank periodically commissions outside research, and employs consultants in specialized areas of sectoral analysis.

These research divisions produce studies designed to provide bank officials with current data on the economic environment in Latin America. A series of Country Studies (about six each year) surveys general economic conditions in the bank's Latin American member nations ranging from macroeconomic updates to in-depth sector analyses. Some of the department's research products are published; others are for internal bank use only. A research bibliography is available upon request. Previously, the Economic and Social Development Department was primarily responsible for these reports. Following reorganization within the bank, responsibility has been spread out within the research departments mentioned above. For information on countries or topics, contact John P. Ferriter, Public Information Officer (202/623-1394).

The center also produces a periodical "Calendar to Future International, Regional Meetings and Seminars Concerned with Economic and Social Development." Scholars may gain access to the center's materials by contacting the department manager or the bank librarian, Benita Weber Vassallo.

3. The Inter-American Development Bank Library is discussed in entry A24. See also entry F11.

4. The bank's unpublished internal reports and records are filed in two separate collections. Both are officially closed to outsiders, but private scholars might gain limited access by contacting appropriate officials. The Secretariat Department maintains a depository of formal policy studies, position papers, and other documents prepared or utilized by the bank's board of directors. Deputy Secretary Oscar Rodriguez-Rozic (202/623-3401) can be of assistance. The Administrative Department operates a Record Center that contains staff-level working papers (communications, memoranda, reports) and bank correspondence with field officers and borrowers. Contact Miriam de Narcho (202/623-3112) for further information. In addition, the bank's Law Library maintains a complete collection of documents and working papers related to each of the bank's loan projects, including project proposals and bank appraisals. Although this collection is only for use of the bank's legal staff, researchers might gain access by securing the permission of the appropriate loan officer. Contact Paulo Renato Souza (202/623-1460) for information.

5.a. The bank's annual report describes the bank's operations, capital resources, and loan projects, by country. It contains a wealth of statistical data on Latin America. Other publications are the banks's annual *Economic and Social Progress in Latin America,* the proceedings of the annual meeting of the board of governors, summaries of yearly roundtables on selected economic and social themes, a monthly newsletter, *IDB News,* and miscellaneous studies on development issues affecting Latin America. Free copies of these publications can be obtained from the Office of Information (202/623-1397).

b. A bibliography, *Publications of the Inter-American Development Bank,* is also available without charge.

6. Index Terms: Development Issues—Aid and Investment; International Economics—International Finance; International Organizations—Regional

See also entries A24 and F11

---

## L8 International Bank for Reconstruction and Development (World Bank)

1.a. 1818 H Street, NW
Washington, D.C. 20433
(202) 477-1234
Fax: (202) 477-6391

b. Not open to the public. Visitors received by appointment.

c. Lewis T. Preston, President

2. The International Bank for Reconstruction and Development, which itself consists of the International Bank for Reconstruction and Development (IBRD), and the International Development Agency (IDA), the International Finance Corporation (IFC), and the Multilateral Investment Guarantee Agency (MIGA) form the World Bank Group. Each subunit of the World Bank Group is discussed below.

### INTERNATIONAL BANK FOR RECONSTRUCTION AND DEVELOPMENT (IBRD)/INTERNATIONAL DEVELOPMENT AGENCY (IDA)

The International Bank for Reconstruction and Development, or World Bank, is an intergovernmental lending institution composed of 177 member nations. According to the bank's 1993 annual report, its goal is to advance economic growth and reduce poverty throughout the world. An essential element of poverty reduction is the country-specific "poverty assessment" (currently 27 countries are evaluated). The assessments help the bank modify its assistance strategies to better target aid to disadvantaged groups within the less-developed countries. The primary way the World Bank aids countries is through loans. Major lending sectors include environmentally sustainable development, which incorporates agriculture, natural resources, environment, transportation, water supply, and urban development; financial sector development, industry and energy, and private sector development; human resources, including education, population, health, and nutrition; and structural adjustment. Lending during fiscal 1993 amounted to more than $23.6 billion; to the poorest countries it totaled nearly $10 billion.

IDA complements the IBRD by supporting economic development in the poorest countries through poverty reduction, economic adjustment and growth, and environmental protection and improvement. IDA uses the "country assessments" to create development strategies for the world's poorest countries in the same way the bank uses them to decide how much assistance to give a country.

Bank departments conduct extensive research activities on international economic affairs. The bank funds contract research, utilizes professional and academic consultants (technical specialists, notably engineers, agronomists, and fiscal experts), and supports research projects in international academic and research institutes. (Two pamphlets, "Use of Consultants by the World Bank and Its Borrowers" and "World Bank Research Program: Abstracts of Current Studies" are available from the Publications Distribution Unit). The information in this entry is based on IBRD's annual report for 1993.

## DEVELOPMENT COMMITTEE

Armeane M. Choksi, Vice-President, Human Resources Development and Operations Policy

The Development Committee works closely with the bank's executive directors to create plans for speeding the development of nations throughout the world. At its semiannual meetings the committee presents papers on factors affecting development, such as resource flows to developing countries, trade policy, the environment, and private-sector development.

## ECONOMIC DEVELOPMENT INSTITUTE (EDI)

Amnon Golan, Director

The objective of the EDI is to mobilize the knowledge and experience accumulated in IBRD and elsewhere in order to strengthen development decision making in the bank's member countries. EDI coordinates training, institution building, and publication programs. During 1993, 152 training activities were carried out in areas such as the republics of the former Soviet Union, South Africa, Vietnam, and the Middle East. Closely integrated with these training activities is the EDI's institution building program. EDI hopes to strengthen the ability of local institutions to train people by uniting local partner institutions with its training programs. For example, EDI helps organize national and regional workshops in cooperation with governments and nongovernmental organizations (NGOs) to improve development programs. In 1993 the EDI held three seminars on

issues related to privatization and restructuring in transition economies. The EDI also prepares and publishes training materials such as case studies, papers, and books on policy analysis and reform. Emphasis is on printed materials, but EDI has begun to transfer its collection onto CD-ROM.

EDI administers several fellowship programs. The World Bank Graduate Scholarship Program supports graduate study leading to a degree in a development-related social science. The McNamara Fellowship Program for nondegree postgraduate study awards approximately 10 fellowships a year to support innovative research in areas of economic development. The EDI, in conjunction with Columbia University in New York City, has designed a master's degree program in development economics and management. The degree involves 12 months of study at Columbia and a 6-month internship at IBRD or International Monetary Fund (LII). Currently, the EDI, with the Africa Capacity Building Foundation, and the African Development Bank (LI) are developing a joint-sponsored program for francophone Africa to be administered by the Center for Studies and Research on International Development in Clermont-Ferrand, France. They are also discussing a program for anglophone Africa at McGill University (Montreal).

## VICE-PRESIDENT FOR DEVELOPMENT ECONOMICS AND CHIEF ECONOMIST

Michael Bruno, Vice-President

A reorganization in 1992 concentrated responsibility for the bank's macroeconomic and sectoral research efforts in the hands of the vice-president. The main areas of emphasis for research are poverty, equity, and social-welfare issues. Work in the areas of environmental analysis and human resource development is increasing. Work on reform of the public sector, development of the private sector, and economic management has also increased since the transition in the republics of the former Soviet Union and Central and Eastern Europe. Support continues to be given to research on financial intermediation, infrastructure, and urban development. Research on structural adjustment, debt, and trade has decreased. Examples of current research are a study of agriculture policies and poverty that assesses women's rights to own land in Africa; a study of income security programs for elderly people; a study of fertility in sub-Saharan Africa; a study examining the least-cost method of reducing pollution in developing countries; an analysis of the effects of fiscal, monetary, trade, financial, and social policies on national growth; and a project assessing the status of the housing sector in over 50 countries.

## INTERNATIONAL FINANCE CORPORATION

(202) 473-9737
Jannik Lindbaek, Executive Vice-President

The International Finance Corporation (IFC), an IBRD affiliate, uses its capital resources to encourage growth of private enterprise and the private sector in developing nations. To this end, IFC finances sound private-sector projects, mobilizes debt and equity financing in the international markets for private companies, and provides technical assistance and advisory services to businesses and governments. The IFC also supports the development of mortgage banks, savings and loan associations, stock exchanges, and other capital-markets institutions that channel domestic savings into productive private enterprises. In 1993, the IFC approved $2.1 billion in spending for 185 projects. The corporation approved projects specific to 54 countries and some with a regional or international focus. Washington staff members function primarily as investment bankers.

## MULTILATERAL INVESTMENT GUARANTEE AGENCY (MIGA)

Glikira Iida, Executive Vice-President

Established in 1988, the MIGA is the youngest member of the World Bank Group. Its objective is to encourage the flow of foreign direct investment to and among developing member nations. It accomplishes this goal by offering political-risk investment insurance coverage to private investors and providing promotional and advisory services to assist its developing member countries in their efforts to attract and retain foreign direct investment. As of March 31, 1994, MIGA had 107 member nations. During fiscal year 1993 MIGA issued 27 contracts totalling $374 million in coverage.

## REGIONAL OFFICES

These offices (Latin America and Caribbean, S. Javed Burki; Africa, Edward V. K. Jaycox; East Asia and Pacific, Gautam S. Kaji; Middle East and North Africa, Caio Koch-Weser; Europe and Central Asia, Wilfried A. Thalwitz; South Asia, D.Joseph Wood) administer the development-assistance projects that IBRD finances each year. The staff—economists, financial analysts, technical specialists (agronomists, et al.), and lawyers—are in daily contact with government and banking officials throughout the world and spend two to three months of each year on data-gathering field missions.

3. See Joint Bank-Fund Library (entry A27).

4. In 1993, IBRD undertook a major review of its disclosure policy to increase the information made public. Under the revised policy, the range of documents released was expanded significantly and public access to those documents was made easier. IBRD established a Public Information Center through which much of the material covered by the revised policy is available.

A new Project Information Document (PID) is available for all projects under preparation. Components of the PIDs include costs and financing, environmental and other issues, and names of government agencies that can provide information on the project. Other information items available to the public include environmental assessments and analyses; environmental assessments and environmental review summaries for IFC-funded projects; environmental data sheets; national environmental action plans; staff appraisal reports; *OED Precis* (a publication of IBRD's independent Operations Evaluation Department, which points out lessons to be learned from IBRD's experience in implementing economic development projects); country economic and sector reports; and sector policy papers.

The Public Information Center is located at 1776 G Street, NW, Washington, D.C. 20433. Requests to the PIC may also be submitted through the Internet, the bank's Paris, London, and Tokyo offices, or other field offices.

5.a. IBRD produces a wide range of free and for-sale publications that are listed in the *Index of Publications and Guide to Information Products and Services*. The Index may be obtained free of charge by writing to World Bank Publications, P.O. Box 7247, Philadelphia, Pa. 19101-9630. *The World Bank Annual Report* reviews bank projects, economic trends in developing countries, capital flows, and the external public debts of over 86 developing countries. *Summary Proceedings of the Annual Meeting* contains texts of addresses and resolutions. More specifically on development, the bank offers three new quarterly publications: *Financial Flows and the Developing Countries,* which reviews the international flow of borrowing, lending, and investing; *Commodity Markets and the Developing Countries,* which tracks recent developments in primary commodity markets; and *Global Outlook and the Developing Country,* which gives decision makers timely insights into the prospects for short-term economic growth in the less-developed nations. Other publications of the bank focus on more general economic trends and their effect on developing countries. These include *Global Economic Prospects and the Developing Countries 1993, Trends in Developing Economies 1993,* and *World Debt Tables 1993–94.*

The World Development Report Series (WDR) spotlights a different development issue each year as it relates to developing countries; the 1994 *WDR* focuses on agriculture. *Social Indicators of Development 1993* contains tables which give country-by-country accounts of selected development indicators for 185 countries. Another book of reference tables is *World Tables 1993.* The most detailed collection of economic data published by the bank, *World Tables* profiles more than 140 countries with up-to-date economic, demographic, and social data. Complementing *World Tables* is *World Bank Atlas 1994.*

For educators, the IBRD publishes a *Catalog of Educational Materials,* which surveys the teaching kits it offers.

b. Almost all IBRD reports are available as software as well as in print. Many are also available on CD-ROM, including the *Compact International Agriculture Research Library.* The bank's bookstore is located at 701 18th Street, NW, Room J-1060, Washington, D.C. 20433 (202/473-2941).

6. Index Terms: Development Issues—Aid and Investment; International Economics—International Finance

See also entry A27

---

## L9 International Center for Settlement of Investment Disputes

1.a. 1818 H Street, NW
Washington, D.C. 20433
(202) 458-1533

c. Lewis T. Preston, Chairman of Administrative Council

2. Created by the Convention on the Settlement of Investment Disputes (ICSID Convention) in 1966 under the auspices of the International Bank for Reconstruction and Development (World Bank) (L8) to provide facilities for conciliation and arbitration of investment disputes between governments and foreign investors. For ICSID to arbitrate or conciliate a dispute one party must be a contracting state (at present 112 states have ratified the convention), and the other party must be a national of another contracting state. The decision to submit to arbitration

of a claim lies with the parties, but once they have agreed to arbitrate, the award of the tribunal is binding. Examples of cases settled in 1993 are S.P.P. (Middle East) Limited v. the Arab Republic of Egypt; Société d'Études de Travaux et de Gestion SETIMEG S.A. v. the Republic of Gabon; and Manufacturers Hanover Trust Company v. Arab Republic of Egypt and General Authority for Investment and Free Zones.

5. The center publishes a semiannual newsletter, *News From ICSID,* which provides information on its activities and on pending disputes, and a biannual, *ICSID Review—Foreign Investment Law Journal,* which reports material on domestic and international law relating to foreign investments. The center also publishes several multivolume series, including *Investment Laws of the World,* a 10-volume series containing the texts of basic investment legislation of various countries, and *Investment Treaties,* a multivolume collection of agreements entered into by countries throughout the world. ICSID publishes numerous booklets relating to itself, including *ICSID Model Clauses, Towards a Greater Depoliticization of Investment Disputes—The Roles of ICSID and MIGA,* and an annual report.

6. Index Terms: Diplomacy and Negotiations; International Economics—International Finance; International Law

---

## L10 International Labor Organization (ILO) (United Nations) — Washington Branch

1.a. 1828 L Street, NW, Suite 801
Washington, D.C. 20036
(202) 653-7652

b. Open to the public.

c. Michael Hansenne, Director-General
Stephen Schlossberg, Director, Washington Office

2. Created in 1919, the ILO today functions as a specialized agency of the United Nations. Its headquarters are located in Geneva, Switzerland, but it maintains 40 field offices around the world, including one in Washington. The goal of the 168 member countries is to improve world labor conditions, raise living standards, and promote economic stability. The Washington office acts as a liaison between the ILO and the U.S. government, the ILO and U.S. employer and labor groups, and the ILO and other UN organizations.

The ILO engages in four main activities: the formulation of international policies and programs to promote basic human rights, the creation of international labor standards, the coordination of extensive programs of international technical cooperation, and the promotion of training, education, research, and publishing activities. The ILO's training activities are partially accomplished through the International Training Center in Turin, Italy. The center is designed to support economic and social development of ILO member nations by training senior and midlevel managers, directors of vocational training institutions, government officials, and leaders of labor and employer groups. Since its inception, the center has trained about 5,000 people from 170 countries.

The ILO also administers the International Institute for Labor Studies, which advances education and research concerning social and labor policy by bringing together government administrators, trade union officials, and industrial experts to study current labor issues.

The ILO, through its Technical Cooperation Program, offers fellowships to scholars from developing countries. Fellowships range from academic programs to seminars to industrial site visits and last from one week to two years.

3. The ILO's main library, which houses the largest labor and social policy collection in the world (over 1 million titles), is located in Geneva. The library in the Washington office brings this collection to the United States through the LABORDOC database, which enables scholars to access 140,000 titles contained in Geneva. For more information about the library see entry A2; for a description of the ILO photographic collection see entry F13.

5. To say that the ILO publishes a plethora of documents would be an understatement at best. Fortunately, it publishes several reference sources to help scholars get a handle on its extensive publications collection. Its *Catalog of Publications* is a useful tool for surveying the types of publications ILO prints. Even more specific are ILO's special lists, such as "Books on Women and Employment," "Books on Occupational Safety and Health," and "Books on International Development." *Spotlight,* a quarterly publication, gives general descriptions of the ILO's most recent publications.

*World Labor Reports,* a four-volume series that discusses every aspect of work including employment incomes, social protection, and industrial relations is an invaluable tool. Another useful tool for international labor researchers is *International Standard Classification of Occupations ISCO-88,* which serves as a model for developing and revising national occupational classifications.

The ILO also publishes several journals. *ILO Washington Focus,* a quarterly, covers key issues involving ILO in the United States, Geneva, and elsewhere. *The World of Work,* published five times a year, focuses on employment and work conditions throughout the world. Recent issues discussed in *The World of Work* were the effects of economic growth on social justice and barriers to women in employment. *International Labor Review,* published six times a year, contains articles, comparative studies, and research by ILO officials on global labor issues. Other ILO journals are *Year Book of Labor Statistics, Bulletin of Labor Statistics, Social and Labor Bulletin,* and *Labor Law Documents.*

6. Index Terms: Conflict Management and Resolution—Unofficial and Nongovernmental Approaches; Development Issues; Human Rights; International Organizations—Labor, —United Nations

See also entries A25 and F13

---

## LII International Monetary Fund (IMF)

1.a. 700 19th Street, NW
Washington, D.C. 20431
(202) 623-7000

b. Not open to the public. Visitors are received by appointment.

c. Michel Camdessus, Managing Director and Chair of the Executive Board

2. The IMF works to promote international currency stability by seeking to eliminate restrictive exchange practices among its 178 member nations and by allocating the fund's monetary resources to assist members in meeting temporary balance-of-payments disequilibria. The fund also reviews trade policy issues in the context of member countries' macroeconomic and structural reform programs.

Twice a year the IMF publishes *World Economic Outlook,* which contains comprehensive analysis of short- and medium-term prospects for the world economy as well as for individual countries and country groupings. This analysis helps to identify areas that might benefit from a change of economic policies. In April 1993, issues examined for the report included the link between trade and growth; the prospects for recovery in the industrialized countries; and the progress made by countries in Central and Eastern Europe in transition to a market economy.

The IMF's departments compile and analyze statistics on international financial and economic conditions. For information specific to a particular region of the world, scholars should contact the relevant regional department. Senior officers of these departments are Africa, Mamoudou Toure; Central Asia, Hubert Neiss; Europe I, Massimo Russo; Europe II, John Odling-Smee; the Middle East, Paul Chabrier; Southeast Asia and the Pacific, Kunio Saito; and the Western Hemisphere, Sterie T. Beza. Little contract research is funded, but the IMF maintains a pool of private international fiscal and central-banking specialists to act as advisers to foreign governments.

## SYSTEMIC TRANSFORMATION FACILITY (STF)

A temporary facility created in 1993, the STF is specially designed to extend financial assistance to members experiencing severe disruptions in their trade and payment arrangements due to a shift from a command to a market economy. Such countries include those in the early stages of transition and as yet unable to formulate a program that could be supported by the fund's existing mechanisms (e.g., the states of the former Soviet Union and the former participants in the Council for Mutual Economic Assistance).

## ENHANCED STRUCTURAL ADJUSTMENT FACILITY (ESAF)

ESAF is a mechanism that allows the fund to get involved in low-income countries by formulating macroeconomic policies and structural reform policies. ESAF accomplishes this goal by providing financial support for programs to liberalize exchange and trade systems, eliminate price controls, reduce the role of agricultural marketing boards, free interest rates, reform public enterprises, and improve local and regional banking structures. The facility also tries to promote a more central role in the international monetary community for the countries that receive its assistance. In 1992–93 eight ESAF arrangements totaling SDR (Special Drawing Rights) 478.2 million were concluded.

## IMF INSTITUTE

Patrick B. DeFontenay, Director

The institute provides training for officials from member countries though residential and longer-term courses at its headquarters and at the Joint Vienna Institute. Shorter courses, seminars, and lecturing assistance are offered in the field at either the national or regional level. Briefings for visiting groups are conducted in Washington, D.C. During 1992–93 the institute offered 13 courses and 3 seminars, 21 external training courses, and 12 seminars for senior officials. The fund finances all costs associated with the institute's training. The rise in need and demand for overseas training has led the institute to collaborate with other donors through cofinancing by local, regional, or multilateral sponsors. An example of such collaboration is the Joint Vienna Institute that was established in September 1992. The Joint Vienna Institute's main purpose is to train officials and private sector managers from former centrally planned economies. In 1992–93, it trained 816 persons.

3. See Joint Bank-Fund Library (entry A27).

4. Fund documents, reports, and other working papers—virtually all confidential—are filed in the Records Division of the IMF's Secretary Department, which maintains a cumulative list of internal fund materials.

5.a. The IMF issues a broad range of publications. The *Annual Report of the Executive Board* reviews IMF activities and surveys the world economy. The *Annual Report on Exchange Arrangements and Exchange Restrictions* reviews developments in the field of exchange controls and restrictions, by country. *Summary Proceedings* is a report of the fund's annual meeting and contains addresses, committee reports, resolutions, and a list of delegates. The biannual *World Economic Outlook* offers analysis of short- and medium-term prospects for the world economy. In January 1993 a special *World Economic Outlook: Interim Assessment* was published. The assessment took account of substantial developments that had occurred since the October release of the *Outlook*. The 16-page *IMF Survey* is issued biweekly and provides a topical report on the fund's activities within the context of developments in national economies and international finance, including all fund press releases, text of communiqués, Special Drawing Rights (SDR) valuations, and exchange rates. *Finance and Development,* a quarterly review of IMF/World Bank activities, offers the general public nontechnical articles on international monetary trends. *Staff Papers* appears quarterly and makes available in-house studies on such subjects as monetary systems, taxation, and inflation. Occasional papers (in 1993 nine were published) cover developments in individual member countries, regional issues, and issues relating to the evolving international monetary system. The *World Economic and Financial Surveys* series publishes papers on topics such as international capital markets, developments in exchange and payment systems, trade, and private market financing for developing countries.

The fund also publishes statistical periodicals. The monthly *International Financial Statistics* contains data on exchange rates, international liquidity, money and banking, international trade, interest rates, etc., by country and region. The *Government Finance Statistics Yearbook* provides data on revenues, expenditures, lending, financing, and debt of central governments. Standardized balance of payments figures for over 100 countries that report their data to the fund are available in *Balance of Payment Statistics Yearbook*.

Recent books published by the IMF include *Foreign and Intratrade Policies of the Arab Countries* (1993), *Improving Tax Administration in Developing Countries* (1993), and *Public Expenditure Management* (1993).

b. An annual publications catalog is available through the fund's Publications Services (202/623-7430).

6. Index Terms: Development Issues—Aid and Investment; International Economics—International Finance; International Organizations

See also entry A27

---

## LI2 International Organization for Migration (IOM)—Washington Mission

---

1.a. 1750 K Street, NW, Suite 110
Washington, D.C. 20006
(202) 862-1826

c. James N. Purcell, Jr., Director General
Frances E. Sullivan, Chief of Mission

2. IOM (*formerly* the Intergovernmental Committee for Migration) is a UN auxiliary organization supported by 49 members and 40 nations with observer status. IOM's primary purpose is to assist in the resettlement of refugees and displaced persons, including voluntary emigrants and repatriots, worldwide. To this end IOM administers a Language and Cultural Orientation Training Program, which trains emigrants and refugees in the language and customs of their countries of destination. For example, the IOM coordinated language training programs in Bangladesh, the Philippines, and Sri Lanka to help migrant workers displaced because of the Persian Gulf conflict. In 1992, 4,978 refugees benefited from IOM language and cultural orientation courses in Europe, Africa, and Southeast Asia.

IOM also assists migrants by supplying medical services. Through predeparture medical examinations, IOM staff ensure that migrants meet the medical qualifications for entry of their countries of destination. IOM is developing an Emergency Response Unit, which will have a ready compilation of basic information on every country. IOM will be able to respond quickly and efficiently to an emergency anywhere in the world.

A corollary to resettlement is IOM's goal of coordinating the world's human resource development. The Migration for Development Program attempts this through the return of scientific, professional, and technical personnel to the developing countries (i.e., in Latin America, Africa, and Asia) from which they migrated. Also, it tries to convince foreign personnel to migrate to developing countries and assist in their development process.

In conjunction with these programs IOM conducts research focusing on the analysis of trends in international migration, national migration policies and legislation, and literature relating to the human resources requirements of individual countries. IOM has added an environmental focus to its research by looking at the effects of migration on the environment, as well as the environment's effect on migration. Other areas of IOM research include foreign direct investment and its relationship to migration, health policies for migrants and refugees, migrants with capital, and present and future migrant pressures.

IOM also holds forums and works in cooperation with other national, regional, and subregional institutions on activities aimed at incorporating the migration variable into development strategies. For instance, in 1992 IOM held seminars concentrating on the integration of qualified African nationals, migration and health, and migration policies and practices.

5. The Public Information Service of IOM is responsible for providing information on current IOM activities, new programs, and projects worldwide. It publishes press releases and a newsletter, the *Monthly Dispatch,* which focuses on IOM's growing involvement in the world (the *Monthly Dispatch* is available in Spanish, English, or French). The service also publishes an annual report that gives a good overview of IOM's objectives and how they are being met. General information brochures such as *Who We Are and What We Do; IOM in Facts* are

useful starting points for scholars conducting research on migration.

IOM also publishes several other journals and newsletters: *International Migration,* a quarterly that focuses on current migration issues; *Migration and Health in the 1990s,* a dedication to the Migration and Health Conference in Brussels, in 1992; *Migration and Health,* a newsletter that provides information on current medical research and policies relating to migration; and *Migration and the Environment,* a brochure that focuses on the environment's relation to migration.

6.   Index Terms: Development Issues—Health; Humanitarian Issues; Refugees

## Organization for Economic Cooperation and Development (OECD)—Information and Publications Center   See entry A39

---

## LI3   Organization of American States (OAS)

---

1.a.  Organization of American States
17th and Constitution, NW
Washington, D.C. 20006
(202) 458-3000

Additional Offices:
General Secretariat
1889 F Street, NW
Washington, D.C. 20006
(202) 458-3754 (Public Information)
(202) 458-3533 (Publications)
(202) 458-6037 (Columbus Memorial Library)

Administration Building
19th and Constitution, NW
Washington, D.C. 20006
Mail: OAS General Secretariat
Washington, D.C. 20006

b.  Open to the public 9:00 A.M.–5:00 P.M. Monday–Friday.

2.   The world's oldest international regional organization, OAS serves as a forum for the negotiation of inter-American agreements and provides technical assistance to Latin American member-governments in the areas of economic, social, educational, scientific, and technological development. The OAS Permanent Council meets in regular deliberative sessions in Washington on the first and third Wednesdays of each month, September through

June. Its meetings are open to the public. Other major OAS deliberative bodies—the General Assembly; the Inter-American Economic and Social Council; the Inter-American Council for Education, Science, and Culture; the Inter-American Commission of Women; the Inter-American Commission on Human Rights; and numerous specialized conferences—convene on an annual basis at rotating sites (including Washington, D.C.) throughout the hemisphere.

The OAS General Secretariat, the organization's permanent support staff in Washington, carries out OAS technical-assistance programs (primarily advisory services and training), conducts research, and produces many publications and unpublished reports. The activities of the various departments of the General Secretariat are described below. Many of these departments periodically contract outside research in specialized scientific and economic areas. The OAS offers a wide range of pre- and postdoctoral fellowships and travel grants (some 1,300 annually) for research and study in virtually every field of the humanities, social sciences, and physical sciences. Fellowship programs are administered by the Scholars Selection Division of Department of Fellowships and Training (202/458-3890).

3.   The Organization of American States Columbus Memorial Library is discussed in entry A38; its map collection in entry D11; its photograph collection in entry F24.

4.   Unpublished OAS research reports remain in the files of the originating offices described below. A partial bibliography has been prepared (see point 5.b. below).

All OAS internal records are eventually housed in the Organization of American States, Records Management Center (B14) and its Voice Archives (E14).

5.a.  The OAS issues an enormous quantity of publications. Its "official records" series includes the annual report of the secretary general; the texts of multilateral treaties, conventions, and agreements; and the resolutions and proceedings of the General Assembly, Permanent Council, and all the OAS specialized conferences and commissions. These records are available on microform.

Technical and informational publications include specialized studies in the fields of economics, regional development, statistics, social affairs, science, law, education, fine arts, and youth affairs.

OAS periodicals include the illustrated, monthly, general-interest magazine *Américas* and the *OAS Chronicle,* a monthly newsletter containing current information on major inter-American events and the texts of important official documents. Other specialized periodicals are discussed below.

b. OAS official documents are indexed in the annual *Documentos Oficiales de la Organización de los Estados Americanos*. OAS publications are listed in the *Catalog of Publications*. One particularly useful publication is *Inter-American Review of Bibliography*, which contains articles, book reviews, and extensive bibliographical information on recent research papers. A section on unpublished OAS technical reports, contract-research studies, reports of seminars and workshops, papers presented by OAS staff members at outside conferences, and studies produced by OAS fellowship-holders can be found in the *Review*.

These publications are available from the General Secretariat's Department of Publications (202/458-3533). Most of the titles of documents, series, books, and reports listed below have been taken from the *Annual Report of the Secretary General 1993-1994*.

## EXECUTIVE SECRETARIAT FOR ECONOMIC AND SOCIAL AFFAIRS

(202) 458-3181

### Department of Regional Development and Environment
This department assists member countries in preparing strategies for the development and preservation of natural resource bases. It provides technical experts to survey and evaluate the resources of underutilized areas, to work out packages of specific development projects, and to draw up comprehensive regional-development plans to attract investment, people, and services into the regions targeted for development. It also assists member countries in planning, promoting, and financing national tourism programs.

### Department of Foreign Trade
The department manages the Foreign Trade System (SICE), which is a computerized data bank with on-line information available. The benefit of this system is that it provides governments and nongovernment agencies with foreign trade information. Sufficient trade information is necessary to make decisions that will result in achieving the development and integration of Latin America.

### Department of Economic and Social Affairs
The department works with member countries on problems related to international trade, transportation, communications, and finance, including the recording and controlling of external debt. It also works with member states and Latin American regional-integration organizations in the formulation and evaluation of public revenue, public expenditure, capital markets, and private investment policies. The department collaborates in setting up tax, budget, capital market, and private investment management and programming systems. Field missions from this department work with national planners, technical specialists, and training institutions of member countries to assist them in developing sound methodologies and institutional bases for formulating and evaluating their national development projects.

The department also provides technical assistance and training to member countries in the design and implementation of strategies and projects to raise the productivity, income, and general welfare of marginal populations in rural areas. Technical advisory field missions collaborate with national planning and development agencies to devise employment schemes that will help to reverse rural-urban imbalances. It also provides technical advisory missions to member states to assist in formulating and carrying out policies and plans on manpower utilization, generation of employment, and labor development.

## EXECUTIVE SECRETARIAT FOR EDUCATION, SCIENCE, AND CULTURE

(202) 458-3141

### Regional Educational Development Program
This program promotes uniform educational standards and improvements in school systems throughout Latin America. It conducts technical-assistance missions and specialized training programs (courses and fellowships), organizes technical conferences, and conducts research. Various specialized units in the department focus on basic education, education for work, and research and higher education. The department publishes studies of Latin American education programs, a series entitled *Status of Educational Planning in Latin America and the Caribbean*, a quarterly entitled *Revista Interamericana de Desarrollo Educativo*, as well as a quarterly journal called *La Educación*.

### Regional Scientific and Technological Development Program
The program promotes the accelerated development of science and technology in Latin America. Its stated goals are institutional development, the upgrading of technically trained personnel, and the dif-

fusion of scientific and technological information. The department supplies direct technical-assistance services to OAS member countries in the form of advisory missions, research and publications programs, advanced courses and specialized conferences, training fellowships and travel grants, modern equipment, and bibliographic materials. Specialized multinational programs focus on sciences and the environment, information and informatics, technology, materials, and microelectronics and data processing.

### Regional Cultural Development Program

The Cultural Heritage Division of this program sponsors conferences and contests to encourage the appreciation and research of Latin American literature, philosophy, history, and other areas of the humanities.

The multinational project on cultural policy and regional studies promotes the formulation of cultural policies, preparation of evaluations, statistics, and laws, and the improvement of cultural administration and planning.

The multinational project on popular culture and education is aimed at human resources training in identifying modes of thought and characteristics of social, political, and economic origins of cultural groups.

The multinational project on preservation and use of the cultural heritage focuses on the preservation of monuments, both historical and artistic. In 1992 it cosponsored a conference with the U.S. State Department and Puerto Rico's Archeological, Anthropological, and Historical Foundation that discussed the environment and archeology in Puerto Rico.

The multinational project on the arts focuses on music and visual arts. In the area of music, the division works closely with music academies and conservatories throughout Latin America to promote music education and the development of orchestras and ensembles. In the area of visual arts, the division serves as a clearinghouse for information on the visual and graphic arts of modern Latin America. It produces films, slide-sets, and video cassettes on Latin American art, artists, and general culture. It also administers the Museum of the Americas, presents rotating exhibitions of Latin American art, and sponsors conferences and traveling exhibits in Latin America.

The divisions for Youth, Physical Education, Recreation and Sports, and Educational, Scientific and Cultural Youth Activities provide technical assistance to youth councils, sports confederations, and voluntary service organizations in member states.

### Department of Fellowships and Training

This department is in charge of selecting fellowship candidates from OAS member countries and is responsible for operating and regulating the training programs and projects under the General Secretariat's division. The department provides fellowships at the graduate level and for specialized studies in such fields as engineering, biology, physics, and economics.

### INTER-AMERICAN COMMISSION OF WOMEN

1889 F Street, NW, Room 880
Washington, D.C. 20006
(202) 458-6084/6085
Fax: (202) 458-6094

Zelmira Regazzoli, President
Linda J. Poole, Executive Secretary

The Inter-American Commission of Women (CIM), an advisory organization of the OAS, promotes women's rights by endeavoring to mobilize, organize, and train women for fuller participation in the political and economic life of their countries. It holds a biennial assembly, sponsors conferences, conducts training seminars, and promotes the creation of women's bureaus within the structure of national governments. It maintains liaison with the UN Commission on the Status of Women and with various national women's rights organizations. The commission's Washington office sponsors an annual student-internship program (primarily for college undergraduates).

The commission houses a collection of its own documents, assembly and conference proceedings, studies, and publications, as well as a small number of legal studies and other books on women. The staff also prepares reports on the political, educational, legal, and heath status of women.

### INTER-AMERICAN COMMISSION ON HUMAN RIGHTS

1889 F Street, NW, 8th Floor
Washington, D.C. 20006
(202) 458-6002
Fax: (202) 458-3992

Oscar Lujan Fappiano, President
Edith Marquez-Rodriguez, Executive Secretary

The Inter-American Commission on Human Rights is composed of seven members elected by the General Assembly of the OAS (but not as government representatives), and a support staff of 10 lawyers.

The commission receives complaints from individuals and organizations regarding alleged violations of human rights and infringements of individual liberties. It then examines the charges, occasionally by means of on-site investigations. When warranted, it addresses official inquiries on behalf of the victims to the national governments involved.

Case files are not open to researchers because of the sensitive nature of the material in them. *The Annual Report of the Inter-American Commission on Human Rights, 1992–1993, to the OAS General Assembly* and its reports on the status of human rights in individual countries (e.g., Haiti) are available to researchers.

6. Index Terms: Development Issues; Human Rights; International Economics; International Organizations—Regional

See also entries A38, B14, D11, E14, F24

---

## LI4 United Nations—Development Program (UNDP)—Washington Office

1.a. 1889 F Street, NW, Ground Floor
Washington, D.C. 20006
(202) 289-8674

b. Open to researchers; appointments recommended.

c. David R. Scotton, Director

2. UNDP was created in 1965 with the merger of the UN Technical Assistance Board and the UN Special Fund. The headquarters of UNDP is in New York City, but the program serves 174 countries throughout the world through 124 field offices, including one in Washington, D.C. UNDP has a two-pronged mission: to help developing countries build their human resources and institutions, their productive use of natural resources, and their planning and managerial capabilities; and to administer a number of special purpose UN funds.

In its attempt to aid developing countries, UNDP coordinates technical assistance programs, establishes regional programs that foster development cooperation between two or more countries in the same area, and provides preinvestment surveys and training to potential investors. In 1992, UNDP received $1.3 billion dollars in donations to help increase third world investment. Examples of UNDP projects are the Development Program for Displaced Persons, Refugees, and Returnees, which attempts to repatriate displaced people and to rehabilitate

war-torn communities, and the Electoral Assistance Unit, which provides technical assistance for electoral processes throughout the world.

UNDP also administers six special UN funds, the largest of which is UN Capital Development Fund (UNCDF) with annual contributions of more than $40 million. UNCDF finances small-scale investments designed to increase economic opportunities for the rural and urban poor. The UN Development Fund for Women (UNIFEM) encourages the inclusion of women in the decision-making process of development planners by directly funding women's projects around the world. Since the fund's beginning in 1975, more than 800 projects have been initiated. The UN Sudano-Sahelian Office (UNSO) assists in the rehabilitation of drought-stricken countries and works to conserve and improve natural productive resources. The UN Revolving Fund for Natural Resources Exploration (UNRFNRE) explores developing countries for minerals and geothermal energy. Since its establishment in 1976, the fund has mounted 28 explorations resulting in the discovery of mineral deposits in Argentina, Honduras, Benin, the Congo, Ecuador, Haiti, Peru, and Suriname. The UN Fund for Science and Technology for Development (UNFSTD) helps developing countries use the latest advances in science and technology, and promotes international networking of scientific and technological institutions. The UN Volunteers Program (UNV) is the fourth-largest volunteer organization in the world. UNV's, of which there are nearly 2,000, work in 114 countries around the world initiating grassroots development projects.

3. The Washington liaison office of the United Nations Development Program maintains a small collection of country proposals and project records relating to United Nations—assisted development programs. These documents are open to researchers, except when governments have placed restrictions on their release. The office staff will also obtain for researchers records on UN development programs from UN headquarters in New York City.

5. In 1990 UNDP began publishing an annual *Human Development Report,* which examines how people participate in the events that shape their lives. It also presents the human development index, a ranking of the countries of the world according to development. To acquire an English edition of the *Human Development Report* (there are also French, Spanish, Italian, and Arabic editions) send a fax to Oxford University Press USA (919/677-1303). UNDP also publishes *World Resource Report,* which presents an up-to-date account of the status

of the world's natural resources. UNDP also publishes an annual report that provides information about its current and proposed programs. The annual report is available from any UNDP office.

6. Index Terms: Development Issues; Humanitarian Issues—Relief Organizations; International Economics; International Organizations—United Nations; Refugees

---

## LI5 United Nations—Economic Commission for Latin America and the Caribbean (ECLAC)—Washington Office

1.a. 1825 K Street, NW, Suite 1120
Washington, D.C. 20006
(202) 955-5613
Fax: (202) 296-0826

b. Open to the public; appointments strongly recommended.

c. Isaac Cohen, Director
Ines Bustillo, Economic Affairs Officer

2. ECLAC's Washington staff of two economists conducts research, represents ECLAC at conferences, provides information, distributes publications, and keeps other ECLAC regional offices abreast of data produced by the United States and international government and financial organizations located in Washington. The staff's research activities encompass a broad range of economic topics, with emphasis on trade and investment and the impact of global and regional trends on the Latin American and Caribbean economies. Recent studies, for example, have analyzed transnational enterprises, the organization of the international commodity market, the global energy crisis and its impact on international trade policy and development assistance, and proposed reforms of the international monetary system.

3. The Washington office maintains a small reference collection of ECLAC documents and research materials for internal staff use. The staff are happy to assist researchers within the limits imposed by their heavy work schedule. The office is not equipped to provide reference services, and it encourages researchers to utilize the full collections of ECLAC publications available at the Library of Congress (A29), Joint Bank-Fund Library (A27), the Inter-American Development Bank Library (for ECLAC technical publications) (A24), and the United Nations Information Center Library (A44).

5. ECLAC publishes an annual *Economic Survey of the United States,* which analyzes bilateral trade agreements and trade relations between the United States, and Latin American and Caribbean countries. A monthly, *CEPAL News,* is available free of charge.

6. Index Terms: International Economics—Integration; International Organizations—Regional; United Nations

**United Nations Information Center** See entry H69

---

## LI6 United Nations—High Commission for Refugees (UNHCR)

1.a. 1718 Connecticut Avenue, NW, Suite 200
Washington, D.C. 20009
(202) 387-8546
Fax: (202) 387-9038

c. Rene van Rooyan, Representative
Barbara Francis, Senior Public Information Officer

2. UNHCR defines a refugee as "any person who . . . owing to well-founded fear of being persecuted for reasons of race, religion, nationality, or political opinion, is outside the country of his nationality and is unable, or owing to such fear or for reasons other than personal convenience, is unwilling to avail himself of the protection of that country; or who, not having a nationality and being outside the country of his former habitual residence, is unable or . . . unwilling to return to it." In 1993, in a global population of 5.5 billion there were 18.2 million refugees and 24 million people displaced in their own land. It is these people UNHCR is charged with protecting and assisting. UNHCR's goals for protection and assistance are to promote international dialogue on refugees that leads to national legislation for their protection, to ensure that refugees are treated in accordance with international human rights standards, to promote the granting of asylum, and to end refugee status through voluntary repatriation or resettlement. To achieve these goals UNHCR uses emergency relief, voluntary repatriation, local integration, resettlement, education,

counselling, rehabilitation, and legal assistance. The 2,400 UNHCR workers in 176 offices in 110 countries worldwide work individually and in conjunction with volunteer and nongovernmental organizations (NGOs) to aid refugees. Funding for this effort comes from a limited subsidy from the regular budget of the United Nations and from voluntary contributions from governments (the United States is UNHCR's largest donor government), NGOs, and individuals.

The Washington, D.C., office acts as the high commissioner's liaison to the U.S. government, government agencies, and NGOs. The office is subdivided into three departments: legal, resettlement, and public information/external affairs. UNHCR does not consider the United States an emergency relief area. The office's activities, therefore, involve resettling refugees in the United States and providing the legal assistance necessary to do so rather than providing emergency assistance. Questions about UNHCR, especially the Washington office, should be directed to Senior Public Information Officer, Barbara Francis.

4. The Center for Documentation on Refugees (CDR) is a computer-based documentation centre that houses UNHCR's internal records. The center, including a library, is located in Geneva, Switzerland. Questions about its resources, or about obtaining a subscription to *Refugee Abstracts* should be directed to 5–7, Avenue de la Paix, 1201 Geneva.

5. UNHCR, through its Public Information Section, publishes *Refugees* (in English, French, German, Italian, Japanese, and Spanish), a magazine that updates the situation of refugees throughout the world. Subscription questions should be directed to P.O. Box 2500, 1211 Geneva 2 Depot, Switzerland (fax: 022/739-8449). The Public Information Section also distributes videos, pamphlets, posters, information kits, bulletins, and a calendar. *Refugee Abstracts,* a quarterly, derives its material from the CDR's document resources. Probably the most useful resource for general information about UNHCR's establishment, goals, and funding is *Information Paper,* available from the Washington office. To obtain information from the Washington office, write to Barbara Francis, Senior Public Information Officer, 1718 Connecticut Avenue, NW, Suite 200, Washington, D.C. 20009 (fax: 202/387-0938). For a complete discussion of issues affecting refugees, see UNHCR's recently published series of reports, *The State of the World's Refugees.* The first report is in print and may be purchased by phone (800/253-6476) or mail (Consumer Sales, Penguin USA, P.O. Box 999, Depart. 17109, Bergenfield, N.J. 07621-0120).

6. Index Terms: Humanitarian Issues—Relief Organizations; International Organizations—United Nations; Refugees

---

## L17 World Health Organization (WHO) (United Nations)—Regional Office for the Americas

1.a. 525 23rd Street, NW
Washington, D.C. 20037
(202) 861-3200
Fax: (202) 223-5971

b. Open to the public. Visitors are required to register at the entrance; appointments are recommended.

c. Hiroshi Nakajima, Director-General
George Alleyne, Regional Director

2. WHO, a specialized agency of the United Nations composed of 183 member countries, provides technical assistance and training to national public health services around the world in such fields as disease eradication and control, health-program development and administration, and environmental sanitation. The organization sponsors seminars and conferences for health administrators, physicians, entomologists, etc., and provides training fellowships to health professionals in some 250 fields.

3. The WHO Library contains approximately 80,000 volumes of technical literature in the field of medicine and public health. It is open to the public with some restrictions. The WHO photograph collection is discussed in F32.

4. Records and correspondence are filed in the WHO—Regional Office of the Americas—Library (202/861-3305).

5.a. WHO publishes an official documents series (which includes an annual report, financial reports, and conference proceedings), and a scientific publications series of technical studies in the fields of biomedical research, disease control, health statistics, nutrition, health-service administration and planning, family health and population dynamics, human resource development, laboratory services, zoonoses and veterinary public health, and vector control.

b. The publication *WHO: Short List of English Titles Available in the Scientific Publications Series* may be obtained from the Publications Office (202/861-3496).

6. Index Terms: Development Issues—Health; International Organizations—United Nations

See also F32

# M

# Associations
# (Academic, Professional, and Cultural)

## Associations (Academic, Professional, and Cultural) Entry Format (M)

1. *Address; Telephone Number(s)*

2. *Chief Official and Title*

3. *Programs and Activities Pertaining to Peace and International Security Studies*

4. *Conventions/Meetings*

5. *Library/Reference Collection*

6. *Publications*

7. *Index Terms* (relevant subject specialties)

### Introductory Note

Associations dealing with subjects within the scope of this Guide are listed in this section. Aside from keeping records of their membership these organizations often sponsor meetings and issue publications. Many of these organizations serve as information clearinghouses and also put scholars in contact with other specialists in their particular field. Some hold library or archival materials.

For associations concerned only with specific geographic areas or individual countries see the geo-graphic volumes in this Scholars' Guides series, which are listed in the Bibliography.

---

### M1   Aerospace Industries Association (AIA)

1.   1250 I Street, NW, 11th Floor
     Washington, D.C. 20005
     (202) 371-8503
     Fax: (202) 371-8573

2.   Don Fuqua, President

3.   AIA is a trade association representing 53 manufacturers of commercial, military, and business aircraft, including helicopters, aircraft engines, missiles, spacecraft, and related components and equipment. AIA is concerned with industry issues, such as economic stability and structural change, cooperation with government on research and development, integrating civil and military technology, and procurement and budgeting. Other issues relevant to the subject area of this Guide include international competitiveness, acquisition reform, and space policy.

5.   The AIA has a small library, open by appointment, with information on procurement, aeronau-

tics, and astronautics. The library also holds trade journals and other reference resources.

6. The AIA publishes a newsletter, 10 times a year. A cumulative subject index is also available. Other publications include *Aerospace Facts and Figures* (annual); *Aerospace Industry Statistical Series; U.S. Aerospace Industry and the Trend toward Internationalization* (1988); and *U.S. Aerospace Industry in the 1990s: A Global Perspective* (September 1991).

7. Index Terms: Arms Production and Acquisitions; Defense Conversion; Military Spending

---

## M2 Alliance for Our Common Future

1. c/o National Peace Foundation
   1835 K Street, NW, Suite 610
   Washington, D.C. 20006
   (202) 223-1770
   Fax: (202) 223-1718

2. Sarah Harder, Leadership Council Chair

3. The Alliance for Our Common Future is an inter-organizational effort of more than 70 organizations and coalitions for the purpose of promoting world justice and peace. It serves as a vehicle for coordinated action in the areas of formulating strategy, identifying priorities, speaking in a unified voice, and acting as a clearing house. The priority areas it has set in recent years include: reducing weapons production and preventing nuclear proliferation; transforming the cold war economy; strengthening the United Nations; and promoting sustainable development. The alliance is governed by a leadership council.

5. The alliance has a small reference collection for its own staff.

7. Index Terms: Defense Conversion; Disarmament; Environmental Issues, Global—Sustainable Development; Proliferation

---

## M3 American Association for the Advancement of Science (AAAS)—Science and Human Rights Program

1. 1333 H Street, NW
   Washington, D.C. 20005
   (202) 326-6600
   Fax: (202) 289-4950

2. Audrey R. Chapman, Director

3. The Science and Human Rights Program is a part of the AAAS Science and Policy Directorate, and is a program of the AAAS Committee on Scientific Freedom and Responsibility. The purposes of the program are to assist scientists whose human rights or academic freedom have been violated; advance the use of scientific methods in documentation and prevention of human rights violations; promote greater support for human rights within the international scientific community; and develop scientific methods for monitoring compliance with human rights standards.

5. The association's resources are solely for the use of its own staff.

6. The program publishes *Directory of Persecuted Scientists, Engineers and Health Professionals* annually and a newsletter, *Report on Science and Human Rights*. It operates an electronic human rights network, called AASHRAN, or Human Rights Action Network. Other publications include *Data Analysis for Monitoring Human Rights,* by Herbert F. Spirer and Louise Spirer (1994); *Caught in the Crossfire: A Mission Report on the Plight of the Peruvian Medical Profession,* by Daniel Salcedo (1993); and *Exploring a Human Rights Approach to Health Care Reform,* by Audrey R. Chapman (1993).

7. Index Terms: Human Rights—Science and Human Rights

---

## M4 American Bar Association (ABA)— Section of International Law and Practice

1. 1800 M Street, NW
   Suite 450-South
   Washington, D.C. 20036-5886
   (202) 331-2239
   Fax: (202) 457-1163

2. Alaire Bretz Rieffel, Director

3. The section is composed of divisions that have committees, a number of which are relevant to peace and international security studies. The Business Law Division has committees on export controls and economic sanctions, international banking and finance, international energy and natural resource law, and international trade. The Comparative Law Division has committees covering the laws of all regions of the world. The Public International Law Division has committees on arms control and disarmament,

aviation and aerospace law, immigration and nationality, international environmental law, international human rights, international law and national
security, and law of the sea.

5.    The ABA's information services department
(202/331-2208) maintains a library that has a substantial collection of ABA publications, including
members' testimony, and policy letters written to offices in both the legislative and executive branches.
Researches may use the library 9:00 A.M.–5:00 P.M.
Monday–Friday.

6.    The section publishes two quarterlies, *Interna-
tional Law News* and *International Lawyer.* Books
and monographs published by the section include
*Report on the International Tribunal to Adjudicate
War Crimes Committed in the Former Yugoslavia*
(1993); *Law and Policy of Export Controls* (1993);
*NAFTA and the Environment* (1994); *The North
American Free Trade Agreement: A New Frontier in
International Trade and the Rule of Law* (1994);
*Counseling Emerging Companies in Going Interna-
tional* (1994).

7.    Index Terms: Arms Control; Environmental Is-
sues, Global; Human Rights—and International
Law; International Economics; International Law;
War Crimes

---

## M5    American Defense Preparedness Association (ADPA)

1.    2101 Wilson Boulevard, Suite 400
      Arlington, Va. 22201-3061
      (703) 522-1820
      Fax: (703) 522-1885

2.    Lawrence F. Skibbie, President

3.    ADPA, founded in 1919, serves as a forum for
policy makers, manufacturers, and researchers on
issues concerning U.S. defense, such as military
requirements, industrial capabilities, and the acquisition process. The ADPA actively works to bring together military users with industry producers. The
ADPA has a Legislative Affairs Division that undertakes advocacy before Congress. The Technical Services Division of the association annually holds over
50 seminars and exhibits on virtually all aspects of
defense programs.

4.    ADPA hosts an annual meeting each spring and
many seminars throughout the year, a number of
which are held in the Washington, D.C., area.

5.    ADPA does not have a library.

6.    ADPA publishes the journal *National Defense*
10 times a year. It also publishes occasional white
papers on current issues relating to the defense industrial base.

7.    Index Terms: Arms Production and Acquisition; Defense Policy, National

---

## M6    American Foreign Service Association (AFSA)

1.    2101 E. Street, NW
      Washington, D.C. 20037
      (202) 338-4045
      Fax: (202) 338-6820

2.    Susan Reardon, Executive Director

3.    AFSA, with 10,300 members, is the professional association of the Foreign Service. Most of its
members are from the State Department (K37),
Agency for International Development (K1), and
United States Information Agency (K41). It also has
members in the Foreign Agricultural Service (Agriculture Department, K2), and the International
Trade Administration (Commerce Department, K7).
The association organizes speakers programs and
conferences on foreign affairs.

5.    AFSA's library consists of 75 years' worth of
back issues of the *Foreign Service Journal.* Scholars
may use the library 9:00 A.M.–5:00 P.M. Monday–
Friday.

6.    AFSA publishes the *Foreign Service Journal.*

7.    Index Terms: Development Issues; Diplomacy
and Negotiations; International Economics

---

## M7    American Political Science Association (APSA)

1.    1527 New Hampshire Avenue, NW
      Washington, D.C. 20036
      (202) 483-2512
      Fax: (202) 483-2657

2.    Catherine Rudder, Executive Director

3.    The majority of APSA is composed of teaching
and research scholars in U.S. universities and colleges. It has over 13,000 members from over 70

countries. Relevant sections include religion and politics; science, technology, and environmental politics; international security and arms control; comparative politics; politics and society in Western Europe; politics and history; and political economy.

4.    APSA holds annual conferences, which are held in Washington, D.C., every few years.

5.    APSA does not have a library.

6.    APSA publishes *The American Political Science Review* and *PS: Political Science and Politics,* both quarterly. It also publishes a number of directories, such as *Directory of Membership* (triennial); *Graduate Faculty Programs in Political Science* (triennial); *Directory of Undergraduate Political Science Faculty* (triennial); *Directory of Political Science Department Chairpersons* (annual); and *Survey of Political Science Departments* (annual).

7.    Index Terms: Arms Control; Collective Security; Defense Policy, National; Development Issues; Environmental Issues, Global; Foreign Policy; International Economics; Political Systems and Ideologies

---

## M8    American Psychological Association (APA)

1.    750 First Street, NE,
Washington, D.C. 20002
(202) 336-5500

2.    Robert Resnick, President

3.    The Committee on International Relations in Psychology of the APA maintains contact with relevant professional societies around the world. In addition, the committee sponsors several initiatives on professional exchanges, student exchanges, family counseling (Soweto, South Africa), and training (in Central America).

4.    The APA occasionally holds its annual conference in Washington, D.C.

5.    The APA maintains a library of approximately 1,100 volumes. Researchers should call for an appointment (202/336-5500). APA maintains Psychological Abstracts Information Services (PsycINFO), a computerized database providing access to international research in psychology and related behavioral and social sciences. Abstracts are entered in PsycINFO and published monthly in *Psychological*

*Abstracts.* For a fee staff can provide bibliographies with abstracts. Researchers may call for information (800/336-4980).

6.    The association publishes *American Psychologist* (monthly), *Developmental Psychology* (bimonthly), *Contemporary Psychology* (monthly), *Journal of Abnormal Psychology* (bimonthly), *Journal of Applied Psychology* (bimonthly), *Journal of Consulting and Clinical Psychology* (bimonthly), *Journal of Counseling Psychology* (bimonthly), *Journal of Educational Psychology* (quarterly), *Journal of Personality and Social Psychology* (monthly), *Professional Psychology* (quarterly), *Psychological Abstracts,* (monthly), and *Psychological Review* (quarterly).

7.    Index Terms: Conflict Management and Resolution—Theoretical Approaches; Psychological Aspects of War and Peace

---

## M9    American Society of International Law (ASIL)

1.    2223 Massachusetts Avenue, NW
Washington, D.C. 20008-2864
(202) 939-6000
Fax: (202) 797-7133

2.    Charlotte Ku, Executive Director

3.    ASIL is a professional association that promotes the study and use of law in international relations. Membership is open to lawyers and non-lawyers. In addition to sponsoring conferences, internationally and within the United States, the society sponsors interest groups that generate activities and publications of their own. There are interest groups on arms control and nonproliferation, the law of armed conflict, Antarctica, dispute resolution in international commercial contracts, indigenous peoples, human rights, international economic law, international environmental law, international organizations, international space law, law in the Pacific region, private international law, wildlife law, women in international law, Southern Africa, and the U.N. decade of international law. The society has also established working groups and committees that deal with the role of law in the post-cold war world and ways to ensure that law is taken seriously in international affairs. Projects include a study of the United Nations in the international legal order, a program of joint study with scholars from the former Soviet Union, a survey of international

law teaching, and studies of major human rights treaties and ocean boundaries delineations.

4. The society sponsors a four-day annual meeting in the spring.

5. The society's library contains an estimated 22,000 items on all aspects of public international law. See entry A3.

6. The society publishes the *American Journal of International Law* and a newsletter. Studies in transnational legal policy published by the society include *The Movement of Persons across Borders,* edited by Louis Sohn and Thomas Buergenthal (1992); *Nonviolent Responses to Violence-Prone Problems: The Cases of Disputed Maritime Claims and State-Sponsored Terrorism,* Bernard H. Oxman and John F. Murphy (1991); and *Legal Aspects of International Terrorism: Summary Report of an International Conference,* John F. Murphy (1980). Books include *U.S. Ratification of the International Human Rights Covenants,* edited by Hurst Hannum and Dana D. Fischer (1992); *The Arab-Israeli Conflict, Volume IV: The Difficult Search for Peace (1975–88),* edited by John Norton Moore (1991); *Law and Force in the New International Order,* edited by Lori F. Damrosch and David J. Scheffer (1991); *Foreign Affairs and the U.S. Constitution,* edited by Louis Henkin, Michael J. Glennon, and William D. Rogers (1990); and *Basic Documents of International Economic Law,* edited by Stephen Zamora and Ronald A. Brand (1990).

7. Index Terms: Arms Control; Conflict Management and Resolution; Development Issues; Disarmament; Environmental Issues, Global; Ethnic and Religious Conflict; Human Rights—and International Law; Humanitarian Issues—Research Organizations; International Economics—International Finance; International Economics—International Trade; International Law; International Organizations; Terrorism

---

## MIO   American Sociological Association (ASA)

1. 1722 N Street, NW
   Washington, D.C. 20036
   (202) 833-3410
   Fax: (202) 785-0146

2. Felice Levine, Executive Officer
   Ruth Searle, Head, Section on Peace and War

3. The ASA is a national association of sociologists that holds its annual meeting each August at differing sites around the United States. The ASA's Committee on International Sociology maintains liaison for ASA with different regions of the world regarding topics such as human rights, international education, and international curriculum. It also helps facilitate international contacts and exchanges. The association's Section on Peace and War maintains teaching resources and syllabuses on related issues, such as military sociology, peace studies, and peacekeeping and its alternatives. The section also makes awards to sociologists and students.

6. The Section on Peace and War publishes a newsletter three times a year. Publications related to the section include *Teaching the Sociology of Peace and War,* edited by John McDougal and Helen Raisz (1991); *Teaching Sociology of Development and Women in Development,* edited by Ali Akbar Mahdi (1991); and *Sociology of Genocide and the Holocaust: A Curriculum Guide,* edited by Jack Nusan Porter (1992). The ASA publishes several journals, including *American Sociological Review,* bimonthly; *Contemporary Sociology: A Journal of Reviews,* bimonthly; *Social Psychology,* quarterly; *Sociology of Education: A Journal of Research in Socialization and Social Structure,* quarterly; *The Journal of Health and Social Behavior,* quarterly; *Sociological Theory,* semiannually; and *Sociological Methodology,* annually. Other publications are a newsletter, *ASA Footnotes* (nine issues per year); a monthly *Employment Bulletin;* and an annual *Guide to Graduate Departments of Sociology.*

7. Index Terms: Development Issues; Peace Theory and Research; Peacekeeping

---

## MII   Amnesty International USA— Washington Office

1. 304 Pennsylvania Avenue, SE
   Washington, D.C. 20003
   (202) 544-0200
   Fax: (202) 546-7142

2. James O'Dea, Director, Washington Office

3. Amnesty International is an international human rights organization, headquartered in London, with over 50 sections worldwide. Amnesty works impartially to protect fundamental human rights

and promote global observance of the UN Declaration of Human Rights. Its principal focus is on release of prisoners of conscience, fair and prompt trials for all political prisoners, an end to torture and execution in all cases and to "disappearances." Approaches to helping political prisoners include long-term adoption of prisoners of conscience; publicizing patterns of human rights abuses; meetings with government representatives; and in urgent cases regarding torture or execution, a network of volunteers who send urgent telegrams demonstrating international concern. The organization does extensive research, collecting and analyzing information from a wide variety of sources, on cases of human rights violations. Its research department is in London. The members and supporters of Amnesty work through a variety of programs, some of them professionally oriented. In addition to local and campus groups, there are urgent action and freedom writers networks, a health professional network, a legal support network, a human rights educators network, as well as individual activities.

The Washington Office serves as a government affairs arm of the U.S. Amnesty section. It is responsible for the legislative program and for relations with Congress, the State Department, and foreign embassies in the United States.

5.　The Washington Office maintains a small library, principally of the organization's reports and other publications. It is open to the public.

6.　Amnesty International publishes a monthly newsletter in English and Spanish. It also publishes an annual report and numerous individual country reports on human rights practices. The Washington Office produces *Human Rights and U.S. Security Assistance,* which reviews the human rights records of countries receiving significant amounts of U.S. security assistance. Other publications include *Amnesty International Handbook* (1992); *Amnesty International Human Rights Plain Language* (1991); *Amnesty International Policy Manual* (1992); *Disappearances: A Workbook* (1981); *Medicine Betrayed—The Participation of Doctors in Human Rights Abuses* (1992); *A Punishment in Search of a Crime,* by Ian Gray and Moira Stanley (1989); *Rape and Sexual Abuse: Torture and Ill Treatment of Women in Detention* (1992); and *The Universal Declaration of Human Rights* (1989, in French, Spanish, Arabic, English, Russian, and Chinese). Amnesty International also produces educational videos.

7.　Index Terms: Human Rights—Monitoring Organizations

## MI2　Arms Control and Foreign Policy Caucus

1.　501 House Annex Two
Washington, D.C. 20515
(202) 226-3440
Fax: (202) 225-0081

2.　Edith B. Wilkie, Executive Director
Sen. James M. Jeffords, Chair
Sen. Joseph R. Biden Jr., Vice-Chair
Rep. Sherwood L. Boehlert, Secretary

3.　The Arms Control and Foreign Policy Caucus is a bipartisan caucus consisting of more than 140 members of the U.S. Senate and House of Representatives. Its goals are to encourage arms control and eventual disarmament, promote and protect human rights, improve relations with the developing world, and strengthen international law and institutions. As an organization it takes no positions on legislative issues. Working through several committees, task forces, and staffs, it seeks to provide weekly legislative publications on foreign and military legislation under consideration in House and Senate committees; expert speakers on foreign and military policy issues; research and advice on relevant legislative strategy; draft amendments, testimony preparation, and letters to the president on policy changes; and timely briefings or meetings on foreign policy or arms control questions.

6.　The caucus issues a bulletin, *The Week Ahead,* on relevant legislation coming to the House or Senate floor. It also issues background papers, fact sheets, and memos on upcoming committee or floor action important to members.

7.　Index Terms: Arms Control; Defense Policy, National; Disarmament; Foreign Policy

## MI3　Arms Control Association

1.　11 Dupont Circle, NW
Washington, D.C. 20036
(202) 463-8270
Fax: (202) 797-4611

2.　Spurgeon M. Keeny Jr., President

3.　The Arms Control Association is a nonpartisan national membership organization that promotes public understanding of effective policies and programs in arms control and disarmament. Its membership has extensive experience in arms control, disarmament, and national security policy. The association seeks public appreciation of the need for positive steps toward limitation of armaments and the implementation of other measures to reduce international tensions and promote world peace.

5.   The Arms Control Association's library consists of a small collection of books and a larger collection of periodicals dealing with arms control issues. Scholars may, with an appointment, use the library 9:00 A.M.–5:00 P.M. Monday–Friday.

6.   The association publishes the journals *Arms Control Today* and *Foreign Policy*; special issues include *Reining in the Arms Trade* (June 1991) and *Nuclear Testing: Time to Call a Halt* (November 1990). Other publications include *Arms Control and National Security: An Introduction*, by the ACA (1989); *Foundation for the Future: The ABM Treaty and National Security*, by Matthew Bunn and the ACA (1990); *The Race for Security: Arms and Arms Control in the Reagan Years*, by the ACA (1987); *Countdown on SALT II: The Case for Preserving Limits on US and Soviet Strategic Forces*, by the ACA and the Ploughshares Fund (1987); *Star Wars Quotes*, by the ACA (1986); *Arms Control, Disarmament, and National Security: An Annual Bibliography*, by the ACA and the Center for the Study of Armament and Disarmament (1987); and *Blundering into Disaster: Surviving the First Century of the Nuclear Age*, by Robert S. McNamara (1986).

7.   Index Terms: Arms Control; Defense Policy, National; Disarmament; Military Science

# MI4  Association of American Geographers (AAG)

1.   1710 16th Street, NW
Washington, D.C. 20009-3198
(202) 234-1450
Fax: (202) 234-2744

2.   Ronald F. Abler, Executive Director

3.   The AAG advances professional study in geography and promotes the application of geographic research in education, government, and business. It has a membership of 7,000 from the United States, Canada, and 50 other countries. In addition to special projects, largely related to education, the association sponsors numerous specialty groups. Relevant group interests include Africa, Asian geography, China, contemporary agriculture and rural land use, cultural ecology, energy and environment, Europe, geography of religions and belief systems, human rights, industrial geography, Latin America, political geography, population, rural development, and Central and Eastern Europe.

5.   The association does not have a library.

6.   The association publishes *Annals of the Association of American Geographers* and *The Professional Geographer*, a quarterly.

7.   Index terms: Development Issues; Environmental Issues, Global; Human Rights; Political Systems and Ideologies

# MI5  Association of Former Intelligence Officers (AFIO)

1.   6723 Whittier Avenue, Suite 303A
McClean, Va. 22101
(703) 790-0320
Fax: (703) 790-0264

2.   Charles A. Briggs, Chair
Lincoln D. Faurer, President

3.   The AFIO promotes public understanding of the continuing need for an effective national intelligence establishment. It supports a number of programs. The National Leadership Forum on Global Challenges conducts two-day seminars for business executives to inform them on conditions in different countries and regions around the world. These seminars are conducted by former intelligence experts on these regions. The association's Academic Exchange Program assists college and university courses in teaching about intelligence. The association also maintains a speakers bureau on intelligence related matters and assists retirees from intelligence agencies to find second careers or further work.

4.   AFIO hosts three or four luncheons each year in the Washington, D.C., area and a two- or three-day annual meeting, which are open to the public.

5.   AFIO has a small library of reference and intelligence material open to members and scholars.

6.   AFIO publishes *Periscope*, a monthly newsletter. Its Academic Exchange Program issues a quarterly newsletter, the *Intelligencer*. AFIO also publishes the Intelligence Profession Series of monographs, which includes *The Central Intelligence Agency: An Overview*, by Lewis Sorley (1990); *Intelligence: What It Is and How to Use It,*

by John Macartney (1991); *The Press and National Security Secrets,* by Tim Hackler (1992); *Estimative Intelligence,* by Harold P. Ford (1993); *From Balloons to Blackbirds: Reconnaissance, Surveillance, and Imagery: How It Evolved,* by Dino A. Burgioni (1993); and *Intelligence Oversight: The Controversy Behind the FY 1991 Intelligence Authorization Act,* by William L. Conner (1993).

7.   Index Terms: Intelligence

---

## MI6   Association of National Security Alumni

---

1.   2001 S Street, NW, Suite 740
Washington, D.C. 20009
(202) 452-5572
Fax: (515) 278-4023

2.   Philip Roetinger, President

3.   The Association of National Security Alumni (originally called the Association for Responsible Dissent) is composed of former members of organizations of the U.S. intelligence community (CIA, National Security Agency, Drug Enforcement Administration, FBI, and military intelligence). The association opposes the use of covert operations, especially those that involve violence, military or paramilitary activity, and propaganda intended to influence U.S. public opinion for the implementation of foreign policy. It also urges greater openness and reform of the information classification system.

5.   The association does not have a library, but it does maintain files on cold war intelligence matters that date from the mid-1980s. It also has all the back issues of the association's newspaper, *Unclassified,* on file. Scholars wishing to use these resources should call for an appointment.

6.   The association publishes a bimonthly newspaper, *Unclassified.*

7.   Index Terms: Defense Policy, National; Intelligence

---

## MI7   Association of Third World Affairs (ATWA)

---

1.   1629 K Street, NW, Suite 802
Washington, D.C 20006

(202) 331-8455
Fax: (202) 785-3607

2.   Lorna Hahn, Executive Director

3.   ATWA brings together individuals from government, business, and other sectors to exchange ideas and promote understanding and new approaches to controversial issues concerning the third world. Its wide-ranging concerns and focus on political, economic, military, and business affairs.

4.   ATWA sponsors meetings and conferences on regional and topical issues. These are frequently held on Capitol Hill and have included "The C.I.S. Needs and Opportunities" (June 1992); "East Asia: Answers for Eurasia?" (October 1992); "The U.N. and the New World: New Tasks, New Structures?" (March 1993); and "The Search for Security in Asia: Economic, Political, and Military Issues" (October 1993).

6.   ATWA publishes a quarterly newsletter, *Third World Forum,* and occasional papers, for example, *After Communism: Democracy, Authoritarianism, Anarchy—or More Communism* (1991). It also publishes conference proceedings.

7.   Index Terms: Development Issues; International Economics; International Politics

---

## MI8   Association to Unite Democracies (AUD)

---

1.   1506 Pennsylvania Avenue, SE
Washington, D.C. 20003
(202) 544-5150
Fax: (202) 544-3742

2.   Charles Patrick, President

3.   The AUD was founded in 1939 as Federal Union to promote world federalism of democracies. In the postwar period AUD was a primary supporter for NATO and the North Atlantic Assembly. Its main goal continues to be world federalism through a union of democracies. It has a strong Atlanticist orientation and focuses on Western Europe, European Union, NATO, and the Conference on Security and Cooperation in Europe.

5.   AUD has a library that is largely devoted to works on federalism.

6.   AUD publishes a newsletter, *Unite!*

7.   Index Terms: Collective Security; International Politics

## M19    Bread for the World Institute on Hunger and Development

1.    1100 Wayne Avenue, Suite 1000
Silver Spring, Md. 20910
(301) 608-2400
Fax: (301) 608-2401

2.    David Beckmann, President

3.    Institute on Hunger and Development is an independent organization that works with Bread for the World, a citizen's movement with more than 40,000 members. The institute, which seeks to strengthen the growing international movement to end hunger and poverty, monitors the hunger situation in developing countries worldwide, with a special emphasis on Latin America and Africa. It is concerned with all causes of hunger, including economic, political, and international, such as foreign debt problems. It pays particular attention to U.S. policy and foreign aid issues.

5.    The institute maintains a small library open by appointment.

6.    The institute publishes an annual report on the state of world hunger, as well as occasional papers and study aids.

7.    Index Terms: Development Issues; Humanitarian Issues—Relief Organizations

## M20    Business Executives for National Security (BENS)

1.    1615 L Street, NW, Suite 330
Washington, D.C. 20036
(202) 296-2125
Fax: (202) 296-2490

2.    Stanley A. Weiss, Chair
Tyrus W. Cobb, President

3.    BENS is a professional association advocating various policies related to U.S. defense. These include reducing the threat of nuclear war, greater control over Pentagon spending, more rigorous weapons testing, increased competition for military contracts, and other military reforms. BENS was active in lobbying for the Base Closing Commission. Current priorities include roles and missions review for the different services, defense conversion, non-

proliferation, and promotion of defense conversion in the former Soviet Union. The association has also sponsored a Commission on Fundamental Defense Management Reform, which has proposed a series of reforms of the Defense Department and the congressional oversight process.

4.    BENS holds an annual Washington Forum.

5.    BENS does not maintain a library.

6.    Publications include a newsletter, *Trendline,* and issue briefs, policy updates, and policy outlooks.

7.    Index Terms: Arms Control; Defense Policy, National; Military Spending

## M21    Citizens Democracy Corps (CDC)

1.    1735 I Street, NW, Suite 720
Washington, D.C. 20006
(202) 872-0933
(800) 394-1945
Fax: (202) 872-0923

2.    Carolyn Stremlau, Acting Executive Director

3.    The CDC mobilizes U.S. private sector expertise and resources to help the economic transition to market economies in Eastern Europe and the former Soviet Union. The main program of the CDC is the Business Entrepreneur Program, which sends volunteers with entrepreneurial skills to give on-site assistance to small and medium businesses, and to institutions that support business development. It also maintains a registry of volunteers willing to work in these regions and a data bank of U.S. organizations currently working there.

5.    The CDC maintains a data bank of over 600 nonprofit organizations.

6.    The CDC publishes *Compendium: U.S. Nonprofit Assistance to Central and Eastern Europe and the Commonwealth of Independent States,* updated annually.

7.    Index Terms: Transnationalism

## M22    Citizens Network for Foreign Affairs (CNFA)

1.    1111 19th Street, NW, Suite 900
Washington, D.C. 20036

(202) 296-3920
Fax: (202) 296-3948

2. Henry H. Fowler, Cochair
Melvin R. Laird, Cochair
John H. Costello, President

3. The CNFA seeks to foster greater engagement among a diverse constituency of the U.S. public and private sectors in foreign policy. It is particularly interested in emerging democracies. It sponsors several economic and development initiatives. The Citizens Network Agribusiness Alliance is a coalition of more than 170 U.S. agribusinesses, food companies, commodity and farm groups, trade associations, and universities that assists, through business-business/people-people partnerships, in enhancing the food supply. These efforts include building food systems to increase availability, quality, and storage, promoting sustainable development and economic growth, helping emerging market economies, and creating trade and investment opportunities. The National Policy Roundtable Program is a public-private sector dialogue that seeks to foster broad-based participation in the foreign policy decision-making process. It focuses on democratization, market reform, sustainable development, technology, and technology transfer. The U.S.-Japan Economic Cooperation Project seeks to increase U.S.-Japanese cooperation in promoting economic development of emerging economies and developing countries. The U.S.-Latin America and the Caribbean Partnership for Mutual Prosperity fosters partnerships that promote the region's growth and aids democratization.

4. The different programs of CNFA host conferences that are frequently held in Washington, D.C.

5. CNFA does not have a library.

6. CNFA publications include *A New Era of Economic Opportunity in the Hemisphere: Latin America, the United States and Japan* (November 1993); *America's Economic Stake in Promoting Market Based Economies in Eastern and Central Europe, the Baltics, and the Soviet Republics* (December 1991); *America's Stake in the Developing World* (Winter 1990); and *The Uruguay Trade Round Reaches a Half Way Point* (November/December 1988).

7. Index Terms: Development Issues—Agriculture; Environmental Issues, Global—Sustainable Development; International Economics—International Trade

---

## M23 Committee on the Political Economy of the Good Society (PEGS)

1. c/o Department of Government and Politics
University of Maryland
College Park, Md. 20742
(301) 405-4117
Fax: (301) 314-9690

2. Stephen Elkin, Chair of Executive Board

3. The national offices of PEGS are located at the University of Maryland's College Park Campus. A nonprofit organization, PEGS seeks to promote and coordinate inquiry and discussion regarding alternative political-economic theories and institutional designs with the hope of eventually restructuring the political-economic systems and institutions of the world to promote and protect the values of liberty, democracy, equality, and environmental sustainability.

4. PEGS conducts colloquia on relevant topics for faculty and students on University of Maryland's College Park Campus.

5. PEGS does not have its own library. See University of Maryland's McKeldin Library, entry A47.

6. The PEGS newsletter is published with the assistance of graduate students interested in political economy.

7. Index Terms: Environmental Issues, Global—Sustainable Development; Political Systems and Ideologies

---

## M24 Consortium on Peace Research, Education, and Development (COPRED)

1. George Mason University
Fairfax, Va. 22030
(703) 273-4485
Fax: (703) 993-1302

2. Barbara J. Wien, Executive Director

3. COPRED is an international nonprofit membership organization housed at George Mason University. COPRED provides a forum for researchers, educators, and activists involved in finding peaceful resolutions to conflict. Individual members include students, K-12 educators, university professors, conflict resolution practitioners, peace activists, and

clergy. Institutional members include colleges and universities, community centers, professional associations, and religious organizations. For more information on becoming a member of COPRED contact Gretchen Reinhardt, Coordinator, Information and Membership Services (703/273-4485).

COPRED is organized into 15 working groups through which members exchange ideas, write for the *Peace Chronicle* and *Peace and Change,* and aid in governing the organization. Examples of working groups are arts and media, conflict resolution, cross-cultural issues, nonviolence, peace action, peace movements, radical/innovative perspectives, and religion and ethics.

COPRED working groups frequently engage in projects. A current project, sponsored by the U.S. Institute for Peace (H73), examines the relation between the fields of peace studies and conflict resolution and develops relevant curricular materials.

4.   COPRED holds regional meetings, skills-building workshops, scholarly presentations, cultural events, and an annual conference. The theme for the 1993 conference in Atlanta, Ga., was nonviolence in a violent world.

5.   COPRED maintains a resource library of peace studies programs around the world. Its holdings consist of files on specific peace studies programs (syllabuses, curricular material, etc.) at universities in the United States and worldwide. COPRED also keeps a roster of current members' research interests and projects, as well as back issues of *Peace Chronicle* and *Peace and Change.* The staff at George Mason's Fenwick Library work in conjunction with COPRED in maintaining and updating a shelf on peace and conflict resolution.

6.   COPRED's *Peace and Change: A Journal of Peace Research* is a quarterly journal that offers articles and essays on topics such as peace education, conflict resolution, and international conflict. *Peace Chronicle* is a bimonthly newsletter published by COPRED that covers the latest developments from COPRED's working groups, reviews of current peace studies literature, and a worldwide calendar of conferences and events.

7.   Index Terms: Conflict Management and Resolution; Peace Theory and Research

---

## M25   Council on Ocean Law (COL)

---

1.   The Decatur House
1600 H Street, NW, Second Floor
Washington, D.C. 20006

(202) 347-3766
Fax: (202) 842-0030

2.   Charles Higginson, Executive Director

3.   COL was founded in 1980 to support the establishment and further development of law for the world's oceans. The council highlights three fundamentals to effective ocean management: a legal order, progressive evolution of international oceans law, and accurate information on all aspects of international oceans law. COL believes that the treaty produced by the UN Convention on the Law of the Sea in 1982 provides the basis of a legal order. Thus, it works to find ways to overcome the obstacles to universal acceptance of the convention. COL strives for the evolution of international oceans law through international forums that monitor agreements on improved vessel safety and pollution control, fisheries conservation, avoidance of terrorism and violence at sea, and the facilitation of marine scientific research. COL attempts to disseminate accurate information concerning international oceans law through forums, conferences, and a newsletter.

4.   COL sponsors evening programs semiannually in Washington, D.C., to encourage debate on current issues of international oceans law.

6.   COL publishes a monthly newsletter, *Oceans Policy News.*

7.   Index Terms: International Law

---

## M26   Federation of American Scientists (FAS)

---

1.   307 Massachusetts Avenue, NE
Washington, D.C. 20002
(202) 546-3300
Fax: (202) 675-1010

2.   Robert M. Solow, Chair
Jeremy J. Stone, President

3.   FAS (*formerly* Federation of Atomic Scientists) is composed of 3,500 natural and social scientists and engineers interested in problems of science and society. Major issues of FAS have been the Anti-Ballistic Missile Treaty, no first use of nuclear weapons, the B-1 bomber, reductions of nuclear weapons and a nuclear weapons freeze, the Strategic Defense Initiative, human rights and scientific cooperation, and energy conservation.

5.   The federation's library consists mostly of periodicals (about 50) on general defense, space, and

foreign policy issues. Researchers may use the library, by appointment, 9:00 A.M.–5:00 P.M. Monday–Friday.

6. FAS publications include *Public Interest Report; Secrecy and Government Bulletin;* and *Arms Sales Monitor.*

7. Index Terms: Arms Control; Defense Policy, National; Deterrence; Human Rights—Science and Human Rights; Military Science

---

## M27  Gray Panthers

1. 2025 Pennsylvania Avenue, NW, Suite 821
Washington, D.C. 20006
(202) 466-3132
Fax: (202) 466-3133

2. d'Layne Kerr-Layton, Program Associate

3. The Gray Panthers is an intergenerational, non-governmental organization that promotes social change. The approximately 40,000 national members of the Gray Panthers attempt to bring about social change by serving on committees and by acting as consultants to the United Nations. Issues of particular importance to the Gray Panthers are economics and tax justice, defense reductions, preservation of the environment, national health care, affordable housing, and antidiscrimination.

4. The Gray Panthers hold a national convention biannually. They sponsored a Peace Summit at the United Nations' University for Peace in Costa Rica.

6. The Gray Panthers publish eight *NETWORK* newsletters a year, and a *NETWORK* newspaper twice a year. Also published is *Gray Panther Media Guide: Age and Youth in Action for Advocacy/Programming/Production Participation* (1983). The organization puts out special reports on issues such as health care and education.

7. Index Terms: Development Issues—Health; Environmental Issues, Global; Foreign Policy; Military Spending

---

## M28  Human Rights Watch (HRW)

1. 1522 K Street, NW, Suite 910
Washington, D.C.
(202) 972-0905
Fax: (202) 371-0124

2. Kenneth Roth, Executive Director
Holly J. Burkhalter, Washington Director

3. HRW is an international human rights organization based in New York with a large office in Washington, D.C. It is composed of five regional divisions, HRW Africa, HRW Americas, HRW Asia, HRW Helsinki, and HRW Middle East. HRW monitors human rights practices of governments and insurgent groups in some 70 countries worldwide. Most of its work focuses on politically motivated human rights abuses, including censorship and bans on association and assembly, closing of religious institutions, and obstacles to travel. It monitors other abuses such as summary executions, torture and cruel conditions of imprisonment regardless of the victim. During times of armed conflict, HRW addresses abuses relating to the laws of war, such as attacks on civilians. HRW publicizes human rights violations and launches international campaigns in an effort to pressure offending governments to cease abusive practices.

HRW also runs five projects on arms transfers, children's rights, free expression, prison conditions, and women's rights. The HRW Arms Project seeks to limit distribution of arms to government and guerrilla movements that practice gross human rights abuses. The HRW Prison Project investigates prison conditions worldwide and promotes compliance with international standards. The HRW Women's Rights Project focuses on violence and systematic discrimination against women committed or tolerated by governments worldwide. The HRW Free Expression Project focuses on the connections between restrictions on freedom of expression and global social problems. The HRW Children's Rights Project opposes state-sanctioned abuses of children worldwide.

5. HRW does not maintain a library, but it does keep a collection of its own publications. A publications list is available upon request.

6. HRW publishes annually *The Human Rights Watch Report World,* as well as over 100 reports of varying lengths. Reports issued in 1993–94 included *Mauritania's Campaign of Terror: State-Sponsored Repression of Black Africans; Final Justice: Police and Death Squad Homicides of Adolescents in Brazil; Detained in China and Tibet: A Directory of Political and Religious Prisoners; Open Wounds: Human Rights Abuses in Kosovo; Arming Rwanda: The Arms Trade and Human Rights Abuses in the Rwandan War; Human Rights Violations in the United States;* and *A Modern Form of Slavery: Trafficking of Burmese Women and Girls into Brothels in Thailand.*

7. Index Terms: Human Rights—Monitoring Organization

## M29  Interfaith Impact for Justice and Peace

1.  110 Maryland Avenue, NE
    Washington, D.C. 20002
    (202) 543-2800
    Fax: (202) 547-8107

2.  James M. Bell, Executive Director

3.  Interfaith Impact for Justice and Peace is a religious coalition of organizations, congregations, and individuals of the Christian, Jewish, and Muslim faith. Through its network of member organizations it provides relevant information to its constituency on numerous issues, and monitors legislative activity and government policy. In addition to a wide range of domestic social issues, Interfaith Impact advocacy touches on numerous international concerns. It seeks to promote international peace through reduction of military spending and its conversion to social needs; it advocates a nuclear test ban and curtailment of nuclear and conventional weapons proliferation. The organization advocates environmental policies promoting sustainable development and trade policies that promote economic opportunities for developing countries. Other issue areas it monitors are U.S. policy toward Cuba, Haiti, and Central America, conflict in the former Yugoslavia, and United Nations peacekeeping efforts.

6.  Interfaith Impact publishes several newsletters: *International Peace Networker; Action,* which advocates constituent contact with Congress on specific legislation; and *Voting Record,* which reports on congressional votes.

7.  Index Terms: Defense Conversion; Development Issues; Disarmament; Environmental Issues, Global—Sustainable Development; Ethnic and Religious Conflict; Foreign Policy; Military Spending; Pacifism and Peace Movements; Proliferation; Regional Conflict

## M30  International Association of Official Human Rights Agencies (IAOHRA)

1.  444 North Capitol Street, NW
    Washington, D.C. 20001
    (202) 624-5410
    Fax: (202) 624-8185

2.  Claude Rogers, President
    R. Edison Elkins, Executive Director

3.  The primary membership of the IAOHRA are statutory human rights and human relations agencies. The goal of IAOHRA is to promote civil and human rights around the world by providing leadership in the development and enforcement of laws protecting civil and human rights. It serves as a clearinghouse for information exchange between human rights agencies around the world. It offers training programs for agency personnel; representation to international, regional, and national government bodies; and technical assistance in defining rights, drafting legislation, establishing human rights commissions and agencies, and building community support for human rights activities.

5.  IAOHRA does not have a library.

6.  IAOHRA publishes a monthly bulletin and regular newsletters.

7.  Index Terms: Human Rights—Monitoring Organizations

## M31  International Development Conference

1.  1875 Connecticut Avenue, NW, Suite 1020
    Washington, D.C. 20009
    (202) 884-8580
    Fax: (202) 884-8499

2.  Paul W. McCleary, Chair
    Robert J. Berg, President

3.  The International Development Conference, held biennially in Washington, is a forum for discussion of U.S.-Third World relations and development issues facing underdeveloped countries. In addition to the conferences, the IDC engages in a series of activities either leading to or derived from the conferences. A chief focus of these activities is policy advocacy and public education. The IDC is a coalition of individuals associated with leading national organizations from a variety of sectors and interests. IDC urges nongovernmental organizations to devote 5 percent of their program resources to public policy advocacy and another 5 percent to public education of global development issues.

4.  The January 1993 conference was on overcoming poverty: global priority. The theme of the January 1995 conference will be achieving global human security.

5.  IDC does not have a library.

6. IDC publishes a quarterly newsletter, *Ideas and Information about Development Education,* and an irregular newsletter, *IDC Policy Bulletin.*

7. Index Terms: Economic Development

## M32  International Society for Intercultural Education, Training, and Research (SIETAR International)

1. 808 17th Street, NW, Suite 200
Washington, D.C. 20006
(202) 466-7883
Fax: (202) 223-9569

2. Zareen Karani Lam De Araoz, President
David Santini, Administrative Director

3. SIETAR International is an interdisciplinary professional organization that promotes interaction and communication among diverse cultures, races, and ethnic groups. It encourages the development of knowledge, values, and skills that enable interaction at the individual, group, organization, and community levels. Members offer services in areas such as team building, conflict resolution, technology transfer facilitation, and cross-cultural counseling. Members include educators, counselors, researchers, consultants, trainers, managers, public servants. They represent education, management, anthropology, psychology, communication, theology, social work, political science, and other disciplines. SIETAR International currently has over 1,800 members in more than 60 countries, and 34 affiliate groups.

5. The Washington Office maintains a library open to SIETAR members.

6. SIETAR International publishes a bimonthly newsletter, *Communique,* a quarterly *International Journal of Intercultural Relations,* and a *Specialist and Consultant Referral Directory.*

7. Index Terms: Conflict Management and Resolution; Ethnic and Religious Conflict; Transnationalism

## M33  Jewish Institute for National Security Affairs (JINSA)

1. 1717 K Street, NW, Suite 300
Washington, D.C. 20006

(202) 833-0020
Fax: (202) 296-6452

2. Ted Dinerstein, President

3. JINSA is a 17,000-member organization that seeks to educate the U.S. public about national security and the defense and foreign policy community about Israel's role in bolstering democratic interests in the Mediterranean and Middle East. JINSA sponsors study trips between the United States and Israel. In addition to member trips, these include an annual trip to Israel for U.S. military leaders to meet with senior Israeli officials; member trips to U.S. bases; and study programs for U.S. military cadets and midshipmen.

4. JINSA sponsors the Gottesman Lecture Series on the Middle East for Military Academies, which focuses on the military situation in the Middle East. It also sponsors the Nathan Golden Lectures, which bring senior Israeli military officers to the United States for lectures at military education institutions. JINSA maintains a luncheon program with presentations and analysis of the U.S.-Israeli security relationship.

6. JINSA produces a number of publications. *Viewpoint* is a periodic analysis on current issues, principally relating to U.S.-Israeli relations and related topics. *The Middle East Media Survey* prints extracts from the Middle Eastern press and is published periodically. *Security Affairs* is a monthly newsletter covering a variety of related issues. JINSA also publishes a monograph series on related issues and *National Security,* a quarterly journal with scholarly articles on a broader range of topics.

7. Index Terms: Defense Policy, National; Foreign policy; Regional Conflict

## M34  Lawyers Alliance for World Security (LAWS)

1. 1601 Connecticut Avenue, NW, Suite 600
Washington, D.C. 20009
(202) 745-2450
Fax: (202) 667-0444

2. Ralph Earle II, Chair
Philip A. Fleming, President
John Parachini, Executive Director

3. LAWS is a nonpartisan association of legal professionals dedicated to stopping weapons proliferation and bringing the rule of law to the New Inde-

pendent States (NIS) of the former Soviet Union. Its membership includes former senior arms control negotiators, international legal scholars, and citizen activists. It engages in several programs such as a joint project with the Washington Council on Non-Proliferation to provide technical support to executive and legislative officials in non-Russian NIS republics in order to prevent nuclear proliferation. The Committee for National Security, an ongoing division of LAWS, conducts a project on chemical and biological weapons control that focuses on public and policy maker education on control and disposal of these weapons. Under the Lawmaking for Democracy Project, LAWS brings parliamentary leaders from the NIS for work-study tours of U.S. legislative and judicial bodies.

4.   The Project on Chemical and Biological Weapons Control sponsors a luncheon briefing series.

5.   LAWS maintains a small resource library for its own researchers' use.

6.   LAWS publishes issue briefs, including *Nuclear Testing and the Non-Proliferation Treaty,* by David A. Koplow (1992); *Strengthening Nuclear Non-Proliferation Security Assurances for Non-Nuclear Weapons States,* by George Bunn (1993); *Who Inherited the Former Soviet Union's Obligations under Arms Control Treaties with the United States,* by George Bunn and John Rhinelander (1992); and *Two Options for the 1995 NPT Extension Conference Revisited,* by George Bunn and Charles N. Van Doren (1992).

7.   Index Terms: Arms Control; Disarmament; International Law; Proliferation

---

## M35   NAFSA: Association of International Educators

1.   1875 Connecticut Avenue, NW
Suite 1000
Washington, D.C. 20009-5728
(202) 462-4811
Fax: (202) 667-3419
Email: INBOX@NAFSA.ORG

2.   Naomi Collins, Executive Director

3.   NAFSA: Association of International Educators is a membership organization whose mission is to strengthen and enrich educational exchange. NAFSA's 7,200 members—from all 50 states and 60 countries—represent some 2,000 colleges and universities, as well as elementary and secondary schools,

public and private agencies, educational associations, exchange organizations, corporations, foundations, community organizations, and individuals.

The association promotes the professional development of its members who work in international educational exchange; establishes and upholds principles of good practice in the field; provides a forum for discussion of issues; and seeks to increase awareness, appreciation, and support for international education and exchange in communities, on campuses, and in government. NAFSA's primary vehicle for achieving these goals is its five professional sections. The Admissions Section deals with recruiting and placing foreign students in U.S. colleges and universities; Administrators and Teachers in English as a Second Language staff ESL programs; the Council of Advisers to Foreign Students and Scholars deals with both counseling programs and administration; the Community Section is composed of professionals involved in community programming for international students; and the Section on U.S. Students Abroad is made up of professionals who arrange exchange programs for U.S. students.

4.   NAFSA holds an annual conference to bring together educators, government officials, business people, and foundation representatives from around the world. Regional groups hold annual conferences in their specific regions of the country. NAFSA also organizes professional development workshops at the regional and national levels.

6.   The *NAFSA Newsletter,* published eight times a year, covers current issues in international education. The *NAFSA Directory* puts the resources of institutions, individuals, government offices, and services together in one book. The *International Educator,* a semiannual, specializes in feature articles and "think pieces." The *Government Affairs Bulletin* tracks changes in legislation and regulations that will affect international educational exchange. *NAFSA Job Registry* keeps members apprised of openings in the field. NAFSA also publishes books, working papers, and reports.

7.   Index Terms: Ethnic and Religious Conflict; Transnationalism

---

## M36   National Academy of Sciences (NAS)

1.   2101 Constitution Avenue
Washington, D.C. 20418
(202) 334-2000
Fax: (202) 334-1597

2. Bruce Alberts, President
E. William Colglazier Jr., Executive Director, Office of International Affairs
Jo L. Husbands, Director, Committee on International Security and Arms Control
Michael Dow, Director, Board on Science and Technology for International Development
Steve Merrill, Executive Director, Board on Science, Technology, and Economic Policy

3. The National Academy of Sciences is a private organization of scientists that serves as an official adviser to the U.S. government on matters of science and technology. The Committee on International Security and Arms Control (CISAC, 202/334-2811) was established to advise the government on security matters. Its functions include engaging similar organizations in other countries in discussions of international security and arms control policy; developing recommendations and initiatives on scientific and technical issues; responding to requests for analysis and information from the government; and writing policy reports. It also conducts dialogues with Russian counterparts. Twenty meetings have been held since 1981. CISAC has plans for contacts with other republics of the former Soviet Union, such as Ukraine, Belarus, and Kazakhstan. It maintains a working group on biological weapons control that, since 1986, has met with Soviet counterparts on the prevention of development, proliferation, and use of biological weapons. Since 1988 CISAC has also met with Chinese scientists and military affairs experts on regional and security issues. In addition, CISAC maintains contacts with the British Royal Society, French Academy of Sciences, and Italian Accademia dei Lincei.

The Office of International Affairs, under the National Resource Council (NRC), which is the working arm of the NAS, maintains a Board on Science and Technology for International Development (BOSTID, 202/334-2633). BOSTID conducts studies and sponsored workshops on the role of science and technology in the social and economic development of Latin America, Asia, and Africa. BOSTID specialists have met with counterparts in developing countries to consider programs relating to education, industrial research, energy, agriculture, natural resources, and appropriate technologies. BOSTID also has advisory panels on technology innovation, international health, natural resources, industrialization, and technological education.

The Board on Science, Technology, and Economic Policy (STEP, 202/334-2200) is an independent board within the NRC whose purpose is to study factors affecting the economic strength of the United

States. As such it is concerned with technology and international trade, international standards and conformity, and international friction and cooperation in high technology development.

5. National Academy of Sciences—National Research Council Library (Pamela C. Pangburn, Manager, 202/334-2125), holding 30,000 volumes and 300 current subscriptions (including the publications of NAS, National Academy of Engineering, Institute of Medicine, and NRC), is open to the public, by appointment, 8:30 A.M.–5:00 P.M. Monday–Friday.

6. CISAC policy reports include *Management of and Disposition of Excess Weapons Plutonium* (January 1994); *The Future of the U.S.-Soviet Nuclear Relationship* (September 1991); *Challenges for the 1990s for Arms Control and International Security* (1989); and *Reykjavik and Beyond: Deep Reductions in Strategic Nuclear Arsenals and the Future Direction of Arms Control* (1988). Other publications of the NAS include *Democratization in Africa,* edited by Sahr John Kpundeh (1992); *Europe 1992: The Implication of Market Integration for R&D Intensive Firms,* by the Office of International Affairs (1991); *Global Environmental Change* (1991); *One Earth, One Future: Our Changing Global Environment* (1992); *The Transition to Democracy: Proceedings of a Workshop* (1991); and *U.S.-Japan Strategic Alliances in the Semiconductor Industry,* by the Committee on Japan, National Resource Council (1992).

7. Index Terms: Arms control; Defense Policy, National; Development Issues; Environmental Issues, Global; Proliferation

## M37 National Association of Evangelicals

1. 1023 15th Street, NW, Suite 500
Washington, D.C. 20005
(202) 789-1011
Fax: (202) 842-0392

2. Robert Dugan, Director

3. The National Association of Evangelicals, with a membership of over 50,000 churches from 72 denominations, maintains a program of Peace, Freedom, and Security Studies that promotes Christian moral guidance for the purpose of understanding national security policy. The program focuses on three major objectives: leadership development; providing material resources, such as study kits, a speakers bureau, and publications; and media relations.

5. The association does not have a library.

6. The association publishes a newsletter, *Washington Insight,* and a bimonthly magazine, *Action.*

7. Index Terms: Defense Policy, National; Religious, Philosophical, and Ethical Concepts of War and Peace

---

## M38 National Association of Manufacturers (NAM) — International Economic Affairs Department

1. 1331 Pennsylvania Avenue, NW
   Suite 1500—North Tower
   Washington, D.C. 20004-1790
   (202) 637-3000
   Fax: (202) 637-3182

2. Jerry J. Jasinowski, President
   Howard Lewis III, Vice-President, International Economic Affairs Department

3. NAM is a trade organization that represents the interests of its 12,000 members. NAM's basic positions in regard to international trade favors export-oriented U.S. policies, multilateral trade talks, increased funding for the Export-Import Bank (K14), and global protection of intellectual property.
   NAM's International Economic Affairs Department is composed of three committees: International Investment and Finance, International Trade, and Technology Policy. Through these committees NAM assists member companies on numerous international issues, including: China's most-favored-nation status, East-West trade, Canada-U.S. trade, export controls, foreign aid, global climate problems, import laws, international finance, international business codes, international taxes, multinational corporations, and nontariff barriers.

4. NAM hosts occasional conferences.

6. NAM publishes a weekly newsletter, *Briefing.*

7. Index Terms: International Economics

---

## M39 National Conference on Peacemaking and Conflict Resolution (NCPCR)

1. George Mason University
   4400 University Drive
   Fairfax, Va. 22030-4444

(703) 934-5140
Fax: (703) 934-5142

2. Linda Baron, Executive Director

3. NCPCR primarily sponsors a biannual conference, held in different locations in the United States, while serving as a forum for peacemaking and conflict resolution. NCPCR promotes the use and acceptance of nonviolent approaches to the conflict resolution and seeks to improve conflict resolution theory and practice. The conference focuses on peacemaking and conflict resolution within the United States, but also serves as a link to similar activities around the world.

5. The National Conference does not have its own library; its staff uses the resources of the Institute for Conflict Resolution and Analysis at George Mason University (see entry J5).

7. Index Terms: Conflict Management and Resolution; Peace Theory and Research

---

## M40 National Organization for Women (NOW) — International Division

1. 1000 16th Street, NW, Suite 700
   Washington, D.C. 20036
   (202) 331-0066
   Fax: (202) 785-8576

2. Marie-Jose Ragab, Director

3. NOW's International Division was founded in 1991 to address the needs of women in the international realm. This division attempts to compensate for the UN's lack of action or mechanisms for meeting the needs of women. NOW conducts research on the effects of foreign policy, international commercial agreements, and international financial treaties on the status of women throughout the world. NOW also works with international nongovernmental organizations, U.S. government agencies, and foreign governments to improve the status of women globally.

4. NOW's International Division sponsors occasional conferences. The one held in Washington, D.C., in 1991 focused on the issues of international violence against women and how to empower women in the global political sphere.

6. NOW publishes a newsletter, the *National NOW Times.*

7. Index Terms: Development Issues—Education; Human Rights; Transnationalism

## **M41**   National Peace Corps Association

1.   1900 L Street, NW, Suite 205
Washington, D.C. 20036
(202) 293-7728
Fax: (202) 293-7554

2.   Charles F. Dambach, President

3.   The National Peace Corps Association (*formerly* the National Council of Returned Peace Corp Volunteers) is the alumni association of individuals who have served in the Peace Corps. Its primary goal is to educate the public about other countries through a network of former volunteers and staff. It also coordinates a network of over 100 affiliated Peace Corps alumni groups with a combined membership of 15,000. Through the Constituency for Sustainable Development, the association is active in policy advocacy on developmental issues.

5.   The National Peace Corps Association does not have a library, but the Washington office of the Peace Corps does (see entry K33).

6.   The association publishes *Worldview Magazine,* quarterly; *Advocacy Bulletin;* and a newsletter, *Group Leader's Digest.*

7.   Index Terms: Development Issues; Environmental Issues, Global—Sustainable Development

## **M42**   National Security Industrial Association (NSIA)

1.   1025 Connecticut Avenue, NW, Suite 300
Washington, D.C. 20036
(202) 775-1440
Fax: (202) 775-1309

2.   James R. Hogg, President

3.   The NSIA, an association of approximately 350 industrial, research, legal, and educational organizations, is devoted to maintaining a close relationship between industry and government in the defense acquisition process. Its work is carried out primarily through 17 committees: expeditionary warfare; undersea warfare; automatic testing; command, control, communications, and intelligence; environment; international; legislative information; logistics management; manpower and training; manufacturing management; procurement; quality and reliability assurance; research and engineering; strike, surface, and anti-air warfare; software and information systems; space; and air-land tactical warfare.

4.   The NSIA holds an annual meeting as well as numerous conferences and symposia throughout the year.

5.   The NSIA does not have a library.

6.   The association publishes a quarterly newsletter, *NSIA News,* and *Annual Report and Directory.*

7.   Index Terms: Arms Production and Acquisition; Defense Policy, National; Military Science; Military Spending; Naval Science

## **M43**   Natural Resources Defense Council (NRDC)—Washington Office

1.   1350 New York Avenue, NW
Washington, D.C. 20005
(202) 783-7800
Fax: (202) 783-5917

2.   Frederick A. O. Schwarz, Jr., Chair
John H. Adams, Executive Director

3.   The NRDC is an environmental advocacy organization that engages in litigation on a wide range of natural resource issues. The NRDC is involved in a number of global projects. In addition to specific site activities (for example, protection of the Clayoquat Sound, British Columbia) NRDC activities include follow-up policy changes to the Earth Summit; cooperation with Canadian and Mexican environmentalists on NAFTA; advocacy regarding U.S. foreign aid to promote environmentally sustainable development; strengthening commitments of industrialized nations to reducing global warming; protection of the earth's ozone layer; and assisting Russian environmental organizations. NRDC is active regarding nuclear weapons issues. These include advocacy of a ban on testing nuclear arms; organizing U.S.-Russian workshops on dismantling nuclear weapons and disposal of nuclear materials; opposition to nuclear proliferation through advocating a halt to the use of weapons-grade plutonium; and advocating curbs on U.S. weapons production. NRDC also does research on nuclear weapons issues.

5.   NRDC does not have a library open to outside researchers.

6.   NRDC publications relevant to peace and international security studies include *One Year after*

*Rio: Keeping the Promises of the Earth Summit: A Country-by-Country Report,* by S. Jacob Scherr, Barrett Frelinghuysen, Rob Burn, Jared E. Blumfeld, and Michelle Benedict Nowlin (June 1993); *Taking Stock: U.S. Nuclear Deployments at the End of the Cold War,* by Greenpeace/NRDC (1992); *Defending the Earth: Abuses of Human Rights and the Environment,* by Human Rights Watch/NRDC (June 1992); *Amazon Crude,* by Judith Kimerling (February 1991). The NRDC also publishes the *Nuclear Weapons Databook* series, which includes: Volume I: U.S. Forces and Capabilities; Volume II: U.S. Nuclear Warhead Production; Volume III: U.S. Nuclear Warhead Facility Profiles; Volume IV: Soviet Nuclear Weapons. Working papers associated with the *Nuclear Weapons Databook* include *United States Nuclear Tests: July 1945 to 31 December 1992* (Working Paper 94–1); *The U.S. Debate over a CTB* (Working Paper 93–5); *Nuclear Alert after the Cold War* (Working Paper 93–4); and *Russian/Soviet Nuclear Warhead Production* (Working Paper 93–1).

7.   Index Terms: Arms Control; Environmental Issues, Global; Proliferation

---

## M44   NETWORK

1.   806 Rhode Island Avenue, NE
Washington, D.C. 20018
(202) 526-4070
(202) 526-4074 (Hotline)
Fax: (202) 832-4635

2.   Kathy Thornton, National Coordinator

3.   NETWORK is a national Catholic social justice lobby with a membership of approximately 10,000 lay and religious members. Its lobbying goals are just access to economic resources; fairness in national funding; and justice in global relationships. Issues include military spending and economic conversion, equitable and sustainable development, and global collaboration. It has a special focus on South Africa, the Philippines, and Central America.

5.   NETWORK maintains a small library of about 500 volumes. Its collection focuses on topics such as Catholic social teaching, war issues, foreign policy issues, and the environment. Scholars may use the library 9:00 A.M.–5:00 P.M. Monday–Friday. NETWORK also has an archive, but it is closed to outside researchers.

6.   NETWORK publishes *Connection,* a bimonthly magazine, and *Networker,* a newsletter.

7.   Index Terms: Development Issues—International Development Policy; Environmental Issues, Global—Sustainable Development; Military Spending; Pacifism and Peace Movements

---

## M45   Peace Links (*formerly* Women against Nuclear War)

1.   747 8th Street, SE
Washington, D.C. 20003
(202) 544-0805
Fax: (202) 544-0809

2.   Betty Bumpers, President

3.   Peace Links was founded in 1982 to educate women about the dangers of nuclear war. Today it is a nationwide nongovernmental organization and network of grassroots individuals who educate communities about global cooperation and nonviolent conflict resolution. For instance, it coordinates citizen exchanges with women of the former Soviet Union, and it administers a leadership skills training workshop for women. Similarly, the Pen Pals for Peace project forges connections between U.S. and Soviet women. Its action network focuses on legislative issues, such as stopping nuclear proliferation, and their implications for women.

4.   Peace Links holds occasional conferences and sponsors educational trips. It also coordinates an annual Peace on Earth Gala.

5.   Peace Links maintains a database listing residents of the former Soviet Union and the United States who are involved in the Pen Pals for Peace program.

6.   Peace Links publishes a newsletter, *Connections.* It also publishes *Action Alert,* reports that appear six times a year and focus on current issues such as the excessive defense budget.

7.   Index Terms: Conflict Management and Resolution—Unofficial and Nongovernmental Approaches; Transnationalism

---

## M46   PeacePAC

1.   110 Maryland Avenue, NE
Washington, D.C. 20002
(202) 543-4100
Fax: (202) 543-6297

2.  Suzy S. Kerr, Executive Director

3.  PeacePAC is an affiliate of the Council for a Livable World (H22) that supports candidates for the U.S. House of Representatives who are committed to nuclear arms control, nuclear disarmament, the prevention of nuclear war, and significant reductions in military spending. The organization maintains a nuclear arms control hotline (202/543-0006), which is a taped message on the status of arms control legislation in Congress.

5.  PeacePAC does not maintain a library that outside researchers can use.

6.  PeacePAC publishes an arms control voting index of U.S. representatives and fact sheets of issues before the Congress.

7.  Index Terms: Arms Control; Disarmament; Military Spending

## M47  Physicians for Social Responsibility (PSR)

1.  1101 14th Street, NW, Suite 700
    Washington, D.C. 20005
    (202) 898-0150
    Fax: (202) 898-0172

2.  Julia Moore, Executive Director

3.  PSR is an organization of over 20,000 health professionals and supporters working in 92 chapters to prevent nuclear war, protect the environment, and reorder national spending priorities. It is the U.S. affiliate of International Physicians for the Prevention of Nuclear War. PSR works toward the following goals: to investigate the medical effects of weapons of mass destruction and environmental degradation; to educate about the realities of the nuclear age and urgent environmental challenges; to promote policies that address the medical consequences of critical environmental threats; to promote policies that shift funding away from weapons production and military facility operations toward cleanup and environmental restoration; to support action in local communities; and to promote international cooperation and communication among physicians and health workers throughout the world.

5.  PSR does not have a library.

6.  PSR is a sponsor of the journal *Medicine and Global Survival* (formerly *PSR Quarterly*); a quarterly newsletter, *PSR Reports;* and a periodic issue briefer, *PSR Monitor.*

7.  Index Terms: Arms Control; Disarmament; Environmental Issues, Global; Humanitarian Issues—Research Organizations; Military Science—Civil Defense and Effects of Nuclear War; Military Spending

## M48  Population Action International (PAI) (*formerly* Population Crisis Committee)

1.  1120 19th Street, NW, Suite 550
    Washington, D.C. 20036
    (202) 659-1833
    Fax: (202) 293-1795

2.  J. Joseph Speidel, President

3.  PAI is a policy-oriented research and advocacy organization promoting international family planning programs. Its research focuses on a range of issues, which include population programs of the World Bank (L8) and the Agency for International Development (K1); barriers to contraceptive development; the environment and sustainable development; and women's education, training, and health care.

5.  Population Action's library contains about 6,500 volumes, over 500 periodicals, and a substantial number of vertical files. Subjects covered include international demography, international family planning, and international women's issues. In contrast to its collection size, the physical size of the library is relatively small. Researchers wishing to use the library (9:00 A.M.–5:00 P.M. Monday–Friday) must make an appointment. Librarian Anne Marie Amantia will make appointments, answer questions over the phone, or send information.

6.  PAI has published country study series on China and India. Booklets issued in 1993 included "Sustaining Water: Population and the Future of Renewable Water Supplies," "Closing the Gender Gap: Educating Girls," "Challenging the Planet: Connections between Population and Environment," "Expanding Access to Safe Abortion: Key Issues," and "1992 Population Picks and Pans." "Youth at Risk: Meeting Youth Sexual Health Needs" appeared in 1994.

7.  Index Terms: Development Issues—Population Policy; Environmental Issues, Global—Sustainable Development

## M49 Population Association of America (PAA)

1.  1722 N Street, NW
    Washington, D.C. 20036
    (202) 429-0891
    Fax: (202) 785-0146

2.  Ina Young, Executive Administrator
    Jennifer Kilroy, Administrative Assistant

3.  PAA is a scientific and professional society for persons interested in all aspects of population, demography, family planning, migration, vital statistics, and related subjects, worldwide. It is affiliated with the American Association for the Advancement of Science (M3) and is represented in the Behavioral Science Division of the National Academy of Sciences (M36).

5.  PAA does not have a library.

6.  PAA publications include the quarterly journal *Demography;* a quarterly newsletter, *PAA Affairs;* and a quarterly bibliographic index to international literature on populations topics, *Population Index.*

7.  Index Terms: Development Issues—Population Policy

## M50 Psychologists for Social Responsibility (PsySR)

1.  2607 Connecticut Avenue, NW
    Washington, D.C. 20008
    (202) 745-7084
    Fax: Call for number

2.  Anne Anderson, Coordinator, National Office

3.  The goals of PsySR focus on preventing war. War prevention and efforts at fostering authentic security include analyzing psychological causes and consequences of war and destructive conflict. PsySR sponsors the Enemy Images Project, which seeks to decrease exaggerated images of the enemy as part of PsySR's examination of psychological mechanisms shaping public attitudes. Other efforts of the organization include analyzing the psychology of the war system; changing attitudes that support the war system; teaching skills of nonviolent conflict resolution and peaceful interpersonal relations; creating a psychological environment conducive to international

cooperation; and promoting the psychological case for a comprehensive test ban treaty. PsySR also produced an educational brochure, "War Trauma and Recovery," on Croatia that has been distributed in former Yugoslavia.

5.  Due to size restraints PsySR cannot open its resources to outside researchers. But the coordinator, Anne Anderson, will answer scholars' questions and provide reference information.

6.  PsySR publishes a newsletter and briefing papers on various relevant topics.

7.  Index Terms: Arms Control; Conflict Management and Resolution—Theoretical Approaches; Peace Theory and Research; Psychological Aspects of War and Peace

## M51 Sierra Club—Washington Office

1.  408 C Street, NE
    Washington, D.C. 20002
    (202) 547-1141
    Fax: (202) 547-6009

2.  Debbie Sease, Legislative Director

3.  The Sierra Club is a conservation organization that promotes environmental concerns. The Washington office engages in direct lobbying to promote legislation. The objectives of its international program include maintenance of biodiversity; protection of tropical forests, which is carried out through the Tropical Forests Campaign; promotion of sustainable development; and protection of natural areas. The club maintains an international population program promoting population stabilization policies. It is also concerned with global warming and energy use. The club's primary international activity is to monitor policies of the International Monetary Fund (L11) and the World Bank (L8) and to advocate funding policies that are environmentally sensitive.

6.  The Washington office publishes a monthly newsletter, *Earthcare Appeals.* The club also publishes a monthly newsletter, *Sierra Club International Activist!* and a monthly magazine, *Sierra.*

7.  Index Terms: Development Issues—Population Policy; Environmental Issues, Global—Sustainable Development

## M52 Society for International Development (SID)—Washington Chapter

1. 1875 Connecticut Avenue, NW, Suite 1020
   Washington, D.C. 20005
   (202) 884-8590
   Fax: (202) 884-8499

2. Stephen F. Moseley, President
   Lawrence R. Goldman, Executive Director

3. SID is an interdisciplinary, nonpolitical, professional association for people interested in international economic, political, and social development. It has members in 130 countries and over 114 national and local chapters. The Washington chapter is the largest, with 1,300 individual and 49 institutional members. SID promotes international cooperation and dialogue on global developmental issues and serves as a network in the international development field. Activity of the society is organized through roundtables on global regions and technical workgroups. Relevant workgroups include agriculture and rural development; culture; environment and energy; human rights; population; refugees and humanitarian affairs; science, technology, and development; and trade.

4. In addition to roundtable and workgroup meetings, there are professional training workshops and an annual chapter conference.

5. SID does not maintain a library.

6. SID publishes a monthly newsletter, *Development Connections;* a quarterly journal, *Development;* and a quarterly newsletter, *Compass.*

7. Index Terms: Development Issues—International Development Policy

## M53 Society of Professionals in Dispute Resolution (SPIDR)

1. 815 15th Street, NW, Suite 530
   Washington, D.C. 20005
   (202) 783-7277
   Fax: (202) 783-7281

2. Valerie Graff, Executive Director

3. SPIDR is an association representing all types of neutral and impartial practitioners engaged in dispute resolution. The goals of the organization are to increase public understanding of dispute resolution procedures; further the acceptability and understanding of the role of neutrals; enhance the skill of mediators and other neutrals involved in dispute resolution; promote recruitment and education of dispute resolution personnel; aid structures and institutions through which dispute resolution services are provided; promote professionalism among neutrals at all levels; sponsor research on innovative resolution techniques; and serve as a clearinghouse for research data in the field. SPIDR conducts its work through committees, which include special committees on law and public policy questions; qualifications; and ethics. It also has committees on international and environmental topics.

4. SPIDR holds an annual conference and numerous regional conferences within the United States.

5. SPIDR does not have a library.

6. SPIDR publishes the quarterly *SPIDR News*. It also has an occasional paper series and publishes conference proceedings. A publications list is available on request.

7. Index Terms: Conflict Management and Resolution

## M54 United Nations—Association of the USA—Washington Office

1. 1010 Vermont Avenue, NW, Suite 904
   Washington, D.C. 20005
   (202) 347-5004
   Fax: (202) 628-5945

2. John C. Whitehead, Chair of the Association
   Thomas B. Morgan, President

3. The United Nations Association of the United States of America is dedicated to strengthening the United Nations system and U.S. participation in that system. The association has more than 30,000 members nationwide and over 170 chapters and divisions. It is headquartered in New York City. The Washington office provides background information and policy analysis on the activities of international organizations to policymakers and the media. The association also sponsors the Global Policy Project, which organizes community based panels throughout the nation to debate and recommend approaches to major issues.

5. The association does not maintain a library.

6. The Washington office publishes a newsletter, *Washington Weekly Report,* and a quarterly, *The Interdependent.* The association publishes a wide array of books, reports, occasional papers, fact sheets, and newsletters. Recent titles include *Whose Collective Security?* by Edward C. Luck and Toby Trister Gati (1992); *Curbing the Middle East Arms Race: Policy Options for the United States and the United Nations,* compiled by Edmund T. Piasecki (1992); *Institutionalizing the Earth Summit: The U.N. Commission on Sustainable Development,* by Kathryn G. Sessions (1992); *Enhancing the Role of the U.N. in Peace and Security,* by James S. Sutterlin (1992); and *Roles for the United Nations after the Gulf War,* by United Nations Association policy analysts (1991).

7. Index Terms: International Organizations—United Nations; International Politics

## M55 United States Catholic Conference (USCC) — Office of International Justice and Peace (OIJP)

1. 3211 4th Street, NE
Washington, D.C. 20017
(202) 541-3199
Fax: (202) 541-3339

2. Drew Christiansen, Director, Office of International Justice and Peace

3. The United States Catholic Conference, a civil corporation of the U.S. Catholic bishops, is the national-level agency for the Catholic Church in the United States. The Office of International Justice and Peace (OIJP) is within the Secretariat of Social Development and World Peace. The staff members of the OIJP advise the U.S. bishops on international affairs, draft policy proposals, and conduct research. The advisers for different regions are Thomas E. Quigley (Latin America, East Asia); Roburt Dumas (Africa); Drew Christiansen (Middle East); and Gerard Powers (Europe and security policies).

5. See Catholic News Service Library (entries B15 and F28) and National Conference of Catholic Bishops' library (entry N38).

6. The OIJP publishes occasional statements on issues concerning international affairs, especially pronouncements of U.S. bishops.

7. Index Terms: Development Issues—International Development Policy; Humanitarian Issues; Religious, Philosophical and Ethical Concepts of War and Peace

See also entries B15, F28, and N38

## M56 Washington Institute of Foreign Affairs

1. 8206 Thoreau Drive
Bethesda, Md. 20817
(301) 469-7223
Fax: (301) 365-0859

2. Armin Meyer, President

3. The Washington Institute of Foreign Affairs is an association of some 300 distinguished public officials, academicians, lawyers, and business executives. Its principal activity is a weekly meeting at which prominent speakers discuss problems in international affairs. These sessions are off-the-record and members may not bring guests.

5. The institute does not have a library.

7. Index Terms: Foreign Policy

## M57 Women in International Security (WIIS)

1. WIIS/CISSM School of Public Affairs
University of Maryland
College Park, Md. 20742
(301) 405-7612
Fax: (301) 403-8107

2. Catherine McArdle Kelleher, President
Carola Weil, Executive Director

3. WIIS is a membership organization whose purpose is to enhance opportunities of women in the fields of foreign and defense policy and international security. Its membership includes men and women from academia, think tanks, the diplomatic corps, the intelligence community, the military, and the private sector. WIIS maintains a data bank of women in the field of international security and serves as a clearinghouse for information in this field. It maintains contact with an affiliated organization in Moscow of Russian women working in international security issues.

4. WIIS hosts an annual Summer Symposium for graduate students in international security. It also convenes conferences and other meetings in the Washington area on an ad hoc basis.

5. WIIS does not have a library of its own. See the University of Maryland's McKeldin Library (A47).

6. WIIS publishes a quarterly newsletter, *WIIS Words,* and *JOBS HOTLINE.*

7. Index Terms: Defense Policy, National; Foreign Policy

---

## M58 Women Strike for Peace (WSP)

1. 110 Maryland Avenue, Suite 302
Washington, D.C. 20002
(202) 543-2660
Fax: (202) 546-0090

2. Edith Villastrigo, National Legislative Coordinator

3. Established in 1961, Women Strike for Peace is a nationwide grass roots advocacy organization in opposition to militarism. It focuses on a worldwide drive for a comprehensive treaty banning nuclear testing, an end to nuclear weapons production, and conversion of the U.S. military budget to domestic programs. Past issues have been opposition to Star Wars, opposition to NATO's multilateral force proposal, support of the 1963 Limited Test Ban Treaty, and opposition to U.S. intervention in Southeast Asia, Central America, and the Middle East. WSP advocates diplomatic methods of international conflict resolution.

5. Women Strike for Peace has a small library including, in particular, material relating to its more than 30-year history.

6. Women Strike for Peace publishes a bimonthly newsletter, *Legislative Alert.*

7. Index Terms: Pacifism and Peace Movements

---

## M59 Women's Action for New Directions (WAND)

1. 110 Maryland Avenue, NE, Suite 205
Washington, D.C. 20002
(202) 543-8505
Fax: (202) 675-6469

2. Arlene Victor, President
Susan Shaer, Executive Director

3. WAND is an advocacy and education organization that promotes reduction in the military budget and increased funding for domestic social programs benefiting women and children. It sponsors the Women Legislator's Lobby (WILL) made up of women federal and state legislators supporting the same agenda.

4. WILL holds an annual conference of women state legislators and women leaders from around the country.

5. WAND keeps some up-to-date resources (such as pamphlets) for scholars' information, but all of its library-worthy materials are sent to the Smith College Library, Northampton, Mass. 01063.

6. WAND publishes a quarterly bulletin.

7. Index Terms: Pacifism and Peace Movements

---

## M60 World Federalist Association (WFA)

1. 418 7th Street, SE
Washington, D.C. 20003
(800) WFA-0123
(202) 546-3950
Fax: (202) 546-3749

2. John B. Anderson, President

3. The WFA is an educational, membership organization that seeks abolition of war and preservation of a livable global environment through the development of world law. The WFA seeks to extend to the world community the principles underlying U.S. federalism.

5. The WFA maintains a small resource collection with a broad focus. Holdings include UN documents, publications of nongovernmental organizations (mostly dealing with disarmament, environmental, and human rights issues), and publications on global governance. Scholars who wish to use the collection should call for an appointment (Rick Panganiban, librarian). The library is open 9:00 A.M.–5:00 P.M. Monday–Friday.

6. The WFA publishes a newsletter.

7. Index Terms: Environmental Issues, Global; International Law; International Organizations; Peace Theory and Research

## M61  World Peacemakers

1.  11427 Scotsbury Terrace
    Germantown, Md. 20876
    (301) 916-0442
    Fax: (301) 916-5335

2.  Bill Price, Director

3.  World Peacemakers, associated with the Church of the Savior, advocates international peace with justice and nonviolence. Issues it is concerned with include U.S. defense and foreign policy and globalization of the U.S. economy. It also is active in the Global Peace Service, a national collaboration of nongovernmental organizations promoting peace.

5.  World Peacemakers maintains a small collection of books on topics such as religion, peace, and international law. Whether scholars may use these resources is determined on a case-by-case basis. Call for permission.

6.  World Peacemakers publishes *World Peacemakers Quarterly.* Other publications include *Handbook for World Peacemaker Groups,* by N. Gordon Cosby, Marilyn McDonald, and Bill Price (1988).

7.  Index Terms: Pacifism and Peace Movements; Peace Theory and Research; Religious, Ethical, and Philosophical Concepts of War and Peace

## M62  World Population Society (WPS)

1.  1333 H Street, NW, Suite 760
    Washington, D.C. 20005
    (202) 898-1303
    Fax: (202) 861-0621

2.  Jarold Kieffer, President
    Frank H. Oram, Executive Director

3.  WPS is an international, interdisciplinary association of scientific and professional "populationists." The organization has members in some 60 countries. It promotes population planning, research, and education in less developed countries, and sponsors an annual or biannual conference at varying international sites.

6.  WPS publishes a newsletter and proceedings of its international conferences.

7.  Index Terms: Development Issues—Population Policy

# N

# Cultural-Exchange and Technical-Assistance Organizations

## Cultural-Exchange and Technical-Assistance Organizations Entry Format (N)

1. *Address; Telephone Number(s)*

2. *Chief Official and Title*

3. *Programs and Activities Pertaining to Peace and International Security Studies*

4. *Conventions/Meetings*

5. *Library/Reference Collection*

6. *Publications*

7. *Index Terms* (relevant subject specialties)

## Introductory Note

Complementing the many research centers and associations listed in sections H and M of this Guide are a number of Washington-area organizations with programs in technical or humanitarian assistance, and in cultural exchanges. Through their involvement in these various programs, staff members in these organizations have acquired a certain level of expertise in the fields covered by this Guide and are often knowledgeable contacts for scholars. In addition, some of these organizations sponsor informa-

tive meetings and issue substantive publications. Frequently they engage in extensive contract work available with the federal government, particularly the Agency for International Development (K1), the State Department (K37), and the U.S. Information Agency (K41).

For technical-assistance and cultural-exchange organizations whose concern is limited to specific geographic areas or individual countries, see the geographic volumes in this Scholars' Guides series listed in the Bibliography.

---

## N1 Adventist Development and Relief Agency International (ADRA)

---

1. 12501 Old Columbia Pike
   Silver Spring, Md. 20904
   (301) 680-6380
   Fax: (301) 680-6370

2. Ralph S. Watts, President and Executive Director

3. ADRA, affiliated with the Seventh-day Adventist Church, operates humanitarian and development-assistance programs throughout the world. In

addition to developing countries in Latin America, Africa, and the Far East, ADRA has begun programs in the former Soviet Union. Activities, which are under the direction of country-program managers in the field, include food, health care, educational, and rehabilitation programs, and construction projects (schools, roads, water systems, and other community projects).

5. ADRA has a small library open to outside researchers by appointment. Contact Audrey Taylor (301/680-5127), 9:00 A.M.–5:00 P.M. Monday–Thursday, and 9:00 A.M.–Noon Friday.

6. ADRA publishes a quarterly magazine and annual reports. Other program information can be obtained from the programs division (301/680-6380).

7. Index Terms: Development Issues—Infrastructure; Humanitarian Issues—Relief Organization

---

## N2  Agricultural Cooperative Development International (ACDI)

---

1. 50 F Street, NW, Suite 900
Washington, D.C. 20001
(202) 638-4661
Fax: (202) 626-8726

2. Ron Gollehon, President

3. ACDI is a nonprofit technical- and management-assistance and training organization created by the leading U.S. agricultural cooperatives and farmer organizations in response to congressional mandates in the Foreign Assistance Act. Since its inception in 1963 it has sponsored projects in more than 70 developing countries. Recently it has begun operations in Eastern Europe and the former Soviet Union. Its mission is to improve the well-being of farmers worldwide by helping agricultural and member-owned organizations increase trade and achieve sustainable economic development. It undertakes projects that improve commercial and credit services to farmers, improve the efficiency of food systems, and respond to the needs of agricultural cooperatives, farm credit systems, autonomous farm-related entities and supporting government agencies in developing countries.

6. ACDI publishes an annual report and a quarterly newsletter called *Cooperative News International,* which contains news on cooperatives, farmer organizations, and other development projects overseas.

7. Index Terms: Development Issues—Agriculture

---

## N3  Air Force Historical Foundation

---

1. 1535 Command Drive
Suite A-122, Stop 44
Andrews AFB, Md. 20331-7002
(301) 736-1959

2. Bryce Poe II, President
Louis H. Cummings, Executive Director

3. The mission of the Air Force Historical Foundation (AFHF) is "to preserve and perpetuate the history and traditions of the U.S. Air Force, its predecessor organizations and of the men who have been devoted to the service." The foundation sponsors annual scholarships and other awards.

4. The AFHF conducts annual symposia, frequently in the Washington area.

6. The AFHF publishes the quarterly journal, *Air Power History.*

7. Index Terms: Military History—Air Force

---

## N4  American Association of University Women (AAUW)—Educational Foundation

---

1. 1111 16th Street, NW
Washington, D.C. 20036
(202) 785-7700
Fax: (202) 872-1425

2. Anne L. Bryant, Executive Director
Tanya Hilton, Director, Educational Foundation

3. The AAUW monitors UN activities and international events involving women's issues and seeks to keep its membership informed. It is an affiliate of the International Federation of University Women (IFUW) in Geneva, Switzerland, through which it maintains contact with university women's organizations in 59 countries worldwide. The main focus of AAUW's international activity is its Educational Foundation. The foundation awards fellowships for full-time graduate or postgraduate study or research in the United States. Six fellowships per year are awarded by AAUW-IFUW and may be used for study in any country other than the recipient's own.

5. The association and foundation maintain a library and an archival collection on issues pertaining to women. Holdings include proceedings of the IFUW and AAUW publications. The library and archive are open by appointment.

6. The AAUW publishes *Outlook Quarterly, Leader in Action* (three times a year), and a number of program reports. A publications list is available upon request.

7. Index Terms: Transnationalism

---

## N5 American Bar Association (ABA)— International Legal Exchange Program

1. 1700 Pennsylvania Avenue, NW, Suite 620
Washington, D.C. 20006
(202) 393-7122
Fax: (202) 347-9015

2. Edison W. Dick, Executive Director

3. The International Legal Exchange Program (ILEX) of the ABA administers three- to six-month training exchanges and internship programs for lawyers, law professors, judges, and other members of the legal profession in the United States and foreign countries. It also arranges seminar programs for foreign legal groups visiting the United States, and briefing trips for U.S. lawyers to foreign countries.

6. Program literature is available.

7. Index Terms: International Law

---

## N6 American Council of Young Political Leaders

1. 1000 Connecticut Avenue, NW, Suite 800
Washington, D.C. 20036-5300
(202) 857-0999
Fax: (202) 857-0027

2. Mimi Weyforth Dawson, Chair
Danny Lee McDonald, President

3. The American Council of Young Political Leaders (ACYPL) arranges bilateral international exchange programs and study tours for delegations of young political leaders and government officials from the United States and foreign countries. The ACYPL's goal is to enhance foreign policy understanding and exposure among rising young U.S. po-litical leaders and their counterparts around the world. ACYPL maintains approximately 20 ongoing bilateral exchanges with counterpart organizations in every region of the world and has conducted more than 500 exchanges in 70 countries. These programs are generally two to three weeks.

4. In conjunction with the U.S. Department of State (K37), the ACYPL annually sponsors a two-day foreign policy conference for all ACYPL nominees and former delegates from across the country.

6. The ACYPL publishes a quarterly newsletter, *Network*. It also publishes its *ACYPL Alumni Directory* annually.

7. Index Terms: Foreign Policy

---

## N7 American Federation of Labor and Congress of Industrial Organizations (AFL-CIO)—Department of International Affairs

1. 815 16th Street, NW
Washington, D.C. 20006
(202) 637-5000

2. Lane Kirkland, President

3. The AFL-CIO Department of International Affairs coordinates the federation's international activities and contacts. The AFL-CIO extends assistance to labor unions internationally through its four labor institutes within the department. They are

African-American Labor Center (AALC)
1400 K Street, NW, Suite 700
Washington, D.C. 20005
(202) 789-1020
Fax: (202) 842-0730
Patrick J. O'Farrell, Executive Director

Asian-American Free Labor Institute (AAFLI)
1125 15th Street, NW, Suite 401
Washington, D.C. 20005
(202) 737-3000
Fax: (202) 785-0370
Kenneth P. Hutchison, Executive Director

American Institute for Free Labor Development (AIFLD)
1015 20th Street, NW
Washington, D.C. 20036
(202) 659-6300
Fax: (202) 872-0618
William C. Doherty, Executive Director

Free Trade Union Institute (FTUI)
1101 14th Street, NW, Suite 300
Washington, D.C. 20005
(202) 842-0322
Fax: (202) 310-5130
Paul Samogyi, Executive Director

AACL and AAFLI are active in Africa and Asia; AIFLD covers Latin America; and FTUI is active in Europe, although its focus is more thematic than geographic.

AFL-CIO assistance focuses on basic union-building skills such as collective bargaining, organizing techniques, occupational safety and health training, nursing and medical care, and mutual assistance projects such as credit unions and cooperatives. The institutes also work in defense of basic trade union rights and to help enable unions to exercise fundamental political rights.

The Department of International Affairs maintains an office in Paris that represents the Federation in Europe. This office carries out the federation's work with the Organization for Economic Cooperation and Development and with the International Confederation of Free Trade Unions in Brussels, and with the International Labor Organization in Geneva. The Department of International Affairs carries out bilateral relations with national union organizations throughout the world. It conducts, with cooperation of the four institutes, many exchanges involving trade union leaders.

5. The AFL-CIO Library is described in A2.

6. The institutes publish quarterly newsletters and occasional updates on current issues. The Department of International Affairs publishes brochures describing the federation's international activities.

7. Index Terms: Conflict Management and Resolution—Unofficial and Nongovernmental Approaches; Development Issues—Education; International Organizations—Labor

---

## N8 American Friends Service Committee (AFSC)

---

1. Davis House
   1822 R Street, NW
   Washington, D.C. 20009
   (202) 232-3196
   Fax: (202) 232-3197

2. James Matlack, Director

3. The AFSC, headquartered in Philadelphia, promotes peace, justice, and reconciliation through development and peace projects in 24 countries. It was originally founded to counsel conscientious objectors and continues to emphasize traditional Quaker concerns regarding disarmament and conflict resolution. Current social and technical-assistance projects aim at fostering local populations' utilization of their own resources. The Washington office monitors legislation and attempts advocacy of AFSC goals based on its experience. Relevant issue areas concern refugees and immigration policy; crisis response and relief efforts; international development policy; and regional conflict.

5. AFSC's archives is located at its headquarters in Philadelphia (215/241-7000).

7. Index Terms: Development Issues—International Development Policy; Humanitarian Issues—Relief Organization; Pacifism and Peace Movements

---

## N9 American Red Cross (ARC)—National Headquarters

---

1. 17th and D Streets, NW
   Washington, D.C. 20006
   (202) 737-8300
   Fax: (202) 783-3432

2. Norman R. Augustine, Chairman
   Elizabeth Dole, President

3. The American Red Cross (ARC) is a humanitarian relief and health education organization. Internationally, the American Red Cross works primarily through the International Federation of Red Cross and Red Crescent Societies and the International Committee of the Red Cross, both based in Geneva, Switzerland. It is affiliated directly with national Red Cross and Red Crescent societies around the world and it is currently active in or giving support to over 40 countries. The Office of International Services (202/639-3318) supervises the donation of supplies, funds, and technical assistance for relief in major foreign disasters and refugee situations. ARC works with other national societies in disaster preparedness, paramedical education, primary health care, first aid, cardiopulmonary resuscitation, and the development of blood centers. It is also involved in technical exchanges. The ACR has offered development assistance to a large number of under-developed countries worldwide. Recent areas of assistance for disaster relief (ranging from floods

to earthquakes) include Bangladesh, Bolivia, Ecuador, Guatemala, Lebanon, Philippines, Turkey, and India. ARC has been active in giving conflict relief in Rwanda, Somalia, and the former Yugoslavia.

5.  Past files of ARC are held at the National Archives and Records Administration (B11). ARC hopes to establish a research center on its history.

6.  In addition to general information sheets on its international services, the national headquarters also has reports on its activities in Somalia and the former Yugoslavia.

7.  Index Terms: Development Issues—Education; Humanitarian Issues—Relief Organization; International Organizations; Refugees

---

## N10   Arca Foundation

---

1.  1425 21st Street, NW
    Washington, D.C. 20036
    (202) 822-9193

2.  Smith Bagley, President
    Janet Shenk, Executive Director

3.  The Arca Foundation (founded as the Nancy Reynolds Bagley Foundation) is a grant-making organization with domestic and international interests aimed at exposing inequities of current policies and changing the status quo. Many of its grants focus on Central America and concern, among other issues, peacemaking, human rights, implementation of UN peace accords in El Salvador, effect of tariff restrictions on living standards in the region, promotion of civil society, and U.S. policy toward the region, especially Cuba and Haiti. Other areas of funding include amelioration of Israeli-Palestinian conflict and World Bank (L8) and International Monetary Fund (L11) lending policies.

6.  Arca publishes an annual report.

7.  Index Terms: International Politics; Regional Conflict

---

## N11   Ashoka: Innovators for the Public

---

1.  1700 North Moore Street, Suite 1920
    Arlington, Va. 22209
    (703) 527-8300
    Fax: (703) 527-8383

2.  William Drayton, Director

3.  Ashoka identifies and grants fellowships to innovative "public service entrepreneurs." In contrast to business entrepreneurs, Ashoka's fellows focus on education, environmental reform, slum development, agriculture, human rights, health care, and other fields of human need. Fellows are provided with living expenses for approximately three years, freeing them for the continuation and expansion of the projects and ideas, which are intended to be replicable. Ashoka sponsors fellows in Mexico, Brazil, Nigeria, Ghana, Ivory Coast, Mali, South Africa, Zimbabwe, India, Nepal, Bangladesh, Indonesia, and Thailand. It is currently planning programs in Eastern Europe, including Poland, Hungary, and the Czech Republic.

5.  Ashoka does not have a library, but it does maintain a resource center with directories and databases of its past and present fellows.

6.  Ashoka publishes an annual profile book of the fellows elected during the preceding year and a newsletter.

7.  Index Terms: Development Issues—Education; Development Issues—Infrastructure

---

## N12   Baptist World Alliance (BWA)

---

1.  6733 Curran Street
    McLean, Va. 22101-6005
    (703) 790-8980
    Fax: (703) 893-5160

2.  Knud Wumpelmann, President
    Denton Lotz, General Secretary

3.  The BWA operates worldwide assistance programs. It provides development assistance, which includes health facilities, vocational training, and schooling. BWA also provides disaster relief such as famine relief and food distribution, refugee assistance, and flood and earthquake relief.

7.  Index Terms: Humanitarian Issues—Relief Organization

---

## N13   CARE USA—Washington Office

---

1.  2025 I Street, NW, Suite 1024
    Washington, D.C. 20006
    (202) 296-5696
    Fax: (202) 296-8695

2. Philip Johnston, President of CARE (Atlanta, Ga.)

Peter D. Bell, Chair

Charles Sykes, Vice-President, Washington Liaison Office

3. CARE USA is a private disaster relief and development organization. It operates self-help programs in more than 50 countries. In addition to programs in developing countries in Latin America, Africa, and Asia, CARE is sponsoring projects in Eastern Europe and the former Soviet Union. Projects focus on food programs, nutrition and health care training, adult education and vocational training, rural development projects, and community self-help. The organization's world headquarters and programming staff are located in Atlanta, Ga. The Washington Liaison Office is a fund-raising and public information unit.

5. CARE does not have a library.

6. An annual report and information pamphlets are available on request.

7. Index Terms: Development Issues—Technical Assistance; Humanitarian Issues—Relief Organization

---

## NI4 Center for International Private Enterprise (CIPE) (Chamber of Commerce of the United States)

1. 1615 H Street, NW
Washington, D.C. 20062
(202) 463-5901
Fax: (202) 887-3447

2. John Sullivan, Executive Director

3. CIPE, one of the four core institutions affiliated with the National Endowment for Democracy (N40), is also affiliated with the U.S. Chamber of Congress. CIPE seeks to encourage the growth of private enterprise principles and assists foreign organizations that contribute to democratic development. The center supports projects worldwide. The program officers for different regions are Howard Wallack (Africa); John Callebaut (Asia); David Lang (Central and Eastern Europe); Keith Miceli and Deborah Soltman (Latin America, the Middle East); and Stephen Deane and Kellyann Szalkowski (Russia and the Newly Independent States).

6. CIPE publishes the quarterly *Economic Reform Today* (in English and Spanish) with a semiannual supplement, *Informal Sector Newsletter*. It also publishes a newsletter, *CIPE in Action*.

7. Index Terms: Development Issues—Education; Development Issues—Infrastructure

---

## NI5 Church World Service/Lutheran World Relief—Office on Development Policy

1. 110 Maryland Avenue, NW
Washington, D.C. 20002
(202) 543-6336
Fax: (202) 546-6232

2. Carol Capps, Director

3. The Office on Development Policy operates on behalf of the Church World Service and Lutheran World Relief. It is an advocacy organization that addresses policy issues relating to causes of injustice, poverty, and hunger worldwide. It monitors agencies such as the World Bank (L8) and the Agency for International Development (KI). It works for policy improvement in several areas: development in Africa and Central America; humanitarian aid amid war; debt relief, including alternative economic restructuring programs; foreign aid reform, including a "demilitarized" U.S. foreign aid program; and peace building and recovery, encompassing U.S. support for peace negotiations and economic reconstruction.

7. Index Terms: Development Issues—International Development Policy; Humanitarian Issues—Research Organization; Pacifism and Peace Movements

---

## NI6 Congressional Human Rights Foundation (CHRF)

1. 1056 Thomas Jefferson Street, NW
Washington, D.C. 20007-3813
(202) 333-1407
Fax: (202) 333-1275

2. David L. Phillips, President

3. CHRF is a private nongovernmental organization dedicated to furthering protection of human rights through strengthening democratic institutions. CHRF is made up of private citizens from business and academia and has a congressional advisory board representing both houses of Congress. The foundation's chief program is the Interparlia-

mentary Human Rights Network, a nonpartisan association of 1,000 legislators in 109 countries. CHRF work focuses on advocacy and communication, such as the interparliamentary exchange of information in order to coordinate international action; parliamentary services, to sustain partnerships between established and emerging democracies; and training and technical assistance, such as assistance in crafting human rights legislation.

5.   CHRF maintains the Global Democracy Network (GDN), a computerized information and communications system providing worldwide access to critical human rights and democracy information. The GDN uses the Internet computer network to access foreign ministry officials, academic institutions, and human rights groups worldwide.

6.   CHRF publishes *Network Update,* a monthly newsletter, and *Reporter,* a monthly briefing paper on specific issues.

7.   Index Terms: Human Rights—Monitoring Organizations; Political Systems and Ideologies

---

## N17   Cooperative Housing Foundation (CHF)

1.   1010 Wayne Avenue, Suite 240
Silver Spring, Md. 20910
(301) 587-4700
Fax: (301) 587-2626

2.   Michael Doyle, President

3.   The CHF provides technical assistance to foreign governments and community organizations in the development of cooperative and nonprofit housing projects for low- and moderate-income families. Activities include advisory and training services in the areas of project planning, construction, land use, finance and management; and preparation of feasibility studies, shelter sector-analyses, and housing policy studies. The organization has assisted local projects in over 80 countries.

5.   CHF maintains an environmental database, primarily for the use of other nongovernmental organizations. The contact person is Rebecca Bailey.

6.   CHF publishes news briefs and program briefs regarding its projects.

7.   Index Terms: Development Issues—Infrastructure

---

## N18   Council for International Exchange of Scholars (CIES)

1.   3007 Tilden Street, Suite 5M
Washington, D.C. 20008-3009
(202) 686-4000
Fax: (202) 362-3442

2.   Jody K. Olsen, Executive Director

3.   The CIES administers, on behalf of the U.S. government, the postdoctoral and professional division of the Fulbright Mutual Educational and Cultural Exchange program for senior scholars. It is affiliated with the American Council of Learned Societies. The council publicizes opportunities for U.S. scholars to lecture, conduct research, or both in nearly 140 countries. It receives and screens applications and selects candidates for awards. It also provides placement and support services to foreign scholars spending time in the United States under the Fulbright program.

6.   Annually issued publications of CIES include *Directory of American Fulbright Scholars* (November); *Directory of Visiting Fulbright Scholars* (October); *Fulbright Scholar Program: Grants for Faculty and Professionals* (April); and an annual report (May).

7.   Index Terms: Transnationalism

---

## N19   Creative Response

1.   9502 Lee Highway, Suite B
Fairfax, Va. 22031
(703) 385-4494
Fax: (703) 273-6568

2.   Mark Sklarow, Executive Director

3.   Creative Response (*formerly* Peace Child Foundation) promotes community service, leadership, and international as well as intercultural understanding between young people through educational programs involving the creative arts. Creative Response has conducted exchanges in more than 30 countries. The foundation coordinates exchanges in the performing arts for thousands of teenagers throughout the world. Students spend four to six weeks in the host country working, sightseeing, performing, and living with local youths and their families. In 1986 the Peace Child Foundation became the

first organization permitted to bring Soviet youths to the United States as apart of a reciprocal exchange. Ongoing exchanges involve participants from Ukraine, Hungary, Russia, Japan, South Africa, Eritrea, Czech Republic, Lithuania, Russia, and Canada, among others.

In addition, Creative Response sponsors the International Youth Leadership Forum, which is designed to assist participants in acquiring the skills necessary to become active and contributing members of the global community. The forum is active on a biannual basis (1995 is the next active year) and incorporates visits to Congress (K8), the State Department (K37), the Environmental Protection Agency (K13), and foreign embassies. Participants in this forum have come from Belarus, Bulgaria, Czech Republic, Georgia, Hungary, Japan, Korea, Russia, and Ukraine.

4.   Creative Response hosts an annual conference on a rotating basis in different U.S. cities; every third year the conference is held in Washington, D.C.

6.   Creative Response publishes a quarterly newsletter, *Update*.

7.   Index Terms: Transnationalism

---

## N20   Diplomatic and Consular Officers, Retired (DACOR) — Bacon House Foundation

1.   1801 F Street, NW
     Washington, D.C. 20006
     (202) 682-0500
     Fax: (202) 842-3295

2.   William W. Lehfeldt, Executive Director

3.   The DACOR Bacon House Foundation was formed in 1985 with the merger of the Bacon House Foundation and the DACOR Education and Welfare Foundation. DACOR is an association of retired U.S. Foreign Service officers that seeks to foster better understanding of foreign relations of the United States. The foundation supports programs that enhance public awareness and foster educated leadership in international affairs. It offers scholastic grants annually in the range of $150,000 in varied projects to encourage careers related to public affairs.

4.   The foundation hosts an annual conference on a timely issue and offers quarterly seminars for area graduate students in international relations. It also sponsors a monthly speakers series on current topics.

5.   The foundation has a small library, largely containing members' works, that is open by appointment.

6.   The foundation publishes the proceedings of its annual conferences; examples of recent titles include *The United States and Latin America in the 1990s* (1991); *The United States and the World Economy* (1992); and *The Future of Foreign Aid* (1993).

7.   Index Terms: Foreign Policy

---

## N21   Episcopal Peace Fellowship (EPF)

1.   P.O. Box 28156
     Washington, D.C. 20038
     (202) 783-3380

2.   Mary Miller, Executive Secretary

3.   The EPF is committed to peace, justice, reconciliation, and renunciation of war and all other forms of violence. The EPF sponsors conferences for Episcopalians engaged in peacemaking; it drafts resolutions and provides education materials for the Episcopal Church on the national, diocesan, and parish levels; it supports members through local chapters; and it counsels young Episcopalians considering conscientious objection to military service and offers them support in dealing with the Selective Service System. The EPF works in coalition with a wide variety of church-related and general peace and justice organizations.

5.   The EPF has a small library, mainly focusing on liberation theology, which is open by appointment.

6.   The EPF publishes a quarterly newsletter. Other literature on the fellowship and its history is available.

7.   Index Terms: Pacifism and Peace Movements; Religious, Philosophical, and Ethical Concepts of War and Peace

---

## N22   Foreign Affairs Assistance Corps (FAAC)

1.   3133 Connecticut Avenue, NW, Suite 702
     Washington, D.C. 20008
     (202) 745-0701
     Fax: (202) 328-0315

2.   Eugene H. Bird, President

3.   The FAAC seeks to assist the newly emerging democracies of Central and Eastern Europe and the former Soviet Union in building democratic institutions and market economies. FAAC has approximately 30 members, many of whom were former diplomats, government officials, and international lawyers and business people. Many have had extensive experience in international, political, economic, and cultural affairs as officers of the State Department (K37), U.S. Information Agency (K41), or the Agency for International Development (KI). FAAC is also affiliated with the newly established Central Asian Development and Investment Foundation, which seeks to bring together leading scholars and others interested in reform in Central Asia.

7.   Index Terms: Development Issues—Infrastructure; Transnationalism

## N23   Forum for Intercultural Communication (FIC)

1.   2400 Virginia Avenue, NW, Suite C-102
Washington, D.C. 20037-2601
(202) 775-7234
Fax: (202) 223-1699

2.   Mauricette Hursh-Cesar, Executive Director

3.   The FIC seeks to improve understanding and working relationships among cultures through exposure to new ideas and technology and through practical experience, study, dialogue, and cultural programs. It conducts four programs. The International Interns Program allows university students to train in the United States and acquire skills in the communications fields. The Folk Arts and Crafts Program fosters appreciation of cultural diversity through workshops, exchanges, and exhibits of indigenous arts and crafts. The Exchange Network promotes exchanges of professionals through a range of conferences, seminars, visitor's programs, study tours, and long-term exchange programs. The Dialogue Center sponsors workshops, seminars, and outreach for policy makers, professionals, and citizen groups on issues of social and economic development. The FIC also maintains a Central and Eastern European Initiative, primarily in Poland, that helps Polish women in business and runs a dialogue program between citizens and local government.

5.   The forum has a small collection of databases that focus on topics such as international and domestic women's issues, education, and commu-

nity development. Scholars may use this collection by appointment.

6.   FIC publishes two newsletters, *Global Women* and *Dialogue Update*.

7.   Index Terms: Transnationalism

**Free Trade Union Institute (FTUI)
See American Federation of Labor and Congress of Industrial Organizations (AFL-CIO)—Department of International Affairs entry N7**

## N24   Fund for Peace

1.   1511 K Street, NW, Suite 643
Washington, D.C. 20005
(202) 783-4130
Fax: (202) 783-4767

2.   James R. Compton, Chair
Nina K. Solarz, Executive Director

3.   The Fund for Peace promotes elimination of war and a just, free, and peaceful world through assistance programs and projects. Key issues include civil and human rights, the free flow of information across U.S. borders, and U.S defense policies. Two major projects that developed with the fund's support are the National Security Archive (B12) and the Center for National Security Studies (H15). The fund has also supported educational and exchange programs, such as a Russian-American exchange of doctoral students. Other organizations it has supported and remains affiliated with are ACCESS (GI) and the Center for Defense Information (H11).

7.   Index Terms: Human Rights; Peace Theory and Research

## N25   Hitachi Foundation

1.   1509 22nd Street, NW
Washington, D.C. 20037-1073
(202) 457-0588

2.   Elliot L. Richardson, Chairman
Delwin A. Roy, President and CEO

3.   The Hitachi Foundation is a grant-making organization whose objective is to help people and institutions adjust to changing global and societal circumstances, help build their problem-solving ca-

pacities, and promote a sense of empowerment and responsibility. In doing this it supports multidisciplinary, cross-ethnic, and collaborative approaches to problems from a grassroots to a global level. The foundation's grants have a strong community orientation, although it very clearly asserts the connection between local, national, and international problems. The foundation awards grants and makes program-related investments in the areas of community development, education, and global citizenship. Efforts within the global citizenship area focus on understanding the complex nature of global communication, changing technology, and environmental degradation; identifying international infrastructure needed for a global system; and promoting greater knowledge of global experience.

6. The foundation assists grantees in the dissemination of their work and occasionally publishes works. Examples include *Defining a New World Order: Toward a Practical Vision of Collective Action for International Peace and Security,* by Alan K. Henrikson, published by the Fletcher School of Law and Diplomacy (1991); and *The Evolving World Order: The State of Deliberations,* by Nigel Gould-Davies, published by the Hitachi Foundation (1993).

7. Index Terms: Transnationalism

---

## N26 Institute for Multi-Track Diplomacy (IMTD)

1. 1133 20th Street, NW, Suite 321
   Washington, D.C. 20036
   (202) 466-4605
   Fax: (202) 466-4607

2. John W. McDonald, Chairman
   Louise Diamond, Executive Director

3. The IMTD sponsors programs of peacebuilding through training, education, and communication in conflict areas around the globe. It seeks to facilitate collaborative projects that encourage peacemaking through participatory, creative, and cooperative actions. The objective of its activities is to put the skills of conflict resolution, intergroup relations, and systems change into the hands of local peacemakers and peacebuilders in projects that generally focus on promoting intercommunal relations or peace leadership training. It is engaged in ongoing work in Cyprus, Israel-Palestine, Liberia, Northern Ireland, the government of Tibet in exile, and with the Unrepresented Nations and Peoples Organizations in the Hague.

4. The Professional Development Program of the institute offers workshops and seminars in areas related to peacemaking and multitrack diplomacy.

6. The IMTD publishes a newsletter, *Peacebuilder.* It has also published *Multi-Track Diplomacy: A Systems Approach to Peace,* by Louise Diamond and John W. McDonald (revised, 1993) and three occasional papers: *Peacemakers in a War Zone,* by Louise Diamond (1993); *Guidelines for Newcomers to Track Two Diplomacy,* by John McDonald (1993); and *How to be a Delegate: International Conference Diplomacy,* by John McDonald (1994).

7. Index Terms: Conflict Management and Resolution; Peace Theory and Research

---

## N27 Institute of International Education (IIE) — Washington Office

1. 1400 K Street, Suite 650
   Washington, D.C. 20005
   (202) 898-0600
   Fax: (202) 842-1219

2. Richard Krasno, President and CEO

3. The IIE administers educational and cultural-exchange programs on behalf of the U.S. and foreign governments, private foundations, corporations, and organizations. Responsibilities encompass the Fulbright Exchange Program, the Hubert H. Humphrey Fellowship Program, and the International Visitor Program sponsored by the U.S. Information Agency (K41). Current programs also include the South Africa Education Program, for scholars and students; the International Human Rights Internship Program; the Energy Training Programs, sponsored by the Agency for International Development (K1); and the National Security Education Program. The last-noted program, the undergraduate portion of which is administered by the IIE, sends U.S. students to study abroad so they may gain global perspectives and deal effectively with foreign policy in future leadership positions. This program also seeks to increase faculty positions teaching relevant subjects in U.S. universities.

4. IIE hosts bimonthly career roundtables related to international education. Reservations are necessary to attend; contact the institute for further information.

6. In addition to publishing a guide to academic-year-abroad programs for U.S. students, IIE annually publishes *Open Doors,* which provides statistics about foreign students studying in the United States; *Funding for U.S. Study—A Guide for Foreign Nationals;* and *English Language and Orientation Programs in the U.S.* To order these publications, or receive a catalog, write to IIE Books, 809 United Nations Plaza, New York, N.Y. 10019-3580.

7. Index Terms: Transnationalism

## N28 International Center—New Forests Project

1. 731 8th Street, SE
Washington, D.C. 20003
(202) 547-3800
Fax: (202) 546-4784

2. William H. Sullivan, Chair
Lindsay Mattison, Executive Director

3. The International Center is a nonpartisan organization that monitors U.S. foreign policy. Its activities include research, overseas fact-finding travel, and hosting foreign visitors.

The center's New Forests Project seeks solutions to rural poverty and deforestation in developing countries. Its people-to-people program promotes agroforestry and reforestation through provision of seeds, training materials, and advice.

*Note:* For other activities of the center see entry H46.

5. The center maintains a small resource collection on international forestry that is accessible to outside scholars.

6. The project publishes *New Forest,* a quarterly newsletter.

7. Index Terms: Development Issues—Technical Assistance; Environmental Issues, Global—Sustainable Development

See also entry H46

## N29 International Foundation for Electoral Systems (IFES)

1. 1620 I Street, NW, Suite 611
Washington, D.C. 20006
(202) 828-8507
Fax: (202) 452-0804

2. Richard W. Soudriette, Director

3. IFES calls on international experts familiar with a wide variety of electoral systems to provide tailored assistance to countries seeking to establish an electoral system or to improve an existing process. In addition to providing direct technical assistance, IFES serves as a clearinghouse for information about all aspects of electoral systems, about individuals expert in these systems, and about commodities essential to administering democratic elections. IFES also offers assistance in civic education to countries and nonpartisan groups seeking information on citizen participation in the voting process, the building and strengthening of civil society, and other aspects of democratic life.

IFES has undertaken election observation and assessment in numerous countries. These include the Baltic states, Belarus, Dominican Republic, El Salvador, Gabon, Georgia, Guyana, Honduras, Liberia, Malawi, Mongolia, Peru, Russia, South Africa, Tunisia, and Venezuela.

5. IFES maintains a library of reference materials and periodicals pertaining to elections. The resource center is open to interested persons for research on specific countries and electoral systems. In addition, IFES maintains a computerized database containing a country-by-country file that includes background information, election dates, names and addresses of election officials, and types of government systems. The database contains additional files with listings of experienced election technicians, country scholars, and potential election observers.

6. IFES publishes a quarterly newsletter and pre-election technical assessments. It has published more than 30 election reports from various countries, including Romania, Estonia, Moldova, and Russia. It has also published five guides to election observation, such as *Guide to Central and Eastern European Election Administration.*

7. Index Terms: Political Systems and Ideologies; Transnationalism

## N30 International Human Rights Law Group (IHRLG)

1. 1601 Connecticut Avenue, NW, Suite 700
Washington, D.C. 20009
(202) 232-8500
Fax: (202) 232-6731

2. Gregory B. Craig, Chair
Reed Brody, Executive Director

3. The IHRLG is an advocacy organization that attempts to empower locally based human rights advocates to promote and protect human rights in their countries; pioneers the development of domestic and international human rights; and seeks justice for the victims of human rights abuses. The IHRLG is affiliated with the International Commission of Jurists in Geneva and has worked in more than 80 countries since 1978. The group sponsors the Rule of Law Program, which assists and trains grassroots human rights advocates in developing countries and emerging democracies. The group's International Advocacy Project seeks to strengthen international and U.S. human rights mechanisms to seek justice for abuse victims through the UN, the U.S. courts, and international forums. The Women in the Law Project works to promote women's rights by strengthening international standards and procedures for protecting women's rights. Countries in which the IHRLG has been active include Burma, Cambodia, East Timor, Haiti, Kazakhstan, Moldova, Paraguay, Romania, and the former Yugoslavia.

6. The IHRLG publishes a biannual newsletter, *The Docket*. Other publications include *U.S. Legislation Relating Human Rights to U.S. Foreign Policy* (1991) and *Guide to International Human Rights Practice*, edited by Hurst Hannum (1992). The group also publishes reports on its activities in various countries.

7. Index Terms: Human Rights—and International Law; International Law

## N31 International Republican Institute (IRI) (*formerly* National Republican Institute for International Affairs)

1. 1212 New York Avenue, NW, Suite 900
Washington, D.C. 20005
(202) 408-9450
Fax: (202) 408-9462

2. R. Bruce McColm, President
John McCain, Chair

3. The IRI (*formerly* National Republican Institute for International Affairs) initiates and supports a wide range of programs to promote and strengthen democratic ideals and institutions in over 50 countries. These programs are nonpartisan but reflect Republican Party principles such as individual free-

dom, equality of opportunity, and the entrepreneurial spirit that fosters economic development. Programs emphasize electoral processes, civic education, mechanics of building political parties, and the legislative process.

6. IRI publishes a quarterly newsletter.

7. Index Terms: Political Systems and Ideologies

## N32 International Research and Exchanges Board (IREX)

1. 1616 H Street, NW
Washington, D.C. 20006
(202) 628-8188
Fax: (202) 628-8189

2. Daniel Matuszewski, President
Herbert Ellison, Chair

3. IREX supports research exchanges between the United States and the countries of Eastern Europe and the former Soviet Union. Its principal purpose is to serve the interests of the U.S. scholarly community. It sponsors a large number of research programs for U.S. scholars and for researchers from abroad. These include individual advanced research opportunities and research residencies; language and development grants, both on-site and at U.S. universities; short-term travel grants; and special projects.

6. In disseminating the practical results of its research programs, IREX has published over 4,200 books, dissertations, and articles. IREX also publishes *News in Brief*, a bimonthly newsletter of activities. A publications list is available upon request.

7. Index Terms: Transnationalism

## N33 International Voluntary Services (IVS)

1. 1424 16th Street, NW, Suite 603
Washington, D.C. 20036
(202) 387-5533
Fax: (202) 387-4234

2. Don Luce, President

3. IVS is a private, nonprofit organization that recruits international volunteer specialists in agriculture, health and nutrition, education, AIDS preven-

tion, and cooperative/small-business development to provide technical assistance for rural development projects in developing countries. The organization supports projects in Bangladesh, Bolivia, Cambodia, Ecuador, Thailand, and Vietnam.

6. The organization publishes an annual report and newsletter.

7. Index Terms: Development Issues—Technical Assistance

## N34 League of Women Voters Education Fund (LWVEF)

1. 1730 M Street, NW
Washington, D.C. 20036
(202) 429-1965
Fax: (202) 429-0854

2. Sherry Rockey, Director of Education Fund

3. The LWVEF promotes public understanding of major public policy issues and encourages citizen participation in government. Internationally, the LWVEF has been active in exchange programs carried out by local branches of the League of Women Voters. These exchanges have taken place with women from the former Soviet Union, Eastern and Central Europe, Latin America, and Africa. LWVEF has provided materials, technical assistance, and networking contacts in the development of democratic institutions in these regions. The main element of the program brings women to the United States for approximately one month to study grassroots organizing, media relations, community relations, and aspects of political organization. Participants are expected to return to their home countries to host conferences and community workshops. The Emerging Democracy Program (Orna Tamches, Program Manager) was established by the LWVEF in 1992 to assist in the development of grassroots institutions in Central and Eastern Europe. The first two projects of this program are: Building Political Participation in Poland and Project Demokracia: Building Coalition Participation in Hungary.

6. The League of Women Voters publishes a quarterly magazine, *National Voter,* which reports on the activities of the Education Fund and the Emerging Democracies Program.

7. Index Terms: Transnationalism

## N35 Legacy International

1. 128 North Fayette Street
Alexandria, Va. 22314
(703) 549-3630
Fax: (703) 549-0262

2. Ira Kaufman, Executive Director

3. Legacy International is a consulting and training organization that helps other internationally oriented organizations manage change in culturally sensitive ways under complex circumstances. Legacy promotes environmentally sound development; peaceful resolutions to ethnic, social, and religious conflicts; and experimental leadership training. Clients include corporations, educational institutions, private foundations, government agencies, and nongovernmental organizations. It has sponsored initiatives in 73 countries. Specific programs Legacy sponsors include Inter-Ministerial Task Force of the Russian Federation; Young Leadership Forum (Jerusalem); Middle East Environment and Development Professional Visitors Program; Islam: East and West; and My Future—My World: Russian-American Curriculum Resource Material Project. Projects address current policy issues and environmental education and promote the development of new coalitions among business, government, nongovernmental organizations, academic institutions, and youth groups.

5. Legacy has a small resource library containing a limited number of works on the environment, associations, Russia, and conflict in the Middle East.

6. Legacy publishes occasional program reports of its activities.

7. Index Terms: Conflict Management and Resolution; Environmental Issues, Global—Sustainable Development; Ethnic and Religious Conflict

## N36 Mennonite Central Committee U.S.— Washington Office

1. 110 Maryland Avenue, NE
Washington, D.C. 20002
(202) 544-6564
Fax: (202) 544-2820

2. Daryl Byler, Washington Representative

3. The Mennonite Central Committee sponsors development projects worldwide. The Washington office, in addition to monitoring legislation and policy developments, maintains contact with numerous nongovernment agencies active in peace and international security issues.

4. The Washington office coordinates seminars throughout the year that bring constituent groups within the church into contact with different parts of the government. They also sponsor inter-Mennonite seminars open to anyone with special interests in the topic under presentation.

5. The committee's library is located at its Akron, Pa., headquarters (717/859-1151).

6. The Washington office publishes a bimonthly newsletter, *Washington Memo,* and an occasional supplement, *Hotline.* The committee also publishes *Peace Office Newsletter.*

7. Index Terms: Development Issues—International Development Policy; Pacifism and Peace Movements

---

## N37 Meridian House International

1. 1630 Crescent Place, NW
   Washington, D.C. 20009
   (202) 667-6800
   Fax: (202) 667-1475

2. Walter L. Cutler, President
   John Michael Dunn, Chair

3. Meridian International Center promotes international understanding through exchange of people, ideas, and the arts, for visitors to the United States from all parts of the globe and for Americans going abroad. It provides services to foreign visitors and resident diplomats, such as cultural orientation and study programs; it conducts international symposia and conferences; and it presents cultural and world affairs programs, exhibits, lectures, and seminars. Meridian presents international art exhibits, as well as concerts and other performing arts programs. Seminars, conferences, and briefings sponsored by the institute address global issues with the participation of U.S. and foreign policymakers, diplomats, journalists, and business and community leaders. It also offers specific training programs for Americans and their families relocating abroad.

6. The Meridian International Center publishes a newsletter.

7. Index Terms: Transnationalism

---

## N38 National Conference of Catholic Bishops (NCCB)

1. 3211 4th Street, NE
   Washington, D.C. 20017
   (202) 541-3000
   Fax: (202) 541-3322

2. Robert N. Lynch, General Secretary

3. The NCCB lends foreign assistance primarily through two bodies: the Secretariat for the Church in Latin America (George Emerson, Executive Director), and the Office for Aid to the Church in Central and Eastern Europe (George Sarauskas, Executive Director). Both bodies are concerned with pastoral, educational, and training programs, evangelization, social ministry, and research.

5. The National Conference of Catholic Bishops' library consists of 10,000 volumes and 120 current periodicals. Its special collections include a Latin American Bishop's collection of 200 volumes and 1,500 NCCB/USCC publications. The library has on-line DIALOG services. Scholars may use the library 9:00 A.M.–5:00 P.M. Monday–Friday. Contact Director, Guy Wilson (202/541-3193) with any questions.

6. A set of guidelines for aid requests is available.

7. Index Terms: Humanitarian Issues

See also entries B15, F28, and M55

---

## N39 National Democratic Institute for International Affairs (NDI)

1. 1717 Massachusetts Avenue, NW, 5th Floor
   Washington, D.C. 20036
   (202) 328-3136
   Fax: (202) 939-3166

2. Kenneth D. Wollack, President

3. The NDI conducts nonpartisan international programs to promote democratic institutions worldwide. It seeks to consolidate existing democratic institutions and nurture peaceful transitions to democracy. NDI has 23 field offices in Africa, Asia, Eastern Europe, Latin America, and Russia and the Commonwealth of Independent States. Since 198

has conducted democratic development programs in more than 60 countries. Areas of NDI activities include political party training; election processes; legislative training; local government reform; civil-military relations; and civic organizations. NDI has approximately a dozen programs in Africa; one in Asia; four in Latin America; and numerous programs in Central and Eastern Europe, and the Commonwealth of Independent States.

4. The institute sponsors periodic World Affairs briefings on NDI programs and on issues related to political developments in individual countries. These meetings are by invitation; the public affairs contact person is Sue Grabowsky.

5. The institute maintains a small library of 2,000 to 3,000 volumes primarily on development of political parties; it also contains recent publications on international politics. The library (Patrick Sheary, Librarian) is open to scholars by appointment. The institute also maintains an archive of retired files of institute programs.

6. NDI publishes a quarterly newsletter, *NDI Reports;* an annual review of program activities; and individual publications on subjects related to its programs. NDI also publishes individual reports, including *Albania: 1991 Elections to the People's Assembly; The October 13, 1991, Legislative and Municipal Elections in Bulgaria* (1991); *Democracies in Regions of Crisis: Botswana, Costa Rica and Israel* (1990); *The Commonwealth of Independent States: Democratic Development Issues and Options* (January 22, 1992); *1990 Elections in the Dominican Republic: Report of an Observer Delegation* (1990); and *Nation Building: The U.N. and Namibia* (1990).

7. Index Terms: Political Systems and Ideologies

---

## N40 National Endowment for Democracy (NED)

---

1. 1101 15th Street, Suite 700
   Washington, D.C. 20005-5003
   (202) 293-9072
   Fax: (202) 223-6042

2. John Brademas, Chair
   Carl Gershman, President

3. NED is a privately operated, government-funded, tax-exempt organization created in 1983 to support democracy through a worldwide grants program. Some grants are provided directly to organizations in foreign countries; others are administered through "core grantees" such as Free Trade Union Institute (N7), the Center for International Private Enterprise (N14), the National Democratic Institute for International Affairs (N39), and the International Republican Institute (N31). The endowment's stated goals are to promote peaceful transition from authoritarianism to democracy, encourage the establishment of civil society within totalitarian systems, empower the poor through the "informal sector," strengthen institutional pluralism in developing countries, and promote democratic culture.

The endowment makes hundreds of grants yearly worldwide. The following are examples of NED interests in different regions of the world. In Burkina Faso, Malawi, Nigeria, and Zaire the endowment has funded human rights groups; in Benin, Burundi, Comoros, Ethiopia, Ghana, Kenya, Madagascar, Mali, Mauritius, Namibia, Rwanda, Seychelles, Tanzania, and Uganda, it has funded seminars, conferences, and education projects on democracy, party politics, and the electoral process. In regard to China the endowment has supported human rights programs, an environmental opposition organization, and a conference on Tibet and Inner Mongolia; it has supported human rights efforts in Cambodia and Vietnam and political development in Mongolia. In Central and Eastern Europe it has been involved in issues of privatization, civic education, institutionalism of democratic values, and building relationships among postcommunist societies. It has supported seminars and conferences on the development of political parties in Russia and the Commonwealth of Independent States, and supported trade unions, privatization, and civil society. In Latin America, NED has sponsored *Conciencia,* a women's group active in Argentina, Columbia, Peru, and other countries. It has promoted market-oriented reforms in Bolivia, Nicaragua, and Paraguay.

4. NED hosts a speakers series that features leading democratic activists on a frequent basis.

5. NED is scheduled to open a library in 1995. Access will be decided on a case-by-case basis (contact librarian, Allen Overland). The majority of NED's library will be information from the nongovernmental organizations that receive its grants.

6. NED publishes *Journal of Democracy* and a newsletter, both quarterly.

7. Index Terms: Human Rights; Political Systems and Ideology

## N41  National Forum Foundation (NFF)

1. 511 C Street, NE
   Washington, D.C. 20003
   (202) 543-3515
   Fax: (202) 547-4101

2. James Denton, President

3. NFF is a public policy institute dedicated to advancing political and economic freedom by providing direct support to democratic groups and enhancing debate on public policy issues. NFF runs Visiting Fellows Program to promote democratic transition in Central and Eastern Europe and the previous Soviet republics of Russia, Ukraine, Kazakhstan, and Kyrgyzistan. Through this program NFF has given more than 250 leaders from these regions and countries fellowships in order to come to the United States and work with their U.S. counterparts in government, journalism, and business management. Another NFF project is the American Volunteers for International Development (AVID). Through AVID, it sponsors qualified U.S. professionals who volunteer to travel to Central and Eastern Europe, Russia, and Ukraine to work with their counterparts in government institutions, private businesses, and independent media organizations.

6. NFF publishes the *NFF UPDATE*.

7. Index Terms: Conflict Resolution and Management; Transnationalism

## N42  National Institute for Dispute Resolution (NIDR)

1. 1726 M Street, NW, Suite 500
   Washington, D.C. 20036
   (202) 466-4764
   Fax: (202) 466-4769

2. Dick Clark, Chair
   Margery F. Baker, President

3. NIDR is a grant-making, advisory, and advocacy organization. It works to increase understanding and acceptance of conflict resolution techniques such as mediation, arbitration, and negotiation. NIDR attempts to make these techniques available to individuals and institutions. In addition to international relations, NIDR has dispute resolution programs in public policy, the courts, higher and professional education, primary and secondary schools, and local communities. Through the international program, NIDR responds to information requests from around the world, administers grants and technical assistance, and undertakes special projects and partnerships. NIDR generally works through local institutions and nongovernmental organizations. The projects under this program have centered on environmental issues. Through a partnership with the UN Institute for Training and Research, NIDR is currently developing training programs in the Czech Republic and Slovakia that will be replicated in 90 countries around the world. It also assists in ethnic conflict problems. For example, NIDR assisted in the development of the first black-led conflict resolution organization in South Africa.

5. NIDR has a library with 8,000 to 9,000 items primarily on conflict resolution, including training material.

6. NIDR publishes a bimonthly newsletter, *Forum*.

7. Index Terms: Conflict Management and Resolution; Ethnic and Religious Conflict

## N43  National Peace Foundation (NPF)

1. 1835 K Street, NW, Suite 610
   Washington, D.C. 20006
   (202) 223-1770
   Fax: (202) 223-1718

2. Richard T. Arndt, Chair
   Stephen P. Strickland, President

3. NPF, with a nationwide membership of approximately 15,000, is the successor organization to the National Peace Academy Campaign, which lobbied for the establishment of the United States Institute of Peace (H73). The NPF's overall mission is to promote peacebuilding and conflict resolution on all levels from local to international. The NPF also served as coordinator for the Alliance for Our Common Future (M2) from 1989 to 1993. The foundation presents biennial Peacemaker Awards. Past recipients are Father Theodore Hesburgh, Javier Pérez de Cuellar, Senators Mark Hatfield and Spark Matsunaga, Betty Bumpers, and Marion O'Malley. Current NPF projects include conflict resolution training programs in Armenia, Central America, Georgia, and Russia. It is also fostering collaboration with three national conflict-resolution educational organizations in establishing conflict resolution training in urban schools in the United States. The NPF also helped create the Armenian Women's

Forum on Peace, Democracy, and Development and facilitated the establishment of the Transcaucasus Women's Peace Dialogue, bringing together women leaders from Armenia, Azerbaijan, and Georgia.

6. The NPF publishes the *Peace Reporter,* a quarterly newsletter. Other publications include *Peacemaking Behavior—Major Research Areas,* by James H. Laue (1986); *Elements of a Peace Plan,* by Paul H. Baldwin (1993); *Summary of National Peace Foundation Observers at the Armenian Vote for Independence, September 1991* (April 1992); and *National Directory: Organizations Concerned with Peaceful Resolution of Arab-Israeli-Palestinian Conflicts* (May 1992).

7. Index Terms: Conflict Resolution and Management; Ethnic and Religious Conflict; Peace Theory and Research

## N44 Nonviolence International

1. P.O. Box 39127
   Friendship Station, NW
   Washington, D.C. 20016
   (202) 244-0951
   Fax: (202) 244-6396

2. Mubarak Awad, Director

3. Nonviolence International is an educational and training organization in nonviolence that assists groups, individuals, and governments to achieve social and political goals through nonviolent action. It offers hands-on training in specific nonviolent actions, such as demonstrations, as well as strategic planning assistance. Nonviolence International supports conflict resolution in numerous areas around the world based on the expertise of its volunteer staff. Types of activities Nonviolence International supports include town meetings among diverse and antagonistic groups, peacemaking teams to conduct nonviolent mass interventions, and third-party alternatives in conflict resolution. Other activities include democratic election organization work. Nonviolence International is particularly active in the Palestinian-Israeli conflict; it also has regional offices in Northern Ireland, Southeast Asia, and Russia.

5. Nonviolence International maintains a database of nonviolent training around the world. It has a small library of theoretical and practical literature on nonviolence.

6. Nonviolence International publishes *Frontline,* a quarterly newsletter and the quarterly, *International Journal of Nonviolence.* It also publishes a how-to booklet series on nonviolence that covers marches, pilgrimages, walks, tax resistance, elections, and other activities.

7. Index Terms: Conflict Management and Resolution; Transnationalism

## N45 Pax World Service

1. 1111 16th Street, NW, Suite 120
   Washington, D.C. 20036
   (202) 293-7290
   Fax: (202) 293-7023

2. Charolett Rhoads, President

3. Pax World Service (*formerly* Pax World Foundation) initiates and supports projects that encourage international understanding, reconciliation, and sustainable development on behalf of world peace and the world's poor. The service works primarily through community-based projects that are both environmentally and economically sustainable. It also promotes the use of a solar powered water purification system. Pax is working to create a permanent funding source for the United Nations. The service sponsors Friendship Tours, international educational ventures exploring peace and reconciliation in areas of conflict as well as issues related to sustainable development.

5. Pax has a small resource collection for the use of its own staff.

6. The organization publishes *Pax Facts,* a quarterly newsletter.

7. Index Terms: Development Issues—International Development Policy; Environmental Issues, Global—Sustainable Development

## N46 Presbyterian Church USA— Washington Office

1. 110 Maryland Avenue, NE
   Box 52
   Washington, D.C. 20002
   (202) 543-1126
   Fax: (202) 543-7755

2. Elenora Giddings Ivory, Director of Washington Office

3. The Washington Office of the Presbyterian Church USA engages in a range of public policy advocacy on domestic and international issues. Global security issues include military budgets, weapons development, nuclear proliferation, arms sales and transfers, regional intervention and low-intensity conflict. In different regional areas such as Latin America, Africa, and the Middle East, the office is concerned with human rights, economic development, fair trade, effective economic aid, and famine. The office is also concerned with environmental issues and healthcare.

7. Index Terms: Pacifism and Peace Movements

---

### N47 Project HOPE (People-to-People Health Foundation) — Center for Health Affairs

1. 7500 Old Georgetown Road, Suite 600
Bethesda, Md. 20814-6133
(301) 656-7401
Fax: (301) 654-0629

2. William B. Walsh Jr., President

3. The People-to-People Health Foundation, with headquarters in Millwood, Va., is a nonprofit corporation that provides educational and training programs in the health sciences in more than 30 countries. Programs, which include medicine, dentistry, nursing, allied health sciences, primary health care, biomedical engineering, health administration and planning, are provided to national ministries of health, universities, medical centers, and public- and private-sector health facilities and health training institutions of developing countries. The Center for Health Affairs is primarily concerned with public policy research and advocacy on health issues generally.

6. Project HOPE publishes a newsletter, *HOPE Today;* a journal, *Health Affairs;* and an annual report.

7. Index Terms: Development Issues—Health

---

### N48 Public Welfare Foundation

1. 2600 Virginia Avenue, NW, Suite 505
Washington, D.C. 20037-1977
(202) 965-1800
Fax: (202) 625-1348

2. Donald Warner, Chair
Larry Kressley, Executive Director

3. Public Welfare Foundation is a grant-making organization supporting programs that provide services or educational outreach to address specific needs within communities, advocate changes in policy and resource distribution addressing such needs, and empower people to achieve needed changes. The general categories of grants are criminal justice, disadvantaged elderly, disadvantaged youth, environment, health, population, and community support. Within these categories, areas of interest include sustainable development, population, immigration, global security, and human rights.

7. Index Terms: Development Issues

---

### N49 Puebla Institute

1. 1319 18th Street, NW
Washington, D.C. 20036
(202) 296-8050
Fax: (202) 296-5078

2. James Finn, Chairman
Nina Shea, President

3. The Puebla Institute is a lay Roman Catholic organization defending freedom of religion worldwide. Puebla Institute documents religious repression and other human rights abuses and mobilizes public support in defense of those persecuted for religious beliefs.

6. The institute has published numerous reports, including *Continued Persecution of Christians in China* (June 1993); *Testimony of Puebla on Nicaragua* (February 1993); *Human Rights in Haiti* (December 1992); *Report of the Democracy Commission: An Examination of the Democratization Process in Nicaragua One Year after Free Elections* (August 1991); *Cuba: Castro's War on Religion* (March 1991); *Haiti: Looking Forward to Elections, An Interim Report* (July 1990). The institute also publishes a quarterly newsletter, *First Freedom.*

7. Index Terms: Human Rights—Monitoring Organizations

---

### N50 RESOLVE—Center for Environmental Dispute Resolution

1. 1250 24th Street, NW
Washington, D.C. 20037-1175

(202) 778-9634
Fax: (202) 293-9211

2. Gail Bingham, President
Christine Pendzich, Director, International
Program

3. RESOLVE—Center for Environmental Dispute
Resolution seeks to facilitate the use of conflict resolution techniques in environmental disputes. RE-
SOLVE's international program was started in 1991
and provides technical assistance and training to
parties involved in environmental conflicts. RE-
SOLVE seeks to build institutional capacity for dispute resolution outside the United States with particular emphasis on Latin America and Central and
Eastern Europe. Its fundamental approach is to
teach basic negotiation and dispute resolution skills
so that concerned parties, familiar with local political and cultural considerations, can adapt them to
their own needs. In its international programs, RE-
SOLVE itself rarely plays an active role in the negotiation as a third party. Training currently centers on
three five-day workshops that use simulations, case
study analyses, and other interactive techniques.
RESOLVE also works with government officials to
institutionalize dispute resolution procedures. The
organization gives technical assistance largely in the
form of consultation on designing a conflict management process or with mediators or government
officials to further the negotiation process. It is also
engaged in outreach activity through public speaking, written materials, and informal consultations.
RESOLVE plans to expand its international program to include transboundary environmental issues and international trade.

6. RESOLVE publishes a newsletter.

7. Index Terms: Conflict Management and Resolution; Environmental Issues

---

## N51  Search for Common Ground

1. 1601 Connecticut Avenue, NW, Suite 200
Washington, D.C. 20009
(202) 265-4300
Fax: (202) 232-6718

2. Randolph Wright, Chair
John Marks, President

3. Search for Common Ground is an independent
organization that seeks to promote recognition of
common interest between opposing parties and

channel conflict toward constructive outcomes.
Search for Common Ground supports several projects. The Initiative for Peace and Cooperation in the
Middle East is an effort to build a comprehensive
process for Mideast peace and security. It includes
several working groups: the Core Working Group,
35 individuals from 7 Arab countries, Israel, Turkey,
and the Palestinian community; the Civil Society
Working Group; the Conflict Resolution Working
Group; the Economics Working Group; and the Security Working Group. Another large project is the
Search for Common Ground in Russia, which seeks
to foster collaborative and nonviolent ways of resolving conflict in Russia. Along with the Iowa
Peace Institute and the former Soviet Academy of
Sciences, this project helped establish the Center for
Conflict Resolution in Moscow. Within this initiative are several projects: ethnic and community conflict resolution; labor mediation; and media productions. Search for Common Ground is also
developing initiatives in South Africa and
Macedonia.

5. Search for Common Ground has a small library
for the use of its own staff.

6. Search for Common Ground publishes the
quarterly *Bulletin of Regional Cooperation in the
Middle East,* which serves as a clearinghouse on
nongovernment cooperation among countries, organizations, and peoples of the Middle East.

7. Index Terms: Conflict Management and Resolution; Ethnic and Religious Conflict

---

## N52  Sister Cities International (Town Affiliation Association of the U.S.)

1. 120 South Payne Street
Alexandria, Va. 22314
(703) 836-3535
Fax: (703) 836-4815

2. Carol Lynn Greene, Executive Director

3. Sister Cities International coordinates exchange and affiliation programs between U.S. communities and cities in other countries. Currently,
there are a total of 1,744 affiliations, including 939
U.S. cities, in a total of 111 countries. The organization's headquarters is located in Tempe, Ariz.

4. The organization hosts an annual conference of
its members.

6. Sister Cities International publishes a quarterly newsletter, *Sister City News;* an annual, *Directory of Sister Cities by State and Country; Sister City Handbook;* and other informational material.

7. Index Terms: Transnationalism

**Smithsonian Institution** See entry K36

---

**N53** Stewart R. Mott and Associates—
Washington Office

---

1. 122 Maryland Avenue, NE
   Washington, D.C. 20002
   (202) 546-3732
   Fax: (202) 543-3156

2. Conrad Martin, Washington Office Contact

3. Stewart R. Mott and Associates is the personal philanthropic organization of Stewart R. Mott. Roughly 20 percent of Mr. Mott's grants have gone toward peace issues, arms control, and foreign policy in recent years; specific issues include military spending, defense conversion, and the arms trades. Other areas of interest are international population and family planning issues.

7. Index Terms: Arms Control—Arms Transfers; Defense Conversion; Development Issues—Population Policy; Military Spending

---

**N54** Student Pugwash USA

---

1. 1638 R Street, NW, Suite 32
   Washington, D.C. 20009-6446
   (202) 328-6555
   Fax: (202) 797-4664

2. Betsy Fader, Executive Director

3. Student Pugwash USA is a national, nonpartisan, nonadvocacy educational organization that fosters commitment among young people to integrate social concerns into their academic, professional, and personal lives. Student Pugwash USA examines the impacts of science and technology in the following areas: peace and security; environment; energy; health and medicine; biotechnology; population and development; information technologies; industrial competitiveness; and issues of access and equity. Student Pugwash USA was inspired by the Pugwash Conferences on Science and World Affairs begun in 1957 in Pugwash, Nova Scotia, and is primarily a stu-

dent organization. It has a mentorship initiative for interaction with concerned professionals. It also sponsors Professional Pugwash, a national network of professionals who engage in interdisciplinary examination of critical issues. The organization holds international conferences approximately every two years at universities across the United States.

4. The organization holds an annual three-day PUGWASHington Seminar in Washington, D.C.

6. Student Pugwash USA publishes a quarterly newsletter, *Tough Questions*. It has also published *The Mentorship Guide: A Directory of Resource People and Advisors in Social Change* (January 1992); and *New Careers: A Directory of Jobs and Internships in Technology and Society* (1993).

7. Index Terms: Peace Theory and Research

---

**N55** United Church of Christ—Office for
Church in Society (OCIS)

---

1. 110 Maryland Avenue, NE, Room 207
   Washington, D.C. 20002
   (202) 543-1517
   Fax: (202) 543-5994

2. Valerie E. Russell, Executive Director
   David Hanson, OCIS Directorate Chair

3. The OCIS of the United Church of Christ monitors legislative issues primarily relating to domestic social issues. Issues on which legislative histories are developed include military spending; Haiti and Haitian asylum seekers; Cuba; the Horn of Africa; expelled Palestinians and the Israel- Palestinian peace process; Cambodia; and the conflict in the Balkans.

5. The United Church of Christ's archives are located in the Phillip Schaff library at the Lancaster Theological Seminary (717/393-0654).

6. In addition to a *Legislative Factsheet*, OCIS publishes a newsletter, *Courage in the Struggle*.

7. Index Terms: Humanitarian Issues—Relief Organizations; Military Spending; Regional Conflict

---

**N56** United Methodist Church—General
Board of Church and Society

---

1. 100 Maryland Avenue, NE
   Washington, D.C. 20002
   (202) 488-5647

2. Bishop Joseph H. Yeakel, President
Thom White Wolf Fassett, General Secretary

3. The United Methodist Church encourages Christian lines of action that assist humankind to move toward a world of peace and justice. The church sponsors research, analysis, and engages in advocacy on Capitol Hill. The church has actively followed the social policies of the United Nations.

5. The General Board does not have a library. Scholars looking for resources on the Methodist philosophy of peace and justice should try the Wesley Seminary library at American University (202/885-8600).

6. The General Board has published a number of booklets on social activism. It also publishes a monthly journal, *Christian Social Action.*

7. Index Terms: Pacifism and Peace Movements; Religious, Philosophical, and Ethical Concepts of War and Peace

---

## N57    United States Committee for Refugees

1. 1717 Massachusetts Avenue, NW, Suite 701
Washington, D.C. 20036
(202) 347-3507
Fax: (202) 347-3418

2. Roger Winter, Executive Director

3. The goals of the U.S. Committee for Refugees center around the defense of basic human rights of refugees, especially regarding the right of nonreturn; the defense of the rights of asylum seekers to fair hearings of their status; and the defense of the right to decent and humane treatment for refugees. The committee publicizes refugee issues through media coverage, congressional testimony, contact with foreign governments and their refugee programs, and contact with the UN High Commissioner for Refugees (L16). It also builds advocacy networks with other organizations around specific refugee issues.

6. The committee publishes *Refugee Reports* monthly. It also publishes issue papers such as *East of Bosnia: Refugees in Serbia and Montenegro* (September 1993); *El Retorno: Guatemalans' Risky Repatriation Begins* (February 1993); *Croatia's Crucible: Providing Asylum for Refugees from Bosnia and Hercegovina* (October 1992). Other publications include *Encouraging Refugee Awareness in the Classroom: A Guide for Teachers* (February 1993).

7. Index Terms: Refugees

**United States Information Agency    See entry K41**

---

## N58    Volunteers in Technical Assistance (VITA)

---

1. 1600 Wilson Boulevard, Suite 500
Arlington, Va. 22209
(703) 276-1800
Fax: (703) 243-1865

2. Harlan Cleveland, Chair
Henry R. Norman, President

3. VITA lends assistance to developing countries through the provision of technical information services and through overseas projects promoting economic growth. VITA has approximately 5,000 volunteers in over 100 countries who assist in inquiries for technical information. VITA's users are businessmen, governments, individuals, private voluntary organizations, schools, and universities. VITA also disseminates information through a weekly Voice of America broadcast. VITA has a global communications program, VITACOMM, consisting of a digital low earth orbiting satellite and terrestrial radio systems, as well as electronic mail/bulletin board systems. VITA's Disaster Information Resource Program serves as a clearinghouse for information on natural and man-made crises to assist relief agencies. VITA conducts a number of field projects that focus on enterprise development, agriculture, rural rehabilitation, renewable energy, and protection of the environment. At present VITA has projects in Afghanistan, Benin, the Central African Republic, Chad, Guinea, Kenya, Madagascar, and Zambia.

6. VITA publishes an electronic newsletter, *DevelopNet News,* available through Bitnet and Internet. It has also published over 200 technical handbooks and manuals. A publications list is available.

7. Index Terms: Development Issues—Technical Assistance; Humanitarian Issues—Relief Organization

**Woodrow Wilson International Center for Scholars (WWICS)    See entry H76**

## N59 World Foundation for Environment and Development (WFED)

1. 3027 Arizona Avenue, NW
   Washington, D.C. 20016
   (202) 364-8276
   Fax: (202) 686-3771

2. Preston T. Scott, Director

3. WFED, headquartered in Washington, D.C., and Oslo, sponsors projects and initiatives designed to improve international understanding of important environmental and development issues. It seeks to contribute to the prevention and peaceful resolution of international environmental conflicts and disputes. It has focused on international conflicts involving river systems, coastal areas, forestry, biological diversity, land resource, and human migration and displacement triggered by environmental degradation. It has held symposia on conflict resolution in Oslo, Jerusalem, and Nairobi. WFED places special emphasis on improving institutional capacity for resolving environmental conflicts and is currently working with the UN Environmental Program on an educational project for dispute resolution and preventive diplomacy.

4. WFED hosts occasional conferences and meetings. In 1993 it sponsored a conference on World Bank (L8) involvement in environmental conflict resolution issues.

6. WFED publications include *International Environmental Conflict Resolution: The Role of the United Nations* (1993) and *Environmental Refugees,* a 1992 conference report.

7. Index Terms: Conflict Management and Resolution; Development Issues—International Development Policy; Environmental Issues, Global—Sustainable Development

## N60 World Learning (*formerly* Experiment in International Living)— Projects in International Development and Training (PIDT)

1. 1015 15th Street, NW, Suite 750
   Washington, D.C. 20005
   (202) 408-5420
   Fax: (202) 408-5397

2. Judy Hendren Mello, President, World Learning

Robert C. Chase, Vice-President, PIDT

3. Projects in International Development and Training (PIDT) is a division of World Learning (*formerly* Experiment in International Living), an international education services organization located in Brattleboro, Vt. PIDT assists local institutions and individuals to carry out community-based, national, regional, and global-based development projects. PIDT works with nongovernmental organizations, educational institutions, and training providers in approximately 60 countries worldwide. Its activities focus on development management, which increases the capability of local organizations to promote economic and social change particularly in regard to health and population matters and management of natural resources. It also sponsors human resource development such as job-related skills, language training, and management training.

7. Index Terms: Development Issues—Education; Development Issues—Technical Assistance

## N61 World Wildlife Fund (WWF)

1. 1250 24th Street, NW
   Washington, D.C. 20037
   (202) 293-4800
   Fax: (202) 293-9211

2. Kathryn Fuller, President

3. WWF is an international conservation organization based in the United States that promotes environmental causes both at home and abroad. It seeks to preserve endangered species and their natural habitats and to maintain biodiversity, especially in the tropical forests of Latin America, Asia, and Africa. The WWF also sponsors the Osborn Center for Economic Development, which assists institutions in developing countries to promote sustainable development.

5. WWF has a library with a collection of 10,000 volumes and 350 journal subscriptions. The main focus of this collection is conservation, including issues such as pollution and hazardous waste. The library is open to the public by appointment, 9:00 A.M. TO 5:00 P.M. Monday–Friday (contact librarian, Carla Langeveld).

6. WWF publishes a bimonthly newsletter, *Focus,* and program literature.

7. Index Terms: Environmental Issues, Global—Sustainable Development

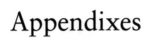

# Appendixes

# I

# Publications and Media

This is a directory of editorial offices of periodicals, as well as of publishing houses in the Washington, D.C., area that publish materials in the areas of peace, international security studies, or both. Each entry contains the basic address information, the name of the editor or publisher, and the name of the sponsoring organization. The researcher is advised that the publications listed here are in addition to relevant newsletters, journals, annuals, and other serials sponsored by the organizations described in sections H–N of this Guide, which are discussed in the entries for these organizations. For instance, the journals *Arms Control Today, Foreign Policy,* and *Washington Quarterly* are described under their parental organizations, Arms Control Association (M13), Carnegie Endowment for International Peace (H9), and Center for Strategic and International Studies (CSIS) (H18) respectively. Similarly, the Smithsonian Institution Press and the Woodrow Wilson Center Press are listed in the entries for their parental institutions (K36 and H76, respectively).

## Alternatives
1875 Connecticut Avenue, NW, Suite 710
Washington, D.C. 20009
(202) 387-6030
Fax: (202) 986-2539
Bill Rice, Editor

## Center for Policy Alternatives
American Council for the UN University Newsletter
4421 Garrison Street, NW
Washington, D.C. 20016
(202) 686-5179
Gerry Glen, Managing Editor

## American Purpose
1015 15th Street, NW, Suite 900
Washington, D.C. 20005
(202) 682-1200

Fax: (202) 408-0632
George Weigel, Editor

## Ethics and Public Policy Center
Anthropology and Humanism Quarterly
4350 North Fairfax Drive, Suite 640
Arlington, Va. 22203
(703) 528-1902
Rick Custer, Managing Editor

## American Anthropological Association
Bridging the Gap
810 First Street, NE, Suite 630
Washington, D.C. 20002
(202) 408-0034
Christie Law, Editor

## Carroll Publishing Company
1058 Thomas Jefferson Street, NW
Washington, D.C. 20007
(202) 333-8620
Robert S. Crossfield, Director, Information Systems

## Church Women Act
110 Maryland Avenue, NE
Washington, D.C. 20002
(202) 544-8747
Fax: (202) 543-1297
Nancy Chupp and Robina Shaw, Coeditors
Church Women United

## Congressional Quarterly Weekly Report
1414 22nd Street, NW
Washington, D.C. 20037
(202) 887-8524
Fax: (202) 785-8784
Rose Gutfield, Managing Editor

## Co-op America
1350 M Street, NW, Suite 700
Washington, D.C. 20036
(202) 872-5307

Fax: (202) 331-8166
Anne Zorc, Editor

**CovertAction Quarterly**
1500 Massachusetts Avenue, NW, Room 732
Washington, D.C. 20005
(202) 331-9763
Fax: (202) 331-9751
Phil Smith and Terry Allen, Coeditors

**Dispute Resolution**
1800 M Street, NW, 2nd Floor
Washington, D.C. 20036
(202) 331-2258
Fax: (202) 331-2220
Mark Donberger, Editor
American Bar Association, Section on Dispute Resolution

**Government Printing Office (GPO)**
Superintendent of Documents
U.S. Government Printing Office
Washington, D.C. 20402
(202) 783-3238
Fax: (202) 275-0019
Michael Dimario, Public Printer

**Interaction**
1325 G Street, NW, Suite 1010
Washington, D.C. 20005
(202) 628-4016
Fax: (202) 628-4018
Don Lesh, Editor
Global Tomorrow Coalition

**Library of Congress—Federal Research Division—Country Studies Program**
3rd and M Streets, SE
Washington, D.C. 20540
(202) 245-5206
Fax: (202) 245-5290
Sandra W. Meditz, Program Specialist

**Livability**
1429 21st Street, NW
Washington, D.C. 20036
(202) 887-5990
Fax: (202) 466-4845
Clint Page, Editor
Partners for Livable Places

**Monitor Publishing Company**
1301 Pennsylvania Avenue, NW, Suite 1000
Washington, D.C. 20004
(202) 347-7757
Fax: (202) 628-3430
David Hurvitz, Publisher
Mary Forschler, Senior Editor (D.C.)

**National Archives and Records Administration (NARA)—Office of the Federal Register**
800 North Capital Street, NW
Washington, D.C. 20002
(202) 523-4534
Martha L. Girard, Director

**New Republic**
1220 19th Street, NW, Suite 600
Washington, D.C. 20036
(202) 331-7494
Fax: (202) 331-0275
Andrew Sullivan, Editor

**Organizer**
739 8th Street, SE
Washington, D.C. 20003
(202) 547-2500
Fax: (202) 546-2483

**Institute for Social Justice**
Panascope
1717 Massachusetts Avenue, Suite 301
Washington, D.C. 20036
(202) 483-0044
Fax: (202) 483-3099
Liz Carlyle, Editor
Panos Institute

**Peace Tax Fund Newsletter**
2121 Decatur Place, NW
Washington, D.C. 20008
(202) 483-3751
Fax: (202) 986-0667
Eirik Harteis, Editor
National Campaign for a Peace Tax Fund

**People and Taxes**
2000 P Street, NW, Suite 600
Washington, D.C. 20036
(202) 833-3000
Public Citizen

**Security Studies**
1727 Massachusetts Avenue, NW, Suite 815
Washington, D.C. 20036
(202) 234-2058
Fax: (202) 265-0799
Amos Perlmutter and Benjamin Frankel, Coeditors

**Sojourners**
2401 15th Street, NW
Washington, D.C. 20009
(202) 328-8842
Fax: (202) 328-8757
Jim Wallis, Editor
Sojourners Fellowship

**TransAtlantic Perspectives**
11 Dupont Circle, NW, Suite 750
Washington, D.C. 20036
(202) 745-3950
Fax: (202) 265-1662
Jane Beckwith, Editor
The German Marshall Fund of the U.S.

**University Press of America**
4720 Boston Way
Lanham, Md. 20706
(301) 459-3366
Fax: (301) 549-2118
James E. Lyons, Publisher

**U.S. News and World Report**
2400 N Street, NW
Washington, D.C. 20037
(202) 955-2000
Fax: (202) 955-2049
Michael Ruby and Merrill McLoughlin,
   Coeditors

**Washington Post**
1150 15th Street, NW
Washington, D.C. 20071
(202) 334-6000
Fax: (202) 334-7400
Leonard Downey, Executive Editor
Jackson Diehl, Foreign Editor

**Washington Times**
3600 New York Avenue, NE
Washington, D.C. 20002
(202) 636-3000
Wesley Pruden, Editor in Chief
Mark Lerner, Foreign Desk

**World Affairs**
400 Albermarle Street, NW
Washington, D.C. 20016
(202) 296-6261
Fax: (202) 537-0287
Joyce Horn, Managing Editor
American Peace Society

# II

# Library Collections: A Listing by Size of Peace and International Security Studies Holdings

*Note:* The size of peace and international security studies holdings in the Washington, D.C., area library collections is difficult to determine. The following table provides estimates only of volumes relevant to peace and international security studies (as defined in the Introductory Note to the A ["Libraries"] section and in Appendix IV) within the holdings of individual libraries. It does not indicate the entire size of holdings, unless all of a library's holdings are relevant to peace and international security studies.

**More than 800,000 volumes:**
Library of Congress (A29)

**100,000–250,000 volumes:**
National Defense University (Defense Department) (A33)
Navy Department Library (A36)
Census Bureau Library (Commerce Department) (A8)
Joint Bank-Fund Library (Library of the International Bank for Reconstruction and Development [World Bank] and the International Monetary Fund [A27])
Pentagon Library (Army Department) (A41)
State Department Library (A43)
Georgetown University—Lauinger Library (A20)
University of Maryland—McKeldin Library (A47)
International Trade Commission—National Library of International Trade (A26)

**50,000–99,000 volumes:**
American University—Bender Library (A4)
George Washington University—Gelman Library (A19)
Howard University—Founders Library (A22)
Inter-American Development Bank (IDB)—Library (A24)
Catholic University—Mullen Library (A7)
National Agricultural Library (Agriculture Department) (A31)
European Union—Delegation of the European Commission—Press and Public Affairs Office (A13)
Labor Department Library (A28)
Senate—Library (A42)

**25,000–49,000 volumes:**
George Mason University—Fenwick Library (A18)
Marine Corps University (Navy Department)—James Carson Breckinridge Library (A30)
House of Representatives—Library (A21)
Marine Corps Historical Center (Navy Department)—Library (B9)
Nitze School of Advanced International Studies (SAIS) (Johns Hopkins University)—Library (A37)
Federal Reserve Board—Research Library (A16)
National Library of Medicine (Health and Human Services Department) (A35)
United States Holocaust Research Institute—Library (A45)

# III

# Bookstores

The following is a selective list of local bookstores that feature materials of special interest to students of international relations in their economic, humanitarian, military, and political aspects. Although the Washington, D.C., area cannot boast truly first-rate academic bookstores, such as exist in New York City, in Cambridge, Massachusetts, or in Oxford, England, scholars usually cite Borders Book Shop, Olsson's Books and Records, Sidney Kramer Books, and (for Russian language materials) Victor Kamkin Bookstore, as offering the widest selection of literature in the social sciences in the nation's capital. Books are also available from the publication offices of the numerous organizations, as noted in entries of sections H, M, and N of this Guide. If a relevant organization operates a bookstore, it is listed below.

### American University Campus Store
4400 Massachusetts Avenue, NW
Washington, D.C. 20016
(202) 885-6301/6307
Fax: (202) 885-6373

### Bick's Books
2309 18th Street, NW
Washington, D.C. 20009
(202) 328-2356
Fax: (202) 667-1630

### The Book Cellar
8227 Woodmont Avenue
Bethesda, Md. 20814
(301) 654-1898

### Booked Up
1209 31st Street, NW
Washington, D.C. 20007
(202) 965-3244
Fax: (202) 298-6555

### Borders Book Shop
11500 Rockville Pike
Rockville, Md. 20852
(301) 816-1067
Fax: (301) 816-8940

18th and L Streets, NW
Washington, D.C. 20006
(202) 466-4999
Fax: (202) 466-2403

### Chapters Literary Bookstore
1512 K Street, NW
Washington, D.C. 20005
(202) 347-5495

### Georgetown University Bookshop
Leavey Center
3800 Reservoir Road, NW
Washington, D.C. 20057
(202) 687-7750
Fax: (202) 687-1925

### George Washington University Bookstore
800 21st Street, NW
Washington, D.C. 20052
(202) 994-6870
Fax: (202) 296-9445

### Government Printing Office (GPO) Bookstore
710 North Capitol Street, NW
Washington, D.C. 20402
(202) 512-0132
Fax: (202) 512-0132

### GPO Bookstore—Farragut West
1510 H Street, NW
Washington, D.C. 20401
(202) 653-5075

**International Bank for Reconstruction and Development (World Bank)    See World Bank Bookstore**

**International Language Center**
1753 Connecticut Avenue, NW
Washington, D.C. 20009
(202) 332-2894
Fax: (202) 462-6657

**International Monetary Fund (IMF)— Publications**
700 19th Street, NW
Washington, D.C. 20431
(202) 623-7430
Fax: (202) 623-7201

See also entry L11

**Lantern Bryn Mawr Book Shop**
3160 O Street, NW
Washington, D.C. 20007
(202) 333-3222

**Maryland Book Exchange**
4500 College Avenue
College Park, Md. 20740
(301) 927-2510
Fax: (301) 209-7118

**National Technical Information Service (NTIS) Bookstore**
5285 Port Royal Road
Springfield, Va. 22161
(703) 487-4604
Fax: (703) 321-8547

See also entry K29

**Newman Book Store**
3329 8th Street, NE
Washington, D.C. 20017
(202) 526-1036
Fax: (202) 526-6725

**News Room**
1753 Connecticut Avenue, NW
Washington, D.C. 20009
(202) 332-1489
Fax: (202) 462-6657

**Olsson's Books and Records**
1307 19th Street, NW
Washington, D.C. 20036
(202) 785-1133

1200 F Street, NW
Washington, D.C. 20007
(202) 347-3686

1239 Wisconsin Avenue, NW
Washington, D.C. 20007
(202) 338-9544
Fax: (202) 342-2342

7647 Old Georgetown Road
Bethesda, Md. 20814
(301) 652-3336

106 South Union Street
Alexandria, Va. 22314
(703) 684-0077

**Organization for Economic Cooperation and Development (OECD) Bookstore**
2001 L Street, NW, Suite 700
Washington, D.C. 20036-4910
(202) 785-6323
Fax: (202) 785-0350

**Pentagon Bookstore**
The Pentagon
Washington, D.C. 20050
(703) 695-0868

**Politics and Prose**
5015 Connecticut Avenue, NW
Washington, D.C. 20008
(202) 364-1919
Fax: (202) 966-7532

**Reiter's Scientific and Professional Books**
2021 K Street, NW
Washington, D.C. 20006
(202) 223-3327
Fax: (202) 296-9103

**Second Story Books**
2000 P Street, NW
Washington, D.C. 20036
(202) 659-8884

4836 Bethesda Avenue
Bethesda, Md. 20814
(301) 656-0170

12160 Parklawn Drive
Rockville, Md. 20852
(301) 770-0477
Fax: (301) 770-9544

**Sidney Kramer Books**
1825 I Street, NW
Washington, D.C. 20006
(202) 293-2685
Fax: (202) 835-9756

**Travel Books and Language Center**
4931 Cordell Avenue
Bethesda, Md. 20814

(301) 951-8533
Fax: (301) 951-8546

**Victor Kamkin Bookstore**
4956 Boiling Brook Parkway
Rockville, Md. 20852
(301) 881-5973
Fax: (301) 881-1637
Victor Kamkin's is the most comprehensive Russian language bookstore in the area.

**Walden Books**
1700 Pennsylvania Avenue, NW
Washington, D.C. 20006
(202) 393-1490

**World Bank Bookstore**
701 18th Street, NW, Room J-1060
Washington, D.C. 20433
(202) 473-2941
Fax: (202) 477-0604

See also entry L8

*Note:* Several major book sales are held each year in the Washington, D.C., area. For scholars, the most significant of these is that of the Association of American Foreign Service Wives, held annually in the fall at the State Department. More than 100,000 books are usually offered, including a large foreign-language section. Also note the Vassar College and Brandeis University book sales, which take place during the spring at varying sites. These book sales are advertised in local newspapers shortly before they occur; notices usually appear for several days in the book review section of the *Washington Post.*

# IV

# Relevant Library of Congress Classification Numbers

As noted in the introductory note to section A ("Libraries"), in analyzing the holdings of the large and general libraries, numbers of titles in the various subject categories were derived primarily through the measurement of library shelflists, on the basis of a Library of Congress formula of 33.8 titles per centimeter of shelflist catalog cards.

Library of Congress classification numbers, used for the shelflist measurements, were chosen for their coverage of the various topics and subtopics germane to peace and international security studies. *Guide to Library of Congress Subject Headings and Classification on Peace and International Conflict*, edited by Judith A. Kessinger (Washington, D.C.: United States Institute of Peace, 1990) served as an important source for the identification of these numbers.

The following classification numbers were selected as pertinent to peace and international security studies in the individual subject areas:

Philosophy: B1–B844, BD10–BD450
Psychology: BF309–BF637, BF697–BF838
Ethics: BJ1–BJ1535
Religion: BL55–BL2223, BM534–BM645, BP50–BP195, BP573.P3, BQ4000–BQ4610, BR115–BR128, BR1600–BR1610, BS680, BS1199, BS1281–BS1285.5, BS2415, BS2417, BS2545, BT70–BT77, BT380–BT382, BT696–BT738, BV629–BV631, BV4627–BV4715, BX1763–BX1795, BX1908, BX7601–BX7795, BX8074, BX8101–BX8143, BX8349, BX8551–BX8593, BX8643, BX9751–BX9793
World History: D13–D888
History—Military Science: U27–U55, U799–U897, V13–V105
Geography: UA985–UA997, UG470–UG474
Anthropology: GN488–494, GN496–499, GN789, GV1101–GV1195, U750–U773, V720–V743
Economic History and Conditions: HB195, HC1–HC94, HC111–HC695

Commercial Policy (including Tariff Policy, Protection and Free Trade): HF1401–HF4040
International Finance (including International Monetary System): HG3811–HG4000
Sociology: HM24–HM299, HV6187–HV6773, HX19–HX970
Political Theory: JC11–JC628
Constitutional History and Administration: JF8–JF2112, JK1–JK2391
Colonies and Emigration: JV1–JV485, JV6001–JV6348
International Relations: JX1–JX1899
International Organizations (including Procedures in International Disputes): JX1901–JX1991 (excludes JX1904.5: Study and Research)
International Law: JX2000–JX5810
Education: JX1904.5, U166–U395, U400–U717, V160–699
Music—Military: M1631–1650, M1675, ML128.M4, ML128.W2, UH40–45
Art and War: N8230, N8260, N9100–N9165, NA490–NA497, NA9325–NA9330, NE955–NE957, NK8475.M5
Military Science: UA10–UA980, UB1–UB890, UD1–UD495, UF1–UF561, UG1–UG590, UG622–UG1435, UG1500–UG1530
Naval Science: V750–V995, VA10–VA750, VB15–VB875, VD15–VD155, VE15–VE157, VE430–VE435, VF1–VF155, VF346–VF395, VG50–VG95, VG500–VG505
Bibliography and Reference: Z5873, Z6207, Z6461–Z6485, Z6721–Z6726, Z6831–Z6836, Z7161.A22–Z, Z7164 (.C7, .C9, .C98, .D2, .E15, .E17, .G45, .I3, .I34, .I39, .I8, .L38, .L6, .M67, .N2, .P19, .P2, .P3, .P79, .P8, .R32, .R34, .R4, .R54, .S67, .T3, .U5, .V55), Z7165, Z7166, Z7809, Z7838.P54, Z7845 (.F8, .M4, .M7, .M8, .S5), Z7853

# V

# Housing, Transportation, and Other Services

This section is prepared to help outside scholars find suitable housing in Washington, D.C. It also contains data on local transportation facilities and information services. Prices quoted are current as of August 1994.

## Housing Information and Referral Service

For anyone interested in leasing an apartment or house, the *Apartment Shoppers' Guide and Housing Directory* (ASGHD), updated every three months, is a valuable source of information. The directory, which quotes current rental prices, terms of leases, and directions to each of the facilities listed, is available at CVS Drug Stores, Safeway Food Stores, and elsewhere in the Washington area. It is published by ASGHD (301/588-7368), located at 8601 Georgia Avenue, Silver Spring, Maryland 20910. The staff provides a housing referral service (for a fee) from 9:00 A.M. to 5:00 P.M., Monday through Friday. The *Washington Post* classified section also has extensive listings of apartment and house rentals.

Listings for housing are also available at the following university housing centers:

American University
Information and Off-Campus Housing Resource
  Center
Mary Grayden Center, First Floor
Washington, D.C. 20016
(202) 885-3270
Hours:
9:00 A.M.–8:00 P.M. Monday–Thursday
9:00 A.M.–5:00 P.M. Friday
Noon–4:00 P.M. Saturday and Sunday

Georgetown University Off-Campus Housing
  Office
100 Harbin Hall
37th and O streets, NW
Washington, D.C. 20057
(202) 687-4560
Hours: 10:00 A.M.–5:00 P.M., Monday–Friday

This office offers listings of apartments and houses in the area. During July and August, use of the facility is restricted to Georgetown students, faculty, and staff.

George Washington University Off Campus Housing Resources Center
Marvin Center, Room 416
800 21st Street, NW
Washington, D.C. 20052
(202) 994-7221
Winter hours:
9:00 A.M.–6:00 P.M., Monday–Friday
10:00 A.M.–2:00 P.M., Saturday
Summer hours:
9:00 A.M.–8:00 P.M., Monday–Thursday
9:00 A.M.–5:00 P.M., Friday
9:00 A.M.–2:00 P.M., Saturday
1:00 P.M.–5:00 P.M., Sunday

This office has listings of apartments and other housing in the Washington area. Open to the public, the office also distributes the Apartment Shoppers' Guide (see above), maps of Washington, D.C., and a Guide to Off-Campus Housing (annual) prepared by the office staff.

Howard University Off-Campus Referral Service
2401 4th Street, NW
Washington, D.C. 20059
(202) 806-5652
Hours: 9:00 A.M.–5:00 P.M. Monday–Friday

Northern Virginia Community College, Annandale
  Campus Housing Board
Student Activities Center
Godwin Building, Room 205
8333 Little River Turnpike
Annandale, Va. 22003
(703) 323-3000
Hours: 9:00 A.M.–5:00 P.M., Monday-Friday

The board maintains a listing of rooms available in private homes.

University of Maryland
Commuter Affairs
1195 Adele H. Stamp Union
College Park, Md. 20742
(301) 314-3645
Hours: 8:30 A.M.–4:30 P.M., Monday–Friday

*Note:* In most cases only listings are available for those not affiliated with the university in question. Other services are usually restricted to students, faculty, and staff.

## Short-Term Housing

For those who intend to stay for a short period of time (i.e. a few weeks to several months), the following facilities may be useful:

International Guest House
1441 Kennedy Street, NW
Washington, D.C. 20011
(202) 726-5808

Rates: $25/day, $160/week (maximum stay is two weeks for international guests, one week for U.S. citizens). Price includes breakfast. Single guests are asked to share a room with another person. The house encourages a nationality quota policy that permits no more than ten Americans or three citizens from any one foreign country at any time.

The Woodner
3636 16thStreet, NW
Washington, D.C. 20010
(202) 328-2800

The Woodner has both unfurnished and furnished efficiency and one-bedroom apartments. Rates are $345 per month and up for an unfurnished efficiency, $445 and up for a one-bedroom apartment. Rates for furnished efficiencies and one-bedroom apartments are $575 and $690 respectively.

## Long-Term Housing

Those wishing to rent an apartment or house for a year or more should consult not only the Apartment Shoppers' Guide and the local university housing offices, but the housing section of the *Washington Post* as well. Home and apartment rents vary greatly from one section to the other in the Washington area. Normally, rents are lower in suburban Virginia and Maryland than in Washington, D.C. One should also remember that it is difficult to find furnished apartments in the Washington area through regular real estate agents. People who need furnished quarters may have to take unfurnished apartments and rent furniture. Again, the *Washington Post* classified advertisements should be checked.

## Transportation

### Within Washington, D.C.

Scholars should be advised that parking space in the nation's capital is limited, and that it is relatively expensive to park at commercial lots (e.g., $4 per hour, maximum $12 per day). It may be preferable, therefore, to use either Metrobus (202/637-7000), Metrorail (subway) (202/637-7000), or taxi to get around the downtown Washington area.

### Between Washington, D.C. and suburbs:

Metrobus and Metrorail (202/637-7000) generally provide the easiest and most convenient route between Washington and its suburbs. Limited parking is available at outlying Metrorail stations in both Virginia and Maryland for those who wish to drive to the Metro. For those commuting into the District from either Virginia or Maryland, car pooling is also a popular option. Commuters should also beware of highways which become exclusively HOV (High Occupancy Vehicle, 3 or more persons) during rush hour, most notably, Route 66.

### To and From National Airport:

Metrorail (202/637-7000) provides service to and from National Airport via both the Blue and Yellow Lines. Washington Flyer also operates a bus service between its terminal at 1517 K Street, NW, and National Airport. The buses run seven days a week. Rates are $8 (one-way) and $14 (round-trip) including loop service between the Washington Flyer terminal and various points throughout the district. Call Washington Flyer (703/685-1400) for schedule information. Please note, Washington Flyer accepts cash only.

## To and From Dulles International Airport:

Washington Flyer operates a bus service between its terminal at 1517 K Street, NW and Dulles International Airport. Buses run seven days a week. Rates, including loop service between the Washington Flyer terminal and various points within the district, are $16 (one-way) and $26 (round-trip). Bus service is also available, seven days a week, between Dulles and the West Falls Church Metro station. Rates for this service are $8 each way. Call Washington Flyer (703/685-1400) for schedule information. Please note that fares must be paid in cash. Door-to-door service is available from Washington Flyer-Dulles Airport Taxi (703/661-8230).

## To and From Baltimore-Washington (Friendship) International Airport:

Airport Connection provides bus service, seven days a week, between their terminal at 1517 K Street, NW and BWI Airport. Rates are $14 (one-way) and $25 (round-trip). Door-to-door service is available, with one day advance notice, for those in Montgomery and Prince George's Counties, Maryland. Rates for this service vary. For further information, call Airport Connection (301/441-2345).

## Taxi:

Fares in Washington, D.C., are based on a congressionally controlled zone system and are reasonable. Taxi fares crossing state lines into and out of Virginia and Maryland are, however, fairly expensive.

## Metrorail System (subway):

The Metro is an economical and efficient means of transportation in the Washington, D.C., area. Metro maps can be obtained at most Metro stations. The system is open Monday–Friday, 5:30 A.M.–midnight, and Saturday and Sunday, 8:00 A.M.–midnight. For routes and schedule information, call (202) 637-7000.

## Metro Buses:

Metrobus, together with Metrorail, links almost every major corner of the greater Washington metropolitan area. For routes and schedule information, call (202) 637-7000.

## Intercity Buses:

The Greyhound/Trailways terminal is located at 1005 1st Street, NE. Call (800) 231-2222 for route and schedule information.

## Trains:

Union Station (50 Massachusetts Avenue, NE) is the terminal for all trains serving Washington, D.C. Located near the Capitol, it is within minutes of the downtown hotel area. For AMTRAK information, call (202) 484-7540.

## Other Services

The Meridian House International, a private, non-profit community organization, offers a diversified program of services to international visitors to the Washington area. Its programs are operated with the support of more than 1,200 volunteers living in the Washington area. (See also entry N37.) The Meridian House has two locations: Main Information and Reception Center, NW, Washington, D.C. 20009 (202/667-6800) and an Information Booth at Dulles International Airport. Multilingual staff and volunteers are available to help the visitor with sightseeing arrangements, hotel accommodations, and bilingual medical assistance. The Meridian House also provides tour brochures, maps, information, and telephone assistance in fifty-five languages, including Russian, while operating twenty-four hours a day, seven days a week. Persons in need of language assistance may call (202) 939-5538. For the foreign student enrolled in U.S. institutions of higher education, it may be useful to contact the Foreign Student Service Council of Greater Washington, 2337 18th Street, NW, Washington, D.C. 20009 (202/232-4979; fax: 202/667-9305). Its staff and volunteers provide home hospitality, sightseeing, and other services to the foreign students (local and transient).

## Other Sources of Information

*Flashmaps! The Instant Guide to Washington* (1994) is an inexpensive, useful, and quick reference book on the city. This, as well as other guides to sightseeing and dining out (e.g., *Bantam Travel Guide,* Washington, D.C., 1990) can be obtained at many area bookstores. Free copies of the metropolitan Washington area map are available from the District of Columbia Department of Transportation and from the Map Office, Presidential Building, Room 519, 415 Twelfth Street, NW, Washington, D.C. 20004. Mail orders must include a stamped, self-addressed, seven-by-ten-inch envelope. The office is open from 8:15 A.M. to 4:45 P.M., Monday through Friday (202/724-4091).

## A Final Word

In general, it costs more to live in Washington, D.C., than in neighboring Virginia or Maryland. For those intending to do research primarily in the city and especially along Metro's Blue and Orange lines, i.e. Foggy Bottom to Capitol Hill, however, the time lost commuting in and out of town and the transportation expense may well make up the difference in rental costs. It may make sense for you to pay to park your out-of-District-licensed car in a parking garage because permits are required for street parking. Temporary permits (six months) are available at the District of Columbia building. A copy of your lease or a note from your landlord is required, along with valid car registration.

# VI

# Federal Government Holidays

Federal government offices are closed on the following holidays:

| | |
|---|---|
| New Year's Day | January 1* |
| Martin Luther King's Birthday | Third Monday in January |
| Presidents' Birthday | Third Monday in February |
| Memorial Day | Last Monday in May |
| Independence Day | July 4* |
| Labor Day | First Monday in September |
| Columbus Day | Second Monday in October |
| Veterans Day | November 11 |
| Thanksgiving | Fourth Thursday in November |
| Christmas | December 25* |

*If date falls on a Saturday, the holiday is on Friday; if the date falls on a Sunday, the holiday is on Monday.

The public areas of the Smithsonian Institution (entry K36) and the General Reading Room of the Library of Congress (entry A29) are open on most holidays.

# VII

# Standard Entry Formats

## A. Libraries (Government, Academic, Public, and Special) Entry Format

1. *General Information*
   a. address; telephone number(s)
   b. hours of service
   c. conditions of access (including availability of interlibrary loan and photocopying facilities)
   d. name/title of director and heads of relevant divisions

2. *Size of Collection*
   a. general
   b. Peace and International Security Studies (if ascertainable)

3. *Description and Evaluation of Collection*
   a. narrative assessment of holdings on Peace and International Security Studies—subject strengths and weaknesses
   b. notable holdings/collections
   c. tabular evaluation of subject strength

| Subject | Number of Titles | Ratings (A–C)* |
|---|---|---|
| Philosophy—War and Peace | | |
| Psychology—War and Peace | | |
| Ethics—War and Peace | | |
| Religion—War and Peace | | |
| World History | | |
| History—Military Science | | |
| Geography—Military | | |
| Anthropology—War and Peace | | |
| Economic History and Conditions | | |
| Commercial Policy | | |
| International Finance | | |
| Sociology | | |
| Political Theory | | |

Constitutional History and Administration
Colonies and Emigration
International Relations
International Organizations
International Law
Education—International Relations and Military
Music—Military
Art and War
Military Science
Naval Science
Bibliography and Reference

A—comprehensive collection of primary and secondary sources (Library of Congress collection to serve as a standard of evaluation)

B—substantial collection of primary and secondary sources; sufficient for some original research (holdings of roughly one-tenth those of the Library of Congress)

C—substantial collection of secondary and some primary sources; sufficient to support graduate instruction (holdings of roughly one-half those of a B collection)

4. *Special Collections*

5. *Bibliographic Aids Facilitating Use of Collection*

6. *Index Terms* (relevant subject specialties)

## B. Archives and Manuscript Repositories Entry Format

1. *General Information*
   a. address; telephone number(s)
   b. hours and days of service

c. conditions of access

d. photocopying facilities

e. name/title of director and heads of relevant divisions

2. *Size of Holdings Pertaining to Peace and International Security Studies*

3. *Description of Holdings Pertaining to Peace and International Security Studies*

4. *Bibliographic Aids Facilitating Use of Collection*

5. *Index Terms* (relevant subject specialties)

### C. Museums, Galleries, and Art Collections Entry Format

1. *General Information*

a. address; telephone number(s)

b. hours and days of service

c. conditions of access

d. photocopying facilities

e. name/title of director and heads of relevant divisions

2. *Size of Holdings Pertaining to Peace and International Security Studies*

3. *Description of Holdings Pertaining to Peace and International Security Studies*

4. *Bibliographic Aids Facilitating Use of Collection*

5. *Library/Archives*

6. *Index Terms* (relevant subject specialties)

### D. Map Collections Entry Format

1. *General Information*

a. address; telephone number(s)

b. hours and days of service

c. conditions of access

d. photocopying facilities

e. name/title of director and heads of relevant divisions

2. *Size of Holdings Pertaining to Peace and International Security Studies*

3. *Description of Holdings Pertaining to Peace and International Security Studies*

4. *Bibliographic Aids Facilitating Use of Collection*

5. *Index Terms* (relevant subject specialties)

### E. Collections of Sound Recordings Entry Format

1. *General Information*

a. address; telephone number(s)

b. hours and days of service

c. conditions of access

d. name/title of director and key staff members

2. *Size of Holdings Pertaining to Peace and International Security Studies*

3. *Description of Holdings Pertaining to Peace and International Security Studies*

4. *Facilities for Study and Use*

a. availability of audiovisual equipment

b. reservation requirements

c. fees charged

d. duplication facilities

5. *Bibliographic Aids Facilitating Use of Collection*

6. *Index Terms* (relevant subject specialties)

### F. Film Collections (Still Photographs and Motion Pictures) Entry Format

1. *General Information*

a. address; telephone number(s)

b. hours and days of service

c. conditions of access

d. name/title of director and key staff members

2. *Size of Holdings Pertaining to Peace and International Security Studies*

3. *Description of Holdings Pertaining to Peace and International Security Studies*

4. *Facilities for Study and Use*

a. availability of audiovisual equipment

b. reservation requirements

c. fees charged

d. duplication facilities

5. *Bibliographic Aids Facilitating Use of Collection*

6. *Index Terms* (relevant subject specialties)

## G. Data Banks Entry Format

1. *General Information*
   a. address; telephone number(s)
   b. hours and days of service
   c. conditions of access (including fees charged for information retrieval)
   d. name/title of director and key staff members

2. *Description of Data Files* (hard-data and bibliographic reference)

3. *Bibliographic Aids Facilitating Use of Storage Media*

4. *Index Terms* (relevant subject specialties)

## H. Research Centers and Information Offices Entry Format

1. *Address; Telephone Number(s)*

2. *Chief Official and Title*

3. *Programs and Research Activities Pertaining to Peace and International Security Studies*

4. *Recurring Meetings Sponsored by the Center/Office* (open or closed)

5. *Library/Special Research Facilities* (including specialized collections and unique equipment; availability to nonmembers)

6. *Publications or Other Media*

7. *Index Terms* (relevant subject specialties)

## J. Academic Programs and Departments Entry Format

1. *Address; Telephone Number(s)*

2. *Chief Official and Title*

3. *Degrees and Subjects Offered*

4. *Programs and Research Centers*

5. *Recurring Meetings Sponsored by Programs/Departments*

6. *Library/Research Facilities*

7. *Publications*

8. *Index Terms* (relevant subject specialties)

## K. United States Government Agencies Entry Format

1. *General Information*
   a. address; telephone number(s)
   b. conditions of access
   c. name/title of director and heads of relevant divisions

2. *Agency Function, Programs, and Research Activities* (including in-house research, contract research, research grants, employment of outside consultants, and international exchange programs)

3. *Agency Libraries and Reference Facilities*

4. *Internal Agency Records* (unpublished materials and aids, indexes, vertical files, etc.)

5. *Publications*
   a. published research products
   b. research bibliographies

*Note:* In the case of large, structurally complex agencies, each relevant division or bureau is described separately, following the description of the organization as a whole, and cross-referenced in the text and in indexes.

## L. International Government Organizations Entry Format

1. *General Information*
   a. address; telephone number(s)
   b. conditions of access
   c. name/title of director and heads of relevant divisions

2. *Organization Functions, Programs, and Research Activities* (including in-house research, contract research, research grants, employment of outside consultants, and international exchange programs)

3. *Libraries and Reference Facilities*

4. *Internal Records* (including unpublished research products)

5. *Publications*
   a. published reports, periodicals, and series
   b. bibliographies

6. *Index Terms* (relevant subject specialties)

**M.  Associations (Academic, Professional, and Cultural) Entry Format**

1.  *Address; Telephone Number(s)*

2.  *Chief Official and Title*

3.  *Programs and Activities Pertaining to Peace and International Security Studies*

4.  *Conventions/Meetings*

5.  *Library/Reference Collection*

6.  *Publications*

7.  *Index Terms* (relevant subject specialties)

**N.  Cultural-Exchange and Technical-Assistance Organizations Entry Format**

1.  *Address; Telephone Number(s)*

2.  *Chief Official and Title*

3.  *Programs and Activities Pertaining to Peace and International Security Studies*

4.  *Conventions/Meetings*

5.  *Library/Reference Collection*

6.  *Publications*

7.  *Index Terms* (relevant subject specialties)

# Bibliography

Listed below are reference sources consulted to identify collections and organizations included in this Guide.

*American Art Directory.* 53d ed. New York: Bowker, 1990.

*American Library Directory 1994–1995.* 47th ed. 2 vols. New York: Bowker, 1994.

Benton, Mildred. *A Study of Resources and Major Subject Holdings Available in U.S. Federal Libraries Maintaining Extensive or Unique Collections of Research Materials.* Washington, D.C.: Department of Health, Education and Welfare, 1970.

Bhatt, Purnima M. *Scholars' Guide to Washington, D.C., for African Studies.* Washington, D.C.: Smithsonian Institution Press, 1980.

Brownson, Ann L., comp. *Congressional Staff Directory.* Mount Vernon, Va.: Congressional Staff Directory, 1959–. Semiannual.

———. *Federal Staff Directory.* Mount Vernon, Va.: Congressional Staff Directory, 1982–. Semiannual.

Cichonski, Thomas J., ed. *Research Centers Directory.* 18th ed. 2 vols. Detroit: Gale, 1994.

Cook, Betsy, ed. *Federal Yellow Book.* Washington, D.C.: Monitor Publishing Company, 1976–. Quarterly.

Daniels, Peggy K., and Carol A. Scwartz, eds. *Encyclopedia of Associations 1994.* 28th ed. 2 vols. in 4 pts. Detroit: Gale, 1993. Annual.

Dillon, Kenneth J. *Scholars' Guide to Washington, D.C., for Central and East European Studies.* Washington, D.C.: Smithsonian Institution Press, 1980.

*Diplomatic List.* Washington, D.C.: U.S. Department of State, May 1994.

*Directory of Oral History Programs in the United States.* Ann Arbor, Mich.: Microfilm Corporation of America, 1982.

*Directory of Postsecondary Institutions, 1991–1992.* Washington, D.C.: National Center for Education Statistics, U.S. Department of Education, 1992.

*Directory of Resources for International Cultural and Educational Exchanges.* Washington, D.C.: U.S. Information Agency, [1992].

Dorr, Steven R. *Scholars' Guide to Washington, D.C., for Middle Eastern Studies.* Washington, D.C.: Smithsonian Institution Press, 1981.

Ehrenberg, Ralph E. *Scholars' Guide to Washington, D.C., for Cartography and Remote Sensing Imagery.* Washington, D.C.: Smithsonian Institution Press, 1987.

*Government Research Centers Directory.* 6th ed. Detroit: Gale, 1990.

Grant, Steven A. *Scholars' Guide to Washington, D.C., for Russian/Central Eurasian/Baltic Studies.* 3d ed., rev. by William E. Pomeranz. Washington, D.C.: Woodrow Wilson Center Press, 1994.

Green, Shirley L. *Pictorial Resources in the Washington, D.C., Area.* Washington, D.C.: Library of Congress, 1976.

Grow, Michael. *Scholars' Guide to Washington, D.C., for Latin American and Caribbean Studies.* 2d ed., rev. by Craig VanGrasstek. Washington, D.C.: Woodrow Wilson Center Press, 1992.

Haines, Gerald K. *A Reference Guide to United States Department of State Special Files.* Westport, Conn.: Greenwood Press, 1985.

Hamer, Philip M., ed. *A Guide to Archives and Manuscripts in the United States.* New Haven, Conn.: Yale University Press, 1961.

Heintze, James R. *Scholars' Guide to Washington, D.C., for Audio Resources.* Washington, D.C.: Smithsonian Institution Press, 1985.

Higbee, Joan F. *Scholars' Guide to Washington, D.C., for Southwest European Studies.* Washington, D.C.: Woodrow Wilson Center Press, 1989.

Jennings, Margaret S., ed. *Library and Reference Facilities in the Area of the District of Columbia.* 12th ed. Washington, D.C.: American Society for Information Science, 1986.

Kessinger, Judith A., ed. *Guide to Library of Congress Subject Headings and Classification on Peace and International Conflict Resolution.* Washington, D.C.: United States Institute of Peace, 1990.

Kim, Hong N. *Scholars' Guide to Washington, D.C., for East Asian Studies.* Washington, D.C.: Smithsonian Institution Press, 1979.

Mayerchak, Patrick M. *Scholars' Guide to Washington, D.C., for Southeast Asian Studies.* Washington, D.C.: Smithsonian Institution Press, 1983.

Meckler, Alan M., and Ruth McMullin, comps. *Oral History Collections.* New York: Bowker, 1975.

*Official Museum Directory.* Washington, D.C.: American Association of Museums, 1993. Annual.

Pitschmann, Louis A. *Scholars' Guide to Washington, D.C., for Northwest European Studies.* Washington, D.C.: Smithsonian Institution Press, 1984.

Rahim, Enayetur. *Scholars' Guide to Washington, D.C., for South Asian Studies.* Washington, D.C.: Smithsonian Institution Press, 1981.

Rowan, Bonnie G. *Scholars' Guide to Washington, D.C., Film and Video Collections.* Washington, D.C.: Smithsonian Institution Press, 1980.

Rowan, Bonnie G., and Cynthia J. Wood. *Scholars' Guide to Washington, D.C., Media Collections.* Washington, D.C.: Woodrow Wilson Center Press, 1994.

Schmeckebier, Laurence Frederick, and Roy B. Eastin. *Government Publications and Their Use.* Rev. ed. Washington, D.C.: Brookings Institution, 1969.

*Serials Directory: An International Reference Book.* 8th ed. 5 vols. Birmingham, Ala.: Ebsco Publishing, 1994.

Thomas, Daniel C., and Michael T. Klare, eds. *Peace and Order Studies: A Curriculum Guide.* 5th ed., Boulder, Colo.: Westview Press, 1989.

U.S. Congress. *Congressional Directory.* 103d Congress, 1993–94. Washington, D.C.: Government Printing Office, 1993. Biennial.

U.S. National Archives and Records Administration. *United States Government Manual, 1993–1994.* Washington, D.C.: Government Printing Office, 1993. Annual.

U.S. National Historical Publications and Records Commission. *Directory of Archives and Manuscript Repositories.* Washington, D.C.: U.S. National Archives and Records Service, 1978.

*Washington 94.* Washington, D.C.: Columbia Books, 1994. Annual.

*Washington Area Library Directory.* Soderton, Penn.: Datamatic Systems, 1992.

*Washington Information Directory, 1993–1994.* Washington, D.C.: Congressional Quarterly, 1993. Annual.

Weber, Olga S. *North American Film and Video Directory.* New York: Bowker, 1976.

Williams, Martha, ed. *Computer-Readable Data Bases.* White Plains, N.Y.: Knowledge Industry Publications, 1982.

# Indexes

# I

# Personal Papers Index

A—Libraries (Government, Academic, Public, and Special)
B—Archives and Manuscript Repositories
C—Museums, Galleries, and Art Collections
D—Map Collections
E—Collections of Sound Recordings
F—Film Collections (Still Photographs and Motion Pictures)
G—Data Banks
H—Research Centers and Information Offices
J—Academic Programs and Departments
K—United States Government Agencies
L—International Government Organizations
M—Associations (Academic, Professional, and Cultural)
N—Cultural-Exchange and Technical-Assistance Organizations

Abshire, David M. B6
Acheson, Dean B11 (RG 59)
Ackerson, Garret G., Jr. B6
Adams, John Quincy B8
Adler, Elmer E. B1
Agan, Arthur C. B1
Alexander, Leo B16
Allen, Martha R. B9
Alsop, Joseph B8
Alsop, Stewart B8
Anderson, Chandler P. B8
Arendt, Hannah B8
Armstrong, John B8
Arthur, Chester B8

Baker, Newton B8
Baker, Ray Stannard B8
Bancroft, George B8
Barbey, Daniel E. B13
Barbour, James B8
Barnes, Milton A18

Baruch, Bernard A33, B6
Bayard, Thomas B8
Beamt, Emil and Erich B16
Belknap, William B8
Bell, John B8
Bellamy, David B9
Berger, Samuel D. B6
Besson, Frank S. A33
Blaine, James G. B8
Bliss, Tasker Howard B8
Bloom, Sally and Samuel B16
Bohlen, Chester B8, B11 (RG 43)
Bonaparte, Charles B8
Borah, William E. B8
Bowen, Russell J. B6
Bradley, Omar N. B8
Braham, Randolph B16
Breckinridge, Henry B8
Breckinridge, Joseph Cabell B8
Breckinridge, William Campbell B8
Brooks, Raymond Arthur B10
Brown, Jacob J. B8
Bryan, William Jennings B8, B11 (RG 59)
Buchanan, James B8
Butler, Benjamin B8
Butler, Smedley D. B9
Byrne, Edmund B8

Cabell, Charles Pearre B1
Calhoun, John C. B8
Camron, Simon B8
Cannon, John Kenneth B1
Caproni, Gianni B1
Carnegie, Andrew B8
Cass, Lewis B8
Cates, Clifton B. B9
Chandler, William B8
Chauncey, Henry B6
Chillson, Charles W. B10

# II

# Library Subject-Strength Index

This index identifies the most useful library collections in the Washington, D.C., area by subject. The evaluations (A, B, and C) presented here are based on the criteria explained at the beginning of section A ("Libraries") of this Guide and summarized below:

A—comprehensive collection of primary and secondary sources (Library of Congress collection to serve as a standard of evaluation)

B—substantial collection of primary and secondary sources; sufficient for some original research (holdings roughly one-tenth those of the Library of Congress)

C—substantial collection of secondary and primary sources; sufficient to support graduate instruction (holdings roughly one-half those of a B collection)

For some libraries, however, a strictly quantitative evaluation would grossly misrepresent the scholarly importance of their holdings. Thus, the quality and nature of holdings in certain collections have called for higher ratings than a purely quantitative appraisal might otherwise suggest. Not to apply this measure of quality would be an injustice to collections and scholars alike.

The subject categories listed below reflect those used in the Library of Congress classification scheme as well as in the tables analyzing major library holdings in section A of this volume. The specific Library of Congress classification numbers constituting each category are listed in appendix IV. The subject headings are listed below in the same order as they appear in section A.

## Philosophy—War and Peace
A collections: A29
B collections: A4, A7, A18, A19, A20, A22, A47
C collections: A3

## Psychology—War and Peace
A collections: A29
B collections: A4, A7, A15, A18, A19, A20, A22, A47
C collections: A3, A11

## Ethics—War and Peace
A collections: A19, A29, A47
B collections: A4, A7, A18, A20, A22
C collections: A3

## Religion—War and Peace
A collections: A29
B collections: A4, A7, A20, A22, A47
C collections: A18

## World History
A collections: A29
B collections: A19, A20, A43, A45, A47
C collections: A4, A7, A18, A22

## History—Military Science
A collections: A29, A33
B collections: A20, A47
C collections: A4, A19

## Geography—Military
A collections: A29
B collections: A33, A41
C collections: A20, A43, A47

## Anthropology—War and Peace
A collections: A29
B collections: A47
C collections: A4, A7, A18, A19, A20, A22

## Economic History and Conditions
A collections: A8, A24, A27, A29
B collections: A1, A4, A10, A12, A19, A20, A28, A31, A41, A43, A47
C collections: A16, A22, A25, A34, A37, A40

# III

# Subject Index

Some of the general subject descriptors (for example, Arms Control) are also broken down by subordinate descriptors (for example, Arms Control—Ballistic Missile Defense). An entry under the general descriptor may subsume materials germane to two or more specific descriptors.

Entries for National Archives and Records Administration (NARA) (B11, D6, E11, F20, and F21) with exceptionally large holdings are provided with their own internal subject indexes under point 3 of each entry.

Entry symbols correspond to the following sections of the text:

A—Libraries (Government, Academic, Public, and Special)
B—Archives and Manuscript Repositories
C—Museums, Galleries, and Art Collections
D—Map Collections
E—Collections of Sound Recordings
F—Film Collections (Still Photographs and Motion Pictures)
G—Data Banks
H—Research Centers and Information Offices
J—Academic Programs and Departments
K—United States Government Agencies
L—International Government Organizations
M—Associations (Academic, Professional, and Cultural)
N—Cultural-Exchange and Technical-Assistance Organizations

Arms Control: A4, A5, A6, A9, A12, A18, A19, A20, A21, A29, A30, A35, A36, A37, A41, A42, A43, A46, A47, B8, B11, B12, C6, F20, F26, G1, H3, H7, H8, H9, H11, H14, H18, H22, H42, H56, H65, H68, H70, H73, H76, H78, K4, K8, K10, K18, K25, K37, M4, M7, M9, M12, M13, M20, M26, M34, M36, M43, M46, M47, M50; Academic Course Offer-

ings J13; Arms Transfers C8, H33, H34, H43, H59, H61, N53; Ballistic Missile Defense H32, H35, H36, H39
Arms Production and Acquisition: B4, E3, F6, H11, H25, H39, H52, H64, M1, M5, M20, M42
Art and War: C1, C2, C4, C9, F21

Collective Security: A29, A33, A37, A41, A43, B1, B3, B4, B6, B8, B11, B12, B13, B14, E11, F16, F17, F22, F24, G1, H1, H28, H68, H73, K3, K5, K10, K29, K37, M7, M18; Academic Course Offerings J1, J2, J4, J6, J11; Regional Alliance Systems A13, A23, F9, H38, L2, L5, L6; NATO H6, H7
Conflict Management and Resolution: A4, A9, A11, A18, A19, A20, A28, A29, A34, A43, A44, A46, A47, B2, B8, B11, B12, B14, E2, E8, F13, F26, F30, G1, H1, H18, H34, H45, H46, H73, M9, M24, M32, M39, M53, N26, N35, N41, N42, N43, N44, N50, N51, N59; Academic Course Offerings J1, J11, J5; Theoretical Approaches J1, J5, M8, M50; Unofficial and Nongovernmental Approaches A2, B2, E2, E8, F3, F13, J1, J5, L10, M45, N7

Defense Conversion: H25, H26, H38, H54, H61, H64, K18, M1, M2, M29, N53
Defense Policy, National: A9, A21, A29, A33, A37, A41, A43, B8, F17, G1, G6, G7, G10, H3, H7, H8, H14, H15, H16, H18, H32, H33, H38, H40, H42, H47, H50, H65, H70, H73, H78, K3, K5, K9, K10, K18, K28, K29, K30, K31, K37, M5, M7, M12, M13, M16, M20, M26, M33, M36, M37, M42, M57; Academic Course Offerings J1, J2, J4, J6, J11, J13; History B1, B3, B4, B6, B9, B11, B12, B13, C3, E1, E4, E6, E11, E13, E15, E16; U.S. Strategic Interests F6, H2, H4, H6, H11, H17, H25, H34, H35, H36, H37, H39, H56, H58, H63, H71
Deterrence: A9, A19, A20, A21, A29, A30, A36, A37, A42, A43, A47, B4, G1, H16, H34, H35, H36, H38, H39, H56, H65, H73, H76, K4, K10, M26

# IV

# Organizations and Institutions Index

Entry symbols correspond to the following sections of the text:

A—Libraries (Government, Academic, Public, and Special)
B—Archives and Manuscript Repositories
C—Museums, Galleries, and Art Collections
D—Map Collections
E—Collections of Sound Recordings
F—Film Collections (Still Photographs and Motion Pictures)
G—Data Banks
H—Research Centers and Information Offices
J—Academic Programs and Departments
K—United States Government Agencies
L—International Government Organizations
M—Associations (Academic, Professional, and Cultural)
N—Cultural-Exchange and Technical-Assistance Organizations

# Contributors

ROBERT W. JANES received a B.A. degree in philosophy from McGill University (1976), M.I.A. (Master of International Affairs) from Columbia University (1985), and a Ph.D. (1991) in government and politics from the University of Maryland. He is currently a Visiting Fellow in the Center for International Security Studies at the University of Maryland. In 1991–92, he held a fellowship in the Center on East-West Trade, Investment, and Communication at Duke University. Dr. Janes's teaching experience has been in the fields of international relations, Russian domestic and foreign policy, and comparative politics. His research interests focus on postcommunist transition in the Baltic Republics, and on the Baltic relations with Russia and the other states of the former Soviet Union. His contributions have appeared in the *Annals* of the American Academy of Political and Social Sciences, *International Journal,* and *Problems of Communism.*

KATHERINE R. TROMBLE received a B.A. in American Studies from Georgetown University in 1994. She was a research intern at the Woodrow Wilson International Center for Scholars, 1993–94. Ms. Tromble has conducted research in U.S. military and ethnic history focusing on the 69th N.Y. State Militia and the development of an Irish-American identity.

Consultant James H. Laue was, until his death in September 1993, professor of conflict resolution in the Institute for Conflict Resolution at George Mason University. From 1975 to 1987, Dr. Laue held appointments as professor of sociology and as director of the Center for Metropolitan Studies at the University of Missouri in St. Louis.

Consultant George H. Quester has been a professor in the Department of Government and Politics at the University of Maryland since 1982. Previously, Dr. Quester taught political science at Cornell University where he also served as director of the Program on Peace Studies from 1970 to 1974 and from 1978 to 1981.

Consultant George S. Weigel is president of the Ethics and Public Policy Center in Washington, D.C. The center aims at strengthening the connection between the Judeo-Christian moral tradition and the public debate over domestic and foreign policy issues. From 1977 to 1984, Dr. Weigel held an appointment as scholar-in-residence at the World without War Council in Seattle.

Series Editor Zdeněk V. David has been librarian of the Woodrow Wilson Center since 1974. He attended Wesleyan University (B.A. 1952), Harvard (M.A. 1954 and Ph.D. 1960), and Rutgers (M.L.S. 1970), and taught historiography and Russian and East European history at the University of Michigan at Ann Arbor and Princeton. Dr. David also served as Slavic Bibliographer at the Princeton University library from 1966 to 1974. He is coauthor of *The Peoples of the Eastern Habsburg Lands, 1526–1918* (1984), and *Bibliography of Works in the Philosophy of History, 1978–1982* (1984) and *1983–1987* (1989). His contributions have appeared in *Canadian American Slavic Studies, Communio Viatorum, East Central Europe, Folia Historica Bohemica, Modern Greek Studies Yearbook,* and *Slavic Review.*